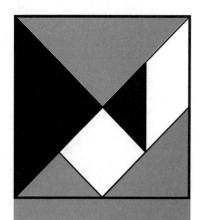

Management Information Systems

A Managerial Perspective

Uma G. Gupta

COURSE
TECHNOLOGY

ONE MAIN STREET, CAMBRIDGE, MA 02142

an *International Thomson Publishing company* I(T)P®

Cambridge • Albany • Bonn • Boston • Cincinnati • London • Madrid • Melbourne • Mexico City
New York • Paris • San Francisco • Singapore • Tokyo • Toronto • Washington

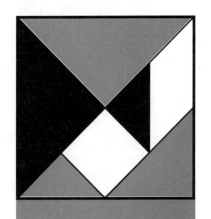

Management Information Systems

A Managerial Perspective

Uma G. Gupta

East Carolina University

West Publishing Company

Minneapolis/St. Paul • New York • Los Angeles • San Francisco

Production Credits

Copyediting: Judith Abrahms

Artist: Gloria Langer

Composition: Parkwood Composition

Interior Design: Merry O'brecht Sawdey/Shade Tree Designs

Proofreader: Jim Bowen

© 1996 by Course Technology
A Division of International Thomson Publishing Inc. — I(T)P®

For more information contact:

Course Technology
One Main Street
Cambridge, MA 02142

International Thomson Editores
Campos Eliseos 385, Piso 7
Col. Polanco
11560 Mexico D.F. Mexico

International Thomson Publishing Europe
Berkshire House 168-173
High Holborn
London WCIV 7AA
England

International Thomson Publishing GmbH
Königswinterer Strasse 418
53227 Bonn
Germany

Thomas Nelson Australia
102 Dodds Street
South Melbourne, 3205
Victoria, Australia

International Thomson Publishing Asia
211 Henderson Road
#05-10 Henderson Building
Singapore 0315

Nelson Canada
1120 Birchmount Road
Scarborough, Ontario
Canada M1K 5G4

International Thomson Publishing Japan
Hirakawacho Kyowa Building, 3F
2-2-1 Hirakawacho
Chiyoda-ku, Tokyo 102
Japan

ISBN 0-314-06805-8

Printed in the United States of America

10 9 8 7 6 5 4 3 2

Photo credits: **3** Michael Newman/PhotoEdit; **9** Michael Newman/PhotoEdit; **39** J3 Learning; **46** Gary Buss/FPG International; **73** Mark Lewis/Tony Stone Images; **87** Hank Morgan/Photo Researchers; **89** Courtesy of AT&T; **91** Courtesy of Epson America; **94** David Parker/Photo Researchers; **99** Courtesy of NEC, Inc.; **115** Matthew Neal McVay/Tony Stone Images; **131** Microsoft; **136** Symantec Corp.; **157** Telegraph Colour Library/FPG International; **171** Telegraph Colour Library/FPG International; **211** Mainstay; **256** Telegraph Colour Library/FPG International; **283** Pilot Executive Software, Inc.; **310** Comshare, Inc.; **313** Federal Express; **325** Telegraph Colour Library/FPG International; **330** Paul Ambrose/FPG International; **357** Jon Riley/Tony Stone Images; **370** John Turner/Tony Stone Images; **389** Roger E. Daemmrich/Tony Stone Images; **431** Walter Hodges/Tony Stone Images; **481** Paul Shambroom/Photo Researchers; **515** D. Young-Wolff/PhotoEdit; **544** Telegraph Colour Library/FPG International; **548** Chuck Keeler/Tony Stone Images; **568** Michael Newman/PhotoEdit.

DEDICATION

To my greatest gift, my daughter,
Priyanka Elizabeth Gupta, for who you are,
and
to all our children,
for the joy, meaning, and purpose they bring to our lives

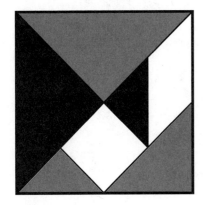

Brief Contents

Part I

Managerial Overview of Information Systems   1

1 ▪ Introduction to Information Systems   3
2 ▪ Information Systems for Managerial Decision-Making   39

Part II

Technical Foundations of Information Systems   71

3 ▪ Computer Hardware   73
4 ▪ Computer Software   115
5 ▪ Telecommunications and Networks   157
6 ▪ Database Design and Management   211
7 ▪ Client Server Computing   256

Part III

Business Applications of Information Systems   281

8 ▪ Decision Support Systems and Executive Information Systems   283
9 ▪ Artificial Intelligence, Expert Systems, and Neural Networks   325
10 ▪ Office Automation   357
11 ▪ Business Information Systems   389

Part IV

Managing the Development and Maintenance of Information Systems   429

12 ▪ System Analysis and Design: Methodologies and Implications   431
13 ▪ Tools for Information Systems Development   481

Part V

Strategic and Managerial Implications of Information Systems   513

14 ▪ Strategic Information Systems   515
15 ▪ Managing Information Resources   544
16 ▪ Computer Security   568

Appendix A ▪ Business Ethics   601
Glossary   613
Index   629

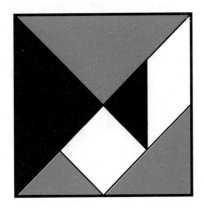

Contents

Preface   xxiii
Acknowledgments   xxix

Part I

Managerial Overview of Information Systems   1

1 ▪ Introduction to Information Systems   3

Learning Objectives   4
Introduction   6
Information Systems Versus Information Technology   8
Computer Literacy Versus Information Literacy   10
Data versus Information   12
Data   *12*
Information   *12*
Characteristics of Information   *12*
The Process of Converting Data into Information   *13*
Why Students Should Study MIS   16
Why Organizations Need Information Systems   17
Meeting Global Challenges   *17*
Capturing Opportunities in the Marketplace   *17*
Supporting Corporate Strategy   *18*
Linking Departments Whose Functions Are Different   *18*
Enhancing Worker Productivity   *18*
Increasing the Quality of Goods and Services   *18*
Information Systems and Organizational Structures   19
The Pyramid Structure   *19*
The Task-Based Structure   *20*
Contributions of Information Systems to Individual, Work-Group, and Organization-Wide Decision Making   21
Potential Risks of Information Systems   23
"Deskilling" of Workers   *23*
Information Overload   *23*
Employee Mistrust   *23*
Increased Competitive Pressure   *24*
Disenchantment with IS   *24*
Challenges in Developing Information Systems   *24*
Security Breaches   *24*
General Systems Theory   25
System Components   *26*

Ethics and Information Systems: A Framework   27
A Framework for Studying MIS   28
Summary   31
Review Questions   31
Discussion Questions   32
Ethical Issues   33
  Case 1: David vs. Goliath ▪ Case 2: Oracle Slapped with Lawsuit
Problem Solving in the Real World   35
  The IRS at Work
References   37
Notes   38

2 ▪ **Information Systems for Managerial Decision-Making   39**

Learning Objectives   40
Introduction   41
Transaction Processing Systems   43
Steps in Processing a Transaction   45
  Data Entry ▪ Validation ▪ Data Processing and Revalidation ▪
  Data Storage ▪ Output Generation ▪ Query Support
Example of A Transaction Processing System   49
Management Information System   49
Example of An MIS   50
Intelligent Support System   52
Decision Support Systems   52
  How a DSS Works
Example of a DSS   54
Executive Information Systems   55
Artificial Intelligence and Expert Systems   56
Example of an ES   57
Office Automation Systems   59
Tapping the Potential of Information Systems   61
Summary   63
Review Questions   64
Discussion Questions   64
Ethical Issues: 65
  Case 1: A Bribery Scandal ▪ Case 2: CIO Under Fire
Problem Solving in the Real World   66
  Case 1: Israeli Discount Bank Delights Customers ▪ Case 2: A Management
  Information System for a Chinese University
References   68
Notes   69

Part II

Technical Foundations of Information Systems   71

3 ▪ **Computer Hardware   73**

Learning Objectives   74
Introduction   75
Fundamentals of Data Representation   76

The Components of a Computer 76
The Central Processor **77**
    The Central Processing Unit
Primary Storage **78**
Secondary Storage 80
    Secondary Storage Devices
Secondary Storage Devices **80**
    Magnetic Disks ▪ *Magnetic Tape* ▪
    CD-ROM ▪ *CD-ROM Features*
Input Devices **85**
    Keyboard ▪ *Mouse* ▪ *Touch Screen* ▪ *Voice Recognition* ▪
    Optical Character Reader ▪ *Magnetic Ink Character Recognition*
Output Devices **89**
    Video Display Terminals ▪ *Printers* ▪ *Sound Boards* ▪
    Other Output Devices
Communication Devices **92**
Types of Computers 93
Supercomputers **94**
Mainframes **95**
Midrange Machines/Minicomputers **96**
Workstations **96**
Microcomputers or Personal Computers **97**
    Components of a PC
Laptops and Notebooks **98**
Hand-Held Computers **99**
Pen-Based Computing **100**
How to Buy a PC 101
Processor **101**
Clock Speed **102**
RAM **102**
Expansion Slots and Buses **103**
Monitor **104**
    Size ▪ *Resolution* ▪ *Tricolor* ▪ *Interlaced Versus*
    Noninterlaced Monitors ▪ *Radiation Level* ▪ *Video Board*

Summary 107
Review Questions 107
Discussion Questions 108
Ethical Issues 108
    Case 1: Bank Looses Money ▪ *Case 2: Electronic Gambling:*
    Winners or Losers? ▪ *Case 3: Questionable Marketing Practices* ▪
    Case 4: Use Keyboards At Your Own Risk ▪ *Case 5: Compaq Is on the Hot Seat*
Problem Solving in the Real World 110
    Case 1: Computer Makeover: From the Stone Age to the Cutting Edge
References 113
Notes 113

4 ▪ **Computer Software** 115
Learning Objectives 116
Introduction 117
Programming Languages 118
Machine Language **118**
Assembly Language **119**

High-Level Languages (3GLs)   *119*
Very High-Level Languages   *119*
Object Oriented Programming   *121*
Visual Programming   *123*
Types of Software   125
System Software   *125*

    System Control Software ▪ *The Operating System and Its Functions* ▪
    Operating System Environments ▪ *Examples of Operating Systems* ▪
    System Support Software ▪ *Systems Development Sofware*

Application Software   *137*

    General Purpose Software ▪ *Application-Dedicted Software*

Selecting Software Packages   143
Investment Criteria for Hardware and Software   144
Ethical Considerations   147
Summary   148
Review Questions   149
Discussion Questions   149
Ethical Issues   150

    Case 1: Is Justice Above the Law? ▪ *Case 2: Software Privacy* ▪
    Case 3: Highway Robbery

Problem Solving in the Real World   152

    Case 1: City of Indianapolis Goes High-Tech ▪

    Case 2: Ryder Rethinks Business Systems

References   155
Notes   155

5 ▪ **Telecommunications and Networks**   **157**

Learning Objectives   158
Introduction   159
Technical Foundations of Telecommunications   160
Part I: Telecommunications Model   162
Telecommunication Channels   162
Providers of Channel Services   *163*

    Common Carriers ▪ *Special Purpose Carriers*

Telecommunication Media   165
Bounded Medium   *165*

    Twisted Pair ▪ *Coaxial Cable* ▪ *Fiber Optics*

Unbounded Media—Wireless Communication   *168*

    Microwave Radios ▪ *Communication Satellites* ▪ *Cellular Phones* ▪
    High Frequency Radio Telephones

Types of Networks   173
Private Branch Exchanges (PBX)   *173*
Integrated Services Digital Network (ISDN)   *174*
Non-telephone Networks   *175*

    Local Area Network (LAN) ▪ *Advantages of LANs*

Wide Area Network (WAN)   *177*

    Advantages of WANs ▪ *Disadvantages of WANs*

Metropolitan Area Networks (MANs)   *179*
Value Added Networks (VAN)   *179*
Network Topologies   179
Bus Topology   *179*

Ring Topology   ***179***
Star Topology   ***180***
Network Architecture   180
Open Systems Interconnection (OSI)   181
Part II: Management Implications of Telecommunications   183
Challenges in Managing Networks   183
    Global Networks
Internet   ***186***
    Information Retrieval Tools ■ *Communication Tools* ■
    Multimedia Information Tools ■ *Information Search Tools*
Electronic Data Interchange (EDI)   ***195***
    Cost of Implementing EDI ■ *Benefits of EDI* ■
    Challenges of Implementing EDI
Summary   199
Review Questions   200
Discussion Questions   201
Ethical Issues   204
    Case 1: Patent Violations ■ *Case 2: Telephone Monitoring: Privacy Breach*
    or Security Measure? ■ *Case 3: Internet Liability* ■ *Case 4: What about*
    Free Speech? ■ *Case 5: Faking on the Internet* ■ *Case 6: Hold that Data,*
    Please
Problem Solving in the Real World   207
    Freddie, Fannie, Ginnie, and EDI
References   209
Notes   209

6 ■ **Database Design and Management**   **211**

Learning Objectives   212
Introduction   213
Data Versus Information   214
Data Hierarchy   216
Methods for Organizing Data in Files   218
Limitations of Traditional Files   220
Introduction to Database Management Systems   221
Advantages of Databases over Traditional Files   ***222***
Disadvantages of Databases   ***223***
Differences Between Databases and Traditional Files   ***224***
The Components of a DBMS   ***225***
    Data Definition Language ■ *Data Manipulation Language* ■
    Data Dictionary
Database Models   ***227***
Hierarchical Data Model   ***228***
    Advantages and Disadvantages of Hierarchical Model
Network Model   ***229***
    Advantages and Disadvantages of Network Model
Relational Model   ***230***
    Advantages of Relational Models ■ *Disadvantages of Relational Models*
Entity Relationship Diagram   233
ERD Symbols   ***234***
Distributed Databases   235
Advantages of Distributed Databases   ***236***

Disadvantages of Distributed Databases   237
Principles of Database Management   238
***Principle 1: Data Resources are Critical to an Organization
    and Must Be Fully Utilized and Protected   238***
***Principle 2: Database Technology Must Be Aligned with Business
    Strategy   240***
***Principle 3: Control and Security Are Important Issues in Databases,
    Particularly Distributed Databases   240***
***Principle 4: It Should Be Easy to Access and Process Data Residing
    in Different Databases   242***
Principle 5: Database Tools Must Be Carefully Selected   242
Summary   244
Review Questions   246
Discussion Questions   246
Ethical Issues   248

    Case 1: Sucker Databases ■ *Case 2: Ad Hoc Reporting May Not Be
So Ad Hoc After All!* ■ *Case 3: Database Fraud* ■ *Case 4: No More
Fraud* ■ *Case 5: Data Privacy* ■ *Case 6: Business as Usual?*

Problem Solving in the Real World   251

    Case 1: Pacific Gas and Electric ■ *Case 2: Becton Dickinson* ■
Case 3 Harper's Freight Is Data

References   254
Notes   254

7 ■ **Client Server Computing   256**

Learning Objectives   257
Introduction   258
What Is Client-Server Computing?   261
Difference Between a LAN Environment and a C/S Environment   263
Developing Client Server Systems   264
Identify the Type of Application   266
Determine Network Requirements   266
Select the Client-Server Architecture   266
Develop the Logical and Physical Design   267
Test, Implement, and Maintain the System   267
Organizational Implications of Client-Server Systems   267
Advantages of C/S Systems   267

    Make Data Readily Accessible to Decision Makers ■ *Reduce Operating Costs* ■
Increase Resource Utilization ■ *Reduce Application Development Time* ■
Increase Organizational Responsiveness

Disadvantages of C/S Systems   272

    Difficult Transition for Many Companies ■ *Massive Retraining is Required*
Lack of Standards ■ *Balancing Act Between Centralization and
Decentralization* ■ *Lower Costs May be Deceptive*

Client-Server Security   273
Guarding Access Privileges   273
Preserving the Integrity of Applications   274
Summary   275
Review Questions   276
Discussion Questions   276
Ethical Issues   277

Case 1: Ethics of Pricing ▪ *Case 2: Beware of Employees*

Problem Solving in the Real World   277

Case 1: Art and Technology Go Hand-in-Hand ▪ *Case 2: United Airlines Takes Off*

References   279

Notes   279

Part III

Business Applications of Information Systems   281

8 ▪ Decision Support Systems and Executive Information Systems   283

Learning Objectives   284

Introduction   285

Steps in Problem Solving   286

What Is a Decision Support System?   288

Applications of a DSS   288

Components of a DSS   292

Database Management Systems   292

Model Management Systems   293

Statistical Models ▪ *Financial and Accounting Models* ▪ *Production Models* ▪ *Marketing Models* ▪ *Human Resource Model* ▪ *Support Tools*

Functions of a DSS   295

Model Building   295

"What If" Analysis   297

Goal Seeking   298

Risk Analysis   298

Graphical Analysis   299

Tools for Developing a DSS   299

DSS Generators   300

DSS Shells   300

Example of a DSS Shell

Custom-Made Software   301

Group Decision Support Systems   301

Single-Computer Systems   303

Keypad-Response Systems   304

Full-Keyboard Workstation Systems   304

Advantages of GDSS   305

Executive Information Systems   307

Characteristics of an EIS   311

Derived Information   312

Drill-Down   312

Critical Success Factors for DSS/EIS   312

Commitment from Top Management   314

Availability of Accurate and Reliable Data   314

Careful Problem Selection   315

Integration of DSS and EIS with Existing Technologies   315

Costs Versus Benefits   315

TPS, MIS, DSS, and EIS   316

Summary   317
Review Questions   317
Discussion Questions   318
Ethical Issues   319
Case 1: Manipulating Decisions ■ *Case 2: Limited Access to Data*
Problem Solving in the Real World   320
Case 1: Amnesty International USA ■ *Case 2: Georgia Power Gains Power Through DSS* ■ *Case 3: Catch the Criminal*
References   322
Notes   323

9 ■ **Artificial Intelligence, Expert Systems, and Neural Networks   325**

Learning Objectives   326
Introduction   327
What Is Artificial Intelligence?   328
Appropriate Areas for an Expert System   331
Application of Expert Systems   332
Components of an Expert System   336
Knowledge Base   336
Inference Engine   339
User Interface   340
Working Memory   340
Explanation Module   341
Knowledge Representation   341
IF-THEN Rules   341
Inferencing Techniques   344
DSS, EIS, and ES   345
Neural Networks   347
How Neural Networks Work   348
Applications of Neural Networks   348
Summary   350
Review Questions   350
Discussion Questions   351
Ethical Issues   352
Case 1: Fighting Fire with Fire ■ *Case 2: Hidden Knowledge* ■ *Case 3: Who's to Blame?*
Problem Solving in the Real World   353
Case 1: Doctors Fight Infections with Artificial Intelligence ■ *Case 2: Moopi Scheduler: The Real Expert*
References   355
Notes   356

10 ■ **Office Automation   357**

Learning Objectives   358
Introduction   359
The Virtual Corporation   360
Types of Office Automation Systems   362
Electronic Publishing and Processing Systems   363
Document Management Systems ■ *Multimedia* ■ *Imaging*

Communication Systems   367

E-Mail ▪ *Fax*

Electronic Meeting Systems   372

Voice Mail ▪ *Audio Conferencing* ▪
Videoconferencing ▪ *Groupware*

Summary   378

Review Questions   379

Discussion Questions   379

Ethical Issues   380

Case 1: Videoconferencing Prisoners: An Ethical Dilemma ▪ *Case 2: Shredding
E-mail: The Iran-Contra Affair* ▪ *Case 3: The Wrath of a Fired Employee*

Problem Solving in the Real World   382

Case 1: A Leading Jeweler Buys into Office Automation ▪ *Case 2: Quintiles
Transnational*

References   386

Notes   387

11 ▪ Business Information Systems   389

Learning Objectives   390

Introduction   391

Functional Information Systems   392

Marketing Information Systems   393

What is a Marketing Information System?   394

Developing Marketing Information Systems   397

Benefits of Marketing Information Systems   398

Manufacturing Information Systems   399

Developing a Manufacturing Information System   399

Agile Manufacturing   400

Benefits of Manufacturing Information Systems   402

Quality Information Systems   403

Benefits of Quality Information Systems   406

Financial and Accounting Information Systems   407

Types of Financial and Accounting Systems   408

Integrated Financial and Accounting Systems   410

Human Resource Information Systems   411

The HRIS and the Competitive Strategy of the Firm   414

Developing an HRIS   414

Geographical Information Systems   417

Developing Cross-functional Systems   418

Summary   420

Review Questions   420

Discussion Questions   421

Ethical Issues   421

Case 1: Vendor-Managed Inventory ▪ *Case 2: The Dangers of
Sharing Information* ▪ *Case 3: False Job Security*

Problem Solving in the Real World   422

Case 1: An All-Star Team: The Tambrands Case ▪ *Case 2: Viacom
International*

References   426

Notes   426

Part IV

Managing the Development and Maintenance of Information Systems   429

12 ▪ System Analysis and Design: Methodologies and Implications   431

Learning Objectives   432
Introduction   434
System Development Life Cycle (SDLC)   436
System Definition   438
System Analysis   438
> *Understanding the Problem ▪ Feasibility Analysis ▪ Establishing Functional Requirements*

System Design and Programming   443
> *System Development*

System Testing and Implementation   445
System Maintenance   446
Limitations of the SDLC   447
Prototyping   448
End-User Development   451
Managing End-User Computing   453
Coordination   453
Support   453
Evaluation   453
Approaches to Managing End Users   454
> *Sink or Swim ▪ The Stick ▪ The Carrot ▪ Support*

Principles for Managing PCs   455
Principle 1: Managing the inventory of PC hardware and software is important   455
Principle 2: Plan, monitor control, and manage the costs of supporting PCs   456
Principle 3: Standardization is the key to effective PC management   457
Principle 4: Ensure that proper and effective performance measures are put in place to assess the productivity gains from PCs   457
Principle 5: Backup of PC files is critical and can affect the very life of an organization   458
Off-the-Shelf Software Packages   458
Advantages of Off-the-Shelf Software   459
Disadvantages of off-the-shelf software   459
Outsourcing   460
Strategic Focus   460
Economic Reasons   460
Market forces   460
Technical Considerations   461
Advantages and Disadvantages of Outsourcing   462
Comparison of Different Methodologies   464
Challenges in Developing Information Systems   465
IS Development in a Global Environment   467
Summary   469
Review Questions   470

Discussion Questions   470
Ethical Issues   471

Case 1: Blue Cross Fails to Take Care of Outsourced Employees ■
Case 2: Minolta Runs Into Outsourcing Snag ■   *Case 3: Trouble at the Office*
of Information Technology, California ■   *Case 4: Moral Minority*

Problem Solving in the Real World   473

Case 1: Doomsday Date ■   *Case 2: Nestle's Global Mix* ■   *Case 3: Crash at*
Denver International ■   *Case 4: Falconbridge Ltd. Soars to New Heights*

References   478
Notes   478

13 ■ Tools For Information Systems Development   481

Learning Objectives   482
Introduction   483
Decision-Making Framework for Selecting IS Tools   483
Envisioning Phase   484
Transition Phase   485
Structured Tools   485
Tools to Analyze and Design Systems   488

Context Diagrams ■   *Data Flow Diagrams*

Tools Represent System Data   492

Entity Relationship Diagram

Tools Represent Processes in the System   494

The Constructs of Structured Programming

Tools for Structured Programming   496

Structure Chart ■   *System Flowchart and Program Flowchart* ■
Decision Tables ■   *Decision Trees*

Tools to Convert Program Specifications into Code   501

Structured English (Pseudocode)

Computer-Aided Systems/Software Engineering (CASE)   502
Advantages of CASE   505
Disadvantages of CASE   505
Summary   507
Review Questions   507
Discussion Questions   508
Ethical Issues   508

Case 1: Anderson in Trouble

Problem Solving in the Real World   509

Case 1: Amtrack Runs with CASE ■   *Case 2: Building Blocks for a New Age*

References   511
Notes   512

Part V

Strategic and Managerial Implications of Information Systems   513

14 ■ Strategic Information Systems   515

Learning Objectives   516
Introduction   517
What Is a Strategic Information System?   518
Examples of SIS   519
Characteristics of Strategic Information Systems   523
Telecommunications   524

Multiple Vendors   **525**
Interorganizational Systems   **526**
Strategic Information Systems (SISP)   527
Strategies for Developing an SIS   528
Is the Project Financially Feasible?   **529**
Is the Project Technically Feasible?   **530**
Steps to Ensure Success of Strategic Systems   **530**
Potential Barriers to Developing an SIS   532
Problem Definition   **532**
Implementation   **532**
Maintenance   **533**
A Classic Tale of a Strategic Information System: SABRE   533
Seek Leverage from Existing Systems   **534**
Use Existing Knowledge to Grasp Opportunities   **534**
Start Early   **535**
Delegate Authority   **535**
Summary   535
Review Questions   536
Discussion Questions   536
Ethical Issues   537

    Case 1: Credit Card Versus Debit Card   ■   *Case 2: Airlines Use Their Muscle*   ■
    Case 3: Patenting Innovation and Creativity

Problem Solving in the Real World   538

    Case 1: Strategic Information Systems Planning for a Hong Kong Hospital   ■
    Case 2: McKesson Water   ■   *Case 3: J. C. Penney*

References   542
Notes   542

15 ■ Managing Information Resources   544

Introduction   546
What is IRM?   546
Principles of Managing Information Resources   548

    Principle 1: The IS department should be managed like any
    other unit or division of business   ■   *Principle 2: The sole purpose of*
    information systems is to help the organization meet its goals and objectives   ■
    Principle 3: IRM is the responsibility of all managers, regardless of their
    discipline or function   ■   *Principle 4: The commitment of top management*
    is the key to realizing the full potential of information systems

Objectives of IRM   550
IRM Functions   552
Technology Management   **553**
Data Management   **554**
Distributed Management   **555**
Functional Management   **559**
Strategic Management   **559**
End User Management   **560**
Summary   561
Review Questions   562
Discussion Questions   562
Ethical Cases   563

    Case 1: Passing the Buck   ■   *Case 2: Fear the FBI*   ■   *Case 3: Inflation is not*
    Welcome

Problem-Solving in the Real World   564

Case 1: TIAA-CREF uses systems to delight customers ▪ *Case 2: Coopers embraces the age of technology*

References   567

Notes   567

16 ▪ Computer Security   568

Learning Objectives   569

Introduction   570

What Is Computer Security?   571

Why Are Computer Systems Vulnerable?   571

Intentional Breaches by Employees   571

Increased System Complexity   572

Choices of System Components   572

Network Vulnerabilities   572

Sophisticated Hackers   574

Complacent Management   574

Types of Computer Security Breaches   575

Accidental or Unintentional Errors   575

Intentional Errors   576

Cracking Passwords ▪ *Breaking into Computer Hardware* ▪ *Software Viruses* ▪ *Legal Implications of Spreading a Virus*

Natural Disasters   579

Security Controls   580

Application Controls   580

Input Controls ▪ *Process Controls* ▪ *Output Controls* ▪ *Storage Controls*

Development Controls   584

Documentation ▪ *Data Security and Reliability* ▪ *Authorization Requirements* ▪ *Separation of Duties*

Physical Facilities Control   586

Personnel Controls   586

Train System Users ▪ *Establish and Communicate Security Policies and Procedures*

Disaster Recovery Plan   587

Developing a Disaster Recovery Plan   587

Summary   592

Review Questions   593

Discussion Questions   593

Ethical Issues   594

Case 1: Monitoring Employees ▪ *Case 2: Worker Privacy*

Problem-Solving in the Real World   596

Case 1: Is it an angel or SATAN in Disguise? ▪ *Case 2: The Clipper Chip* ▪ *Case 3: The Jury Is Out on Clipper*

References   597

Notes   598

Appendix A ▪ Business Ethics   601

Glossary   613

Index   629

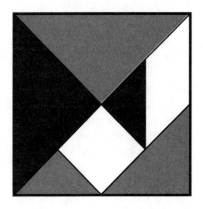

Preface

"T he Future Belongs to Those Who Can Create Real Change," says a recruiting ad run by consultants Deloitte & Touche in the *New York Times.* Students who can become "change agents" will be the IT equivalent of the star quarterback.[1] Robert Sullivan, dean of the business school at Carnegie Mellon University in Pittsburgh, emphasizes that all students should develop a critical perspective and understanding about the potential and challenges of information systems and technologies so that they can "understand, anticipate, push, and lead IT strategy in the 21st century."[2] In order to supply businesses with students who will meet the above challenges and play a dynamic role in shaping corporate America, many business schools are revamping their curriculum and, in almost all cases, the revised curriculum places an increased emphasis on information systems and technologies and the globalization of business markets. Although there is some debate about the ideal balance between technology and management in the university curriculum, most faculty agree that information is a key currency in facilitating organizational change.

It is probably difficult to identify an academic discipline that is more intensely dynamic, fast-paced, profound, and revolutionary than computers and information systems. The sphere of influence of information systems and technologies is vast and ever expanding, as it effortlessly eliminates the barriers of time and space and has a far-reaching impact on the way we receive, process, and share knowledge and information. The days when a few experts sat in a cool room with blinking lights on mammoth machines is long gone. Today, the ability to handle all aspects of information and computer technology is nearly equated with the three basic skills of reading, writing, and arithmetic.

The purpose of *Management Information Systems: A Managerial Perspective* is to present an up-to-date, multifaceted, and exciting view of the world of information systems in the "new curriculum." This book accentuates the relevance and contribution of information systems not only to the growth and success of a business, but also to our personal lives. Given that the home computer market is one of the fastest-growing segments of the computer industry, the notion that computers and information systems are only for "techies" is archaic. Wherever possible, the book presents real-world examples that highlight the influence of computers and information systems on our personal lives, thereby encouraging the student to see the usefulness and the pervasive nature of this technology.

This book presents an exciting view of the field of information systems by blending technical concepts with contemporary and practical issues associated

[1]Winkler, Connie, "Putting B-Schools to the Test," *InformationWeek,* August 8, 1994, pp. 26–34.
[2]Ibid.

with the management of computer technologies. Rather than discussing technology for the sake of technology, the book integrates technical discussions with managerial concepts and real-world examples and presents the student with a lively and exciting view of the field. The text is highly readable and is replete with examples, both domestic and global, that show how information systems have helped organizations achieve their organizational goals. Examples cover a wide range of industries including agriculture, health care, education, retailing, law enforcement, publishing, banking, government, and entertainment. Global regions examined include China, Canada, Hong Kong, Mexico, South Africa, Singapore, Switzerland, France, Italy, India, and Israel, to name a few. Such a broad and global view of information systems and technologies is designed to help the student realize that computers and information systems are tools that, like any other tool, can be applied with creativity and talent to *any* field of study, be it art, science, engineering, business, law, or medicine. The global examples illustrate that the application of information systems to solve complex problems has universal appeal. As globalization becomes the norm, students are being challenged in schools around the country to become more aware of business practices in foreign countries; this book addresses this issue from a technological perspective.

While many of the examples stress the power and potential of information systems, the book also provides some examples of how poorly designed information systems can cause more problems than they solve. Several discussions throughout the book allude to the difficulty in designing and developing truly integrated, seamless, customer-focused systems with the intent of helping the student realize that successful information systems take time, money, outstanding technical people, good management, and long-term commitment to design and develop.

Another unique feature of this book are the ethical issues at the end of each chapter which often provide for fascinating class discussion. Every ethical issue case in the book is a "real world" case; many cases discussed in the book are pending in U.S. courts of law. The questions at the end of each ethical case are open-ended, thus allowing the instructor to introduce important ethical concepts as part of class discussion. Appendix A provides an ethical framework and theoretical basis for these discussions.

Finally, the book is written so that the instructor has the freedom and the choice to select the material that he or she would like to cover in class. The pedagogy facilitates dividing class time between discussions.

A Central Theme

The central theme of this book revolves around four key ideas:
1. IS and IT are critical resources that can have a strategic impact on an organization.
2. IS and IT should enable change and enhance business processes.
3. The globalization of corporate America creates new challenges for end users and knowledge workers.
4. Ethics should be an integral part of the University curriculum.

Strategic impact of IS and IT   Information systems have evolved from being support systems to being strategic systems. The innovative use of technology has helped companies achieve a leadership position in their industry by generating new products and services or by enhancing existing products and services. On the other hand, companies that continue to treat information systems as a backroom function have languished and, in some cases, become bankrupt as they failed to understand and capitalize on the importance of IS and IT.

Examples include Blockbuster's national inventory management system that is often cited as a key element in the company's continued success and Reader's Digests customer database that makes the company one of the most successful retail marketers. These and other examples are used throughout the book to emphasize that regardless of the discipline or functional area that a student may pursue, information will be the common thread that links units inside and outside the organization.

IS as a change agent and enabler of business processes   The new currency that drives organizations is information. On that account, students must be taught how to use information to introduce change in the organization, to improve and enhance existing business processes, and to introduce new processes that will help the organization achieve its goals. This theme emphasizes the importance of aligning business needs with technology goals, since companies that put technology before business needs are often doomed to fail from the start. For example, the book explains how the financial giant Fannie Mae uses Electronic Data Interchange to re-engineer its operations, how Campbell Soup has developed an automated sales and marketing system that allows it to be highly responsive to customers needs, and how the UCLA Medical School uses client server technologies to facilitate decision-making in a university environment.

Globalization of corporate America and its significance for end users Universities around the country are placing increasing emphasis on international education and global awareness. Information systems and technologies play a key and vital role both in the content and the delivery of such a curriculum. The global examples in this book give the student an understanding of information systems. More importantly, creative and ambitious thinking, coupled with leading-edge technologies, has sometimes led to effective solutions to complex human problems. For example, the United Nations has used IS to bring together families torn apart by the ravages of war. Computer technologies played a key role in the first historic democratic elections held in South Africa.

Ethical Dilemmas

In recent years the IS profession has had to come to grips with a growing number of business scandals and moral issues. Today many computer-related court cases are breaking new ground, primarily because society has never had to deal with these questions before. Besides integrating ethical considerations throughout the chapter, where appropriate, we present a number of real-world ethical issues and dilemmas at the end of each chapter. Quite frequently, there are no right or wrong answers to these issues, and the primary purpose of this exercise is to help the student come to grips with some sensitive issues in the business environment.

Organization of the Book

This book is divided into five main parts:

Part I: Managerial Overview of Information Systems

Part II: Technical Foundations of Information Systems

Part III: Business Applications of Information Systems

Part IV: Managing the Development and Maintenance of Information Systems

Part V: Strategic and Managerial Implications of Information Systems

Part I of the book has two chapters. The first chapter, *Introduction to Information Systems,* provides a broad overview of IS and introduces the student to general systems theory. The framework for discussing ethical cases and issues is also presented in this chapter and further elaborated on in Appendix A. Chapter 2, *Information Systems for Managerial Decision-Making,* introduces the student to different types of information systems such as TPS, MIS, DSS, EIS, ES, and Office Systems. The chapter highlights the importance of "information stewardship" versus "information ownership" as the key to tapping into the full potential of IS.

Part II, *Technical Foundations of Information Systems,* lays the technical foundation for the material covered in this book and is made up of five chapters. Chapters 3 and 4 cover computer hardware and software. Since many students may be considering buying a PC, Chapter 3, *Computer Hardware,* provides a detailed discussion of several factors that students should consider before buying a PC. Chapter 4, *Computer Software,* not only covers the major categories of software but also identifies different financial and nonfinancial criteria that companies should take into account before investing in computer hardware and software.

Chapter 5, *Telecommunications,* is divided into two parts. The first part lays the technical foundation and gives extensive coverage to technical terms and concepts. The second part of this chapter gives a flavor of the managerial challenges that network administrators face and expounds on the complexity of developing global telecommunication systems. This chapter also gives extensive coverage to the Internet and its implications for business. The World Wide Web, Telnet, FTP, Gopher, Archie and web browsers are a few of the topics covered in this section. Many hands-on examples about the Internet are provided at the end of this chapter.

Chapter 6, *Databases,* covers some of the traditional topics in databases. Many examples highlight how critical databases are to the success of an organization and, in some cases, can even solve some nagging societal problems. For example, the state of Massachusetts uses databases to target dead-beat parents, while food banks around the country rely on databases to match volunteers with the needs of their organization.

Chapter 7, *Client Server Computing,* provides coverage of one of the hottest topics in the IS community today. As organizations engage in downsizing and end users demand more from their systems, client-server computing is likely to become the norm for the way business is done. This chapter is groundbreaking and hence is likely to evolve in future editions.

Part III, *Business Applications of Information Systems,* has four chapters. Chapter 8, *Decision Support Systems and Executive Information Systems,* provides a broad overview of these two technologies while Chapter 9, *Artificial Intelligence,*

Expert Systems, and Neural Networks, lays the foundation for intelligent support systems. Chapter 10, *Office Automation Systems,* begins with a discussion of virtual corporations and emphasizes the growing importance of oral and written communication tools for employee productivity. A detailed discussion of groupware, Lotus Notes in particular, is also provided. Finally, Chapter 11, *Business Information Systems,* emphasizes the importance of building integrated, cross-functional systems. Although the chapter provides a description of information systems in each functional area, the importance of building cross-functional systems is emphasized and suitable examples are provided.

Part IV, *Managing the Development and Maintenance of Information Systems,* consists of two chapters, both of which relate to designing and developing information systems. Chapter 12, *System Analysis and Design: Methodologies and Implications,* discusses five different development methodologies: SDLC, prototyping, off-the-shelf software, end-user computing and outsourcing. Extensive discussion of the pros and cons of outsourcing is also provided. IS development in a global environment is discussed and some examples of developing global information systems are provided. The problems associated with application backlogs and runaway systems are outlined and some recommendations are provided. Chapter 13, *Tools for Information Systems Development,* identifies different tools and techniques, both traditional and modern, used to develop information systems. Computer Aided Software Engineering (CASE) is giving extensive coverage in this chapter.

Finally, Part V of the book, *Strategic and Managerial Implications of Information Systems,* is made up of three chapters. Chapter 14, *Strategic Information Systems,* describes different types of strategic information systems. The ability to use existing systems and technologies in new and innovative ways has often been at the heart of some of the most successful strategic systems; this theme is emphasized throughout this chapter. Chapter 15, *Information Resources Management,* emphasizes the importance of managing and protecting information like any other resource in the company, such as manpower, machines, materials, and money. The chapter provides examples to show how IRM can help an organization achieve its goals and identifies several functions and principles for managing information resources. Finally, Chapter 16, *Computer Security,* covers the issues related to computer security and its importance to the survival of a business. Some of the weak links in information systems are identified and classified into different types of security breaches. Security controls and the importance of taking measures to prevent virus infection are also discussed.

There are a number of interesting and distinctive features in this book. Each chapter begins with an opening vignette that describes an organization or business entity that uses the technology or key concepts covered in the chapter, thus helping the student focus on the integral elements covered in the chapter. For example, Chapter 5 opens with a discussion of how New York public schools are using telecommunications to link their students with experts around the world. Chapter 9 shows how air traffic controllers for the Federal Aviation Administration rely on expert systems to help them be better prepared for contingencies and natural disasters.

Each chapter begins with a clear set of learning objectives that will help students to identify the key concepts covered in the chapter. The learning objectives also help faculty to determine what aspects of the chapter they would like to emphasize. The summary at the end of each chapter is designed around these learning objectives.

There are two types of examples in each chapter: **Business Realities** and **Global Perspectives.** Business realities focus on U.S. companies and demonstrate the applications of concepts or technologies covered in the chapter. Global Perspectives, on the other hand, focus on international companies and highlight some of their unique problems and characteristics.

The book makes extensive use of graphics, figures, and photo exhibits to convey the concepts covered in the chapter. The figures are sometimes designed to present the material, while at other times they help to summarize some of the key concepts covered in a given section. Review questions are very thorough and designed with the intention of helping the student study for the exam and understand the material covered in the chapter. Therefore, the number of review questions in some chapters, such as telecommunications, is higher than average. The discussion questions are designed with the intent of giving the student a more in-depth understanding of the concepts and in some cases, involve establishing contact with local companies and IS managers. Such questions give the student a better understanding of how information systems influence business processes.

Ethical Issues at the end of each chapter gives students an opportunity to think about how they would act in a variety of business situations and also to take into account some of the ramifications on business, its employees, and society at large when ethical principles are compromised.

Finally, **Problem Solving Cases** at the end of each chapter are cases that are longer than **Business Realities** and designed to help the student gain a better understanding of the concepts covered in the chapter. Some of these cases are global cases, thus promoting a better understanding of international information systems.

Key terms are margin definitions that run throughout the text. The margin term helps to draw the attention of the students to key terms that they should become familiar with. Finally, a glossary is provided at the end of the book to serve as a reference.

Three outstanding videos also accompany the book. The first includes profiles on the following companies: *First Bank System Information Systems, Boeing Computer Services Overview,* and *American Greeting: Information Processing Control Center.* The second video includes segments on thirteen Blue Chip programs. Companies profiled include *Alliance Rubber Company, Kenda Systems, Triad Protective Services,* and *Video Lottery Consultants.* The third video introduces students to the functions of the Internet, the resources found on the internet, and how the Internet is being used today.

Supplementary Material

The Test Bank consists of true/false and multiple-choice questions. Each chapter has a large number of questions, with approximately 50 to 75 true/false questions and 30 to 75 multiple-choice questions. Such a wide range of questions gives the instructor the ability to tailor the exam to meet the unique needs of his or her class.

The Instructor's Manual provides answers to all the review questions, discussion questions, ethical cases and problem-solving cases listed at the end of each chapter. I strongly believe that the Instructor's Manual should *not* be a simplistic extension of the textbook. Instead, the Instructor's Manual should enhance the role of the instructor in the classroom. The Instructor's Manual has real-world examples in addition to the ones that are already given in the book, thus allowing the instructor to take additional examples to class without expending too much time and effort.

Appreciation

I would like to acknowledge the meticulous reviews of the following reviewers for this book: Douglas Boch, Southern Illinois University; William Bullers, University of New Mexico; Chandler Bush, University of North Carolina; Chou Hong Chen, Gonzaga University; Gary Clark, Sinclair Community College; Eli Cohen, Eastern New Mexico University; Allen Corbett, University of South Carolina; Mohammad Dadashzadeh, Wichita State University; Barbara Denison, Wright State University; George Easton, San Diego State University; Eugenia Fernandez, Butler University; Dale Gust, Central Michigan University; Charles Hardwick, University of Houston-Clearlake; Tom Hilton, Utah State University; Jack Hogue, University of North Carolina-Charlotte; Bharat Jain, Towson State University; John Johnson, University of Mississippi; Peter Kirs, Florida International University; Albert L. Lederer, University of Kentucky; Helen Ligon, Baylor University; Pat Llosan, John Carroll University; Jane Mackay, Texas Christian University; Sathi Makesh, University of New Orleans-Lakefront; Mary Meredith, University of Southwest Louisiana; Rodney Pearson, Mississippi State University; Floyd Ploeger, Southwest Texas State University; Laurie Rattner, University of New Mexico; John Schillak, University of Wisconsin-Eau Claire; C.A.P. Smith, University of Montana; Raphael Solis, California State University-Fresno; Jack Thornton, East Carolina University; Bindisanavale Vijayraman, University of Akron; William Wagner, Villanova University; Diane Walz, University of Texas-San Antonio; Michael Wolfe, West Virginia University.

Acknowledgments

A book of this nature is often the product of the time, effort, and dedication of a large number of people, many of whom always remain in the background. I would like to begin by thanking the tireless efforts of many people at West Educational Publishing. This book would have never seen the day of light without the sustained efforts of Rick Leyh, my editor. Through the many ups and downs that I went through as I wrote this book, he stood behind me and my efforts like a solid rock. His unwavering trust and faith in my abilities to successfully complete this project served as a quiet, yet consistent, motivator throughout this process. I realized as I wrote this book that his reputation in the industry as a giant of a man is so well earned and well deserved. Thank you, Rick.

Alex Von Rosenberg, Editor, began the development work for this project and was always there to help. His unperturbed attitude even in the face of sliding downhill helped to put things in perspective. Sara Schroeder, my developmental editor, was paramount to the success of this book. Her superior organizational skills, great attitude, and willingness to go the extra mile was instrumental in keeping the book on track. She never compromised on quality and her sense of commitment to her work was inspiring. May all authors be blessed with such developmental editors!

Brenda Owens, my production editor, was a godsend. First, she managed the copy editing process and kept the lines of communication open between the copy editors and me. When things got rough, Brenda's superb negotiating skills helped all parties to put things in perspective and continue with the task at hand. She had the ability to coax and cajole, push and plead, all at the same time! Her commitment to quality can be seen from cover to cover of this book. She was delightful to work with and always had my interests at heart. I owe a great deal to Brenda for her fine contributions.

Finally, many students worked on this project as part of their assistantships or work-study programs. James Baran (who also co-authored the Test Bank with me) worked meticulously in designing and creating the wonderful figures and graphics in this book. The transparency masters and the PowerPoint presentation are also his work. While getting an MBA he volunteered to work on this book and his contribution has been immense and noteworthy. He had many opportunities to "slip away" but he stuck with it and gave it his all. Tracy Tyson, my work-study student of several years, organized and managed many different aspects of this book. Her superb organizational skills and people skills played a key role in completing the project on time. She never let anything slip by that did not match her high standards of quality and workmanship. I cannot imagine doing another book without James Baran or Tracy Tyson!

Nora Tucker, my departmental secretary, acted as the manager for the many different elements that must come together to make a book of this magnitude a success. She single-handedly managed the copyright process for the numerous examples and cases used in this book. She supervised the preliminary production of the Test Bank and played an instrumental role in putting together the Test Bank. She never let anything slip through the cracks and often was there to point out any errors or omissions on my part, thereby improving the quality of the book. I can honestly say that I could not have successfully completed this book without Nora Tucker.

I would also like to thank my students who were willing to experiment with the first draft of this book. Their frank comments and enthusiasm for the book inspired me to complete this project.

Finally, I would like to thank my family, friends, and colleagues for their unwavering faith and their immense support through the years that it has taken to complete this project. In particular, I would like to acknowledge my daughter, Priyanka, who has been a source of inspiration to me. Her great love of learning and her eagerness to explore the world around her provide lessons for all of us entering the world of information systems and technologies.

Uma G. Gupta

Managerial Overview of Information Systems

Chapter 1
Introduction to Information Systems

Chapter 2
Information Systems for Managerial Decision Making

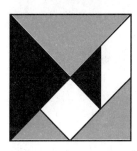

Introduction
to
Information
Systems

Contents

Learning Objectives
Technology Payoff: A Corn-Seed Company Goes High-Tech
Introduction
Information Systems Versus Information Technology
Computer Literacy Versus Information Literacy
Data Versus Information
    Data
    Information
    Characteristics of Information
    The Process of Converting Data into Information
Why Students Should Study MIS
Why Organizations Need Information Systems
    Meeting Global Challenges
    Capturing Opportunities in the Marketplace
    Supporting Corporate Strategy
    Linking Departments Whose Functions Are Different
    Enhancing Worker Productivity
    Increasing the Quality of Goods and Services
Information Systems and Organizational Structures
    The Pyramid Structure
    The Task-Based Structure
Contributions of Information Systems to Individual, Work-Group, and
    Organization-Wide Decision Making
Potential Risks of Information Systems
    "Deskilling" of Workers
    Information Overload

Employee Mistrust
Increased Competitive Pressure
Disenchantment with IS
Challenges in Developing Information Systems
Security Breaches
General Systems Theory
System Components
Ethics and Information Systems: A Framework
A Framework for Studying MIS
Summary
Review Questions
Discussion Questions
Ethical Issues
Case 1: David versus Goliath
Case 2: Oracle Slapped with Lawsuit
Problem Solving in the Real World
The IRS at Work: "You Know Who You Are, and So Do We."
References
Notes

Learning Objectives

Information has become the lifeline of many companies all over the world. Without timely and accurate information, many businesses would come to a screeching halt, because information is one of the key factors in good decision making. Since we live in an information-driven society, all students, regardless of their major, must have a good understanding of information systems and their potential impact on our personal and professional lives.

In this chapter, we provide a broad overview of information systems and the vital role they play in shaping corporate America. The difference between information systems and information technologies is outlined; some key terms that lay the foundation for later chapters are defined. The importance of systems theory to the study of information systems is emphasized.

After reading and studying this chapter, you should be able to

- Understand the significance of management information systems to organizational decision making
- Distinguish between information systems and information technologies
- Know the difference between data and information
- Distinguish between computer literacy and information literacy and understand the importance of both to organizations
- Understand systems theory and its relevance to the study of information systems

TECHNOLOGY PAYOFF

A Corn-Seed Company Goes High-Tech

Most people would be surprised to find that a farm-seed company is a leader in information technology. They shouldn't be, according to Tom Urban, chairman, president and CEO of corn-seed producer Pioneer Hi-Bred International. Sitting in an office the size and color scheme of a corn patch, Urban patiently but pointedly notes that the farm industry has a long tradition of embracing technology. "Agriculture has achieved 35 to 40 percent annual gains in productivity at times," he says, "Manufacturing pales in comparison."

Many large airlines and banks also pale in comparison to Pioneer when it comes to information systems. Pioneer's systems have given the company a formidable edge in R & D, operations and marketing—an edge that the company has parlayed into dominance of the corn-seed business.

Among those who find Pioneer's technology-driven performance stunning is Harvard Business School professor Warren McFarlan, an expert in the application of information technology for competitive advantage. McFarlan was so impressed when he visited Pioneer six years ago that he joined the board of directors. "Everyone thinks that the corn-seed business means wallowing in the mud," he says. "But Pioneer is absolutely the most high-tech company I'm associated with. In many ways it's similar to an aerospace company."

Corn-seed breeding isn't rocket science—it's harder. At its core is the dauntingly complex world of plant genetics. From its founding in 1926, the Des Moines company has pioneered the production of hybrid corn, which is obtained by mixing and matching different strains of ordinary varietal corn, each of which has been inbred or fertilized with its own pollen for several generations until its genetic characteristics are well established. When two different inbred lines are cross-fertilized, the result is a hybrid corn that is often exceptionally sturdy and imbued with the best characteristics of each parent.

The challenge in hybrid corn breeding is to discover which pairs of inbred corn lines produce the best offspring. Pioneer's corn breeders can choose from tens of thousands of inbred lines which can be paired in billions of different combinations. The only way to determine which pairs will produce winning hybrid strains is to cross-breed as many as possible and observe the offspring carefully for desirable traits. Thus, large-scale experimental breeding is the game in the hybrid-seed business. And no one breeds on a larger scale than Pioneer, which creates some 70,000 experimental hybrids each year at 90 testing stations scattered around the world.

But Pioneer's real challenge is not so much to produce all of these experimental hybrids as it is to sort through them and decide which 12 or so of the 70,000 will end up winners. To make this determination, Pioneer has turned to an array of information systems which comprise about a third of the company's information technology budget—to oversee the complex process of bringing the hybrids from the experimental stage to the market. The process starts when testing station researchers examine the growing new plants and enter data on 20 different characteristics including size, moisture content, durability, and insect and disease resistance—into book-sized, hand-held computers made by Norand. The data are transferred via modem to a large DEC system computer at headquarters. The Comprehensive Research Information System (CRIS) compiles data from the testing stations and makes them available to all researchers through their local computers.

Researchers from around the world then debate via E-mail which approximately 5,000 hybrids should be advanced to the company's greenhouses and then which 25 of these foundation hybrids should be sent to growers to plant in more than half a million, on-farm test plots around the world. The time advantage is crucial. Farmers base their corn-seed buying decisions largely on which seed yields the most bushels per acre. Pioneer seed currently holds a seven-bushel-per-acre, or five percent edge over its competition—up from 2.2 bushels in 1982. Pioneer owes much of that edge to the time savings that CRIS has helped bring about. The company now brings the hybrid seed from initial test to market in six years instead of 12, while its competitors are only down to eight years. Better seed inventory and process management have saved the company $4 million per year, while a software program that tracks 60,000 contract workers will save the company between $2 million and $3 million per year.[1]

Information technology (IT) is not just the sum of its inscrutable jargon; it is an aggregate business tool about which business people had better know at least a digestible minimum.

—Peter Keen

Introduction

Management information systems are a broad class of systems that provide decision makers with the information necessary to make effective decisions in a world that has almost overnight become an "electronic showroom." Such systems are competitive tools that allow organizations to create new, innovative products and services quickly, efficiently, and effectively. As our opening example shows, computers and information systems are playing a vital role in the growth of Pioneer Hi-Bred into one of the most successful agricultural companies in the world. They are helping the company in many ways, such as reducing the time it takes to bring goods to market and improving inventory management. Throughout this book, you will encounter many other examples that illustrate how information systems and technologies are changing the world around us. Information systems and their growing influence on all aspects of business are the subject matter of courses on management information systems.

The field of **management information systems** (MIS) is the study of information and its impact on the individual, the organization, and society. Quite often, when we think about information systems we think of computers. Although computers are at the heart of today's information systems, a number of important social, organizational, behavioral, and ethical issues also surround the study of information systems. An appropriate analogy is the field of medicine. Medicine and its branches revolve around the human body and its various parts and functions. Similarly, today's information systems revolve around a business and its various components, such as people, products, and procedures. MIS is an interdisciplinary field; many other fields of study influence it, as shown in Figure 1–1. Areas that continue to influence the field of MIS include

Management information systems
The study of information and its impact on the individual, the organization, and society. Also, systems that create, process, store, and retrieve information.

- *Computer science:* theories and methods of computation, efficient data storage and access, and their impact on information
- *Political science:* the political impact and uses of information, both within and outside the organization
- *Psychology:* cognitive models of human reasoning and behavior as they relate to information
- *Operations research:* scientific models that enhance decision making and make use of information to solve complex problems
- *Linguistics:* languages and human communications and their influence on the creation and use of information

FIGURE 1-1

The field of MIS has been shaped and influenced by a number of other fields. Some of these fields are identified here.

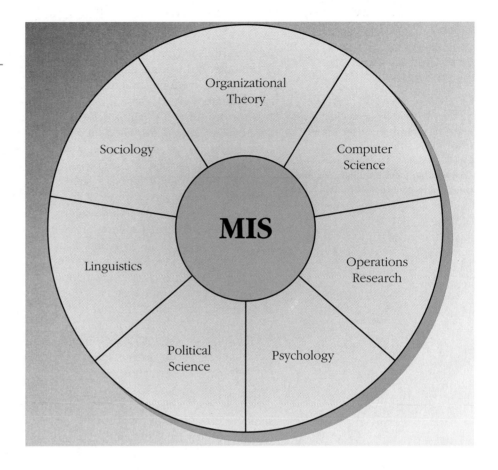

Formal system

A system that is designed and developed using well-established guidelines and principles. It helps to coordinate and to establish communications among different functional units and meet the overall information needs of a business

* *Sociology:* principles governing society as it relates to shaping information policies and principles
* *Organization theory and behavior:* the nature and characteristics of organizations and their effect on the way human beings use information to make decisions

MIS is a system that creates, processes, stores, and generates information within and outside an organization. A system is a collection of parts that work together to achieve a common goal. Later in this chapter, we provide a more detailed description of systems and their characteristics. The primary goal of MIS is to support organizational decision making, though it has many other uses, such as designing and developing new products, ensuring the quality of goods and services, preventing theft and pilferage, and so on. We provide examples of different uses of MIS throughout this book.

Information systems can be formal or informal. **Formal systems** are designed and developed using a set of well-established organizational policies, procedures, and principles to coordinate and facilitate communication between different functional units and the processes they support, and to meet the overall information needs of the business. The social, economic, and regulatory environment of a business fosters the development of formal systems. These systems can be manual or automated. In a manual system, information is collected, processed, stored, and disseminated by manual methods, such as keeping records with paper and pencil. A ledger book is a good example of a manual information system. In a computerized system, similar tasks are performed with the help of computers. In this book, we focus on the study of computerized formal information systems.

Informal systems, on the other hand, do not follow any formal or preestablished rules for collecting, processing, storing, or disseminating data. Employees create informal systems when they need information that is not readily available through formal systems. Informal systems are powerful; they thrive in many organizations and can play a useful role as long as they are not the results of dissatisfaction with existing formal systems, in which case they become divisive and unproductive. A good example of an informal information system is office gossip, in which people try to acquire information through conversations with others. Recognize that informal systems are neither worse nor better than formal systems; they simply meet a different kind of need.

Table 1–1 presents the two common meanings of the term *MIS*.

The rest of this chapter covers a number of concepts. In the next three sections, we compare and contrast some terms that are commonly used in the study of information systems. They are

- Information systems (IS) versus information technologies (IT)
- Computer literacy versus information literacy
- Data versus information

Next, we explain why it is important for students to have a good understanding of MIS and how such an understanding is related to job opportunities and career growth. We then discuss why organizations need information systems to survive in today's competitive market and outline the role of computers in organizational decision making. We also discuss the impact of information systems on the structure of an organization and explore the role and contribution of information systems in facilitating individual, work-group, and enterprise-wide decision making. Some potential risks and pitfalls associated with computers are also outlined. The chapter concludes with a discussion of general systems theory.

Information Systems Versus Information Technology

We have defined an information system (IS) as a broad, generic class of systems that create, process, store, and disseminate information. Formal **information systems (IS)** facilitate organizational decision making. They are guided by sets of policies, principles, procedures, and resources. Various social, technical, and environmental factors influence the design and development of such systems.

Information technologies (IT), on the other hand, are tools and techniques that support the design and development of information systems. They include hardware, software, databases, telecommunications, and client-servers. Companies that can integrate various technologies to achieve business goals are often very successful. For example, American Greetings Corporation is a company that successfully uses technologies to capture new markets. This $1.7 billion Cleveland-based company launched a line of "electronic cards" that allows cus-

---

Informal systems
Systems created by ad hoc, informal work groups to support information needs that cannot be met by formal systems. These are powerful systems that meet unique needs and thrive in many organizations.

Information system
A system that creates, processes, stores, and retrieves information. The input to such a system is data; processed data becomes information.

Information technologies
Tools and techniques that support the design and development of information systems; these include hardware, software, databases, telecommunications, and client-servers.

TABLE 1–1
The two contexts in which the term MIS is used

MIS as a *field* of study	MIS is an interdisciplinary field that is influenced by computer science, political science, psychology, operations research, linguistics, sociology, and organizational theory.
MIS as an information *system*	MIS is a broad class of systems that provides information to facilitate organizational decision making.

tomers to create and send greeting cards from their computers. The company's goal is to build a $500-million electronic-card business through innovative uses of computer technologies. The ability to use technologies effectively is a key factor in business success today.[2]

Information systems and information technologies go hand in hand. Unfortunately, some organizations equate buying the latest technology with using technology effectively. However, technologies by themselves are just that: technologies. In and of themselves, they do nothing for the organization. It is only when technology is integrated with business goals and objectives that its full potential can be achieved. Figure 1–2 illustrates the point that technology requirements and decisions should be based on business needs and constraints. This kind of decision making requires several skills, such as the following:

- Vision, foresight, and an innovative approach to the firm and to the industry in which it operates.
- Willingness to take meaningful risks while acquiring new technology

FIGURE 1-2

Business needs and opportunities should drive technology decisions and not the other way around. Technology decisions should also be shaped by technology requirements, business constraints, and technology trends.

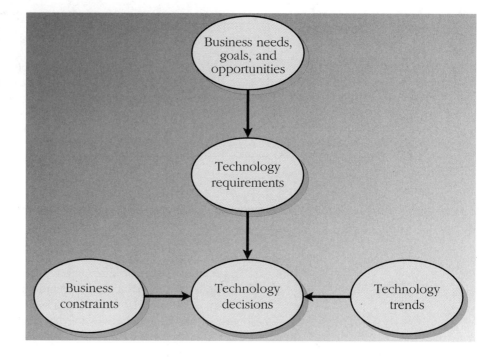

♦ Discipline in putting the needs of the business before the power of technology
♦ The ability to align business goals with what the technology can do
♦ Willingness to put the customer at the center of all technological acquisitions and developments

Computer Literacy Versus Information Literacy

Manufacturing and service organizations depend on information to keep business running smoothly. What kinds of skills and knowledge do people need in this information-intensive setting? They need two kinds of knowledge: computer literacy and information literacy. Let us take a closer look at these two kinds of literacy.

Computer literacy
Working knowledge of computers, their components, and their functions.

Computer literacy is knowledge of how a computer and its components work. A computer is a tool designed to mimic and complement the intellectual abilities of a human being while overcoming some of the inherent limitations of the human brain. The components and functions of a computer are discussed in Chapter 3.

Information literacy
The ability to create and use information systems to achieve a competitive advantage. It includes computer literacy, business acumen, and problem-solving skills.

Information literacy, on the other hand, is the ability to use information to one's advantage. Information literacy *includes* computer literacy, along with problem-solving skills and business acumen. For example, a jeans manufacturer, Marithe and Francois Girbaud, located in Greensboro, North Carolina, uses information systems to efficiently generate designs for its jeans. The company uses a software called Computer Aided Design that allows designers to design and modify jeans quickly and efficiently and thereby create products that closely match the needs of its customers. The PC-based system allows the company to electronically transmit computer generated images and designs of its jeans from its office to retailers and other customers around the country. Before the software was installed, if any change had to be made to a design, the designer had to go back

TABLE 1–2
Difference between computer literacy and information literacy

Computer literacy	Knowledge of computers, their components, and their functions.
Information literacy	Information literacy has four characteristics: business acumen, understanding the organizational mission, knowledge of information technologies and problem-solving skills. Refers to the ability to use information to achieve organizational goals.

to the drawing board and redo the design entirely. Today the company can hold telephone discussions with buyers about the quality and preference of designs and if the customer wants to modify a design, it can be done with a few simple keystrokes. Information literacy has helped the company to increase its productivity, reduce operating costs, and foster better customer relations.

In summary, computer literacy is knowledge of how computers function, whereas information literacy is the ability to use computers in innovative and meaningful ways to solve business problems. Table 1–2 summarizes the differences between computer literacy and information literacy; Figure 1–3 shows that

FIGURE 1–3

Computer literacy is a working knowledge of computers and computer programs. Information literacy is the ability to use information systems to find solutions to business problems. As this figure shows, computer literacy is only a small part of information literacy.

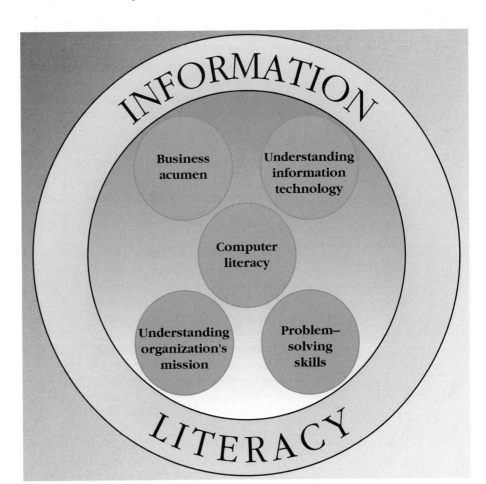

computer literacy, business acumen, and problem-solving skills are all essential to information literacy.

Data Versus Information

Data

Data
The raw material from which information is generated. Data appear in the form of text, numbers, figures, or any combination of these.

People sometimes use the terms *data* and *information* interchangeably, but data and information are different. **Data** can be text, numbers, audio, video, images, or any combination of these. There are many ways to collect data, including surveys, interviews, the use of sensors, the reading of documents, and even the monitoring of brain waves. Sophisticated voice-activated technology is already available that allows people to store data by simply speaking into a computer. In its raw form, data may or may not be useful to the decision maker; quite frequently, data must be processed to become useful.

Information

Information
Data processed and converted into a form that is useful to the decision maker. Facts, principles, knowledge, experience, and intuition are applied to convert data into information.

When we process data and convert it into a form that is useful and meaningful to the decision maker, it becomes **information.** Human beings apply facts, principles, knowledge, experience, and intuition to convert data into information. Only then does it become useful for making decisions. Note, however, that it is difficult to place a dollar value on information. Also, information is time-dependent, since its value and usefulness often decrease with time.

Let us look at an example of data versus information. Efforts are under way to create a national information system that would allow employers to determine whether a job applicant is qualified to work in the United States, simply by keying the applicant's social security number into a computer system. The system compares the social security number with other relevant data, such as the candidate's immigration status and work permit.[4] Here, data (social security number) is converted into information (work eligibility) that an employer can use to make hiring decisions.

Characteristics of Information

All good information has the characteristics discussed below.

Subjectivity   The value and usefulness of information are highly subjective, because what is information for one person may not be for another. For example, even small changes in the price of a stock can be meaningful to a stockbroker, because these changes may influence buying and selling decisions. However, to a layperson, a stock price may be just a number, with little or no meaning.

Relevance   Information is good only if it is relevant—that is, pertinent and meaningful to the decision maker. For example, suppose a plant manger is trying to determine why a certain machine breaks down frequently. For that plant manager, the number of units that the machine has produced in the last 5 years is probably not relevant to the problem at hand.

Timeliness   Information must be delivered at the right time and the right place to the right person. In the above example, if the manager gets information about the causes of machine failure a year after requesting it, the information is not timely and hence is probably not useful. Many organizations produce large volumes of reports without regard to *when* the information is needed; this greatly diminishes the value of their reports.

Accuracy   Information must be free of errors, because erroneous information can result in poor decisions and erode the confidence of users. Note, however, that accuracy is a relative concept; its meaning varies from context to context. For example, great precision is not required in predicting the number of customers at a restaurant, but is critical for a space mission.

Correct Information Format   Information must be in the right format to be useful to the decision maker. For example, if a manager wants to know the total sales of Product X last year, the most appropriate format is an annual summary of sales figures for that product. The format should be such that it can be applied directly to the problem at hand without further processing.

Completeness   Information is said to be complete if the decision maker can satisfactorily solve the problem at hand using that information. Although completeness of information is highly desirable, often complete information is not available. Managers are compelled to make decisions even when their information is incomplete; this is particularly true for problems that require intuition and judgment. However, if most, though not all, of the essential information necessary to make a decision is available, the decision maker may view the information as essentially complete.

Accessibility   Information is useless if it is not readily accessible to decision makers, in the desired format, when it is needed. Advances in technology have made information more accessible today than ever before; however, there is also a downside to this development. Sometimes managers feel overwhelmed by the large volumes of information that are readily available to them. Also, if information is easily accessible, it may fall into the wrong hands; this can seriously jeopardize the company. Hence there should be a balance between accessibility and security of information. In the chapter on computer security (Chapter 16), we discuss some methods for achieving information security in an organization.

The Process of Converting Data into Information

How is data converted into information? The steps in this process may include the following:

- Collection
- Classification
- Sorting, adding, merging, and so on
- Summarizing
- Storing
- Retrieval
- Dissemination

Depending on the task at hand, some or all of the above steps may be required to convert data into information. Let us look at each of these steps.

A GLOBAL PERSPECTIVE
The United Nations

Information systems and computer technologies are playing a major role in reuniting 40,000 children with their families from which they were separated during the Balkan war, and in managing one of the largest refugee crises since World War II. The United Nations High Commissioner for Refugees, Electronic Data Systems, and Bull HN Information Systems have formed a team to develop an innovative information system that will collect, process, and distribute information about refugee children to 4 million people displaced from Bosnia, Herzegovina, Croatia, and other parts of the former Yugoslavia. "This is the first time, as far as we know, that high technology has been used to address a refugee situation," says one United Nations representative.

The information system, known as *Operation Reunite,* allows social workers to fill out refugee profile forms in the field and send them to Paris, where the information is keyed into a database. Workers then scan the photographs of children into the system, which matches requests for missing children with existing data on children in refugee camps. The system then prints the information on missing children and distributes it to many refugee sites, radio stations, and television stations across Europe to match parents with their children. Currently, data on approximately 500 children resides in the system; the United Nation hopes eventually to have information on more than 3,000 refugee children.[5]

When data on missing children is matched with data on parents, it becomes useful information that allows refugee camp personnel to bring families together.

The first step is to collect data through surveys, interviews, sensors, documents, newspapers, or any other appropriate means. (Data collection can sometimes be a very tedious, time-consuming, and labor-intensive process. Hence managers should carefully assess the time and cost of data collection.) Next, data is classified and sorted to arrange it in a meaningful form. For example, data about students can be sorted alphabetically, based on their last names, for easy retrieval. Sometimes the process may include steps other than sorting, such as adding values, merging files, and so on. When processed data becomes information, it can be condensed and summarized to make it more useful to the decision maker. The information is then stored carefully for future use. (Without proper storage decision makers may find it difficult to retrieve the information when they need it; also, the information may be damaged if it is not properly stored.) The different ways to store information are covered in Chapter 3 (Computer Hardware). Finally, information must be disseminated or distributed in the right format, at the right time, to the right place, and to the right people if it is to be useful.

It is important to note that simply executing all of the steps discussed above does not guarantee that data will become information. If the processing is inaccurate or inappropriate, its output may be useless to the decision maker. The principle "GIGO"—Garbage-In-Garbage-Out—refers to bad data or to bad processing.

Figure 1–4 shows how data is collected and processed before it becomes information.

Let us look at a real-world example in which data is converted into information. The Massachusetts Department of Revenue (see box) converts data from an individual's tax and employment records into information that helps government employees track and identify "deadbeat dads." The state collects data on men who are accused of defaulting on their child support payments, and classifies and sorts the data based on factors such as the name of the employer or the residential

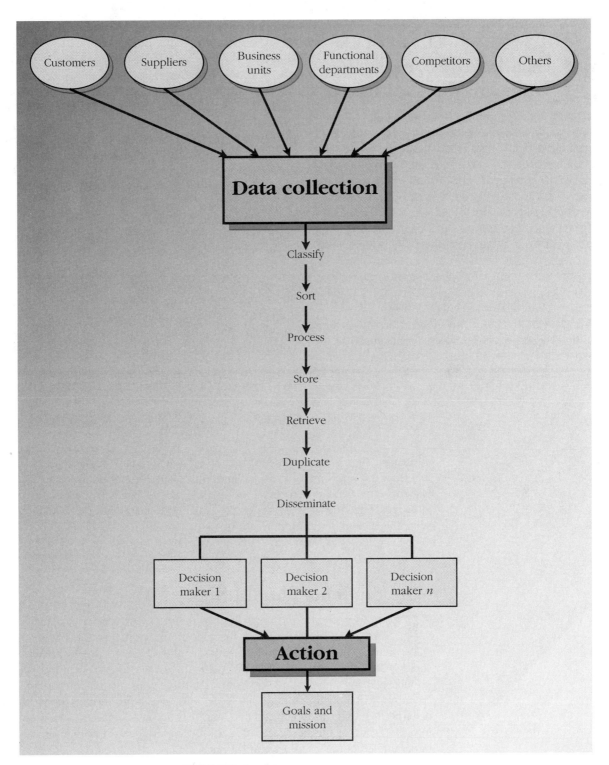

FIGURE 1-4

Data are collected from different sources and processed using a series of steps. Processed data become information. Decision makers use information to achieve the goals and the mission of the organization.

Dialing for Deadbeat Dads in Massachusetts

Nationally, 15 million parents owe almost $20 billion to 17 million children! While the statistics are staggering, until recently very little was done about this sorry state of affairs. However, the Massachusetts Department of Revenue (DOR) is using its information systems to track "deadbeat dads" and collect child support payments.

The DOR collects data on fathers who owe child support payments and matches this data with incoming data on new hires. If a match is found, the state tells the employer's payroll office how much money must be withheld from the father for child support payments. Agency workers use tax data to ensure that a father pays child support even when he changes jobs.

Here, data is processed and converted into useful information. The processing includes collecting data on "deadbeat dads," classifying and summarizing the data,

sorting or merging data on these fathers with other relevant data such as tax information, and finally storing the data and disseminating it to the proper decision makers.

The results of using information systems to track "deadbeat dads" have been tremendous. In just 2 years, the state has boosted its child support and alimony compliance rate from 59% to 78%. (Compare Massachusetts with some other states, which have been able to show only a 1% improvement in their collections.) The system is so successful that it earned awards for the state from both the Ford Foundation and the American Management Association. Massachusetts is encouraging other states to tap into its database, and is asking for permission to tap into the databases of other states as well, to further reduce the problem of "deadbeat dads."

This is a good example of converting data into information to facilitate decision making. It also shows the usefulness of information literacy, the ability to use computers and information systems to achieve organizational effectiveness.[6]

address of such a man. This information is then summarized, stored, and disseminated to the appropriate agencies and employers throughout the state. Note that tax and employment records alone are of limited value to the decision maker. However, once the state processes the data, it becomes useful information, which serves as a catalyst for further action.

Next, let us explore why students must have a good foundation in information systems.

Why Students Should Study MIS

Today, every student, regardless of his or her area of specialization, must have a solid foundation in the theory and principles of information systems. There are several reasons for this. First, in an information-based society, the primary output of organizational workers consists of information and knowledge. As the complexity and sophistication of managing businesses increase, global and international economic pressures mount, political forces reshape the world in which we live, and technology becomes intricately woven into the fabric of business, knowledge of computers and information systems is becoming essential for most employees.

Also, computers and information systems are already an integral part of our everyday lives: we use them in libraries, in banks and at home. For example, PIDEAC (Personal Identification and Entry Access Control), a company based in Yellow Springs, Ohio, has developed a system that encodes information about the shape of a person's hand and stores it on a plastic card's magnetic strip. The card has many different uses. Users can gain access to anything from a bank's ATM to a high-security building by entering the card in a computer and placing their hands on the computer screen. The system compares the size and shape of the user's hand with the data encoded on the card. When a match is found, it gives the individual access to the system. PIDEAC even allows for minor changes due to hand injuries or swelling.

The benefits of such a card are enormous and there are many different uses of this kind of technology. For example, financial institutions, telephone companies, and businesses can prevent unauthorized use of their facilities through this type of identification card. Since there is only one hand print that will match with the hand print on the card, this technology will reduce, if not eliminate, the fraudulent use of other types of cards, such as credit cards.

Finally, more and more Americans are buying computers for their home; in 1993 alone, American consumers bought 5.85 million personal computers at an estimated value of $7 billion! Industry analysts predict that eventually two-thirds of American homes will own a personal computer. Hence, proficiency with computers and information systems will be essential in both our personal and professional lives.[7]

In the next section, we look at why organizations depend on information systems for their growth and survival.

Why Organizations Need Information Systems

Today, few if any medium- or large-sized companies can survive without computers and information systems. In this section, we identify some reasons why organizations need information systems.

Meeting Global Challenges

The world has become a small place; the competition faced by a business is no longer limited by national boundaries. Companies therefore strive to produce high-quality goods and services that can compete in world markets. Though globalization can bring many benefits, such as increased profits and market share, the challenges of running a global company are also significant. If the company is to be successful, it must effectively coordinate and control products, people, and procedures around the world. This requires a great deal of timely, accurate, and reliable information.

Capturing Opportunities in the Marketplace

Successful companies are those that can identify and take advantage of opportunities in the marketplace and can continue to do so over the long run. Information systems that allow a company to identify strategic growth opportunities in the marketplace are known as strategic information systems (SIS). These systems have catapulted some companies to the top of their industries, leaving their competitors far behind. Chapter 14, which covers strategic information systems, describes many companies whose success is directly attributable to such systems.

Supporting Corporate Strategy

Companies use three basic strategies to compete successfully in the marketplace:

- They stay ahead of the competition by providing goods and services at a lower price than their competitors.
- They produce highly specialized or unique goods and services that allow them to stand apart from their competitors.
- They find a market niche and focus on meeting the needs of this special group.

These three strategies are not mutually exclusive; a company can use them in combination. Regardless of the strategy a company uses to stay ahead of the competition, information systems and technologies play an important role in the implementation of business strategies. This book describes many companies that use information systems to cut costs, improve productivity, create unique and innovative products and services, and better serve customers.

Linking Departments Whose Functions Are Different

Some years ago, departments or units with different functions in a business, such as accounting, finance, marketing, manufacturing, and human resources, were viewed as separate business entities. Often the efforts of these departments were not coordinated; this resulted in inefficiencies and lost opportunities for the company. Today, most companies treat these apparently different departments as parts of a cohesive unit whose members must work together to achieve the overall goals of the business. This is not always an easy task, because the goals of some units may conflict with those of others. However, information systems can bring different functioning units together by coordinating their tasks and functions.

Enhancing Worker Productivity

The pervasiveness of computers and information systems in business has made them essential tools in many tasks, such as managing the shop floor, evaluating the performance of employees, tracking customers, reordering items, and generating the payroll. Computers and information systems can therefore have a significant impact on a company's bottom line.

Increasing the Quality of Goods and Services

Quality is a leading concern for top and middle managers around the world, regardless of the products or services that their companies produce. Total quality management (TQM) is one of the most popular and most widely used approaches for enhancing quality in an organization. Quality-oriented efforts and decisions are highly information-intensive, so computers help a company achieve its quality goals by providing the right information to the right people at the right time. An enterprise-wide effort is required to improve quality; this often involves coordinating the tasks and decisions of many departments and units, sometimes located all over the world.

We have now examined some reasons why students must have a good foundation in information systems and how organizations use these systems to achieve their goals. Next, we will look at organizational structures and the information needs of managers at different levels in these structures.

Information Systems and Organizational Structures

Managerial decisions are made within the structure of an organization, where an **organizational structure** identifies, among other things, the level of responsibility or authority and the scope of control that employees of the organization have. There are two types of organizational structures: the pyramid, or hierarchical, structure and the task-based structure.

The Pyramid Structure

One of the most popular organizational structures is the traditional **pyramid, or hierarchical, structure,** in which the chief executive officer (CEO) and the top managers are at the top of the pyramid and nonmanagerial employees (staff) form its base. Middle managers fall somewhere between top management and staff. Let us take a closer look at these three levels.

Lower-level managers are responsible for the day-to-day operations, activities, and transactions of an organization, which may include inventory control, payroll, processing sales transactions, and keeping track of employee work hours. They are responsible for the short-term performance of the company and mostly perform **structured** tasks, which are routine, are easily understood, and do not require intuition or judgment. For example, calculating the simple interest on a loan is a structured task. Usually, the information necessary to solve structured problems is readily available and easily applicable to the given problem.

The next layer in the hierarchical organization comprises of middle managers, who coordinate, control, and monitor various activities in an organization and act as liaison between operational managers and top managers. The tasks performed by middle managers are partly structured and partly ambiguous, or unstructured; hence these tasks are called **semistructured.** Semistructured tasks include assessing the impact of different marketing strategies on product sales, determining the impact of an increase in operational costs on company profits, appraising the impact of a new tax law on return on investments, and so on.

Finally, the top layer of the pyramid consists of top managers, who establish the vision and the long-term goals of the organization and chart its overall course. The decisions of top managers tend to be **unstructured**—that is, decisions that rely heavily on intuition, judgment, and experience. Unstructured decisions include assessing the way competitors may react to a new marketing strategy, predicting the impact of changes in the global economy, developing global competitive strategies, and so on. Sometimes it is difficult even to simply identify the kind of information needed to solve unstructured problems. The relevant information may be incomplete, inconsistent, or unavailable. Table 1–3 compares the nature and the information needs of structured (operational), semistructured (tactical), and unstructured (strategic) tasks.

Three factors—sources of information, degree of judgment, and time span of information—influence the way managers in a hierarchical organization use information.

Organizational structure
Identifies the level of responsibility, authority, management, and scope of control of employees in the organization. There are two types of organizational structure: pyramid and task-based.

Pyramid structure
The pyramid structure is an organizational hierarchy with the CEO at the top and non-managerial employees at the bottom. Middle managers are somewhere between top management and non-managerial employees.

Structured tasks
Tasks that are routine, are easily understood, and do not require intuition, judgment, or experience. Lower-level managers often engage in structured decision making.

Semistructured task
Tasks that are partly structured and partly ambiguous, or unstructured. Semistructured tasks are often performed by middle managers.

Unstructured task
A task that relies heavily on intuition, judgment, and experience. Top and middle managers often engage in unstructured decision making.

TABLE 1–3
The nature and scope of information and its use at different levels in the organization.

Information Characteristics	Level of Decision Making		
	Operational	Tactical	Strategic
Time frame	Short-range	Medium-range	Long-range
Source	Internal	Internal and external	External
Nature	Detailed	Mostly summary	Summary
Level of certainty	Certainty	Some uncertainty	Uncertainty
Risk Level	Low risk	Medium risk	High risk
Judgment	Very little	Some judgment	Extensive judgment
Dependence on information systems	High	Moderate	Low to moderate
Dependence on internal information	Very high	High	Moderate
Dependence on external information	Low	Moderate	Very high
Need for online information	Very high	High	Moderate
Use of historical information	High	Moderate	Low
Use of "what-if" information	Low	High	Very high

Top and middle managers are more likely to be heavy users of external information—that is, information generated outside the firm by entities such as government, laws, regulations, competitors, and stockholders—than lower-level managers. In exercising their judgment, top and middle managers rely more on knowledge and intuition to solve problems than lower-level managers, since top managers perform unstructured tasks while lower-level managers perform structured tasks. Top managers make strategic and tactical decisions that address long-range questions such as "Where should our organization be 3 to 5 years down the road and what should we do to get there?" and "What should we do to stay ahead of the competition?" Lower-level managers, on the other hand, need information to address short-term problems such as number of units to be produced, how to eliminate defective parts, number of transactions generated, number of hours worked by part-time employees, and so on. Figure 1–5 shows the three management levels in a pyramid structure and identifies the kinds of decisions that are made at each level.

The Task-Based Structure

Task-based structure
A structure in which a group of people required to accomplish a given task are brought together based on their skills rather than on their places in the organizational hierarchy.

Another type of organizational structure is called **task-based organization,** which brings together a group of people, based on their skills, to accomplish a given task, without any consideration of their level in the organization. A good example of a task-based team is one that is assembled to perform surgery. A

FIGURE 1-5

The pyramid structure divides management into three layers: strategic, tactical, and operational. Different types of information systems are designed to meet the needs of these three levels. The source of information (internal or external), the degree of judgment used, and the time span of the information may vary from one level to the next.

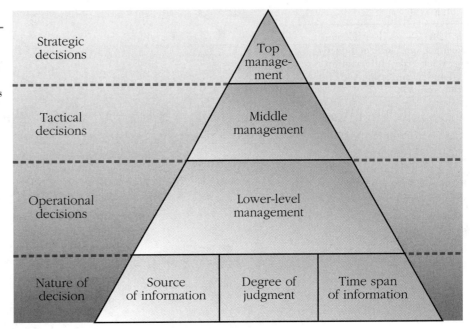

group of medical specialists and physicians comes together to accomplish the task, regardless of their levels within the structure of the hospital.

Task-based organizations also work well for companies that operate in highly dynamic business environments. For example, Intel, a leading manufacturer of computer chips, frequently uses the task-based approach to draw people from a wide variety of disciplines to manage and run its business projects. Intel describes the work of a task-based organization as similar to "planning and executing a play in football before regrouping, with substitutions or perhaps an entirely new line-up, and running another play." The company used the task-based approach to attract professionals from a variety of disciplines, such as marketing, manufacturing, and law, to produce and implement the $80 million marketing campaign for its powerful chip, the Pentium. Although later the chip was found to have some technical problems, the marketing campaign itself was highly successful.[9] The success of task-based teams depends a great deal on the ability of the teams to share and disseminate information, so computers and information systems play a vital role in such organizations.

Contributions of Information Systems to Individual, Group, and Organization-Wide Decision Making

A primary reason for the sustained growth of information systems in organizations is that they support and enhance the making of individual, group, and enterprise-wide decisions. We refer to information systems that support individual, group, and organization-wide decisions as personal infor-

FIGURE 1-6

This figure shows the differences among personal information systems, work-group information systems, and organization-wide information systems.

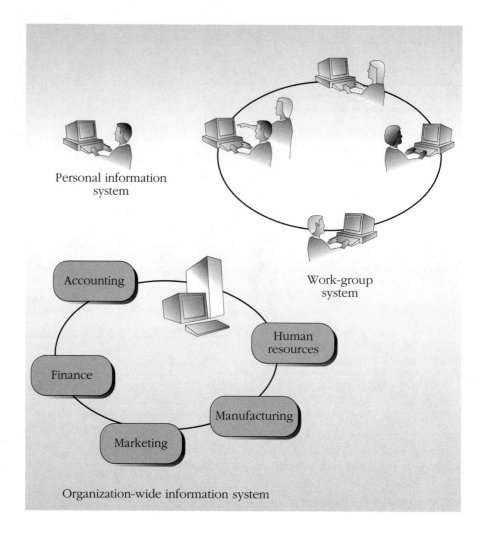

Personal information system

Work-group system

Organization-wide information system

Personal information systems
Systems that support the information needs of individual decision makers for solving structured, semistructured, and unstructured problems. PCs are a good example of such systems.

Work-group information system
A system designed to support group decision making. Such systems promote the free flow of information among group members.

Organization-wide systems
Systems that provide overall, comprehensive, long-term information about the entire organization. These systems integrate information from multiple sources to present a complete view of the organization.

mation systems, work-group systems, and organization-wide systems, respectively. Figure 1–6 shows the differences among these three types of systems.

Personal information systems (PIS) are those that support the information needs of individual decision makers for solving structured, semistructured, and unstructured tasks. For example, a manager may use a PIS to calculate the total amount due on a set of invoices (structured decision), to analyze market trends over the next 5 years (semistructured), or to evaluate the impact of a competitor's marketing strategy (unstructured).

Many important decisions in an organization are made by a group of individuals; **work-group information systems (WIS)** support group decision making. For example, launching a new product requires team effort and free sharing of information among group members; the WIS is designed primarily to support such activities. Work-group systems are covered in Chapter 8.

Information systems that provide comprehensive long-term information about the entire organization are called **organization-wide information systems (OWS).** A good example of such a system is one that responds to customer

	Number of Users	Tasks	Size of Computer
Personal Information Systems	Single	Individual-based	Small
Work-Group Systems	Group	Group-based	Medium
Organization-wide Systems	Larger groups	Organization-wide	Medium/large

TABLE 1–4
This table compares the three groups of information systems.

queries. If a customer wants to know the status of his or her order, an employee will need information on product availability (manufacturing), product discounts (marketing), payment policies (finance), quality issues (damaged items), and so on. This employee will need the ability to integrate information from different departments; the OWS provides the tools necessary to achieve this integrated view.

Table 1–4 summarizes some key differences that distinguish personal, work-group, and organization-wide systems.

Potential Risks of Information Systems

Although, as we have seen, organizations derive many benefits from information systems and technologies, sometimes the same systems and technologies can have negative effects on people and organizations. Therefore, organizations should take all possible precautions to make sure that information systems will not hinder their growth and progress. This section outlines some problems that can arise from information systems.

"Deskilling" of Workers

Introduction of new technologies, especially for purposes of automation, sometimes render obsolete the existing skills of some workers. Many industries, such as the automobile, defense, and insurance industries, have gone through periods of massive layoffs because of intense automation efforts. So, while computerization can increase operational efficiency and improve profits, sometimes it is also the root cause of work-force reduction.

Information Overload

Today, as information systems become more sophisticated and user-friendly, reports can be generated easily and quickly. However, this improvement also has its downside, because excessive amounts of information can overwhelm managers who must digest it and use it to make decisions, a phenomenon called information overload.

Employee Mistrust

When organizations introduce information systems, employees sometimes fear that computers will eventually replace them. Unless they are assured that their jobs are not in danger, they may well view information systems with skepticism.

Further, some companies use computers to monitor the activities of employees, which may also cause mistrust and dislike of computers.

Increased Competitive Pressure

A few years ago, when computers were expensive, many companies (small businesses in particular) that could not afford to invest in these machines found themselves slowly and steadily being pushed out of the marketplace by larger companies that invested heavily in computers and information systems. Although price is no longer an issue today, computers can be a boon or a bane for a business, depending on whether it can successfully deploy them or not. Companies that can use computers effectively to solve problems may be very successful; those that cannot may find themselves pushed out of the market by competitors that are more technologically sophisticated.

Disenchantment with IS

In recent years, the CEOs of many corporations have become disenchanted with computers and information systems because of poor returns from investments in these systems. Though there can be many reasons for this, including investments in inappropriate technologies or poor applications of good technologies, poor returns can obscure the true value of computers and information systems. Many CEOs are now questioning the value of information systems and technologies to their organizations by raising questions such as "How do I measure the return of our investment in IS and IT?" and "What is the true value of IS and IT in achieving organizational goals?" In the coming years, the MIS field will experience close scrutiny of its ability to deliver on its promises.

Challenges in Developing Information Systems

Although there are many successful information systems, building these systems is one of the most difficult and challenging tasks facing IS personnel. In spite of the large number and variety of development tools available today, few companies develop systems on time and within budget. In Chapter 12 (System Analysis and Design) and Chapter 13 (System Development Tools), we discuss these issues.

Security Breaches

When companies introduce new and sophisticated technologies, they must also find new ways to protect these assets from theft, pilferage, and security breaches. However, the more sophisticated the technology, the more difficult and expensive it is to protect it, so sometimes computers and information systems actually increase the operating costs of an organization.

Table 1–5 presents some characteristics of companies where information systems and technologies are viewed as an asset versus those of companies that consider them a liability.

In summary, like other tools, information systems have their advantages and disadvantages, and an awareness of the pros and cons of IS is the first step toward being an effective user and manager of these tools. The next section describes the principles of general systems theory, which is used extensively throughout this book to discuss IS concepts.

TABLE 1–5
Characteristics of companies where IT is viewed as an asset and those where it is considered a liability.

Issue	IT Is an Asset	IT Is a Liability
Are we getting value for our money?	Return on investment (ROI) is difficult to measure, but IT's contribution is perceived as worthwhile.	Organization is unhappy with IT as a whole.
How important is IT?	Stories of strategic use of IT are seen as interesting and instructive.	Stories of strategic use of IT are viewed as "irrelevant" to the firm.
How do we plan for IT?	IT thinking is an inherent part of business thinking.	IT thinking is done by specialists only.
Is the IS function doing a good job?	The performance of IS is not under debate.	There is cynicism about the track record of IS.
What is the CEO's vision of the role of IT?	CEO sees IT as having an important role in the transformation of the firm.	CEO sees a limited role for IT within the firm.

Source: Earl, Michael J., and David F. Feeny, *Sloan Management Review,* "Is your CIO adding value?", Spring 1994, pp. 11–20.

General Systems Theory

The world in which we live is full of systems. Human bodies, business organizations, and galaxies are all systems. Although systems theory may appear a bit abstract, we study it for a number of important reasons. It lays the foundation for many IS concepts and provides a structured and systematic approach to defining and understanding certain vital problems. Here, we address two important questions: "What is a system in relation to the study of management information systems?" and "What are some characteristics of systems?"

A **system** is a collection of parts that work together harmoniously to achieve specific goals. A system normally has subsystems and functions within an environment. Units within a system that share some or all of the characteristics of that system are called **subsystems.** An entity is a system or a subsystem depending on the perspective of the user. For example, we can view the accounting department as a subsystem of the entire organization or we can view the same accounting department as the system and the tax section within that department as the subsystem.

The world outside the system is called the **environment;** the system can be viewed as a subsystem of the environment. For example, a business organization is a system that functions within the confines of the environment known as society. The environment greatly influences the behavior of the system by imposing various constraints on it—such as limitations on financial resources, competitive forces, market conditions, and economic factors—but a single system can rarely influence the behavior of its environment. We use logical, rather than physical, boundaries to separate a system from its subsystems or from its environment. Logical boundaries change from time to time and differ from one system to another.

Every system has a set of dynamic goals that should be attainable, preferably measurable, and communicated to all units within the system. Figure 1–7 shows a subsystem, a system, and the system's environment (or suprasystem). It shows

System
A collection of interrelated parts that work together in harmony to achieve one or more common purposes.

Subsystem
A unit within a system that shares some or all of the characteristics of that system.

Environment
The world surrounding the system. The system is a subsystem of the environment.

FIGURE 1-7

A system usually has one or more subsystems and an environment. The boundaries separating one from the other are logical, not physical, boundaries.

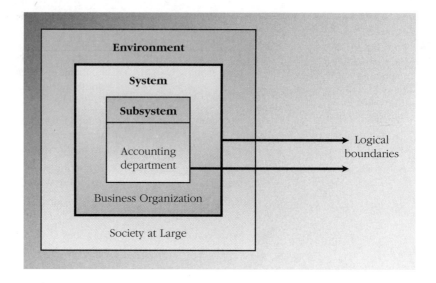

the accounting department as a subsystem of the business organization, which in turn is a subsystem of the environment, or society at large.

Open system

A system with a feedback mechanism that promotes the free exchange of information between the system and external entities.

Closed system

A system that neither transmits any information to the outside world nor receives any information from the outside world. There are few, if any, closed systems in the real world.

System Components

A system has five primary components: *input* (machines, manpower, raw materials, money, time, and so on), *processes* (policies, procedures, and operations that convert data into information), *output* (information in the right format, conveyed at the right time and place to the right person), *feedback* (data about the performance of the system), and *control* (processing the feedback and taking the necessary action). Figure 1–8 shows the system's components and how they work together to achieve the overall goals of the system.

A system with a feedback mechanism is called an **open system;** a **closed system** is one that does not receive feedback. In an open system, such as a busi-

FIGURE 1-8

A system has inputs, processor, output, feedback, and control. The processor adds value to the input and converts it into output. The feedback mechanism provides input to the control unit about the performance of the system. If there are any deviations between expected performance and actual performance, the control unit makes modifications to the system.

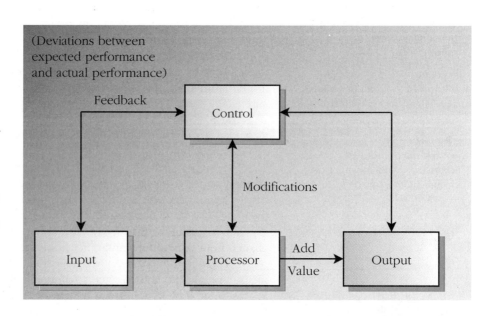

ness, there is a free and unrestricted flow of information among the subsystems, the system, and the environment. A closed system, on the other hand, does not receive or process any input from the external environment. All systems are open to some extent; there are very few, if any, fully closed systems in the world.

In an open system, feedback from the system becomes input to the control unit, which processes the feedback and identifies the course of action, if any, to be taken. Control includes rules, guidelines, principles, and measures that eliminate or reduce the difference between actual performance and desired performance. Control may be tangible or intangible, qualitative, or quantitative, explicit or implicit, simple or complex, written or oral, and formal or informal. When the control unit detects a discrepancy or deviation, it triggers the system to modify its behavior according to preestablished rules; then the process of feedback-control-modification repeats itself.

Here are some characteristics of systems:

- Every system has a purpose.
- Most systems have five components: input, processes, output, feedback, and control.
- Systems are made up of subsystems, whose goals are referred to as subgoals.
- The goals of a system are more important than the subgoals of its subsystems.
- Subsystems are guided both by their individual goals and by their relationships with other subsystems within the system.
- Subsystems must work together in harmony to achieve system goals.

Ethics and Information Systems: A Framework

Ethics is the study of right and wrong behavior as it applies to oneself, to others, and to organizations that are implicitly or explicitly engaged in decision making. An organization must have a social conscience; it must be sensitive to the moral dilemmas of its employees and managers, since organizations make a significant contribution to the ethical conscience of a nation.

In the words of Professor O. C. Ferrell,

> The problem with most ethics education in this country today is that we are taking the wrong approach. We are trying to make individuals more ethical when we need to try and make organizations more ethical. You can take the best person in the world and put [him or her] in a company where there is a culture of dishonesty and that person will have to do what is expected if he or she hopes to keep the job.

Organizations must provide employees with clear guidelines for conduct and encourage them to uphold high ethical standards in their everyday business practices. As the growing presence of advanced technologies poses new ethical dilemmas and challenges for the business community, it is important to prepare students to face these challenges. Note that ethical dilemmas are not about legal issues but about moral issues—distinguishing right from wrong. There are three sources that can be used to assess ethical behavior.

- The laws and regulations that specify codes of conduct
- The explicit ethical guidelines established by an organization
- The ethical and moral code of conduct of an individual

TABLE 1-6
The Ten Commandments of
Computer Ethics

Ten Commandments of Computer Ethics

1. Thou shalt not use a computer to harm other people.
2. Thou shalt not interfere with other people's computer work.
3. Thou shalt not snoop around in other people's computer files.
4. Thou shalt not use a computer to steal.
5. Thou shalt not use a computer to bear false witness.
6. Thou shalt not copy or use proprietary software for which thou hast not paid.
7. Thou shalt not use other people's computer resources without authorization or proper compensation.
8. Thou shalt not use other people's intellectual output.
9. Thou shalt think about the social consequences of the program thou art writing or the system thou art designing.
10. Thou shalt always use a computer in ways that demonstrate consideration and respect for thy fellow humans.

This book addresses ethical issues in relation to information and information-related issues. Table 1–6 shows a set of ten commandments, established by the Computer Ethics Institute to guide IS managers.[10] Appendix A provides a structural framework for analyzing and interpreting ethical situations in an organizational setting.[11]

A Framework for Studying MIS

This book is about the study of concepts, principles, and technologies of formal, computerized, organizational information systems. We will address five important questions that lay the foundation for a good understanding of the field of MIS:

1. What is MIS? Why is it important to study MIS? How does MIS support organizational decision making?
2. What building blocks and technologies are required to build information systems? How can these different technologies be linked?
3. What are the different types of information systems that managers use to enhance organizational decision making?
4. What are some tools, techniques, and methodologies that help organizations design and develop robust and reliable information systems?
5. How can an organization use information systems to be competitive in the marketplace and what should it do to protect its assets from theft, pilferage, and break-ins?

These five questions are answered in the five parts of this book: Part I, A Managerial Overview of MIS; Part II, Fundamentals of Information Technologies; Part III, Information Systems for Managerial Decision Making; Part IV, Managerial Issues in System Design, Development, and Maintenance; and Part V, Strategic Benefits and Management of Information Systems and Computer Security. Figure 1–9 shows the overall structure of the book.

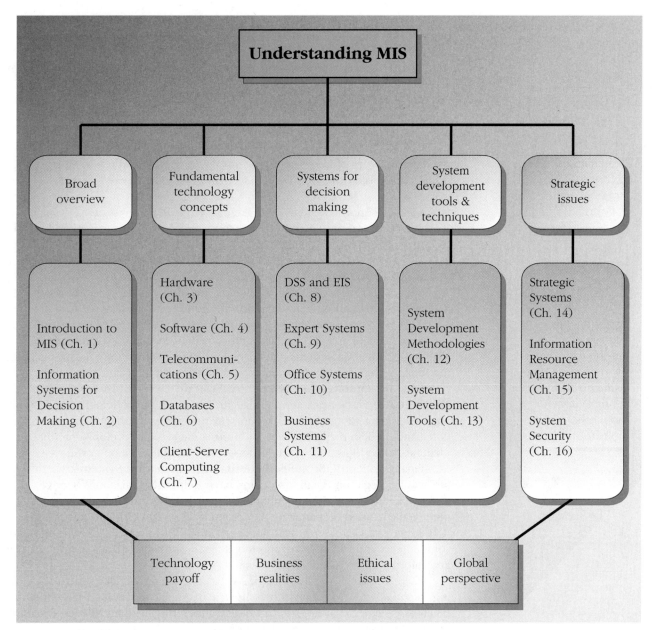

Understanding MIS

Broad overview	Fundamental technology concepts	Systems for decision making	System development tools & techniques	Strategic issues
Introduction to MIS (Ch. 1)

Information Systems for Decision Making (Ch. 2) | Hardware (Ch. 3)

Software (Ch. 4)

Telecommuni-cations (Ch. 5)

Databases (Ch. 6)

Client-Server Computing (Ch. 7) | DSS and EIS (Ch. 8)

Expert Systems (Ch. 9)

Office Systems (Ch. 10)

Business Systems (Ch. 11) | System Development Methodologies (Ch. 12)

System Development Tools (Ch. 13) | Strategic Systems (Ch. 14)

Information Resource Management (Ch. 15)

System Security (Ch. 16) |

Technology payoff	Business realities	Ethical issues	Global perspective

FIGURE 1–9

This figure gives a broad overview of the layout and contents of this book.

Part I, **A Managerial Overview of MIS,** explains what MIS is and how it supports organizational decision making. Chapter 2 introduces different types of information systems, such as Transaction Processing Systems, MIS, and Intelligent Support Systems, and shows how these systems support organizational decision making.

Part II, **Fundamentals of Information Technologies,** examines different technical building blocks for information systems. It is made up of five chapters.

Chapter 3 provides an overview of computer hardware. Chapter 4 gives an overview of software. Chapter 5 covers networks, which link different computers that are geographically dispersed and have revolutionized the way we do business. A database is a repository of internal and external data that drives organizational decision making; Chapter 6 covers databases and related issues, such as how to build, maintain, and manage databases. Finally, Chapter 7 covers client-server computing, which is a recent and growing trend in the way organizations process and disseminate information.

Part III, **Information Systems for Managerial Decision Making,** covers the different types of information systems that managers can use to enhance organizational decision making. These information systems are as follows:

+ Decision support systems and executive information systems (Chapter 8), which support middle and top managers making semi-structured and unstructured decisions
+ Artificial intelligence and expert systems (Chapter 9), which help organizations to capture and retain the knowledge and experience of experts
+ Office automation (Chapter 10), which includes various types of systems that facilitate oral and written communication in the workplace.

Finally, in Chapter 11 (Business Information Systems), we discuss the vital role that information systems play in various business functions, such as accounting, finance, marketing, management, manufacturing, and quality control.

Part IV, **Managerial Issues in System Design, Development, and Maintenance,** discusses some tools, techniques, and methodologies for designing and developing robust and reliable information systems. Chapter 12 covers traditional and modern methodologies for information system development; Chapter 13 identifies some tools and techniques used to build information systems.

Finally, in Part V, **Strategic Benefits of Information Systems,** we describe the way strategic information systems have helped organizations survive, grow, and even outsmart the competition (Chapter 14). Information resource management is the process of managing the information resources in an organization and is the focus of Chapter 15. And in Chapter 16 (Computer Security), we identify some threats and risks that organizations face in protecting their computers, data, and information from thieves and unauthorized users.

Each chapter of the book begins with an opening vignette, under the heading *Technology Payoff,* that shows how a particular technology has influenced businesses. Each chapter also includes, under the heading *Business Realities,* many real-world descriptions of companies that show how information systems and technologies can be used to acquire a competitive edge in the marketplace. In *Global Perspectives,* we present examples of information systems from around the world, ranging from those that reunite children and families separated by the misfortunes of war to those that allow farmers to access information from research laboratories. Finally, *Ethical Cases,* included at the ends of some chapters (wherever appropriate) present ethical dilemmas that IS managers face in a world that is becoming increasingly dependent on technology.

Summary

- **The significance of management information systems to organizational decision making.**

  Today, MIS has become a vital resource for organizations around the world. Sometimes the term *management information systems* is used to refer to the field of information systems; at other times, the term refers to the system that creates, processes, stores, and retrieves information. MIS is an interdisciplinary field that has been influenced by other fields, including psychology, computer science, and linguistics. Although the computer is at the heart of today's information systems, a number of important social, organizational, behavioral, and ethical issues surround the study of MIS.

  There are a number of reasons why every student, regardless of his or her major, must be well versed in the fundamentals of information systems. Today we live in an information-based society; the growth and survival of many businesses all over the world depends on computers and information systems. Therefore, many employers expect their new hires to be proficient in the use of computers and information systems. Also, computers are becoming commonplace in many homes; hence it is important for individuals to have a working knowledge of computers and information systems.

- **The difference between information systems and information technologies**

  An information system is a tool that creates, processes, stores, and disseminates information to help managers make decisions. Information technologies, on the other hand, are technologies that support the design and development of information systems. Technologies by themselves are just that: technologies. In and of themselves they do nothing for an organization. It is only when technologies are carefully integrated into an existing business environment and are guided by business needs and opportunities that they yield significant results.

- **The difference between data and information**

  Data is the raw material from which information is generated. It can appear in the form of text, numbers, figures, or any combination thereof. Information, on the other hand, is processed data and can be used to make decisions. When data is processed and is presented in a form that is useful and meaningful to the decision maker, it becomes information. Some of the steps involved in converting data into information are collecting, classifying, sorting or merging, summarizing, storing, retrieving, and disseminating data.

- **The difference between computer literacy and information literacy**

  Computer literacy is a working knowledge of computers, their components, and their functions. Information literacy, on the other hand, includes computer literacy as well as the ability to create and use information in innovative ways to solve organizational problems, to enhance business acumen, technological knowledge, and a clear understanding of the business and its goals.

- **Systems theory and its relevance to the study of information systems**

  A system is a collection of interrelated parts that work together in harmony to achieve one or more common purposes. A system has five basic components: inputs, processes, outputs, feedback, and control. If a unit within a system has the characteristics of a system, it is referred to as a subsystem. Every system works within the confines of its environment. Most systems have a feedback-and-control mechanism that ensures that the system's actual performance matches its expected performance.

 Review Questions

1. Describe the *field* of MIS. Why is MIS an interdisciplinary field? What are some of the fields that have shaped and influenced MIS?

2. What are the two common meanings of the term *MIS?* Discuss the meaning of MIS as an information system.

3. Identify some reasons why all students, regardless of their majors, must have a good background in information systems. Can you think of some reasons why MIS is relevant to your area of specialization?

4. Who is a knowledge worker? Why is information

vital to the productivity of a knowledge worker? Identify a knowledge worker in any profession and list a few of such worker's information needs.

5. What is the difference between information systems and information technologies? Can one exist without the other?

6. Is the registration system at your university an example of an information system or of information technology or of both? Discuss.

7. Identify two reason why it is important for users and managers to recognize that information technologies do not operate in a vacuum but are, rather, a part of the social fabric.

8. What is the difference between computer literacy and information literacy? Suppose a student designs and implements an information system for a video store. Is this an example of computer literacy, of information literacy, or of both?

9. In today's business world, computer literacy alone is not enough. Discuss.

10. What is the difference between data and information? Identify some activities in the process of converting data to information. Identify any three characteristics of information that were important to you in selecting the school of your choice.

11. Consider the global example (see box) of the United Nations. Is this an example of computer literacy, of information literacy, or both? Explain your answer. Also, identify at least three pieces of data in this example and show how data becomes useful information.

12. What is the difference between the pyramid structure and the task-based structure? Which do you think is more effective? Does your university have a pyramid structure or a task-based structure of management?

13. Define the following terms from system theory: *system, subsystem, environment, feedback,* and *control.* Identify any system in your university; describe the system, its subsystems, and its environment.

 Discussion Questions

1. Consider your university as a system. Identify any subsystem in this system. Also, identify and describe the environment in which the university operates. What are some of the inputs, processes, and outputs of your system? What kind of feedback and control mechanism would be appropriate for this system?

2. Packard Bell, a market leader in PCs, develops and markets computer systems for the home buyer. Packard Bell's "designer PCs" feature integrated speakers, which facilitate voice-activated commands, and easy-to-use software; some models even have television, FM-radio, stereo, fax, and telephone-answering capabilities. Identify three desirable features (besides those listed above) that are important to you in your home PC.

3. Quite frequently we hear about layoffs as a result of automation and computerization. However, State Industries, Inc., a Tennessee-based, $350-million water heater manufacturer, has managed to retain and even to create jobs through the use of information technologies. In 1985, many companies were moving their manufacturing facilities to Mexico, where labor costs were one-tenth those of the U.S.

State Industries, on the other hand, stayed in the U.S. and developed a state-of-the-art, automated manufacturing facility to cut operating costs. Today, robots, automated devices, and sophisticated information systems have helped the company stay ahead of its competition.[12]

a. Would you consider the above example to involve information literacy, computer literacy, or both? Identify two information technologies that State Industries is using.

b. Identify a company in your area where layoffs have occurred as a result of computerization. Provide some reasons why computerization may result in layoffs.

4. Give an example of a personal information system in manufacturing and one of a work-group system in accounting and finance. Study the systems found in any small business and classify them as personal, work-group, or enterprise-wide systems.

5. Identify a company that has felt the negative effects of computers and information systems; list the negative impacts. Identify a company that has become a market leader because of its use of information systems.

6. Identify any field of study other than business and show how systems theory can be used to better understand and solve problems in this field.

7. Describe the control and feedback mechanism that your teacher uses in this course to assess and evaluate your class performance and his or her performance as a teacher.

 ETHICAL ISSUES

Case 1: David versus Goliath: a landmark case in computer ethics and practices.

(An excerpt from McWilliams, Brian, "Defying the Giant," *ComputerWorld,* May 8, 1995, pp. 82–84.)

On July 1, 1975, Catamore Enterprises made history in Rhode Island's 7th District Court when a family-owned jewelry manufacturer was awarded $11.4 million in damages from IBM, by far the largest suit of its kind at that time. Though the jury's verdict was ultimately overturned on appeal and the two parties settled out of court, *Catamore v. IBM* became a landmark in computer ethical practices and laid the foundation for consumer practices in the then evolving computer industry.

"We never expected to lose the case," says Nicholas Katzenbach, former U.S. Attorney General and IBM's general counsel at the time. "But we lost, and we lost big." It was not the dollar value that shocked IBM (the amount was less than a day's profit for IBM), but the company's reputation for honesty and integrity that worried IBM. Ironically, it was IBM that picked the fight, suing Catamore for $68,000 in unpaid systems rent. Catamore counter sued for $26 million, charging IBM with fraud, negligence and breach of contract.

Many outsiders viewed the case as a fight between David and Goliath: IBM, the world's most powerful corporation at the time, represented by the most prestigious law firm in Rhode Island (Edwards and Angel), the biggest law firm in New York (Caravath, Swain and Moore), and IBM's extensive legal staff, headed up by Nicholas Katzenbach, versus Catamore Enterprises, whose lead counsel, 27 years old, was trying his first civil suit and was just three years out of law school.

How the story goes:

Prior to 1967, Catamore sold jewelry through wholesale distributors; but in 1967 Catanzaro, president and founder of the company, traveled across the country to sell his then new merchandising concept: automatic replenishment. In exchange for agreeing to put a Catamore jewelry display case in its stores, a retailer could turn over all ordering and inventory management to Catamore. Retailers fell in love with the idea and orders began to pour in. The company's paper-based production control and inventory system could not handle the projected 300 percent increase in business and it was at this time that Maurice Davitt, Catanzaro's old university fraternity brother who was then working for the local IBM branch office, suggested automating the system.

Davitt promised that along with leasing IBM hardware, IBM would customize production control software to meet the jeweler's unique information needs. This was not unusual, as IBM often packaged its products (hardware and software) to provide customized solutions to customers. When Catanzaro entered into a signed agreement with IBM in September 1968, he had actually entered into two contracts: the written contract for the lease of IBM's hardware and an *oral* contract for the production of control software. IBM agreed the complete system would be delivered and installed by January 1,1970.

Catanzaro then proceeded to invest in the new system by buying land to build a new plant, and hiring managers, salespeople and factory workers to manage the new facility. The company also followed IBM's expert advice and converted its existing inventory numbering system into one that could be more easily automated.

For its part, IBM directed an inexperienced systems engineer trainee to develop a flow chart of Catamore's product system, while Davitt moved on to become manager of IBM's Providence branch office. In a November 1969 letter to Catanzaro, the representative who took over the account assured Catamore that the "system design was 90% complete." The company, however, had

(Continued on next page)

to sign another services agreement and pay $5,000 to cover the 10 percent of work left on its system. Because unbundling was accompanied by a 3 percent reduction in monthly hardware lease rate, Catanzaro took the change more or less in stride. In court, however, IBM claimed that the services agreement effectively nullified the oral agreement for software.

Two years after the order was placed, the system was nowhere near completion. Catamore stopped payment on its lease agreement. As retailer's orders poured in that fall, the lack of a functioning inventory system caused major chaos and proved disastrous for the jeweler. Orders were lost or filed incorrectly and employees, unable to keep up with the demand, simply ignored orders as they poured in. Irate customers canceled orders while loyal customers who agreed to give the company another chance found that things did not improve even the following year. The company was losing its most loyal customers to the competition. For the first time in many decades, the company lost money; but even more damaging was the loss of its good reputation and the opportunity to break into a lucrative market.

See you in court

In court, IBM's attorney's blamed system delays by saying that the reason the system was not yet functioning was because the company failed to implement the automation plan that IBM had suggested. It also argued that while IBM provided education, training and systems design, developing the code was part of Catamore's responsibility. Catanzaro argued that he had contracted with his data processing vendor for a production control system, not a piece of hardware.

The turning point in the trial, according to some observers, came late in May as IBM was presenting its case. Christo (Catamore's lawyer) brought in Warren Hume, an IBM vice president and management committee member, to comment on IBM's sales and contract policies. For hours, Christo tried to find an opening in Hume's armor, but the polished executive said little that strengthened Christo's case. On the second day of questioning, as he jabbed away at Hume about IBM's integrity, a gift landed in Christo's lap. "I have put in motion millions of dollars worth of IBM assets on the basis of an oral conversation," boasted Hume. "I'll guarantee you if the president of AT&T calls me up, I'll put it in motion. We don't have to sign a lot of contracts to do it. . . That's what I call credibility."

Christo just looked at the judge and said, "Sounds like an oral agreement to me."

The verdict

The six-member jury in IBM v. Catamore labored for 11 days to arrive at the following verdict: In the case of IBM v. Catamore, we find in favor of IBM. Catamore must pay the $68,000 in back rent. But then the words that forever altered the vendor/user power balance: In the counter suit of Catamore v. IBM, we find in favor of Catamore and award $11.4 million in damages. "You could have knocked us over with a feather," Cipolla remembers.

IBM filed an appeal with the U.S. Court of Appeals for the First Circuit in which a three-judge panel ruled in September 1976 that the case must be retried. The two companies agreed to an out-of-court settlement. The case is considered a landmark in computer industry because, according to Ed Langs, an attorney at Brooks and Cushman in Southfield, Michigan, "Catamore put the fear of God into hardware vendors.[13]

1. Explain the main issues behind this landmark case.
2. Do you feel that IBM should have honored its agreement, oral or otherwise?

Case 2: Oracle slapped with lawsuit

A $30 million lawsuit was filed in October 1995, against Oracle Corporation and Larry Ellison, president and chief executive officer, for wrongful firing, breach of contract and other misdeeds described as "a conflict of interest" between Ellison's personal investments and his database company. The suit was filed by Terry Garnett, former senior vice president of worldwide marketing at Oracle. Mr. Garnett alleges that Ellison asked him to channel interactive television business to a new company, Human Nature Interactive, Inc., while Garnett was trying to drum up the same kinds of deals for Oracle. Garnett, a four-year veteran at Oracle, was fired for questioning the legality of that request, the suit claims.

An Oracle spokesman countered that Garnett proposed the Human Nature start-up idea to Ellison. Further, "neither Mr. Ellison nor Oracle ever made assurances that implied or promised either Mr. Ellison's or Oracle Corp.'s cooperation" in Human Nature. Bob Kin, an analyst at New York brokerage house S. G., Warburg & Co., shrugged off the suit. "Oracle's has been on a roll, and it seems like they are the target for lawsuits because of it." Garnett's suit seeks $30 million for punitive and compensatory damages, loss of salary, stock options and benefits.[14]

1. If Mr. Ellison did in fact try to channel interactive television business to his new company, Human Nature Interactive, Inc., while Mr. Garnett was trying to drum up the same kinds of deals for Oracle, do you think that this was ethically wrong on the part of Mr. Ellison?
2. Do you believe the argument that an upcoming company often faces lawsuits from jealous competitors?

 PROBLEM SOLVING IN THE REAL WORLD

IRS at Work: "You Know Who You Are, and So Do We"

In 1985, the state of New York ran an ad touting a crackdown on tax dodgers. A stern taxman stood in front of a computer and warned, "You know who you are, and so do we." The ad was in large part a bluff. But the tax collectors aren't bluffing now. The IRS really does have some good computers and are getting more.

Example: In 1991, an Internal Revenue Service criminal investigator was sitting at his computer in Flint, Michigan, searching a database of suspicious bank deposits of cash. The name, John E. Long, appeared on his screen. At the next desk, another agent who was sorting paper criminal referral forms from banks saw the same name. "Just by looking at the computer screen, we knew we had a case," said supervisory special agent Leonard Nawrocki—and what a case. Building on those leads, the IRS got Long, his son-in-law and their wives to pay more than $12 million in back taxes, interest, penalties, and forfeitures. It even collected a down payment by seizing a 50-foot yacht and $1.4 million of currency. The two men are serving 21-month terms in prison camps, after which their wives will do shorter terms.

What happened? The family, which is the largest promoter of country folk art shows in the nation, didn't book the cash it collected for admissions. Instead it deposited into its corporate accounts only the checks it received from renting booths, publishing a magazine, and so on. Result: The Longs reported that their business was losing money, when in fact it was quite profitable.

But the computer knew better. An agent pulled reports of 63 suspicious cash deposits of under $10,000 made by Long and his son-in-law at eight banks. He then subpoenaed the bank's records—the Longs didn't even know this was happening—and entered into his PC the data on 2,000 deposits the family had made into 37 accounts. Computer sorting established which accounts contained

(Continued on next page)

skimmed money and which assets were purchased with unreported cash and thus subject to forfeiture.

Until recently, the tax department's computers couldn't do much more than badger the average-salaried Joe about exaggerated deductions or dividends and interest omitted from his return. The computers were inept at finding folks who didn't file or omitted income—except when that income was shown on a 1099 or W-2 that could be matched to the 1040. That is, the huge underground economy remained largely untouched. By the IRS' own estimate there are 500,000 self-employed individuals making over $25,000 who don't even file returns. These non-taxpayers evade $7 billion a year in federal individual income taxes—to say nothing of Social Security taxes and state taxes. "With computers, failure to file is almost suicidal. If you are involved in commerce of any sort, it's only a matter of time until you get caught. That was not true five years ago."[15]

The state and federal tax cops are also cooperating to an unprecedented degree. In its St. Louis district, the IRS is looking for prosperous non-filers by matching its list of taxpayers against holders of Missouri drivers' licenses, aged 25 to 62. It will pick those ripe for audit by matching the non-filers with currency reports, ownership of expensive cars, boats and airplanes, and professional licenses.

Ever heard of the Currency & Banking Retrieval System? This database stores information from banks, businesses, and professionals who file forms whenever there's a cash transaction of $10,000 or, in the case of banks, a pattern of "suspicious" smaller deposits. This database is a goldmine for the tax cops: One random sample found that 21% of people who made big-ticket cash purchases (of cars and other items) hadn't filed 1040s. Among those who had filed: a California taxpayer who claimed a $300 earned income credit while paying $17,000 cash for gold bullion.

In 1993 agents tapped into the cash transactions database 130,000 times to pull data on 2 million taxpayers. The objective, says IRS Chief Compliance Officer Philip Brand: "We want to move our examinations from verification of deductions to economic reality. I could always question that you claimed $5,000 for business expenses. Now I can say, this person is showing only $6,000 a year net profit and that's (business expenses) not the level of his lifestyle. Before, we had to go through a very complex field investigation to find that out."[16]

All this, of course, raises disturbing questions about invasion of privacy and the brute power of the state. There is always the risk that computer-generated information will be handled by poorly trained people who harbor resentment against those who are better off. And in civil tax cases the taxpayer is presumed wrong until he proves otherwise. Thus innocent people can be forced to spend large sums to defend themselves against unreasonable demands by the tax people—concede our case or face costly legal bills. Thus many taxpayers pay computer-generated bills they believe they don't owe, accountants and lawyers say. Still another problem of the new computer era is taxpayer confidentiality. An internal IRS audit released last year disclosed that in the Southeast region alone, 368 IRS employees were suspected of snooping into the finances of relatives, neighbors, and even celebrities. The IRS, of course, maintains that it does everything possible to ensure taxpayer privacy and is working to build more safeguards into its computers. But with 56,000 employees having access to taxpayer information via computers, abuses are inevitable—part of the price Americans must pay for big government![17]

1. Describe the problem that the IRS is trying to solve. How important are information systems to achieving the goals of the IRS?
2. Give an example of an information system that the IRS is currently using to track tax evaders. What are some technologies that drive these systems?
3. Give an example showing how the IRS converts data into useful information. Identify the data in this case and show the steps that convert the data into information.
4. Do you believe that your privacy is being violated by the IRS? What measures do you think the IRS should take to prevent abuse of confidential data?
5. Is the Currency and Bank Retrieval System an example of information literacy, of computer literacy, or of both? Explain your answer.

References

Alavi, Maryam and Patricia Carlson. "A Review of MIS Research and Disciplinary Development." *Journal of Management Information Systems* 8, no. 4 (Spring 1992).

Baker, Daniel B., Sean O'Brien Strub and Bill Henning. *Cracking the Corporate Closet,* in Association with the National Gay & Lesbian Task Force Policy Institute, HarperCollins Publishers, 1995.

Budapest, Zsuzsanna E. *The Goddess in the Office,* HarperCollins Publishers: San Francisco, CA, 1995.

Branscomb, Anne Wells. *Who Owns Information?* HarperCollins Publishers, 1995.

Cash, James I., Warren McFarlan, James L. McKenney, and Linda M. Applegate. *Corporate Information Systems Management,* 3rd ed. Homewood, IL: Irwin, 1992.

Clark, Thomas D., Jr. "Corporate Systems Management: An Overview and Research Perspective." *Communications of the ACM* 35, no. 2 (February 1995).

Cowan, John. *The Common Table,* HarperCollins Publishers, 1995.

Cowan, John. *Small Decencies,* HarperCollins Publishers, 1995.

Dosick, Rabbi Wayne. *The Business Bible,* HarperCollins Publishers, 1995.

Epictetus. *A Manual For Living,* HarperCollins Publishers: San Francisco, CA, 1995.

Feeney, David F. and Blake Ives. "In Search of Sustainability: Reaping Long-term Advantage from Investments in Information Technology," *Journal of Management Information Systems* 7 (Summer 1990): 27–46.

Gorry, G. A. and M. S. Morton. "Framework for Management Information Systems." *Sloan Management Review* 13, no. 1 (Fall 1971).

Gurbaxani, Vijay and Seungjin Whang. "The Impact of Information Systems on Organizations and Markets." *Communications of the ACM* 34 (January 1991): 59–73.

McFarlan, F. Warren, James L. McKenney, and Philip Pyburn. "The Information Archipelago—Plotting a Course." *Harvard Business Review* (January–February 1983a).

McKenney, James L. and F. Warren McFarlan. "The Information Archipelago—Maps and Bridges." *Harvard Business Review* (September–October 1982).

McKinnon, S. M. and Bruns, W. J. Jr. "The Information Mosiac," Harvard Business School Press, 1992.

Michael J. Mandel. "The Digital Juggernaut," *Business Week* (Special Issue: Information Revolution), May 1994.

Niederman, Fred, James C. Brancheau, and James C. Wetherbe. "Information Systems Management Issues for the 1990s." *MIS Quarterly* 15, no. 4 (December 1991).

Oz, Effy. "Ethical Standards for Information Systems Professionals: A Case for a Unified Code," *MIS Quarterly,* December 1992, pp. 423–433.

Pinsonneault, A. and K. L. Kraemer. "The Impact of Information Technology on Middle Managers," *MIS Quarterly,* September 1993, pp. 271–292.

Roach, Stephen S. "Services Under Siege—The Restructuring Imperative." *Harvard Business Review* (September–October 1991).

Scott Morton, Michael, ed. *The Corporation in the 1990s.* New York: Oxford University Press, 1991.

Notes

1. Freedman, David H. "Top Seed", *Forbes ASAP,* March 29, 1993, pp. 43–44, 46.
2. Icing, Julia. American Greetings puts cards on PCs, *Computerworld,* July 18, 1994, p. 40.
3. Wilson, Linda. "PCs Make a Fashion Statement," *InformationWeek,* March 29, 1993, p. 15.
4. Betts, Mitch. National ID system proposed for immigration job tracking," *Computerworld,* August 8, 1994, p. 6.
5. Anthes, Gary. "Tech Firms help U.N. reunite families," *Computerworld,* April 11, 1994, p. 40.
6. Earls, Alan R. "Dialing for deadbeats," *Computerworld,* June 27, 1994, p. 130.
7. Kirkpatrick, David. "How Pcs will take over your home," *Fortune,* February 21, 1994, pp. 100–104.
8. "Practical Palm Reader." *CIO* January 1993, p. 22.
9. Deutchman, Alan. "High Tech Superstars", *Fortune,* October 17, 1994, pp. 197–206.
10. Computer Ethics Institute, Washington, D.C.
11. *Advanced Instructional Module on Business Ethics,* prepared by Susan J. Harrington, Kent State University. *Supplement to Organization Challenges* by Debra L. Nelson and James Campbell Quick, West Publishing Company, 1994.
12. Adapted with permission from Hoffman, Thomas, *Computerworld,* "Automation Preserves Jobs at Manufacturer", August 9, 1993, p. 58.
13. McWilliams, Brian. "Defying the Giant," *Computerworld,* May 8, 1995, pp. 82–84.
14. Nash, Kim S. "Oracle slapped with lawsuit, *Computerworld,* Oct. 31, 1994, p. 6.
15. IRS Chief Compliance Officer, Philip Brand.
16. Ibid.
17. Novach, Janet. "You know who you are, and so do we," *Forbes,* April 11, 1994, pp. 88–92.

2

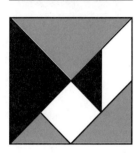

Information Systems for Managerial Decision Making

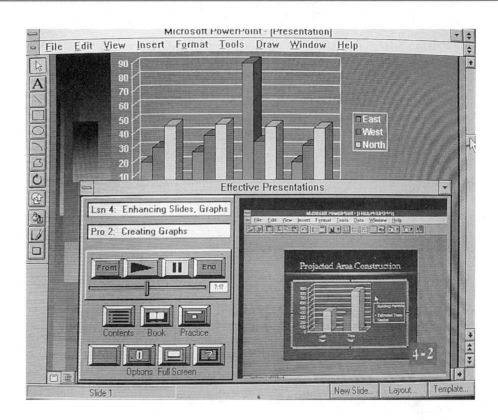

Contents

Learning Objectives
Technology Payoff: The Genesis Project of American Express
Introduction
Transaction Processing Systems
  Steps in Processing a Transaction
    Data Entry
    Validation
    Data Processing and Revalidation
    Data Storage
    Output Generation
    Query Support
  Example of a Transaction Processing System
Management Information Systems
  Examples of Management Information Systems
Intelligent Support Systems
  Decision Support Systems

39

How a DSS Works
Example of a Decision Support System
Executive Information Systems
Artificial Intelligence and Expert Systems
Example of an Expert System
Office Automation Systems
Tapping the Potential of Information Systems
Summary
Review Questions
Discussion Questions
Ethical Issues:
Case 1: A Bribery Scandal
Case 2: CIO Under Fire
Problem Solving in the Real World
Case 1: Israel Discount Bank Delights Customers
Case 2: A Management Information System for a Chinese University
References
Notes

Learning Objectives

The nature and scope of information required by managers at different levels in an organization varies considerably; therefore, organizations require different types of information systems to meet their needs. In this chapter, we provide a broad overview of four different types of information systems and the roles that they play in organizational decision making. The four types are transaction processing systems, management information systems, intelligent support systems, and office automation systems.

An organization can select and implement one or all of these systems to meet its particular information needs. Although these are four distinct systems, we emphasize the importance of integrating them in order to realize their full potential. After reading and studying this chapter, you should be able to:

- Understand why different types of information systems are necessary to facilitate organizational decision making.
- Understand why transaction processing systems are the lifeline to a company's data.
- Understand the role of management information systems in decision making.
- Describe the nature and scope of intelligent support systems and explain how they support high-level decision making.
- Understand how office automation systems can enhance communications and productivity in the workplace.
- Identify success factors that help to make use of the potential of different types of information systems.

TECHNOLOGY PAYOFF

The Genesis Project of American Express

The primary objective of the Genesis Project, the mammoth $100-million global transaction processing system used by American Express, is to enhance customer service. The overall goal of this system is to efficiently process the transactions that take place whenever customers use the American Express card anywhere in the world. Genesis helps American Express cut operating costs, speed payments to merchants, and make card transaction data available to sales representatives.

The new transaction processing system replaced five separate, inflexible, and complex systems that once provided merchants with sales information. In one stroke, Genesis eliminated many technical and geographical barriers that sales representatives and customers had frequently encountered when using the old system.

Genesis is flexible and reliable; it provides valuable information to merchants and sales representatives. For example, merchants can now get reports on when they requested payments from American Express and when American Express made the payments. They can also receive reports on the global shopping patterns of customers in order to better target their advertising dollars.

Genesis has helped American Express become "information-rich." In spite of the huge volumes of data that credit card companies collect, quite often they are "data-rich" but "information-poor." In other words, although companies collect a great deal of data, very few use the data to achieve a competitive edge in the marketplace. Genesis provides American Express with a significant advantage in the marketplace. Today, competitors such as Visa and MasterCard are overhauling their transaction processing systems in order to remain competitive with American Express.[1]

Those of us in the information industry are so busy making history that we may sometimes forget to stop and think about the scope and significance of the very changes we are making.

—John Young, Ex-CEO of Xerox Corporation

Introduction

In the last few decades, the field of information systems has come a long way. Creative and innovative ideas from entrepreneurs, scientists, and engineers have contributed to the explosive growth of information systems and their applications. Computers and information systems function at the core of entire industries, such as space, medicine, automobiles, communications, sports, entertainment, and education. Today the processing power of computers that once occupied entire buildings can literally be held in the palm of one's hand. Data-processing chips have become powerful yet inexpensive and have steadily found their way into our homes and offices. Software (the set of instructions necessary for performing a given computer task) has become so versatile and so user-friendly that even elementary school children can use it. In fact, computers are likely to become such an integral part of our daily lives that the Council on Competitiveness, a nonprofit, nonpartisan group, anticipates that by the early part of the 21st century, *all* Americans will be able "to access information and communicate with one another easily, reliably, securely, and cost-effectively."[2] Many organizations are also tapping the versatility and power of computers by designing and developing systems tailored to meet their specific needs.

An increasing number of managers rely on computers and information systems to make decisions. As you may recall from Chapter 1, managers at different levels in an organization make different kinds of decisions (operational, tactical, and strategic), so that the kinds of information necessary to support their decisions are also different. Accordingly, different types of information systems are designed to meet the various information needs of managers, as shown in Figure 2–1. For example, the Genesis project of American Express (see box) shows how a special type of information system helps managers analyze company transactions.

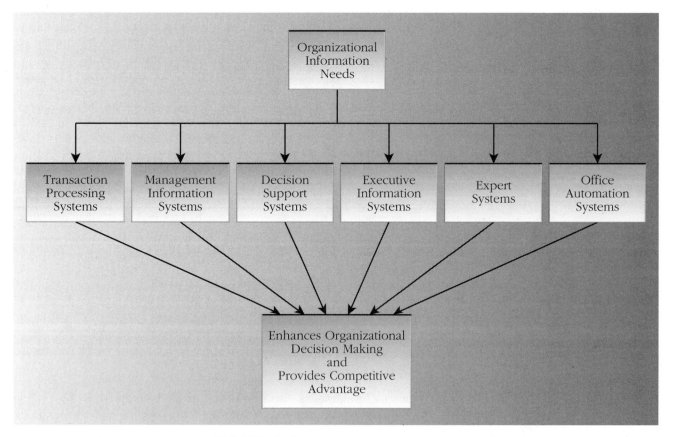

FIGURE 2–1

Often a company needs several types of information systems. The six types of information systems shown can work together to enhance organizational decision making.

There are four types of information systems:

- Transaction processing systems (TPS)
- Management information systems (MIS)
- Intelligent support systems (ISS), which consist of decision support systems (DSS), executive information systems (EIS), and expert systems (ES)
- Office automation systems (OAS)

The types of information systems used by an organization depend on its information needs. One organization may rely only on a transaction processing system for its information needs; another may use all four types of systems. Note, however, that no one system is superior to another. Further, different types of systems must be integrated to promote the free flow of information within and outside the organization.

This chapter is organized as follows: The next six sections cover the above mentioned systems. The chapter concludes with a discussion on how to make use of the full potential of these different systems.

Transaction Processing Systems

Transaction processing systems (TPS)

Information systems that record internal and external transactions. A TPS meets the needs of operational managers; the output of the TPS becomes the input to an MIS.

Transaction processing systems were among the earliest computerized systems. Their primary purpose is to record, process, validate, and store transactions that take place in the various functional areas of a business for future retrieval and use. A **transaction processing system (TPS)** is an information system that records company transactions (a transaction is defined as an exchange between two or more business entities). Let us look at a simple example of a business transaction. McDonald's, which sells a large number of hamburgers every day, orders raw materials from its suppliers. Each time the company places an order with a supplier, a transaction occurs and a transaction system records relevant information, such as the supplier's name, address, and credit rating, the kind and quantity of items purchased, and the invoice amount. Note that transactions can be internal or external. When a department orders office supplies from the purchasing department, an internal transaction occurs; when a customer places an order for a product, an external transaction occurs. A TPS supports these tasks by imposing a set of rules and guidelines that specify how to record, process, and store a given transaction. There are many uses of transaction processing systems in our everyday lives, such as when we make a purchase at a retail store, deposit or withdraw money at a bank, or register for classes at a university. Almost all organizations, regardless of the industry in which they operate, have a manual or automated TPS.

A TPS is the data lifeline for a company because it is the source of data for other information systems, such as MIS and DSS. Hence, if the TPS shuts down, the consequences can be serious for the organization. A TPS is also the main link between the organization and external entities, such as customers, suppliers, distributors, and regulatory agencies.

As shown in Figure 2–2, transaction systems exist for the various functional areas in an organization, such as finance, accounting, manufacturing, production, human resources, marketing, quality control, engineering, and research and development. Until a few years ago, many companies viewed the

FIGURE 2–2

Data must be processed to become useful information. This figure shows the six steps involved in processing a transaction.

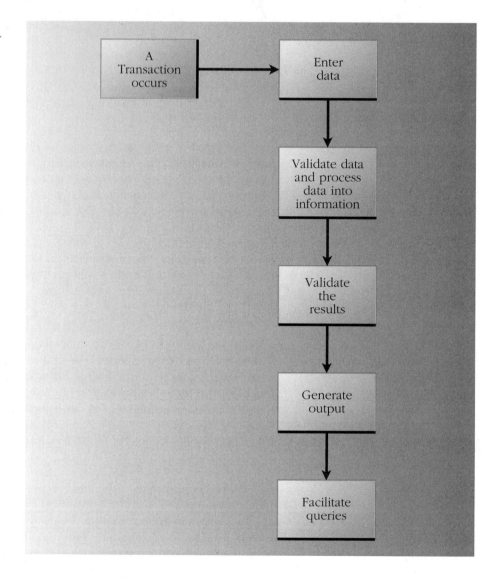

TPS for each business function as a separate entity with little or no connection to other systems in the company. Today, however, many companies are trying to build cross-functional TPS to promote the free exchange of information among different business units. This is a desirable goal, but is still very difficult to achieve.

Let us look at an example of a real-world TPS. CareNet, the TPS of Travelers Insurance Company (see box), is an advanced system that records and processes insurance-related transactions. Filing and processing insurance claims is a highly information-intensive process in which every step generates new data or modifies existing data. CareNet allows the company to accurately capture this data and disseminate it at the right time to its 7 million clients. The information generated by CareNet is useful both to employees of Travelers Insurance and to its clients. A Travelers employee can access the system and look at the latest transaction; an authorized client can also access CareNet to study the status of his or her insurance claim. This system, therefore, spans organizational boundaries and provides information to both internal and external entities.

Steps in Processing a Transaction

The six steps in processing a transaction are:

1. Data entry
2. Data validation
3. Processing and revalidation
4. Storage
5. Output generation
6. Query support

Source document

The document that is generated at the source where the transaction occurs. A sales receipt is an example of a source document.

Data Entry   To be processed, transaction data must first be entered into the system. There are a number of input devices for entering data, including the keyboard and the mouse. Other input devices are covered in Chapter 3. Documents generated at the point where a transaction occurs are called **source documents** and become input data for the system. For example, when a customer returns an item at a store, the sales receipt becomes the source document for the transaction "return item for refund." An ATM receipt for a bank transaction becomes the source document for balancing a checkbook.

Data validation   Data validation is an essential step in transaction processing. It ensures the accuracy and reliability of data by comparing actual data with predetermined standards or known results. There are two steps in validation: error detection and error correction. *Error detection* is performed by one set of control mechanisms; *error correction* is performed by another.

BUSINESS REALITIES
Travelers Insurance Company

CareNet, a TPS used by Travelers Insurance Co., a $11.3-billion company based in Hartford, Connecticut, is considered to be one of the most advanced transaction systems in the health care industry. It took more than 100 programmers working over 18 months and more than 11 million lines of code to develop this sophisticated system.

The business of providing insurance is highly information-intensive. The company is required to disseminate accurate and timely information to a large number of decision makers and regulatory agencies. This is no small task and it requires the use of sophisticated information systems and technologies.

CareNet stores and analyzes data that is generated during each step of the claim processing cycle, from the sale of an insurance product to the filing and paying of claims. Some of this information becomes input to other systems in the company. The system updates and maintains detailed records for the company's 7 million clients.

One of the special characteristics of CareNet is that it is easily accessible both to employees and to clients. For example, any authorized employee, located anywhere in the country, can access the data residing on CareNet and obtain information on the latest transaction. But what is interesting about this system is that even the company's corporate customers can access CareNet directly and view insurance data on *their* employees. For example, the human resources manager at Company A can access the system and view the claims filed by one of Company A's employees.

Such ready access to information has not only gained Travelers high marks in customer service, but has also helped the company retain its leading position in the highly competitive insurance business.[3]

Some commonly used error detection procedures are checking the data for appropriate format (text, numbers, etc.), checking for aberrations (values that are too low or too high), and checking for missing data, invalid data, and inconsistent data. The term *missing data* refers to fields that are missing a mandated data value. For example, if the number of hours worked by a part-time employee is missing on a payroll form, that is a missing-data error. *Invalid data* is data that is outside the normal range. For example, if the number of hours worked by a part-time employee is 72 hours per week instead of the normal 20 hours, then we have invalid data. Finally, the term *inconsistent data* means that the same data item assumes different values in different places without a valid reason. For example, if payroll records show that an employee worked 25 hours, but the employee log shows that the same employee worked 35 hours, then we have inconsistent data. Although sophisticated validation techniques can detect many errors, some human errors are difficult to detect. For example, if a data entry clerk enters 12 work hours instead of 21 for a part-time employee, the system will not be able to detect this error.

Error correction procedures are designed to ensure that all errors have been corrected and that no new errors have been introduced during the process. The kind of error correction technique used depends on the type of error and the nature of the application. Some simple error correction measures include allowing only authorized people to correct errors, maintaining an updated record of individuals authorized to make corrections, maintaining a log of revised (corrected) data values, and establishing a paper trail showing the nature and the source of each error and the techniques that were used to correct it. This paper trail, showing who corrected the errors and when and how the errors were corrected, is sometimes called an **audit trail.**

Audit trail
A trail showing who corrected each error and when and how each error was corrected.

Online transaction processing (OLTP)

Data are processed as they are created; since there is no time lag between data creation and data processing, the information in an online system is always current.

Batch processing

There are two ways to process transactions: batch processing and online processing. In batch processing, transactions are accumulated over a certain period of over time, such as a day, a week, a month, or a quarter, before they are processed.

Transaction file

A file that contains information about transactions that are processed as a batch and that occurred in a given period of time.

Master file

A permanent record of all transactions that have occurred in a company.

Data Processing and Revalidation   Once the accuracy and reliability of the data are validated, the data are ready for processing. There are two ways to process transactions: online and batch mode.

Online transaction processing (OLTP) is the almost instantaneous processing of data. The term *online* means that the data input device is directly linked to the TPS and therefore the data are processed as soon as it is entered into the system. The input device may be at a remote location and be linked to the system by networks or by telecommunications systems.

Since there is little or no time lag between data creation and data processing in an online system, the information is always current. Some examples of online transaction processing are ATM transactions, student registration for classes, and order tracking. The processing of flight reservations is another good example of an online system in which data are processed as it is input into the system. A travel agent checks for seat availability, using the data in a central computer system, and immediately notifies the customer as to the status of his or her ticket. Once the reservation is made, the airline system immediately updates its files and sends a confirmation to the travel agent. Online processing is possible because of storage media, such as disks, that process data in a random order. The relationship between storage media and types of processing is discussed in Chapter 3.

The second type of processing is **batch processing,** in which transactions are accumulated over time and processed periodically. Batch processing may be done on a daily, weekly, or monthly basis, or any other time period appropriate to the given application. For example, a company may process the travel expenses of its employees on a monthly basis, whereas sales may be processed at the end of each day.

A **transaction file** contains information about a group of transactions that occurred in a given period of time. It is processed using techniques such as sorting, merging, and so on. Once the transaction file has been processed, the next step is to update the **master file,** which is a permanent record of all transactions that have occurred. Each time the master file is updated with information from the transaction file, a new master file, including most current transaction data, is generated.

Although until the early 1960s batch processing was the only method for processing data, today there are other methods. However, batch processing continues to be a popular method because it is often the most sensible and practical approach. For example, batch processing lends itself well to payroll operations, since paychecks are generated periodically. Processing jobs in batches also results in more efficient use of computer resources. Finally, quality control is sometimes easier in batch processing, since errors detected at the end of a batch can be rectified before the next batch is processed.

However, one of the disadvantages of batch processing is that there is a time lag between data creation and data processing, so that the information in the files may not be up to date. Compare the master file of a batch processing system with the master file of an online processing system. In batch processing, updates to the master file are made periodically; in an online system, the master file is updated continually. Another disadvantage of batch processing is that some errors may be detected only after the batch has been processed, in which case the entire batch has to be processed again, whereas in online processing, the error can be detected as soon as it appears.

Which type of processing is better? That depends on the user's needs. If a user needs periodic updates on system transactions, batch processing is ideal; if a user needs up-to-the-minute information, online processing is necessary. Also, the decision regarding the processing method varies from one organization to the next. One company may do batch processing of its inventory while another may use online processing for its inventory management.

Regardless of the type of processing used, once it is complete, the output should be validated for accuracy and reliability. Therefore, validation should be done both before the data is processed (to check input validity) and after the data is processed (to check output validity).

Data Storage   Processed data must be carefully and properly stored for future use. Data storage is a critical consideration for many organizations because the value and usefulness of data diminish if data are not properly stored. The kind of processing and the type of storage medium are, to some extent, related issues. For example, magnetic tape is often used to store data that is batch-processed. However, online transaction processing cannot be done on magnetic tape; it relies on other types of storage media, such as magnetic disks. Storage and storage devices are covered in Chapter 3.

The next step in the processing of a transaction is to output the results of the transaction to the decision maker. Note that storage and output may not always occur in the same order. We can output the results of the transaction to the decision maker and then store them, or store the result and then output them to the decision maker.

Output Generation   Once data has been input, validated, processed, revalidated, and stored, the output can be communicated to decision makers in two ways:

* Documents and reports
* Forms: screens or panels

Documents are a popular output method. They can be processed further, either to generate additional information or to present the same information in a different format. Some examples of documents are invoices, paychecks, purchase invoices, sales receipts, and job orders.

What is the difference between documents and reports? In the IS literature, a document is usually a record of one transaction, whereas a report is a summary of two or more transactions. For example, the manager of a retail store may receive an invoice (i.e., a document) from a supplier indicating the quantity and type of each item ordered and the total cost of the order. A report, on the other hand, may summarize all the invoices from a given supplier. (Nevertheless, these terms are often used interchangeably.)

Computer output need not always be presented in hard-copy form (such as reports, documents, and printouts), but can also appear on computer screens and panels. Such soft-copy presentations are known as forms.

Query Support   The last step in processing a transaction is querying (asking questions of) the system. Query facilities allow users to access data and information that may otherwise not be readily available. For example, a sales manager may query the system for the number of damaged items in a given store.

Now let us look at a real-world example of how a transaction is processed.

Example of a Transaction Processing System (Genesis)

Genesis (see page 41) is a TPS that records American Express card transactions from all over the world. Let us take a look at how Genesis processes a customer transaction. When a customer uses the American Express Card, details of the transaction, such as customer name, account number, card expiration date, description of items purchased, date of purchase, invoice amount, merchant's name, address, and so on are input into the system. The merchant may either mail this data to American Express, where an operator enters the data into Genesis through an input device, such as a keyboard, or directly inputs the data if the merchant's computer system is linked to the Genesis system.

After the data has been input, the next step is to validate the input. This process may include checking for missing data (such as the customer account number), invalid data (such as an alphanumeric customer name), and inconsistent data (such as a mismatch between total invoice amount and individual item values). Genesis has several error correction mechanisms that automatically correct an error and sends an error report to the merchant.

The next step is to process the data. Genesis batch-processes the monthly billings to customers, while credit card debits and balances are processed online. The output of the system is then validated and error control mechanisms are activated to rectify errors, if any.

Genesis then stores the output for future retrieval and use. The results are also output to managers at American Express and to merchants, in the form of reports or documents detailing the shopping patterns of customers, the dates of payment to merchants, the total dollar value of each transaction, and so on.

Finally, managers at American Express can query the system to receive information on different variables, such as total payments made to merchants the previous day. Both merchants and managers at American Express greatly value the contribution of Genesis to their decision-making process. It links managers with the external environment, which includes customers, merchants, and regulatory agencies, and provides input to other information systems at American Express.

Table 2–1 summarizes the characteristics of a TPS.

Management Information Systems

Management information systems (MIS) are general-purpose, well-integrated systems that monitor and control the internal operations of an organization. They provide middle managers with vital information necessary to make tactical decisions and to assess the impact of daily operations on the long-range goals of the company.

The input to an MIS comes primarily from the TPS and other sources within the company. The output of an MIS takes the form of summary reports and exception reports. A **summary report** accumulates data from several transactions and presents the results in condensed form. For example, a bank manager may get a summary report listing the total dollar amounts of deposits and withdrawals made the previous day. A sales manager may get a summary report giving the number of units of each product sold in the preceding month. An **exception report,** on the other hand, is a report that outlines any deviations from expected output. The primary purpose of an exception report is to draw the attention of middle managers to any significant differences between *actual* performance and *expected*

Management information systems (MIS)
Well-integrated systems that meet the tactical information needs of middle managers. These systems generate summary and exception reports.

Summary report
A report that summarizes data from several transactions. This is one of the outputs of an MIS.

Exception report
A report that identifies data that appear to be exceptional, where an exception is the difference between actual performance and expected performance.

TABLE 2–1
A transaction processing
system (TPS) records
transactional data. This
table summarizes the
characteristics of a TPS.

Characteristics of Transaction Processing Systems

♦ A TPS records internal and external transactions for a company. It is a repository of data that is frequently accessed by other systems.
♦ A TPS performs routine, repetitive tasks. It is mostly used by lower-level managers to make operational decisions.
♦ Transactions can be recorded in batch mode or online. In batch mode, the files are updated periodically; in online mode, each transaction is recorded as it occurs.
♦ There are six steps in processing a transaction. They are data entry, data validation, data processing and revalidation, storage, output generation, and query support.

performance. A sales manager may study an exception report that lists all sales personnel who sold less than $20,000 or more than $80,000 in the preceding month. Reports of both kinds should always be succinct, accurate, timely, reliable, verifiable, and readily usable.

What are some differences between a TPS and an MIS? First, the primary goal of a TPS is to record and process transactions that take place in the company, while the primary goal of an MIS is to produce summary and exception reports used in tactical decision making. Second, the output of a TPS becomes the input to an MIS, and although the TPS is not the only source of data to the MIS, it is a primary source. Figure 2–3 shows that transaction data are input into a TPS and that the output of a TPS becomes the input to an MIS. Finally, a TPS helps managers primarily with operational or day-to-day decisions, while an MIS helps managers make tactical decisions over a longer period of time, such as a year or more. Both systems must work in harmony in order to meet the known or anticipated information needs of the company.

Examples of Management Information Systems

Home Depot, a $7.1-billion company based in Atlanta, is a leader in the $115-billion home improvement industry. Home Depot credits the customized MIS inventory system in each of its 218 stores as one of the major factors in its sus-

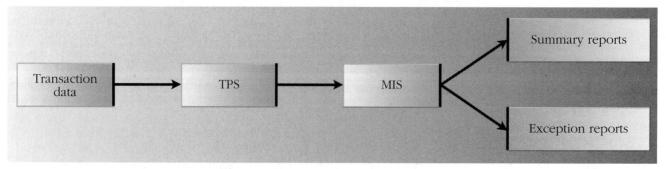

FIGURE 2–3

TPS and MIS must work together to meet the information needs of an organization. The output from a TPS becomes the input to an MIS, which produces summary and exception reports.

Ucar Carbon

Ucar Carbon Company is a major producer of graphite electrodes, supplying them to the steel industry. Managers at Ucar rely on an MIS to help with product pricing, delivery schedules, and inventory management. The summary and exception reports produced by the system play an important role in helping the company reduce operating costs, cut inventory, and increase customer service.

Before the system was installed, it took 12 clerks, sometimes working as long as a week, simply to provide customers with basic pricing and delivery information on Ucar's different products. The process was so frustrating that customers began to take their business elsewhere. Ucar rectified the problem by building an information system that provides customers with timely and accurate information and allows managers to be proactive in their decision making.

Today, the new system handles 80% of customer queries with just three employees. It can generate pricing information and delivery schedules within a few minutes on any of Ucar's diverse line of products. Summary and exception reports keep managers abreast of important product information, which allows them to be highly responsive to customer queries. The system has helped Ucar to slash inventory by $15 million, because managers no longer maintain large buffers of stock to meet possible demand.[4]

tained growth. The system captures data about local market conditions and consumers, identifies the type and quantity of items to be ordered, and electronically transmits purchase orders to suppliers, thus relieving managers of unproductive paperwork. Managers use the reports generated by the system to develop local inventory policies and advertising methods.

Another company that has made effective use of MIS is Ucar Carbon Company (see box). A few years ago, the company had an antiquated information system that was slow to respond to the information needs of its managers. Company sales people found it difficult even to perform simple tasks such as providing customers with price quotes and delivery schedules for different products. It took several people, working for several days, to draft a price and delivery schedule for the company's products.

Ucar installed a new MIS that provides pricing and delivery information and summary and exception reports, within a few minutes, on all company products. Before the system was installed, since managers did not know whether a product was available or, if it was, when it could be delivered to the customer, they often kept inventory buffers to avoid stock-outs. The timely and accurate product information provided by the new system has significantly reduced inventory stock pile-ups and operating costs.

Management information systems are used not only in the U.S. but throughout the world. Even countries with limited financial resources understand the importance and vitality of information systems to their national economies. For example, China is investing huge sums in computers and information systems in an effort to become technologically sophisticated (see Global Perspective box). At the Bao Steel plant in China, MIS is responsible for payroll, administrative functions, and inventory management.

In the next section, we discuss the third category of information systems, Intelligent Support Systems (ISS). While TPS and MIS meet the information needs of operational and tactical decisions, ISS support tactical and strategic decisions.

Intelligent Support Systems

Intelligent support systems (ISS)
Systems designed to assist intuitive decision making. Decision support systems, executive information systems, and expert systems fall into this category.

Intelligent support systems (ISS) are systems that facilitate decisions requiring the use of knowledge, intuition, experience, and expertise. Systems that fall into this category are

- Decision support systems (DSS)
- Executive information systems (EIS)
- Artificial intelligence (AI) and expert systems (ES)

Such systems are called intelligent support systems because they support the knowledge-intensive activities of managers, which require the application of theoretical knowledge and practical experience. ISS are ideal for decisions that require the use of theoretical knowledge, such as theorems and principles, and of practical knowledge, such as intuition, experience, and judgment. In this section, we give a broad overview of ISS and its role in organizational decision making. Later chapters provide a more detailed view of each system.

Decision Support Systems

Decision support systems (DSS)
Computerized systems that provide managers with internal and external data and decision-making models that facilitate semi-structured decision making.

Decision support systems (DSS) are interactive, well-integrated systems that provide managers with data, tools, and models to facilitate semistructured decisions or tactical decisions. As you may recall, a tactical decision is partly structured and partly unstructured. An example of a tactical decision is bidding on a contract. Part of the task is structured—for example, considering standard operational costs and overheads—while part is unstructured, since the bidder must take into account the way competitors may bid on the same contract. DSS provide the decision maker with a set of tools and techniques that can be "mixed and matched" in creative ways to solve semistructured problems. It automates the routine and repetitive elements in a problem while simultaneously supporting the use of intuition and judgment.

 A GLOBAL PERSPECTIVE
Unisys Goes to China

As impatient travelers besiege an airport ticket counter in a southern China boomtown, a harried clerk scribbles seat assignments on boarding passes and jots down passengers' names on a sheet of paper. On good days, he gets help with such chores from a mainframe computer in Beijing that runs China's reservation system. China is planning to invest between $50 billion and $100 billion in both infrastructure and information systems and is seeking the help of western companies, such as Unisys, to achieve this goal.

Unisys, which set up shop in China in 1979, is playing an active role in helping the Chinese government develop some of the following information systems:

- A nationwide airline reservation system, with 2,000 terminals in 30 cities, is likely to be the largest online computer network in China. This system will display computerized flight information and will automate many administrative functions.
- At Bao Steel, the nation's second largest steel mill, a MIS helps process payroll, administrative functions, and inventory management.
- The China Meteorological Administration is developing a new weather radar system that will improve the locating and forecasting of hurricanes, lightning, and other severe weather conditions. It is similar to the one at the U.S. National Weather Service.[5]

Some problems for which DSS are ideally suited are location selection, identifying new products to be marketed, scheduling personnel, and analyzing the effect that price increases for resources have on profits.

How a DSS Works   A DSS accesses and processes large volumes of internal and external data and integrates them with various decision-making models. Internal data are often downloaded from the TPS or from other information systems. (Downloading means moving data from a larger system, such as a mainframe, to a smaller system, such as a PC.) External data may come from a wide variety of sources, such as the Dow Jones, *The Wall Street Journal,* or other external databases maintained by government agencies or private companies.

The data are then integrated with models to produce alternate solutions to a problem. (A model is a physical or conceptual representation of reality.) Most decision makers use conceptual models to support decision making. Some examples of models include calculating mortgage payments, determining overall course grades, assessing the amount of air pollution, and predicting population growth. Figure 2–4 shows how a DSS integrates internal and external data with different models to produce alternative solutions to a given problem.

The alternatives generated by a decision maker can be further analyzed using "what-if" analysis, which assesses the impact of changes made to input or output variables. For example, product pricing is a complex decision that takes into account a number of internal factors such as material costs, production costs, labor costs, and external factors such as competitor pricing and product demand. A DSS can present a manager with different pricing alternatives and help answer "what-if" questions such as these: "What if the price of raw materials increases by 3.6% a year?" "What if demand for a product increases by 10%?" "What if a competitor reduces its price for a similar product by 20%?"

FIGURE 2–4

A DSS is a type of intelligent support system that integrates internal and external data with various decision-making models in order to produce alternative solutions to a given problem. It also allows managers to ask "what-if" questions and to perform goal seeking.

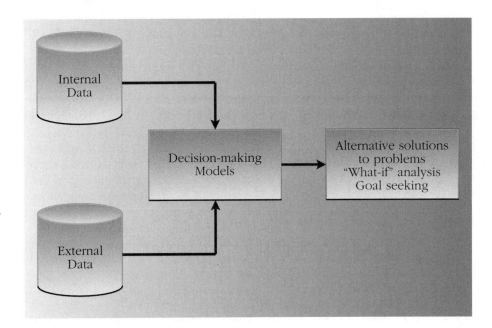

A DSS also allows managers to perform *goal-seeking,* which specifies the actions a manager should take in order to accomplish a certain goal. For example, suppose the goal of the company is to increase sales of Product A by 10%. A DSS can help a marketing manager decide on the course of action to take regarding operating costs, product pricing, advertising, and other related issues in order to achieve the goal.

Another interesting feature of DSS is that an individual or a group of individuals can use them. DSS that support group decision making are called **Group decision support systems (GDSS).** In most organizations, decisions of any significance are made collectively by a group, not by a single person. GDSS are a set of interactive, well-integrated systems that facilitate and support group decision making. Note that DSS is a tool that facilitates the *process* of decision making more than simply solving a given problem. We explore these concepts further in Chapter 8.

Group decision support systems
Decision support systems that support group decision making are known as group decision support systems.

Example of a Decision Support System

Jewish Hospital Health Care Services (see box) deploys several DSS to support tasks such as cost accounting, productivity analysis, nurse scheduling, forecasting, and planning. For example, the hospital uses a DSS to prepare contract bids for its services. Preparing a contract is a semistructured task that involves some structured, routine activities (such as assessing the cost of a certain service) and some unstructured activities (such as assessing a competitor's strategy). Preparing a bid requires the decision maker to take into account both internal and external data; internal data may consist of cost and profit figures, manpower requirements, and overhead costs, while external data may include factors such as state and federal taxes, regulatory requirements, and so on. The system then integrates these data with different decision models, such as financial and accounting models, manpower planning models, business intelligence models, and project evaluation models, to arrive at a solution. The DSS also helps decision makers answer "what if" questions such as these: "What if the price of materials increases?" "What if the new health plan comes into effect?" "What if competitors reduce their prices by

B U S I N E S S   R E A L I T I E S
Jewish Hospital Healthcare Services

Jewish Hospital Healthcare Services (JHHS) is a regional health care provider in Louisville, Kentucky, that owns and manages seven health care facilities with a total of 1,000 patients and 3,500 employees. It uses several DSS, in cost accounting, productivity analysis, and nurse scheduling, to perform tasks such as accounting, forecasting, planning, and communications.

For example, a cost-accounting DSS combines internal and external data to prepare bids on contracts and services that the hospital provides to outside parties. The system helps the hospital to determine pricing policies for a variety of products and services by taking into account a large number of internal cost factors and external competitive factors.

The hospital also has a DSS that helps managers schedule nurses for different shifts. Scheduling nurses is a very complex task, since a large number of factors, such as education level, training, special skills, overall attitude, and patient requirements, must be taken into account before the schedules can be devised.[6]

5%?" By addressing a number of "what-if" scenarios, decision makers become better prepared to respond to changes in the marketplace. It also helps decision makers to engage in goal-seeking. For example, what should the pricing be if the hospital wants to bid 3% lower than the winning bid last year?

Executive Information Systems

Executive information systems (EIS)
User-friendly and interactive computer-based systems, designed to meet the information needs of top managers.

A second type of ISS, used primarily by top management, is the **Executive information system (EIS).** It is a user-friendly, interactive system, designed to meet the information needs of top management engaged in long-range planning, crisis management, and other strategic decisions. As you may recall from Chapter 1, strategic decisions are unique, nonrepetitive, and future-oriented decisions, which address long-term issues such as emerging markets, merger and acquisition strategies, new-product development, and investment strategies. Such systems assist in the making of decisions that require an in-depth understanding of the firm and of the industry in which the firm operates.

The primary difference between a DSS and an EIS is that the goal of an EIS is not so much to generate alternatives for a given problem as it is to integrate data from different sources and present it in a useful format to the decision maker. An EIS is user-friendly and almost intuitive to use; it has excellent menus and graphic capabilities. Another special characteristic of an EIS is its **drill-down**

Drill-down
A feature that allows the user to get information at any desired level of detail from an EIS.

capability, which is the ability of the system to provide information at any level of detail desired by the decision maker. For example, the CEO of a company may want the monthly sales of Product X for the entire company. Next, the CEO may want a breakdown of sales figures on a regional basis or on a store-wide basis. The drill-down facility can provide both.

Chapter 8 provides a detailed discussion of EIS. Table 2–2 summarizes the characteristics of DSS and EIS.

TABLE 2–2
Characteristics of decision support systems and Executive Information Systems, both of which are intelligent support systems.

Characteristics of Decision Support Systems (DSS) and Executive Information Systems (EIS)

- DSS and EIS are intelligent support systems designed to provide middle and top managers with information necessary to make decisions that require intuition and judgment.
- Both DSS and EIS are intuitive, interactive, user-friendly systems that augment the decision-making capabilities of a manager. They are menu-driven and often have excellent color and graphic capabilities.
- Both systems use internal and external data to solve problems. Managers at this level tend to rely more on external data than on internal data.
- A DSS also uses various decision-making models to provide managers with alternative solutions to a given problem. An EIS provides managers with information integrated from a variety of sources.
- Both systems are equipped with decision-making tools such as "what-if" analysis and goal seeking. In addition to these tools, an EIS is equipped with drill-down capabilities.
- A DSS can support both individual decision making and group decision making. Decision support systems that support group decision making are referred to as group decision support systems (GDSS).

EIS Spreadsheet

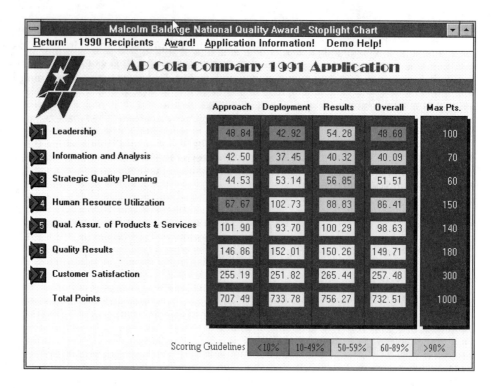

Malcolm Baldrige National Quality Award - Stoplight Chart					
Return! 1990 Recipients Award! Application Information! Demo Help!					

AP Cola Company 1991 Application

	Approach	Deployment	Results	Overall	Max Pts.
1 Leadership	48.84	42.92	54.28	48.68	100
2 Information and Analysis	42.50	37.45	40.32	40.09	70
3 Strategic Quality Planning	44.53	53.14	56.85	51.51	60
4 Human Resource Utilization	67.67	102.73	88.83	86.41	150
5 Qual. Assur. of Products & Services	101.90	93.70	100.29	98.63	140
6 Quality Results	146.86	152.01	150.26	149.71	180
7 Customer Satisfaction	255.19	251.82	265.44	257.48	300
Total Points	707.49	733.78	756.27	732.51	1000

Scoring Guidelines | <10% | 10-49% | 50-59% | 60-89% | >90% |

Artificial Intelligence and Expert Systems

Artificial intelligence (AI)
A branch of computer science whose goal is to design and develop machines that emulate human intelligence. AI attempts to endow machines with capabilities and characteristics that would indicate intelligence in a human being.

Expert systems (ES)
Software designed to capture the knowledge and problem-solving skills of a human expert. An expert system has three main components: a knowledge base, an inference engine, and a user interface.

The third type of ISS is **artificial intelligence (AI),** a branch of computer science whose goal is to design and develop computer systems that emulate human intelligence. AI attempts to endow machines with capabilities and characteristics that would indicate intelligence if found in a human being.

Expert systems (ES) are a branch of AI. These systems incorporate the knowledge and problem-solving skills of a human expert, such as a physician, a nuclear scientist, or an automotive engineer. When the Exxon tanker accident resulted in a massive oil spill in Alaska a few years ago, Exxon management tapped into the expertise of oil experts from all over the world. An expert system would have been ideal for this problem.

Expert systems are good at solving semistructured and unstructured problems and can solve problems that require theoretical knowledge and practical experience. More important, they help organizations acquire and retain knowledge that is vital to the competitiveness and the success of the company.

An expert system has three main components: a knowledge base, an inference engine, and a user interface. Figure 2–5 shows these three components. The knowledge base, as its name implies, serves as a storehouse of knowledge and experience gathered from experts in a given field, including facts, theorems, and principles related to a given area of knowledge or field of study. For example, an expert car mechanic would be the source of knowledge for an expert system designed to solve car problems. Once the expert's knowledge is acquired, it is translated into a language that the computer can use; this process is called *knowledge representation.*

The second component of an expert system is the inference engine, which uses rules of behavior and interrelationships between different pieces of knowl-

FIGURE 2–5

An expert system, which conveys the knowledge and experience of a human expert, consists of three main components: a knowledge base, a reasoning mechanism, and a user interface. The knowledge base is the repository of knowledge; the inference engine provides rules and guidelines for applying that knowledge.

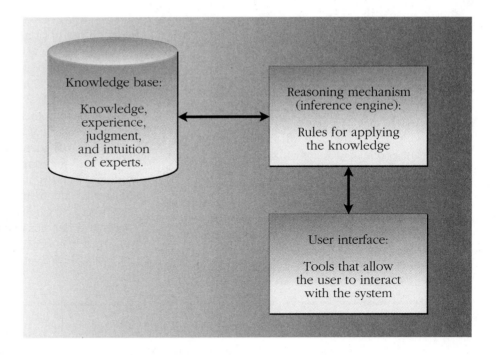

edge to solve the given problem. It selects the appropriate knowledge, applies it to the problem, and resolves any conflicts that may arise in the process.

Finally, the user interface consists of tools, such as menus, graphics, and explanation facilities, that help users to interact with the system. Of particular importance is the explanation module in an expert system, which provides explanations as to how a problem was solved and how the knowledge was used to solve the problem. The explanation module can also serve as a valuable training tool for novices in the field, because it provides step-by-step instructions on how to solve a problem. These and related concepts are explored in Chapter 9.

Example of an Expert System

Some years ago, Merced County, in California, used a manual screening system for processing welfare applications, which resulted in significant delays and huge error rates. Today, the county's new expert system carefully uses the collective knowledge of many experienced social workers in the county to process applications. The system is more effective than social workers because it applies the knowledge consistently, does not forget any rules or regulations, and is not moody or biased. The benefits of using the expert system have been dramatic for Merced County. Processing time has dropped by more than 50%, staff efficiency has increased, and turnover rates have decreased by two-thirds. More importantly, processing errors and welfare fraud have dropped significantly, which has saved the county millions of dollars. Another significant advantage of the system is that it can be used to train new social workers in processing welfare applications.[7]

An expert system is ideal for this application, because processing welfare applications requires knowledge of state and federal laws and intuition and judgment about the credibility of the applicant. A social worker should not apply rules

BUSINESS REALITIES
Kaiser Foundation Health Plan

An expert system is helping Kaiser Foundation Health Plan, Inc., based in Oakland, California, to improve office productivity by helping office workers evaluate if an applicant is qualified for membership in the company's health plan. Before the system was installed, workers often wrote down information about applicants on scratch pads, which was then transferred to index cards. The process was so cumbersome and tedious that almost 15 workers had to handle each application, and it took anywhere between four to six weeks to process a single application. The company was concerned that this was affecting its reputation and that customers were dissatis-fied with the poor and lengthy turnaround time.

An investment in an expert system has turned this situation around for the company. Using Trinzic Corporation's Aion Development System (DS) rule-based expert system, the company has codified rules that medical staffers and other professional workers use to review and process client applications. The system, dubbed System for Individual Marketing and Review (SIMR), has cut in half the time it takes to process applications. Further, users can add some of their own rules that may reflect their judgment in processing an application (such as number of cigarettes an individual smokes and so on). The system handles about 80% of individual applications with approximately 28% resulting in immediate acceptances and 12% in immediate rejections.[8]

blindly and rigidly but should be sensitive to the circumstances of the applicant. This usually comes from experience, not just from textual knowledge.

The knowledge base in this expert system is a compilation of the knowledge and experience of several highly qualified social workers and legal consultants. It includes federal and state welfare laws, tax policies, and related information. This knowledge is represented in the system as a set of IF-THEN rules, which specify the actions that the system should take if a certain set of conditions are met. These rules are then applied to determine whether an applicant qualifies for welfare.

The biggest advantage of this expert system is that it is a storehouse of the knowledge and experience of many social workers. Under the manual system, the county had to rely on the knowledge of each individual social worker, who might or might not be well versed in all the rules and regulations that govern welfare. This can lead to the inconsistent application of rules and policies, since rules may be interpreted differently by different social workers. The new system uniformly applies the collective knowledge of a group of experts to each case, thus providing consistency in the quality of decisions. We will revisit this example in Chapter 9 and explore some of the technical details of this system. Table 2–3 summarizes the characteristics of expert systems.

TABLE 2–3
The study of expert systems is a branch of artificial intelligence. An expert system is an intelligent support system. Some of the main characteristics of expert systems are shown here.

Characteristics of Expert Systems

- An expert system is a program designed to capture the knowledge and problem-solving skills of a human expert. Expert systems are a branch of artificial intelligence.
- Expert systems handle problems that require knowledge, intuition, and judgment.
- Expert systems, unlike DSS and EIS, can replace decision makers.
- An expert system has three main components: the knowledge base, which stores the knowledge, the inference engine, which stores the reasoning principles used by the expert, and the user interface, which allows the user to interact with the system.
- Expert systems are not designed for any one level of management; their primary function is to disseminate expertise throughout the organization.

There are several differences among the three types of ISS discussed in this section. For example, a DSS is intended for middle managers who solve semistructured problems, while EIS is intended for top managers who solve unstructured problems. Expert systems, on the other hand, are not for managers at any specific level; they are simply designed to assist in the solution of complex semistructured and unstructured problems.

The goal of both DSS and EIS is to facilitate and enhance the quality of decision making. The goal of expert systems, on the other hand, is to gather and apply organizational knowledge for problem solving. A DSS uses both data and models to solve problems and present alternatives, while an EIS integrates data and presents it in a useful format to decision makers. While DSS and EIS do not replace managers, expert systems have, in some cases, displaced knowledge workers.

Office Automation Systems

Office automation systems (OAS)
Systems that are designed to increase the productivity of clerical workers and knowledge workers and enhance communication in the workplace. Examples of OAS are word processing, desktop publishing, voice mail, e-mail, videoconferencing, and multimedia systems.

The fourth type of information system found in organizations is **Office automation systems (OAS).** These are systems that support the automation of various managerial and clerical activities. The primary goals of office automation are to enhance communication in the workplace and increase the efficiency and productivity of knowledge workers and clerical workers. Office automation systems include

* *Word processing:* Creating written documents, such as letters, memos, and term papers, on the computer
* *Desktop publishing:* Using software with sophisticated publishing capabilities to create documents
* *E-mail:* Sending mail electronically from one computer to others
* *Voice mail:* Storing, accessing, retrieving, and distributing messages using the telephone
* *Videoconferencing:* Using group-oriented systems that allow users located in different parts of the world to engage in face-to-face communication
* *Image retrieval and storage:* Conversion of paper documents into electronic files and images for easy retrieval and processing
* *Facsimile transmission, or fax:* The transfer of written or pictorial information over phone lines to users anywhere in the world
* *Electronic meeting systems:* Systems that bring together people who are geographically separated to facilitate face-to-face group meetings

Chapter 10 provides a detailed discussion of each of these systems. Figure 2–6 shows how knowledge workers and clerical workers can use OAS to increase productivity.

How do office automation systems help increase productivity and decrease operating costs? Take, for example, United Technologies, a manufacturing conglomerate in Hartford, Connecticut. The company uses videoconferencing to allow employees to register for courses at several different universities across the country and to get specialized training in areas vital to the success of the company. Videoconferencing also allows employees to meet face-to-face with experts from all over the world without leaving their offices. Thus, office automation has helped the company reduce its training costs while increasing the productivity of its employees.

An office automation system (OAS) is designed to increase productivity and enhance communications in the workplace. This figure identifies some tools and systems that may be part of an OAS.

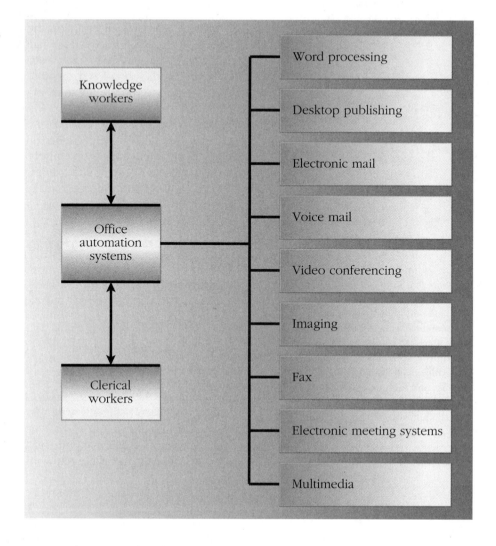

Multimedia systems
Systems that can store, retrieve, and process various types of media, such as text, graphics, image, full-motion video, audio, and animation.

Another example of OAS is Motorola's office automation package, Site Connect, which helps reduce the nagging problem of "phone tag." Site Connect alerts users to important phone calls and electronic messages even when they are away from their offices. Tools such as these simplify tasks in the workplace and enhance communication between employees.

An emerging area in OAS is **multimedia systems,** which are well-integrated systems that store, retrieve, and process different types of data, such as text, graphics, images, full-motion video, audio, and animation. Multimedia systems allow users to create, process, share, and display information in a broad variety of formats. For example, a student or a manager can use a multimedia system to make an impressive business presentation. The student can use text to display a company's mission statement, graphs and charts to show its financial performance, and video to show some highlights of the city where the company is located—all accompanied by the music of Beethoven!

Another example of the use of multimedia is the Simon Wiesenthal Center, which uses multimedia to sensitize people to the atrocities that arise from discrimination and hatred. The museum houses a multimedia system that integrates text, maps, graphics, music, photos, and film footage from around the world to educate visitors about the atrocities of hate and violent crimes. The museum is a showcase of leading edge multimedia systems that give visitors a historical perspective of human right violations.[9]

In summary, there are four broad categories of information systems:

- Transaction Processing Systems (TPS)
- Management Information Systems (MIS)
- Intelligent Support Systems (ISS), that includes Decision Support Systems (DDS), Executive Information Systems (EIS), and Expert Systems (ES)
- Office Automation Systems (OAS)

Table 2–4 summarizes the characteristics of the four types of information systems.

In the next section, we look at some factors that help organizations capture the full potential of their information systems.

Tapping the Potential of Information Systems

Information is not innocent."[10] Delivering high-quality, timely information to decision makers is not as easy as it may seem. Today, most firms understand the critical nature and the high value of information as a business resource and emphasize the importance of the free flow of information within and out-

TABLE 2–4
Characteristics of the various types of information systems.

Type of System	Input	Processing	Output	Users	Examples
TPS	• Transaction-related data	• Uses procedures and rules • Repetitive tasks • Control-oriented	• Summaries of transactions	• Lower-level managers	• Sales Transactions • Credit card payments • Insurance claims
MIS	• Output from TPS • Other internal data	• Measures and monitors operational performance	• Summary and exception reports	• Middle-level managers • Quarterly travel reports	• Monthly production reports • Safety violation reports
ISS (DSS, EIS, ES)	• Internal and external data and models • Knowledge and experience	• Interactive, ad hoc reporting • Generates alternatives	• Alternatives • Analysis reports	• Top managers • ES: Knowledge workers	• Investment portfolios • Enterprise-wide performance • Plant expansion
OAS	• Data and information	• Formatting • Summarizing • Displaying	• Documents • Graphics • Multimedia	• Knowledge and clerical workers	• Fax • Multimedia • Video-conferencing

side the organization. In spite of this understanding, few firms are able to gather and deliver timely and accurate information to their decision makers.

> Today, in fact, the information-based organization is largely a fantasy. Despite forty years of the Information Revolution in business, most managers still tell us that they cannot get the information they need to run their own units or functions.
>
> As a recent article by the CEO of a shoe company put it: "On one of my first days on the job, I asked for a copy of *every* report used in management. The next day, twenty-three of them appeared on my desk. I didn't understand them. . . . Each area's reports were Greek to the other areas, and *all* of them were Greek to me." [It was as if] each part of the organization had a separate political domain, with its own culture, leaders, and even vocabulary.[11]

One of the primary reasons why organizations fail to be effective users of information is their inability to manage the politics of information. Quite often, companies treat politics as peripheral, not essential, to the task of building an information-based organization. "Only when information politics is viewed as a natural aspect of organizational life and is consciously managed will true information-based organizations emerge."[12]

Popular theories propagate the idea that new systems and technologies create a free flow of information in an organization. However, empirical evidence suggests just the opposite: The more emphasis the company places on information, the less likely managers are to share information, because managers view information as a source of power and indispensability. "When information is the primary unit of organizational currency, we should not expect its owners to give it away."[13]

Another reason why companies are not able to realize the full potential of their systems is that they approach information management from a technological perspective rather than from a human one, and assume that technology will resolve all problems. Frequently this is not the case, because "no technology has yet been invented to convince unwilling managers to share information or even to use it. Put another way, information flow does not make an organizational culture less hierarchical and more open; rather, democratic cultures make possible democratic information flows."[14] Hence, acquiring or developing information systems is not sufficient. Organizations must also carefully address the human issues that come with these systems. There are two ways to achieve this goal.

First, technology that is easily understood and well integrated—that is, systems that can talk to one another should be used. This alone will bring a uniform face to information and present the same information in the same way to everyone in the organization. Many major U.S. corporations, including Du Pont, IBM, and American Airlines, are making substantial efforts to build integrated systems. While the benefits of integrated systems may seem obvious, very few companies have such systems.

Second, the responsibility for collecting, maintaining, and interpreting information should not rest with just one person in the organization, because this gives undue power to that person. Instead of information *ownership* by a few individuals, companies should institute information *stewardship,* which makes all employees responsible for the proper creation, quality, use, and sharing of data and information.

Summary

- **Different types of information systems are necessary to facilitate organizational decision making.**
  Managers at different levels in an organization make different kinds of decisions (operational, tactical, and strategic); therefore, the information systems necessary to support these decisions are also different. The types of information systems that an organization uses depend on its information needs. One organization may use only a TPS, while another organization may use all of the systems we have discussed to meet its information needs. Note, however, that no one system is superior to another and that different types of systems must be integrated to promote the free flow of information within and outside the organization.

- **A TPS is the data lifeline of a company.**
  A TPS records the company's transactions. When an internal or external transaction occurs, it changes old data or creates new data. In either case, the system must carefully record and process this transaction. There are six steps in processing a transaction. They are data entry, data validation, data processing and revalidation, storage, output generation, and query support. Almost every organization, regardless of the industry in which it operates, has a TPS, which may be either manual or automated. Most of the information used by managers to make operational decisions originates within the TPS. Hence, such a system is the data lifeline for an organization.

- **MIS plays a vital role in decision making.**
  The term MIS refers to a group of information systems that produce summary and exception reports. Middle managers use these reports to make a wide variety of decisions. Often these systems are general-purpose information systems that monitor and control the internal operations of an organization and serve as a vital link between top management and lower-level management. The output of a TPS often becomes the input to an MIS, so both systems must work together in order to meet the information needs of operational and middle managers.

- **Intelligent support systems support high-level decision making.**
  Intelligent support systems support and enhance unstructured decisions that require intuition and judg-

ment. Three types of systems fall into this category: decision support systems (DSS), executive information systems (EIS), and expert systems (ES). Both DSS and EIS are very user-friendly, interactive systems that help to meet the particular information needs of middle and top managers, respectively. DSS combine internal and external data with decision-making models to generate alternatives to problems, while EIS are intuitive systems that provide top managers with a wealth of information that is necessary to make strategic decisions. ES is another type of ISS. It focuses on storing and using the knowledge and experience of a human expert. The system stores the expert's knowledge in its knowledge base and the reasoning principles of the expert in its inference engine.

- **Office automation systems help to enhance communication and productivity in the workplace.**
  Office automation systems support the automation of various managerial and clerical activities. The primary goal of OAS is to enhance communication in the workplace and increase the efficiency and productivity of knowledge workers and clerical workers. Some office automation systems are word processing, desktop publishing, e-mail, voice mail, videoconferencing, image retrieval and storage, facsimile (fax) transmission, and electronic meeting systems. Another class of OAS includes multimedia systems that create and process different types of media, such as text, graphics, video, images, and audio.

- **Certain success factors help to realize the potential of different types of information systems.**
  Although many organizations have information systems, few seem to be able to make full use of these systems. Two factors are critical to the success of information systems: First, it is important to plan and develop integrated systems so that all employees get a consistent view of information. Second, organizations should promote the idea of information stewardship rather than information ownership. This will improve the flow of information while ensuring that each individual is responsible for the quality and timeliness of the information.

Review Questions

1. Why does an organization need different types of information systems to meet its information needs? Does an organization need *all* the different types of systems that we have discussed in this chapter or does it depend on the information needs of the organization? Discuss.

2. What is a transaction processing system and how does it support operational decision making? Why is a TPS often considered the data lifeline of an organization?

3. When you deposit your paycheck in a bank, a transaction takes place. Describe the six steps in processing a transaction and show how they apply to your bank deposit.

4. A middle manager receives a monthly report on the number of hours worked by the employees in his unit. A top manager receives a report on accidents that occurred on the factory floor because of safety violations. Which of these two is a summary report and which is an exception report? Discuss.

5. Identify three reasons why an organization may need ISS. Describe any two differences among TPS, MIS, and ISS.

6. What is a DSS and what are its three main components? Suppose a company uses a DSS to decide where it should build a new plant. What kind of internal and external information would be necessary to make this decision? What are some models (financial, statistical, etc.) that would be useful in this context?

7. Identify any three decision-making models that managers may use (financial, statistical, quality models, and so on).

8. What is an ES and what are its three main components? Who are some of the primary users of an ES?

9. Identify any two types of problems that can be solved using a DSS, an EIS, and an ES.

10. Identify at least four office automation systems. Identify any two goals of OAS.

11. What is a multimedia system? How can a multimedia system enhance communication in the workplace? Give an example of a business presentation in which multimedia can be used.

12. What are the two schools of thought about the impact of information systems on middle-management jobs? Discuss.

13. What are some steps that an organization can take to realize the full potential of its information systems?

 Discussion Questions

1. Consider the example of Merced County's use of expert systems to process welfare applications and detect welfare fraud. What are some pieces of knowledge that you might find in the knowledge base of this system?

2. Identify any company in your area that has laid off employees and downsized its managerial staff. Find out if information systems and technologies are among the causes of the layoff.

3. Our opening example describes Genesis, a TPS used by American Express. Explain how Genesis provides American Express with a competitive advantage and why this system can be viewed as a lifeline to the company's data.

4. What is the difference between information ownership and information stewardship? How would information stewardship help a company to make better use of its information systems?

ETHICAL ISSUES

Case 1: A Bribery Scandal

A former IS manager at a New York state agency is being investigated by the state's inspector general for allegedly accepting bribes from computer vendors as well as performing other unethical practices. Robert B. Quick, ex-assistant IS director at New York's Substance Abuse Services Division in Albany, allegedly accepted up to $8,000 in 1991 from computer salesmen who donated the money to a scholarship fund set up in his late son's name. Quick was later demoted and has since resigned his position. The computer salesmen represented Oracle Corp., Digital Equipment Corp., General Electric Co., and Data General Corp.

The state inspector's office charges that the largest contributors to the fund were two Data General (DG) salesmen, who donated a total of $1,000. The DG salesmen, who have since been fired, also allegedly discussed making large cash payments to an independent consultant who advises the state in the procurement process.

DG subsequently won the $1 million contract. However, that award was rescinded in March, 1993, as part of the ongoing investigation. DG also agreed not to participate in any New York state general office procurements until March 31, 1993. A spokesman for DG says the company averages about $2 million in annual sales from New York state.[15]

1. What are the ethical violations in this case?
2. Identify all of the participants in this situation who violated moral and ethical guidelines.

Case 2: CIO under Fire

After years of legal wrangling, S. C. Johnson and Son Inc. has extracted a monetary settlement from its former chief information officer and senior VP, Laurance T. Burden, whom the consumer goods manufacturer accused of profiting from an elaborate contractor kickback scheme. The other two defendants in the case are an executive recruiter, Milton Wood, and an IS consultant, Arthur Shack, both of whom also agreed to the settlement. The suit charges that Burden hired the two defendants for various projects at grossly inflated fees. The suit says that a portion of those fees was funneled to Burden through Shack's businesses. Alleged payments from Shack to Burden totaled $238,777. The suit also charges that Burden secretly invested company funds in a software development project, then hired Wood to discredit it so that Burden could later buy it at less than fair-market value.

While all details of the settlement were not made public, it is understood that Burden, who was at Johnson Wax from October 1988 to March 1991, would contribute a substantial amount to the settlement payment to be made to Johnson Wax, with the other two defendants making contributions.[16]

1. While Mr. Burden is clearly at fault in this situation, it is evident that there are several loopholes in the organization that allow an individual to commit these violations. What are some steps that the company should have taken to prevent unethical behavior on the part of its employees?
2. There is nothing wrong with the philosophy. "You scratch my back and I will scratch yours," particularly in the business world. Discuss.

PROBLEM SOLVING IN THE REAL WORLD

Case 1: Israel Discount Bank Delights Customers

Imagine if you could walk into your bank and log on to a computer terminal that lets you buy and sell stock, print out a history of all your credit card purchases, check foreign exchange accounts, and engage in other financial transactions without the help of a bank manager. Israel Discount Bank (IDB), Israel's third largest bank, provides such sophisticated online services to its customers and is considered to be one of the most customer-oriented banks in the world.

Although some of the technologies used by Israeli banks may be a little conservative, these banks are highly successful in using technology to delight their customers. IDB, for example, uses online kiosks (linked together by networks) to provide customers with automatic access to more than 40 kinds of financial service transactions, including account statements, money transfers, real-time stock market quotes, automatic check deposits, and monitoring of different funds. The kiosks communicate in three languages: Hebrew, Arabic, and Russian (tens of thousands of Israelis have emigrated from the former Soviet Union).

Customers log on to the kiosks using their credit cards or self-service cards. The kiosks are completely menu-driven, and if a customer has problems using the kiosk, a bank representative is always available. Customers can get a hard copy of any information from a nearby printer. The services provided by these kiosks are so sophisticated that a banking system specialist commented, "It's far ahead of what you would find in London, Paris, or New York." IDB embraces the philosophy of serving the customer.

The innovative use of information technologies has had a significant impact on bottom-line profits for IDB. Before the kiosks were put into place, the bank had to mail monthly bank statements to every customer. Printing, envelope packaging, and mailing the statements to each customer was a costly affair. Today, the kiosks automatically print statements; statements are mailed only to customers who do not use kiosks. This allows the company to save almost 50% on postage, and the customer gets the statement quicker.

Past applications of computers have been so successful that the bank continues to invest in information systems and technologies. IDB hires more than 200 software developers, engineers, and other IT staff at a total cost of nearly $10 million each year, and spends an equal amount on hardware and maintenance. Automation has not resulted in layoffs, but instead has allowed employees to become more productive and to perform more challenging tasks. In fact, IDB's success has been so great that other banks all over the world are developing similar systems.

1. What kind of system is the online kiosk at IDB? Discuss.
2. In spite of a conservative approach to technology, IDB has a reputation for delighting customers. What do you think are some reasons why IDB has been so successful with its IT applications?

3. IDB is exploring new technologies. You have been hired to investigate and determine whether IDB should invest in ISS. Prepare a presentation of your case for the bank's board of directors.[17]

Case 2: A Management Information System for a Chinese University

China, as a developing socialist country, has only recently begun to apply modern management principles and techniques, especially in its state enterprises. In particular, information systems are still somewhat new and are used more at the operations level than at the strategic level, and even there they are not very widespread.

China, like many other developing countries, faces a number of obstacles while attempting to introduce and implement information technologies. Some of the roadblocks to computer applications include inadequate telecommunications systems, lack of sophisticated and comprehensive data-gathering systems, lack of trained users, and infrastructure limitations (such as shortage of power). For example, although the Chinese government is actively involved in developing a modern telecommunications system for the entire country, only major cities have modern telephone services. These problems are further complicated by China's lack of hard currency to purchase expertise and technology in world markets.

Against this background, let us look at a fairly sophisticated MIS at a Chinese university. Shenzhen University has approximately 6,000 students and 600 faculty members, whose primary mission is to serve the scientific, technical, economic, and managerial needs of the Shenzhen Special Economic Zone.

A few years ago, the university had developed information systems for many applications, such as information retrieval, faculty management, student registration, and financial management. However, these systems could not share data or messages. This resulted in inflexibility and data redundancy (i.e., the same data was stored in different systems).

The university embarked on developing a system that would address some of these issues and cover all aspects of university management. The following goals were set for the system:

1. The system should meet the growing needs of users.
2. The system should be dynamic and adaptable to advances in hardware and software technologies.
3. All applications on the system should be fully integrated.

The new system, called the University Management Information System, is made up of the following subsystems:

Financial Management System: This is one of the most successful subsystems of the university system. The Finance Management Office uses this system to monitor and control the university's finances and also for general accounting purposes. This subsystem also manages the monthly payroll for university personnel, prepares financial reports for the president, and monitors the university's bank accounts. What formerly required the efforts of several people, working for many days, can now be accomplished in a few minutes by the computerized system.

(Continued on next page)

Teaching Affairs System: This subsystem creates and maintains student records and information about curriculum, class scheduling, and enrollments. Each department in the university enters the grades of its students into this system so that accurate records of students can be maintained.

Student Job Appointment Guide System: This subsystem provides valuable information to graduating students about potential employers in the area. The system keeps an up-to-date record of job openings, salary trends, and market needs.

Other subsystems of the university's MIS include the *Management System for the Communist Party* (a system that maintains party rosters and records of time spent in party activities, including the study of communist theory), the *Device and Maintenance System* (which maintains an inventory of all teaching and research equipment and their maintenance schedules), the *Comprehensive Inquiry System* (which provides orientation information for newcomers to the campus), the *President's Inquiry System* (which provides the president of the university with any information, including sensitive information, needed for the smooth and efficient running of the university), the *Science and Technology Research Management System* (which keeps records of all grants, funds, and donations to the university for research), the *Sports Activities Management System* (which maintains records for all intramural sports and activities, assigns people to teams, matches teams, and stores the results of games), and the *Environment Protection and Safety System* (which maintains records of losses and damages related to university facilities, lost and found articles, and student and faculty records for law enforcement purposes).

Shenzhen University completed the entire system in record time, at a total cost of about $270,000, which is quite low compared to the costs of other MIS projects in China. The primary reasons for the system's success are believed to be (1) clear and concrete goals and (2) excellent management of the project.[18]

1. Why is the university's system an MIS? Identify at least three characteristics of this system that classify it as an MIS.
2. Although the *President's Inquiry System* is classified as a subsystem of the MIS, system developers feel that it would be more appropriate as an EIS. Do you agree? Discuss and identify at least three reasons why this subsystem should be developed as an EIS. What are some characteristics that this system should have?
3. Describe three summary reports and three exception reports that this MIS could generate that would be useful for decision makers at the university.

References

Barua, Anitesh, Charles H. Kriebel, and Tridas Mukhopadhyay. "An Economic Analysis of Strategic Information Technology Investments." *MIS Quarterly* 15, no. 5 (September 1991).

Betts, Mitch. "ATM Pioneer Reaps Market Share, Income." *ComputerWorld,* January 20, 1992.

Cash, J. I. and Benn R. Konsyski. "IS Redraws Competitive Boundaries." *Harvard Business Review* (March–April 1985).

Cash, James I., F. Warren McFarlan, James L. McKenney, and Linda M. Applegate. *Corporate Systems Management,* 3d ed. Homewood, IL: Irwin, 1992.

Clemons, Erik K. "Evaluation of Strategic Investments in Information Technology." *Communication of the ACM* (January 1991).

Clemons, Erik K. and Michael Row. "McKesson Drug Co.: Case Study of a Strategic Information System." *Journal of Management Information Systems* (Summer 1988).

Copeland, Duncan G. and James L. McKenney. "Airline Reservation Systems: Lessons from History." *MIS Quarterly* 12, no. 3 (September 1988).

Feeney, David F., and Blake Ives. "In Search of Sustainability: Reaping Long-Term Advantage from Investments in Information Technology." *Journal of Management Information Systems* (Summer 1990).

Hopper, Max. "Rattling SABRE—New Ways to Compete in Information." *Harvard Business Review* (May–June 1990).

Ives, Blake and Michael R. Vitale. "After the Sale: Leveraging Maintenance with Information Technology." *MIS Quarterly* (March 1986).

Keen, Peter G. W. *Shaping the Future: Business Design Through Information Technology.* Cambridge, MA: Harvard Business School Press, 1991.

Notes

1. Caldwell, Bruce. "Trouble in the Beginning," *Information Week,* January 4, 1993, pp. 18–19.
2. Schatz, Willie. "A Cooperative, Productive Future," *Computerworld,* May 23, 1993, p. 30.
3. Perry, Linda. "Handle with CareNet," *Information Week,* April 6, 1992, p. 15.
4. Caldwell, Bruce. "Steeled for a New Century," *Information Week,* April 26, 1993, p. 50.
5. Knox, Andrea. "Unisys set to capitalize on China's chaos," *Austin American-Statesman,* August 8, 1994 C2.
6. Butters, Sandy and Sean Eom. "Decision Support Systems in the Health Care Industry," *Journal of Systems Management,* 43(6), June 1992, pp. 28–31.
7. Appleby, Chuck. "Client Server is the County Line," *Information Week,* April 20, 1992, pp. 38–40.
8. Ballou, Malinda-Carol. "Expert System Modernizes Kaiser," *Computerworld,* November 14, 1994, p. 121.
9. Pitt, Alexander. "The Sights and Sounds of Hate," *Information Week,* March 1, 1993, p. 53.
10. Davenport, T. H., R. G. Eccles, and L. Prusak. "Information Politics," *Sloan Management Review,* Fall 1992, pp. 53–65.
11. Ibid.
12. March, J. G. *Decisions and Organizations* (Cambridge, Massachusetts: Basil Blackwell, 1988).
13. Davenport, T. H., R. G. Eccles, and L. Prusak. "Information Politics," *Sloan Management Review,* Fall 1992, pp. 53–65.
14. Pfeffer, J. *Power in Organizations,* New York: Harper Business, 1986.
15. McGee, Marianne Kolbosuk. "DG Snared in Bribery Scandal," *Information Week,* October 12, 1992, p. 13.
16. Bartholomew, Doug. "CIO Suit Settled," *Information Week,* August 1, 1994, p. 20.
17. Greenbaum, Joshua M. adapted with permission from "Taking it to the Streets," *Information Week,* August 8, 1994, pp. 40–41.
18. Qirui, Ying, Zhu Mingxue, and Therold E. Bailey. Adapted with permission from "A management information system for a Chinese university," *Information & Management,* 1993, pp. 283–288.

Technical Foundations of Information Systems

Chapter 3
Computer Hardware

Chapter 4
Computer Software

Chapter 5
Telecommunications and Networks

Chapter 6
Database Design and Management

Chapter 7
Client-Server Computing

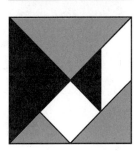

Computer Hardware

Contents

Learning Objectives
Technology Payoff: Knocking Down Barriers
Introduction
Fundamentals of Data Representation
The Components of a Computer
    The Central Processor
    The Central Processing Unit
    Primary Storage
    Secondary Storage
    Secondary Storage Devices
      Magnetic Disks
      Magnetic Tape
      CD-ROM
    Input Devices
      Keyboard
      Mouse
      TouchScreen
      Voice Recognition
      Optical Character Reader
      Magnetic Ink Character Recognition
    Output Devices
      Video Display Terminals
      Printers
      Sound Boards
      Other Output Devices

      Communication Devices
    Types of Computers
      Supercomputers
      Mainframes
      Midrange Computers/Minicomputers
      Workstations
      Microcomputers
        Components of a PC
      Laptops and Notebooks
      Hand-Held Computers
      Pen-Based Computing
    How to Buy a PC
      Processor
      Clock Speed
      RAM
      Expansion Slots and Buses
      Monitor
        Size
        Resolution
        Tricolor
        Interlaced Versus Noninterlaced Monitors
        Radiation Level
        Video Board
  Summary
  Review Questions
  Discussion Questions
  Ethical Issues
    Case 1: Bank Loses Money
    Case 2: Electronic Gambling—Winners or Losers?
    Case 3: Questionable Marketing Practices
    Case 4: Use Keyboards at Your Own Risk
    Case 5: Compaq is on the Hot Seat
  Problem Solving in the Real World
    Case 1: Computer Makeover: From the Stone Age to the Cutting Edge
  References
  Notes

Learning Objectives

In this chapter we provide a broad overview of computer hardware, which includes the physical computer and its peripheral components. Input, output, and storage devices, along with different types of computers, are identified and described in this chapter.

After reading and studying this chapter, you will be able to

♦ Identify and describe the main hardware components of a computer system and describe its primary functions.

♦ Compare and contrast different types of computers: supercomputers, mainframes, minicomputers, workstations, microcomputers, and portables.

Knocking Down Barriers

Mike Ward, 47, an accomplished engineer at Intel Corp. in Hillsboro, Oregon, cannot use his hands anymore. In fact, Ward, who has amyotrophic lateral sclerosis, has lost control of all his muscles, except his eyes. He cannot speak or move. Ward breathes through an artificial ventilator, requires around-the-clock nursing, and is artificially fed.

In spite of these handicaps, Ward holds a full-time job and communicates with his family and his peers using an eye-tracking computer system. The Eyegaze Computer System enables Ward and other disabled people to perform basic functions such as speech synthesis, typing, using a telephone, and controlling their surroundings (turning on lights, appliances, and so on) by staring at control keys displayed on a computer screen.

This system is based on principles used by the U.S. Air Force to track a pilot's eye movements when he or she is sighting targets. A video camera positioned below the monitor tracks the eye movements of the user, while an infrared device mounted in the center of the video lens illuminates the eye and provides a bright image of the pupil. Sophisticated software identifies and predicts the location of the user's gaze on the screen. The system is so precise that a user can activate a key as small as 5/8 of an inch across by staring at the key for about one-fourth of a second. The computer screen flashes to indicate that the key has been "pressed" and performs the action associated with the key.[1]

I regard information technology as a precocious teenager: full of energy, irreverent, unpredictable, a source of both joy and heartache—and frequently in need of close supervision.
　　　　　—Kent ("Oz") Nelson, Chairman and CEO of United Parcel Service

Introduction

Every day, in one form or another, our personal and professional lives are touched by computers. Our description of Mike Ward, the disabled engineer, shows how computers can help people reach their full potential. A recent study, entitled *Report on the Effectiveness of Technology in the Schools (1990–1992),* found that students who use computers feel better about themselves, learn faster, contribute to a more cooperative learning environment, communicate better with teachers and peers, and achieve more than nonusers.[2]

A computer is designed to increase the productivity of an organization and to enhance the decision-making capabilities of knowledge workers. It is a workhorse that effortlessly and accurately performs repetitive tasks that are tedious and difficult for the human mind—tasks such as sorting through large volumes of information, performing long and complex calculations, and analyzing complex scientific or mathematical data, all in the blink of an eye. On the other hand, even the most sophisticated computers cannot *think*. Intelligence and creativity are still exclusive and endearing qualities of the human mind. Thus memory, search, and processing are difficult tasks for the human mind, but very simple tasks for the computer. On the other hand, humans possess creativity, vision, leadership, and common sense, but computers don't. Thus, human beings and computers complement each other in powerful ways.

In Chapter 1, we explained that computers are devices that convert data into information. In this chapter, we identify and describe the actual physical components of a computer system, which are known as hardware. We examine their primary functions, and look at the different types of computers.

Fundamentals of Data Representation

How are data represented in a computer? All data—numbers, letters, symbols, graphs and images—are represented in a computer by strings of binary digits, or **bits**. A bit is the smallest unit of data in a computer. It is represented by a 1 (to indicate the presence of an electronic signal) or a 0 (to indicate the absence of an electronic signal). A unique combination of eight bits, referred to as a **byte**, represents each character in a computer. The letter *P*, the number *7*, and the symbol *!* are each represented in a computer by eight bits.

The two most important characteristics of hardware in a computer system are *speed* (the rate at which the computer can process data and instructions) and *size* (the amount of memory required to store the data and instructions). Computer processing time is measured in millionths of a second; the number of instructions processed per second is expressed in MIPS (millions of instructions per second).

Size, or memory capacity, is measured in bytes. A thousand bytes (1,024 bytes, to be exact) is called a kilobyte (kB). A megabyte is approximately one million bytes (MB); a gigabyte is about a billion bytes (GB), and a terabyte is about a trillion bytes. Table 3–1 summarizes the units of time and size used to describe a computer.

The Components of a Computer

The modern computer system consists of five basic components:

* The central processor (central processing unit and primary storage)
* Secondary storage

Bit
An electronic signal that denotes a zero or a one; the smallest unit of representation in a computer.

Byte
A byte is made up of eight bits. Each character requires a byte of memory to be represented in the computer.

TABLE 3–1
Summary of key time and size units for a computer. These units are often used to measure computer performance.

Unit	Amount of Memory
Byte	8 bits
Kilobyte (kB)	1,000 (10^3) bytes*
Megabyte (MB)	1,000,000 (10^6) bytes
Gigabyte (GB)	1,000,000,000 (10^9) bytes
Terrabyte	1,000,000,000,000 (10^{12}) bytes

* This is an approximation. Actual value is 1,024 bytes.

- Input devices
- Output devices
- Communications devices

Figure 3–1 shows these five components and the way they are interrelated. Each of these components is described below.

The Central Processor

Central Processing Unit (CPU)
Also referred to as a microprocessor, this is a critical computer component that directs the flow of information among various input and output devices. The CPU is made up of the ALU and the control unit.

The central processor consists of the central processing unit (CPU) and primary storage.

The Central Processing Unit   The **central processing unit (CPU)** (called the *microprocessor,* in smaller computers) is a critical component that determines the capabilities of a computer. It directs the flow of information between various

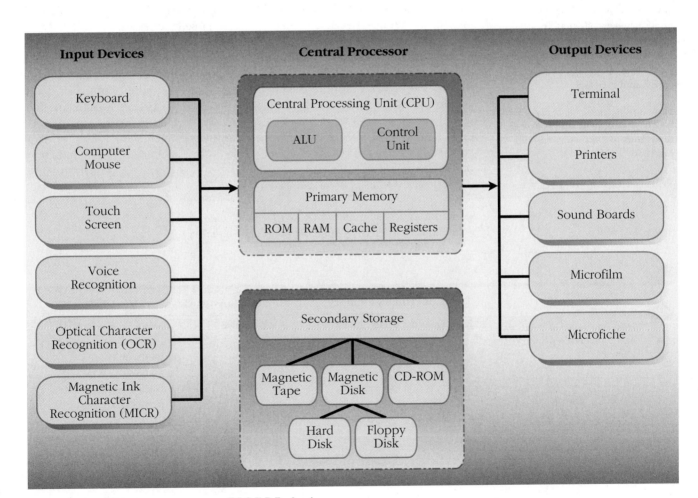

FIGURE 3–1

A computer system has five components: the central processor, secondary storage, input devices, output devices, and communication devices (which are optional). This figure shows the four necessary components.

Arithmetic-Logic Unit (ALU)
The part of the CPU that performs fundamental arithmetic and logical operations.

Control unit
The control unit is a part of the CPU that accesses data and instructions stored in the computer memory and transfers them to the ALU.

Primary storage
The computer's main memory is called primary storage and is part of the central processor. It is made up of memory cells that are used to store data and instructions temporarily. There are four types of primary memory: RAM, ROM, cache, and registers.

Semiconductor
A chip that is made up of several thousands of transistors fused together.

input and output devices. The CPU consists of two main parts, the arithmetic-logic unit (ALU) and the control unit. (See Figure 3–1.)

The **arithmetic-logic unit (ALU)** performs fundamental arithmetic operations, such as addition and subtraction, and logical operations. The CPU directs all mathematical and logical calculations to the ALU.

The **control unit** accesses the data and instructions stored in the computer and transfers them to the ALU. (An instruction tells the computer how to perform a given task.)

Primary Storage

Primary storage is made up of memory cells, which are used temporarily to store data and instructions. Each cell in primary storage consists of one byte and can hold one character. As with mail slots at the post office, each cell has an *address.* While the data or instructions in cells may change during data processing, the addresses remain constant. The computer knows where each piece of information resides, because it keeps track of all cell addresses.

What is primary storage made of? Primary storage consists of several electronic components called **semiconductors,** or chips. Each chip holds several thousand transistors, or circuits; each transistor represents the binary state of a bit (on/off, zero/one). Chips are classified according to the number of transistors or circuits etched on them. A chip with a small number of circuits is called an integrated circuit (IC). As the number of circuits on the chip increases, it is referred to as a large-scale integration (LSI), very large-scale integration (VLSI), or ultra-large-scale integration (ULSI) chip. See Table 3–2 for a summary of different types of memory.

There are four types of primary memory:

♦   Random access memory (RAM) *(volatile memory)*
♦   Read-only memory (ROM) *(nonvolatile memory)*

TABLE 3–2
Different types of volatile and nonvolatile primary memory.

Types of Primary Memory	Volatile/Nonvolatile	Description
RAM (random access memory)	Volatile	Memory in which data and instructions are stored temporarily.
ROM (read-only memory)	Nonvolatile	Memory in which some basic instructions are permanently stored.
Cache memory	Volatile	Memory used to complement RAM. Speeds up retrieval of data and instructions.
Registers	Volatile	Memory used in the ALU and control unit to hold data, instructions, and addresses.

FIGURE 3-2

The contents of a RAM cell before and after a power failure. RAM is volatile and hence loses its contents after a power failure.

Random Access Memory (RAM)
A type of primary memory that resides in the CPU and temporarily stores data and instructions.

Volatile memory
Memory that loses its contents when the power is switched off or fails.

Read-Only Memory (ROM)
Nonvolatile memory that resides in the CPU and cannot be changed except with special equipment or by the hardware vendor. Programs and instructions that are frequently used are etched in ROM.

Programmable Read Only Memory (PROM)
Programmable Read Only Memory. Customized data and instructions, which are non-erasable, etched on a chip using special equipment.

Erasable Programmable Read Only Memory (EPROM)
Erasable Programmable Read-Only Memory: a computer chip with pre-programmed instructions. The instructions etched on this chip can be erased and reprogrammed using ultraviolet rays.

Cache memory
A type of primary memory that is designed to increase the efficiency of the CPU. It is made up of memory cells that are used to store data and instructions temporarily.

Registers
A type of special storage that holds data values, programming instructions, and memory addresses. Registers are located in the ALU and the control unit; they are volatile units of memory designed to increase the efficiency of the CPU.

An empty address in RAM.

00000000000000000000000000000000000000000

Before power failure: An address with "Hello" stored in it.

00010010101000101010001000110011111100100

Oops! RAM after a power failure.

00000000000000000000000000000000000000000

- Cache memory *(volatile memory)*
- Registers *(volatile memory)*

The computer can read and write instructions to **random access memory (RAM),** whose primary purpose is to temporarily store data and instructions. (See Figure 3–2.) RAM loses its contents when the power is turned off or fails; hence it is also called **volatile memory.** The word *random* in the term *random access memory* means that the computer can randomly access any memory cell, without accessing all cells in sequence.

While the computer can write instructions to RAM, it can only read from **read-only memory (ROM).** Programs and instructions that are frequently used, but not frequently changed, are "burned in," meaning etched into ROM, by the hardware vendor. ROM is nonvolatile memory; it does not lose its contents when the power is turned off or fails.

There are two variations of ROM: PROM and EPROM. In **PROM (programmable read-only memory),** data and instructions are permanently etched on the chip, using special equipment. Once the instructions are etched on the PROM, they cannot be erased. In **EPROM (erasable programmable read-only memory),** the instructions etched on the chip can be erased and rewritten, using ultraviolet rays.

The third type of primary memory is **cache memory** (*cache* is pronounced *cash*). The CPU searches cache memory for data and instructions before it searches RAM. Since cache memory is physically located closer to the CPU than is RAM, the computer can retrieve information from cache memory more quickly. Cache memory is more expensive than other types.

The fourth type of primary memory is a **register,** which is a type of special storage that holds data values, programming instructions, and memory addresses. A typical computer has between 10 and 20 registers. Registers are found in the ALU and the control unit; they are volatile units of memory, designed to increase the efficiency of the CPU. The types of registers include *accumulators,* which accumulate the results of various mathematical calculations, *address registers,* which hold the addresses of memory cells, *instruction registers,* which hold instructions waiting to be executed, and *general purpose registers,* which hold various types of data.

Motherboards for PCs

Secondary storage
Nonvolatile memory that resides outside the CPU on devices such as magnetic disks and tapes. Data is stored on secondary storage devices, retrieved, and put into primary memory, where it is processed, and then is transferred back to secondary storage. There are two types of secondary storage: sequential storage and direct-access storage.

Sequential storage
Data that can be accessed and retrieved only in the order in which it was entered.

Direct access
Also known as random access. A type of secondary storage in which any record can be directly accessed; this type of storage is essential for online systems.

Magnetic disk
Storage medium which provides direct access to data for both large and small computers.

Secondary Storage

Because primary storage alone is inadequate to meet the information needs of an organization, we need **secondary storage,** which is nonvolatile memory that resides outside the central processor on devices such as magnetic disks and tapes. Since data must reside in primary storage before it can be processed, the computer transfers data from secondary storage to primary storage before processing begins.

There are two types of secondary storage: sequential storage and direct-access storage. In **sequential storage,** data can be accessed and retrieved only in the order in which it was stored in the system. For example, if a file contains 100 names, the 98th name can be accessed only by reading the 97 names that precede it. **Direct-access storage,** on the other hand, can retrieve data in any order and is essential for online systems where information must be processed as it arrives. With direct-access storage, the computer could directly access the 98th name without searching the 97 names preceding it.

Secondary Storage Devices   Today, developers of storage devices are embracing the principle that storage devices should be as small as possible and work as fast as possible. Although considerable progress has been made in secondary storage, many experts believe that the revolution in data storage has just begun. In this section, we look at some popular secondary storage devices: magnetic disk, magnetic tape, and CD-ROM.

Secondary Storage Devices

Magnetic Disks   **Magnetic disks,** a popular storage medium for both large and small computers, provide direct access to data. Such devices are called direct

A Sense of Humor, Please!

Even computers can be fined and held in contempt of court. That is precisely what a federal bankruptcy judge, one with a sense of humor, did to a Nationsbank Corporation computer. The judge fined it 60 Mb of memory for sending erroneous bills to two customers.

The case began when the computer sent a dunning letter to John and Margaret Vivian in Miami Lakes, Florida, even though a bankruptcy court had excused them from paying their debts. The bank apologized to the Vivians, but the computer continued to send the couple dunning notices for the next 2 months. The couple were terribly upset and requested the court to stop these letters, adding that they would next take the matter to a federal judge.

Judge Cristol said this letter had "truly established, beyond all reasonable doubt, that Mr. and Mrs. Vivian have no sense of humor," cited the computer for contempt of court, and fined it "50 Mb of hard drive memory and 10 Mb of random access memory." Nationsbank's attorneys responded by sending the court a hard disk and nine computer chips, which together exceeded the amount of the fine.[3]

Floppy disks

These are 5.25-inch or 3.5-inch storage diskettes made of polyester film with a magnetic coating, used mostly on microcomputers. They are reliable and portable and have fairly large memory capacities (between 720 kB and 2.88 MB). The 3.5-inch size is currently the most widely used.

Hard disk

A secondary storage device that actually consists of several disks, a read/write head mechanism, and an electronic drive interface.

access storage devices (DASD). Magnetic disks are essential for online systems, where data has to be stored and retrieved almost instantaneously. They come in two forms: floppy disks and hard disks. **Floppy disks** are 5.25-inch or 3.5-inch diskettes, made of polyester film with a magnetic coating. They are used mostly on PCs and other microcomputers. They are popular because they are reliable and portable, and have fairly large memory capacities (between 720 kB and 2.88 GK). Today, most floppy disks come in the 3.5-inch format and can hold about 1.44 MB. However, even smaller disks (1.3 inches), with larger storage capacities, are beginning to replace 3.5-inch diskettes.

Hard disks are made up of several "hard" disks or rigid platters (each hard disk usually has about 11 disks), a read/write head mechanism, and an electron-

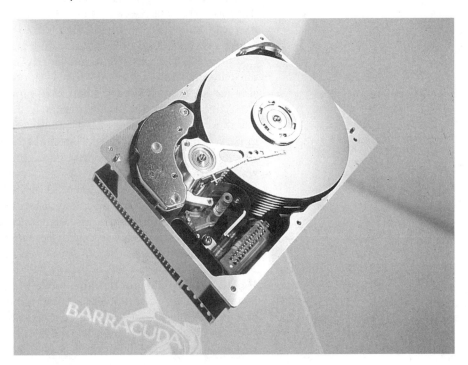

Hard Disk

BUSINESS REALITIES
Home Depot

What do a superstore retail chain, an athletic footwear and apparel manufacturer, and a hotel video-services provider have in common? They all use magnetic disks to cut costs and improve business performance. The number of bits per inch that can be recorded on a disk has increased by 60% annually over the last 4 years. In fact, disks that are 3.5 inches or 5.25 inches across can match or even exceed the capacity of a typical mainframe disk, which measures 8 to 25 inches across. Today, the most capacious 3.5-inch disk is IBM's Starfire, which stores 5.25 gigabytes of information. Compare these with the first disk ever shipped, IBM's Ramac 350 (manufactured in 1956), which had a capacity of 5 megabytes and measured 24 inches across.

The business benefits of good storage technologies can be impressive, as Home Depot, a superstore chain based in Atlanta, found out when it saved about $1 million in computing costs last year alone. With 3,030 super-

stores in the U.S. and 11 in Canada selling do-it-your-selfers and builders everything from penny nails to lumber, the $10-billion Home Depot is the biggest chain of its kind in North America. Accordingly, its storage needs are tremendous. It has a total of 1.3 terabytes of storage capacity (a terabyte equals 1,000 gigabytes); this storage capacity is expected to grow by 40% to 60% over the next year. The company uses storage subsystems of 9-gigabyte drives from EMC Corp. of Hopkinton, Massachusetts.

Home Depot estimates that advanced storage systems have saved it about $1 million over the past year by letting it delay computer upgrades. This is because the new disks allow data to be accessed and processed faster. Specifically, disk access time has been cut by about 70%, from 19 milliseconds to about 6 milliseconds; computer processing is about 40% faster; power and cooling needs have been cut from 4,000 feet to 700. "I could put a bowling alley in where I used to have to put my DASD [direct-access storage device]," says a company spokesman. In all, total operating costs for running the storage area of the computer room have dropped by 80%.[4]

ic drive interface. Hard disks access data more quickly and efficiently than floppy disks and are highly reliable. Large computer systems may use multiple hard disks to store data. Decisions about storage devices must be made carefully as they can influence the productivity of an organization. For example, Ceridian Corp., provider of payroll and accounting services, found that simply by using faster hard disks it was able to generate twice as many checks, thus boosting productivity. Another example is Home Depot (see box), which achieved considerable reduction in its storage costs by using advanced magnetic disks.

Magnetic disks have both advantages and disadvantages. The advantages are that they allow direct access to data and are effective storage devices. Hard disks, in particular, have quick access rates and fairly large storage capacities (between 20 megabytes and 7.5 gigabytes). Also, online systems simply cannot function without magnetic disks.

One disadvantage of magnetic disks is that they are more expensive than other storage media. Also, magnetic disks are not always reliable; if they "crash," the data residing on them is usually destroyed. Finally, the speed and performance of magnetic disks is considerably slower than the CPU (this is also true of other secondary storage devices).[5]

Magnetic tape

A popular secondary storage device, primarily used for storing historical data or for keeping backups of important files. It is a sequential storage device.

Magnetic Tape   **Magnetic tape,** once a popular secondary storage device, is now mostly used in computers for storing historical data or for keeping backups of important files. However, in recent years, network administrators and PC users have also been using magnetic tape as secondary storage. Magnetic tape is a sequential storage medium that is well suited to batch applications. It is a low-cost, portable, and fairly reliable storage device that holds large volumes of data and information. When carefully handled, magnetic tape can be used many times. The primary disadvantage of magnetic tape is that it does not allow random access, although for some applications this may not be a disadvantage. Also, magnetic tapes require careful handling and must be kept in a controlled environment at all times.

CD-ROM
Compact Disk-Read Only Memory, a special kind of optical disk that has excellent storage capabilities and stores different kinds of data, such as text, pictures, audio, and video.

CD-ROM **CD-ROM (compact disc–read-only memory)** is a special kind of optical disc on which data are recorded, using laser devices, and read using CD-ROM drives. CD-ROMs, which are used in both small and large computers, are relatively inexpensive and have excellent storage capacities (between 440 megabytes and 1 gigabyte), almost 300 times that of a floppy disk.[6] For example, an entire encyclopedia can be stored on a single CD-ROM! Most CD-ROMs are read-only disks, particularly well suited for storing static data such as historical facts and figures. Telephone directories and dictionaries are well suited to the CD-ROM medium.

A recent trend in CD-ROMs is CD-Erasable (CD-E). A group of hardware manufacturers led by Philips Electronics North America Corp. in San Jose, California, is developing drives and discs that will allow users to read, write, and rewrite CD-E discs and also read data contained on CD-ROM discs. This is a big improvement over today's CD-ROM drives that allow users to read only from discs or to write to a disc only once. The CD-Erasables are expected to be fairly inexpensive (about $25) with 650 MB capacity.[7]

A special characteristic of CD-ROM is its ability to store different kinds of data, such as text, pictures, animation, sound, video, and graphics. Many industries, such as travel, entertainment, finance, and motion pictures, have enthusiastically embraced the CD-ROM technology because of its ability to integrate different types of data. CD-ROMs have also helped companies increase productivity and reduce operating costs.

For example, when the General Services Administration converted to CD-ROM, it realized significant benefits in terms of reduced storage space and increased productivity. The GSA ensures that the government receives uninterrupted telecom services. Given the size of the U.S. government, a single copy of monthly phone bills amounts to approximately 1.1 *million* pages, or hundreds of boxes of computer printouts. Further, because of government regulations, the agency couldn't throw any of the bills away. The government realized that it was time to find a better way to process bills and decided to convert to optical disks. The agency now receives the million-page phone bill on a half-dozen 5.25-inch CDs. As a result, the GSA can store in 4 inches of shelf space what used to fill 400 boxes. Invoices are processed faster and more efficiently and GSA personnel can respond to billing questions in seconds rather than in days. The conversion has also paid off for the environment, saving 2,148 trees and 312 barrels of oil per year![8]

CD-ROM is also playing an integral role in interactive advertising, which enables manufacturers, retailers, and advertising agencies to reach consumers, advertise products, and sell goods. Many consumers are using CD-ROM drives to access product information and to get detailed information on a variety of products. For example, a PC-based CD-ROM produced by auto-maker Ford, called the Ford Simulator, allows potential buyers to compare colors, engine sizes, options, and payment plans for Ford's entire line of 25 cars and light trucks and targets

Write-Once, Read-Many (WORM)
A special kind of CD-ROM: Write-Once, Read-Many. An optical disk that can be written to once, but read many times.

the advertiser's dream demographic group: 25- to 45-year-old, college-educated, upwardly mobile users, who spend a lot of time on their PCs.[9]

WORM (Write-Once, Read-Many) is a special kind of CD-ROM where data, once recorded, cannot be erased without special equipment. WORM is an excellent storage medium for archives and backups. Rewritable optical disks are available, but they require special laser equipment to rewrite the contents of the disk.

CD-ROM Features What features should a user look for when buying a CD-ROM drive for his or her computer? Although most CD-ROM drives look deceptively similar, their features can vary widely. Five features to look for in a CD-ROM drive are

- ◆ Access time
- ◆ Sustained throughput rate
- ◆ Sound card
- ◆ Interfaces
- ◆ Buffer

Access time is the speed at which data can be transferred from the CD-ROM to the computer. Early CD-ROM drives transferred data at the rate of 150 kB per second; with double-speed CD-ROM drives, data can be transferred at 300 kB per second. Double-speed CD-ROMs can run at double or single speed. A triple-speed CD-ROM transfers data at 450 kB per second; a quad-speed CD-ROM transfers data at 600 kB per second and can run at single, double, or quadruple speed.

Sustained throughput rate is the amount of data that the drive can consistently provide. An access time of 250 to 270 milliseconds and a throughput rate of 300 bits per second is sufficient to run most CD-ROM software.

CD-ROM Drive

Another useful feature in a CD-ROM is a *sound card,* a device that plugs into an expansion slot in the CPU and allows the computer to produce and record sound and access voice data.

There are three types of *interfaces* for connecting a CD-ROM drive to a PC: SCSI, proprietary, and IDE.

SCSI (pronounced scuzzy, this acronym stands for "Small Computer System Interface") supports a wide variety of devices and allows up to seven devices to be connected to the computer using a single adapter. A proprietary interface costs much less than SCSI, but forces the user to use the drive sold with the interface and does not allow the user to add other devices to the computer. While SCSI is technologically the richest and most versatile interface, proprietary interfaces offer a low-priced alternative to SCSI. The third type of interface is IDE, which allows devices other than hard disks to be easily plugged into an IDE cable. The ATAPI (AT Attachment Packet Interface) specification is part of the Enhanced IDE standard. It is cheaper than SCSI.

The fifth feature that influences the performance of a CD-ROM is the size of the CD-ROM drive's *buffer,* a virtual space, much like RAM, where information can be stored temporarily until the drive is ready to send it to the CPU. The bigger the buffer, the better. Buffers can range in size from 32kB to 1 MB.[10]

Storage is a critical function for any organization, since data loss can cause serious financial repercussions for the company. Hence, a good understanding of data storage and its organization implications is essential for IS managers.

Input Devices

From the relatively simple devices of the 1950s, 1960s, and 1970s, to the ultra-sophisticated devices of the 1990s, input and output devices have come a long way. In this section, we look at some popular input devices (which allow us to enter data into a computer). Figure 3–1 shows some commonly used input devices.

Keyboard
Most common and popular method of inputting data into a computer.

Keyboard Most students are familiar with the **keyboard,** which is one of the most common and popular methods of inputting data into a computer. The keyboard is linked to the CPU, which is also linked to a video display terminal (VDT), or computer screen, that can display the keyboard input.

Mouse
A hand-held "point-and-click" input device that can be moved over a smooth surface to control the position of the cursor on the screen. Pressing the mouse buttons executes different commands.

Mouse Macintosh computers popularized the **mouse,** a hand-held "point-and-click" device that can be moved over a smooth surface to control the position of the cursor on the screen. (See the box that gives a brief history of the inventor of the mouse.) A mouse is connected to the computer by a cable; the user can press the left and/or the right button on the mouse to execute various commands. Mice are popular input devices for terminals that use a graphical user interface (GUI)—that is, one that shows various options by using menus and graphics.

Touch Screen
An input device that allows users to execute commands by touching a specific location on the screen.

Touch Screen A **touch screen** is an input device that allows users to execute commands by touching a specific location on the screen. Touch screens are popular, easy to use, intuitive, and inexpensive. They are used in fast-food restaurants, video stores, and entertainment parks. For example, at Disneyland, visitors can get information on various entertainment programs offered at the resort by simply touching a menu on a computer screen. At Grace Hospital, in Morgantown, North Carolina, doctors enter patient data using touch screens.

BUSINESS REALITIES
Douglas Engelbart, Inventor of the Mouse

If you tried to reduce Douglas Engelbart's role in the computer revolution to just 10 words—father of the mouse, creator of windows, pioneer of hypertext—you would not diminish his importance even slightly. Engelbart, now 69 years old, is one of the great humanizers of the modern era's defining technology. Since he first began working at the Stanford Research Institute (later SRI International) in the mid-'50s, Engelbart was motivated by the idea that the computer, made accessible to ordinary citizens, would become a tool needed to make effective decisions in a free society. In the punch-card age, he had a vivid sense of just what the computer would mean to the future. "Here was something on the same order as writing, the printing press, agriculture," he has said.

To Engelbart, ease of operation was not an end, but a means to expand human intelligence. "People need a new eloquence and skill," he says. "They need to be able to explore new avenues of process knowledge." Every time we pull down a menu from the top of the computer screen or edit access files, we are in his debt.

Douglas Engelbart's achievement in the history of information technology is far more than a story of mouse and man. Yet the brilliant little device with the cute name (it was originally called the X-Y Position Indicator for a Display System) changed the relationship between computer and user. With a point and a click, what had been an unwieldy grind of keystrokes and codes became an intimate, interactive communication. The graphical interface concepts linked to the mouse later inspired crucial work at Xerox that would later lift Apple to a new level of success. Without Engelbart's innovative staff at Xerox's Palo Alto Research Center, there might never have been a "computer for the rest of us."

Ironically, the mouse was one of this inventive scientist's few profitable patents. Many of his breakthroughs, he says, "came at a time when software processes weren't deemed patentable. But wealth wasn't his goal. "I made a conscious decision at the age of 25 that money would be secondary to what kind of contribution my work would make." After a pause, Engelbart goes on. "Sometimes, though, I think I've overdone the *pro bono* idea. You get way out on the frontier and eventually you think, 'Maybe it's time to back out. Is it really necessary for me to be this cold and hungry'?"

Currently, Engelbart heads the Bootstrap Institute in Fremont, California, which he founded to improve computers and the human organizations increasingly dependent on them. Despite the rapid growth of the technology he helped create, he is far from sanguine about the future. "I still feel we're missing the boat," Engelbart says. "It took a long time for people to understand how printing would change civilization, but we don't have that kind of luxury today. The planet's problems are too complex. Wasted time could be disastrous."[11]

Hallmark Cards is one of the largest greeting card producers in the world (more than 11 million cards per day), with sales of $2.3 billion per year (45% of the card market). The company uses touch screens in its 1,200 in-store kiosks, all over the world, that allow card buyers to design and print their own customized cards. Hallmark's touch-screen kiosk contains a computer, a CD-ROM, and a printer. Using the touch screen, the computer gathers answers to questions such as "Who is the card for?", "What is the occasion?", and "Is the recipient male or female?", then prints a customized card on the printer.

Even users with little or no computer background can easily enter information using touch screens. The only disadvantage of touch screens is that the kind of data that can be entered is limited, since only options that are available on the screen can be selected.

Voice recognition
An input device that responds to the human voice to execute computer commands.

Voice Recognition   **Voice recognition** devices recognize and execute a set of instructions based on voice commands. In a voice recognition system, the human

Computer Voice Recognition

speech is first converted into a digital pattern and is then compared to a set of pre-recorded patterns. If a match is found, the command is executed. Although voice recognition systems have inherent appeal and have been available for several years, until recently they were fairly limited and hence not commercially viable. Today, they have become fairly common; it is estimated that in the near future voice recognition will be a standard feature in many computers.

Until recently, voice recognition systems required users to speak slowly and distinctly. But Dutch manufacturer Philips Electronics NV has introduced a new program that allows users to speak at a natural pace and also translates dictation into word-processing documents and PC commands. The program carefully studies how a specific user speaks. Then, it allows the user to scan the document for incorrect words and make necessary corrections. Based on these corrections, the system records how the user pronounced the word so it doesn't make the same mistake twice.[12] Also, we are beginning to see the integration of computers, voice recognition technology, and telephones. Today, commercial products that combine the above technologies are available, giving managers what is called a "virtual secretary." This "virtual secretary" can answer telephone calls, place calls, direct incoming calls to any number, put through high priority calls, and take messages.[13]

For example, the Long Island Lighting Co. (LILCO) and AIL Systems Inc., of Deer Park, New York, have developed a wearable computer with voice recognition capabilities for company technicians. The 7-pound device includes a computer that is strapped to a belt, a display unit positioned close to the eye that functions as a PC screen, and a microphone that carries verbal commands to the computer unit. The voice recognition system thus frees workers from being tied to a keyboard.

BUSINESS REALITIES
The U.S. Postal Service

The U.S. has 6% of the world's population, but generates 40% of its mail. The U.S.P.S. has 29,000 post offices, 682,000 employees, and a budget of $49 billion. It is spending billions of dollars to modernize its operations; over the past decade, it has adopted a variety of information technologies, from mammoth machines that read and sort the mail to networks that carry mail images, to enhance productivity and reduce operating costs.

The U.S.P.S. faces an awesome challenge: to make machines and computers handle 166 billion items a year, given that no two items are exactly alike. In an effort to face some of these challenges, it is using OCRs to process letters. The work is done in three tiers. At the top, envelopes with neatly typed or printed ZIP codes pass through OCR equipment, which reads the ZIP codes and applies the corresponding bar codes. In the second tier, the envelopes are sorted according to zip code; the third tier uses special equipment to add two digits to the nine-digit ZIP codes and sort the mail into the exact sequence of addresses on neighborhood mail carrier's route. These automation efforts, and others, boosted the productivity of the U.S.P.S. by 4% last year.[14]

DHL Worldwide Express is using voice recognition systems to help customers track packages using their telephone keypads. When a customer enters the airbill number on the keypad, an automated voice provides information regarding the package, such as the time the package was delivered, the name of the person who signed for the package, and the time when the package cleared customs. Customers can even ask the system to fax them a delivery statement. Today, almost 65% of DHL's customers use the interactive voice system.[15]

In spite of its many advantages, there are also some disadvantages to voice recognition systems. Experts say that as users begin to "talk or even yell" at their computers, they may become burdened with sore throats and hoarseness of their vocal chords. New users, in particular, tend to "speak louder to make sure the systems understands!" In other words, users may now be exchanging typing injuries for voice injuries; the problem is even more acute for those with stress, smoking, or allergies. In fact, some users are seeking the help of speech therapists to learn correct posture, breathing, and relaxation techniques. Speech therapists recommend the following measures to avoid voice injuries:

- sip water frequently
- sit up straight (or stand)
- relax the neck
- move shoulders and jaw
- speak softly and in a conversational tone
- take frequent rests[16]

Optical Character Recognition (OCR).
An input device that scans data from paper documents and converts it into digital form. The most widely used OCR is the bar code scanner, which scans patterns of bars printed on different products.

Optical Character Reader (OCR)   An **optical character reader (OCR)** scans data into a computer from paper documents and converts it into digital form. Documents such as utility bills, insurance premiums, and credit cards are ideal OCR applications. The most widely used OCR is the bar code reader, which scans a pattern of bars printed on products in grocery stores and department stores. The pattern of the bars represents information about the product that can be used for managing inventory and sales. Bar code scanners are extensively used in many companies around the world. For example, Toyota Vehicle Processors, a

Magnetic Strip Reader

subsidiary of Toyota, uses bar code scanners to achieve just-in-time shipments of thousands of automobile parts to the parent company (see box). The U.S. Postal Service also uses OCR to enhance office productivity (see box).

Magnetic Ink Character Recognition (MICR)
A device that can read magnetic characters found on a document; it reads data, but does not process data. Used primarily in banks.

Magnetic Ink Character Recognition   **Magnetic ink character recognition (MICR)** was developed primarily for the banking industry, to increase the speed, efficiency, and accuracy of check processing. MICR input devices automatically read characters printed at the bottom of a check, such as the account number, the type of account, the name of the bank, and so on.

Output Devices

Output devices are used to output data and information generated by a computer.

Video Display Terminals   The technical term for a computer screen is *video display terminal*. The terminal uses a cathode ray tube (CRT) to shoot a stream of electrons onto the computer screen. This allows us to see text and images on the screen. (A detailed description of VDTs is provided later in this chapter, under the section on PCs.)

Printers   Printers are based on three different types of technology: dot matrix, inkjet, and laser.

Dot matrix printer
The cheapest printer. It uses a rectangular array of 9 or 24 printing wires, or pins. The pins strike a ribbon and when the ribbon presses against the paper, it forms a character.

The cheapest in terms of price and operational costs is the **dot matrix printer,** which uses a rectangle of 9 or 24 printing wires, also called pins. The pins strike a ribbon; and when the ribbon is pressed against the paper, it forms a letter. A 24-pin printer can print 24 dots per character while a 9-pin printer can print only 9 dots per character. Thus, the higher the number of pins, the better the quality of print. Printing speed is measured in characters per second (cps).

A GLOBAL PERSPECTIVE
Toyota Vehicle Processors

Suppliers the world over are striving for just-in-time deliveries and Toyota Vehicle Processors, Inc. (TVPI) of Northlake, Ill., is no different. TVPI is the Toyota subsidiary charged with supplying Toyota plants in Japan with components bought in the United States. It is responsible for consolidating shipments arriving from scores of suppliers, located mostly in the East and Midwest, and forwarding them in a timely fashion to their Japanese destinations.

More than 50 parts suppliers feed TVPI-Northlake with components for inclusion in vehicles made in Japan. Toyota realized early on that requiring daily direct shipments from suppliers to Japanese factories was impractical. Instead, it uses sixty-four truck routes to pick up parts from between one and eight suppliers

and ensures that each truck is fully loaded before arriving at the facility for drop-off.

Each truck route has a designated arrival window at TVPI and the system directs each arriving driver to a specific dock among the 124 doors located at the facility. Hand-held, bar code scanners identify the items in the truck, which are then off-loaded in one of eight designated areas and kept there for about 2 hours before production. The information about shipments is then sent electronically to factories in Japan. This is the key concept behind Toyota's system of "Heijunka," or the leveling of production, which implies a smooth and consistent flow delivery of materials needed for that production. "The essence of the system involves shipping a little bit a lot, says TVPI's Fortenberry. "By sending out shipments a little at a time, the parts make the three-day rail trip and the two-week ocean voyage and arrive in Japan just-in-time."[17]

Inkjet
A printer that uses a print head nozzle to spray drops of ink that form characters on a page.

Laser printer
A high-end computer printer, capable of printing 600 dpi or more.

For example, the Epson LQ-570+ is a 24-pin printer that can print 75 to 337 cps. Clearly, printers with higher cps are more desirable.

Dot matrix printers can use either rolls of printer paper or single sheets and come with features such as letter quality (better quality print than regular dot matrix) and quiet (makes less noise than the regular dot matrix). The market leaders for dot matrix printers are Epson, Panasonic, Citizen, Lexmark, Okidata, and Star Micronics.[18]

Inkjet printers use a print-head nozzle to spray drops of ink that form characters on the page. Inkjets lie somewhere between dot matrix printers and laser printers in terms of price and print quality; they are also quieter than dot matrix printers. While most inkjet printers print in black, a few models also print in color. The only drawback is that inkjets have high operating costs—about 4 to 8 cents per page. Hewlett-Packard's Deskjet is one of the most popular inkjet printers.[19]

Laser printers are the high-end computer printers. They can print 600 dots per inch (dpi) or more. The industry standard for a laser printer is 300 dpi, a far cry from the dot matrix printer's 24 dots per character. The 600-dpi models are sophisticated printers whose output is of the same quality as that of a magazine or newspaper. Laser printer speed runs from about 4 ppm (pages per minute) to 16 ppm; network printers are even faster.[20] See Table 3–3 for a summary of the characteristics of the three types of printers.

Some companies are using printers to increase their productivity. For example, a Phoenix-based subsidiary of Banc One Corp. is using a laser printer to help speed bank-customer lines, keep track of transactions with more precision, and prevent check forgeries. The bank uses a laser printer and specialized software to generate checks. The checks bear the bank's logo, the customer's authorized signature, and MICR generated information on specially treated paper that, when

Laser Printer

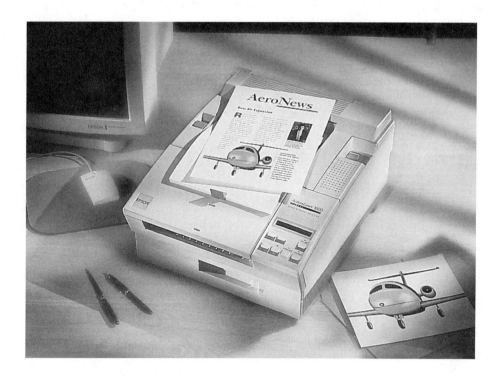

photocopied, produces the word *void* on the copy. The printer has helped the bank trim the time it takes for generating bank checks and money orders by more than half. Also, passwords and limited access to the printer have helped to reduce the possibility of fraud and theft often associated with handling preprinted checks.[21]

Sound Boards   Sound, generated by a sound board, can add a new dimension to many computer applications, from computer games to business applications. Speakers are an important part of a sound board; the board is only as good as its speakers. There are three important factors to consider when selecting a sound board. They are the sampling rate, the amount of data stored in each sample, and the MIDI capability.

Most sound boards can sample at 44.1 kHz, which is the number of times each second (in this case, 44,100 times) that the sound board takes a "snapshot" of incoming or outgoing sound. While sampling rates of 11 to 22 kHz are adequate for recording and playing speech and sound effects, they are inadequate for music and other sophisticated audio.

Sound boards are designated as 16- or 8-bit boards. This designation refers to the amount of data stored in each sample; higher numbers create more realistic sound. For complex audio, such as music, 16-bit sound is necessary, while 8-bit is adequate for speech and other simple sounds. Although lower data rates are much more efficient in their use of disk space, they introduce some background noise into sound recordings.

Musical Instrument Digital Interface (MIDI), another important consideration in sound boards, is a music-industry standard for creating and storing electronic representations of musical scores. MIDI files consist of instructions that tell the

TABLE 3–3
This table summarizes the characteristics of the three types of printers.

Type of Printer	Features
Dot matrix	Cheapest type of printer. Uses pins to press on a ribbon to make characters. Noisiest type of printer.
Inkjet	Higher-quality output, usually 300 dpi. Uses a nozzle to spray ink onto page. Can produce 2 to 8 ppm. Can print documents in color. Considered quiet compared to dot matrix printer. More expensive to operate, at 4 to 8 cents per page.
Laser	Highest-quality output, 300 to 600 dpi, comparable to magazine output. Can produce from 4 ppm to 16 ppm or more.

sound board which notes to play and on what "instruments." With its small file sizes and distortion-free playback, MIDI is especially useful in presentations and is frequently used to provide music for games and titles.[22]

Other Output Devices   Many libraries use microfiche and microfilm, which can store large volumes of information in a small amount of space and are also relatively inexpensive. An entire issue of a newspaper, such as *The New York Times,* can be stored on a piece of microfilm that is only a few inches long. Unlike microfilm, which is stored on a file, a microfiche is stored on a 3 × 5 inch index card and can hold several hundred pages of output.[23] Microfiches are ideal for outputting information related to transaction processing applications, such as invoices, checks, and accounts receivable.

Communication Devices

In this section, we take a brief look at communication devices, which are covered in detail in Chapter 5. Communication devices allow users separated by time and distance to communicate electronically and can transmit text, images, graphics, voice, and video. Some basic communication devices are *terminals* (to input and output data), *communication channels,* such as telephone lines and cables, and *communication processors,* such as modems (which enable the transmission of data over telephone lines). These devices, along with communication software, enable companies to electronically send and receive information all over the world.

Let us take a closer look at modems, a popular communication device. A modem, short for *mo*dulator-*dem*odulator, is a device that converts digital signals into analog signals and vice versa. Telephone lines transmit analog signals. Hence, if two computers are to communicate over telephone lines, the sending computer's digital signals must first be converted into analog signals, and at the other end reconverted into digital signals so that the receiving computer can recognize and accept the signals.

Faster modems, although more expensive, result in lower long distance charges because they take less time to transmit data. The speed with which a modem sends and receives data is measured in **bits per second (bps).** Older

Bits per second (bps)
A measurement used to describe the speed at which a communication device sends and receives data.

modems transfer data at 300 to 2400 bps; newer models transfer data at rates ranging from 9,600 bps to 28,800 bps. (Some are even faster.) A 14,400-bps modem with data compression capabilities can effectively transmit at 57,600 bps.

Many modems also come with fax capabilities; these are called faxmodems. Such modems can send or receive documents to or from any standard fax machine and offer several advantages over standard fax machines. First, it is much easier to send a document to a number of recipients over a faxmodem than over a fax machine, since the pages need not be repeatedly fed into the fax machine. Second, using special software, it is possible to convert a fax received over the modem into a computer file. Documents received through a fax machine must be rekeyed or scanned into the computer to become digital files.[24]

In summary, there are five components in a computer: central processor, secondary storage, input devices, output devices, and communication devices. Although all computers have these five components, computers are classified into different categories based on their size and processing speed. In the next section we discuss different types of computers.

Types of Computers

Computers can be classified into different types based on memory size and processing speed. In this section, we describe the following types of computers: supercomputers, mainframes, midrange machines, workstations, microcomputers, laptops, hand-held computers, and pen-based computers. Figure 3–3 shows the classification of different types of computers into organization-wide, work-group, and personal information systems. Supercomputers and mainframes are organization-wide systems; midrange computers and workstations are work-group systems; all other types of computers are personal information sys-

FIGURE 3–3

Computers can be classified into different types based on their memory size and processing capabilities. Supercomputers and mainframes support organization-wide activities; midrange computers and workstations support group activities; and PCs and laptops support individual activities.

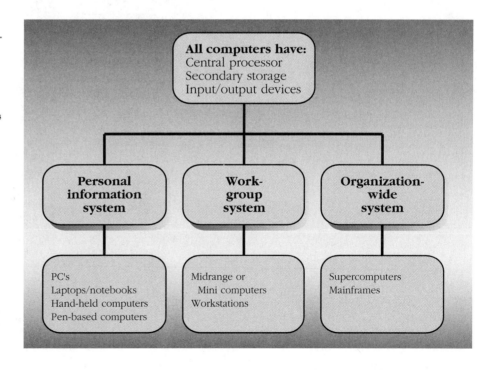

tems. Recall from Chapter 1 that organization-wide systems provide an overall information view of the entire enterprise, work-group systems allow groups of decision makers to process and exchange information, and personal information systems are designed to meet the information needs of individual decision makers.

Supercomputers

Supercomputers are the fastest and largest computers available today; they are used in a wide variety of applications. For example, the University of Oklahoma uses a supercomputer at the Pittsburgh Supercomputing Center to forecast severe storms; with its help, weather experts can now extend the forecasting period from 30 minutes to 4 or 5 hours. Supercomputers have large memories and high processing speeds; they can process up to a billion instructions per second. They are used for processing very large files and performing large-scale mathematical calculations. In fact, supercomputers are used for such intense computing that they are enclosed in frames containing liquid coolant to prevent them from melting down.

Most supercomputers have two characteristics in common. One is the ability to recover automatically from failures (fault tolerance). Also, unlike conventional computers, which have a single processor which processes one instruction at a time, supercomputers have multiple processors (or CPUs) that process multiple instructions at a time; this is known as **parallel processing.** Some business appli-

Supercomputers
The fastest and largest computers available today, with large memories, high processing speeds, and multiple processors.

Parallel processing
The processing of more than one instruction at a time. Multiple processors (or CPUs) are required for parallel processing.

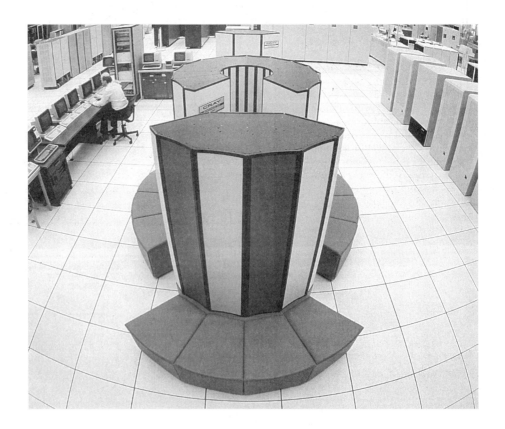

The Cray Supercomputer

cations to which parallel processing is ideally suited are resource optimization, image processing, graphics, and financial portfolio analysis. For example, parallel processing is helping drug companies reduce the time it takes to market a drug. Currently it takes about 12 years and $350 million to develop a new cancer drug, but with the help of parallel processing machines, drug companies can cut this time in half.

Fault-tolerant computers use a backup mechanism to automatically isolate and reconfigure hardware that fails during system operation. Companies that require highly reliable computer systems use fault-tolerant computers. For example, European banks use fault-tolerant systems because of their reliability and their ability to process huge volumes of data. In the U.S., the Securities and Exchange Commission (see box) also uses fault-tolerant computers to analyze massive amounts of financial data that U.S. corporations submit to the Commission. The White House has recently installed four high-security fault-tolerant computers for a wide variety of applications.

The primary disadvantage of supercomputers is their high cost. Supercomputers cost between $250,000 and $3 million; the software that runs on them is also very expensive. This is one reason why today there are fewer than 200 supercomputers in the United States. Table 3–4 shows other applications of supercomputers.

Fault-tolerant computers
A computer with a backup mechanism to automatically isolate and reconfigure hardware that fails during systems operation.

Mainframes

A **mainframe** is a large, general-purpose computer with a large memory and excellent processing capabilities. Mainframes, which are frequently organization-wide systems, take their name from the "main frame" that once housed the CPU. They are ideal for transaction processing, financial applications, payroll, investment analysis, weather forecasting, airline reservations, and other applications that require massive computations and large-scale processing. Unlike PCs, which serve only one user, mainframes serve many users at the same time.

Mainframe
A large, general-purpose computer with extensive memory and high processing speed. Mainframes are enterprise-wide systems that are ideal for transaction processing.

T A B L E 3 – 4
This table shows some applications of supercomputers and their market share.

Application	Total Sales ($M)
Scientific research and R&D	119.8
Classified defense	40.3
Geoscience and geo-engineering	26.0
Design engineering and analysis	21.4
Economic and financial modeling	18.8
Imaging	13.7
Simulation	12.6
Biological and chemical engineering	9.1
Business/professional	6.8
Software engineering	5.5

Data: International Data Corp.

After nearly a decade of pilot tests and volunteer filings, about 500 U.S. companies today electronically file their financial data with the Securities and Exchange Commission (SEC). The Electronic Data Gathering, Analysis, and Retrieval system, or *Edgar,* as it is popularly called, was designed to replace the huge volumes of paper that the SEC receives each year from U.S. corporations. Using Edgar, corporations can now file their data on tape or on floppy disks. Edgar analyzes the data and applies the same error checks that SEC personnel apply when analyzing company data.

At the heart of Edgar is a pair of fault-tolerant computers. Fault-tolerant computers are necessary for this application because any computer downtime while a company's financial data is being processed can adversely affect the organization's financial well-being. A delay by the SEC can cause the company to postpone a public stock offering, which in turn could adversely affect market conditions. The two fault-tolerant computers at the SEC ensure that the computer never fails and that all transactions are completed in time.[25]

Greyhound Lines Inc. is investing in a $4-million mainframe reservation system, dubbed Trips. Trips allows passengers to reserve tickets in advance while giving Greyhound managers the vital information necessary to organize travel routes, set ticket prices, and allocate resources during peak travel times. Trips also provides customers with fare and scheduling information and allows sales representatives to make ticket reservations for customers over the phone. This mainframe-based system is a significant improvement over the current system, in which Greyhound passengers buy tickets at the point of departure and seats are available only on a first-come, first-served basis. "Right now," explains a Greyhound spokesman, "we don't know how many passengers will be traveling on a bus until minutes before the bus leaves."[26]

One of the main disadvantages of the mainframe is that it is expensive to purchase, operate, and maintain. Mainframes often require customized software and highly trained computer personnel to run and operate them. In spite of this disadvantage, mainframes have been in use since the late 1950s and continue to be used for a wide variety of applications.

Midrange Machines/Minicomputers

In the 1970s, Digital Equipment Corporation (DEC) introduced the concept of a midrange computer, or minicomputer, called the VAX. **Minicomputers,** which are typical work-group systems, are small yet powerful multiuser systems with excellent memory capabilities and processing speeds. Although they are slower than mainframes and often have less memory, these workhorses can deliver considerable "bang for the buck." The introduction of midrange computers allowed American corporations that were unable to afford mainframes to enter the age of computing. Thorn EMI of London (see box) uses midrange computers for a number of business functions, such as processing royalties and analyzing market data.

Workstations

Workstations lie somewhere between midrange computers and PCs (covered in the next section). They can be used by individuals or by groups. They are faster

Minicomputer
A small, powerful multiuser system with excellent memory capabilities and processing speed. It is less powerful than a mainframe but more powerful than a PC.

Workstations
Machines that are faster and more sophisticated than PCs and are equipped with a number of productivity tools that increase their efficiency.

A GLOBAL PERSPECTIVE
Thorn EMI of London

Thorn EMI, the London-based music conglomerate, is playing a simpler song these days: one that requires new information systems. Two years ago, Thorn EMI decided to sell most of its subsidiaries, including its security-systems and defense businesses, and began to focus on the music industry. As part of that effort, the $6.2-billion company last year consolidated several U.S. and Canadian startup record labels into EMI Record Group North America, based in New York.

Getting those operations, which handle artists as diverse as Garth Brooks, Megadeath, and Frank Sinatra, to work together necessitated the design of new information systems. Although there had been very little IT investment during the past 15 years, the company is now investing tens of millions of dollars in information systems. That could give EMI a distinct advantage in the music business.

The AS/400 (a midrange computer) will manage EMI's financial, distribution, and royalties functions, which were previously handled by an IBM 3090 mainframe in Los Angeles. The AS/400 will run financial software, an order-entry and distribution system, and a royalties system. EMI will use the data collected at retail counters to help artists sharpen their sense of who buys their records. Although most retailers and consumer-goods manufacturers have for years used systems to link production forecasts with consumer demand, "that concept is still foreign to the music industry."[27]

and more sophisticated than PCs and are equipped with a number of productivity tools that increase their efficiency. Advances in microprocessors and sophisticated software have significantly increased the capabilities of these machines and today some workstations are handling tasks that ran on supercomputers and mainframes as little as 2 years ago. Further, their low cost makes them an attractive alternative to the PC. SPARC stations from Sun Microsystems, IBM RS/6000s, Hewlett-Packard's Series 700, and DEC's Alpha-based Model 3000 are some popular workstations.

Engineers, designers, architects, and film-industry animators are heavy users of workstations. For example, at Du Pont, in Wilmington, Delaware, about one in five workstations is a high-end machine used for simulation and molecular modeling. Pitney-Bowes uses workstations to model advanced office products before they are manufactured.

Microcomputers or Personal Computers (PCs)

Microcomputer
Also known as personal computers (PCs). A compact, powerful, and versatile machine with memory and processing capabilities.

Microcomputers, also known as personal computers (PCs), are regarded by many as one of the greatest inventions in history. They have completely revolutionized the way American corporations do business. Although the memory size and processing capabilities of microcomputers are less than those of mainframes and midrange computers, advances in hardware technology have made the PC a compact, powerful, and versatile machine. In fact, recent advances in hardware technology have equipped many microcomputers with the same, or even better, memory and speed capabilities than the mainframe of a few years ago—with the result that many companies, such as Texas Commerce Bank (see box), are replacing their mainframes with PCs to run sophisticated applications.

The PC market is growing at an explosive rate. According to International Data Corp., a Framingham, Massachusetts, research firm, companies spent nearly $30 billion on PC hardware alone in 1992,[29] and that figure is expected to increase slightly in the coming years.

BUSINESS REALITIES
Texas Commerce Bank

When Texas legalized branch banking in 1987, one of the goals of Texas Commerce Bank was to improve its loan approval process. In order to provide managers with all the information necessary to make good loan decisions, the bank realized that it would have to provide managers with access to seven different mainframe-based systems (credit bureaus, internal loan processing, credit card systems, and so on), requiring each officer to have five terminals on his or her desk.

The bank switched to PCs that would be linked to the bank's mainframe computers. The decision proved to be sound. The bank has doubled the volume of its business without increasing its staff, has increased the number of new product and service offerings, and has reduced the number of errors in the loan approval process. A personal loan approval that used to take up to 2 days can now be processed in under 3 hours. What is more impressive is that virtually no paper is generated under the new system.

As can be seen from this example, PCs are powerful and versatile machines that can help an organization achieve its goals.[28]

Components of a PC   The basic units of a PC are the system unit, the video display terminal (VDT), a keyboard, and a mouse.

The system unit is the rectangular metal box that houses the processor, where data are input, processed, stored, and retrieved. This unit also contains primary memory, disk drives, a power supply, and outlets for connecting input and output devices. The VDT provides users with images of data, instructions, and output. The keyboard and the mouse are the most popular input devices for microcomputers.

When the components of a PC are customized to meet the particular information needs of the user, the process is called **configuration.** For example, a user may choose to have a system that has built-in fax capabilities, while another user may require a communication device, such as a modem, installed in the unit.

In fact, **"plug-and-play"** is emerging as the central theme in computing today. The term refers to the ability of users to plug in different hardware and software components and customize their PCs to meet their own personal information needs. "Plug-and-play" embeds PCs with limited intelligence, as it automatically installs and configures different computer components. It allows users to install or remove devices from PCs, dock and undock notebook computers from docking stations, and run different kinds of software on different types of desktop machines manufactured by different vendors. A new standard, referred to as Desktop Management Interface (DMI), was created by a consortium of more than 300 computer hardware and software vendors so that "plug-and-play" eventually has become commonplace. DMI provides users with a number of benefits, such as systems that are easier to use and provide a better way to manage the computing resources of an organization.[30]

In the next section, we discuss some of the considerations that a user should take into account when buying a PC.

Laptops and Notebooks

Laptops and notebooks provide mobile computing technology. These are computers that are battery-operated and hence can be used any time and anywhere. Laptop computers are small enough to fit on the lap of a user; notebook com-

---

Configuration
The customization of a PC to meet the information needs of a particular user.

"Plug-and-play"
A standard that allows different brands of hardware and software components to be "plugged in" and "play" on the same computer system. It allows users to run different kinds of software on different types of desktop machines from different vendors.

Laptops and Notebooks
Computers that are battery-operated which provide mobile computing technology to be used any time and anywhere. Laptops are small enough to fit on the lap of a user; notebook computers are even smaller.

A Laptop Computer

puters are even smaller. Some popular mobile computing devices and applications are shown in Table 3–5.

The primary differences between a laptop and a notebook are size and weight. Notebooks are smaller than laptops and weigh less. However, both are equipped with powerful microprocessors, graphic capabilities, adequate memory size, and mouse-driven input. Some laptops and notebooks even have fax capabilities, CD-ROM drives, and optical storage devices and can be linked to various input and output devices.

The portability of laptops and notebooks has increased the productivity of many workers, particularly field workers and those who travel extensively. For example, sales representatives for United Airlines use notebooks to provide better customer service and attract new customers. Formerly, it was difficult for sales reps to retrieve customer information because it was hidden in the company's corporate database. Today, every sales representative has a notebook computer that is linked to the corporate database, so information can be retrieved almost instantaneously. Reports that once took 4 to 6 weeks to arrive can now be obtained in a matter of a few minutes, thus enhancing the timeliness and the quality of decisions.[31]

Hand-Held Computers

Hand-held computer
A computer that is smaller than notebooks and used primarily to collect field data.

Hand-held computers are even smaller than notebooks. They are primarily used to collect field data. For example, archaeologists at a dig site in Jordan use hand-held computers to gather information about centuries-old artifacts. The New York City transit police use hand-held computers to apprehend criminals. When a suspect is apprehended, a police officer uses a hand-held computer to do a background check on the individual. Each hand-held computer holds more than 1,200 records and provides police officers with timely, and sometimes life-saving, information.

TABLE 3–5
Some popular mobile computing devices and applications are shown in this table.

	Weight	Description	Typical User
Pocket organizers	Less than 1 pound	Shirt-pocket-size machine for organizational applications.	A mobile user who does not need communications capabilities.
Hand-held computers	Less than 1 pound	8086-based machines that contain an inexpensive docking station.	Field service person with data entry applications.
Personal digital assistants	Less than 3 pounds	A powerful hand-held communications-intensive device with a focus on ease of use.	Mobile users who desire two-way communications, for either business or personal use.
Subnotebooks	Less than 4 pounds	A device with full PC functionality but with a reduced keypad and screen and no floppy drive.	User with non-RAM-heavy applications.
Pen-based devices	Less than 6 pounds	A device with an input stylus, using either the PenPoint or the Pen Windows operation system.	Field service person with data entry applications.

Source: Rood, Stephen, "After You Buy, How Small Can You Get?," *Computerworld,* June 28, 1993, pp. 112–113.

Pen-Based Computing

Pen-based computing
Portable computers that use an electronic writing pad and a light-sensitive pen to input data into a computer. The writing is converted into digital input and stored in a file in the computer.

Pen-based computing refers to portable computers that use an electronic writing pad and a light-sensitive electronic pen, thus freeing users from the constraints of a keyboard. When the user writes on the pad, the writing is converted into digital input and stored in a file in the computer. Pen-based computing is becoming increasingly popular because most people are comfortable using a pen. It is particularly useful for sales and service representatives, insurance agents, retail suppliers, delivery people, inventory clerks, and health care providers, who are often on the move.

Pen-based computing is revolutionizing the way companies record data and conduct business. For example, ADP Automotive Claims uses pen-based computers to estimate auto claims and develop collision estimates. The company's pen-based system, Audapoint PenPro, collects and stores data and images on parts and labor costs for most modern cars. If a car has a damaged front end, say, the system guides the estimator from the bumper to the grille, headlights, radiator, fan, and other parts, and helps assess the cost of the damage. The system automatically tallies the costs of parts and assembly, along with related labor expenses, and uses the same logic that an automotive expert would use in the estimation process.[32]

Table 3–6 summarizes the characteristics of different types of computers.

T A B L E   3 – 6
This table compares the characteristics of different types of computers.

	Parallel	**Super**	**Mainframe**	**Mini**	**Micro**
Size	Huge	Huge	Large	Medium	Desktop
Number of processors	Thousands	4–16	1–4	1	Single chip
Users	Multi	Multi	Multi	Multi	Single
Environment	Special (liquid cooling)	Special (liquid cooling)	Special (air conditioning)	Not necessary	Not necessary
Cadding	Special platform	Special platform	Special platform	no	no
Clock speed	>100 MHz	>100 MHz	>50 MHz	>10 MHz	>10 MHz
MIPS	>1 billion	>500 million	>100 million	>10 million	>1 million
Software	Special parallel processing software	Special vector processing software	Multiuser software	Multiuser software	Single-user software
Applications	Defense/space	Simulation defense/space	Commercial	Commercial	Commercial and home use

How to Buy a PC

For those of us who do not already own a PC, the task of buying one can be daunting. The microcomputer world is changing so rapidly that even technical wizards sometimes find it difficult to keep up with all the changes and advances taking place in this field. However, it is very important to know what to look for when buying a PC. In this section, we identify some technical considerations to take into account before buying a PC.

Six important factors must be considered while buying a PC: its processor, its clock speed, its RAM, its secondary storage, its expansion slots, and its monitor.

Processor

The processor (the CPU) determines the overall processing capabilities of the computer. The current generations of processors or chips are the 286, the 386, the 486, and the Pentium. They descended from the 8086 chip; all of these were developed by Intel Corp. The higher the processor's number, the faster the processor. For example, a 386 is faster than a 286 and a 486 is two to three times faster than a 386.

Intel's Pentium is one of the newest and most powerful processors on the market. This chip is much more powerful than its early predecessors (the Pentium represents a 90% increase in performance over the 486 chip).[33] It is capable of delivering processing speeds in excess of 100 million instructions per second and can execute two instructions per system clock cycle, as compared with the single-instruction capability of the fastest 486 chip. As the price of Pentium chips continues to drop, they are likely to overtake the 486 chip and become the industry's predominant processor.

The PowerPC uses a rival chip family, jointly developed by IBM, Motorola, and Apple Computer. It uses a new technology called **RISC (Reduced Instruction Set Computing),** which processes instructions more quickly than older chips. This is because while older chips contain a vast number of instructions to handle nearly every task that a computer carries out, RISC chips contain only those instructions that are fundamental to operating the computer. RISC also contains instructions that can be used to create other instructions.[34]

What are some considerations that a buyer should take into account in selecting the right processor, or CPU? The choice of CPU depends primarily on three factors:

♦ The average volume of data that the computer is likely to process
♦ The complexity of the operations it will perform
♦ The importance of speed

A buyer should analyze the volume and complexity of work that is likely to be done on the computer. The greater the volume and complexity of the applications, the more powerful the CPU should be. Another factor is the importance of speed to the user. Although most of us like fast computers, speed comes at a certain price. Hence, users must determine the applications for which speed is critical and recognize those for which speed is only desirable, not essential. For example, in a word processing application, speed may not be a critical factor, whereas in an application that runs the factory floor, speed may be critical.

The fastest processor, the Pentium, is appropriate whenever high speeds are important, as in network applications and complex mathematical calculations on large amounts of data. A 486DX will serve the same needs as the Pentium CPU, although the processing speed will be slower. However, it is an ideal machine for word processing, business graphics, and processing data for small and medium-sized companies.[35] Of course, any increase in the performance of the processor implies an increase in price, although the costs of computer components are generally decreasing over time.

Clock Speed

The second factor to be evaluated is the clock speed, or the speed of the processor, measured in megahertz (MHz). Clock speed can vary between 25 MHz and 100 MHz, and is sometimes even higher. The higher the clock speed, the faster the computer. In computer advertisements, the clock speed is usually indicated after the processor. For example, *486/33* indicates that the computer has a 486 processor with a 33-MHz clock speed.

RAM

The third consideration is the amount of RAM in the system, represented in megabytes. The simple principle to follow is "the more, the merrier." That is, the more memory the computer has, the better off the user will be. All application programs (such as Word, Excel, and so on) and all files use RAM. Today, many

Reduced Instruction Set Computing (RISC)
A new technology used by the PowerPC which processes instructions more quickly than older chips. It contains only those instructions that are fundamental to operating the computer.

applications require more RAM than they did a few years ago, since they have grown larger and more complex. Additional RAM can be added to the computer's motherboard.

The speed of RAM, measured in nanoseconds (billionths of a second), measures the average time it takes to access a piece of information. Speed ratings of 60, 70, and 80 nanoseconds are common; a lower speed rating means faster information retrieval.[36]

Expansion Slots and Buses

The fourth consideration is the number and type of expansion slots in the computer. **Expansion slots** allow users to add features and capabilities to their computers, such as memory, sound cards, video cards, faxmodems, and other input and output devices. For example, a user can increase the amount of RAM by adding a memory card to an expansion slot or can add an I/O (input/output) device, such as a CD-ROM, using an expansion slot.

The *expansion bus* is the type of electrical connection used in an expansion slot. The original IBM PC used an expansion bus called the PC bus, which allowed the CPU to communicate with peripherals (such as printers) at a rate of 8 bits per second. When the expansion bus of the IBM AT was increased to 16 bits per second, the industry embraced the 16-bit architecture and it became the Industry Standard Architecture (ISA) bus.

The ISA bus accommodates expansion boards designed for both the older 8-bit bus and the 16-bit ISA expansion boards. Since the ISA bus can transmit only 16 bits of data at a time at a speed of 8 MHZ,., IBM created a new 32-bit bus, called the Micro Channel Architecture (MCA) bus, which runs at speeds in excess of 8 MHz (about 10 MHz). The major problem is that MCA is not backward-compatible with ISA. To overcome this problem, the Extended Industry Standard Architecture (EISA) 32-bit bus was developed.[37]

Although the speed of microprocessors continues to increase at a rapid rate, I/O processing continues to be considerably slower than the CPU. This is particularly true for PCs, in which graphics and disk access can take a long time and thereby slow down CPU performance. One of the latest developments that help to overcome this bottleneck and enhance the performance of the CPU is local bus technology.

A **local bus** gives peripherals direct access to the PC's CPU rather than having them arbitrated by ISA, EISA, or MCA I/O expansion buses. The local bus provides a 32-bit bus that operates at the same speed as the CPU; this provides a fourfold increase in performance over the EISA bus design, which is limited to an 8-MHz operating speed. Theoretically, a local bus could allow a peripheral to send and accept data at the full speed of the 386 or 486 CPU across a 32-bit data bus.

The **Small Computer System Interface** (SCSI), the most popular bus today, is an 8-bit parallel I/O bus that "hides" the internal structure of the peripherals from the host computer. Vendors generally use a high-speed bus to connect CPUs with memory and a SCSI bus to connect I/O devices and peripherals. Up to eight SCSI devices, including the host computer, can be attached to the bus. However, only one pair of devices can communicate at a time. SCSI is favored over other bus types because the specifications of SCSI are widely distributed, making it easy to manufacture SCSI devices. Further, the SCSI specifications group devices into types, which makes it easy for vendors to develop SCSI bus controllers for new

Expansion slots
Allows users to add features and capabilities to their computers, such as memory, sound cards, video cards, faxmodems, and other input and output devices.

Industry Standard Architecture (ISA) Bus
Type of electronical connection used in an expansion slot which transmits only 16 bits of data at a time at a speed of 8 MHZ and allows the CPU to communicate with peripherals.

Local bus
Gives peripherals direct access to the PC's CPU rather than having their signals arbitrated by ISA, EISA, or MCA I/O expansion buses.

Small Computer Systems Interface (SCSI)
The 8-bit parallel I/O bus that "hides" the internal structure of the peripherals from the host computer and is the most popular bus today.

devices. Device types include direct-access devices (disk drives), sequential-access devices (tape drives), printer devices, processor devices, write-once, read-many (WORM) devices, and read-only, direct-access devices. Therefore, a new device driver for the host computer does not have to be developed for each new device.[38]

The current SCSI standard, finalized in 1986, defines a bus that supports transfer speeds of up to 5 MB/second. SCSI uses a 3-bit addressing scheme in which each device is assigned an address of 0 through 7; address 7 has the highest priority. Communication between devices occurs when the initiator, typically the host computer, originates a request and the target, such as a device controller, performs the task requested. The SCSI standard allows all devices to communicate with each other.

Monitor

The fifth consideration in buying a PC is the monitor, or video display terminal (VDT). Quite frequently, buyers pay a great deal of attention to processing speed, memory, storage capacity, and other computer capabilities, but overlook the importance of monitors. But having the right monitor can greatly influence the comfort level, productivity, and health of the user.

Six factors affect the quality of a monitor. They are

- Size
- Resolution (sharpness)
- Tricolor
- Interlaced or non-interlaced
- Radiation levels
- Video boards

Size   Like TV screens, monitors are measured diagonally. A 15-inch monitor is adequate for most tasks, including word processing and accounting, although a 17-inch monitor is much easier on the eyes. Nineteen- and 21-inch monitors are mostly used for desktop publishing or graphics. Another consideration is the shape of the monitor, which can be flat or curved. A flat screen reduces image distortion, especially at the edges, but is more expensive than a curved screen. Many monitors currently in use are curved monitors.[39]

Resolution
The sharpness of an image. It is determined by the number of pixels on the screen.

Resolution   Two more important considerations in selecting a monitor are its **resolution** and dot pitch. Resolution refers to a monitor's capacity for displaying pixels (short for picture elements), which are tiny illuminated points on the computer screen that affect the resolution or sharpness of screen images. Resolution is usually expressed in two numbers, for example, 640 by 480. The first number is the horizontal number of pixels and the second is the vertical number of pixels. Most standard 14-inch screens have 640-by-480 resolution, which implies that there are 640 columns and 480 rows of pixels on the screen. The higher the resolution, the sharper the letters and graphics will be on the screen. Common resolutions are 640 by 480, referred to as VGA (Video Graphics Array), and 1,024 by 768 (Super VGA). A monitor's *dot pitch* refers to the shortest distance between two pixels of the same color; the shorter the distance, the better the image. Monitors have dot pitches ranging from 0.25 millimeters to 0.39 millimeters.[40]

Tricolor   Tricolor is the ability of the monitor to display colors that the human eye can recognize (about 16.7 million colors). Colors are represented on the screen by bits per pixel: the greater the number of bits per pixel, the greater the number of colors. For example, a monitor should have a minimum of 24 bits per pixel in order to display 16.7 million colors. Most VDTs have 8 bits per pixel, and hence can display approximately 256 colors.

Interlaced Versus Noninterlaced Monitors   There are two types of monitors: interlaced and noninterlaced. An interlaced monitor makes two passes in order to draw a full screen of text or images. This produces a flicker on the screen—especially when running high-resolution graphics—which can cause eyestrain. Noninterlaced (NI) monitors make a single pass to draw a full screen of text and images; this produces flicker-free images, which are easier on the eye. However, noninterlaced monitors are more expensive than interlaced monitors.[41]

Radiation Level   The radiation level is another matter to be considered when selecting a monitor. Several years ago, Sweden's labor department set a standard (known as the MPR-II standard), now adopted internationally, for the maximum amount of electromagnetic radiation a monitor can emit. Since not all monitors in the U.S. meet this standard, radiation level may be an important consideration while selecting a monitor.[42]

Video Board   The type of video board (also called a video card or graphics adapter) used with the monitor is also important. Monitors work in tandem with a video board, which fits in an expansion slot on the motherboard. VGA and SVGA boards use analog signals and can create up to 16.7 million different hues (the number of colors depends on the number of bits used by the board). For example, VGA boards use 4 bits to create colors and consequently can display only 16 colors. Some SVGA boards, however, use 15, 16, or 24 bits, and are therefore able to display many colors. The more colors a video board can display, the more expensive the board. Standard SVGA video boards (256 colors) are suitable for most business applications.

SVGA video boards, which have higher resolutions and higher refresh (redrawing) rates than VGA boards, typically display a maximum resolution of 1,024 by 768 pixels, compared to a maximum VGA resolution of 640 by 480 pixels. SVGA boards can redraw an image on the screen at least 70 times per second, as compared with VGA boards, which redraw the screen 60 times per second. Because of lower refresh rates, VGA video boards sometimes suffer from screen flicker.[43]

A summary of the important considerations for choosing a monitor is given in Table 3–7(a).

These are the technical considerations that must be taken into account when buying a PC. Another issue that many customers grapple with is "With all the technological changes that are taking place, when is a good time to buy a PC?" This is a difficult question to answer, particularly because of the steady and rapid decline in hardware prices. In 1992, a PC with a 386 chip, 2 megabytes of RAM, and a 40-megabyte hard drive cost somewhere between $1,000 and $2,000. By

TABLE 3–7 (a)
Some technical considerations to take into account while buying a PC monitor.

Feature	Description
Size of Screen	Sizes range from 13 inches to 21 inches, measured diagonally.
Resolution	Resolution is measured in pixels; the higher the numbers the crisper the image. 640 by 480 VGA 1,024 by 768 SVGA
Dot Pitch	Dot pitch refers to the closeness of the pixels; the closer the better. Range from .25 mm to .39 mm.
Interlaced/ noninterlaced	Refers to the number of passes necessary to display an image. Interlaced requires 2 passes while noninterlaced requires only 1, which is easier on the eyes.
Radiation	Radiation levels should meet the MPR-II standard.

1996, a Pentium chip with 32 megabytes of RAM and at least a 1,000-megabyte hard drive will be available for the same amount. Thus, it seems inevitable that hardware prices will continue to drop and hence it is futile to wait for the "lowest price." One way to overcome this problem is through system upgrades. An **upgrade** is the process of combining some parts of an existing PC with some new components. Upgrades allows users to create better systems from existing systems, and the cost may be lower than that of a new system.

Some nontechnical considerations to take into account when buying a PC are shown in Table 3–7(b).

Upgrade
The combining of parts of an existing PC with new components to enhance the PC's performance.

TABLE 3–7 (b)
This table identifies other considerations to take into account when buying a PC.

Nontechnical Considerations in Buying a PC

Shop at the end of a quarter: Hardware and software vendors sometimes overstock their products at retail stores. At the end of a quarter, stores often cut prices in order to move extra merchandise.

Don't insist on advertised prices: In fact, store prices may sometimes actually be lower than advertised prices.

Don't be afraid of "old" models: Changes may be only incremental or cosmetic, and prices on discounted computers are usually deeply discounted.

Don't be seduced by an excess of preloaded software titles: Market researchers find people are impressed by programs they never use but pay for anyway.

Be skeptical of hard sells in stores: The salesperson may sometimes steer you to products that carry higher commissions.

Don't judge a computer by its name: Identical models of a particular machine often bear different names.

Source: Wall Street Journal, September 12, 1994, p. B1.

Summary

- **The main hardware components of a computer system and their primary functions.**

  A computer has five main components. They are the central processor, secondary storage, input devices, output devices, and communication devices. The central processor, which consists of the CPU and primary storage, is also referred to as the microprocessor. It processes data, converts it into information, and manages the overall functioning of the computer. The CPU consists of the ALU and the control unit. While the ALU processes arithmetic and logic operations, the control unit accesses the data and instructions stored in the computer and transfers them to the ALU. Primary storage temporarily stores data and instructions, is made up of semiconductors, and is volatile. There are four types of primary storage: RAM, ROM, cache, and registers.

  Secondary storage is nonvolatile memory that resides outside the CPU. Some popular secondary storage devices are magnetic tapes, disks, and CD-ROM. Input and output devices are essential to move data in and out of the computer. Some popular input devices are the keyboard, the mouse, touch screens, voice recognition, OCR, and MICR. Some popular output devices are monitors, printers, microfiche, and microfilm. Finally, the fifth component of a computer is its communication devices, which facilitate communication with other computers.

- **Different types of computers.**

  Computers can be classified into different types based on their memory size and processing speed.

- **Supercomputers** are the largest and fastest computers available today; they have large memories and high processing speeds and are capable of processing up to a billion instructions per second. A **mainframe** is a large general-purpose computer whose large memory and excellent processing capabilities make it ideal for applications that require massive computations and large-scale processing. **Minicomputers** are small, powerful, multiuser systems with excellent memory capabilities and processing speeds; although they are slower and often have less memory than mainframes, they are excellent workhorses. **Workstations** lie between midrange computers (minicomputers) and personal computers; they are faster and more sophisticated than PCs. They are fairly powerful machines that can be used both by individuals and by groups (if they are networked). **Personal computers** are versatile machines that are used for a number of business applications. Finally, there are laptops, notebooks, hand-held computers, and pen-based computers, all of which are battery-operated and hence can be used anywhere, at any time.

Review Questions

1. Explain how data are represented in a computer. What are the two important hardware considerations in representing data in a computer system?
2. Identify the time and space units of a computer. What does MIPS stand for?
3. Identify the five basic components of a computer system and briefly describe their functions.
4. Describe the central processor and its two main elements.
5. Identify any two differences between primary storage and secondary storage. Identify at least two reasons why we need secondary storage.
6. Identify the four types of primary storage and briefly describe each type.
7. What is the difference between RAM and ROM? What are the two types of ROM?
8. What are the differences between volatile and nonvolatile memory? Give at least two examples of each.
9. There are two types of secondary storage: sequential storage and direct-access storage. Briefly describe each type.
10. Describe a CD-ROM and its characteristics. What are some applications of CD-ROM technology?

11. Name and describe any two input or output devices.

12. Computers are classified into different categories based on memory size and processing speed. Identify the different types of computers discussed in this chapter, from the most powerful to the least powerful.

13. Describe parallel processing. What is the difference between a parallel-processing machine and a PC?

14. What is the difference between a workstation and a PC?

15. What are some technical considerations that a user should take into account when buying a PC?

16. What are three factors that influence the performance of a CPU?

17. What are some factors that should be taken into account when selecting a computer monitor?

 ## Discussion Questions

1. For many IS managers, the proliferation of PCs in their organization is a mixed blessing. With advances in user-friendly software, users are now capable of developing their own systems to meet their particular information needs. But as PCs proliferate in an organization, managers are concerned that they may be losing control over the use of PCs in their organizations.

   Managers are taking two different approaches to manage the proliferation of PCs. Some are taking a conservative approach by authorizing employees to use only limited software packages, such as spreadsheets and word processors, and those only from certain vendors. In fact, some organizations are so strict about this policy that employees who are found using unauthorized software can be fired. Other managers believe that the full power and potential of PCs can be achieved only by giving users full freedom to develop their own applications on whatever software packages that they choose.

   a. What are the two approaches for managing the growth of PCs in an organization? Which approach would you advocate and why?

   b. What are some of the pros and cons of each approach?

2. Computer downtime in most businesses is costly and unproductive; in the case of hospitals, it can be life-threatening. In 1992, computer downtime cost U.S. hospitals about 23 million staff hours and $466 million in wages, according to a survey of hospital IS executives. It also had other negative effects, such as lowered quality of patient care, delayed admissions and treatment, and increased patient dissatisfaction.

   As hospitals increase their dependency on computers, computer downtime will become an even more critical issue. More than 95% of those polled expect the systems to become increasingly vital in the next few years. In addition, 90% anticipate 24-hour online availability for key applications such as laboratory, radiology, pharmacy, nursing, admissions, discharge, and bedside computing functions.[44]

   a. What type of computer(s) do you think is best for hospitals, given the critical nature of hospital tasks?

3. Identify some special hardware that provides the disabled with easy access to computers.

 ## ETHICAL ISSUES

Case 1: Bank Loses Money

When a major Texas state agency purchased 25 pieces of computer equipment, little did it realize that a year later it would end up with "50 non-working machines from the original vendor, 25 machines that work from a new vendor, and a legal dispute on its hands." Problems started a few weeks after installation of 25 PCs, when five machines broke down and were sent back to the vendor for repair. The vendor fixed the five machines and provided instructions on how to fix other machines. When problems persisted with the remaining machines, the vendor sent 25 replacements. However, the replacements had the same problem. By then, a year had passed and the machines were no longer covered under warranty. Fed up with the whole state of affairs, the manager purchased 25 machines from a different vendor. The agency is now holding the 50 machines hostage (25 replacements and 25 old PCs that the vendor claims to have fixed) and the dispute is in litigation.[45]

a.   Discuss how this situation could have been avoided. Are there any ethical violations in this case?
b.   What measures should organizations take to avoid such legal disputes?

Case 2: Electronic Gambling—Winners or Losers?

Computers provide significant advantages to both organizations and individuals. However, sometimes there is also a downside to this wonderful technology, as gambling opponents are finding out. People opposed to gambling fear that computers have made it easier, and sometimes more fun, for people to "electronically gamble," and believe that new computer and network technologies are ushering in a dangerous era of electronic wagering. "With interactive TV, you'll be able to stay in your house, sell your car, and destroy yourself gambling without getting out of bed," says one opponent.

For example, computerized Keno and video poker games, 800- and 900-call services, multimedia racetrack systems, and interactive gaming channels are all examples of the growing trend toward electronic gambling, which is expected to transform the $329 billion gambling industry into a huge digital monster. As computer gambling becomes popular and commonplace in bars, restaurants, homes, and even airplanes, many worry that it will affect those who can least afford it.

On the other hand, supporters of computer gambling argue that computerized gambling brings in billions of dollars in nontaxed revenue to state and local governments. They believe it is a wonderful form of entertainment and that those addicted to gambling will continue to gamble, computers or no computers. Many states are actively exploring the possibility of generating revenues through computerized gambling.[46]

a.   Identify the pros and cons of electronic gambling.
b.   Do you believe that it should be popularized, without regard to the problems that it may cause for compulsive gamblers?

Case 3: Questionable Marketing Practices

The world of computer hardware is changing at such a rapid pace that many managers have difficulty keeping up with the changing technology. Often, they are bombarded by invitations from hardware vendors to upgrade their existing equipment. However, some experts in the field point out that often such upgrades are quite unnecessary and primarily benefit the vendor. Also, computer vendors often give "freebies" like modems (a modem is a device that helps to connect two computers). However, these modems are often slow and buyers who get "hooked" by such deals will often have to invest money to make their computers and the "free tools" truly functional.

In other cases, vendors falsely advertise at prices that are too good to be true, simply to draw the customer into the store. Once the customer shows interest in buying the product at the advertised price, the salesperson reveals that the prices do not include basic elements such as computer memory or a monitor. This is similar to asking, "Oh, you want wheels with that car?"[47]

a.   Many industries practice this form of marketing. Do you find any ethical violation in such practices?

Case 4: Use Keyboards at Your Own Risk

In the last few years, many users have complained of hand injuries caused by long hours at the keyboard, such as carpal tunnel syndrome (once headlined as "the asbestos case of the 1990s") which causes numbness and pain in the wrist and arm. Although many computer users have filed lawsuits against computer vendors, they have not been very successful in their prosecution efforts. Further, the U.S. House of Representatives recently (April, 1995) passed product liability reform legislation that caps punitive damages at $250,000 and limits lawsuit filings to within 15 years of a product's introduction.

Although more than 2,000 law suits have been filed around the country, only two have actually gone to jury trial and the verdict was not favorable to users. On March 8, 1995, a jury in Hastings, Minnesota, found IBM not guilty for the disabling injuries of former school registrar, Nancy Urbanski. Although prosecutors argued that IBM should have warned customers, IBM counterargued that items such as keyboards, tennis rackets, and

(Continued on next page)

tools can be harmful if overused and hence no special warning is required. In 1994, Compaq Computer Corp. also successfully argued in a state court in Houston that there is no scientific evidence that its keyboard was to blame for a legal secretary's crippling wrist injury.[48]

a. Do you believe that vendors should be held liable for keyboard injuries? Can an employer be held liable for the same?
b. Is it fair for an employee to file for workers' compensation for keyboard injuries?

Case 5: Compaq Is on the Hot Seat

Recently, Compaq filed suit against Packard Bell Electronics, Inc., one of its most aggressive competitors, alleging unfair and deceptive trade practices. The suit, filed by Compaq in U.S. District Court in Wilmington, Delaware, accused Bell of false and misleading marketing of the company's products and their capabilities, and

patent infringement on desktop and notebook products. Compaq also charged Bell of disassembling components from returned products and reusing them in its "new" products. However, some in the industry believe that this may just be Compaq's way of attacking a competitor who is fast becoming a leading vendor in the computer industry. "Compaq wants to succeed in the consumer market, and [the company feels] threatened by Packard Bell in the consumer and small business markets," said Jennifer Munson, an analyst at WorkGroup Technologies, Inc. in Hampton, N.H.[49]

a. How should a competitor deal with such allegations? Is it an ethical strategy on Compaq's part to create doubts in the mind of Bell customers?
b. Is there anything wrong with using quality, reusable parts in new products, without notifying customers?

 ## PROBLEM SOLVING IN THE REAL WORLD

Case 1: Computer Makeover: From the Stone Age to the Cutting Edge

Christopher Carey, president of DataTec Industries, a $50-million-per-year company that helps retailers link different electronic systems, had an inkling that the company's computer systems were badly overloaded and underpowered. However, it wasn't until the company lost a major customer over repeated bill errors that he realized how severe the problems were. Since then, DataTec has been transformed into a savvy technology user. The change surprises no one more than Carey, a self-described technophobe who once asked "Why do we need computers?" and is now the head cheerleader for the computer overhaul at DataTec.

This is the story of DataTec's bumpy journey from the technological stone age to the technological cutting edge. It offers insight into businesses that have outgrown their existing systems or have failed to get the most out of them. The moral of this story is that fixing hardware problems can cost a fortune and may well pose a new round of technology headaches, but without hardware investments, a company can easily lose its business edge and eventually become obsolete.

When It Started

Carey bought DataTec in 1976, when the company had just nine employees and less than $500,000 in revenues. By 1990, he had built it into a company with 300 employees and $31 million in revenues, and employees often worked 12-hour days just to keep up with business. But with growth came a whole new set of problems related to automation.

DataTec suddenly found itself burdened with a mismatch of stand-alone personal computers, because computer-related purchases had not been centralized and each department had bought its own computers without considering other existing systems. The result: None of the 200 computers in the eight field offices could exchange information, nor could the computers in the field communicate with those at the company headquarters.

For years, DataTec had been told by customers, directly and indirectly, that it had serious billing problems. Disparate systems led to frequent errors in invoicing, scheduling field crews, and balancing inventory. Bills showed up late, were outdated or incomplete, or were simply in error. One customer, after heaping praise on DataTec's service and support in a written survey, listed just one gripe: "Your billing sucks!"

Quick Fix

About 6 years ago, the company tried a quick-fix approach to these problems by spending $100,000 to update its existing system, hoping that the upgrade would last for at least 10 more years. DataTec outgrew it in less than 2 years; the end of that system came quickly and brutally, Carey recalls, when someone walked into his office and calmly announced, "The file is full," referring to DataTec's main office computer. "We had failed miserably," says Carey.

By 1991, the billing problems had festered, souring the relationship between DataTec and a longtime million-dollar client. Despite DataTec's repeated promises to fix the problems, they continued month after month, creating rising tension with the customer. "All of a sudden they forgot that we'd done a quality job for them," Carey recalls. "They just knew that they were spending hours a day talking to us about invoice problems." The big account walked out in disgust in 1991 and officers of DataTec snapped to attention. In retrospect, Carey says, the incident was the kick that DataTec needed.

Problems! Problems!

A subsequent top-to-bottom review of DataTec's internal systems revealed what managers at DataTec already knew: a hodgepodge of computers, which ranged from late-1980s 286 machines to newer 486 speedsters; outdated processing techniques, backed up by voluminous manual systems employing paper and pencil, all of which were pitifully inadequate to meet the day-to-day demands of the business. Computers were causing a lot of problems at DataTec!

The review found that invoices took too long to get out the door: typically 10 days to 2 weeks, compared with the norm of same-day invoicing. The error rate, about 15%, was far higher than the accepted norm of less than 1% among top companies. DataTec lost thousands of dollars because it was late in collecting overdue payments and its poor billing system was turning away customers. In fact, the computer system was so lame that DataTec couldn't even be sure it had turned a profit on a given project until 2 months after it had been completed. That was because job costing was taking a staggering 60 days or more to complete, far longer than the 1-week turnaround time at comparable companies. Inventory was

(Continued on next page)

still being tracked by paper and pencil. Carey still cringes when he remembers the time he bought $50,000 worth of special-order equipment for a job, only to discover later that DataTec had a "warehouse filled with it" in Chicago.

Since the computers in different field offices were not linked to each other, account information often had to be re-entered by hand into each field-office computer. Updates weren't easily shared with other offices, leading to foulups in handling large national accounts. "The process of getting information on customers was just so convoluted and difficult," Carey says, "we multiplied by five times the complexity of doing a job."

In Search of a Solution

DataTec's old patchwork of systems, including the various Band-Aid solutions installed over the years, can be likened to "racing in the Indy 500 in a souped-up Pinto." DataTec's Pinto is now being replaced with a sparkling new Maserati: the company plans to spend more than $1 million over the next 24 months to install an advanced computer system that will connect its eight field offices in the U.S. and abroad with corporate headquarters in New Jersey. The overhaul also includes replacing the fax machines in DataTec's fleet of 200 installation trucks with portable computers so road crews can transfer customer information to and from DataTec's central system.

The centerpiece of DataTec's $1-million computer system is an AS/400 mini-computer system from IBM, which will house all of the company's core business applications, including accounts payable, inventory, sales, and operations data, and will be linked to the 200 computers in DataTec's seven field offices. The system will allow DataTec to reduce job costing from the current 10 days to less than 48 hours and will reduce the time it takes to complete an invoice from five days to just one. Perhaps even better than that, DataTec finally has an information system that can expand just as rapidly as the company, which expects to break $60 million in revenue next year.

The downside of buying the new system is that the company had to scrap virtually all of its previous accounting and inventory programs and re-enter thousands of lines of data to use the new system. An ancient high-speed printer had to be retired. And while the AS/400 was state-of-the-art when DataTec installed it last November, just 5 months later IBM announced a new version that delivers up to 65% better price performance.

The company plans to upgrade when it needs the extra power. "I'm happy to spend the money, [although it is] a much bigger commitment than I ever anticipated." When DataTec first started looking at overhauling its computer systems about 2 years ago, Carey says, "I thought it would take a few months and cost about $150,000. Boy, was I wrong!"[50]

1. What were some signs that the existing system at DataTec was beginning to crack?
2. Why did DataTec finally decide to invest in a new system? Briefly describe the hardware of the new system.
3. What are some lessons that managers can learn from DataTec's experience?

References

Bartlett, Mel W., Stephen M. Omohundro, Arch D. Robison, Steven S. Skiena, Kurt H. Thearling, Luke T. Young, and Stephen Wolfram. "Tablet: Personal Computer in the Year 2000," *Communications of the ACM* 31, no. 6 (June 1988).

Bell, Gordon. "Taking Note of Multimedia." *Information Week,* March 16, 1992.

Maglitta, Joseph. "IS at O.J. City," ComputerWorld, May 15, 1995, p. 1, 90–91, 94.

Markoff, John. "Supercomputing's Speed Quest," *The New York Times* (May 31, 1991).

Peled, Abraham. "The Next Computer Revolution," *Scientific American* 257, no. 4 (October 1987).

Press, Larry. "Compuvision or Teleputer?" *Communications of the ACM* 33, no. 3 (September 1990).

Notes

1. Hoffman, Thomas. "Knocking Down Barriers," *Computerworld,* August 30, 1993, p. 28.
2. McPartlin, John P. ed. "PCs Are a Student's Best Friend," *InformationWeek,* April 5, 1993, p. 44.
3. Betts, Mitch. "Rogue Computer Fined for Contempt," *Computerworld,* April 5, 1993, p. 2.
4. Adhikari, Richard. "Joining the Gbyte Club," *InformationWeek,* October 24, 1994, pp. 56–60.
5. Laudon, Kenneth C. and Jane P. Laudon, "Management Information Systems: Organization and Technology," 3d ed, Macmillan Publishers.
6. Ouellette, Tim. "CD Gets All-in-one Format," Computerworld, May 8, 1995, p. 20.
7. "Small Is Beautiful," *Chief Information Officer,* May 15, 1994, p. 14.
8. Ibid.
9. Walker, Clinton. "Interactive Ads," *InformationWeek,* October 3, 1994, pp. 25–60.
10. Desmond, Michael, and Melissa Riofrio. "Best CD-ROM Drives and Sound Boards," *PC World,* December 1994, pp. 154–186.
11. Edwards, Owen. "Douglas Engelbart," *Forbes ASAP,* October 10, 1994, p. 130.
12. Hayes, Mary. "Philips Invites Free Speech," *InformationWeek,* October 24, 1994, p. 73.
13. Wildstrom, Stephen H. "This secretary really listens," *Business Week,* April 24, 1995, p. 19.
14. Anthes, Gary H. "Postal Service Sorts through Automation," *Computerworld,* October 4, 1993, p. 26.
15. Stahl, Stephanie. "DHL Agent Keeps Track," *InformationWeek,* July 25, 1994, p. 76.
16. Betts, Mitch. "Voice Strain Plagues Some PC Users," *Computerworld,* April 24, 1995, pp. 1 & 12.
17. Anthes, Gary H. "Postal Service Sorts through Automation," *Computerworld,* October 4, 1993, p. 26.
18. McCune, Jenny C. "Home Based Warriors," *Success,* Vol. 41, 3, April 1994, pp. 42–47.
19. Ibid.
20. Ibid.
21. "Banc One's Time-Saver," *InformationWeek,* September 26, 1994, p. 45.
22. Desmond, Michael, and Melissa Riofrio. "Best CD-ROM Drives and Sound Boards," *PC World,* December 1994, pp. 154–186.

23. Senn, James A. "Information Systems in Management," *Wadsworth Inc.,* 1990, pp. 173–174.

24. Brooks, Richard C., and Harlan L. Etheridge. "Hardware Checklist," *CA Magazine,* May 1994, pp. 47–51.

25. Anthes, Gary H. "SEC Electronic Filing System in High Gear," *Computerworld,* April 5, 1993, p. 59.

26. McPartlin, John P. "Greyhound Gets on Fast Track," *InformationWeek,* January 25, 1993, p. 13.

27. Caldwell, Bruce. "EMI Puts Processes In Tune," *InformationWeek,* October 17, 1994, p. 48.

28. Fitzgerald, Michael. "PCs are Money in the Bank," *Computerworld,* March 15, 1993, p. 39.

29. *InformationWeek,* January 6, 1992, p. 10.

30. Vijayan, Jaikumar. "Plug and Play Makes Strides," *Computerworld,* November 7, 1994, p. 46.

31. McMullen, John. "United Keeps Service 'Insight,'" *InformationWeek,* August 17, 1992, p. 42.

32. Bartholomew, Doug. "Damage Control," *InformationWeek,* July 11, 1994, p. 32.

33. Brooks, Richard C. and Harlan L. Etheridge. "Hardware Checklist," *CA Magazine,* May 1994, pp. 47–51.

34. Baum, David. "Power MAC Migration," *Infoworld,* May 9, 1994, p. 67.

35. Holzinger, Albert G. "What You Get Is What You See," *Nation's Business,* October 1994, p. 61.

36. Ibid.

37. Ibid.

38. McNutt, Dinah. "Basic SCSI," *UNIX Review,* September 1993, pp. 23–28.

39. Ibid.

40. Brooks, Richard C. and Harlan L. Etheridge, "Hardware Checklist," *CA Magazine,* May 1994, pp. 47–51.

41. Ibid.

42. Ibid.

43. Ibid.

44. McPartlin, John P. "Downtime May Be Hazardous to Health," *InformationWeek,* April 12, 1993, p. 60.

45. Leinfuss, "A Comedy of Errors," *Computerworld,* July 12, 1993, p. 127.

46. Maglitta, Joseph. "High-tech Wagering: Jackpot or Jeopardy?" *Computerworld,* February 7, 1994, Vol. 28, No. 6, pp. 1, 28–29.

47. Pulleyn, Chris. "Ethics and High-tech Marketing," *Marketing News,* Vol. 28, No. 19, September 12, 1994, p. 4.

48. Betts, Mitch. "Keyboard Lawsuits Lose Ground," *Computerworld,* April, 3, 1995, p. 44.

49. Vijayan, Jaikumar. "Playing Hard Ball in Court," *Computerworld,* April 17, 1995, p. 8.

50. Cauley, Leslie. "Computer Makeover: How DataTec Industries Is Moving From Stone Age to the Technological Cutting Edge," *Wall Street Journal,* Monday, June 27, 1994.

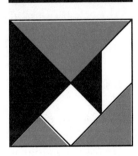

Computer Software

Bill Gates, President of Microsoft

Contents

Learning Objectives
Technology Payoff: Kentucky Fried Chicken
Introduction
Programming Languages
    Machine language
    Assembly language
    High-Level Languages (3GLs)
    Very High-Level Languages
    Object-Oriented Programming
    Visual Programming
Types of Software
    System Software
      System Control Software
      The Operating System And Its Functions
      Operating System Environments
      Examples of Operating Systems
      System Support Software
      System Development Software
    Application Software
      General Purpose Software
    Application-Dedicated Software

115

Selecting Software Packages
Investment Criteria for Hardware and Software
Ethical Considerations
Summary
Review Questions
Discussion Questions
Ethical Issues
    Case 1: Is Justice Above the Law?
    Case 2: Software Piracy
    Case 3: Highway Robbery
Problem Solving in the Real World
    Case 1: City of Indianapolis Goes High-Tech
    Case 2: Ryder Rethinks Business Systems
References
Notes

Learning Objectives

Software is the detailed set of instructions given to a computer so it can perform various tasks. In this chapter, we identify and describe different types of software and their functions. Operating systems, which are a special type of software that manages the computer system, are also discussed. Issues related to the use and management of software in organizations are presented. After reading and studying this chapter, you will be able to

* Understand the concept of programming and identify the different generations of programming languages
* Describe different types of system software and application software
* Discuss the structure and functions of an operating system and identify different types of operating systems
* Identify some managerial issues related to hardware and software investments

TECHNOLOGY PAYOFF

Kentucky Fried Chicken

Kentucky Fried Chicken (KFC) in Louisville, Kentucky, uses customized software to provide outstanding service to its customers in an industry where competition is stiff, to say the least. Although KFC added 44 stores in the U.S. last year, sales were flat at $3.4 billion. KFC officials believe that what was missing was a plan to expand the first commandment of the fast-food industry: "Customer convenience comes first." In an effort to retain existing customers and attract new ones, KFC has developed a home delivery system for domestic and international markets that allows customers to call a KFC restaurant and have food delivered at home.

KFC has spent millions of dollars (the company won't say exactly how much) to create an information system that can support home-delivery service for its 3,905 overseas restaurants and eventually for restaurants in the U.S. KFC piloted the home-delivery programs in Malaysia, Singapore, Puerto Rico, and the Middle East, where there are fewer restaurants and a pressing need to update antiquated hardware systems. The company uses networked 486 PCs and customized software, which includes UNIX and DOS-based applications, in its home-delivery system.

Since hundreds of customers could conceivably place phone orders within a short period of time, KFC developed a central system that sorts the information and reroutes delivery instructions to the right outlets. For example, when a customer in Puerto Rico calls KFC for a bucket of chicken, the operator records the order on a PC. Then the name, address, and phone number of the customer are sent to a delivery dispatcher, who transmits the order to the restaurant closest to the customer's home. The restaurant then prepares the food and delivers the order.

The home-delivery system has specialized software that monitors the volume of chicken sold at each site and generates a report if sales are higher or lower than a predetermined average. Managers review the data throughout the day and accordingly make plans for food preparation. This is a considerable improvement over the old system in which sales volumes were calculated only once a day, giving managers very little information with which to make operational decisions.

On the administrative side, international KFC sites use the system to monitor employee attendance, process marketing information, and track inventory to help corporate managers evaluate the performance of individual restaurants. Effective systems can be developed only if hardware and software are brought together in meaningful ways. KFC used customized PC-based software—software designed to meet its particular needs—to develop its customer-oriented sales and delivery system.[1]

As a great social leveler, information technology ranks second only to death. It can erase cultural barriers, overwhelm economic inequalities, even compensate for intellectual disparities. In short, high technology can put unequal human beings on an equal footing, and that makes it the most potent democratizing tool ever devised.

—Sam Pitroda, telecommunications consultant

Introduction

Both hardware and software are necessary to build an information system. In the last chapter, we studied various types of computer hardware and their functions. In this chapter, we identify various kinds of software and describe the critical role that software plays in helping an organization meet its information needs. Behind the many success stories of computers lies the power of software, or programs.

The story about KFC shows how the company is using hardware and software to provide outstanding customer service. The company developed its own software to create a central system that sorts customer requests and reroutes delivery instructions to the right outlets for quick, easy delivery. The software also monitors sales volume, generates reports, monitors employee attendance,

Program

A set of instructions given to a computer to accomplish various tasks. Written in a special computer language, called programming language.

processes marketing information, and tracks inventory. KFC's information system uses DOS and UNIX, two popular operating systems, which are discussed later in this chapter.

Systems such as KFC's are driven by programs. A **program** is a set of step-by-step instructions given to a computer to have it perform various tasks. Programmers write software using special languages, called programming languages. The process of writing programs is referred to as programming.

In the 1950s, more than 70% of the cost of a computer system was spent on hardware. Today, hardware accounts for less than 15% of system costs; customized software accounts for about 85%. Although inexpensive, mass-produced software packages are available off the shelf, software development continues to be a major challenge for many organizations. There are many reasons for this.

First, the complexity and sophistication of software has increased manyfold over the past decade. Today, computers are used in a wide variety of fields for a number of complex tasks such as automating the factory floor, helping doctors perform surgery, conducting scientific research, and exploring space. The software that performs such tasks is highly complex and takes many people years to develop. Second, coding and testing software is time-consuming and labor-intensive, and recent studies have shown that writing software is one of the more complex and creative activities of the human mind. Third, since it takes many years of extensive training to become an expert in software development, experienced programmers are expensive to hire and are often in short supply. Fourth, a software application is never fully complete, because users function in a dynamic environment in which their information needs are continuously changing. Hence, software has to be frequently updated and maintained.

Programming Languages

Programming language

A special kind of computer language, with its own syntax and grammar, that is used to write software.

A **programming language** is a computer language, with its own syntax and grammar, which is used to write software. There are two types of programming languages: procedural and nonprocedural languages. A **procedural language** is one that explains, step by step, *how* a given task is to be accomplished. A **nonprocedural language,** on the other hand, focuses on *what* needs to be done, without specifying exactly how it is to be done. For example, suppose a CEO is interested in finding the top five stores in her company in terms of sales. In a nonprocedural language, the CEO would simply tell the computer what needed to be done: "Determine the five stores with the highest sales." The computer would automatically figure out how to get this information. In a procedural language, on the other hand, the CEO would have to give specific instructions to the computer as to how it should retrieve and process this information. The CEO would have to tell the computer where to find the data, how to process the data, and how to format and output the data. Although early programming languages were completely procedural, today there are several powerful and user-friendly nonprocedural languages, such as Focus.

Procedural language

Language that explains in a step-by-step sequence *how* a given task should be accomplished.

Nonprocedural language

Language that focuses on *what* needs to be done, without specifying exactly *how* it should be done.

Machine Languages

Machine language

Language written at the primitive level of binary arithmetic. It was the first generation of computer language and was tedious and error-prone.

In the early years of the computer revolution, programs were written at the primitive level of binary arithmetic, in **machine language.** Machine language, the first generation of computer languages, was tedious, error-prone, and machine-dependent—that is, programs written on one type of machine could not be executed on other types of machines without rewriting all the code. Note, however, that machine language is the only language that a computer can understand and execute, and hence programs written in all other programming languages must first be converted or translated into machine language before the programs can be executed.

Assembly Language

Assembly language, which uses meaningful abbreviations of words, or mnemonics, to represent basic computer instructions, emerged in the early 1950s. It is viewed as the second generation of computer languages. Although assembly language is machine-dependent, it was an improvement over machine language because it used words such as *add* and *sub* (for subtract) instead of the 0s and 1s used in machine language. Assembly language is converted into machine language by a program called an **assembler.**

High-Level Languages (3GLs)

Between the mid-1950s and the 1970s, a new set of languages, called **high-level languages (HLL),** or 3GLs (third-generation languages), emerged. They were a big improvement over assembly language and machine language. 3GLs were English-like; they were called high-level languages because what took several lines of code in machine language or assembly language could be written using a single instruction in a 3GL and this greatly enhanced the programming process.

3GLs are *machine-independent* languages; that is, they are portable from one type of machine to another, although, like other languages, a 3GL must be converted into machine language before it can be executed. The conversion from 3GL to machine language is done using a program called a **compiler,** which is a system software product that reads a program written in a 3GL and converts it into machine language. Some popular high-level languages are BASIC, COBOL, FORTRAN, and C. Although high-level languages were a considerable improvement over earlier languages, considerable training and experience are required to program in 3GLs.

Very High-Level Languages

Very high-level languages, or 4GLs (fourth-generation languages), began to emerge in the late 1970s. They were designed primarily to overcome some of the

---

Assembly language
A language based on mnemonics, or meaningful abbreviations of commands, such as *add*, *load*, and so on. It was the second generation of computer languages.

Assembler
A program used to convert assembly language into machine language.

High-level languages
Computer languages that improve on assembly language and machine language because they are English-like and require fewer instructions.

Compiler
A system software product that reads a program written in a high-level language and translates it into machine language.

Very high-level languages
Also called 4GLs (fourth-generation computer languages), these are efficient, user-friendly, and English-like languages.

Instruction	Comment
mov a,01h	;put the number 1 in A
mov [1000h],a	;store in memory location 1000h
mov a,02h	;put the number 2 in A
mov [1001h],a	;store in memory location 1001h
mov a,03h	;put the number 3 in A
mov [1002h],a	;store in memory location 1002h
go 0000h	;set IP back to start of program

Assembly Language

limitations of high-level languages. 4GLs are nonprocedural languages, in which the user need only specify what task must be done, not how it should be done. This greatly simplifies the process of developing applications.

Some examples of fourth-generation languages are SQL, FOCUS, and SAS. Fourth-generation languages are efficient, user-friendly, easy to learn, and very English-like. Table 4–1 gives brief descriptions of some popular third- and fourth-generation programming languages.

One of the primary advantages of a 4GL is that it is easy to use; it allows even nonprogrammers to develop fairly complex applications. This not only reduces the cost of development, but also reduces the time it takes to develop systems. People knowledgeable in 4GLs are in high demand; it is estimated that the average salary of programmers with 4GL skills is 7% to 12% higher than that of programmers with only traditional programming skills.[2] In the last few years, many organizations have switched to 4GLs in an effort to reduce their programming staffs and decrease software development costs, although 3GLs continue to be popular.

For example, the Sante Fe Railroad's Corwith Yard in Chicago was in desperate need of a computer system to track its complex and growing "piggyback" operations. Although the company had a detailed plan to computerize the piggyback operations, its programmers on the West Coast were busy with many other projects. Corwith finally asked four middle-level managers with no programming experience to become 4GL programmers. In less than three months, the first part of the system was operational; before long, it was adapted for use in other Santa

```
/****************************************************************************/
/*      Function Name:          ARVW002A_set_user                       */
/*      Description:            This function validates that the user   */
/*                              logged in is a valid clerk.             */
/****************************************************************************/
void ARVW002A_set_user( )
{
        static int usr_rtrn_cde;
        set_fct_CCR("ARVS002", "ARVW002A", "ARVW002A_set_user");

        strcpy(ARVW002A.tkt_aud_id, getenv("LOGNAME"));

        clear_results(THREAD_2);

      usr_rtrn_cde = sybase_procedure(THREAD_2,
   "mgt",
   "s_get_clerk_s_0102",
   "%S",
   ARVW002A.tkt_aud_id,
   "%S %S %S %S %S",
   t_clerk.tkt_aud_id,
   t_clerk.tkt_clk_phn_num,
   t_clerk.tkt_aud_nme,
   t_clerk.sect_id,
   t_clerk.wg_suprv_usid);
```

TABLE 4-1
Some popular high-level and very-high-level languages.

BASIC: BASIC is an acronym for Beginners' All-Purpose Symbolic Instruction Code, a program developed at Dartmouth College in 1964 by John Kemeny and Thomas Kurtz. It is usually the first computer language that novice programmers learn. BASIC is a procedure-oriented, general-purpose language that is widely used for commercial and scientific applications. It is flexible and easy to learn, but is not portable.

FORTRAN: FORTRAN is an acronym for FORmula TRANslation. The program was developed by IBM in the mid-1950s. Like BASIC, FORTRAN is a general-purpose, procedure-oriented language. It is widely used for scientific and engineering applications and number crunching. A large number of languages developed after FORTRAN have been influenced by its structure. However, it lacks flexibility in input/output operations.

COBOL: COBOL is an acronym for Common Business-Oriented Language. The program was developed at the Pentagon in 1959, the product of a joint effort by the federal government and the computer industry. COBOL is the dominant language of the business world and many industries use thousands of lines of code written in COBOL. It is easy to learn and has an English-like structure. It is excellent for processing large data files and performing repetitive tasks.

PASCAL: PASCAL was developed by Niklaus Wirth of the Federal Institute of Technology in Zurich, Switzerland, in 1968. It is named for the seventeenth-century French mathematician Blaise Pascal. PASCAL is widely used for business and scientific applications. The language is easy to learn and allows a programmer to structure programming problems. PASCAL is a popular language in computer science courses, because it lays the foundation for a structured programming framework.

C Language: C is a general-purpose language. It is called C because it was an improvement over another language called B that was developed at AT&T Bell Labs in the early 1970s. C was developed by Brian Kerninghan and Dennis Ritchie. It is closely associated with the UNIX system since the C language was developed on UNIX. Although UNIX was initially written in assembly language, Dennis Ritchie later rewrote UNIX in C language. In a short time C has become an extremely popular language and is now widely used in system development applications and for commercial uses. C is a concise language that provides a high level of modularity.

Fe yards. The finished system has helped the company save more than $100 million per year.

If 4GLs are so efficient and user-friendly, why aren't all programs written in 4GLs? Companies have already invested millions—in some cases, billions—of dollars in their software systems. Many of their programs were written in BASIC, COBOL, FORTRAN and other third-generation languages. It is difficult, if not impossible, and financially impractical to rewrite all these programs in 4GLs. Hence, while new systems may be developed using 4GLs, companies must continue to update and maintain systems that were written in earlier languages.

Object-Oriented Programming

Object-oriented programming (OOPs)

A powerful type of programming language that enhances the productivity of programmers and reduces software development time. Another significant benefit of OOPs is code reusability.

Object-oriented programming, also known as OOPs, is another kind of programming language that has become increasingly popular in recent years. It enhances the productivity of programmers and reduces software development time. OOPs is an innovative approach to the design and programming of computer software, in which systems are modeled using chunks of programming and

4GLs

```
WHILE LOOPTEST = FALSE DO
        AT 12,72 INPUT PRNTCHEK STR USING "I"
        IF PRNTCHEK NE "y" and PRNTCHEK NE "n" THEN
            AT 14,10 OUTPUT "Please enter y or n"
        ELSE
            AT 14,10 OUTPUT"
            LOOPTEST = TRUE
        ENDIF
ENDWHILE

IF PRNTCHEK = "y" THEN
        E.OPRN = TRUE; CLEAR
        CONSULT #A
        E.OPRN = FALSE
ENDIF

IF PRNTCHEK = "n" THEN
    AT 16,10 OUTPUT "Your printer is not ready. Would you like"
    AT 17,10 OUTPUT "to output the trace to the screen? (y/n)"
LOOPTEST = FALSE
```

Code reusability

A significant benefit of OOPs that allows the same piece of code to be used for different applications.

data called *objects*. Each object includes programming code that specifies how it should behave, how it should manipulate data, respond to messages from other objects, and send messages of its own.

The principal benefit of OOPs is **code reusability,** which means that the same piece of code can be used for different applications. (The idea of reusability is something that designers have known and practiced for many centuries: even complex systems can be easily assembled by using a set of well-defined existing components, rather than by building them from scratch.) Compare this with the traditional approach, in which code was written from scratch for every new application. For example, a print function in a word processing program does the same thing as a print function in a spreadsheet program. However, without code reusability, the same print function must be written twice—once for each application.[3] Software reuse dates back to 1944, when a Defense Department programmer wrote a routine to compute a mathematical function. Today, code reusability has become not only desirable but essential in many software development environments. It is estimated that half of the code required for most applications already exists and that an estimated 40% to 60% of all new code can come from software libraries of reusable components.[4]

For example, Raytheon, in Lexington, Massachusetts, has had a software reuse program in place since 1976. The company has perfected the art of reusability to the point where 80% to 90% of the code for new business applications comes from reusable components. Over the years, Raytheon has built a library of nearly 2,000 reusable software modules—that is, chunks of reusable code that can be used over and over again for a number of basic business functions. Not only can applications be developed much faster using reusable code, but maintenance also becomes easier because reusable code is standardized and widely understood.[5]

Another company that uses object-oriented programming to cut down application development time and customize applications to meet local needs with-

Scotiabank, which operates branches in Canada and 45 other countries developed a banking sales and services system using object-oriented design and programming concepts. The application is designed to help new customers choose savings accounts and keep demographic information on individual and commercial customers. This, in turn, helps salespeople better market the bank's investment, loan, and other bank products by matching the individual's needs to the company products. The system replaced a "paper and pencil" approach and "the common sense of our employees," said Drew Brown, manager of systems development. Scotiabank has spent more than $250,000 educating its employees on object-

oriented concepts. The bank is hoping that the move to object-oriented technology will help to cut application development time by half or more and that code reusability will significantly increase once people become trained in object-oriented concepts. However, the company estimates that it will be able to reap the benefits only after three or four years because of a big learning curve for object programming.

The company also uses object-oriented databases that allow each branch to customize its database (a repository of data) to meet local needs. For example, not all branches offer the same loan, investment, and other programs, and hence it is important that computer applications also take these differences into account. Customized, local databases help each branch to keep detailed data relevant to its community, while passing on relevant corporate information to headquarters.[6]

---

out having to build each application from scratch is Scotiabank (see box). The company, however, fully recognizes that object-oriented programming takes time to learn and only expects to reap the full benefits of this technology in three to four years.

Another benefit of OOPs is that it lowers the amount of testing required. If components in a system have been thoroughly tested in other applications, they need not be tested with the same degree of rigor in a new application. This improves product quality and the timeliness of product delivery. Also, OOPs software is easier to update than software written in traditional languages because often only some aspects of an object have to be modified. Objects can inherit attributes from a parent object, so that only the differences have to be modeled. For example, Shearson Lehman Brothers uses OOPs to model its securities products; when it offers a new product, programmers simply alter an existing securities model to reflect the particular features of the new one.[7] Many other companies have increased their productivity by reusing code (see box).

Although OOPs has many benefits, it still has some limitations and bottlenecks. First, many experts feel that OOPs technology has been oversold as a panacea for all software development problems, with the result that many customers are often disappointed by its yields. The benefits of OOPs cannot be reaped in the short run, but only in the long term, as more OOPs code is generated and reused. Further, the full benefits of OOPs can be achieved only if a company is willing to start from scratch, rather than making gradual transitions from existing code. This is something that many firms are reluctant to do.

Visual Programming

Visual programming
Programming languages that allow the user to visualize code and its impact on the system.

The term **visual programming** refers to programming languages that allow users to visualize their code and its impact on the system, thus helping them to create powerful and less error-prone applications in less time. For example, a product called Prodea Synergy, from Prodea, of Eden Prairie, Minnesota, allows users to

BUSINESS REALITIES
Code Reusability

Many companies have increased their productivity and cut development costs simply by reusing existing code. For example, the Pentagon believes it could save $300 million annually if it increased software reuse by just 1%. GTE Data Services, in Tampa, Florida, has gained a 20% to 40% productivity increase from its repository of 960,000 lines of COBOL, C, assembler, and PC spreadsheet code. Each year, GTE's chief information officer raises the target percentage for reused software for the company so that more benefits can be achieved through reusability.

Another company that has successfully implemented code reusability is the Canadian National Railway, whose programmers wrote 10,600 lines of code for a freight-car optimization system, of which 137,600 lines came from existing code, thus completing the complex application in less than 8 person-months.[8]

automate the flow of information among different software products, such as word processors and spreadsheets, to create an integrated application. Users themselves can use the package to create a program that performs fairly sophisticated tasks. The program allows a user to download competitors' advertised prices from an external database. It then compares the competitors' prices with those of the user's company and graphically displays comparisons of the prices. The visual program also allows the user to fax the results to the board of directors, which can then recommend a course of action. In visual programming, instead of writing many lines of code, the user clicks on various icons and achieves the same effect. PowerBuilder Enterprise is another popular visual programming package that allows users to visually manipulate data and perform sophisticated data analysis.

```
Sub ReadFile( )
        Sheets(1) .Activate
        Dim CurrentRecord As EmployeeRec
        ' Get a filename
        Filename = Application.GetOpenFilename
        ' Get a valid file number.
        iFileNum = FreeFile
        ' Open the file for random access
        Open Filename For Random As iFileNum Len = Len(CurrentRecord)
        Do Until EOF(1)
                iCount = iCount + 1
                ' Read record.
                Get iFileNum, iCount, CurrentRecord
                ' Display it in the worksheet.
                With ActiveSheet
                        .Cells(iCount, 1) = CurrentRecord.FName
                        .Cells(iCount, 2).Value = CurrentRecord.MInitial
                        .Cells(iCount, 3).Value = CurrentRecord.LastName
                        .Cells(iCount, 4).Value = CurrentRecord.ID
                        .Cells(iCount, 5).Value = CurrentRecord.Password
                End With
        Loop
        ' Close the file
        Close iFileNum
End Sub
```

Visual BASIC

One of the most popular visual programming languages is Visual BASIC, a programming language developed by Microsoft. It is designed to allow users and developers to easily integrate Microsoft Windows applications and is one of the fastest ways to develop Windows applications. Visual BASIC serves as a common macro language for Access, PowerPoint, Word, and Excel; this feature can reduce the development time for many applications.

When Bankers Trust switched to Visual BASIC to manage its large and constantly changing investment portfolios, the time required to develop new applications dropped significantly. Sun Hydraulics is also using visual programming to manage its online catalog inventory and to navigate its huge parts catalog. Visual programming reduces application development time and gives end-users the ability to create their own tools. Harley-Davidson has used visual programming to create Trademark Wizard, a database program that tracks the company's licensed merchandise.[9]

In summary, the programming languages that are used to create software have come a long way since the early days of machine language.

Types of Software

Software can be classified into two broad categories: system software and application software. System software performs computer-related tasks, such as managing input and output devices; application software performs people-related tasks, such as human resources and marketing. A more detailed discussion of these two types of software follows.

System software can be divided into three categories: system control software, system support software, and system development software. Application software can be divided into two categories: general purpose software and application-dedicated software. Figure 4–1 shows the relationships among hardware, system software, and application software.

System Software

System software and its marginal definitions are shown alongside.

System software performs the basic functions necessary to start and operate a computer. It controls and monitors the various activities and resources of a computer and makes it easier and more efficient to use the computer. System software is classified into three categories:

- *System control software* (programs that manage system resources and functions)
- *System support software* (programs that support the execution of various applications)
- *System development software* (programs that assist system developers in designing and developing information systems)

System Control Software   **System control software** includes programs that monitor, control, coordinate, and manage the resources and functions of a computer system. The most important system control software is the operating system.

The Operating System and its Functions   An **operating system** is a complex set of software modules that manages the overall operations of a computer. It is a

System software
Software that performs the basic functions necessary to start and operate a computer.

System control software
Programs that monitor, control, coordinate, and manage the resources and functions of a computer.

Operating system
The most important system control software, it refers to a complex set of software modules that manage the overall operations of a computer.

FIGURE 4–1

The relationships among hardware,
system software, and application
software

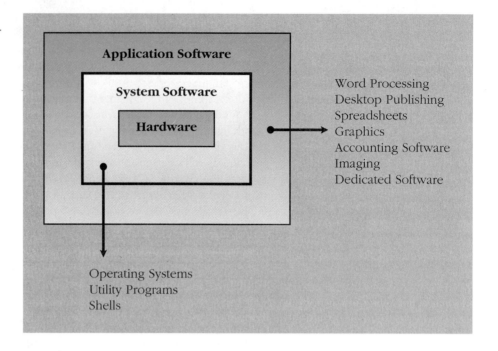

master control program that acts as a manager, a housekeeper, and a traffic cop for the computer system. Depending on the type of computer (mainframe, personal computer, and so on), the operating system performs a number of functions, such as allocating resources for running different software programs, tracking the use of different computer resources, ensuring optimal utilization of various resources, and acting as an interface between the user and the computer. Application programs, such as word processors and spreadsheets, run under the supervision of the operating system.

An operating system loads programs, performs and manages input/output operations, manages files, monitors and manages the use of computer memory, allocates resources for various computer functions, and resolves conflicts. Some of these functions are carried out only by organization-wide systems and work-group systems, such as mainframes and minicomputers; others are performed by personal information systems, such as PCs. Let us take a look at some of these functions.

The operating system loads programs to be executed into primary memory and sends a message to the user when the execution is completed. It also notifies the user of any errors in the system or errors that it encounters during program execution.

The operating system allocates and manages input/output (I/O) devices and provides I/O instructions, such as "start printer" and "rewind tape," to various programs. It is the operating system that provides access to different I/O devices and "releases" these devices when a task is completed so they can be used by other programs. If user intervention is necessary because of a loose printer cable connection or lack of paper in the printer, it sends a message to the user.

Another function of an operating system is to manage files; a file is a place in computer memory where data and instructions are stored. The computer reads,

FIGURE 4-2

In a system with no multiprogramming capabilities, the operating system is completely dedicated to executing one program at a time. In a multiprogramming environment, the operating system executes several programs concurrently. This increases the efficiency of the CPU, the memory, and the input/output devices.

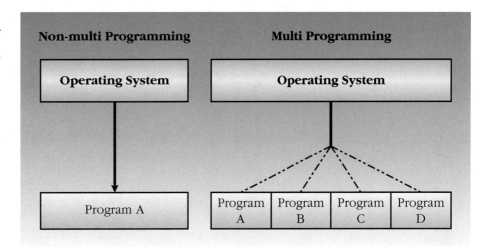

creates, deletes, merges, and renames files and performs other file-related tasks with help from the operating system.

The operating system also manages hard-disk storage so that users can create, execute, save, and retrieve various applications. Hard-disk storage management is an important consideration in ensuring the efficient utilization of computer memory.

Managing computer resources such as the CPU, primary memory, secondary storage, I/O devices, and other peripherals is another function of the operating system, as the resources in a computer system must be carefully synchronized. Operating systems for organization-wide systems and work-group systems track the use of computer resources for cost accounting and statistical purposes. Statistics on resource use can help managers to better plan, implement, and coordinate strategies that will lead to full utilization of existing resources. For example, if usage statistics show that computer memory is overutilized while the CPU is underutilized, a manager can improve operational efficiency by expanding computer memory.

Finally, conflict resolution is an important function of an operating system for mainframes. When resolving a resource conflict, the operating system serves as an arbitrator by taking into account factors such as the criticality of the application and the priority of the user, and allocates resources accordingly. It ensures that limited system resources, such as the CPU and the I/O devices, are allocated among different programs according to predetermined criteria. For example, a payroll program often gets higher priority than a program that calculates employee travel expenses; the chief financial officer may get higher priority than a part-time worker.

Table 4-2 presents a summary of the functions of an operating system.

Multiprogramming

A computing environment in which a number of users can run multiple programs on a single-CPU computer at the same time.

Operating System Environments **Multiprogramming** emerged in an effort to address the wide discrepancy between the processing speed of the CPU and input/output devices. The CPU is many, many times faster than input and output devices and hence, while an input/output operation was being executed the CPU sat idle. This is a tremendous waste of computer resources and multiprogramming helped to overcome this bottleneck and increase the efficiency of computer operations.

TABLE 4-2
A summary of some of the
important functions of an
operating system.

Function	Description
Load programs	Moves programs to be executed into primary memory and indicate when program execution is complete.
Manage I/O operations	Enables and manages the use of multiple I/O devices. Ensures the efficient utilization of I/O devices.
Manage files	Allows application programs to read and write files. Performs other file-related operations such as copying, deleting, moving, and so on.
Manage memory	Allocates memory so users can create, execute, and retrieve different applications. Ensures that memory is fully and efficiently utilized.
Detect errors	Brings system and execution errors to the attention of the user so that timely action can be taken.
Allocate resources	Manages all computer resources, including the CPU, primary memory, secondary storage, and I/O devices and other peripherals.
Monitor resource use	Tracks use of computer resources for cost accounting and statistical purposes. Mostly done for enterprise-wide systems.
Resolve conflicts	Acts as an arbitrator among competing programs, taking into account factors such as the criticality of the application or the priority of the program.

A multiprogramming environment works in the following way: A number of programs to be executed are kept in primary storage. The operating system selects and begins execution of the first instruction or element in the first program. When it encounters an I/O instruction, the operating system hands off the instruction to the I/O device. While the I/O device is processing the instruction, the CPU selects the next program from the program queue and begins execution of the second program. When the I/O processing of the first program is complete, the operating system notifies the CPU, which then switches back to the first program and continues execution until another I/O activity is encountered. This greatly increases the utilization of the CPU and ensures that the slow processing speed of I/O devices does not affect CPU utilization. Therefore, in a multiprogramming environment the CPU switches between multiple programs, although at any given time the CPU is executing only one program.[10]

Time-sharing environment
A way of allowing different users to use the CPU at the same time.

Multiprogramming is similar to a **time-sharing environment** in which different users get a slice of the CPU's time. In time-sharing, like multiprogramming, the CPU is not dedicated to one user but many users. However, the CPU is so fast that users are unaware that the CPU is switching between different users because of the tremendous speed with which the CPU processes instructions. Time-sharing systems were developed so that users could interface in an interactive or conversational mode directly with the CPU through dumb terminals. When the user types in a processing request, the CPU processes the request and sends a response, where necessary, to the user's terminal. Time-sharing greatly facilitated testing code and developing system applications because users could locate and correct errors in a matter of a few minutes, instead of having to wait for hours to get some CPU time.[11]

Multiprocessing system
A multiuser system in which a number of processors, or CPUs, process data and instructions.

A **multiprocessing system** has several processors, or CPUs. Multiprocessing is ideally suited for complex and computationally intensive operations that require a large amount of processing. Note that multiprogramming and multiprocessing are not mutually exclusive. Table 4–3 provides a brief description of multiprocessing and multiprogramming.

Today there are many types of operating systems on the market. Some are designed for microcomputers and workstations; others are targeted for mainframes and minicomputers. In the next section, we look at some popular operating systems.

Examples of Operating Systems MS-DOS, Windows, Windows NT, UNIX, and OS/2 are the most popular operating systems for PCs. While some of these operating systems, such as MS-DOS, are exclusively for PCs, other operating systems, such as UNIX, are available for both large and small computers.

DOS (Disk Operating System) MS-DOS is a popular operating system for machines based on Intel processor chips. It is a single-user system—that is, only one user at a time can use the computer. DOS has been in use for many years and the Windows operating system (covered below) is built on DOS. The commands in DOS are somewhat cryptic and not very user-friendly. Table 4–4 shows some commonly used DOS commands. Two important files in DOS are CONFIG.SYS and AUTOEXEC.BAT. A CONFIG.SYS file contains commands that set up various parameters for your system. Each time you start your system, DOS searches for a CONFIG.SYS file; if it finds one, it uses the commands there to configure your system. After searching for the CONFIG.SYS file, DOS searches for an AUTOEXEC.BAT file. If DOS finds an AUTOEXEC.BAT file, it uses the commands there to further define the way it starts your system. In other words, the AUTOEXEC.BAT file sets certain parameters that facilitate using the computer. If an AUTOEXEC.BAT file is not included, then the user will be in the default mode when he or she starts the computer. For example, if a user wants to open a word-processing application each time he or she starts the computer, the command for this would be included in the AUTOEXEC.BAT file.

Windows The Windows operating system, developed by Microsoft, expands on the DOS operating system; users can activate programs from Windows using icons (or symbols). An icon is a picture on the screen that represents an action or application that the computer can implement. Windows is a graphical user interface (GUI), that uses the point-and-click method (i.e., the use of a mouse to point at

TABLE 4–3
Two types of operating system environments and a brief description of each.

Operating System Environment	Description
Multiprogramming	Multiple users can run multiple programs on a single-CPU computer at the same time. The CPU switches between programs; however, at any given time it is executing only one program.
Multiprocessing	A multiprocessing system has a number of processors that process data and instructions, unlike systems that have only one CPU. Ideally suited for complex and computationally intensive operations that require extensive processing.

TABLE 4-4
Some popular DOS
commands.

Command	Description	Examples
CD	Allows you to switch between subdirectories. CD changes the current directory and allows you to access any subdirectory.	cd\reports cd\reports\annual cd monthly cd\
CHKDSK	Analyzes the directories, the files, and the file allocation table on the designated or default drive and produces a disk and memory status report.	chkdsk chkdsk a: chkdsk/f
COPY	Allows you to copy files. You can copy files from one diskette or hard disk to another, from one directory to another, and so on.	copy a:\friday c:\ copy c:\mon 　c:\reports copy a:*.* c:\reports copy Monday c: 　tuesday
DEL	Allows you to remove one or more files from a hard disk or diskette.	del Friday del C:*.* del c:\reports*.*
DIR	Allows you to see what files are on a disk. The DIR command lists all files and subdirectories in a directory. For each file, the system displays the name, the size (in bytes), and the date and time you last changed the file. DIR also displays the total number of files and the amount of free space (in bytes) on the disk.	dir dir c: dir\reports dir *.wyz dir >prn
DISKCOPY	Allows you to make a copy of a complete diskette on another diskette of the same size and formatted capacity.	diskcopy a: b: diskcopy
DOSSHELL	Allows you to start or return to the DOS Shell from the DOS command prompt.	dosshell
FORMAT	Allows you to prepare a diskette or hard disk for use on your system. FORMAT checks the disk for defects and prepares it to hold information. Warning! If you format a diskette or hard disk that already contains data, all the data is erased.	format a: format a: /s
MEM	Displays the amount of used and free memory, allocated and free memory areas, and all programs loaded in the system.	mem mem /c /p
RENAME	Allows you to change one or more filenames and/or extensions. Renaming a file does not change the contents of the file.	rename memos 　letters rename c:memos 　letters rename *.old *.new

an icon or menu item and click on it) to execute different commands, such as the file commands *open, close, delete,* and *move.*

In Windows, each application appears in its own window. For example, word processing can appear in one window, a spreadsheet in another window, and a graphics program in a third. A user can easily move between windows to

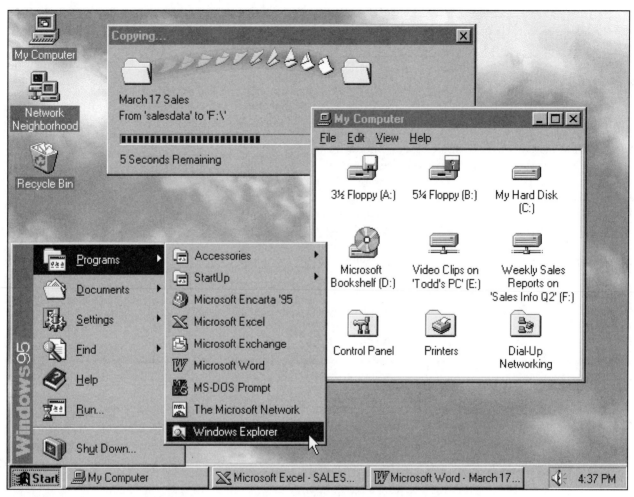

Windows 95

switch applications. Further, Windows is a highly integrated environment, in which different applications have the same "look and feel," so users familiar with one application can easily work in other applications. For example, in Windows the symbol for closing a file or a document is the same in a word-processing application or in a spreadsheet application. Many companies now use Windows as their operating system. For example, Boston Chicken uses Windows-based PCs for applications such as customized forecasting, scheduling, and inventory management.

Windows 95, also known as Windows Version 4.0, is in many ways similar to Windows. Yet it is a radical departure from Windows in that it is independent of DOS and allows for "plug-and-play," unlike Windows. Like Windows, Windows 95 represents programs with icons; when a user clicks on an icon, the system recognizes and opens the application associated with it. For example, suppose you have a file called RESUME.DOC in Windows 95. If you simply click on the file, Windows 95 automatically recognizes that this is a word processing file and opens the word processing program. Windows 95 is a powerful operating

BUSINESS REALITIES
National Football League

In 1993, the NFL's Management Council, the collective bargaining entity for the team owners, selected Windows NT as the operating system for its new Player Compensation Management System (PCMS). One of the responsibilities of the Council is to track the salary of each player on every team in the country to ensure that no team exceeds a league-wide compensation cap. In plain language, that means the Council must make sure each team spends no more than $34.6 million next season on player compensation. Compliance is important to ensure that all the teams are evenly matched when it comes to competing for the best players.

Sifting through complex contract language and league rules that govern the salary cap is one of the primary functions of the new compensation system. The new system allows decision makers to examine and ana-

lyze data in various ways. For instance, data such as every compensation transaction that has taken place in a player's career, the number of players a particular sports agent handles, or the number of games in which a player was active last season can be retrieved using a few keystrokes. Even the NFL's public relations department has found uses for the system, such as being able to tell reporters instantly how many players in the league played at a particular college.

The NFL selected Windows NT as the operating system for this application because of its power, flexibility, and ease of use. Once Windows NT was selected, the race was on to get the PCMS online by February 18, 1994, the date when players whose contracts had expired would become free agents. "Basically, we crammed two years' worth of work into six months," a spokesperson for the NFL said. This was made possible partially because of a sophisticated and user-friendly operating system.[12]

---

system that enhances the speed and performance of the PC. It takes up about 20 MB of hard disk storage and uses 8 MB of RAM.

Windows NT   Windows NT is another new and powerful operating system from Microsoft, with multitasking and multiprocessing capabilities. It processes data in 32-bit chunks (unlike earlier versions of Windows, which process data in 16-bit chunks), resulting in increased speed and efficiency. Windows NT is ideal for large business applications that run in a networked environment; it provides mainframe-like capabilities on a microcomputer. It can support multiple processors and has excellent I/O device support. Although Windows NT can run on 486 (or more powerful) PCs, it is better suited for workstations and minicomputers, because it requires 20 MB of RAM and occupies 40 to 45 MB of disk space. NFL selected Windows NT as its operating system because of its many features (see box).

UNIX   Although the UNIX operating system was developed by AT&T's Bell Labs in 1969, it is only in the last decade or so that it has become popular. Today it is widely used in a number of important business applications. UNIX is a powerful, interactive, multiprogramming, multitasking (allows users to perform multiple tasks simultaneously), multiuser operating system that is highly portable (i.e., it works on a number of types of computers).

Wells Fargo Bank's wholesale services group, a company that provides cash management and related services to large U.S. businesses and financial institutions, chose UNIX as its operating system because of its portability and reliability. Applications dealing with the group's core businesses, totaling almost $20 billion in daily transactions, run under UNIX. Another UNIX user is Western Publishing (see box).

One of the disadvantages of UNIX is that there are many different versions of UNIX and this can sometimes get confusing. Also, UNIX, compared to other operating systems, is cryptic and not very user-friendly. However, its advantages far outweigh its drawbacks and UNIX has become a mainstream operating system for many businesses.

OS/2 IBM's OS/2 (Operating System/2) is a 32-bit operating system that supports multitasking and can run programs written for OS/2 as well as for other operating systems, such as DOS and Microsoft Windows, thus reducing the need to learn several operating systems. Its 32-bit capability makes it faster than DOS and it is an ideal, sophisticated operating system for applications that require networking and multimedia features, such as playing sound files or movies. OS/2 offers a number of small applications, called *applets,* such as time scheduling, appointment calendars, and card games. The OS/2 version of Windows has most of the features found in Windows 95, yet requires only 4 megabytes of RAM.

In late 1994, IBM introduced its long-awaited new version of OS/2, dubbed OS/2 Warp. Since a dearth of brand-name applications that can run on OS/2 has always been OS/2's Achilles' heel, IBM has effectively addressed the problem by ensuring that there are more than 2,500 applications that run on OS/2. Further, Warp can also run all the applications written for DOS and Windows, thus greatly increasing the number of applications available to users who choose the OS/2 operating system. OS/2 Warp comes bundled with 12 OS/2 applications, collectively known as BonusPak, which includes a word processor, spreadsheet, personal information manager, and easy access to the Internet and other on-line services.[14]

BUSINESS REALITIES
Western Publishing

Western Publishing is well known for its Little Golden Books, a popular series of children's stories that has been in print for over 50 years. The company chose UNIX because it is one of the most robust, mature, and reliable operating systems and delivers on almost every front: networking capabilities, flexibility, and volume of applications. "We always look for the best application first, and then (and only then) we bring in the technology that supports it. Very often, that supporting technology is UNIX, which directly contributes to our bottom line."[13] Western Publishing uses UNIX in a number of departments, ranging from sales forecasting to telemarketing, because UNIX delivers an outstanding price/performance ratio, is easy to upgrade, and is highly portable.

Applications in the telemarketing group at Western Publishing point to the power of UNIX. This 16-person department plays a critical role in marketing various product lines, including children's books, games, toys, videos, and books on tape. In the past, it relied solely on a word processing system and traditional card files to track sales contacts and prepare orders. The system was not integrated with other applications in the company, so information that decision makers received was often outdated. The company found the best software to automate this marketing function and used UNIX as the operating environment for it.

Today, the publisher states that UNIX improves the flow of data in the department and throughout the company. Since it was installed, telemarketing has boosted the department's sales contracts by a full 30 percent and personal productivity has increased by roughly 35 percent. Very recently, when the workload in telemarketing increased, the scalability (ability to move up to a more powerful version) of UNIX came to the rescue, enabling the company to upgrade in a fast, easy, and cost-effective manner.[15]

BUSINESS REALITIES
Travelers Insurance

A couple of years ago, case managers handling workers compensation claims at Travelers Insurance Co.'s 50 or so remote sites were buried in paperwork. Case workers had a difficult time tracking the claims that they were processing and often were not able to answer the queries that their corporate clients had on claims filed by their employees. When a claim was in question, it was often difficult to provide information that is essential for good negotiation. "If you went to a remote office, you could typically see a case manager with paper files for dozens of active claims spread over his desk. They needed immediate access to those paper files to manage a claim to its full resolution," says Paul Reid, information systems director in Travelers' PC Claim Systems Division.

In late 1993, Travelers launched one of the compa-

ny's largest application development projects, called the Workers' Comp Case Manager Workstation. The new, OS/2-based application is used by virtually all of the 1,600 employees and allows a case worker to quickly access, process, and track claims and even uncover trends and identify future product needs. The application generates a daily to-do list, calendar, and an inventory list of cases that can be easily sorted by case number or employee name. The new system is also integrated with the company's Customer Service Information System and other Windows-based desktop productivity applications, such as word processing and spreadsheet applications, allowing case managers to view all applications, side by side, on one screen.

The system has proved very beneficial to Travelers. Workers who once handled 30-case workloads can now typically handle 100 cases and this has not only had a significant impact on worker productivity but also improved customer satisfaction.[16]

In recent years, several companies are using OS/2 for developing company-wide applications. For example, Travelers (see box) developed an OS/2-based case processing application for insurance claims and First Union National Bank is a heavy user of OS/2 (see box).

In summary, operating systems are the most important type of system control software; they perform a number of basic functions. Table 4–5 provides a brief summary of the different types of operating systems. Clearly, no one operating system is superior to another, since a number of factors, such as number and criticality of applications, number of users, and network requirements, must be taken into account in selecting an operating system. Also, note that it is possible to use more than one operating system on a computer. A user may run some applications using, say, the Windows operating system, and other applications under some other operating system, such as UNIX.

In the next section, we cover the second type of system software: system support software.

System support software
Programs that support the smooth execution of various programs and operations of a computer.

Utility programs
Programs that perform routine, repetitive tasks. Utility programs make it easier to use the computer.

System Support Software   **System support software** is software that supports, or facilitates, the smooth and efficient operation of a computer. There are four major categories of systems support software: utility programs, language translators, database management systems, and performance statistics software.

Utility programs are among the most popular types of system support software. They perform tasks such as formatting disks, locating free space on a disk, retrieving lost or damaged files, sorting and merging data, converting files from one format to another, backing up important files, and providing online help.

As you may recall, all programs must be translated into machine language for the computer to understand and execute them. Language translators are sup-

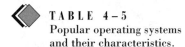

TABLE 4-5
Popular operating systems
and their characteristics.

Operating System	Characteristics
DOS	A single-user system. Commands are somewhat cryptic and not very user-friendly.
Windows	Uses icons to execute programs. Uses point-and-click method to execute commands. Applications appear in windows on the monitor. A highly integrated environment, in which different applications have the same "look and feel."
Windows NT	Has multitasking and multiprocessing capabilities. Processes data in 32-bit chunks. Ideal for large business applications that run in a network environment.
UNIX	Powerful, interactive, multiprogramming, multitasking, multi-user, operating system. Highly portable.
OS/2	This 32-bit operating system supports multitasking, making it faster than DOS. It can run programs written for OS/2 or for other operating systems such as DOS and Windows.

port programs written specifically to convert a programming language (assembly language, high-level language, or very high-level language) into machine language. As you may recall, language translators that translate assembly language into machine language are called assemblers. Language translators that translate an *entire* program written in 3GL or 4GL into machine language before program

---

BUSINESS REALITIES
First Union National Bank

In spite of the growing popularity and the extensive marketing of Windows by Microsoft, First Union National Bank has never lost faith in IBM's OS/2 operating system and continues to use it. The bank first looked at the test copies of OS/2, Version 1.0, in 1986, and soon after declared it the standard operating system for all applications at First Union. Since then, First Union has deployed nine commercial and imaging applications under OS/2. The bank now has approximately 6,000 OS/2 desktop systems; that figure could swell to 10,000 in the next year or two.

Two new projects, called the Commercial Banking Solution (CBS) and the Corporate Call Center (CCC), also use OS/2. CBS allows loan officers to begin the loan process in the field using notebook computers. The managers can then send documents back to the home office, where they are routed to several workers through a program that features an "in basket" and an "out basket," allowing workers to route documents to the next worker when they are finished with it. "The end result is that we turn business around faster and get our relationship managers out more with customers."[17]

Corporate Call Center (CCC) allows customers to call a single number to get answers to questions about basic bank services and products. The application, which resides on an OS/2-based workstation, intelligently routes hundreds of thousands of calls over the course of a year to the support personnel who can best answer the questions. In the long run, OS/2 has proven to be an outstanding operating system for First Union. "The technology people here have come and thanked me for sticking with OS/2," says the bank's director of information systems.[18]

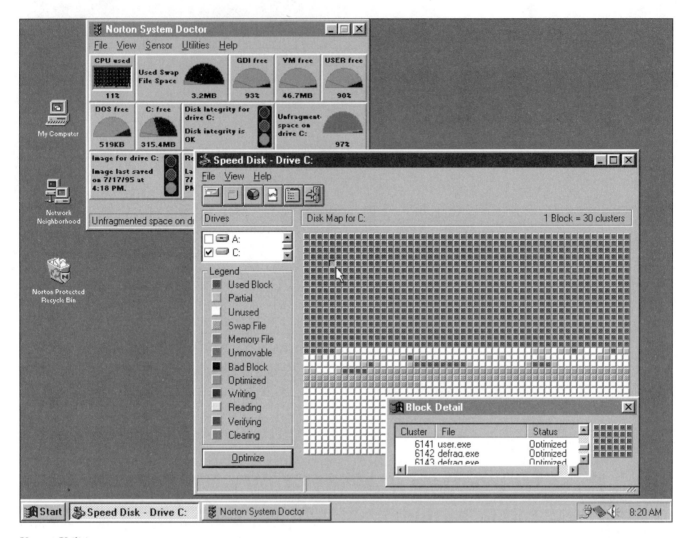

Norton Utilities

Interpreter
A system software product that translates and executes one statement at a time.

execution are called compilers; language translators that translate a statement and execute it before translating the next statement are called **interpreters.**

Data is at the heart of an information system. In Chapter 6, we will take a detailed look at database management systems, which help us to create, manage, and maintain data. The operating system too has certain basic data management features. Database management systems are unimportant system support software.

Another example of system support software for organization-wide systems is software that monitors the performance of a system by collecting data about various computer activities such as idle CPU time, utilization of different I/O devices, amount of memory used by programs, and amount of time users are logged onto the system. By collecting data on system performance, managers can take action to ensure full utilization of their systems.

System development software
Software packages and programs that assist programmers and system analysts in designing and developing information systems.

Shell
A set of tools and techniques that allows developers to build the prototype of a system.

Application software
Software designed to perform people-related tasks such as word processing, graphics, and so on.

General-purpose software
Software that is mass-produced for a broad range of common business applications, such as word processing.

Word processing
A computerized way to create, edit, and manage text.

System Development Software **System development software** helps system developers design and build better systems. An example is computer-aided software engineering, or CASE, a collection of programs that assist developers in developing an information system. CASE is covered in Chapter 13. Shells are also system development software; a **shell** is a set of tools and techniques that allows developers to build a prototype (or model) of a system. A shell contains some essential system features that can be customized to meet the needs of the user. For example, shells can be used to build expert systems, decision support systems, and executive information systems.

Application Software

Application software is designed to perform people-related tasks such as payroll, inventory, and sales analysis. The United Nations uses application software to meet its information needs (see box). There are two types of application software: general-purpose (designed for general applications, such as payroll and so on) and dedicated software (designed for specific applications, such as the space shuttle). Table 4–6 lists different types of general-purpose application software; Table 4–7 lists some commercial application software.

General-Purpose Software **General-purpose software** is mass-produced for a broad range of common business applications such as word-processing, graphics, payroll, and accounting. Some popular general-purpose software programs are discussed below.

    Word processing is a computerized way to perform a task that has existed for centuries: text creation and management. It is used by many organizations all over the world to save time and money and facilitate communication. Word pro-

 T A B L E 4 – 6
Types of general-purpose application software.

Type of Application Software	Description
Word processing	Computerization of the creation and management of documents. Allows easy correction and manipulation of text.
Desktop publishing	Produces documents such as memos and pamphlets. Has many of the features of word processing along with more sophisticated text and graphics capabilities.
Spreadsheets	Electronic calculators used for extensive number crunching, such as financial analysis, budget preparation, and other numerical analysis. Also used for "what-if" analyses.
Computer graphics	Provides for the creation and management of sophisticated graphics, charts, and figures. Often comes with extensive color capabilities and clip art.
Accounting software	Automates accounting functions, such as general ledger, accounts payable, and accounts receivable. Often can be interfaced with other financial systems, such as payroll, budgeting, and so on.
Imaging	Scans text and graphics from paper documents and converts them into digital images.

A GLOBAL PERSPECTIVE
The United Nations

When the United Nations General Assembly gathers its 184 member nations under one roof, the power and expansiveness of this world body is evident. But under the surface, that united front crumbles in the computer room, where tracking down specific information on even one U.N. employee may prove formidable. "We now have more than 20 different systems between 20 and 30 years old that do not talk to each other, so we have not been able to get updated information on employees and finances," explains Gian Piero Roz, chief of a $47 million project now under way to consolidate and automate administrative functions at the UN Secretariat in New York.

Working with Price Waterhouse consultants, the United Nations has created the Integrated Management Information System (IMIS), a large and sophisticated piece of application software, which currently serves about 400 users. Eventually, the new information system will be extended to Secretariat branches in seven other nations and to the United Nation's 20 or so peace-keeping missions worldwide, bringing the number of users to 2,100.

Currently, several IBM mainframes in New York contain information on more than 20,000 U.N. employees, including payroll figures, cost-of-living allowances, and school costs, all of which vary by location and job title. Since this information is not centrally located, administrators have to search manually through multiple databases that often contain duplicate information, some of which are out of date. This makes it difficult for the United Nations to determine its cash flow at any given time. The financial management of the United Nations is further complicated by its international scope. The accounting department administers an annual budget of $3 billion, encompassing 90 different currencies, thus making the task of converting expenses to U.S. dollars a mind-boggling one. Expenses are liquidated in a master budget using U.S. currency.

One of the biggest advantages of the IMIS software is that it provides a uniform face to data and hence, different U.N. organizations in different countries can view and analyze data across organizations—something that until now has been an impossible feat. Besides cost and time savings that such standardization brings, it allows managers to easily retrieve and effectively analyze data.

The first phase of IMIS involved the implementation of a personnel information system. The application software for this system covers recruiting, hiring, promotions, and moving of U.N. employees throughout the world. Since most U.N. employees have never worked with an automated system, it was imperative that the new software be highly user-friendly. The second phase involved the automation of the entitlement system, which includes special benefits such as housing subsidies, medical insurance, and educational allowances for overseas staff. This piece of software involves complicated formulas for each country and must be frequently updated as living expenses of different countries change. This module of IMIS uses an object-oriented expert system called proKappa that is designed to work in both English and French, the official U.N. languages. This component of IMIS will improve decision making as it will let decision makers know if funds are available before making a commitment to expend them.

Two key characteristics of IMIS, which will accommodate many users accessing different sensitive employment information, are its security and its modularity. The modularity allows users to customize the system to meet local requirements and regulations. So, for example, if hazardous duty pay in dangerous peace-keeping regions needs to be added to the entitlements system, the entire entitlements program does not have to be updated or rewritten, only the local software module. IMIS also allows U.N. employees to distill information that was previously inaccessible, such as a query about a population or how many people met a certain criteria.

The remaining software components of IMIS are a financial system and a payroll and budget preparation system. "(The IMIS) was a strategic decision by the U.N.' says Gian Piero Roz.[19]

TABLE 4–7
Application software packages and the operating systems on which they run.

Type of Application	Software Package	Vendor	Operating System
Word Processors	Word	Microsoft	DOS, Windows
	WordPerfect	WordPerfect	DOS, OS/2, Windows
	Ami Pro	Lotus	DOS, Windows
Spreadsheets	Lotus 1–2–3	Lotus	DOS, OS/2
	Excel	Microsoft	Windows
Graphics	Power Point	Microsoft	OS/2, Windows
	Freelance Graphics	Lotus	OS/2, Windows
	Photo Shop	Adobe	Windows
Desktop Publishing	Publisher	Microsoft	DOS, Windows
	Printshop	Broderbund	DOS, Windows
Accounting	Peachtree Accounting	Peachtree	DOS, Windows
	In the Black	Microrims	Windows
	DacEasy Accounting	DacEasy	Windows
	MYOB Accounting	Teleware	Windows
	Simply Money	Kiplinger	Windows
Integrated Packages*	Microsoft Works	Microsoft	DOS, Windows
	Claris Works	Claris	Windows

*Packages that combine a number of capabilities, such as word processing, spreadsheets, and graphics.

Desktop publishing
The production of office documents such as memos, price sheets, technical manuals, invoices, and newsletters.

Spreadsheets
Programs that are used for applications involving numerical analysis, number crunching, graphical output, and "what-if" scenarios.

Computer graphics
The graphical display of computerized information.

cessing programs allow for easy correction of errors and text manipulation. Microsoft Word and WordPerfect are two very popular word processing packages.

Desktop publishing (DTP) has many of the features found in word processing packages and is used to produce office documents such as memos, price sheets, technical manuals, invoices, and newsletters. Desktop publishing packages have more sophisticated graphical features than do word processing packages. They have excellent text manipulation capabilities and color presentation graphics; these features can be used to produce high-quality documents. Desktop publishing provides WYSIWYG (What You See Is What You Get), which allows the user to see on the screen what the document will look like when it is printed.

Another type of general-purpose software is **spreadsheets,** which are used for tasks that require number crunching, such as financial analysis, budget preparation, and grade calculation. Spreadsheets can sort and analyze data, create charts, graphs, and figures, and perform "what-if" analysis to assess the impacts of changes to input variables.

The first electronic spreadsheet was VisiCalc, introduced in 1978 for Apple II computers. Since then, the spreadsheet has become an essential tool for professionals. In the early 1980s, Lotus introduced its versatile, easy-to-use Lotus 1–2–3 for the IBM PC. Today, there are other powerful spreadsheet packages on the market, such as Microsoft's Excel.

Although many word processing and spreadsheet packages are capable of producing graphics, sometimes users need sophisticated tools to draw complex figures and graphs. **Computer graphics** is the graphical display of computerized information; there are many sophisticated graphics packages. For example, CorelDRAW, a popular computer graphics program, offers many advantages over the more basic graphics packages included in word processing applications.

CorelDRAW offers extensive text-handling and precision-drawing features, powerful paint and photo retouching applications featuring numerous image-enhancing filters, and even animation programs that let you create both simple and complex animations.

Accounting software

General-purpose software that helps companies automate their accounting functions.

Accounting software is another type of general-purpose software, which helps companies automate their accounting functions. The main modules of an accounting system are General Ledger, Accounts Payable, Accounts Receivable, and Fixed Assets. These can be interfaced with other financial products, such as payroll, budgeting, and inventory management software, to produce an integrated accounting package.

For example, Globex is an electronic futures trading network that uses accounting software to link brokers in New York, Chicago, and Paris with the Chicago Mercantile Exchange and the Chicago Board of Trade. Traders use this program to electronically buy and sell financial products and to receive timely and accurate financial information on various transactions. Accounting software packages are flexible; they can be used for other applications. Budget Rent-A-Car uses an accounting software package to keep track of losses resulting from damaged or wrecked vehicles.

Imaging software

Programs that scan data and information and convert them into digital images.

Imaging software uses scanners to scan paper-based documents, then converts the data into digital images. Imaging software is increasing in popularity because of its many benefits. These include reduction of floor space when fewer paper documents are stored, decreases in copying costs, and fewer problems with lost or misplaced data. In fact, imaging software is becoming so popular that business analysts forecast that by 1996 imaging will be a $12-billion to $15-billion market in the U.S. alone; the worldwide figures are expected to be much higher.

Companies are using imaging for a number of tasks. For example, JBS and Associates uses imaging software to auction items. Before the imaging system was installed, buyers had to sort through roughly 2 million pages of documents to get

Computer Clip Art

BUSINESS REALITIES
Delivering the Goods

Staying home waiting for a furniture delivery or appliance repair truck to arrive is a major complaint for many customers. Not knowing when they will show up or *if* they will show up is a problem that consumers would like to see go away. But, thanks to new software, many service companies are taking the responsibility of delivering goods and services more seriously and are able to give customers better estimates of delivery times. Desktop mapping software and sophisticated logistics algorithms and formulas are now being used to estimate arrival time within a two-hour range, rather than saying "sometime during the day." Although both companies and customers would like to see a shorter interval for the estimated time of delivery, this is very difficult to do. "You never know when you'll run into a truck inspec-

tion station or a spiral staircase in the home," said Bill Mooradian, operations manager at Mooradian's Furniture, Inc. in Troy, NY.

The software, which runs under Windows, is provided by Avon, Connecticut-based RoTec. Maps embedded in the software show the geographical location of each customer. The software then uses this information to calculate the travel time based on the actual road network rather than "as the crow flies." Furthermore, the PC can change the route in order to accommodate last-minute changes if a customer needs to revise the schedule. If the trucks are outfitted with mobile computers and satellite positioning devices, the maps can even show the exact location of the truck and any problems that it may face in keeping the assigned schedule. If the trucker runs into a problem, then the customer can be immediately notified. The result has been a significant increase in delivery productivity and enhanced customer satisfaction.[20]

---

the details on a specific item. Today, imaging software allows a buyer to retrieve the electronic image of an item in a matter of a few seconds, resulting in major savings in terms of time and money. Another imaging application is used in law enforcement: officials are using imaging software to catch criminals by capturing images of their fingerprints. While the human eye can only see about 60 shades of gray, imaging software allows officers to see 256 or more shades of color in a fingerprint, thus increasing the chances of catching a criminal.

Another example of imaging is the one at the University of Pennsylvania Medical Center in Philadelphia for patient billing. In the past, since patient records were often misplaced or lost, the medical center often was not able to collect all the money that was owed to it. When the Minolta Corp. imaging system was installed in June, 1994, the center was able to process a larger number of claims with the result that it is likely to generate 10 times more annual residual revenue.[21]

In the next section, we discuss the second type of application software: dedicated software.

Application-dedicated software
Specialized or customized applications designed to meet the particular information needs of an organization.

Application-Dedicated Software The second type of application software is **application-dedicated software,** which includes specialized or customized applications designed for very specific purposes. For example, software designed to cater the delivery of goods and services to a customer's doorstep is highly specialized (see box). Such a program cannot easily be modified and adapted for other applications, because it is designed to perform a specific task. The National Aeronautics and Space Administration (NASA) also uses a large number of sophisticated, complex, and mission-critical, application-dedicated programs in its space shuttles. Some space missions have used programs that consist of more than 14 million lines of code, written in 15 different languages and running on 170 different computers. Overall, it takes about 6,000 person-hours to develop application-dedicated software for a single space flight. NASA also uses application-dedicated software for a variety of other activities such as training astronauts, simulating flight conditions, controlling the shuttle in space, monitoring the vital signs of astronauts, and generating and processing data gathered in space. In fact, a NASA software team is placed on standby during a space launch so that in case of any program difficulties during flight, the programmers can immediately correct the problem.

U.S. Postal Service rate hikes often hit businesses hard. For example, in the last rate increase, third-class postage jumped 14% and second-class postage jumped more than 19%. One way by which companies are trying to reduce their mailing costs is through the use of innovative, dedicated software that ensures the accuracy of mailing addresses, adds bar codes to letters for easy sorting at the post office, and even presorts mail for postal discounts. The savings resulting from such efforts can be quite significant. For example, ITT Hartford saves approximately $135,000 a year on its 23 million mass mailings through the use of such software. Chase Manhattan Bank NA in New York also uses software to presort bulk mailings, verify nine-digit ZIP codes, and add postal bar codes.[22]

The Minneapolis police department uses application-dedicated software in its computer-aided dispatch system, which retrieves and analyzes information from 911 calls. The system, called RECAP (Repeat Call Addressing Policing), captures the identity of the caller and provides it to the police officer. Using RECAP, police found that 10 percent of the addresses in the city accounted for nearly 60 percent of the calls for police intervention in domestic violence. Working with people in the communities that generated the most calls, police officers found ways to solve community problems. In one short period, 75 of 105 calls were made from one building and involved a single apartment. Overall, RECAP helped the woman in that apartment seek help in an alcohol treatment program and averted future calls. Overall, RECAP has helped police analyze 400,000 emergency calls and gain a better understanding of callers and their problems.

Another example of application-dedicated software is logistics software which helps companies handle the flow of goods and services from one location to another. Companies are using logistics software in order to cut costs, minimize inventory, and reduce the time it takes for goods, services, or information to reach their destinations. Two broad categories of technologies are used in logistics operations. Transactional-software products, the first category, track inventory, follow the movement of vehicles, and provide various information capture, storage, and manipulation capabilities. Decision-support tools, the second category of software, helps users determine where to locate a facility, which type of shipping carrier to use for a particular product, and the most efficient routes.

At Robert Bosch Ltd., the British subsidiary of the Germany-based automotive- and industrial-equipment supplier Bosch Group, customized logistics software helps manage the 3,000 orders the company receives daily from over 400 customers. The software helped the company to cut the number of people needed to pick an order from three to one. Other companies use logistics software that incorporates maps to show users the precise position of products, customers, vehicles, streets, retailers, etc. Nordstrom Valves uses dedicated software to increase sales and emphasize the high quality of its products (see box, page 144).

Pennsylvania Hospital uses application dedicated software to monitor the health of patients from their homes. A computer on one end of the line answers medical questions and even records the vital signs of the patient on the other end.

The software, developed by Purdue University, automatically reports the information to the patient's doctor who looks for any changes that may signal the need for on-site medical care. This system is being touted as another way to keep health care costs down by limiting hospital visits or stays for non-critical patients.[23]

Another example of dedicated software is UVB-Ware software, which provides information on ultraviolet rays and their negative effects. It makes specific forecasts on ultraviolet levels and sunburn times for specific locations, time of year, and time of day, based on seasonal ozone trends calculated from 13 years of data gathered by NASA's Nimbus-7 satellite. The UVB-Ware package measures UV intensity levels and displays the results on a scale of 1 to 10, with sunburn times calculated as the number of minutes of exposure that will cause the first reddening on untanned Caucasian skin. There is also a reference section that suggests basic precautions and recommends protective products.[24]

Selecting Software Packages

One of the decisions that information systems managers frequently face is whether to write or buy software. In the last few years, this decision has become even more complex and challenging because today there are so many powerful and versatile off-the-shelf programs available for a wide variety of tasks. Software selection is a critical decision that can have serious financial implications and can affect the productivity of employees. Hence, in this section we look at some steps in selecting software.

The first step is to put together a team of people from different functional areas in the organization that will be affected by the selected software. These people will play a vital role in the selection process. Depending on the size of the project, the team may consist of three to ten people. The team approach not only helps to build consensus, but also reduces the possibility of showing favoritism to one vendor and other ethical violations.

The next step is to determine the features and functions that the software should have in order to meet the requirements established by the users. This is often a very difficult task. Requirements must be clearly specified; no detail should be missed. For example, it is not sufficient to say that the software should have graphic capabilities. The specifications should list the kind of graphics, the colors, and the print capabilities that are needed. Specifications are at the heart of successful software selection. Without them, the target becomes a moving one; further it will be difficult to assess the performance of the group: "Did the group select the best software that meets the specifications?" The team should also determine in this step the type of computer (mainframe, mini, micro, and so on) and the platform (IBM, Hewlett-Packard, Sun, Digital, and so on) on which the software will run. This selection process is influenced by a number of factors, such as existing systems, budgetary considerations, performance requirements, and future trends.[25]

The next step is to request and acquire information about different software packages that can meet the established specifications. Besides contacting vendors directly, many managers will question their peers in other companies about the quality and reliability of various products. Other sources of product information include trade shows, product demonstrations, industry association meetings, consumer reports, and vendor references. Once product information has been obtained, the team should do a cost analysis. Clearly, the cost considerations are different for make-versus-buy decisions. Also, this is a good time to take stock of the skills and talents available in-house to write the software. Information gathered from different sources should be carefully scrutinized. Then the team should make a recommendation whether to write or buy the software.

If the decision is to buy the software, the team should start negotiations with the vendor. Contractual arrangements must be drawn up for warranties, software licenses, training, updates, modifications, and maintenance. The larger the investment, the more closely the agreements must be examined. Some considerations that a company should take into account when investing in hardware and software will be discussed in the next section.

Investment Criteria for Hardware and Software

Today, the number of hardware and software choices available to IS managers has increased exponentially; with this growth, the complexity of investment decisions has also increased. According to U.S. government figures, the amount of money spent on information technologies accounts for about half of all durable-equipment spending, totaling about 2.7 percent of U.S. corporate revenues, and even these figures are said to be on the lower side.[26] In this section, we look at some criteria that organizations use to make such decisions.

Investments in information systems and technologies include the acquisition of hardware, software (both off-the-shelf products and those developed in-house), networks, and other computer-related systems and technologies. The term *investment criteria* refers to measures or standards that an organization uses to make computer-related investment decisions. There are several reasons why

BUSINESS REALITIES
Nordstrom Valves

Nordstrom Valves doesn't cut corners when it comes to the pipeline valves it manufactures and sells to the oil and natural gas industries. "In terms of both features and price, we are the Cadillac of our industry."

Nordstrom implemented an interactive software program in 1991 to provide both salespeople and customers with the information to make better decisions. The company's sales force typically works with customers' engineers during the design phase of a project so that the customers can specify the kinds of valves they need up front. However, the company found that its sales cycles were as long as a year and that its prices were often 15 to 25 percent higher than those of competing valves. Nordstrom wanted a system that would respond to the initial qualms that customers had about

its higher prices by demonstrating how the quality built into its valves could actually save the customer money in the long run.

The company developed a sales and marketing program to demonstrate the features and benefits of its products. The system compares the prices of the company's valves against its competitors' prices by taking into account the cost of maintaining valves of lower quality. Without this program, conducting such an analysis required Nordstom's salespeople to create a mathematical model and crunch the numbers with calculators. That took so much time that by the time the calculations were done, the customer had lost interest. The original marketing program has been translated into Spanish for use throughout Nordstrom's sizable Latin American market. "Once we demonstrate the program, we encourage customers to load it onto their hard drives. It is a marketing tool that helps both the company and the customer reap the benefits of high quality."[27]

TABLE 4–8
The extent to which each of various investment criteria is used in organizations for making hardware investment decisions.

Criteria	Percentage of Companies Using Criteria
Financial Criteria	
Discounted Cash Flow (DCF)	
1. Net Present Value	49
2. Internal Rate of Return	54
3. Profitability Index Method	8
Other Financial	
4. Average/Accounting Rate of Return	16
5. Payback Method	61
6. Budgetary Constraints	68
Management Criteria	
7. Support of Explicit Business objectives	88
8. Support of Implicit Business Objectives	69
9. Response to Competitive Systems	61
10. Support for Management Decision Making	88
11. Probability of Achieving Benefits	46
12. Legal/Government Requirements	71
Development Criteria	
13. Technical/System Requirement	79
14. Introduce/Learn New Technology	60
15. Probability of Project Completion	31

Source: MIS Quarterly, September 1992, p. 341.

investment criteria are critical. First, the kind of criteria that an organization uses (or does not use) will influence the process of system selection. For example, depreciation and its impact on net assets is an important consideration in investment decisions for most organizations (see box). Second, without criteria, it is difficult to measure the return on investment (ROI) in information systems. ROI is an important measure of success for most investment decisions. Table 4–8 shows some criteria that organizations use to make IS and IT investment decisions and the extent of use of each criterion.

One of the most popular financial criteria used in investment decisions is the cost-benefit analysis model, in which the costs and benefits associated with an investment are analyzed mathematically. Frequently, companies will invest in a system or project only if its benefits exceed its cost unless other factors, such as social responsibility, outweigh financial considerations.

Another way of assessing the value of long-term capital-intensive investments is known as capital budgeting. Capital budgeting is based on the principles of cash flow, on the time value of money, and on discounted cash flow (DCF) techniques. There are six widely used capital budgeting models: payback method, return on investment (ROI), cost/benefit ratio, net present value, profitability index, and internal rate of return (IRR). (See any introductory finance text for a more detailed look at these concepts.)

B U S I N E S S   R E A L I T I E S

Data Processing versus the "Bean Counters"

IS managers and financial officers are at loggerheads over the rapid pace of technological change. Technology's latest burden is product depreciation schedules. The typical depreciation cycles of five years or longer are no longer appropriate for computers, particularly PCs, given that new products are introduced every 6 to 9 months. IS managers often find themselves pitted against accountants who don't want earlier models to be treated as obsolete before they are fully depreciated.

The main obstacle to changing accounting rules is the Internal Revenue Service (IRS), which imposes a mandatory 5-year depreciation cycle on computer equipment. Some companies even keep two sets of books: one, for tax accounting purposes, that uses IRS-mandated depreciation cycles, and another, for corporate accounting, that uses more aggressive depreciation schedules.

Vendors are helping IS managers with their depreciation dilemmas by offering upgradable equipment, which does not fall under the 5-year depreciation law. This is lightly referred to as "Velcro serial numbers," because the serial number of the machine remains the same but the internal parts of the machine are changed in order to postpone obsolescence.[28]

Using financial criteria alone for investment decisions has certain inherent limitations. It encourages managers to "stretlch" the figures to fit the need, thus creating a "numbers game." Second, since many benefits of information systems are intangible, it is sometimes difficult to isolate and accurately measure the dollar value of these benefits. Third, indirect organizational costs of IS are often difficult to estimate, so these can distort the numbers. Finally, different departments within an organization may use different methods to measure costs and benefits creating difficulties in assessing the true value of an information system. This is not to say that financial analysis is not useful, but that numbers should be tempered by the consideration of qualitative factors.

For example, at Garrett Co., a publishing and printing firm, every IS project is decided on the basis of its ROI. On the other hand, Tribune Co., in Chicago, invested in a large marketing system without doing any ROI analysis because top management had a "gut feeling" that the project was essential to the future of the company. In other words, qualitative factors outweighed financial considerations.

Many companies establish standards, policies, and procedures to coordinate, control, and manage their investments in technologies. James Cash, a professor at Harvard Business School, has developed a model that provides organizations with guidelines for establishing policies and procedures for IS and IT decisions. (See Figure 4–3).

When a technology is well understood and widely accepted, the policies and standards that guide the use of that technology should also be well established and there should be no ambiguity in the minds of users about the uses, applications, and processes that guide that technology. The lower left quadrant of Figure 4–3 illustrates this point.

When newly developed technologies are introduced in an organization, managers must establish new standards, policies, and procedures that will guide the use of these technologies, because they may pose challenges and opportunities different from those of mature technologies. Policies and procedures that guide emerging technologies should be loose and should encourage innovation and experimentation. New technologies should not be subjected to the same policies established for mature technologies (see the top right-hand corner of Figure 4–3).

FIGURE 4-3

FIGURE 4-3

James Cash's model, which provides a framework for investments in information technologies.

		Technologies	
		Mature	**Emerging**
Control	**Loose**	Poor fit: inefficient operations	Good fit: encourages experimentation, learning, adaptation
	Tight	Good fit: helps ensure consistent, secure, efficient operation	Poor fit: may stifle innovation

In general, investments in information systems and technologies should not be arbitrary or ad hoc, but should follow well-thought-out criteria and be guided by sound policies and procedures.

Ethical Considerations

There are ethical considerations that organizations should take into account when buying or installing software. The most important of these is the prevention of illegal copying of software. Copying software is illegal, violates U.S. copyright laws, can result in dire consequences for the firm and the employee, and can lead to prolonged and expensive legal battles. In fact, a single copyright infringement may result in civil damages of up to $100,000. One of the most pressing concerns facing software vendors is the illegal copying and use of software by employees who use the software at home and by companies that make illegal copies of the software. When a company buys a piece of software, it often signs a license or agreement with the software company to install that software on a given number of computers. For example, a company may pay a licensing fee to install a single copy of a word processor on 10 computers. Copyright violations occur if a single-user copy of a piece of software (software that is licensed for use on only one computer) is installed on several computers or if the company installs an illegal copy of a piece of a licensed software (software that is licensed to another company). Either violation could result in an injunction or a court order to search the company's premises and seize illegal copies. It is estimated that the software industry lost $12.8 billion in 1993 alone because of illegal copying.[29]

There are several measures that an organization can take to ensure that it is not violating any software copyright laws. In particular, organizations must ask three questions to ensure that it is obeying the law:

1. Does the company have a published and well-understood policy statement that educates employees about software copyright infringement and pro-

hibits them from making or accepting unlicensed copies of software?

2. Is there a set of original user manuals at each computer where a software product is installed?

3. Are the purchase, installation, and license registration of all software controlled at a central point in the company?

If the answer to any of these questions is "No," the company may be violating software copyright laws.

Here are several steps an organization can take to ensure that employees do not violate any copyright laws:

*   Educate all employees and managers about copyright infringement.
*   Make one individual, or one group, responsible for acquiring software for the entire organization.
*   Conduct regular audits of company software. The Software Publishers Association (SPA) has a free software packet called SPAudit that searches all computer systems for about 700 products sold by SPA members.
*   Keep a careful record of all documentation and records related to the purchase, legal ownership, and registration of purchased software.
*   Destroy illicit copies of software and delete illicit copies from all computers.

 # Summary

*   **The concept of programming and the different generations of programming languages.**
    A program is a set of step-by-step instructions given to a computer so it can perform various tasks. Programmers are people who write, test, and install software, using special languages called programming languages; the process of writing programs is referred to as programming. Today, many end-users also develop programs, thanks to advances in computer hardware and software.

    There are two types of programming languages: procedural and nonprocedural. Procedural languages specify the way a certain task must be accomplished; nonprocedural languages simply specify what needs to be done. There are four generations of programming languages: machine language, assembly language, high-level languages (3GLs), and very high-level languages (4GLs). Each generation of languages improved on earlier versions in terms of the number of lines of code required for a given procedure, user-friendliness, and efficiency.

*   **Different types of system software and application software.**
    System software performs the basic functions necessary to start and operate a computer; it controls and monitors the activities and the use of resources in a computer. System software can be classified into three categories: system control software (programs that manage system resources and functions), system support software (programs that support the execution of different applications), and system development software (programs that assist system developers in designing and developing information systems). The most important type of system control software is the operating system.

    Application software can be classified into two categories: general-purpose and application-dedicated software. General-purpose software is designed for a broad range of business applications, such as word processing, desktop publishing, graphics, accounting, and imaging. Application-dedicated software includes specialized or customized applications designed to meet the specific information needs of an organization.

*   **The structure and functions of an operating system and the different types of operating systems.**
    An operating system is a complex set of software modules that manages the overall operation of a computer and acts as manager, housekeeper, and traffic cop for a computer system. Some of its functions are loading programs, performing and managing input/output operations, managing files, managing computer memory, detecting errors, allocating resources, monitoring

resource use, and resolving conflicts. The most popular operating systems for PCs are DOS, UNIX, Windows, and OS/2.

♦ **Some managerial issues related to hardware and software investments.**

One of the most pressing concerns that organizations face is the illegal copying and use of software by their employees, which violates copyright laws and can result in dire consequences both for the firm and for the employee. The Software Publishers Association (SPA), the copyright-enforcement arm of most major U.S. software vendors, prosecutes violators. Some simple, yet effective, measures that an organization can take to protect itself from copyright violations include educating employees and managers, assigning responsibility for software purchases to only one person or group, conducting regular audits of company software, and keeping a careful record of all documentation related to software purchase and license.

 Review Questions

1. What is a program? Why do we need both hardware and software to build an information system?
2. What are the four generations of programming languages? Give an example of a language from each generation and identify some of the improvements between the generations.
3. What are the two major types of software? What is the primary purpose of each?
4. Identify the most important type of system control software. Can a computer function without system control software? Discuss.
5. Identify any two differences between 3GLs and 4GLs. Give an example of each.
6. What is an operating system and what are its primary functions? What are some operating systems that can be used on PC-based systems?
7. Name any three operating systems for PC-based

environments and briefly describe each system. Are these systems mutually exclusive?
8. What is the difference between multiprogramming and multiprocessing? Can you do multiprocessing on your PC? Discuss.
9. Identify any two advantages of multiprogramming. How is it related to the idea of time-sharing?
10. What is object-oriented programming and what is its greatest benefit? How does code reusability affect software development?
11. What is application software? What is the primary difference between general-purpose software and dedicated software? Can you give an example of each? Identify one or two popular packages for each type.
12. What are some measures that organizations can take to prevent software copyright infringements?

 Discussion Questions

1. Slowly and inexorably, the buying habits of most purchasers of PC software are undergoing a radical change. Microsoft, IBM, Novell, and a variety of third-party vendors are promoting electronic software distribution systems that will encourage customers to purchase software directly from the vendor rather than through a reseller.

    The advent of electronic delivery systems, along with the growing interest in CD-ROM as a medium for storing software, promises to change the buying habits of most PC users. Instead of purchasing floppy disks loaded with an individual software package, the user will be able to purchase a number of software packages on a single CD-ROM disk.

    Customers can browse through a CD-ROM that contains all the products that a given software vendor offers. When a customer decides to purchase a specific package, he or she can call the software vendor, which will provide the customer with a password that will allow him or her to access the software directly from the CD-ROM. The sale will then be recorded using an electronic delivery system.[30]

    a. If you were planning to set up an electronic software distribution system, what kind of hardware and software would you need to implement this system? What kind of an operating environment would be suitable for this application (multiprocessing, multiprogramming, or both)?

2. Software meters are programs that monitor the use of applications such as spreadsheets, word processors, or databases and are based on the principle of "concurrency," which means that a company need only buy as many licenses for a program as it has people using the program at one time. For example, a company with 100 WordPerfect users, evenly split between the day and night shifts, would need only 50 licenses to stay within the federal law that governs these agreements. And because all 50 copies would probably not be in use at the same time, the organization might need even fewer. Metering programs can ensure that there are no more concurrent users than licenses, or vice versa.

For software vendors, metering is a mixed blessing. On the one hand, metering should reduce corporate software piracy, which vendors claim costs them billions of dollars a year; on the other hand, metering allows companies to buy fewer licenses, which means lower revenues for the vendors. For users, metering promises lower software expenditures. A report function gives information technology managers a running tally of who is using what and how much additional software might be required to meet the company's needs and remain legal. "The whole motivation has always been for companies to know what their people are doing and how many people are doing it at the same time as a way to reduce costs." Metering programs cost between $500 and $900.[31]

a. Why are software meters a mixed blessing for software vendors?

b. What are some benefits that an IS manager can derive from software meters?

3. Video-Cart of Chicago dispenses electronic coupons through grocery carts. Electronic coupons have a number of advantages over the traditional paper coupons. They require no clipping and saving; a customer cannot forget a coupon at home; and store managers find that electronic coupons help to move products almost 80% faster.

Video-Cart is a special shopping cart that has a series of electronic sensors. These receive preprogrammed messages from store aisles; the messages are displayed on a screen that is built into the cart. When the cart approaches an item for which a coupon is available, a message indicating the brand name, the product, and the associated coupon savings flashes on the screen. Shoppers who choose the product push a button on the screen and the software in the Video-Cart records the value of the coupon and stores it in memory. At checkout time, the value of the coupon is electronically transferred to the point-of-sale (POS) system at the checkout counter. The software in the VideoCart also gathers sales information about various products; this information helps manufacturers target future promotions according to customer, store, or geographical location. Electronic coupons also help reduce coupon fraud by making sure that coupon savings go into effect only when the correct product is scanned.

a. What are some of the functions that Video-Cart performs?

b. Is this an example of application-dedicated software? Discuss.

 ETHICAL ISSUES

Although computers provide many significant benefits to humanity, they also cause many ethical dilemmas. For example, illegal copying of software is a major problem for software publishers. A study by the Software Publishers Association (SPA) illustrates just how widespread the problem is: "Thieves last year stole as much business software as McDonalds sold hamburgers," says Ken Wasch, executive director of SPA in Washington, D.C. Software revenues lost to thieves around the world totaled $7.4 billion last year, he says. In recent years, the number of lawsuits against software vendors has risen; experts believe that this trend is likely to continue. In this section, we look at some ethical issues related to software.

Case 1: Is Justice Above the Law?

In August 1992, the House Judiciary Committee recommended that Attorney General William P. Barr appoint an independent counsel to investigate alleged criminal conduct by the Department of Justice in its dealings with the Washington-based software firm Inslaw, Inc. High-level Justice Department officials were accused of being involved in contract violation, coercion, and theft of Inslaw's program Promis.

In 1982, Inslaw had agreed to install Promis in 94 U.S. Attorneys' offices over three years at a total cost of $10 million. High-level officials of the Justice Department had allegedly taken possession of the software and distributed it illegally to law enforcement agencies around the world, had deliberately ignored Inslaw's proprietary rights, and had colluded to violate the contract with Inslaw. To make matters worse, investigators found that friends of officials in the Justice Department were allowed to sell the software for a profit, resulting in losses of millions of dollars for the software company. When Inslaw threatened to take action, the Justice Department carried out a campaign of litigation and intimidation intended to drive Inslaw, a small company with fewer than 55 employees, out of business. The Justice Department is responsible for leading the charge against people who engage in ethical violations; in this case it stands accused of serious ethical violations.[32]

a. What are some ethical violations in this case?
b. What steps can a company such as Inslaw take to protect itself from such injustices?

Case 2: Software Piracy

The SPA, on behalf of Lotus, Microsoft, and WordPerfect, conducted a surprise raid on two branches of a property management company on the West Coast for alleged violation of software copyright laws. Although the company had a policy against software copying, employees of the company were violating software copyright laws and hence the company is likely to face criminal charges.

In a separate case, Lotus and Novell filed criminal charges against a married couple in Singapore after the pair was found guilty of trademark and copyright infringement in a civil suit. The software companies obtained a court order freezing $900,000 in personal assets belonging to the couple, who reportedly sold thousands of illegal copies of software throughout Southeast Asia.

a. If a company has a well-publicized written document outlining its policies against software piracy, that company should be protected from infringement liabilities. In such a case, if an employee is caught violating software piracy policies, the employee should be sued, not the company. Discuss.
b. What is considered illegal in this country may or may not be considered illegal in other parts of the world. The U.S. should not impose its ethical standards on other countries. Comment.
c. The personal possessions of an individual should not be taken even if that individual is found guilty of ethical violations. Discuss.

Case 3: Highway Robbery?

Software publishers are calling software piracy "information highway robbery." In two separate cases, college students were accused of illegally distributing copyrighted software over the Internet, a worldwide system of interconnected networks. While software piracy is not a new problem, the magnitude of the Internet gives it new dimensions.

In what prosecutors say could be the largest software piracy case ever, David LaMacchia, a 20-year-old junior at the Massachusetts Institute of Technology, is being accused of computer fraud for his involvement in the distribution of more than $1 million worth of illegal software. He is charged with running a public bulletin board, accessible via the Internet, on which copyrighted software, such as Excel and WordPerfect, was uploaded and downloaded by subscribers. (A public bulletin board is an electronic space on the Internet that users can access for information processing and retrieval.)

While there is no question that copyrighted material was illegally distributed on LaMacchia's computer, it is not clear whether he actually copied the software himself. One issue here is whether or not the computer owner is responsible for what others do on his or her computer. "It is not at all clear that a system operator who neither controls what is placed on the system nor profits one cent from any copyrighted software that others download from the system has committed any crime."[33]

(Continued on next page)

Software is potentially accessible to 20 million people on the Internet and with the exponential growth of the Internet comes the prospect of exponential growth in the trafficking of illegal software. It is estimated that software publishers lose an estimated $12 billion to software piracy annually.

The second case involves Daniel Goldwater, a 20-year-old student at Brown University who is facing similar charges.[34]

a. If LaMacchia did not profit from pirated software, he should not be penalized. Discuss.

b. The argument that LaMacchia should not be held liable if he did not copy the software himself promotes and encourages software piracy. Discuss.

c. "If copyrighted software is available on the Internet, I don't see anything wrong in copying it." Discuss.

PROBLEM SOLVING IN THE REAL WORLD

Case 1: City of Indianapolis Goes High-Tech

People are demanding better service these days, not only as consumers but as taxpayers. In Indianapolis, Mayor Stephen Goldsmith is using information technology to cut through bureaucratic constraints and upgrade the city's infrastructure, enhance public safety, and improve services—all without raising taxes.

When Goldsmith took office in January 1992, he shook up the local government by forcing departments to compete against private firms for the city's service contracts. Henceforth, contracts would go to the group, public or private, that could provide the best services at the best price. Goldsmith realized that in order for his program to succeed, he would have to radically improve the quality and accessibility of information, both within the city government and between city hall and taxpayers. He focused on three areas: First, he knew that for the various departments to enter bids against outside contractors, they needed better information about the cost of providing services. Second, he believed that city employees were in the best position to offer improvement ideas, so an effective and dependable means of communication between constituents and government offices was required. Third, he felt that meaningful information should be made readily available to decision makers. For example, city officials did not have the necessary cost data for many functions that the government provided. "We had no idea how much it cost to mow a park or to fill a pothole," says Goldsmith. "Without that information, it's awfully hard to know whether you're doing something good, and it's impossible to know if you're competitive with the private sector."

The administration implemented an activity-based costing (ABC) system, a technique for allocating both direct and indirect costs to specific jobs, products, and customers. The city chose a customized PC-based software package that calculates labor, equipment, materials, and overhead to identify the cost of each service. With this data, management was able to access the city's performance in providing a particular service and determine whether a contract for that service should be put up for bids from the private sector. If a job is going out for bids, management and employees look at the figures provided by ABC and identify ways to perform that job more efficiently.

For instance, the government has already outsourced 60 percent of the city's trash collection, but to reduce costs, the Department of Public Works has decided to put 85 percent of the collection services up for bids. City employees who were performing the job evaluated their procedures and decided to restructure routes and reconfigure staffing, resulting in an increase of daily pickups from 800 to 1,200 per route. This forced contractors to lower their prices and let the city retain its 40 percent of the services. As a result, the city is saving $15 million over a 3-year period.

The administration has improved its information flow with citizens as well by conducting polls, surveys, and neighborhood meetings. The Mayor's Action Center provides a single number for citizens to call with all of their questions, complaints, and concerns. The center handles about 15,000 calls a month about problems ranging from sewer backups to abandoned vehicles. When service representatives receive a call, they enter the data into workstations that run a help-desk program. The software's diagnostic capabilities guide the representatives in recording information; if the call requires human intervention, the system automatically sends the request to a fax machine or printer in the appropriate department. In the past, it could take up to 4 weeks for a request to make its way to the right person in the right department. Now, with calls coming into one place and with automatic routing built into the system, the appropriate areas receive requests immediately, resulting in faster response to citizens' requests.

Because of the mayor's progress, Indianapolis will see $100 million in savings over a 5-year period. This includes a $65 million saving from having the private sector manage the city's wastewater-treatment plants. Over 50 services have been turned over to the private sector, including the billing of sewer services and the management of the city's golf courses. By cutting operating costs, the government can invest more money in the city's streets, bridges, and sidewalks, thereby enhancing public safety. Goldsmith says, "Every major improvement takes a high dose of information."[35]

1. Describe the type of software that is used in the ABC system.
2. What role do you think software has played in implementing the mayor's goals for the city?
3. "Every major improvement takes a high dose of information." Discuss.

Case 2: Ryder Rethinks Business Systems

Joe Roberts refuels and services 80 trucks every day at Ryder Systems' maintenance yard in Holt, Michigan. Unlike most fueling attendants, however, Roberts is also a data-entry clerk. As Roberts refuels each truck, he plugs a hand-held instrument into the truck's onboard computer to retrieve information that helps Ryder keep track of its vehicles.

Ryder Commercial Leasing and Services has recently implemented a $33-million truck maintenance and tracking system that will help the Miami company maintain and manage vehicles throughout much of the Midwest and the South. Eventually, the system will keep tabs on the company's 170,000 vehicles at 915 locations throughout North America.

(Continued on next page)

Formerly, Ryder's various information systems presented more than one face to many of its 11,000 customers, which include retailer Home Depot and hotel chain Marriott International. Further, revenue from truck fleet leasing over the past 6 years had plateaued and the prospect of generating additional income was limited by existing business processes. Dennis Klinger, Ryder's V.P. of Information Services, said "We couldn't squeeze costs and improve performance by doing the same old things."[36] The company decided to restructure itself and developed a master plan toward this end.

The master plan called for the company to integrate disparate field, district, and headquarters information systems that had often created "islands of information." The result: a system that will allow users to share data with 1,000 local service centers, 76 district offices, and the company's Miami headquarters.

Under the new maintenance system, a mechanic or attendant in Florida will be able to access the maintenance history of a truck that was serviced in Michigan a week earlier.

The system works as follows: When servicing a truck, the service representative inserts a probe from a hand-held computer into a button-shaped data-carrying device that is mounted on the side of each vehicle's cab. The computer records the amount of fuel pumped, oil used, and other pertinent information, all of which was previously transcribed by hand.

This gives attendants time to perform additional routine checks and to clean the trucks more thoroughly. The touch memory button tracks a vehicle's fueling and service history. "The button is like a file cabinet with room for extra files."

Another new system at Ryder is the shop management system, written in COBOL, which automatically schedules vehicles for maintenance or repair. The system matches the job with the mechanic best qualified to perform the task. It also updates the maintenance histories of all vehicles in the fleet and monitors inventory levels at Ryder locations. The system can automatically submit warranty claims, process payroll data, and even order parts electronically from 20 suppliers. By the end of 1995, the company hopes to hook up with 130 additional vendors.

Another interesting system at Ryder is Simplified Asset Management (SAM), which gathers information from a variety of systems in order to assess how the company is putting its fixed assets to use. For instance, using the system, the company could decide 18 months before a truck lease expires when best to dispose of the vehicle. "In essence, we have a profit-and-loss statement for every truck." The SAM system will reduce the time district managers need to collect data on the vehicles they manage from 2 workdays to 15 minutes.[37]

1. Three software systems have been identified in this case: a truck maintenance system, a shop management system, and the Simplified Asset Management system. Describe the type of software required for each application.
2. Would you recommend a multiprocessing environment for these applications? Discuss.
3. The shop management system was written in COBOL. Identify some advantages and disadvantages of COBOL.

References

Apte, Uday, Chetan S. Sankar, Meru Thakur, and Joel E. Turner. "Reusability-Based Study." *MIS Quarterly* 12, no. 3 (September 1988).

Haavind, Robert. "Software's New Object Lesson." *Technology Review,* February/March 1992.

Joyce, Edward J. "Reusable Software: Passage to Productivity?" *Datamation* (September 15, 1988).

Korson, Timothy D. and Vijay K. Vaishnavi. "Managing Emerging Software Technologies: A Technology Transfer Framework." *Communications of the ACM* 35, no. 9 (September 1991).

Littlewood, Bev and Lorenzo Strigini. "The Risks of Software." *Scientific American* 267, no. 5 (November 1992).

Nerson, Jean-Marc. "Applying Object-Oriented Analysis and Design." *Communications of the ACM* 35, no. 9 (September 1992).

Notes

1. Hayes, Mary, "KFC's Delivery Challenge," *InformationWeek,* July 18, 1994, pp. 58–59.
2. Baum, David, "4GL Skills," *Computerworld,* December 13, 1993, p. 121.
3. Nash, Kim S., "Toronto Bank Rolls into Object Mode," *Computerworld,* March 16, 1995, p. 69.
4. Betty, Greg and Tony Dimnik. "Object-Oriented Programming Revolutionizes Software Development," *Management Accounting,* May 1993, pp. 50–53.
5. Ibid.
6. Anthes, Gary H. "Software Reuse Plans Bring Paybacks," *Computerworld,* December 6, 1993, pp. 73, 76.
7. Ibid.
8. Kessler, Andy. "Fire Your Software Programmers-Again," *Forbes ASAP,* August 1994, p. 23.
9. Ibid.
10. Deiotel, Harvey M. "An Introduction to Operating Systems," Addison-Wesley Publishing Company, Reading, Massachusetts, Revised First Edition, p. 11.
11. Ibid.
12. Johnson, Stuart. "NFL adds Windows NT to roster," *Computerworld,* April 25, 1994, pp. 1 and 41.
13. Vecchione, Anthony and Mary Hayes. "Warp Factor," *InformationWeek,* October 24, 1994, p. 12.
14. Brantingham, David. Director of Computer Operations and Technical Service, Western Publishing, Racine, Wisconsin.
15. Brantingham, David. "No Single Solution," *CIO,* May 15, 1994, p. 32.
16. Scannell, Ed, "Travelers Reduces Risk of Claims Errors," *Computerworld,* February 1, 1995, p. 74.
17. Headley, Jeff, a systems architect at First Union.
18. Scannell, Ed. "OS/2 pays dividends to faithful bank user," *Computerworld,* September 26, 1994, pp. 34, 36.
19. Valigra, Lori. "U.N. Shackled by 30-year-old Mainframe System," *InfoWorld,* February 21, 1994, p. 61.

20. Betts, Mitch. "Software Combo Cuts Delivery Guesswork," *Computerworld,* March 27, 1995, p. 40.

21. Hoffman, Thomas. "Medical Center Finds Cure for Ailing Billing System," *Computerworld,* March 27, 1995, p. 49.

22. Betts, Mitch. "Postal Software Helps Firms Beat High Rates," *Computerworld,* March 6, 1995, p. 61.

23. McPartlin, John. "Good Health: Just a Phone Call Away," *InformationWeek,* April 12, 1993, p. 64.

24. McPartlin, John. "Let the Sunshine Software In," *InformationWeek,* April 12, 1993, p. 64.

25. Hollander, Nathan. "Selecting Software," *Software Magazine,* Oct. 1992, p. 6.

26. Bacon, C. James. "Use of Decision Criteria in Selecting Information Systems/Technology Investments," *MIS Quarterly,* September, 1992, pp. 335–352.

27. Santosus, Megan. "New Value Systems," *CIO,* October 1, 1994, p. 80.

28. Halper, Mark. "Faster Product Cycles at Odds with Accounting Firms," *Computerworld,* June 7, 1993, p. 24.

29. "The Price of Piracy," *InformationWeek,* May 16, 1994, p. 10.

30. Vizard, Michael. "Bye-bye, VAR?," *Computerworld,* June 7, 1993, pp. 37 and 43.

31. Fisher, Lawrence, M. "Software Meters May Help Firms Cut Costs and Stay Legal," *Austin American Statesman,* August 22, 1994, p. 6.

32. Soat, John, and McPartlin, John P. "Is Justice Above the Law?," *InformationWeek,* August 17, 1992, p. 15.

33. Silvergate, Harvey, LaMacchia's attorney.

34. Stahl, Stephanie. "Highway Robbery?," *InformationWeek,* April 25, 1994, p. 17.

35. Hitchcock, Nancy. "Stretching City Limits," *CIO,* August 1994, pp. 54–55.

36. Klinger, Dennis, Ryder's Vice President of information services.

37. Chabrow, Eric R. "Ryder Rethinks Business Systems," *InformationWeek,* September 26, 1994, pp. 48–50.

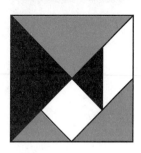

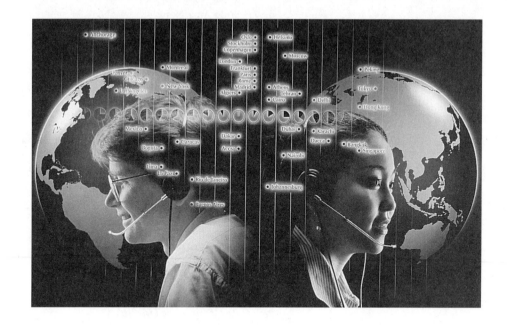

5

Telecommunications and Networks

Contents

Learning Objectives
Technology Payoff: New York State Schools
Introduction
The Technical Foundations of Telecommunications
   Part I: The Telecommunications Model
   Telecommunication Channels
   Providers of Channel Services
      Common Carriers
      Special-Purpose Carriers
Telecommunication Media
   Bounded Media
      Twisted Pairs
      Coaxial Cable
      Fiber-Optic Cable
   Unbounded Media (Wireless Communication)
      Microwave Radio
      Communication Satellites
      Cellular Phones
      High-Frequency Radio Telephones
Types of Networks
   Private Branch Exchanges (PBXs)
   Integrated Services Digital Networks (ISDNs)
   Nontelephone Networks

              Local Area Networks (LANs)
              Advantages of LANs
              Wide Area Networks (WANs)
              Value-Added Networks (VANs)
Network Topologies
     Bus Topology
     Ring Topology
     Star Topology
Network Architecture
Open Systems Interconnection (OSI)
Part II: Management Implications of Telecommunications
     Challenges in Managing Networks
          Global Networks
     The Internet
     Electronic Data Interchange (EDI)
Summary
Review Questions
Discussion Questions
Ethical Issues
     Case 1: Patent Violations
     Case 2: Telephone Monitoring: Privacy Breach or Security Measure?
     Case 3: Internet Liability
     Case 4: Faking It on the Internet
     Case 5: Hold That Data, Please
     Case 6: Electronic Bookstore or Telephone Directory
     Case 7: Existing Copyright Act Must Go!
Problem Solving in the Real World
     Case 1: Freddie, Fannie, Ginnie, and EDI
References
Notes

Learning Objectives

Telecommunications links people and electronic devices that are geographically separated. This chapter provides a broad overview of telecommunications and its operating principles, emphasizing its vital role in business decision making and in our personal and professional lives. Internet and other online services are discussed in detail. After reading and studying this chapter, you should be able to

* Understand the importance of telecommunications to business organizations
* Explain the characteristics of telecommunication channels and media
* Describe the role of common and special-purpose communication carriers
* Describe different types of networks
* Describe different types of network topologies
* Understand the significance and the implications of Internet
* Describe Electronic Data Interchange (EDI) and its implications for business

TECHNOLOGY PAYOFF

New York State Schools

Both visionaries and corporate executives are concerned that in the coming decade the U.S. may face a severe shortage of knowledge workers skilled in telecommunications and information technology, both of which are vital elements in the global marketplace. Educators have been encouraged to implement programs that teach these subjects.

New York's State Education Department has translated this call into a vision of the 21st century classroom, in which students and teachers will have instantaneous access to global information through the use of computers that are linked together by telecommunications. New York's Board of Regents has embarked on a Long-Range Plan for Technology that calls for New York's 4,000 public school buildings and 186,000 classrooms to acquire telecommunications equipment by the end of the century.

"Our global society has created this technological revolution, and unless we meet the needs of all our student populations, we will soon have electronic ghettos," says William Mulvey, a technology and communications teacher at Geneva High School in Geneva, New York.

Under the New York State plan, each classroom will have four PCs or workstations for students. The PCs will be linked to the teacher's workstation and to a laser printer. Each school will also be equipped with a CD-ROM-based multimedia system that will allow students to electronically process and retrieve text and graphics. It is anticipated that students who are provided with a high-tech learning environment will become more familiar with the applications and benefits of telecommunications.[1]

The development and effective use of telepower is perhaps the single most important key to strategic success of American society in the next century.
—Joseph N. Pelton, Director of the Advanced
Telecommunications Research Center

Introduction

Technology has made the world a small place. Today, it is easy to "reach out and touch someone," no matter where in the world that person lives. Information, which is being created at a rate that is 200,000 times faster than the growth of the human population, can easily be accessed and delivered, usually within a few seconds, between any two points on the planet. Human ingenuity and the development of computer technology have made telecommunications one of the most powerful technologies of our times.

In our story of the New York State schools, we have seen how telecommunications is expected to help the learning process by making a wealth of information easily accessible to students and teachers. Teachers can communicate with other teachers all over the world and participate in a free exchange of ideas. Telecommunications can link schools, universities, research institutions, industry, and government; it will eventually create what amounts to a "national brain."[2] Telecommunications, the backbone of tomorrow's "global school," is an agent of change so powerful that it dictates corporate management styles, shapes business trends, facilitates new alliances in global markets, and creates new market dynamics. Telecommunications will continue to alter the way we live and do business, and even the way we think.

We are witnessing the power of telecommunications in our everyday lives. For example, coffeehouses in San Francisco are using networks to help people communicate with each other. The network, called SF Net, was designed by a local computer consultant, who installed screens and keyboards in coffeehouse tabletops that link patrons of more than a dozen cafes in San Francisco. Users pay 50 cents for 20 minutes of electronic conversation with patrons of similarly equipped coffeehouses. Conversations are arranged by topic, including politics, books, and philosophy. The network is a great way to make dates. "You don't need to worry about rejection," said Amber Clisura, who met her boyfriend through SF Net, although sometimes "they sound cool on the board, but then you meet them and it's not pretty!"[3]

Automated Teller Machines, airline reservations, live broadcasts, remote health care, space exploration, medical research, and learning at a distance are made possible through telecommunications. Therefore, it is not surprising that employers expect their new hires to have a working knowledge of telecommunications and its applications.

The Technical Foundations of Telecommunications

Telecommunications
The transmission of data (text, images, voice, graphics, etc.) over different media from one set of electronic devices, also referred to as nodes, to another set of electronic devices that are geographically separated.

Telecommunications refers to transmitting different forms of data (i.e., text, images, voice, graphics, etc.) over different media from one set of electronic devices, also referred to as nodes, to another set of electronic devices that are geographically separated. Although students frequently think that telecommunications has something to do with telephones, *tele* simply means "at a distance" and is derived from the Greek word for "far away."

Telecommunications is similar to human face-to-face communications in that there is a sender, a receiver, a message, and a medium through which the message is transmitted. Although the words *telecommunications* and *networks* are often used interchangeably, some writers define **networks** as the systems that transmit data, and telecommunications as the sending and receiving of data. In this book, however, the two terms are used interchangeably.

Network
A system that transmits data to and from a number of locations that are geographically dispersed.

This chapter is divided into two parts. Part I provides a technical overview of telecommunications while Part II discusses the impact and implications of telecommunications on the business community. Figure 5–1 lays the foundation for the discussion that follows.

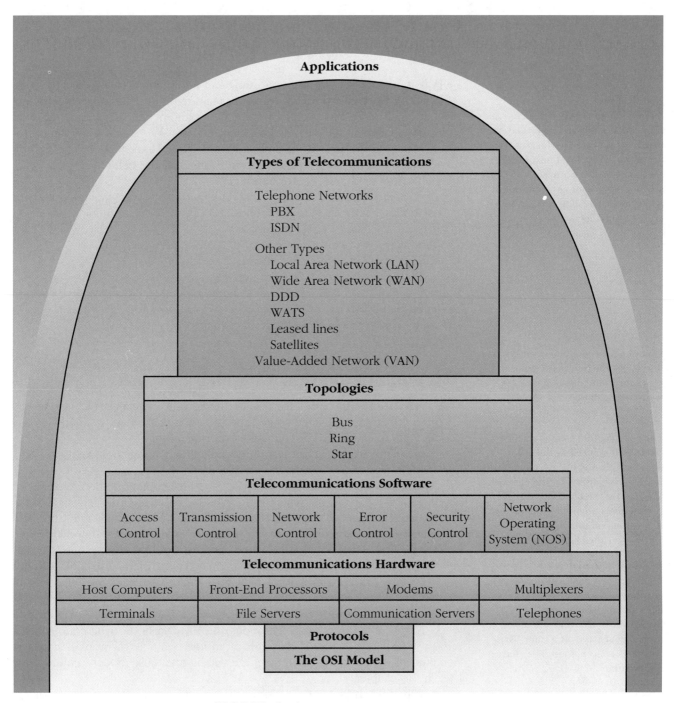

Applications

Types of Telecommunications

Telephone Networks
  PBX
  ISDN

Other Types
  Local Area Network (LAN)
  Wide Area Network (WAN)
  DDD
  WATS
  Leased lines
  Satellites
Value-Added Network (VAN)

Topologies

Bus
Ring
Star

Telecommunications Software

Access Control	Transmission Control	Network Control	Error Control	Security Control	Network Operating System (NOS)

Telecommunications Hardware

Host Computers	Front-End Processors	Modems	Multiplexers
Terminals	File Servers	Communication Servers	Telephones

Protocols

The OSI Model

FIGURE 5–1

The OSI model and protocols lay the foundation for telecommunications.
Both hardware and software are used to develop and implement a network and this chapter addresses different hardware and software elements. Topologies are different ways of arranging the devices on a network. Finally, there are different types of networks that are used to support a variety of network applications.

Part I: The Telecommunications Model

The telecommunications model has several basic components:

1. A computer to receive, process, and send information, called the host computer. A **host computer** is usually a mainframe or a fairly large computer that sends and receives data over a network and performs a number of other important functions, such as checking the data for accuracy, sending error messages to the user if an error is found during transmission, and coordinating and controlling all data transmissions over the network.
2. Devices to send and receive information.
3. Telecommunications channels that link geographically separated devices using media such as telephone lines and cables. Telecommunications channels are discussed in the next section.
4. Various types of computer hardware. (See Table 5–1.)
5. Various types of computer software. (See Table 5–2.)

Figure 5–2 shows the basic components and their connections. We have covered input and output devices in Chapter 3, so we will now look at the next item in our component list, telecommunication channels.

Telecommunication Channels

A **channel** is the part of the telecommunications system that constitutes the link between message source and message destination. A channel is any conduit along which data can be transmitted.

Telecommunications channels are identified according to transmission rate, transmission mode, and transmission direction.

Transmission rate is the capacity of a telecommunication channel; it depends on the bandwidth, which is the difference between the highest and the lowest frequency carried over the channel. The greater the bandwidth, the more information can be transmitted simultaneously over the channel. Bandwidth can be classified into three categories: voice-band, or low-speed (transmission rates vary between 300 bits per second (bps) and 9,600 bps), medium-band (9,600 bps to 256,000 bps), and broad-band, or high-speed (256,000 bps to a very large number, usually in the billions).

Transmission mode is the mode in which data are transmitted over the network. There are two modes: synchronous and asynchronous. Synchronous transmission transmits a group of characters at a time, while asynchronous transmission transmits one character at a time. We will discuss these modes in more detail later in this chapter.

Finally, **transmission direction** is the direction in which data is transmitted. Transmission direction is categorized in three ways: simplex, half duplex, and full duplex. In **simplex mode,** a data communication device can either send or receive data, but cannot do both, so transmission occurs in one direction only. Simplex transmission takes place on news wires that carry information to various newspapers. News wires can only send information to newspapers, not receive information from them. Another example of simplex transmission is television broadcasting, which moves only from the TV station to the TV set.

Host computer
A large computer, often a mainframe, that sends and receives data over a network and performs a number of important functions, such as checking the data for accuracy, relaying error messages, and coordinating and controlling all data transmissions over the network.

Channel
Part of a telecommunication system that forms the link between message source and message sink for transmitting data.

Transmission rate
The capacity of a communication channel, measured as the difference between the highest and lowest frequencies carried by the channel. The greater the bandwidth, the greater the amount of information that can be simultaneously transmitted over the channel.

Transmission mode
There are two modes of data transmission over a network: synchronous and asynchronous. Synchronous transmission moves several characters at a time; asynchronous transmission, one character at a time.

Transmission direction
There are three directions in which data can be transmitted: simplex, half duplex, and full duplex.

Simplex
Term for a data communication device that can either send or receive data, but cannot do both.

TABLE 5–1
Some computer hardware used in telecommunication systems.

Front-End Processor
A minicomputer that acts as a buffer between the client device and the host computer. The goal of the front-end processor is to increase the operating efficiency of the network by taking care of routine tasks such as coordinating peripherals and ensuring error-free transmissions.

Modem
A device that converts digital signals into analog and back. An abbreviation of **mo**dulator/**dem**odulator. Analog transmissions, such as the human voice, are sent in waves, while computer data are represented using digital signals in the form of binary digits, such as 1s and 0s. (See Figure 5–8.)

Multiplexer
Multiplexing is the process of transmitting two or more messages over a single channel; a device that performs multiplexing is called a multiplexer. A multiplexer collects signals from several terminals, interweaves the signals, and transmits them over a single channel.

Frequency Division Multiplexing
A type of multiplexing format in which a channel with a large bandwidth is divided into subchannels and each subchannel carries individual analog signals, which are then bound together. At the receiving end, the bound signals are separated into individual signals.

Time Division Multiplexing
Multiplexes digital signals. Although only one device transmits signals at any given time, the high speed of the transmission device gives the impression that several signals are being transmitted simultaneously.

Switch
A computer or electronic device that determines the data transmission path by making connections. Switches can control the transmission path across national or local networks.

Bridge
A device that links two or more *compatible* networks, allowing information to be sent between users on different networks.

Gateway
A device that links two or more *incompatible* networks. For instance, gateways enable PCs on LANs to access a mainframe computer.

Half duplex
A data exchange device in which two parties alternate sending data. In half-duplex mode, when one party has completed a transmission, control of the channel switches to the other party, allowing it to transmit data.

Full duplex
A data exchange device in which both parties can send and receive information at the same time.

Data communication carriers
Telephone and telecommunication companies that provide telecommunication services to move data. There are two types of carriers: common carriers and special purpose carriers.

In **half-duplex mode,** the sender and the receiver can *alternate* sending data. An example of a half-duplex device is a walkie-talkie. Both parties can send and receive data, but only one of them can send at a given time. In half-duplex mode, when one party has completed a transmission, control of the channel switches to the other, who can then transmit.

In **full-duplex mode,** both parties can send and receive information at *the same time*. An example of a full-duplex device is the telephone, on which both parties can speak and be heard at the same time.

Providers of Channel Services

Telephone and telecommunication companies that move data and information from one location to another are called **data communication carriers.** There are two types of carriers: common carriers and special-purpose carriers.

TABLE 5–2
Some telecommunication software.

Access Control Software

Establishes access between different devices, terminals, and computers in the network and checks the transmission speed (low, medium, or high), transmission mode (synchronous or asynchronous), and transmission direction (simplex, half duplex, or duplex). Access control also includes functions such as automatic dialing and redialing of telephone numbers and the enforcement of access restrictions.

There are two forms of access control: centralized and decentralized. In centralized control, a host computer controls access between different devices on the network; hence, if the central unit is down, the whole network is down. In decentralized, or distributed, control, any device on the network can communicate directly with any other.

Terminal Emulation Software

Software that enables a microcomputer to behave like a specific terminal when it interacts with a mainframe.

Transmission Control Software

Software that controls the transmission of data over the network.

Network Control Software

Software that controls, coordinates, and manages the overall operations of the network. The network operating system is central to network control software; it has many of the same functions and features as the operating systems discussed in Chapter 4. It establishes priorities for data waiting to be transmitted, routes messages, checks for any errors in the transmission, and maintains statistics on system use.

Error Detection and Correction Software

Ensures that errors, caused by power surges or other problems, are detected and corrected.

Security Software

Prevents unauthorized access to data and monitors the use of the network. Performs encryption when necessary; encryption refers to a security measure that scrambles a message before it is sent over the network and descrambles it at the other end.

Common carrier
A company that furnishes voice and data communication services both to businesses and to the general public. AT&T, MCL, Sprint, GTE, and ITT are common carriers.

Common Carriers A **common carrier** is a company that furnishes communication services to businesses and to the general public and is regulated by state and federal agencies. For example, companies such as AT&T, MCI, Sprint, GTE, and ITT are common carriers that offer long-distance voice and data communication services.

Special-purpose carriers
Also known as value-added carriers. Companies that add value to the basic communications services provided by a common carrier by providing E-mail, videoconferencing, correction of transmission errors, backup services, and network management.

Special-Purpose Carriers **Special-purpose carriers,** or **value-added carriers,** are companies that add features to the basic communication services provided by a common carrier. They lease communication services provided by common carriers and add amenities such as E-mail, videoconferencing, correction of transmission errors, solution of compatibility problems between different computer systems and terminals, backup services, and network management. Special-purpose carriers generally charge their clients a basic monthly fee; additional charges are levied based on volume and type of use. One of the most popular value-added carriers is CompuServe, an international network that provides access to over 1,700 online products and services such as travel, shopping, entertainment, and games.

T A B L E 5 – 3
A summary of the key points covered in this section.

How are data transmitted?	Data are transmitted over channels using various media.
What are the characteristics of channels?	**Transmission Speed** 　Bits per second 　Bandwidth **Transmission Direction** 　Simplex 　Half Duplex 　Duplex **Transmission Mode** 　Synchronous 　Asynchronous
What are the different types of media over which data is transmitted?	Bounded Media 　Twisted-Pair Cables 　Coaxial Cables 　Fiber-Optic Cables Unbounded Media 　Microwave Radios 　Communication Satellites 　Cellular Phones 　High-Frequency Radio
Who provides these services?	Common Carriers Special-Purpose Carriers

Telecommunications media
The means by which data are transmitted. There are two types of media: bounded and unbounded.

Twisted pair
Two insulated stands of copper wire twisted together. When a number of twisted pairs are grouped together and enclosed in a protective sheath, they form a cable. Twisted-pair cable, one of the most popular telecommunication media, is used for phone lines and computer networks.

Coaxial cable
Consists of a central conducting copper core, surrounded first by a layer of insulating material and then by a second conducting layer of braided wire mesh. Used extensively in the cable television industry and in computer networks covering short distances.

Fiber-optic cable
Consists of thousands of hair-thin strands of glass or plastic, bound together inside a glass cylinder that is covered by a protective sheath. Fiber-optic cable carries data signals in the form of modulated light beams. It is virtually free from all forms of electronic interference.

Telecommunications Media

Telecommunications media are the links over which data are transmitted. There are two types of telecommunications media: bounded and unbounded.

Bounded Media

In a **bounded medium,** the signals are confined to the medium; they never leave it. The three most popular types of bounded medium are "twisted-pair" wires, coaxial cable, and fiber-optic cable.

Twisted Pairs　A **twisted pair** consists of two insulated strands of copper wire, twisted together. An ordinary cable consists of a number of twisted pairs, grouped together and enclosed in a protective sheath. Twisted-pair cable is one of the most popular telecommunications media for phone lines and computer networks.

Coaxial Cable　**Coaxial cable** consists of a central conducting copper core, surrounded first by a layer of insulating material and then by a second conducting layer of braided wire mesh. A layer of nonconductive insulation, called a jacket, also covers the wire to make it weather-resistant and usable both on land and under water. Coaxial cable is extensively used in the cable television industry and over short distances in computer networks.

Fiber-Optic Cable　**Fiber-optic cable** consists of thousands of hair-thin strands of glass or plastic, called the core, bound together inside a glass cylinder, which

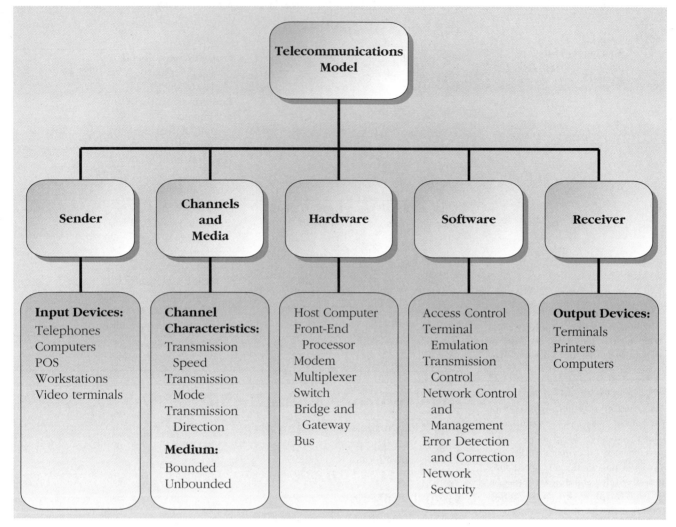

FIGURE 5-2

The five main components of a telecommunications system.

is covered by a protective sheath known as the cladding. Fiber-optic cable carries signals in the form of modulated light beams. It has become very popular because it is smaller, lighter, and faster than twisted-pair or coaxial cable. Further, since it does not radiate energy or conduct electricity, it is noninductive, and hence is virtually free of all forms of electrical interference. Finally, fiber-optic cable can handle high transmission rates—up to almost 2 billion bps, whereas, twisted-pair cable can handle only about 100 million bps.[4]

For example, the American Association of Retired Persons (AARP), a non-partisan, nonprofit organization with 1,200 employees, 34 million members, and 400,000 volunteers, uses fiber optics to link its two data processing centers, one at its Washington headquarters and one in California. It processes voice and video in real time, and provides videoconferencing capabilities. AARP uses networks to run its membership information processing system and its financial systems, which include about 20 LANs, 1,355 PCs, and 400 laptops at 15 sites all over the country. The network allows AARP volunteers to obtain research and publications online from area offices within 48 hours, instead of the usual 6 weeks.

Communication networks and databases, packed with information on members and volunteers, help to keep AARP's volunteer lobbyists up to date and vocal regarding legislation that affects health insurance, social security, or other related matters, so that they can be a powerful force at election time.[5]

One of the few disadvantages of fiber-optics technology is that it is more expensive than twisted-pair, although in recent years this price difference has narrowed. For example, when the Richardson Independent School District asked for bids to equip a test building, it found the total cost of twisted-pair cables pair to be $17,526, whereas the total cost of fiber optics was $23,898.[6] In any case, many organizations are willing to pay high prices for fiber optics, because its long-term benefits far outweigh its higher cost.

For example, Anderson Cancer Center uses a fiber optic network to share valuable medical knowledge with experts across the country. About a decade ago, the center began using networks and today all eight of Anderson's buildings are hooked up through fiber optics. The networks keep Anderson's directors at the main campus in touch with other managers at its research and government sites across Texas, and its research center in Orlando, Florida. One of the most powerful applications of the network is the imaging system which scans patient magnetic resonance images (MRI's) into a computer and allows physicians throughout the hospital to track and monitor a patient.

Figure 5–3 shows a twisted pair, a coaxial cable, and a fiber optic cable.

FIGURE 5–3

The three types of popular bounded medium: twisted-pair cable, coaxial cable, and fiber-optic cable.

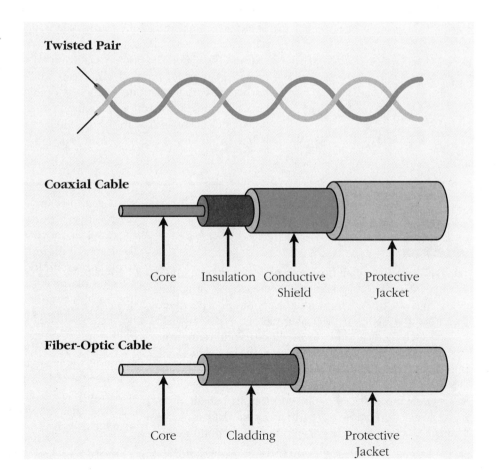

Unbounded Media (Wireless Communication)

In an unbounded, or wireless, medium, the signals are not confined to the medium. Wireless media propagate signals through the atmosphere, the ocean, and outer space. Wireless communication makes a mobile office easier to implement: airline passengers can keep in touch with their offices through the use of wireless phone, fax, and E-mail services and can even access online information services from the air—or from anywhere.[7]

Another example of wireless communication is the $94 million W. M. Keck telescope. The eight-story, 270-ton structure was designed using computer modeling and analysis; the 10-meter, 14.4-ton mirror is made up of 36 small hexagonal mirrors that were carved with unprecedented accuracy using computers. Each of the 36 mirrors in the telescope is fitted with sensors that send information about the positions of the planets over the network to 12 computers located in different parts of the country. The computers assess the data about the different planetary positions and send commands to motors that nudge the 6-foot, 880-pound mirrors into positions from which they can register planetary positions with great accuracy. The Keck telescope is the product of ingenuity and advanced computer technology. The telescope makes about 10 to 20 observations per night; each observation takes up about 32 megabytes. The data are written to magnetic disks at the telescope site and transmitted continuously over the network to optical discs located at Keck headquarters.[8]

Eight hospitals in the Buffalo, New York area, along with the State University of New York at Buffalo, are partners in a high-speed fiber-optic network that facilitates sharing valuable medical data and tracking the health of patients in the region. The Fiber Distributed Data Interface (FDDI) network allows health care providers to share clinical databases and an extensive online medical library known as Hubnet. Hubnet, which is operated by the university, provides members with the equivalent of 6.5 million pages of medical data from sources all over the world. Compared with the providers' former capability, the new technology is like expanding a highway from one lane to eight.[9]

BUSINESS REALITIES
Value Health, Inc.

Today, 7% to 10% of all hospitalizations for people under the age of 65 occur when a patient takes a drug that aggravates an underlying medical condition. The figure increases to 14% for people over the age of 65. To help reduce such medication-induced illnesses and reduce the cost of prescription medicines, one major health care provider is turning to wireless technologies. Value Health, a health care provider for Ford Motors, uses wireless messaging services to link doctors to patient pharmaceutical information stored in a central data bank. As a result, doctors make better-informed prescription decisions at the point of care and can choose from a list of the health plan's discounted medications.

Such a move is a considerable improvement over the former prescription system, under which a physician wrote a prescription and gave it to the patient, who took it to the pharmacy. The pharmacist entered the prescription into the system, but there were very few checks to determine whether the medication could harm the patient. However, using wireless technologies and accessing a patient database, doctors can check the prescription against the patient's records to determine whether there is a therapeutic conflict before they prescribe any medication. The doctor can also access a database that shows the prices of different products and select a less expensive drug.[10]

Value Health, Inc. is another health care provider that is relying on wireless technologies to enhance the quality of patient care (see box).

It is predicted that within the next few years, the number of wireless computing devices (estimated to number about 7.5 million today) will equal the number of stationary desktop PCs (about 9 million). "Whole new business structures will be created around these mobile technologies. Companies will come up with innovative ways to compete for efficiency that are based around these data communications architectures."[11] Emerging applications of wireless technology are shown in Figure 5–4.

There are four types of wireless communication. They are microwave radio, communication satellites, cellular phones, and high-frequency radios.

Microwave radio

A popular unbounded medium that uses radio signals to transmit large volumes of voice and data traffic.

Microwave Radio   **Microwave radio** is a popular unbounded medium that uses radio signals to transmit large volumes of voice and data traffic. The tall towers with large horns and/or disk antennas that we see across the country are devices for line-of-sight (LOS) ground transmission and transmission between ground stations and satellites. This is how it works: the antenna on a microwave radio converts the short wavelength of the transmitted signal into a beam that provides a much greater signal strength at the receiving end, without requiring increased transmitter power.

Microwave radios are useful for connecting networks that are only short distances apart. For example, the Keystone Group Inc. uses microwave technology to link their offices that are on opposite sides of the Charles River. The company

FIGURE 5–4

Some of the popular applications of wireless technology.

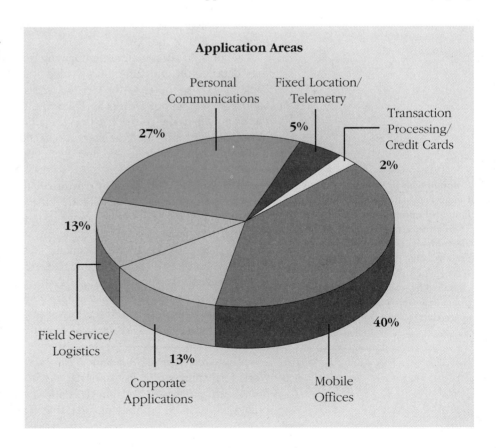

FIGURE 5-5

Microwave radio is an unbounded medium. The tall towers send line-of-sight (LOS) transmissions.

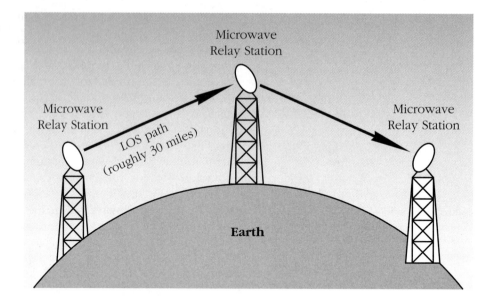

found that a conventional leased phone line would cost $20,000 for the connection fee and an estimated $1,000 in monthly operating costs. In addition, a leased line could handle only about 1.5 Mbps (mega bits per second), whereas the company's network traffic was close to 10 Mbps. Microwave radio, on the other hand, required only a one-time payment of $30,000 and could easily meet the communication needs of the company.[12]

Schools, in particular, are embracing microwave technology because it transmits data, voice, and full-motion video for a fraction of the cost of fiber-optic cable. This was the case for George Araya, technology specialist at the Desert Sands Unified School District in Palm Springs, Calif. He states, "For 10 cents on the dollar versus the cost of fiber-optic cabling, we were able to link all 21 schools in our district for a one-time cost of $500,000, compared with an estimated $5.5 million for comparable leased-line connections."[13]

Communication satellite systems Commercial satellites that are launched into geosynchronous orbit at an altitude of about 22,300 miles above the equator. These are powered by solar panels and carry different types of signals, such as standard television programs, telephone transmissions, and high-speed data.

Communication Satellites **Communication satellites** are launched into geosynchronous orbits at an altitude of about 22,300 miles above the equator. Objects orbiting at 22,300 miles move at the same rate at which the earth rotates, and thus are stationary with respect to the surface. Satellites are powered by solar panels. They carry a variety of signals, such as standard television broadcasting, telephone transmissions, and even high-speed data. Surface stations all over the world use *dish antennas* to transmit data to communication satellites, which amplify the signals and transmit them to other surface stations. Since there is some delay between the transmission and the arrival of data, satellites cannot be used for real-time data processing. (Figure 5–6 shows a satellite receiving and transmitting signals.)

The Great Atlantic & Pacific Tea Co. (A&P) uses a $10-million satellite network for a number of its supermarkets, to approve fund transactions, such as debit card purchases and check authorizations. Using bar-code scanners and point-of-sale (POS) equipment, A&P tracks its inventory and even entertains cus-

Satellite Dishes

tomers by providing news and entertainment on terminals at checkout counters.[14] Carnival Cruise Lines is another company that has made use of satellite technology to enhance customer satisfaction and its bottom line profits (see box).

Cellular phones
As a cellular phone moves through space, each cell, or geographic area, through which it passes contains a base station with a radio transmitter, a receiver, an antenna, and a computer. The user's calls are handled using radio waves with a unique set of frequencies that are assigned to each cell.

Cellular Phones **Cellular phones** are wireless personal telephones. A cellular system partitions geographical areas into cells; each cell has a base station with a radio transmitter, a receiver, an antenna, and a computer. Instead of having one high-power base station for a given geographical area, cellular phone technology uses a low-power transmitter attached to each cell (a smaller area), thus greatly increasing the number of frequencies available to mobile phone customers. Incoming calls are transmitted to a user's telephone with radio waves, using a unique set of radio frequencies for each cell, while a central computer and other communication devices send, receive, track, and manage calls and handoffs from one cell to another. Figure 5–7 shows how these cellular divisions work.

UPS has launched a nationwide cellular tracking system, called TotalTrack, that has equipped the company's 55,000 vehicles with state-of-the-art cellular technology. The company can find out the status of any air or ground package at a moment's notice; delivery status can be confirmed in a matter of seconds.

High-frequency radio telephones
Uses radio waves to transmit information over great distances. High frequency signals radiate from an antenna using ground waves and sky waves.

High-Frequency Radio Telephones **High-frequency radio telephones** use radio to transmit information over great distances. High-frequency signals radiate from an antenna using two paths: a ground wave that follows the earth's surface and a sky wave that bounces between the earth and the ionosphere. The ground wave can communicate over distances of up to 400 miles; the skywave can reach points up to 4,000 miles away, with a path reliability of over 90%.

FIGURE 5–6

Communication satellites, powered by solar panels, serve as relay stations for stations all over the world.

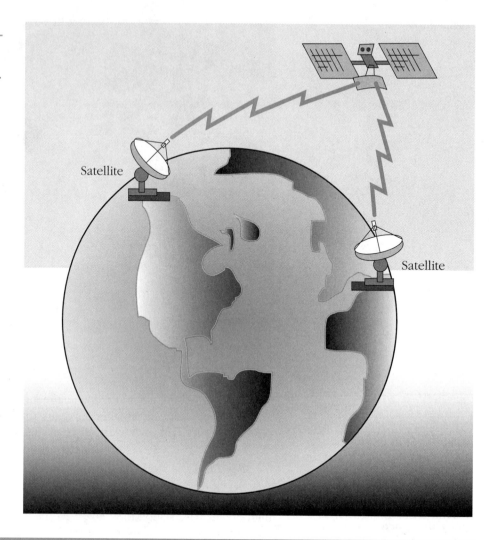

BUSINESS REALITIES
Carnival Cruise Lines

The only thing missing on Carnival Cruise Lines was cash. Customers did not have access to their ATMs and therefore were running out of money on board. It is estimated that 65% of cruisegoers run out of cash on the fifth day of a 7-day cruise. What Carnival needed was a data link between ATMs on their ships and a host bank on land. Recently, Carnival turned to satellite technology and became the first cruise line to provide shipboard ATMs.

The cruise line already had a satellite connection to carry digitized voice signals so that passengers could call their friends and families. The 64-Kbps satellite link is now a dedicated connection that accommodates eight voice lines and one data link. Each ship is connected to an enterprise-wide network with a Sun Microsystems SPARC station-10 server. The new ATMs are located on the promenade decks.

Before the satellite connection, vacationers used their credit cards for most of their expenditures on the cruise line. However, some activities, such as gambling at the casino, day trips, and tips to crew members, require cash. When vacationers ran out, the activity at casinos and other profitable centers dropped considerably, resulting in losses for the cruise line.

The response to the ATMs has been positive and they have increased the revenues of the company considerably, so it is placing ATMs on the rest of its ships.[15]

F I G U R E 5 - 7

Cellular technology partitions geographical areas into cells in which
low-power transmitters are used to
send incoming telephone signals.

(Adapted from AT&T Technology, vol.
6, no. 4, 1991)

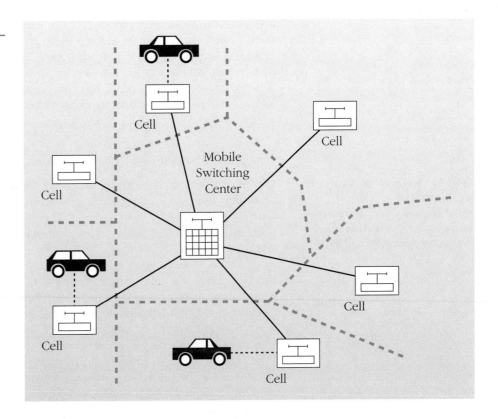

Types of Networks

How do common carriers and special-purpose carriers provide communication services? Some methods for providing communication services
are private branch exchanges (PBXs), integrated services digital networks (ISDNs), local area networks (LANs), wide area networks (WANs), and
value-added networks (VANs).

Private Branch Exchanges (PBX)

Private branch exchange (PBX)
An electronic switching device (or a
special computer) that provides
connections between the company's
telephone lines and those of the
local telephone company.

A **private branch exchange (PBX)** is an electronic switching device (or a special computer), located within the company, that automatically switches calls
between the company's telephone lines and those of a local telephone company.
It is a small telephone exchange that is owned by the organization, as opposed
to the large public telephone exchanges owned by telephone companies.

A PBX performs a number of functions, such as call routing, call forwarding,
redialing, storing, tracing the origins of calls for statistical purposes, and automatically determining the least expensive route for a long distance call. Networks that
carry only voice and data from PBXs are referred to as PBX-based networks; those
that integrate voice, data, and images are referred to as integrated services digital
networks (ISDNs); they are covered below.

Today, PBXs are becoming an integral part of the "smart office" with their ability to coordinate, control, and communicate data among various devices on the network. For example, suppose a user wants to fax a word processing document that

resides on the user's computer. A PBX can retrieve this document, automatically dial the fax number, and fax the document. Another major advantage of a PBX is that it requires only a telephone jack to become operational, unlike telecommunication devices that require extensive wiring or rewiring of existing facilities. The primary disadvantage of a PBX is that it can cover only a small geographical area, unless it is connected to other PBXs or to value-added networks. Also, since PBXs use only telephone lines, they cannot handle large volumes of data.

Integrated Services Digital Network (ISDN)

Integrated Services Digital Network (ISDN)
Digital network which uses commercial telephone systems that allow users to transmit voice and data.

Carriers can also provide communication services using **the ISDN,** a digital network that uses the commercial telephone system to provide users with a wide array of telecommunication services. The ISDN relies on a set of international-standard interfaces that allow users to transmit data and voice, in digital form, over telephone lines.

ISDN is viewed as a critical technology that will change the way we store, process, and receive information. Its growth has accelerated greatly in the last few years and it is likely to become the international standard for data and voice communications. One of the primary reasons for the growing popularity of ISDN is that it is a digital network, whereas today's telephone lines are analog. Analog signals must be converted into digital form before a computer can interpret them. (The human voice, for instance, is an example of an analog signal.)

What are the benefits of a digital network? First, it eliminates the need for a modem to convert analog signals into digital signals and vice versa. Second, ISDN uses the coaxial or fiber-optic cables already used in telephone networks, so it does not require any rewiring. (Of course, new digital telephone equipment is required to replace the existing analog telephone.) Finally, ISDN promotes uniformity and standardization through a set of standard interfaces established by the International Telegraph and Telephone Consultative Committee to promote connectivity, flexibility, and manageability. Although the standards for some of these services are continuing to evolve, many regard ISDN to be at the heart of a global information revolution.

ISDN revolves around five key principles: openness, modularity, communications-based intelligence, network management and control, and integrated products and services.

Openness means that all ISDN products will be standardized, which will allow users to mix and match products from different vendors. Without openness, an organization can be tied to one vendor because only products from that ven-

FIGURE 5-8

A modem converts digital signals from a computer into analog signals that can be carried over telephone lines. At the receiving end, the analog signals are converted into digital signals that a computer can interpret.

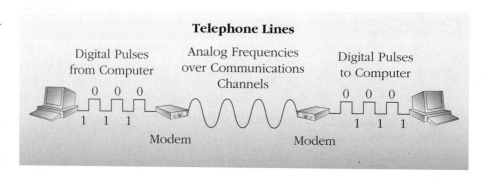

Telephone Lines

Digital Pulses from Computer   Analog Frequencies over Communications Channels   Digital Pulses to Computer

Modem   Modem

dor will work on its network. Standardization also brings order and uniformity to the complex, and often chaotic, task of developing a network.

Modularity allows an organization to upgrade or replace any part, or module, in a network without replacing the entire network. Since the entire network is built as a set of standard modules, organizations can "mix and match" different modules as their needs change.

Communications-based intelligence means that the network has intelligence built into it, providing users with a way to configure their network connections to meet their requirements.

Network management and control is one of the most complex and challenging tasks that IS managers face. Part II of this chapter is devoted to managerial issues of telecommunications.

Integrated products and services allow the use of a wide variety of products and services on the network, such as voice networking, data networking, telemarketing, teleconferencing, crisis management, and electronic order entry.

Northwest, the world's fourth largest airline, has realized huge savings by using ISDN to link its seven reservation centers. The ISDN routes customer calls to the appropriate reservation center based on the time of day, the day of the week, and the volume of calls; if a call is not answered promptly, ISDN can reroute it to another agent or another center. The airline also plans to use ISDN to deliver client account information to the reservation agent in an effort to avoid redundant questions and improve customer service.

However, there are also some drawbacks to ISDN. Experts say that ISDN installation prices which are now in the $150 range must drop to the $40 range if the technology is to attain widespread use and the Federal Communications Commission is developing guidelines to establish a more coherent nationwide pricing structure. Today, for example, users on the East Coast pay per-minute rates for ISDN, while Californians are charged on "rates miles," which clock the geographic distance that the voice or data transmission travels. And even rates within a given region vary considerably. For example, Nynex charges 1 cent a minute in New York but as much as 55 cents a minute in Maine. Finally, although ISDN lines can carry four times the amount of data as a standard phone line, only about 65% of phone switches nationwide are ISDN-capable.[16]

Nontelephone Networks

Local Area Networks (LANs) A **local area network (LAN)** is a network that links a number of independent electronic devices located within a moderate-sized geographic area, usually with a radius of 1 to 10 miles. LANs are used primarily to connect devices within buildings and offices so that knowledge workers can share data, information, messages, software, and even peripherals, such as printers. Hence, a LAN is owned by a single organization.

Devices on the LAN have a **peer-to-peer relationship,** in which all of them have equal status and privileges, as compared to a master-slave relationship, in which a central computer controls all the other devices on the network. LANs use telecommunication media, such as twisted-pair, coaxial cable, and, in recent years, fiber optics and wireless communications.

Physically connecting computing devices to a LAN requires one of three systems: Ethernet, token ring, and AppleTalk, although in recent years wireless LANs are becoming popular (see box on KMart).

BUSINESS REALITIES
KMart Corporation

KMart uses wireless communication to move mission-critical data to and from its main computer. Employees are equipped with wireless data terminals that look like guns. Each "gun" has an alphanumeric keyboard, a small display monitor, a laser bar-code scanner, and a radio unit. The gun is basically a hand-held computer with a pistol grip. The wireless LAN is so powerful that in less than 7 seconds, data make the 100,000-mile round trip from a KMart store to a computer at KMart headquarters in Troy, Michigan, passing through eleven computers and eight networks along the way. An employee equipped with a "gun" can thus get information about a specific item in less than a minute.

In particular, transaction-processing wireless networks that rely on radio-frequency communication to transmit critical data on a real-time basis are revolutionizing the way many businesses process information. In spite of the tremendous potential of radio-frequency (RF) wireless LANs, IS managers are often accused of being slow to embrace this technology.

"RF LANs aren't part of the sexy, high-profile world of corporate information and decision-support technology. Instead they support the down-and-dirty world of operations, commonly the purview of all those manufacturing types."[17]

Ethernet
A popular system that connects computers using coaxial cables. A typical Ethernet network has a maximum speed of 100 megabits per second (Mbps).

Token ring
A frequently used arrangement of connecting computer equipment using twisted-pair cable.

AppleTalk
A networking capability that is built into all Macintosh computers and can be used on twisted-pair wiring, coaxial cable, or fiber-optic cable, although it is most commonly used on twisted-pair.

Baseband
Transmits digital signals directly over the network; can transmit only one signal at a time. It is one of the most common forms of transmission used in LANs. Both token-ring and Ethernet Systems use baseband transmission.

Broadband
Transmits multiple streams of analog signals over the network using frequency division multiplexing. Useful for transmitting large amounts of data over long distances.

An **Ethernet** network is a standard way of connecting computer equipment using coaxial cables. A typical Ethernet network has a maximum speed of 10 Mbps. The new Fast Ethernet will operate at 100 Mbps or more. This system was jointly developed by DEC, Intel, and Xerox.

A **Token-ring network** is another standard way of connecting computer equipment. It uses a special type of twisted-pair cable. Early token ring networks had a maximum speed of 4 Mbps; new ones have a maximum speed of 16 Mbps. This system was developed by IBM.

AppleTalk is a networking system that is built into all Macintosh computers. Though AppleTalk can be used on twisted-pair, coaxial, or fiber-optic cable, it is most commonly used on twisted-pair. AppleTalk is much slower than an Ethernet or token-ring network, with a top speed of 230 Kbps.

Unlike other types of networks, which use common carriers for transmitting data, a LAN uses a private communication system. There are two different ways of transmitting signals on these private communication systems: baseband and broadband. **Baseband** technology transmits *digital* signals directly over the network; it can transmit only one signal at a time. Baseband is the most common form of transmission used in LANs. Token-ring and Ethernet networks both use baseband transmission. **Broadband,** on the other hand, transmits multiple streams of *analog* signals over the network at the same time, using frequency division multiplexing (see Table 5–1 for a more detailed explanation of this term), and hence is suitable for transmitting large amounts of data over long distances. Broadband is usually used to connect separate LANs, such as those at universities and in larger corporations.

There are some differences between a LAN and a PBX. LANs carry only data; PBXs carry both voice and data. Unlike a PBX, a LAN is not part of a telephone system. LANs require wiring; PBXs use the existing wiring of the telephone system.

Advantages of LANs The power and versatility of LANs have made them commonplace in both large and small organizations. LANs that link PCs to mainframes allow users to access, process, and share large volumes of data and resources, without being burdened by the problems and expenses associated with mainframes. LANs often reduce computing costs by allowing users to share resources. For example, it is unnecessary to buy a laser printer for each user when a LAN can be used to link several users to one printer. An organization can store its word processing or spreadsheet package on its LAN so that any user on the network can access the software. Thus a single copy can be accessed by many users. LANs also facilitate organizational communications through the rapid dissemination of files, programs, and messages. For all these reasons, LANs have been instrumental in cutting costs, improving productivity, and enhancing customer service.

The National League for Nursing, a major Washington lobbying organization for health care reform, credits a part of its success to LANs. Hundreds of PCs installed on three LANs in the league's New York headquarters download data from a central mainframe to local PCs, giving members access to information on nursing schools, patient management techniques, and political news related to health care. Applications including membership services, nursing school accreditation, accounting, and research are also available on the LAN. Besides providing members with valuable and timely data, networks are estimated to have saved the league 30% of its annual IS expenditures.

At Kenwood USA Corp., a privately held, $400 million consumer stereo and audio distributor, an average of 100 customer claim forms came in each day. Each form contained up to 32 individual claims, ran 12 pages, and sometimes was even handwritten. In 1990, in an effort to shift to a paperless environment, the company acquired a $350,000 LAN-based image processing system that linked 80 computers, multiple scanners, and optical disks to the company's mainframe computer. The new system scans customer claims and product warranty claims into the computer, and if a match is found, the claim is paid immediately.

Wide Area Networks (WANs)

Wide-area networks (WANs)
Networks that span large geographical areas, sometimes even countries; used for data and voice communications.

A **wide area network (WAN)** is a network that spans wide geographical areas, sometimes even countries, for data and voice communications. The primary difference between a LAN and a WAN is that a WAN covers greater geographical distances than a LAN; also, unlike a LAN, which is usually owned by a single organization, a WAN is owned both by the organization and by a common or special-purpose carrier. It is predicted that data traffic over WANs will grow by 20% in the 1990s, making them an integral part of corporate IS.

There are several ways to set up a WAN. They are direct distance dialing (DDD), wide-area telephone service (WATS) lines, leased lines, and satellites.

Direct distance dialing (DDD)
Network that transmits voice and data.

Direct distance dialing (DDD) is one of the easiest ways to set up a WAN, since it uses the services of the local telephone company and a long distance carrier, such as AT&T, to transmit voice and data. Although DDD is simple and easy to use, long distance data communications can become expensive and are error-prone. Another limitation is that DDD is restricted to sites that are linked by a telephone network, although most business locations in the world do meet this requirement.

Wide area telephone service
Similar to DDD except the organization pays flat monthly fee if the service is used or not.

Wide Area Telephone Service (WATS) is similar to DDD, except that the organization pays a flat monthly fee whether it uses the network or not.

Leased lines
Telephone lines are leased to organizations for its exclusive use in setting up WANs.

Leased lines are another alternative to setting up WANs; telephone lines are leased to an organization for its exclusive use. A leased line is a dedicated line between two specific locations; it tends to be less error-prone than a public telephone line, although it is more expensive.

Satellite communications
Satellites which companies lease or purchase used to transmit data.

Satellite communications, which can also be used in WANs, can be leased or purchased from companies, such as AT&T. Satellites are a good choice for organizations that have many remote locations and moderate data transmission needs. They are a relatively inexpensive way to transmit data.

The U.S. Marine Corps uses WANs to provide On-Line Books, a computerized storage and retrieval system that allows the user to browse through more than 234,000 books from the comfort of his or her home, office, or foxhole! Using a computer and a modem, a marine can request any book from the collection and can receive an electronic copy over the network. The network itself includes mainframes and PCs that are connected by LANs, which in turn are linked to Marine Corps headquarters in Quantico, Virginia, by leased lines and satellites. The Marine Corps also uses a WAN to link about 640 servers, 20,000 microcomputers, 32 minicomputers, and 33 mainframes in the U.S., Europe, Japan, the Philippines, Korea, and Saudi Arabia. The network connects bases and battlefields all over the world and helps the Marine Corps manage its logistics, manpower planning, training, and intelligence activities. The network has proven indispensable in the fast deployment of information, equipment, and personnel.

Many organizations and institutions, such as the Center for Disease Control, rely on networks to meet their communication needs. The center, which monitors the health status of citizens around the world, gathers massive amounts of data on the health of Americans and literally monitors the health of the world, such as famine in South Africa, cholera in South America, or AIDS in the United States. Over the last several years, the CDCs 7,000 staff members have become increasingly dependent on a WAN to access and analyze large volumes of scientific data residing on different computers around the globe and to send and receive more than 10 million electronic messages a year.[18]

A major university in Madison, New Jersey, under a $4.5 million computer initiative, has provided each of its 400 staff members and 2,100 graduate and undergraduate students with a PC, a printer, and basic software. (Individual computer equipment was an essential component of the project). Information-sharing was provided by a network with voice, data, and video capabilities. One year and $3.2 million later, students, faculty, and administrators could all communicate through extensive E-mail and voice mail applications. Every PC is linked to the library; in addition, users have access to a variety of off-campus networks, databases, and library services.

Advantages of WANs   WANs have many of the same advantages as LANs, which we will not repeat here. Clearly, one advantage of WANs over LANs is that they can link sites that are farther apart.

Disadvantages of WANs   Although WANs have many significant benefits, they also pose some challenges. In particular, managing WANs is a very difficult task; this is why network administrators are paid huge salaries and are in short supply. One IS manager writer wryly commented, "When you thought your job couldn't get any harder, you suddenly inherit a wide area network. Your first inclination is to run. Your second is to sign up for primal scream therapy. After the panic subsides, you realize what you already knew: You can't escape.[19]

Since no two WANs are the same, there are few guarantees that a network environment will function smoothly. Further, when things go wrong, it is difficult to identify the source of the problem, because so many elements come together in so many different ways to make the network operational. Adding to the challenge is the onslaught of a wide and growing variety of network products from vendors and changing services from carriers.

Metropolitan Area Networks (MANs)

Metropolitan area networks (MANs) are high-bandwidth WANs that link electronic devices distributed over a metropolitan area. They are used for LAN-to-LAN connections, high-speed data transmission, backup network facilities, full-motion video, and image transmission.

Value-Added Networks

Value-added networks (VANs) are public data networks that add value to the basic communication services provided by common carriers by offering specialized services, such as access to commercial databases and software, correction of transmission errors, establishing compatibility between previously incompatible computers and terminals, E-mail, and videoconferencing. A subscriber to a VAN service pays a monthly fee depending on its level of use; VANs present an attractive alternative for companies that want to receive the benefits of telecommunications without investing large amounts of capital in hardware.

Network Topologies

Topology, put simply, is the geometric configuration of devices on a network. There are three popular network topologies: bus topology, ring topology, and star topology.

Bus Topology

Bus topology is the connection of all computers on the network through a single circuit to a central channel, or communication bus. Signals that are transmitted over the channel are called messages. Each message is transmitted to all the computers on the network, although only the targeted device will respond to the message. Each device has an address that is used by other devices to send messages to it.

The primary advantage of bus topology is that it is easy to add devices to the network or remove them without affecting network performance. Another advantage is that if one of the devices on the network fails, the network is not affected, since the bus topology does not rely on a central host computer. The disadvantage, however, is that the performance of the network decreases as the number of messages increases, since each node has to check every message whether or not the message is addressed to it.

Ring Topology

Ring topology arranges the devices on the network in a circular array. Instead of relying on a host computer, the ring network transmits a message to all the

---

Metropolitan area networks (MANs)
High-bandwidth WANs that link electronic devices distributed over a metropolitan area and are used for LAN-to-LAN connections, high-speed data transmission, backup network facilities, full-motion video, and image transmission.

Value-added networks (VANs)
Public data networks that add value to basic communication services provided by common carriers by providing additional services, such as access to commercial databases and software, correction of transmission errors, e-mail, and videoconferencing.

Topology
The physical configuration of devices on a network. There are three popular network topologies: bus, ring, and star.

Bus topology
All computers on the network are connected through a single circuit to a central channel, or communication bus; each message is transmitted to all computers on the network, although only the targeted device will respond to the message.

Ring topology
An arrangement whereby networked computers are arranged in a ring. The ring network transmits a message to all the nodes between the sending node and the receiving node.

nodes between the sending node and the receiving node. Each computer can communicate directly with any other computer on the network by specifying the address of the device; the processing and control functions are distributed among all devices on the network. If a node fails, the message is rerouted around it.

Star Topology

With **star topology,** one of the oldest network topologies, a central host computer receives messages and forwards them to various computers on the network. For one node to communicate with another node on the network, the central controller establishes a circuit, or dedicated path, between the two. The most common use of star topology is in PBXs: the PBX is the central controller and the telephones are the nodes.

Star topology is useful in environments in which some tasks are centralized and others are decentralized, so many business applications work well with star topology. An advantage of star topology is that it can be readily expanded by adding nodes to the host computer. However, if the host computer fails, the entire network comes to a standstill. Also, if the distance between the nodes and the central computer is very large, the cost of sending a message over the network increases significantly. Figure 5–9 shows the three topologies.

Network Architecture

A network—a LAN, WAN, or VAN—supports a large number of very different devices, such as servers, workstations, terminals, printers, fax machines, and modems. The ability to coordinate all these devices gives networks great flexibility and power.

A **network architecture** is a set of standards, or protocols, for telecommunication hardware and software. A network architecture is intended to maximize modularity, user-friendliness, reliability, and ease of network maintenance. The network architecture must establish standards for all its elements: the hardware, the software, and the user interface.

What are protocols? In international relations, protocols are guidelines for behavior and communications between nations. Similarly, in telecommunications, **protocols** are rules and formats that are established to ensure efficient and error-free electronic communication. Protocols range from very simple rules that show how an electric connection should be established between two networks to very complex rules that establish international guidelines for the exchange of ideas, programs, and messages.

A protocol has three major components: a set of characters that mean the same thing both to the sender and to the receiver, a set of rules for timing and sequencing messages, and a set of methods for detecting and correcting errors. Hence the primary functions of protocols are to accurately identify each device in the communication path, to ensure that each message is transmitted accurately to the correct destination, and to detect and correct errors as they occur. Some popular protocols are TCP/IP (Transmission Control Protocol/Internet Protocol), Systems Network Architecture (SNA), System Application Architecture (SAA), XMODEM, YMODEM, and Kermit.

The simple network management protocol (SNMP) is a popular network architecture. For example, a network manager can use SNMP to get statistics about

Star topology
An arrangement whereby a central host computer receives messages from computers on the network and passes them to others on the same network. The most common example of star topology is the PBX.

Network architecture
A set of standards, or protocols, for telecommunication hardware and software.

Protocols
Rules and formats that ensure efficient and error-free electronic communication.

The three popular network topologies: bus, ring, and star.

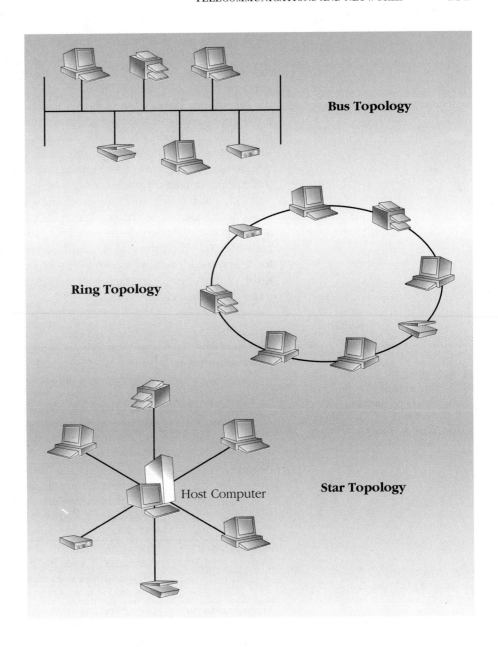

Bus Topology

Ring Topology

Host Computer

Star Topology

the various devices and applications that are on the network. Using SNMP management, a manager can disable a network component that is malfunctioning so that the rest of the network can continue to operate smoothly.

Open Systems Interconnection (OSI)

Open systems interconnection (OSI)
Network architecture that uses a seven-layered functional approach.

One of the most widely used network architectures is the **open systems interconnection** (OSI), developed by the International Standards Organization (ISO). The OSI is popular because it uses a seven-layered functional approach to achieve the primary goals of network architecture: modularity, simplicity, flexibility, and openness. The various tasks associated with network communication are distributed among the seven functional layers; each layer is responsible for a set of tasks and is guided by a set of protocols. The OSI model is still evolving, and many leading computer manufacturers have expressed their commitment to it.

The seven layers of the OSI model, starting with the topmost layer, are the application layer, the presentation layer, the session layer, the transport layer, the network layer, the data link layer, and the physical layer. Table 5–4 identifies the seven layers of an OSI model and the functions of each. An understanding of the OSI model (or of any other popular network architecture) is fundamental to understanding telecommunications.

One year after launching a global effort to consolidate more than 100 telecommunications networks, Citicorp has standardized its networking platforms and protocols. Citicorp developed a single global backbone for all its company networks, based on the OSI standard, allowing the bank's products and services to be accessed from any location on the network, anywhere in the world.[20] One result of this effort is an impressive $60-million cost reduction, some $10 million more than originally estimated.

TABLE 5–4
The OSI model, one of the most popular network architectures, is made up of seven functional layers, described here.

Application Layer	An end-to-end protocol, in the sense that a direct link is established between the sending device and the receiving device. Facilitates the use of network application programs, such as E-mail. By adhering to a set of protocols (embedded in the software), users can communicate with one another, regardless of the terminal or the hardware platform on which the application resides.
Presentation Layer	Ensures the smooth transmission of information. It receives the input from the sending device, attaches a header to it, and sends the information to the session layer. Any decryption (opposite of encryption) is also done in this layer. This layer uses an end-to-end protocol.
Session Layer	Primary responsibility is to establish or terminate links between computers. If a file has to be transferred between two computers, the session layer ensures smooth transmission. This layer uses an end-to-end protocol.
Transport Layer	Uses an end-to-end protocol to ensure the smooth transfer of data over the entire transmission path, from the sending device to the receiving device. It receives data from the session layer, performs the necessary services, such as multiplexing, and passes the data to the network layer.
Network Layer	Receives the data from the transport layer and adds a header that identifies the data path. The data, along with the path that they should take, become the data frame that is handed over to the data link layer.
Data Link Layer	Receives data, in the form of frames from the network layer. Puts boundaries around the data frames, sends them to the physical layer, and acknowledges receipt of data.
Physical Layer	Composed of hardware to effect actual connection between hardware components.

Part II: Management Implications of Telecommunications

So far, in this chapter, we have looked at the technical foundations of telecommunications. In this section, we look at the management implications of telecommunications and analyze the way it has completely revolutionized the way companies all over the world do business. It is very difficult to exaggerate the impact and implications of telecommunications on our personal and professional lives. In fact, the claims made for this technology in the literature often seem understated.

Many firms—even entire industries—have been altered by it; new businesses have evolved, while some traditional business habits have simply died. Business' dependence on electronic communications is on the rise because the technology has become as easy as dropping a letter into a mailbox. Businesses no longer have to rely only on television or other news media to sell their products and services; they can now use telecommunications to go into the homes of many American families and directly solicit their business. In fact, businesses that do not actively participate in this revolution will be left behind by a journey that is bound to be exciting and challenging.

However, with power come problems and the challenges posed by this technology are almost as large and significant as the technology itself. In the areas of commerce spurred by telecommunications, appropriate laws and regulations are only now evolving; every related case that comes before a court of law is therefore groundbreaking in some sense. This technology is raising issues of privacy, freedom of speech, and other fundamental rights and complex and intricate problems in this area must be resolved in order to tap into the full potential of this technology.

In this section, we look at three primary areas of telecommunications that have greatly influenced businesses: challenges in managing networks, the Internet and electronic commerce, and electronic data interchange (EDI).

Challenges in Managing Networks

One of the most critical and challenging issues confronting network administrators is finding a way to efficiently manage the organization's networks and telecommunication systems. In a survey conducted by Deloitte & Touche, telecommunication managers at 800 North American organizations called network management *the* most important technical issue they face.[21] In fact, many network managers feel that it is much easier to build a network than to manage one, and the more critical the network is to the smooth operation of the organization, the greater is the challenge of managing it. As distributed systems become the norm and security violations become more commonplace, network management becomes even more critical, particularly because in spite of all their technological sophistication, telecommunication environments are fragile.

One of the biggest difficulties of managing a network is the lack of tools for centralized and automated network management, which would allow administrators to collect information about the performance of their networks and to prevent problems before they occur. In the absence of such tools, network administrators often spend considerable time putting out fires rather than delivering high-quality network services and ensuring the full utilization of the network.

Why is network management so critical for the organization? Because network management often has a direct and significant impact on profits, productivity, customer satisfaction, and overall decision making. Network failures can cause losses of millions of dollars; in extreme cases, they can result in bankruptcy. Revenue losses resulting from network problems averaged approximately $3.8 million per company in 1993, compared to $650,000 in 1989, according to a survey of 106 LAN managers by Infonetics, Inc.[22]

Organizations that are successful in network management seem to adhere to certain principles. First, successful organizations appear to have a long-range focus on developing open, seamless, and integrated systems—systems that are not dependent on one vendor, but instead can take a "plug-and-play" approach. As an organization's network expands, an open system allows the firm to link its more remote sites into the network without in any way sacrificing accuracy, reliability, or control.

Second, successful organizations recognize that networks are vital to productivity, to profits, and sometimes even to survival. They continue to invest in the maintenance of the network, and have clear and well-understood policies on user policies and procedures. Such companies often encourage the use of networks to further the achievement of their goals. Network managers in such companies are often encouraged to take a proactive approach to meet changing information needs and to seek network solutions by combining the services of both public and private networks.

Third, top managers in these organizations have a good understanding of the power of telecommunications and its strategic role in achieving overall organization goals. Though they do not participate in the technical decisions, they play a very active role in determining how networks will be used in the organization. The CEO and the CIO work hand-in-hand so that network investments are closely aligned with business goals.

Finally, well-managed networks are also secure networks. In recent years, network security has become one of the top concerns for IS managers and CEOs around the world. (Chapter 16 covers computer security.)

In summary, good network management must:

- establish lines of communication among different network administrators
- develop standards throughout the organization for the use of network resources and applications
- establish corporate security policies that ensure that critical or proprietary data are well protected; ensure that network configuration is carefully documented, distributed to all network managers, and updated frequently
- establish backup procedures for all corporate data and strictly enforce backup policies
- eliminate or at least reduce redundancies in company databases.[23]

Global Networks Though managing domestic networks is difficult, managing global networks is many times more difficult, not simply because of their size and technical complexity, but also because a number of uncontrollable factors, such as poor infrastructure, monopolistic rules and regulations, and a different set of business ethics, come into play.

Many companies operating in global markets fully realize the importance of establishing global networks. A local presence in the countries where they operate is fundamental to their success; further, the best way to acquire and coordinate accurate and timely information from business units in different countries is through global networks.

Toyota (see box) relies on its global networks to get information from its manufacturing and research facilities all over the world. As with domestic networks, global networks can be public or private.

Setting up global networks is an enormous technical and social challenge for many companies. First, telecommunication agencies in other countries, particularly developing countries, tends to be governed by monopolistic and bureaucratic systems. A phone connection that takes a day or so in the U.S. may take months, even years, in another country, and even then it may not work properly 24 hours a day. For U.S. managers who are used to an excellent infrastructure, including reliable roads, telephones, and power, working in some countries can be a daunting task. Second, some countries have very strict guidelines as to what can be transmitted over communication channels, and in some cases the information is even monitored by government agencies. Says one global network administrator, "Our business is handicapped by telecommunications policy, not by technical problems. At times, you just shake your head and disbelieve what you've heard." For reasons such as these, global networks may not be utilized to the fullest extent. Finally, many U.S. managers are discovering first hand that the rest of the world is not as technologically advanced as the U.S. and Europe, so that technological expansion in a foreign country may be severely limited. Thus,

---

A GLOBAL PERSPECTIVE
Toyota

The most successful automobile exporter in Japan, Toyota, firmly believes that information systems are critical to the achievement of ambitious quality and service goals. It is no wonder that the company gets rave reviews from automobile and business quality experts around the world. "Toyota, operationally, is the most amazing thing on the planet," says James Womack, former research director of MIT's International Motor Vehicle Program and lead author of *The Machine That Changed the World.* An unusual feature of Toyota is that although the company fully embraces technology, workers at Toyota's factories and at its suppliers' facilities still rely on index cards, called *kanbans,* and other simple tools to make important decisions affecting the production process.

Since increasing global pressure from Japan's trading partners and a strong yen have inflated Toyota's costs, it no longer manufactures cars exclusively in Japan. Today, the company has become global in the true sense of the term. It no longer relies only on local Japanese suppliers, but also has suppliers and manufacturing facilities in America and Europe; the company conducts research and development in California and Belgium, and even imports American-made Camrys into Japan.

With such a global presence, Toyota knows that global networks are vital to its survival and uses the technology to gather worldwide sales data, forecast production requirements, and transmit purchase orders and production schedules to its suppliers all over the world. It also uses EDI (discussed at the end of this chapter) to supplement the traditional *kanbans* and to communicate with its distant suppliers.

Currently, its network includes 6-Mbps to 12-Mbps links among the company's three main offices, Toyota City, Tokyo, and Nagoya, as well as 64-Kbps to 6-Mbps connections to its major suppliers, factories, and sales offices throughout Japan. AT&T provides data links between Toyota's U.S. sales organization and its Tokyo office. Future plans include connecting U.S. suppliers to the network and upgrading it to include multimedia capabilities, such as multimedia catalog car sales. The automaker is also planning to sell cars to Asian consumers through the Internet.[24]

a manager may be aware of a more powerful tool or technology, but may be compelled to choose a less attractive alternative.

In spite of these many challenges, companies are building global networks. They are coming up with creative solutions, such as forming alliances with telecommunication carriers in different countries or building private networks. They are aware that in the coming years, as the world becomes a smaller place and electronic commerce becomes commonplace, global networks will be a necessity.

The Internet

". . I think the Internet is one of the rare, if not unique, instances where 'hype' is accompanied by understatement, not overstatement. I estimate that the Net (or whatever it is called) will have 1 billion users by the year 2000. I don't think we know what has hit us."
Nicholas Negroponte, Director, MIT Media Lab.

If the Internet were a stock it would be considered a market phenomenon, with sustained doubling growth and no apparent end in sight to the upward spiral. Recent Internet numbers are stunning. Between January 1993 and January 1994 alone, the number of nodes grew from 1,313,00 to 2,217,000, an impressive 69% increase. Over 70 countries have full Internet connectivity and about 150 have at least E-mail services.[25]

Internet
Also called the Net. Long distance network that links computers.

No discussion of telecommunications would be complete without discussing the **Internet,** referred to by its millions of users as the Net. The Net evolved from ARPANET, a research network created and subsidized in the 1960s by the Defense Department and the National Science Foundation (NSF) to link research institutions and government agencies around the world to exchange information on a wide range of topics. Although the original ARPANET no longer exists, its design and architecture laid the foundations for the Internet.

The Net, one of the oldest long distance networks in the country, is a network of networks. It links approximately 1.5 million computers, attached to more than 13,000 networks, in 100 or more countries.

Businesses use the Net for a number of tasks, such as sharing files, sending E-mail, and selling goods and services. Fewer than 1% of major companies today are *not* attached to the Internet.[26] In fact, the Internet has become such an integral part of the corporate landscape that it is generating a number of entrepreneurial opportunities and highly specialized jobs: there are Internet explorers, security experts, technicians, librarians, trainers, and other service providers. In fact, the Internet is becoming so common that many employers expect their new hires to have a working knowledge of it.

Think of the Internet as a huge repository of information on almost every topic imaginable. People all over the world can search the net for information, add new information, and exchange views on different topics. The Internet is an electronic web that connects people and businesses that have access to networks and allows them to send and receive E-mail and to participate in a number of other activities, around the clock. In fact, the Internet is so huge, with such a wide variety of features, that there are few, if any, experts in the world who know everything about it.

Thus in spite of its enormous power and potential, no one really owns the Internet, although some segments of it may have their own funding and guidelines.

TABLE 5–5
Life on the Information
Superhighway

Sept. 1, 1969:   The first connections are made in the construction of ARPANET, the U.S. Advanced Research Projects Agency's computing network.

October 1972:   The first public demonstration of ARPANET is given at a conference in Washington, D.C.

October 1984:   The Computer Fraud and Abuse Act becomes law, making unauthorized access to computers used by the federal government or for interstate and international commerce a felony.

1987:   The National Science Foundation creates the backbone of the National Research and Education Network. The Internet as we know it is born.

Feb. 11, 1991:   The term *information superhighway* first appears in the popular media as the Bush administration approves Senator Al Gore's idea of developing a high-speed national computer network.

January 1992:   Senator Gore's High Performance Computing Act is signed into law. It will provide $3 billion, with $1 billion in new funding over a 5-year period, to develop a high-speed computer network and support more R&D in high-performance computing.

Dec 16, 1993:   Yes, Virginia, there really is a Santa Claus. Delphi Internet Services offers E-mail service to Santa at the North Pole. Santa's box gets 800 messages in 4 days.

January 1994:   MCI announces its plan to spend $20 billion over a 6-year period to construct an international information highway.

July 21, 1994:   McDonald's runs the first online ad in a 6-week campaign on America Online.

October 1994:   The White House "home page" debuts on the Internet. An estimated 1,300 people per hour take multimedia tours of the nation's capital. The biggest draw: sound bytes of the Clintons' cat, Socks, meowing online.

November 1994: CommerceNet, a consortium of companies starting to do business on the Internet, receives the Pacific Bell California Research and Education Network (CalREN) Award, a $520,000 grant to facilitate Internet connectivity and electronic commerce.

Sources: Business Week, The New York Times, The Wall Street Journal, Time, Fortune, CNN Transcripts, *The Internet For New Users* by Daniel P. Dern, *Electronic Messaging News, Computerworld,* and the White House media office.

The primary workings of the Internet are funded by the National Science Foundation (NSF); the Internet Engineering Task Force (IETF), a committee of scientists and experts, provides technical supervision, standards, and guidelines for the Net. Any network (remember, the Internet is simply a network of networks) connected to the Internet must abide by the standards established by the Internet Architecture Board (IAB).

In recent years, the term **information superhighway** has been used frequently in the media and in the computer literature. Although there is no precise or universally acceptable definition of the information superhighway, it has three primary characteristics:

Information superhighway
A network of networks that is fully scalable, with no central controlling entity, and does not determine the user's profile.

*   It has no central controlling entity.
*   It is fully capable of handling an increase in the number of users and an increase in the volume of traffic. This is often referred to as the *scalability* of the technology.
*   It does not determine the profile of the user. The user can be a machine, an individual, or any business entity.[27]

Since the Internet has all the above three characteristics, it can be viewed as an excellent model of the information superhighway.

In spite of its many advantages, one of the most-cited disadvantages of the Internet is its inadequate security, because much of the information available over the Net can easily be accessed by dishonest people. The Net was originally used by universities and large corporations to exchange information; "hackers" were far less numerous. Today, however, with the commercialization of the Net, more and more businesses are entering cyberspace—and in their wake come problems of data misuse or theft. (Internet security is addressed in detail in Chapter 16, Computer Security.)

Another problem is that many employees are "surfing the net" for fun rather than for business purposes. Many companies have established Internet access policies specifying that employees must make *productive* use of the Internet, not waste the time and resources of the organization playing computer games, writing to friends, or accessing information on their favorite topics. Companies are establishing written policies on privacy concerns that employees may have when they realize that they are being monitored by the organization.

Should employees be allowed to surf the Net in search of creative ideas or should they be limited to using the Net strictly for business purposes? We discuss these and other related ethical questions at the end of this chapter.

Linking to the Internet In recent years the Internet has undergone explosive growth, primarily because of the exponential growth in PCs, both at work and in the home. Today, 70% of PC sales are targeted at the home market. Andy Grove, CEO of Intel (which makes Pentium and other chips for the PC market), points out that every 2 years the U.S. makes as many PCs as have existed in all preceding years. Before the spread of PCs, the Internet could be accessed only if an

---

BUSINESS REALITIES
The State of Utah

The State of Utah's computer bulletin board has been swamped with calls ever since it was set up in May 1995. The bulletin board system (BBS) had 1,000 calls in its first day of operation and has received an average of 300 calls per day since then, resulting in a high telephone bill for the state's toll-free 800 number. "What we've introduced is a way to give citizens faster access to current information about the state, and it's much easier for the public to voice their concerns," explained Utah Gov. Michael O. Leavitt.

The BBS allows citizens to access information posted by various state agencies, including state job openings, consumer tips, press releases, air-quality reports, speeches, regulations and the state budget. The BBS links all state agencies and allows them to freely exchange information so that each agency knows what the other is doing.

Clark Development's PCBoard BBS software is at the heart of the system, which acts as a gateway to the Internet. This allows BBS to send and receive Internet E-mail at no cost. That is controversial, however, because it could be viewed as unfair competition with for-profit Internet access providers. Therefore, the state may at some point decide to limit the scope of its Internet traffic to government destinations only.

The Utah Public Access BBS is actually the first tier in the state's information infrastructure. The second tier is UtahNet, a WAN that allows direct log-in so that state employees don't need a modem. The futuristic third tier, called Smart Utah, will let businesses conduct electronic commerce, access state databases, and handle regulatory affairs over a state information highway.[28]

organization was a site or node on the Net. Today, one can access the Internet through a company's connection or through commercial online services (discussed below) or simply from a home PC. Further, there are a number of PC-based interfaces that facilitate interaction with the Net. For example, Cyberdog, a Macintosh-based tool, allows users to directly access the Internet even without quitting an application, such as word processing. It also allows them to link and update their documents with information from the Internet.[29] Such user-friendly interfaces are another reason for the increased usage of the Internet.

Today, there are a number of commercial online service providers, such as CompuServe, Prodigy, and America Online. It is estimated that there are approximately 6 million users of commercial online services; this number is expected to grow to more than 13 million by 1998. CompuServe claims to have 2 million subscribers, mostly businessmen; Prodigy claims 2 million, including more women and children than CompuServe; America Online claims 1 million subscribers—a younger, more consumer-oriented crowd.[30] (Table 5–6 provides a listing of these online services and their contact numbers.)

Connection to the Internet opens the door to a vast world of information and communications that resides in files on host computers, including any computer that follows the TCP/IP protocol. (A protocol, as we stated earlier, is a set of rules and standards that ensures the compatibility of different network equipment and components.) Finding a file on the Internet is similar to finding the location of an individual in a city: the user needs the file's address. Addresses are the key to receiving and sending information on the Internet. All individual Internet addresses follow the same two-element pattern: the person's userID, followed by an @, followed by the name of the person's *host computer* (including that of the domain in which it resides). An Internet service provider gives addresses to individuals and organizations that register with it. Let us look closely at the elements of an Internet address.

The address uniquely identifies the individual or the organization that the user is trying to reach. For an individual, the name is made up of two parts separated by the character @. For example, if Joe Green is accessing the Net from his home, using his American Online (AOL) account, his Internet address might be joe@aol.com. "aol" identifies the host computer or network; ".com" indicates the domain in which AOL resides. (".com" stands for commercial sites, ".edu" is for educational institutions, ".mil" is for military ones, and so on.) If Joe Green is connecting to the Internet from, say, a machine in the computer science department at New Mexico State University, his address might be jgreen@cs.NMSU.edu. jgreen is his *userID;* cs.NMSU.edu, which identifies the host computer, is known as the *host name.*

TABLE 5–6
Online Services

Provider	Number of Subscribers	Information Number
America Online (AOL)	1 million	(800) 827–6364
Prodigy	2 million	(800) 776–3449
CompuServe	2 million	(800) 848–8199
E-World	1 million	(800) 775–4556

Source: Booker, Ellis, "Get Wired," *Computerworld,* December 26/January 2, 1995, p. 30.

Thus, all Internet addresses have the following format or some slight variation thereof:

userid@name-of-the-computer.name of division/department.name of the institution/organization.type of institution or organization (Note that there are no spaces between the different elements in an Internet address.)

For example, let us take the Internet address

hford@hollywood.fanclub.columbia.com

The userid is *hford* (Harrison Ford); the name of the computer which receives the mail is *hollywood* which is part of the *fanclub* (department) at *Columbia Pictures* (organization), a commercial entity.

Some of the important and popular tools on the Net are discussed below. These include

* Information retrieval tools (ftp and Gopher)
* Communication tools (E-mail, telnet, Usenet)
* Multimedia information tools (World Wide Web)
* Information search tools (WAIS, Archie, Veronica)

Each of these is briefly discussed below.

Information Retrieval Tools

ftp
File transfer protocol allows users to send or receive files from a remote computer.

ftp **File transfer protocol** (*ftp*), which was one of the first tools on the Internet, allows users to move files, such as text, graphics, sound, and so on, from one computer to another. It is a command that activates a type of client-server relationship (client-server systems are discussed in Chapter 7). *Ftp* works as follows: The user first uses the software on his or her machine (or service provider), called the client, to gain access to the remote machine, called the server. The user's client program communicates with a program on the remote computer, to either upload, or send, files to the remote computer or download (receive) certain requested files from it.

Another popular way to retrieve files is by using what is called an *anonymous ftp server*. In this case, the user logs on to the server using the special user ID *anonymous*. If the server then asks for a pass-word, the user types in his or her user ID. Freeware and shareware—programs that are available at no cost on the Net—can be obtained through anonymous *ftp* servers. Although it is easy to retrieve the information once the site is located, sometimes it is difficult to locate an *ftp* site or identify the files available on that site.

Gopher
A menu-based interface that provides access to information residing on Gopher sites.

Gopher The second type of information retrieval tool available on the Internet is **Gopher,** a menu-based interface that provides easy access to information residing on special servers, called Gopher sites. Although Gopher performs primarily the same tasks as the *ftp* command, its interface is much more user-friendly and it provides additional functions, such as links to other Internet services. By selecting an item on the Gopher menu, users can move, retrieve, or display files from remote sites. The menu also allows users to move from one Gopher site to another, where each site provides different information. The entire Gopherspace (which refers to the interconnected Gopher servers) can be easily expanded by adding more servers.

A GLOBAL PERSPECTIVE
Internet Responds to Earthquake in Japan

Minutes after a devastating earthquake hit the Kobe and Kansai region of Japan, Internet activist Kenji Rikitake in Osaka sent E-mail to friends and associates worldwide. "I don't think you can send food or water to Kobe just now, but you can help people in Kobe by sending support to Japan Red Cross," Rikitake wrote in another E-mail message, sent 19 hours after the quake. Rikitake's notes went straight to Tony Rutkowski, executive director of the Internet Society in Reston, Virginia, who forwarded them to many other users. About 10% of the group's 4,500 members are in Japan, and the city of Kobe—the epicenter of the deadly quake—had hosted the Internet Society's first INET conference in 1992, according to Rutkowski.

In addition to radio and television news, computer users worldwide received a steady flow of reports about the earthquake over the Internet. Within a week, dozens of online informational sites were created in Japan. A number of World Wide Web pages in Japan offered up-to-the-minute news and photographs of the disaster, which claimed more than 4,000 lives.[31]

Communication Tools   Communication tools facilitate written communications and in this section we discuss three types of communication tools: E-mail, Telnet and Usenet.

E-mail
Source used to send messages or files electronically.

E-mail   **E-mail,** which refers to sending messages or files electronically, was one of the first Internet tools. (A detailed discussion of E-mail is provided in Chapter 10, Office Automation.) (see box on earthquake in Japan).

Telnet
A command that connects the user to a remote machine located anywhere on the Internet. This allows the user to type commands to the remote machine, such as activating a program.

Telnet   **Telnet** is a command that connects the user to a remote machine which may be located anywhere on the Internet and the user can then type commands to the remote machine, for example to change directories in search of certain files. While the *ftp* only allows users to move or transfer files, the services that *Telnet* provides depend on the services provided by the host machine, which may include much more than simple file transfers. For example, some servers are dedicated to the playing of board games, such as chess or go.

Usenet
Provides users with electronic discussion groups or forums for gathering information on a wide variety of topics.

Usenet   The **Usenet** is a network that provides users with discussion groups, or forums. A user posts an article to a chosen newsgroup on the Usenet, where each newsgroup is devoted to a particular topic such as politics, the environment, gun control, surfing, and so on. The article is routed only to those sites that have expressed an interest in receiving information on the topic.

Many find the Usenet to be helpful for gathering information on a variety of topics. For example, vendors monitor the technical forums on the Usenet closely to answer technical questions that customers may have and to stomp out any misinformation or rumors about their company or its products. For instance, the calculation error in Intel Corp.'s Pentium microprocessor was first discussed on an Internet Usenet newsgroup. Another popular application on Usenet is downloading new or upgraded software from vendors and obtaining quotes for products and services. IS managers are also tapping into the Usenet to search for potential employees. One IS manager posts particularly thorny technical problems on the

Usenet in the relevant discussion groups and then makes an offer to individuals who gave some of the best replies.[32] (see box on state of Utah on page 188).

Multimedia Information Tools

World Wide Web (WWW)

A hyper-text based Internet tool that allows users to display documents stored on any server on the Internet.

World Wide Web   The **World Wide Web (WWW)** is one of the newest and most popular hypertext-based Internet tool. It allows users to access and display documents and graphics stored on any server on the Internet. In 1989, Tim Berners-Lee, a computer scientist at the CERN particle physics lab in Switzerland, designed WWW as a tool to help an international group of physicists exchange findings and information related to their research. It became popular only in late 1993, when WWW software was delivered for desktops that used popular operating systems, such as Windows, allowing users easy and friendly access to the Internet. Some WWW terms are shown in Table 5–7.

There are many interfaces to the WWW, such as Mosaic, a GUI-based hypertext browser, and Netscape, that allows users to easily navigate the Internet and access its many services. These easy-to-use interfaces are playing an important role in popularizing the Internet, and many companies that once shied away from the Net are now making use of these interfaces to create their own Web pages (discussed below). According to Michael J. Walsh, president of Internet Info., in Falls Church, Virginia, the number of companies with *.com* addresses (which indicate a commercial site) is expected to double within the next year, primarily because it is now easy to use the Internet and gain 24-hour access to customers all over the world.

Home page   The World Wide Web has also spawned new services, known as service providers, that provide a multitude of services on the Web. For example,

◆ **T A B L E 5 – 7**
World Wide Web Terms

CGI	Common gateway interface. A specification for a communication interface between external systems and a Web server.
HTML	Hyper-Text Markup Language. A text formatting language used to create Web pages.
HTTP	Hyper-Text Transport Protocol. The communications protocol between a Web server and a client.
Image Map	A text file that defines regions using graphics files (usually GIF files) that users can click on to navigate.
MIME	Multipurpose Internet Mail Extensions. An Internet standard for sending and receiving multimedia E-mail.
Server-Side	A Web server feature that lets HTML pages be parsed "on the fly," filling in parts of the page with information from external files.
S-HTTP	Secure Hyper-Text Transport Protocol. An extension of HTTP that provides communication and transaction security for Web clients and servers.
SSL	Secure socket layer. A transport mechanism developed by Netscape Communication for transmitting secure data over a network.
URL	Uniform resource locator. An address that specifies the location of a Web page.

Home page
An electronic description of an individual, institution, or organization. Home pages can be accessed through the Internet.

a Web service provider can help a company establish a **home page** on the Net, an electronic description of the company and its products and services, similar to a catalog or a brochure. Just as catalogs should be attractive and grab the interest of customers, the home page should also be attractive and encourage the user to further explore the company and its products. It can cost from $300 to $10,000 per page of information; for interactive home pages (where the user and the system can interact), the cost per page can be higher.[33]

Basic requirements to set up a home page include an Integrated Services Digital Network (ISDN) line, software to generate Hypertext Markup Language (HTML), which is the graphical interface to the Internet, and a PC or Unix server that has between 16M bytes and 32M bytes of RAM and runs at 100 Mhz or more.

Many companies are setting up home pages to attract new customers. For example, GE Plastics found that as soon as it set up a Web page, it was getting approximately 12,000 potential inquires each month about its products. Before the page was set up, it took nearly 3 days to respond to customer queries; now customers can get information within a few minutes. The company firmly believes that setting up a Web page has given it a competitive advantage. Further, the cost of setting up a Web page was much lower than that of printing pamphlets and mailing catalogs to customers. The advantages of a Web page are so great that, as one spokesperson said, "You simply can't lose. There is nothing equivalent [to the Net]."

Security APL is an example of another company that relies on the Internet to enhance internal and external communications (see box).

In 1995, when statewide elections were held in California, tens of thousands of voters accessed a World Wide Web server that contained poll reports culled every five minutes from the state's Election Web Server. The California Voter Foundation, a nonprofit organization in Sacramento, launched the California Online Voter Guide, a Gopher site that contains biographies, position papers, press releases and E-mail addresses of candidates running for statewide office. Clinton's 1992 presidential campaign was notable for making his E-mail address public, and the White House recently established its own World-Wide Web Home Page (try whitehouse.gov).[34]

BUSINESS REALITIES
Security APL

Every day, an IBM RS/6000 server at Security APL, Inc., in Chicago processes a half million inquiries from across the worldwide Internet, spitting out stock quotes that are under 15 minutes old. The Quote Server, as it is called, is one of the most popular landing sites on the Internet (www.secapl.com/cgi-bin/qs).

Security AP has used the power of the Internet to leverage new and existing businesses, more than any other financial services company. It has also launched a fee-based service called Portfolio Accounting World-Wide, or PAWWS, that offers a comprehensive and growing portfolio management and accounting system to customers who have access to the Internet. The portfolio service includes automated links to Securities and Exchange Commission (SEC) archives, corporate home pages, news and on-line stock trading services, such as the Net Investor.

Use of the Internet is widespread throughout the company. In fact, each of the firm's 90 employees, who work in offices in Chicago, Jersey City, N.J., Boston and San Diego, maintain their own hypertext home pages which are accessible to company employees and external clients.[35]

TABLE 5-8
Highway Rules: A Summary of Bell Atlantic's Customer Privacy Policy.

1. Collect only the consumer information that is necessary for current and add-on services.
2. Disclose personal information only for limited purposes, such as long distance billing, fraud prevention, and law enforcement.
3. Tell consumers how information about them is used and how it can be corrected. Allow them to "opt out" of marketing lists.
4. Use advanced computer security techniques and ensure that employees comply with the privacy code.
5. Participate in U.S. and international government proceedings to resolve privacy issues.
6. Evaluate privacy implications before new services are offered.

Source: Betts, Mitch, "What You Don't Know," *Computerworld,* December 26, 1994/January 2, 1995, p. 28.

United Parcel Service (UPS) is another company that has set up an "electronic storefront" on the Internet—on CompuServe and Prodigy, the commercial online service providers. The home page allows users to arrange for UPS package pickups and deliveries. The company is confident that the page will increase business from existing customers and will also attract new customers who are avid users of the Net. "Our competitors aren't online yet, and that gives us an edge where we can generate some allegiance to our service," says a UPS spokesperson.

1–800–Flowers, a small business in the flowers-by-wire industry, found that setting up shop on CompuServe not only attracts more business (5% of the firm's $100 million in revenue is generated by online orders), but has also saved the company 10% to 30% by replacing direct mailings and telemarketing.

Although there are many advantages to a home page, some experts are worried that the Internet may simply become a "de facto national post office," and may become heavily commercialized. As more and more businesses start using the Net to sell their products and services, the Net may not be capable of handling the expanded volume of traffic. Ray Hoving, chairman of the Society for Information Management's (SIM) National Data Highways Advisory Council, is concerned about the technical, administrative, and security issues that will arise as traffic on the Net continues to increase.

Information Search Tools

Archie An information search tool for the Internet that identifies and indexes all files on anonymous ftp servers; user must know the file name, or at least part of it.

Archie The tools discussed in this section help users locate information on the Net. For example, **Archie,** one of the first information search tools developed on the Internet, periodically searches anonymous ftp servers that participate in the Archie database and identifies *all* files on these servers. It then creates a central index of all files available on anonymous ftp sites and creates a central database that users can access to locate information.

Users who have the Archie software, or who can use the Telnet command to connect to an Archie server, can access this database. The only disadvantage is that the user must know at least part of the filename in order to be able to search for the file. When the desired file is located, the servicer identifies the file's address and the user can use the ftp command to access and retrieve the file.

Though Archie is a very useful tool for locating files, it must be noted that not all anonymous ftp sites participate in the Archie database, and therefore, the database is not a comprehensive one.

Veronica

An Internet-based, information search tool that locates all files on participating Gopher servers. User need not know the filename to retrieve the file.

Veronica **Veronica** is a search tool designed specifically to locate all files on Gopher sites and it is listed under *Other Gopher and Information Servers* on the Gopher menu. Users who have access to a Gopher server and a Veronica server can then access the database. Note however, that some Gopher servers may choose not to participate in the Veronica Service. One of the biggest advantages of Veronica over Archie is that the user does not have to know the filename; phrases descriptive of the search area will do.

Wide Area Information Server (WAIS)

A search system that accesses servers all over the world to locate files on specific topics and identify their addresses.

WAIS **WAIS (Wide Area Information Server),** pronounced "ways," is a search system that accesses servers all over the world to locate requested files. The WAIS database has an index of keyboards that helps users to locate files in topic areas of interest to them. When given the keywords, WAIS returns the addresses where the files are located. The user can then use one of the other services discussed above to download the files. If a particular file is not found on a given WAIS server, the server will automatically direct the query to other WAIS servers on the Net.

Electronic Data Interchange

Electronic Data Interchange (EDI)

A direct computer-to-computer exchange of data over a telecommunications network.

Electronic data interchange (EDI) is a direct computer-to-computer exchange of data. The data found in business documents, such as purchase invoices or bills of lading, are transmitted from one computer to another over a telecommunication network. EDI is replacing the physical exchange of documents and can save time and money by eliminating the need for rekeying data, thereby reducing input errors, eliminating unnecessary handling and copying of documents, and increasing the productivity of employees. An EDI transaction is simply an exchange of flat files between trading partners that have established a communication link. Frequently, the services of a value-added network (VAN) may also be required. EDI software may be implemented on a variety of platforms, from PCs to mainframe computers such as Hewlett-Packard's HP 3000, DEC's VAX 6000, and IBM's AS/400 and ES/9000 mainframes.

For example, Harper Group, Inc., a $430-million, San Francisco based shipping company founded in 1898, relies on EDI for its market success. Harper distributes, ships, and tracks goods for customers, such as Procter & Gamble, by arranging air transport, ocean carriers and truckers, and ensuring that shipments are on time and within budget. The company carefully tracks shipments by attaching to each container a bundle of duty and tariff forms, reams of customs documentation (electronic and paper-based), and a host of accounting papers required by each nation. "We're determined to be an information company. We don't own ships or trucks, but we've always had information. That's the asset we have to market." In 1990, Harper established EDI and linked more than 500 customers to its IBM 3090–300E mainframe and its AS/400 minicomputer in San Francisco. The links transmit bills of lading, waybills, invoices, and other documentation and allow customers to check the status of their shipments. "That electronic conversation with Harper is an absolute must for us. If anything, we want Harper to provide us with even more information," says one customer.[36]

EDI is not a new technology. It got its formal start in the transportation industry as early as 1975; the grocery industry followed with an EDI project in 1978. In 1979, ANSI assigned the Accredited Standards Committee (ASC) X12 organization the responsibility of establishing EDI standards across industries. Today, there are more than 160 published X12 transactions; each transaction is a type of business document, such as a purchase order or an invoice.

All that is needed to implement EDI on a PC is a modem, a printer, and EDI software. In the simplest form of EDI, transactions are typed directly into the PC and they can be printed at the other end. But the true power of EDI can be achieved when EDI software is integrated with internal systems that handle only information relating to manufacturing, marketing, accounting, finance, and other functional areas.

Costs of Implementing EDI   The costs associated with implementing EDI fall into six general areas: software, hardware, VAN charges, software interface, program maintenance, and process reengineering. Some estimates of these costs are provided below; these costs can vary significantly from one organization to the next.[37]

- **Software:** EDI software can range from $500 for PCs to $100,000 for main-frames. Annual software maintenance typically costs 10 percent to 15 percent of the purchase price.
- **Hardware:** Costs vary depending on the type of computers used.
- **VAN Charges:** Users should expect from $25 to $200 in VAN startup costs. Monthly fees of $3 to $50 and use fees of 10 cents to 50 cents per 1,000 characters transmitted or received are usual in the industry.
- **Software Interface:** Integrating EDI software with existing applications can be expensive, because it often requires the development of a customized interface. This is one of the primary reasons smaller firms are often reluctant to implement full-blown EDI systems.
- **Program Maintenance:** These costs include software maintenance, technical support, and personnel training; they vary from one organization to another.
- **Organizational Changes:** A significant (and sometimes hidden) cost of EDI implementation is the change that it creates in an organization. Quite often these changes raise the fundamental question, "Why do we do business the way we do?" The answers may lead to significant (and costly) organizational changes and such costs are difficult to estimate.

Benefits of EDI   EDI is a powerful technology because it can create partnerships where none existed and can replace sluggish bureaucracies with responsive organizations. It is one of the most successful efforts in recent years to reduce operating costs and increase worker productivity. In some cases, it has changed the relationship between suppliers and customers from one of caution and mistrust to one of cooperation and collaboration. EDI is so powerful that it is viewed as a "glue technology that binds businesses together in the value chain from raw materials to finished products.[38]

The benefits of EDI may be divided into three groups: direct, indirect, and strategic.[39] Direct benefits include decreased operating costs and increased productivity. RCA, one of the early adopters of EDI, found that the number of purchase orders it generated decreased by a factor of 5 when it switched to EDI. Since up to 25% of the cost of a transaction is associated with data entry and re-entry, savings from EDI have been tremendous. Indirect benefits come from using EDI to re-engineer business practices. EDI enables businesses to identify and implement the most efficient way to conduct business. In many cases, EDI has prompted much-needed changes in inventory policies and accounting practices. GE Transportation Systems, for example, used EDI to develop a better inventory policy and eliminated an acre of warehouse space, realizing significant savings. Before EDI, the company maintained a large inventory because this was the only way to meet customer demand. By establishing EDI links with its leading customers, GE can find out their needs and modify its production schedule accordingly. Finally, EDI can yield strategic benefits in the marketplace. By allowing suppliers to access sales data, Wal-Mart Stores in Bentonville, Arkansas, ensures that there are no stock-outs by shifting to its suppliers the task of ensuring that its shelves are fully stocked. This, in turn, has increased sales and enhanced customer satisfaction.

Singapore is a big believer in EDI and its benefits (see box). Many countries around the world use EDI to promote business transactions.

RJR Tobacco, owner of Salem and Winston cigarettes, with estimated sales of $9 billion, uses EDI for almost 90% of its purchasing transactions. The company, which purchases more than $1-billion in materials from suppliers around the world, reduced the processing cost of a purchase order from $75 to a mere 93 cents and lead time for purchases from three weeks to less than an hour with the help of EDI! The company has also integrated EDI with other key applications in the company. For example, a manufacturing information system automatically generates a purchase order when stock reaches a certain level, and the order is then sent via EDI to suppliers, thus eliminating mailing costs and time delays.[40]

A GLOBAL PERSPECTIVE

Singapore Sings EDI's Praises

While the benefits of electronic data interchange (EDI) are being debated in the U.S., the technology has become a standard in Singapore, a Southeast Asian island nation renowned for its industriousness. TradeNet, Singapore's mainframe-based EDI system, was created in 1989 to help local firms process customs declarations. Six years later, the system serves 3,500 companies and handles more than 95% of Singapore trade declarations. About 70,000 messages are processed through TradeNet daily. Switching to EDI is estimated to have saved Singapore's government and businesses about $600 million per year. The change has also greatly cut the time it takes for key documents to

be approved. "It is now possible for a single electronic document to be sent to all relevant government agencies and returned with the necessary approvals within 15 to 30 minutes," says a spokesperson for TradeNet.

The EDI network has also helped Singapore become one of the world's busiest ports as a result of its links with trade networks in the Netherlands and the U.S.

TradeNet provides a wide range of trade information, such as company profiles, global trade leads, and foreign exchange rates. Over the past year, EDI documents for the export of rice and timber, which was previously handled manually, have been added to the system. "The future of EDI in Singapore is exciting. Like most success stories here, the accomplishments will be driven by minds open to change and a passion for excellence."[41]

Aetna Life & Casualty Co. relies on EDI to make checking into a hospital a little easier for its patients. Since January, 1994, the Hartford, Connecticut company has been operating an immediate-response EDI application that lets hospitals know in six seconds whether a patient has insurance coverage, the extent of the coverage, and the amount of co-payment. The system also verifies insurance eligibility, which could otherwise take anywhere from a five-minute phone call to simply not verifying the information. The system works as follows. The hospital runs a patient's health card through a credit card reader or enters the information manually. The EDI inquiry travels from the hospital across a network to an Aetna facility that quickly looks up the information on a mainframe and returns the eligibility status back to the hospital.[42]

Another example of a company that has successfully used EDI to increase sales is Dannon (see box).

Challenges in Implementing EDI   Quite often, the more powerful the technology, the greater are the challenges in implementing it. First, EDI requires the careful integration of several applications that may reside on incompatible platforms, and application integration is an expensive proposition. Second, with EDI, employees have to adapt to new ways of doing business, so the learning curve can be frustrating. Auditors must learn to process documents electronically; the legal department must get used to the idea of finalizing contracts without signatures and so on. Third, training, which is at the heart of successful EDI, can be both costly and difficult. Fourth, internal and external resistance to EDI can

BUSINESS REALITIES
Dannon Co.

As many supermarkets and dairy manufacturers are becoming more and more technologically sophisticated and savvy, they are increasingly using EDI systems as marketing weapons to determine which products are top sellers and which are languishing on valuable shelf space. In a highly competitive and cost conscious industry, technology seems to be one powerful way of understanding the needs of the customer and delivering the right goods at the right time and place.

The Dannon company, famous for its yogurt, has embraced EDI systems in an effort to leverage its abilities to reduce paper-based order processing, invoicing errors and costs, while streamlining efficiency between the production and delivery of goods. The company realized the importance of linking its finished goods inventory with the EDI network in order to accomplish the above goals.

Prior to installing the EDI, Dannon relied on fax-based purchase orders and invoice transmissions between itself and its wholesale food brokers. However, that process required Dannon's customer service representatives to manually key in customer orders and invoice amounts, a cumbersome and mistake-prone undertaking. By linking 20 of its leading trading partners to its EDI network, the company expects to reduce its labor and fax-based communications costs by $300,000 to $500,000. EDI will also help the company deliver the goods to supermarkets in a more timely manner.

The company also recently installed invoicing and purchase order software for the EDI network. Using OrderNet, Dannon can drop an invoice into a customer's mailbox that can be retrieved and responded to via modem. To help facilitate electronic funds transfer between Dannon and its brokers over the EDI network, the yogurt giant is working out a contract with Citibank NA for transfer services. The company also plans to eventually connect its order-entry and finished goods inventory manufacturing systems with the EDI network.[43]

jeopardize its implementation. Finally, EDI sometimes creates power struggles as the traditional relationship between suppliers and customers is altered.

In some cases, EDI has shifted the responsibility of inventory management from customer to supplier. This new and revolutionary concept, referred to as "vendor-managed inventory," requires a supplier to closely monitor the inventory of its customers and make sure that there are no stock-outs. Suppliers are thus working harder to get and retain the business of their customers. As at Wal-Mart, the vendor must make sure there are no stock-outs of its product at the purchaser's store. This has some powerful implications for EDI participants. "For suppliers who do get the call to manage a retailer's stock, this sudden shift in responsibility and risk is like jumping into a cold pool early in the morning," observes Robert Salerno, partner in charge of the retail consulting practice at Coopers & Lybrand in New York.[44]

This practice has created a great deal of tension, since some retailers insist on compliance with EDI standards within 6 weeks, levy penalties on suppliers who fail to meet the deadline, and sometimes even threaten to drop suppliers who refuse to participate in vendor-managed inventory. For example, Ralph's Grocery Co., in Los Angeles, levies fines on its suppliers for unreadable bar codes. After the first violation comes a warning; after the second, a $500 fine; subsequent offenses cost $1,000 each. Some suppliers are upset about such "bullying" tactics but dare not complain to the retailer for fear of being dropped.[45]

Suppliers who buy into the concept of vendor-managed inventory often have no choice but to invest heavily in EDI so they can capture sales data at the point of transaction and feed the data back to their forecasting and production systems. The biggest challenge in developing such systems is that each customer has its own hardware, software, and data requirements, thus forcing suppliers to customize their systems for each customer. Nabisco, for example, has developed different systems for six of its major clients. This has led some industry experts to question the idea that EDI promotes partnerships.

"Mega-retailers have the leverage to be bargain-hunting consumers. Despite talk about data sharing, integration, and partnerships, retailers and suppliers can get only so close. After all, the basic rules of capitalism call for arm's-length transactions between buyers and sellers, which implies some adversarial tension. Realistically, we're not likely to get to a point in the next 10 years where it's one big, happy, sharing family."

 **Summary**

♦ **Understand the importance of telecommunications to business organizations.**

This chapter emphasizes the importance of telecommunication technology to business organizations. There are many examples in this chapter that show how businesses around the world use telecommunications to enhance organizational productivity and increase market share. The key idea behind telecommunications is connectivity, i.e., the ability to link computers and people that are geographically dispersed.

Many of you will be working in a networked environment and therefore it is important to fully understand and appreciate the potential of this technology.

♦ **Explain the characteristics of telecommunication channels and media.**

A channel, as you may recall, is the part of the telecommunications system that constitutes the link between message source and message destination. In other words, it is the pipeline along which data are transmitted. There are three characteristics that help to identify channels: transmission rate, transmission mode, and transmission direction.

Telecommunications media, on the other hand, are the links over which data are transmitted and there are two types of telecommunications media: bounded and unbounded. In a bounded medium, the signals are confined to the medium and never leave it. Examples of bounded medium are twisted pair wires, coaxial cable, and fiber optics. In an unbounded medium, signals are propagated through the atmosphere, the ocean, and outer space. Examples of unbounded medium are microwave radio, communication satellites, cellular phones, and high-frequency radios.

* **Describe the role of common and special purpose communication carriers.**

Companies that move data from one location to another are called carriers and there are two types: common carriers and special purpose carriers. Common carriers are regulated by state and federal agencies and furnish communication services to businesses and the general public. Special purpose carriers or value-added carriers add features, such as e-mail, videoconferencing, and error-correction, to the basic communication services provided by common carriers.

* **Describe the different types of networks.**

There are five types of networks: private branch exchanges (PBXs), Integrated services digital network (ISDNs), Local area networks (LANs), Wide area networks (WANs), and Value-added networks (VANs). A PBX is an electronic switching device located in the company that automatically switches between the company's telephone lines and that of the local telephone company and therefore, acts like a small telephone exchange. The ISDN is a digital network that uses the public telephone network that allows users to transmit data and voice, in digital form, over telephone lines. A LAN is a network that links a number of independent electronic devices located within a moderate sized geographic area. It is primarily used to connect devices within a building or office. A WAN, on the other hand, spans wider geographical areas than a LAN. It is often owned by both the organization and a common or special purpose carrier. VANs are public data networks that add value to the basic communication services pro-

vided by common carriers by offering specialized services. A subscriber to a VAN service pays a monthly fee depending on the level of use.

* **Describe the three types of network topologies.**

The three types of network topologies are bus, ring, and star topology. A topology is the geometric configuration of a network. In a bus topology, computers on the network are connected through a single circuit to a central channel. The targeted device alone will respond to the message, although each message is transmitted to all the computers on the network. In a ring topology, the network devices are configured as a circular array. Each computer can communicate directly with any other computer on the network. Finally, in a star topology a host computer receives messages and forwards them to various computers on the network.

* **Understand the significance and implications of Internet.**

The Internet is a network of networks that serves as a storehouse of information on diverse topics and is often cited as an excellent model of the information superhighway. It allows millions of people all over the world to exchange and share ideas and information, and send messages to one another, around the clock. Some important tools on the Net are information retrieval tools (ftp and Gopher), communication tools (E-mail, Telnet, and Usenet), multimedia tools (World Wide Web), and information search tools (WAIS, Archie, and Veronica). Many companies set up a "home page" on the Net which allows potential or existing customers to electronically view the products, services and other company-related news.

* **Describe Electronic Data Interchange (EDI) and its implications for businesses.**

EDI refers to a direct computer-to-computer exchange of data found in many business documents. The data are transmitted over a telecommunication network and this eliminates the need for rekeying data. Although EDI has been around for a long time, in recent years, many corporations are using EDI as a way to reduce processing errors and cut operating costs. EDI is a powerful technology because it can create meaningful partnerships and replace sluggish bureaucracies with responsive organizations.

 **Review Questions**

Technical Foundations

1. What is meant by telecommunications?

2. What are the basic components of a telecommunication system? In particular, what is a host computer?

3. What is a channel and what are its three characteristics? Briefly describe each characteristic.

4. What are the three types of transmission direction? Can you give an example of each?

5. What is the difference between common carriers and special-purpose carriers? When would an organization choose a special-purpose carrier over a common carrier?

6. What is the difference between bounded and unbounded media? Identify the three types of bounded media and the four types of unbounded media.

7. Why is fiber-optic cable becoming one of the most popular bound media?

8. What are some reasons why wireless media are revolutionizing the way organizations do business? Identify and describe at least two types of unbounded media.

9. How does a cellular phone system work? What are some reasons for the growing popularity of cellular technology?

10. Identify the five different types of networks. Explain how a PBX works and identify one or two advantages and disadvantages of this type of network.

11. What does ISDN stand for? Is ISDN a digital or an analog network? What are some advantages of ISDN?

12. What are the five key operating principles of ISDN? Briefly describe each principle.

13. What do LAN, WAN, and VAN stand for? Describe a LAN and explain what is meant by a peer-to-peer relationship.

14. Briefly describe Ethernet, Token Ring, and AppleTalk.

15. Does a LAN use a common carrier or a private communications channel for transmitting data? What is the difference between baseband and broadband?

16. If you were a network manager, how would you decide whether a LAN, a WAN, or a VAN is most suitable for your company?

17. What are some differences between a LAN and a PBX? Identify any two advantages of LANs.

18. What is a WAN? What are some different ways of setting up a WAN?

19. Identify and describe the three types of network topology.

20. Define network architecture. What are the three characteristics of a protocol and why do we need protocols? Name any one popular protocol.

21. List the seven layers of an OSI model and give a brief description of each layer.

Managerial Foundations

22. Explain why telecommunications is changing the way companies do business.

23. What are some of the challenges that network administrators face? What are some managerial characteristics of organizations that are most successful in network management?

24. What do we mean by a global network? What are some unique challenges that companies face when establishing a global network?

25. What is the Internet? How did it evolve?

26. What are some of the characteristics of the information superhighway? Is the Internet a good example of the information superhighway?

27. Explain one of the primary reasons why the use of Internet has increased in the last few years. What are some ways of connecting to the Internet?

28. What are the two elements of an individual's Internet address? Briefly describe each element and its primary purpose.

29. What kind of services do *ftp* and Gopher provide? What is the primary difference between them?

30. What kind of service does *Telnet* provide?

31. Describe the World Wide Web (WWW). How did it evolve? What is one of the most popular interfaces for accessing the Web?

32. What kind of services do Archie, Veronica, and WAIS provide? What, if any, are the differences among them?

33. What is a home page? What are the advantages of setting up a home page on the Web?

34. What is EDI? What impact does it have on business productivity?

35. What are some of the costs associated with implementing EDI?

36. Identify some of the challenges that organizations face when implementing EDI.

 Discussion Questions

1. As a network manager, you are responsible for the selection of a suitable network for your company. The first step in selecting a network is to determine the information and network requirements of the organization. You must then determine the location of the network, the traffic on the network, and the

performance requirements of the network. Regarding location, you must ask: Where will the network be installed and what is the geographic area that must be covered? What services will be provided by common and special-purpose carriers in this location? Regarding traffic: What kind of data will be transmitted over the network (data, voice, graphics)? What is the volume of data that will travel over the network? What are the peak and low periods for the traffic? Regarding performance: What is the average required response time? What levels of accuracy and reliability are required? How critical are the data that are transmitted over the network? What kind of security and backup measures should the organization have?

When the requirements have been determined, the next step is to identify hardware and software that will meet them. This is not an easy task, given the large number of products that are available. Moreover, you must make sure that the system can be upgraded as the needs of the organization change. Compatibility with existing systems is also a key issue.

Although a number of companies use traditional cost-benefit analysis in making decisions, technology decisions must also take into account strategic advantage, quality of customer service, and company image. This is particularly true for networks.

Set up a meeting with an administrator at your university and find out how the university selected its network.

2. Dr. Pepper/7-Up believes that if a technology does not help to push another soda bottle out the door, that technology has no meaning for the company: "Innovation is how well you solve a business problem, not how much money you burn on fiber." Do you agree? Discuss.

3. You have been assigned the task of linking three business units, located in New York, Los Angeles, and Orlando. What type of network and what medium would you recommend for this application and why?

4. The organization of today is more global than ever before. Economic and political forces are shaping the way organizations do business. Global networks allow companies to increase their global presence and achieve better control over their world-wide markets. However, developing and implementing global networks is a very difficult task, particularly in developing countries where telecommunications is still in its infancy. Tariffs and regulatory problems, restrictive national laws and regulations, lack of sophisticated technology, hardware and software incompatibility, inadequate utilities, and poorly trained employees are a few of the challenges of developing global networks.

Some companies, such as Texas Instruments, overcome some of these problems by building their own private networks; others use special-purpose carriers to manage their networks. Network outsourcing (hiring third parties to develop, implement, and manage the network) is also becoming an attractive alternative for many organizations that do not have enough in-house expertise to develop their own global networks.[46]

Identify a company that has a global network in a developing country. Identify some of the problems that the organization may have faced in developing and implementing the network.

5. Many leaders are concerned that the U.S. is lagging behind other countries in telecommunications, particularly because Japan and Europe are ahead of the U.S. in terms of developing long-range telecommunications policies and in implementing the "telepower mandate." In Europe, the European Commission has a broad-based long-term research program; of the member nations' total research dollars, more than 40% are devoted to telecommunications. In Japan, in 1984, the Ministry of Post and Telecommunications and the Ministry of International Trade and Industry created 40 "key technology centers," using both public and private monies and expertise to develop a strong telecommunications base. The U.S., on the other hand, seems to lack long-range policies that will encourage the development of telecommunications technology.

Many IS experts believe that one way to increase the commitment of policy makers to information systems and technology is to attract students to IS careers. What are some measures that you would recommend to attract students to careers in telecommunications?

6. Talk with a local PC network administrator and a mainframe network administrator about their primary job functions. Identify any differences between the two.

Talk with the local PC administrator and identify some of the challenges of managing a PC network.

7. Remote LAN access is a hot topic in telecommunications. According to a recent Forrester Research report, investments in mobile LAN solutions are expected to increase from $529 million in 1994 to $2.8 billion by 1997. One of the primary benefits of remote LAN is access to mail. For example, at MCA/Universal Studios, remote LAN allows executives to stay in touch through E-mail. But with remote access come several problems, ranging from the monitoring of system use to the tracking of software licensing. In particular, security is a major concern. The most common security measures are dial-back, in which the modem calls back the person requesting access and checks his or her authorization, and varying levels of password protection.

Identify two other simple security measures that network administrators can take to protect remote LANs.

8. Marin County in California has set up an Internet system that permits all public and private organizations to share information. The new network, called the Marin Information and Data Access System (MIDAS), is built around a countywide fiber-optic network and each organization is a node on the network and can communicate with any other node. Since MIDAS was installed, all communication between Marin County and the outside world is taking place via the Internet. Participants say that in addition to improving communications, MIDAS has fostered a new level of cooperation and collaboration among disparate organizations that previously were not accustomed to working with one another.

MIDAS comprises of the following:

- Marinet Libraries Consortium, which provides all users on the MIDAS network with on-line database access to three city libraries as well as the county library.
- Marin Cities and County Public Access System, which provides dial-up and Internet users with access to schedules, agenda and minutes of city council and board of director meetings.
- Home Care Consortium, which provides an automated registry of in-home workers to assist with personal care and household chores, coordinated by two government agencies and multiple private nonprofit agencies.

- Marin Property System Title Company Access System, which uses a special access menu for title companies to display on demand the property information needed for title searches.[47]
   a. If you lived in Marin County in California, explain how Midas may be useful to you.
   b. "MIDAS has fostered a new level of cooperation and collaboration among disparate organizations that previously were not accustomed to working with one another." Explain how the Internet can facilitate team work.

9. The following are Internet addresses. Identify the user ID and the domain in each of the addresses and describe the kind of organization that the user belongs to:
   a. dcgupta@ecuvm.cis.ecu.edu
   b. joeblow@aol.com
   c. marshal@.ibm36.foreign.DOD.mil

10. Ask your instructor for his or her Net address and send an E-mail to your instructor. Request acknowledgment that the mail was received. (Note: Since each E-mail package is different, the commands required to do this exercise will vary from one system to the next.)

11. If you are interested in viewing all the known Gopher servers, you can do so by accessing the address gopher.tc.umn.edu. You can then browse through this list of Gopher servers and pick the one that is appealing to you. Browse through the list of Gopher servers, select one that is of interest to you, and write a one-page summary on the selected Gopher site.

12. gopher.internic.net is an excellent Gopher site for beginners on the Internet. It provides a wealth of information on the Internet. From the main menu, select InterNIC Information Services and then select Beginners: Select Here.[48]

13. One of the most popular Gopher sites is metaverse.com. an archive of music and video. Access this server and select the menu "woodstock." Write a brief summary of your findings.

14. Access the address gopher.exploratorium.edu, "a museum of science, technology, and human perception located in the Palace of Fine Arts in the Marina district of San Francisco." You will find a vast amount of information on science and culture. Describe your findings.

15. If you would like to find some jokes and good humor, access Usenet site rec.humor.funny. This

group is estimated to have more than 340,000 readers. Could you have found this site without Usenet?

16. misc.jobs.misc is another popular Usenet group for people looking for a job. Describe some features of Usenet.

17. From Archie, access alt.music and alt.fan, two very popular information groups that provide a wealth of information on music and fans of people, things, places, and so on, respectively. There are a whole range of choices that you can select from each of these groups. Briefly describe Archie.

ETHICAL ISSUES

The greatest benefit of networked computing is its promise of widespread access to data and processing power. However, that expanded access can also be a network managers worst nightmare. Network intrusion is on the rise and, alarmingly, most of the breaches are committed by insiders, people who know the security measures taken by the organization and know ways to beat those measures. Some ethical issues in telecommunications are presented below.

Case 1: Patent Violations

With the rapid proliferation of hardware technology on a worldwide basis, the question of who invented what–and when—is a critical one that organizations must carefully address. Roger Billings and his International Academy of Science sued Novell, one of the largest network vendors in the country. In December 1991, Billings claimed that Novell copied one of his ideas for distributed computing and used it in its NetWare product. Billings is demanding $220 million in lost royalties.

Novell senior VP and general counsel David Bradford maintains that "the suit is without merit," and that the case should be dismissed before trial. He argues that even if everything Billings claims were true, the court could still rule Billings's patent invalid because similar technology existed before Billings applied for his patent.[49]
1. What role should patents play in the development of IS products and technologies?

Case 2: Telephone Monitoring: Privacy Breach or Security Measure?

During the 1980s, hackers Lenny DiCicco and Kevin Mitnick were convicted for breaking into DEC's internal network. They did it by controlling about 50 telephone switches, including some in Chicago and Manhattan, and were able to shut down all DEC's telephone service. There are many telephone hackers who can easily penetrate corporate phone networks and cause serious damage by accessing and/or destroying valuable corporate data and incurring thousands of dollars' worth of phone charges.

The telephone system is the weakest link in network security. Some measures that companies are taking to prevent telephone breakins are full-time monitoring of the telephone system, obtaining insurance to limit security breaches, and end-to-end data encryption. (See Table 5–7).
1. If the network administrator monitored your telephone calls, would you consider that a breach of privacy or would you support it in the interest of security? Discuss.

Case 3: Internet Liability

The Internet is the most widely used network in the world. Unfortunately, when employees are given free access to the Internet, organizations can run into legal and ethical problems.

For example, a company can be held legally liable for what its employees do and say on the Internet. If an employee divulges trade secrets, or engages in copyright infringement, the company may be held responsible. Mary J. Cronin, author of *Doing Business on the Internet,* indicates that the controversial statements or the politically unpopular views of an employee can affect the image and status of a company. One way to attack this problem is to impose strict rules stating that all messages posted on the Internet must clearly specify whether the employee is expressing his or her views or those of the organization.

1. What are some measures that an organization can take to minimize its liability on the Internet?

Case 4: Faking It on the Internet

A 15-year-old Utah boy was charged with defrauding as many as 13 Internet users of $10,000 in a scam that investigators called highly effective. Ironically, the boy's mother and grandmother had bought him a computer so he would stay at home and stay out of trouble.

Allegedly, the boy established an account with a commercial online service, giving a fake name and address and other fabricated personal information. He then posted advertisements for computer parts on the Internet and used E-mail to send the ad to other Net users. The ad indicated that customers must pay for C.O.D. deliveries with cashier's checks addressed to a postoffice box. Customers were mailed an empty box or a box containing one diskette. When customers realized that they had been taken, it was too late, since one cannot stop payment on a cashier's check.

The boy also got the credit card number of another subscriber by impersonating an employee of the online service provider and telling the user that the provider had lost his records. He then used the stolen credit card number to buy computer parts. This boy will be prosecuted as a juvenile for second-degree theft and computer and credit card fraud. Under state law, adults can be imprisoned for 5 years to life for these charges.[50]

1. What, if any, are the ethical violations in this story?
2. What measures can be taken on the Internet to avoid such crimes?

Case 5: Hold That Data, Please

The information superhighway has made it easy for marketers to compile detailed information on how consumers use online services—on their hobbies, their music preferences, their favorite movies, their vacation spots, their dream automobiles, and so on. Such detailed data on an individual's consumption patterns are invaluable to marketers, who often spend large sums on promotions and advertising directed at special audiences. But privacy advocates warn that this is a quick route to trouble; it can often cause customers to abandon companies that sell data about them to other companies without their express permission. Companies may even find themselves in court for such violations of consumer privacy.

For example, America Online was chastised recently by Representative Edward J. Markey (D-Mass.) for trying to sell its subscriber data in the direct-marketing industry and earn huge profits. Today, in order to avoid the privacy trap, many companies are hiring consumer advocates and consulting legal experts before selling data. Consumers are insisting that they should be notified in advance that data are being collected on them. They are also demanding a voice in the decision as to how the data will be used and they want to review and correct the data whenever necessary. On the other hand, some marketers say, "If you give them a big enough discount to divulge their life story and a say in how that information will be used, they will go along."[51]

1. What role, if any, should consumers play in monitoring and controlling the sale of consumer-related data?
2. Do you believe that consumers would be more willing to share data about themselves if companies paid them for the data? Discuss.

Case 6: Electronic Bookstore or Telephone Directory?

In November, 1994, Prodigy Services Co., provider of on-line services, and one of its subscribers were sued for $200 million over a message posted on its Money Talk bulletin board that called a particular stock offering a criminal fraud. The note, allegedly written by codefendant David Lusby of Key West, Florida, disparaged a public stock offering by New York securities firm Stratton Oakmont, Inc. Prodigy is likely to fall back on the 1991 case against CompuServe in which a federal judge ruled that the service provider was not liable for messages on its network because it was like an electronic bookstore with no editorial control over content. But the Prodigy case has a new twist.

Lusby worked at Prodigy as a software manager until 1991 and allowed at least 30 employees to use his "house" account for internal purposes. Lusby claims he did not write the message in question and that it must have been written by someone using his old Prodigy account. (The courts may charge Prodigy for negligence in not retiring an expired account.) Ultimately, the court will have to decide whether the proper metaphor for

(Continued on next page)

Prodigy is a newspaper that has editorial control or a bookstore or telephone company that does not have control. The Prodigy suit may be the precedent-setting case for on-line libel.

The posting of libelous messages is one of the greatest nightmares of information service providers and organizations with E-mail capabilities. Liability for employee misbehavior stems from a body of corporate law called the "Law of agency." Many companies are taking a proactive role in limiting their liabilities from employee misbehavior.

Johnson Controls in Milwaukee wrote a draft policy, dated Jan. 20, 1994, for internal and external electronic-mail networks. The policy prohibits the following activities:

* Operating a business for personal gain, searching for a job outside Johnson Controls, sending chain letters or soliciting money for religious or political causes.
* Offensive or harassing statements, including "disparagement of others based on their race, national origin, sex, sexual orientation, age, disability, religious or political beliefs."
* Sending or soliciting sexually oriented messages or images.
* Disseminating or printing copyrighted materials (including articles and software) in violation of copyright laws.

Joseph Rosenbaum, a technology lawyer in New York, NY, said firms can help insulate themselves by answering three simple questions:

* Is there a guideline?
* Do employees know about it?
* Is it enforced?

Simply putting a disclaimer at the bottom of the message stating that the views are that of the individual sending the message and not the company may not be sufficient in a court of law. "Disclaimers will be just one factor, and they may not sway the court," said Dan L. Burk, an expert on cyber-law at the George Mason University School of Law in Fairfax, VA. On the other hand, "if the message was completely outside the scope of the employee's work—in a realm lawyers call 'detour and frolic'—then the employer will not be liable.[52]

1. Who do you think is to blame in this case: Prodigy or Mr. Lusby? Why?

2. Identify some measures that your organization has taken to prevent ethical violations on the Net.

Case 7: Existing Copyright Act Must Go!

MIT student David LaMacchia escaped conviction on criminal charges that he ran an electronic bulletin board that others used to illegally upload and download more than $1 million in copyrighted software. U.S. District Court Judge Richard Stearns ruled that the old federal wire fraud law under which LaMacchia was indicted was not applicable in this case. Successful use of the wire fraud law against LaMacchia would have served to "criminalize. . .the myriad of home computer users who succumb to the temptation to copy even a single software program for private use," Stearns wrote in his decision. While LaMacchia escaped a fine and a federal prison term, his alleged behavior won no support from the court. "If the indictment is to be believed, one might at best describe his actions as heedlessly irresponsible and at worst nihilistic, self-indulgent and lacking in any fundamental sense of values," Stearns wrote.

He also said current copyright law could not be used against the MIT student because its criminal provisions require showing that copyright infringement was made "for purposes of commercial advantage or private financial gain," something LaMacchia was not alleged to have done. It is expected that the U.S. Department of Justice will seek changes to the Copyright Act to make it easier to prosecute those who facilitate software copyright infringement without directly profiting from it. "The LaMacchia case points out that we need a legislative fix to enable us to prosecute unethical bulletinboard operators," said Ken Wasch, executive director of the Software Publishers Association in Washington. He estimated that software piracy costs vendors $7.5 billion a year worldwide, and $1.5 billion in the U.S. Wasch said the requirement in the current copyright law that infringers must benefit financially to be prosecuted is flawed. "The issue is not what the bulletin board operator gains, it's what the copyright holder loses."[53]

On the other hand, opponents argue that the current law simply does not make any sense. Says Ken Wasch, executive director of the Software Publishers Association in Washington "Suppose I advertise, through various means, a service for thieves. I will appear at the back door of, say, a sporting goods store at midnight. I'll bypass alarms and hold the door open, and anyone responding to my solicitation is free to walk in and take what he wants. I don't profit from this. I am motivated by the belief that some capitalist pig created the goods therein, and thus they should be free to the people. Only the lunatic fringe would say I wouldn't be committing a crime. But this is pretty much what an MIT student is alleged to have done in allowing thieves to cart away more than $1 million worth of software, free of charge. Instead of standing at the door, David LaMacchia

posted the software on a bulletin board and exhorted anyone to copy it. He knew it was wrong and tried to cover his tracks. He got caught." [54]

1.   What, if any, are the loopholes in the U.S. copyright law?

2.   Do you think that LaMacchia got the punishment that he deserved?

PROBLEM SOLVING IN THE REAL WORLD

Case 1: Freddie, Fannie, Ginnie, and EDI

Freddie, Fannie, and Ginnie: they sound like the names of small children. But the huge companies bearing those nicknames are the Federal Home Loan Mortgage Corp. (Freddie Mac), the Federal National Mortgage Association (Fannie Mae), and the Government National Mortgage Association (Ginnie Mae). These companies are among the fiercest of competitors in an $825 billion market for mortgages. But these arch-rivals are collaborating on a project to standardize the flow of data in the mortgage industry, a project that will touch all sectors of the industry, including borrowers, lenders, mortgage service providers, and even Wall Street firms.

Cash Flow

Freddie Mac and Fannie Mae are chartered by Congress and are publicly held corporations, established to ensure a flow of funds from the capital markets to mortgage lenders. They buy mortgages from banks and savings institutions, group them into pools, and sell shares on Wall Street as mortgage-backed securities. Ginnie Mae has the same mission but is part of the federal government, under the U.S. Department of Housing and Urban Development. Last year, Freddie, Fannie, and Ginnie bought mortgages worth $534 billion.

The three agencies have teamed with the Mortgage Bankers Association of America (MBA) to develop EDI standards governing the creation, servicing, and selling of these mortgages. The goal is to make it easier, faster, and cheaper to get information from lenders (who typically maintain three sets of interface systems, one each for Freddie, Fannie, and Ginnie) so they can better manage their operations.

Numerous parties are involved in a mortgage—in its origination, closing, monthly servicing, possible sale, and eventual payoff. A considerable volume of paper submitted by home buyers when applying for mortgages triggers a flood of data in the form of credit reports, employment verifications, appraisals, title searches, and so on. "The whole industry exists to exchange information," says

(Continued on next page)

Mark Fleming, operations vice president at Freddie Mac in Vienna, Virginia. "That's our business; we don't produce anything except information." Unfortunately, much of that information remains on paper, and the intercompany electronic interfaces that do exist must be built on a custom basis for each party because of the lack of standards. "Loan organization is very paper-intensive," says David Barkley, director of EDI customer service at Freddie Mac. "Those guys are ecstatic if a credit report is faxed."

Transaction Approval

Freddie, Fannie, Ginnie, and the MBA have established a Lending Task Group under the X12 Finance Committee of ANSI; it is working to develop a set of EDI standards. The mortgage industry has now received X12 approval for the first three of a dozen or so mortgage transaction sets, and implementation has begun at some lender sites. Officials at Freddie Mac say they are just beginning to do a cost-benefit analysis for the project. However, recent industry surveys already predict that banks and other lenders may be able to trim the costs of dealing with the three agencies by 40% as a result of the EDI standards. Though lenders may see their lives greatly simplified as a result of EDI, it will also create some difficulties for the three agencies, says Fleming. "In the past, we could add or change data whenever we wanted to without getting permission or having to conform to dates or definitions. Now we'll have to anticipate needs and changes much further in advance. That's a little scary; it's an internal challenge."

Building Steam

The mortgage industry's EDI project has a bit more behind it than automating and standardizing data flow. It will greatly increase the amount of information that now accompanies the loans that Fannie Mae, Freddie Mac, and Ginnie Mae buy from lenders. Currently, the three agencies get summaries of the loan data, but an official at Freddie Mac said that in the first phase of the EDI project alone, the number of data elements per loan will jump from 30 to 114. The extra data bear on the credit worthiness of borrowers and on the characteristics of their properties—from details on loan applications, credit reports, and appraisals.

"Sooner or later we knew the information was going to be asked for," said Brian Hershkowiz, associate director of the Mortgage Bankers Association of America, which represents 2,600 firms that originate, sell, or service mortgages. "Whoever owns the loan is entitled to this information." Freddie Mac, Fannie Mae, and Ginnie Mae hope to develop AI systems that will allow them to use these additional data to do a better and faster job of evaluating mortgages. The data-hungry AI programs would not be practical without EDI, says Fleming.[55]

1. Describe the project on which Freddie, Fannie, and Ginnie are collaborating; explain the purpose of this project.
2. Why is EDI being proposed as the solution to some of the common problems faced by these three companies? What are the advantages and disadvantages of EDI?
3. What impact will this project have on the mortgage industry?

References

Benjamin, Robert I., David W. DeLong and Michael S. Scott Morton. "The Realities of Electronic Data Interchange: How Much Competitive Advantage?" Management in the 1990s Working Paper 88–042. Sloan School of Management, MIT, 1988.

Bliss, William L. "Can Existing Networks Facilitate Global Monitoring?" *Security Management,* June 1994, pp. 98–99.

Hall, Wayne A. and Robert E. McCauley. "Planning and Managing a Corporate Network Utility." *MIS Quarterly* (December 1987).

Hammer, Michael and Glenn Mangurian. "The Changing Value of Communications Technology." *Sloan Management Review* (Winter 1987).

Keen, Peter G. W. *Competing in Time.* Cambridge, MA: Ballinger Publishing Company, 1986.

Schwarzkopf, Albert B., Brenda L. Burroughs and Michael G. Harvey. "The Role of the Information Center in Multinational Corporations," *Multinational Business Review,* Spring 1995, pp. 82–92.

Notes

1. Panettieri, Joseph C. "NY Schools Launch Major Law Project," *InformationWeek,* August 10, 1992, p. 24.
2. Ibid.
3. Anonymous. "The Coffee Connection," *CIO,* October 15, 1992, p. 14.
4. Klett, Stephen P., Jr. "Fiber May Make More Cents," *Computerworld,* February 21, 1994, pp. 49, 54.
5. O'Leary, Meghan. "Mature Technology," *CIO,* July 1992, pp.48–56.
6. Klett, Stephen P., Jr. "Fiber May Make More Cents," *Computerworld,* February 21, 1994, pp. 49, 54.
7. O'Leary, Meghan. "Mature Technology," *CIO,* July 1992, pp. 48–56.
8. Anthes, Gary, "Network Helps to Focus Giant Eye on Heaven," *Computerworld,* March 11, 1992, pp. 71, 75.
9. Betts, Mitch. "N.Y. Hospitals Join Forces," *Computerworld,* Dec. 13, 1993, p. 56.
10. Radosevich, Lynda. "PDAs To Assist Doctors, Pharmacies," *Computerworld,* March 21, 1994, p. 77.
11. Thyfault, Mary E. "On the Same Wave Length," *InformationWeek,* January 18, 1993, p. 32.
12. DiDio, Laura. "School Districts Give Microwave Top Marks," *Computerworld,* February 13, 1995, p. 78.
13. Ibid.
14. "A&P: Everything Network," *InformationWeek,* June 15, 1992.
15. Weinberg, Neal. "Satellite Links Let Cash Flow Out to Sea," *Computerworld,* May 8, 1995, p. 56.
16. Fitzgerald, Michael. "ISDN Costs May Fall," *Computerworld,* May 15, 1995, pp. 1, 117.
17. Sharp, Kevin R. "Out of Sight, Out of Mind, Out of Luck," *Computerworld,* October 11, 1993, pp. 89–90.
18. Stahl, Stephanie, "Home Remedy for CDC Networks," *InformationWeek,* May 17, 1993, p. 22.
19. Hart, Julie. "When You Inherit a WAN," *Computerworld,* December 6, 1993, p. 129.
20. Hoffman, Thomas. "Citicorp Reaps Net Benefits," *Computerworld,* Mar. 15, 1994, p. 6.
21. Travis, Paul. "If Not Now, WAN?" *InformationWeek,* Mar. 8, 1993, p. 28.
22. Horwitt, Elisabeth. "The Cost Of Doing Business With LANs," *Computerworld,* Feb. 7, 1994, pp. 53–54.

23. Baum, David. "What Mainframes Can Teach You," *Computerworld,* Jan. 10, 1994, p. 89.
24. Alter, Allan, E. "Toyota," *Computerworld,* The Global 100, May 1, 1995, p. 19.
25. Goodman, S. E., L. I. Press, S. R. Ruth, A. M. Rutkowski. "The Global Diffusion of the Internet: Patterns and Problems," *Communications of the ACM,* August 1994, pp. 27–31.
26. Jones, Katherine. "Castle Internet Under Attack, *Client/Server Computing,* April 1995, pp. 37–38, 42, 44.
27. Brandel, William. "The Five Million Channel Man," *Computerworld,* December 26, 1994/January 2, 1995, p. 34.
28. Betts, Mitch. "Citizens Swamp Utah Bulletin Board," *Computerworld,* November 7, 1994, p. 64.
29. Picarille, Lisa. "Apply Cyberdog Fetches Info Over the Net," *Computerworld,* May 8, 1995, p. 2.
30. Sullivan-Trainor, Michael. "Down to the Cybermall," *Computerworld,* December 26, 1994/January 2, 1995, p. 25.
31. Booker, Ellis. "Japan Internet Sites Report on Disaster," *Computerworld,* January 23, 1995, p. 12.
32. Booker, Ellis. "IS Staffs Take the On-line Plunge," *Computerworld,* May 15, 1995, p. 59.
33. Wilder, Clinton. "Plugging Into the Web," *InformationWeek* April 3, 1995, pp. 42–44, 48, 50, 54.
34. Booker, Ellis and Mitch Betts. "Democracy Goes On-line," *Computerworld,* October 31, 1994, pp. 1, 123.
35. Booker, Ellis. "Financial Services Spread Across Web," *Computerworld,* May 15, 1995, p. 12.
36. Garner, Rochelle, "Harper's Freight Is Data," *InformationWeek,* June 20, 1994, pp. 32–33.
37. Drummond, Rik. "Preparing For EDI: Do the Benefits Justify the Costs?" *Network Computing,* September 1993, p. 168.
38. Dearing, Brian. "The Strategic Benefits of EDI," *The Journal of Business Strategy,* January/February 1990, pp. 4–6.
39. Ibid.
40. Stahl, Stephanie. "EDI is Habit Forming RJR Tobacco," *InformationWeek,* January 11, 1993, p. 14.
41. Mesher, Gene. "Singapore Sings Praises of EDI," *InformationWeek,* April 11, 1994, p. 70.
42. Radosevich, Linda. "Network Eases Pains of Hospital Visits," CIO, May 30, 1994, pp. 59–60.
43. Hoffman, Thomas. "Dannon adds EDI to Its Culture," *Computerworld,* July 18, 1994, p. 64.
44. Betts, Mitch. "Manage My Inventory or Else!" *Computerworld,* January 31, 1994, pp. 93–95.
45. Ibid.
46. Betts, Mitch. "The Headache Continues," *InformationWeek,* Oct. 12, 1992, pp. 60–64.
47. Klett, Stephen P. "California County Network Employs the MIDAS Touch," *Computerworld,* November 21, 1994, pp. 57, 62.
48. Pike, Mary Ann. "Using the Internet," 2nd ed., *Que Publishers,* IN., p. 1061.
49. Violino, Bob and Joseph C. Panettieri. "Hey, Novell, See You In Court," *InformationWeek,* Feb. 14, 1994, p. 14.
50. Anthes, Gary. "Juvenile charged with Internet Crimes," *Computerworld,* May 8, 1995, p. 12.
51. Betts, Mitch. "What You Don't Know," *Computerworld,* December 26, 1994/January 2, 1995, p. 28.
52. Betts, Mitch. "On-line Libel Lawsuits Looming," *Computerworld,* November 28, 1994, pp. 16–17.
53. Anthes, Gary H. "Wire Fraud Law Falls Short," *Computerworld,* January 9, 1995, p. 16.
54. Laberis, Bill. "A Crime That Pays," *Computerworld,* January 9, 1995, p. 34.
55. Anthes, Gary H. "Rivals Team Up for EDI," *Computerworld,* March 15, 1994, p. 64.

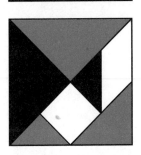

6

Database Design and Management

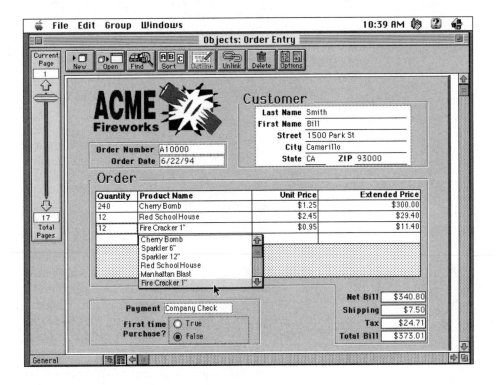

Contents

Learning Objectives
Technology Payoff: Reader's Digest
Introduction
Data Versus Information
Data Hierarchy
Methods for Organizing Data in Files
Limitations of Traditional Files
Introduction to Database Management Systems
    Differences Between Databases and Traditional Files
    The Components of a DBMS
        Data Definition Language
        Data Manipulation Language
        Data Dictionary
Database Models
    Hierarchical Data Model
    Network Model
    Relational Model
Entity Relationship Diagram
    ERD Symbols
Distributed Databases
Principles of Database Management

Summary
Review Questions
Discussion Questions
Ethical Issues
    Case 1: Sucker Databases
    Case 2: Ad Hoc Reporting May Not Be So Ad Hoc After All!
    Case 3: Database Fraud
    Case 4: No More Fraud
    Case 5: Data Privacy
    Case 6: Business as Usual??
Problem Solving in the Real World
    Case 1: Pacific Gas and Electric
    Case 2: Becton Dickinson
    Case 3: Harper's Freight Is Data
References
Notes

Learning Objectives

The purpose of this chapter is to provide a broad overview of databases and to emphasize the importance of timely and accurate data in organizational decision making. Database management systems (DBMS) are vital tools that create, process, store, and disseminate data for decision makers at all levels in an organization, so the study of databases is basic to understanding information systems. The various components of a database are described; the benefits of databases are outlined. The concept of distributed databases is also introduced.

    After reading and studying this chapter, you should be able to

- Understand the role of data in a business and the importance of being able to quickly retrieve and process data
- Describe a data hierarchy and its elements
- Describe different methods of representing data in files
- Describe and discuss the importance and functions of a DBMS
- Describe the three components in a DBMS

TECHNOLOGY PAYOFF

Reader's Digest

At the Reader's Digest Association, the Reader's Digest Customer Information Management System (CIMS) is designed to help the company target the right customers by ensuring that "the right people get the right mail." *Reader's Digest* has always been highly successful in targeting its customers, thanks to a 23-year old database system that tracks the likes and dislikes of 100 million customers worldwide. CIMS, an update of the existing database system, is based on a relational database designed to achieve the company's goal of increasing customer response rates and lowering mailing costs.

This is how the system works: The company buys mailing lists of potential customers from a variety of sources and gathers relevant data on existing and potential customers. Next, different sources are researched and customer surveys are used to gain a better understanding of each customer. Once the data on the customer is gathered and entered in the database, it is used to target product offerings. For example, if a customer subscribes to a book series about Japan, the company considers that the customer may have interest in Asia and sends information about Asian products to the customer. Based on customers' purchases, the database is frequently updated. The database is also used by market planners to target customers for new publications. "We're trying to take some of our great products and great ideas and move them around the world faster."[1]

The company has consolidated 17 data centers into three: one in North America, one in Europe, and one in the Far East. These data centers, all patterned after the $20-million Pleasantville facility, will house IBM mainframes running sophisticated databases.

In short, databases help *Reader's Digest* to maintain a leadership position in the highly competitive magazine market.[2]

If data cannot be correctly understood, it cannot be combined with other information. Instead, it is just data pollution.

Computer Graphics World

Introduction

Databases are vital to many firms. Without them, some companies simply cannot function. Poorly managed and maintained data can threaten the very existence of an organization; while well-managed data systems can provide a significant edge in the marketplace. For example, the story of Reader's Digest shows how databases provide decision makers with valuable data that targets the right customers and identifies their needs. By using its databases effectively, *Readers Digest* can be a more responsive company.

Accurate and timely data are the backbone of good decisions, regardless of the business. A manager must decide on the price of a firm's product, based on cost factors and market conditions. A stockbroker must decide, based on investment data, how and where to invest. A banker must decide, based on credit reports, whether to approve a loan. A student must decide what university to enroll in and what classes to take, based on certain data. The Defense Mapping Agency's Digital Nautical Chart project uses data, such as an area's port facilities or underwater obstructions, to guide ocean navigation for vessels in the U.S. Navy, U.S. Coast Guard, and Merchant Marine fleets.

Another example of the need for data to make good decisions is buying a home: buyers base their decisions on factors such as price, interest rate, neighborhood, schools, and so on, and the primary business of some companies is to provide home buyers with the data that they need to make sound decisions. For example, shopping for a home can be a tiresome and frustrating experience for some people. Home View Realty Search Services provides potential buyers with comprehensive data about properties that allow buyers to view external and internal shots of a piece of property, view the entire neighborhood, or even a section of the town in which the property is located, using factors like price, style of house, location, number of bedrooms, bathrooms, school district, taxes, and other relevant factors.

In all these cases, data are the driving force behind good decisions, and therefore the ability to gather, store, process, and retrieve data in a timely manner is vital to the health of an organization. Data that are well managed can save an organization time and money, increase market share, capture new markets, improve customer service, increase productivity, and enhance decision making. For example, in order to successfully manage its gas plant on Scotland's North Sea coast, Mobil Oil created a huge database of technical drawings, called a digital image processing system (DIPS), which allows staff at different locations to access, modify, and update the drawings. Providing easy access to accurate and reliable data has not only increased productivity, but has also greatly simplified the design, construction, and daily operations of the gas facility. Another example is food banks (see box) that rely on databases to match the skills of volunteers to volunteer jobs and to identify and track homeless people. Prisons around the country are also relying on databases and other innovative technologies to make prisons more secure (see box).

In fact, data are such a valuable resource that the primary business of some companies is to generate, process, and safeguard the data of other organizations. For example, Neodata collects and processes a wealth of data about consumers so that client companies can successfully market their products. The ability to gather and process data is big business.

Data Versus Information

Although the terms *data* and *information* are sometimes used interchangeably, they have distinct implications in the study of information systems. As you may recall from Chapter 1, when data are processed,

---

BUSINESS REALITIES
Food Banks

Many food banks act as regional pantries for hundreds of homeless people all over the country. They distribute food donated by manufacturers, farmers, restaurants, hotels, and other sources to 150,000 soup kitchens, shelters, and day care centers located in their localities.

Food banks and hunger agencies use databases for a variety of tasks. For example, many food banks use databases to match more than half a million volunteers with shelters and soup kitchens in their neighborhoods,

particularly between Thanksgiving and Christmas. The Olive Branch Mission in Chicago also uses a database to track the homeless while Second Harvest uses a database to find volunteers with special skills for homeless agencies.

"We want to allow the food banks to pass information back and forth. A computer allows small staffs to do a lot of important things, rather than just keeping records, like drumming up more food donors. A nonprofit has to run every bit as businesslike as a private-sector company, and to do that, you need darn good data," says John Muller, Data Processing Manager at Second Harvest in Chicago.[3]

BUSINESS REALITIES
The Prison System

While there is often a lot of discussion in the media about the need for more and more prison systems, rarely is any coverage given to the advanced technologies that are used in some of the existing prison facilities. In fact, prisons are often said to be ahead of corporate America in their ability to deploy leading-edge technologies. Why do prisons need technologies? "You're dealing with all sorts of strange situations. An inmate might go out for medical treatment and a look-alike brother might try and come back in. Or a friend comes in for a visit and an inmate tries to leave." In fact, on many prison bids, contractors often give IS an important place on the negotiating table.

For example, biometrics is being deployed in the security systems of some prisons that are managed by CCA, the largest and fastest growing private prison management firm in the country. Biometrics is the science of measuring unique physical characteristics, such as retina scanning, handprint scanning, and voice-pattern monitor-

ing. In prisons with high traffic, CCA uses biometric hand scanning on prisoners and visitors. When a prisoner or visitor or contract worker enters a prison, his or her hand is scanned by a biometric device that creates a unique, nondigital number associated with the biometric measurement of the handprint. In retina scanning a light beam emitted by the scanner bounces off the retina and then returns to the scanner, where blood vessel patterns are digitized and recorded. The number, along with a digitized photograph of the person, is logged into a digital database. The visitor or worker must go through the same scanning process when he or she leaves the prison. The two images (at the time of entry and exit) are then compared to ensure that the same person who entered the facility is leaving the facility. Since the database system was installed many attempts to dupe jail guards have been detected and stopped.

Technologies have also made prisons more secure. For example, inmates wear electronic wristbands that are scanned at different locations throughout the prison and stored in a database. Guards can then access the database to know the location of a given prisoner at any point in time.[4]

they become information. For example, the following alphanumeric characters may not be very meaningful to a car buyer:

0100HONDA09171992IIIO4ATPSPW6925001

On the other hand, when this data is processed and the output below is produced, it becomes meaningful information to the decision-maker:

MAKE	TYPE	YEAR	PRICE
Honda	2 Doors	1994	$20,955

The once-meaningless data becomes information when it is processed and presented to the decision maker in a meaningful way. Note, however, that only when the input (data) is accurate, timely, and reliable will the output (information) be useful and reliable. The popular GIGO principle (Garbage-In-Garbage-Out) was formulated as a warning about data because bad data cannot provide useful information, no matter how much it is processed. For example, errors in data entry can result in multiple payments for the same invoice (see box on Costly Data Entry Errors), resulting in huge (and avoidable) losses for the company. The information that is generated from error-prone data is also likely to be of very limited value. There are many other disadvantages to poor data quality. Time spent checking the quality of data is entirely unproductive. Some organizations are spending 30% to 40% of IS time on data correction and revision;[6] and this is an enormous waste of resources. Firms should, therefore, continuously monitor the

Costly Data Entry Errors

As companies search for places to cut costs, they may be shocked to learn that they are losing large amounts of money by paying suppliers twice for the same invoice. The combination of data entry errors and inadequate accounts-payable software means that, on the average, 0.1% of a company's payments are duplicates. That 0.1% may seem small, but spread over the whole U.S. economy, it amounts to $3.5 billion in duplicate payments each year.

The cause can be as simple as paying both the packing slip and the invoice, or can be caused by mis-takes in data entry that defeat the software's error-checking routines. For example, most invoice-processing software packages can flag duplicate payments to a single vendor, but only if there is an exact match in the data. For example, if a hyphen is dropped in the invoice number, or if a vendor's name is spelled in a different way, the computer will not catch a duplicate payment. Errors include adding or deleting zeros, using the letter O instead of zero, or even inserting an extra space between characters. Data entry errors occur because massive amounts of data are processed by a large number of people, many of whom lack proper training and are paid the minimum wage.[5]

quality of data, establish a continuous process of data improvement, and educate users about the impact of low-quality data on bottom-line profits.

For data to be useful in decision making, it must meet three criteria: it must be accessible to the people who need it; it must be well organized, cross-referenced, and efficiently managed; and it must be easy to create, update, and maintain.

For example, the Los Angeles Department of Public Social Service (see box) uses data to detect fraudulent claims. From the success of the system, it is apparent that the data is easily accessible to decision makers, is well organized, and is effectively cross-referenced with data in other counties.

Data Hierarchy

Data and information are stored in computer files for processing, retrieval, and dissemination. If data files are not carefully organized and managed, decision makers will not be able to find the data when they need it.

Los Angeles Department of Public Social Service

The Los Angeles Department of Public Social Service (DPSS) has lost millions of dollars paying fraudulent claims. The agency turned to database technology to solve this problem and curb its losses. In 1991, the agency invested in the $9.6-million Automated Fingerprint Image Reporting and Match (AFIRM) system, which allows clerks at the 14 county DPSS offices to scan the fingerprints of each applicant and find out if the applicant is already receiving aid from other social service agencies. Images of the applicant's fingerprints are sent to a central database that contains the fingerprints of applicants from all 14 county offices; if a match is found, it confirms a fraudulent claim. The process takes about 5 minutes, compared with the many months taken by manual searches. The accuracy rate of the database is an impressive 95%.

The system catches approximately 30 people a month who are trying to double-dip and beat the system. The system went live in June 1991; in the 6 months following its installation, 3,011 cases of existing fraud were detected, saving the county $5.4 million. In the next year or so, AFIRM is expected to save the county $20 million.[7]

While many organizations are good at collecting data, only few organizations are good at *managing* their data and making it accessible to decision makers in a timely and useful manner.

The data in a computer system is organized in a hierarchy, referred to as the **data hierarchy chain.** The hierarchy, in ascending order, includes bits, bytes, fields, records, files, and databases. Figure 6–1 shows the relationships among these elements.

A bit, as you may recall, is a value that represents the presence or absence of an electronic signal and is represented as a 1 or 0—an on-off switch. Eight bits make up a byte and a byte is required to represent a character (numeric, alphabetic, and so on) in a computer. For example, we need four bytes to represent the name *Mary* in a computer. Since each character, such as *M,* is represented using 8 bits, the word *Mary* requires 32 bits.

A meaningful grouping of characters or bytes is referred to as a **field.** For example, Mary's last name, first name, and phone number are three fields. A group of interrelated fields is called a **record.** Thus, Mary's last name, first name,

Data hierarchy chain

The data stored in a database is organized in a hierarchy: databases, files, records, fields, bytes, and bits.

Field

A meaningful group of characters. A record consists of fields; a field is made up of bytes.

Record

A group of interrelated fields. A collection of records is a file.

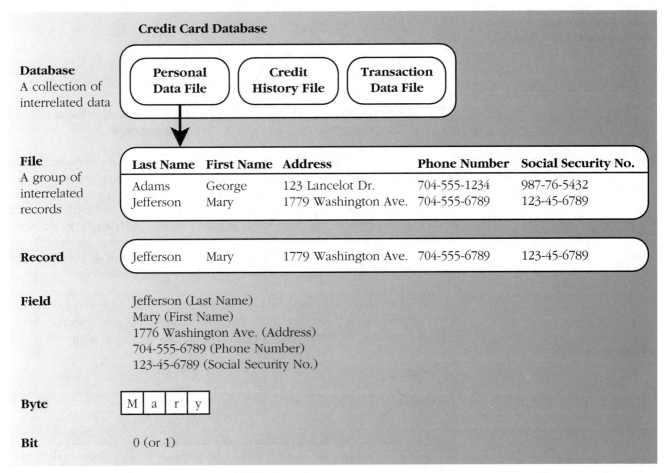

FIGURE 6–1

The data hierarchy. A database is made up of records, records consist of fields, fields contain bytes, and bytes are made up of bits. This example shows part of a database for a credit card company.

Entity
A person, place, thing, or idea about which data is gathered.

Attribute
Each column in a relational table represents a field, also referred to as an attribute. Attributes are characteristics of an entity.

Key field
A field that is a unique identifier.

File
A file is a collection of records of the same type grouped together.

Database
An integrated repository of logically related data that facilitates easy access and processing of data.

Sequential file organization
The use of unique keys to sequentially store the contents of a file in the same sequence in which they were collected. Sequencing must be done before the file is created.

social security number, phone number, and home address can make up a record because they constitute relevant data about Mary. Another way to look at a record is to view it as a description of an **entity** (e.g., Mary). An entity can be a person, a place, a thing, or an idea. The characteristics of the entity are called **attributes.** In our example, Mary can be described by using attributes such as her phone number, social security number, gender, and so on; the value of each attribute can be found by referring to the relevant field (recall that Mary's last name is a field). Each record must contain at least one field that uniquely identifies the entity. For example, since there may be many Marys at ABC Company, we need a unique identifier (such as social security number), referred to as a **key field,** to make each record unique.

A collection of records of the same type that are grouped together, such as the collection of employee records at ABC Company, is called a **file.** A collection of interrelated files is a **database.** The personnel data file, the employee benefits file, and the employee salary file are a group of interrelated files that provide information about employees, and hence can be brought together as a database. On the other hand, an organization's inventory file, employee benefits file, and suppliers' addresses file would not make a good database because these files are not interrelated.

Methods for Organizing Data in Files

There are a number of methods to organize data in files. The choice of the method depends on factors such as storage media, access methods, processing techniques, and so on. In this section, we look at three ways to organize files: sequential file organization, direct file organization, and indexed-sequential file organization.

Figure 6–2a shows how sequential files are organized. In **sequential file organization,** records are written and stored on a secondary storage device (such as a magnetic tape or magnetic disk) in the same sequence in which they were collected. The records are arranged in order using a unique key (such as social security number) and are physically adjacent to one another. For example, employee records can be arranged in ascending order by their social security numbers. Although sequentially organized files can be stored in different types of storage media, magnetic tape is the most popular storage medium for this type of data organization.

In order to retrieve or process a record, the file is sequentially processed from the beginning, using the order in which it was created, say social security number, until the desired record is located. This implies that data sequencing and

FIGURE 6–2A

In sequential file organization, if we want to retrieve Record 199, records 1 through 198 must be read first.

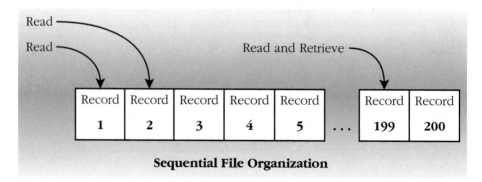

Sequential File Organization

Record 199 To be Located → Unique Key → Hashing Algorithm

Direct-file organization

Record	Record	Record	Record	
122	**372**	**199**	**412**	. . .

ordering must be done before the file is created, because the ordering of the data cannot be changed when the file is processed. Further, when records are modified, the entire file must be rearranged. This can be a time-consuming task.

In spite of its limitations, sequential file organization is well suited to batch processing applications, such as payroll. This method uses very little storage space and is useful for applications in which records have to be retrieved in the same order every time the file is processed.

Figure 6–2b shows the orientation of direct file organization. In contrast to sequential organization, **direct file organization** allows data to be retrieved quickly in a random manner, regardless of the way in which the data was originally stored. In this method, the unique key that is used to organize files (such as social security number) is converted directly to a memory address, using a mathematical formula called a **hashing algorithm.**

The magnetic disk is ideally suited to this type of file organization and many applications today use some form of direct file organization. They are particularly well suited to quickly retrieve a single record, although sequential processing of direct files can be time-consuming.

Figure 6–2c portrays indexed-sequential file organization. In **indexed-sequential file organization** data are stored in a sequence (similar to the sequential method), but in addition an index is created that shows the memory address of each piece of data. Like a book index, which shows the page location

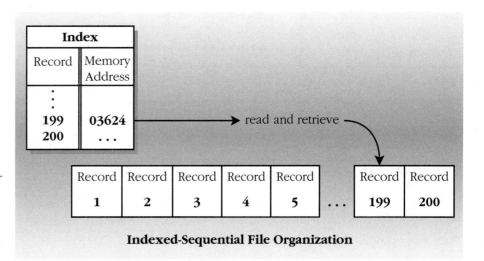

Indexed-Sequential File Organization

of each given topic, a file index shows the memory address or physical location of each piece of data, making it easier and quicker to access data. Note that the difference between direct file organization and this method is that direct files use a hashing algorithm to directly retrieve the record, whereas the indexed-sequential system refers to an index to determine the location of a record in memory. Table 6–1 summarizes the three ways in which files can be organized.

Limitations of Traditional Files

Although in the early days of the computer revolution data was stored and processed using file processing systems, today databases are strongly preferred because of the many disadvantages of file processing systems. In a file processing system, each file is independent of (or unrelated to) other files, and hence data in different files can be integrated only by writing customized programs. Further, the data and the application that uses the data are so tightly interwoven that any change to the data requires changing all the programs that use the data. This is because each file is "hard-coded" with specific information about each piece of data, such as data type, data length, and so on. Therefore, when the data changes, all programs that access the data have to be modified to reflect the changes to the data. In many instances, since it is difficult even to identify all the programs that use that data, quite often this is done on a trial-and-error basis.

Figure 6–3 shows how in a file processing system, each functional area of the business generates separate data files.

For example, suppose we have two files: one containing the names of salespeople and their sales commissions, and another file containing names, home addresses, and telephone numbers of the salespeople. In a file processing environment, a customized program must be written to generate a report that identifies the sales commission and the phone number of each salesperson.

Data redundancy
Occurs when data are duplicated in different files.

Another disadvantage of a file processing system is **data redundancy,** or duplication of data, in which the same data resides in several files. This causes problems such as wasted storage, difficulty in updating and maintaining files, and inconsistency of data values. In our example, note that the names of the salespeople appear in both files. Data duplication not only results in wasted computer resources, but can also create gross inconsistencies in the definition of terms, leading to poor decisions. For example, if work-in-progress is defined differently in two databases, then depending on the database that a manager accesses, the value of a variable may be very different, although there should be only one value for this variable. Finally, data duplication may compromise the integrity of the

TABLE 6–1
Before the evolution of databases, data was stored in independent files. Three ways to organize files are sequential, direct, and indexed-sequential.

File Type	File Organization
Sequential	Data is stored sequentially, based on a unique key. Data can be accessed only in the order in which it is stored.
Direct	The memory address of the data is identified using the hashing algorithm and this speeds up the process of retrieving the data.
Indexed-Sequential	Data is stored based on a unique key and can be accessed directly. The location of the data is identified using an index.

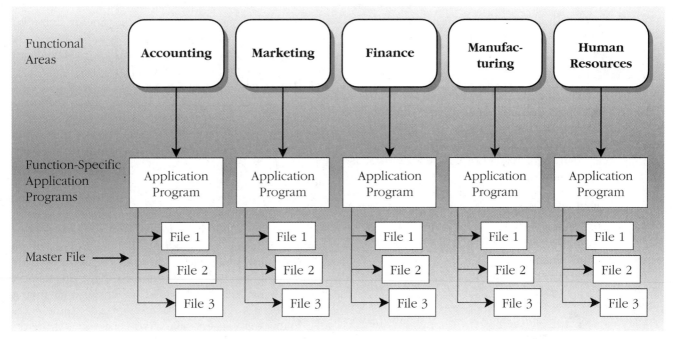

FIGURE 6–3

In a file-oriented environment, each functional area in the organization creates, processes, and disseminates its own files. Function-specific application programs, such as payroll and inventory, generate separate files. These files do not communicate with each other.

data, since one file may be updated while another file containing the same record may not be updated. As organizations grow in size and the volume and complexity of their data increase, files become more difficult to maintain and less reliable.

A database overcomes many of the limitations of file processing systems, so today many organizations use databases to create, process, and disseminate data. For example, the Houston Astros use databases to track the injuries and treatments of players (see box). Unlike file processing systems, in which files are independent, a database is a collection of interrelated files. Files are dependent on the application programs that use them while databases are independent of the application programs that access and process the files.

Introduction to Database Management Systems

In this section, we describe the primary functions of a DBMS.

A database is an integrated repository of logically related data, organized in such a way as to facilitate easy accessing and processing of data. Database systems require the use of direct access storage devices.

Database management systems (DBMS) are support programs that work in conjunction with the operating system to create, process, store, retrieve, control, and manage data. Table 6–2 describes the primary functions of a DBMS. The DBMS acts as an interface between the application program (say, payroll) and the data in the database (say, employee records). Hence, if a user wants to retrieve the social security number of an employee, the DBMS locates the data and dis-

Database management system (DBMS)

A set of programs that act as an interface between application programs and the data in the database. Support programs that work with the operating system to create, process, and manage data.

B U S I N E S S   R E A L I T I E S
Houston Astros

Today, baseball teams are looking for innovative ways to improve the batting average of the players and the most recent addition to the tool set designed to improve efficiency is computer technology. The Houston Astros, for example, are using a Microsoft Corp. Access 2.0 database to track player injuries throughout their six minor-league teams and its 100-plus game season. Since many players sign a contract when they are 18, the probability of suffering injuries over the entire career is quite high and it is critically important to keep track of these injuries and their treatments.

Trainers were having a problem in tracking the different injuries of different players. Before the new system was installed, trainers used hand-written notes to keep track of the injuries and the treatments players received. The manual system was tedious, error-prone, and inefficient. Even more important, such a system could become embarrassing, and even damaging, in case of a lawsuit. Also, keeping track of injuries and treatments is vital in order to plan and estimate when an injured player would return to the lineup. Improper tracking of injuries could seriously harm the player and result in lost games. On the other hand, it could also result in keeping a good player off the field.

The Access database is loaded on notebook computers and tracks players' injuries and treatments. Trainers can easily access the notebooks and access or update records on players. Under the new system, when a player is injured, a detailed description of the injury along with the treatment given to the player is entered into the database.

The system, which took only six months to build, has provided the Astros with some significant benefits. First, the information is up-to-date and accurate. Second, trainers can gain ready access to information on any player at any time. Third, there is consistency in the information that is shared among different trainers. Finally, it has helped the team to ensure that injured players do not return too soon or too late to the game. "I couldn't tell you in dollars and cents terms if there is a direct monetary return on this system. But if it keeps your talent healthy, then it is definitely worth its cost," says Pat Murphy, systems analyst for the Astros.[8]

---

plays it for the user. Compare this with traditional file processing, in which the user must specify both the data and the location of the data!

Advantages of Databases over Traditional Files

Data independence
A system that lets a user access data based simply on the contents of the data and its associations with other data, without knowing the physical location of the data.

One of the primary advantages of a DBMS is **data independence,** which means that a user can access a piece of data based simply on its contents and its associations with other data, without being burdened with the question "What is the physical location of this data?" For example, a sales manager can retrieve the entire record of a salesperson in his or her region based just on that person's social security number (or any other unique key), without worrying about where that data is located. Also, a DBMS allows the user to retrieve all records associated with that social security number, such as number of sales made by the salesperson, total amount of each sale, and so on, even if the data is changed or relocated, making databases more user-friendly and less error-prone than other systems.

Further, in a DBMS, the physical organization of the data is independent of the program that uses that data. Hence, if data is physically relocated, the programs that use that data do not have to be modified, making it considerably easier to maintain the database. Also, data redundancy is considerably reduced, since there is no need to store the same data in different locations. Accessing and processing data is considerably more effective in a DBMS than in traditional files; this is a significant advantage, particularly for large databases.

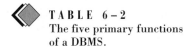

TABLE 6-2
The five primary functions
of a DBMS.

Define, create, and organize a database.	Establish the logical relationships among different data elements in a database and define schemas and sub-schemas using the data definition language (DDL).
Input data.	Enter data into the database through an input device, such as a data screen, a touch screen, or a voice-activated system.
Process data.	Process and manipulate data using the data manipulation language (DML).
Maintain data integrity and security.	Limit database access to authorized users.
Query database.	Provide decision makers with information they need to make dependable decisions. Query the database using Structured Query Language (SQL).

Disadvantage of Databases

The primary disadvantage of a database is that it requires considerable outlay of resources. Mainframe hardware is expensive and although today there are a number of PC-based databases, multiple copies of the software, combined with training, can become an expensive proposition.

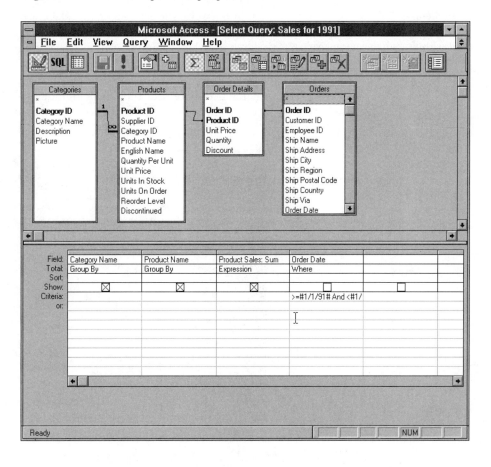

Access Query Output

Differences Between Databases and Traditional Files

Let us take a look at why the location of data has to be specified in a file processing environment, whereas a database automatically retrieves the data. The primary reason for this difference is that in a DBMS, the logical and physical views of the data are separate, whereas in a file processing environment, the logical and physical views of the data are tightly interwoven.

The **logical view** of data presents the logical relationship between different data elements in a database; the **physical view** shows how the data are physically stored in a storage medium. A decision maker is concerned only with the logical relationship between data, and hence must not be burdened with storage issues. For example, a payroll administrator simply wants to view the relationships among gross pay, taxes, other deductions, and net pay, and is not interested in the memory locations of the data.

A **schema** is a *logical* description of each piece of data and its relationships with other data elements. Note that a schema simply identifies the data (say, social security number) and the relationships among different pieces of data (say, social security number and employee name), but not the actual values of the data (say, 999–99–9999). Hence, the schema is simply a description of the following elements: name of the data (e.g., customer name or credit card number), the type of data (e.g., customer name is alphabetic), and the number of positions assigned to the data (e.g., name cannot be more than 20 characters long). Figure 6–4 presents a graphical view of a schema.

A **subschema** is a subset of a database that is used by a particular program or application. For example, a marketing manager would look at a subschema to view the sales commissions of salespeople in the company. When the user defines the schemas and subschemas, they are automatically generated by the DBMS. Schemas and subschemas increase the efficiency of databases and make them much more user-friendly than traditional files. Table 6–3 summarizes the differences between flat files and relational databases.

Logical view
The logical relationships among data elements in a database.

Physical view
A view that shows how data is physically stored in a storage medium.

Schema
A logical description of each piece of data in the database and its relationship with other data elements. It does not identify the actual value of the data.

Subschema
A subset of the fields and records in a schema. Subschemas provide a user-oriented view of the database.

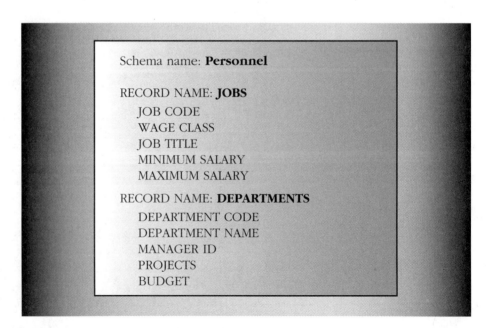

Schema name: **Personnel**

RECORD NAME: **JOBS**
    JOB CODE
    WAGE CLASS
    JOB TITLE
    MINIMUM SALARY
    MAXIMUM SALARY

RECORD NAME: **DEPARTMENTS**
    DEPARTMENT CODE
    DEPARTMENT NAME
    MANAGER ID
    PROJECTS
    BUDGET

FIGURE 6–4

A schema.

TABLE 6-3
The differences between flat files and relational databases.

Flat-Files	vs.	Relational Databases
• Store data in one-dimensional files.		• Store data in two-dimensional tables.
• Store, organize, and retrieve information from one file at a time.		• Store, organize, and retrieve information from tables in which information is linked by a common column or field.
• Leave the management of data relationships to the applications that access the data.		• Establish relationships between files with foreign keys and views within the database itself.
• Require the programmer to write code for data management functions.		• Have a database engine that handles different functions
• Are typically created and maintained by application programs.		• Are typically created and maintained by database administrators.
• Are often associated with older programs on mainframe and midrange systems.		• Are popular on UNIX processors and powerful servers within a client/server architectural framework.

The Components of a DBMS

A DBMS has three main components. They are the data definition language (DDL), the data manipulation language (DML), and the data dictionary.

Data Definition Language The contents of a database are created using the **data definition language (DDL).** It defines the relationships between different data elements and serves as an interface for application programs that use the data. For example, if a payroll program needs the social security number of an employee, the DDL defines the logical relationship between the social security number and the other data in the database and acts as an interface between the payroll program and the files that contain the social security numbers.

Data Manipulation Language Data is processed and updated using a language called the **data manipulation language (DML),** whose commands process, update, and retrieve data. It allows a user to query a database and receive summary reports and/or customized reports, for instance, a list of the top five salespeople in the company. The DML is usually integrated with other programming languages, many of which are 3GLs and 4GLs, in order to implement sophisticated database functions.

 Structured Query Language (SQL) is a nonprocedural language that deals exclusively with data: data integrity, data manipulation, data access, data retrieval, data query, and data security. SQL, developed by the American National Standards Institute (ANSI), is primarily a query language that allows users to elicit responses from their databases to specific queries, both on mainframes and on PCs. SQL has helped to bring some standardization to relational systems so that users can transfer their experience from one database system to another without going through a steep learning curve.

 Today, most DBMS products use some version of SQL, whose primary purpose is to allow users to query a database and generate ad hoc reports that provide customized information. The box on Ciba International shows how SQL helped the company to reduce its application development time. The box on Indy 500 shows how a database helps race car drivers to develop winning strategies.

Data definition language (DDL)
A language that is used to create and describe the data and define the schema in a DBMS. It serves as an interface for application programs that use the data.

Data manipulation language (DML)
The language that processes and manipulates the data in the database. Allows the user to query the database.

Structured Query Language (SQL)
A database language that allows users to query a database and receive ad hoc reports or planned reports.

A GLOBAL PERSPECTIVE
Ciba-Giegy International

Ciba-Giegy International AG, the Swiss chemical giant based in the U.S., decentralized its IS operations in 1990. Since then, the firm has been able to provide users with greater access to corporate data, particularly through the use of SQL-based software tools.

Ciba-Giegy programmers are using Information Builders, Inc.'s EDA/SQL fourth-generation language (4GL) software to download financial data from the company's IBM DB2 and other midrange and mainframe databases to Lotus Development Corp.'s 1-2-3 and other PC software packages. Financial controllers within the company then use the decentralized applications to determine whether the financial goals of the company are being met.

The 4GL software has enabled the company to access the data from a wide variety of database systems without having to develop new databases for its distributed systems. Decentralizing the financial reporting would have been enormously expensive. The company expects to save more than five years of application development time through the use of SQL tools on just one application. Over the years, the company expects to reap much greater rewards from other applications.[9]

There are four basic operations in SQL: Select, Update, Insert, and Delete. The Select statement allows users to query the database for specific information; Update, Insert, and Delete allow users to update the data, insert new data, and delete existing data, respectively.

Users can ask two kinds of questions in SQL: static questions and dynamic questions. Static questions are routine, standard questions that, once defined, can be repeatedly used and are appropriate for generating weekly, monthly, and quar-

BUSINESS REALITIES
The Indy 500

Although the Indianapolis 500 has always featured the latest and greatest automobile technology, in recent years, the racing teams on the Indy car circuit are turning to information systems and computer technology to win the race. Computers are used in every aspect of the sport now; while some teams buy their own computer equipment, others receive it from major car companies in exchange for sponsorship or help in research. Data about the performance of the car is one of the key ingredients that helps the driver to win the race. For example, the Newman-Haas Racing Team, partly owned by actor Paul Newman, gathers nearly 60 megabytes of data during a typical race.

A case in point is Bettenhausen Motorsports. The racing team outfits driver Stefan Johansson's car with various standard sensors that feed information on a real-time basis to a notebook computer used by engineers in the pit, who then can communicate with the driver through speakers and microphones built into the driver's helmet. During pit stops, drivers such as Mario Andretti get updates on their cars based on data analyzed on the notebook computers. Data typically monitored by racing teams include fuel use, internal temperature and pressure, and ride height.

"The data gathered during the race plays a lot bigger part than what you'd think in setting up the car," says Brent Harvey, data acquisition engineer at Bettenhausen. For example, the data acquired from the car can be used to adjust wheel loads and make the car "feel" better to the driver. The data gathered during the race is carefully studied and analyzed in order to devise better winning strategies.[10]

Report writers
Software packages that allow users to generate static questions.

Data dictionary
A component of a DBMS that describes the data and its characteristics, such as location, size, and type of data. It is an electronic document.

terly reports. Software packages that generate static questions are sometimes referred to as **report writers.** Dynamic questions are those that are ad hoc and specific to the decision maker. Today, most query tools allow users to ask dynamic questions.

Data Dictionary   The third component of a DBMS is the **data dictionary,** which is an electronic document that contains data definitions and data use for every piece of data in an organization. Every organization, whether small or large, needs a tool to describe, identify, locate, control, and manage each piece of data in the organization and to ensure consistency and standardization in the use of the data throughout the organization.

A data dictionary describes data and its characteristics, such as location, size, and type; it identifies the origin, the use, the ownership, and the methods of accessing and securing data. (See Table 6–4.) The DBMS uses the data dictionary to address all questions pertaining to data, such as definitions, storage locations, use, and access privileges. Data is created, stored, and updated in the data dictionary using DDL. For example, a serious accounting blunder during the 1991 Gulf War was traced to inconsistencies in the data dictionary, which offered different figures for the number of submarines at sea. The term *submarines* was defined differently in different data dictionaries; that created the error. A good data dictionary would ensure consistent definitions of data across different databases, and if there were a change to the data, it would also identify all the databases affected by the change.

Database experts emphasize that it is important to standardize both *data terms* and *process terms* in the data dictionary. For example, at Aetna Life & Casualty Co. of Hartford, Connecticut, although the way it defines the data term "participant" is identical in different systems, the term means different things to Aetna's different business units. When the same data has different business and technology applications, such inconsistencies can cause major problems for decision makers. Aetna is taking measures to standardize its data terms and its process terms.[11]

Database Models

Database model
Represents the logical relationships among data elements in the database. Popular database models are hierarchical, network, and relational.

1–1 (one-to-one)
A relationship between two entities.

A **database model** is a way of organizing data and its interrelationships. There are three such models. They are hierarchical models, network models, and relational models.

Before we look at the different types of models, let us look at three types of relationships. A **1–1 (one-to-one)** relationship indicates a unique relationship between two entities. For example, the relationship between name and social security number is a 1–1 relationship because each person has only one social security number and vice versa. Other 1–1 relationships are that between a pres-

TABLE 6–4
An example of two data items in the data dictionary for an employee database.

Data Name	Data Type	Min. Length	Max. Length	Data Location	Access
Employee Name	Alphabetic	2	25	File A	Common
Social Security Number	Numeric	0	9	File A	Privileged

ident and a country, that between a student and his or her grade in a given course, and that between a child and its biological mother.

In a **1–M (one-to-many)** relationship, an entity can have multiple relationships with other entitles in the database. For example, a mother can have many children, but each child can be traced to only one mother; in a given course, a teacher has many students, but each student has only one teacher for that course; Delta Flight 3065 has many passengers, but each passenger has only one flight number. These are all examples of one-to-many relationships.

Finally, in an **M–M (many-to-many)** relationship, every entity can be related to a number of entities. Each airport has many airlines that use its facilities and each airline has access to many airports; each credit card company has many customers and each customer may have many credit cards; each teacher has many students and each student may have many teachers.

One-to-many (1–M)
A relationship in which each node can have only one parent, but can have multiple children.

Many-to-many (M–M)
A relationship in which a record can have multiple parents and multiple children.

Hierarchical Data Model

Hierarchical model
A model in which the logical relationships among data elements are represented as a hierarchy using 1–M relationships.

In a **hierarchical model,** the *logical* relationships among various data elements are represented as a hierarchy, similar to an organizational chart, and a given data element can be accessed only by going through the proper hierarchy. Each "box" in the hierarchical model is a record, sometimes referred to as a node; the topmost node is referred to as the *root node.* The relationship between different nodes is sometimes referred to as a parent-child relationship; in a hierarchical model, each node (except the root node) has exactly one parent. In other words, the data elements in a hierarchical model are well suited for a one-to-many (1–M) relationship with other data elements in the database, because each parent can have a number of children. Note that the hierarchical model can also be used to represent relationships other than the 1–M relationship, although this is not recommended. An example of a hierarchical DBMS is IBM's Information Management System (IMS).

Figure 6–5 shows a hierarchical data model of a university registration system. The root node is the university, which is made up of a number of schools (business, arts, engineering, and so on). A school is on the first level in the hierarchy. Each school, in turn, has a number of departments. For example, the business school has MIS, marketing, accounting, finance, and economics departments. The departments are the second level in this hierarchy. Each department offers different courses—for example, the MIS department offers MIS 1025, MIS 2023, and so on—so courses are the third level; finally, on the fourth level are the students registered in each course.

Pointers
Data stored by a computer to establish links between records.

How does the computer retrieve records from the hierarchy? This is done through **pointers,** which are pieces of data that identify the links between different records. The data nodes in a hierarchical database are linked to one another through a series of pointers, one of which is attached to the end of each record in the database. For example, each department in the business school has a series of pointers that point to all the courses offered by that department. Each course, in turn, has pointers to the students registered in that course.

Advantages and Disadvantages of Hierarchical Model   The hierarchical model is ideally suited for problems in which the data elements have a natural hierarchical structure or flavor, such as problems with a large number of structured and routine requests. However, this model also has some disadvantages. In the absence of a natural hierarchical structure among data elements, the model may hinder the

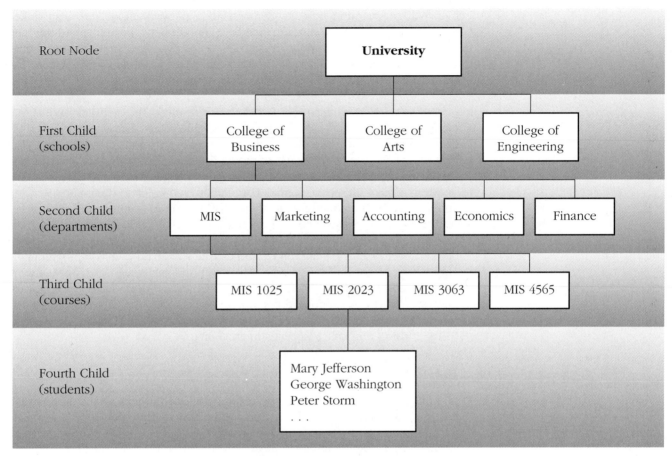

Root Node			University		
First Child (schools)		College of Business	College of Arts	College of Engineering	
Second Child (departments)	MIS	Marketing	Accounting	Economics	Finance
Third Child (courses)		MIS 1025	MIS 2023	MIS 3063	MIS 4565
Fourth Child (students)		Mary Jefferson George Washington Peter Storm . . .			

FIGURE 6–5

A hierarchical database for a university registration system. Notice the similarity between the hierarchical model and an organizational chart. The root node (University) has no parents, but has many children. In order to access the node Peter Storm, data elements above it, starting with University, must be accessed.

modeling process rather than facilitate it. Second, data values stored at a lower level cannot be accessed without accessing data values above them, making this method of retrieval time-consuming, especially for large databases. Third, this model has a rigid structure in which the relationships between different elements must be clearly identified before development begins, and any changes to the model require major programming effort. Hence, a hierarchical data model may not always be flexible enough to accommodate the dynamic data needs of an organization.

Network Model

Network model

A model in which the relationships among data elements are represented by M–M relationships. It is a variation of the hierarchical model.

In a **network model,** each record in a database can have multiple parents—that is, the relationships among data elements can be many-to-many (M–M relationship). For example, each student can attend many classes and each class can have many students, so that there is a M–M relationship between students and classes. The network model is a variation of the hierarchical model; databases can be translated from hierarchical form to network form and vice versa. Like those in hierarchical data models, data elements in a network model are also linked through pointers. The main difference between the network model and the hierarchical model is that in a network model a child can have a number of parents, whereas in a hierarchical model a child can have only one parent. Figure 6–6 shows the M–M relationships among airports and airlines.

Advantages and Disadvantages of Network Model   The network model has many advantages. Its structure promotes flexibility and data accessibility, since data elements at a lower level can be accessed without accessing the data elements above them. The network model is efficient, is easy to understand, and can be applied to many real-world problems that require routine transactions. The disadvantages of the network model are that it is complex to design and develop and it has to be fine-tuned frequently so that relationships among different pieces of data are true representations of the real world. Like the hierarchical model, the network model requires that the relationships among all data elements be defined before development begins, and changes often demand a major programming effort. Further, for large databases, operation and maintenance of the network model are time-consuming and expensive. Neither the hierarchical model nor the network model can support ad hoc queries.

An example of a network DBMS is Integrated Database Management Systems (IDMS), from Computer Associates International.

Relational Model

The third type of data model is the relational model, in which data is represented using two-dimensional tables, called **relations** or **flat files,** which are made up of columns and rows. Each column represents a field, also referred to as an attribute; each row represents a record, also referred to as a **tuple.**

Today, the most popular type of DBMS is the relational DBMS, because of its many advantages. The biggest advantage of the relational model over others is that it can relate data in a table to data in any other table as long as the two tables (or files) *share at least one common attribute*. This is a simple yet powerful idea, one that has made the relational model almost a database standard. Today, there

Relational model

Two-dimensional tables made up of columns and rows. Each column represents a field and each row a record. One of the most popular database models.

Tuple

Each row in a relational database represents a record, also called a tuple.

FIGURE 6–6

In a network data model, there can be a many-to-many (M–M) relationship among data elements. In this figure, each airport has many airlines that use its facilities, and each airline uses many airports.

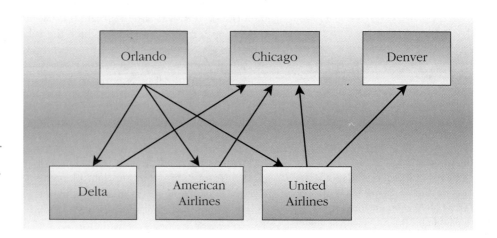

are many popular microcomputer relational databases, such as dBASE IV and Paradox (from Borland International), and Oracle (from Oracle Corporation).

Figure 6–7 shows an example of a relational database with three tables: School, Faculty, and Course. This example will be used to discuss some basic concepts. There are three basic operations in a relational database: *select, project,* and *join.* The *select* operation selects all records in a table that meet a certain criterion, such as selecting core courses (Core Course = "Yes"). The *join* operation joins, or links, two or more tables, if the information requested by the user is not found in one table. For example, in order to determine all core courses taught by a certain faculty member, the information has to be gleaned from two tables: School and Faculty. The third operation, *project,* creates a subset of columns (or a new table) designed to meet the information needs of the user, such as the time and meeting place of every core course. This is one of the most powerful features of relational databases, since it allows data to be easily retrieved and analyzed from a number of tables at the same time.

There are many relational databases in the real world. For example, a major auto company has installed a relational database system on its IBM mainframe which holds data on 400 test-driven vehicles and provides on-line information and statistics about the wear and tear of different components and systems. The database can be accessed by almost 300 engineers in 11 North American manufacturing plants and allows managers to generate summary reports of hundreds of test results and recommend suitable changes to the vehicles. Access to the right data at the right time by the right people has increased the company's ability to analyze vehicle performance by almost 284 percent.

FIGURE 6–7

A relational database with three tables: School, Faculty, and Course. These tables are sometimes called *relations.* Each column (e.g., Course No.) is a field and each row (e.g., MAN 4140) is a record, or tuple.

School Table

School	Department	Dept. Chair	Course No.	Core Course
Business	Marketing	Sheila Stuart	MAR 4530	Yes
Business	Management	Angela Williams	MAN 4140	No
Engineering	Materials	Peter Chen	EMA 3110	No
Arts	Music	Michael Jones	AMI 2140	Yes

Faculty Table

Faculty Member Name	Social Security No.	Faculty Member ID	Course No.
Wheatly	940-00-1111	3624	MAN 4140
Jones	362-62-6222	1014	EMA 3110
Bailey	111-11-1111	4636	EMA 3110
Vanden	333-33-0000	1099	AMI 2140

Course Table

Course No.	Teacher Name	Meeting Time	Place
MAR 4530	Lewis	6:00 p.m.	BH 310
MAN 4140	Wheatly	9:30 a.m.	GCB 220
EMA 3110	Bailey	10:00 a.m.	ART 149

Some popular relational databases are Access (Microsoft), dBase IV and Paradox (Borland), and DB2 (IBM).

Advantages and Disadvantages of Relational Models   The relational model has many advantages, but its most appealing quality is its great simplicity. First, users can easily relate to tables and hence find the data structure in a relational model easy to understand and implement. Second, users are not burdened with issues such as storage structure and access strategy because a relational database automatically addresses these issues. Third, the relational model is flexible and can integrate data and information from multiple files. Fourth, the relational model supports ad hoc queries; this feature is important if users are to be able to use the full power of the database. Finally, in a relational model, new data elements can easily be added and old ones deleted or updated without any significant design changes to the database.

The relational model is not without its drawbacks. It is slow by comparison with other data models, since it has to access data from different tables, and this can become tedious, particularly for large databases. However, with advances in hardware and software, this limitation is being overcome. Another disadvantage of large relational databases is their data redundancy (data duplication), since the same data are likely to be stored in several tables. Despite these drawbacks, relational models continue to grow in popularity. Table 6–5 summarizes the advantages and disadvantages of the three data models.

You may have observed that dealing with large databases is difficult for all three data models discussed above. This is not so much a limitation of these models as it is a problem with large databases. The largest databases are already breaking records: IRI's homegrown database takes up about 1.7 terrabytes; Nynex's Market Intelligence Tracking and Analysis System (MITAS) occupies more than 400 GB; and UPS's Delivery Information Automated Lookup System (DIALS) is passing 1.5 terrabytes.

TABLE 6–5
The advantages and disadvantages of the three types of data models.

Data Model	Advantages	Disadvantages
Hierarchical	• Some problems lend themselves to this model • Easy to understand • Continues to be widely used	• Difficult to access values at lower levels • Changes to the model require extensive programming
Network	• Easy access to data • Flexible	• Complex to design and develop • Large models consume a great deal of computer memory
Relational	• Widely used • Easy to understand • Provides excellent support for ad hoc queries • Users need not consider issues such as storage structure and access strategy	• Relatively slow to execute for large databases • Data redundancy

Most databases are considered large when they reach tens of gigabytes in size. For example, Information Resources, Inc.'s (IRI) proprietary database of supermarket data, fed by supermarket scanners at more that 3,000 stores, is almost 2 terrabytes in size and continues to grow at a rate of 100 GB per month.[12] The company uses the consolidated database to track 1 million products nationwide, allowing its customers, including food and soap manufacturers, to pinpoint regional buying patterns. However, such large databases can quickly become unwieldy. One way to handle this problem is to break the data down into "slices" of 10 GB to 20 GB, such that each slice groups relevant data. However, the task of dividing data is not an easy one and the concept of a slice should be carefully defined. The $276-million firm uses artificial intelligence programs to determine a slice and help users navigate the jumbo-size database. Further, large databases use multi-million-dollar mainframes that require a staff of hundreds to maintain the system and the database and maintenance is very expensive on large databases.

Entity Relationship Diagram

Entity relationship diagram (ERD)

A graphical tool that identifies and represents the entities in an enterprise or system and the logical relationships among those entities.

An **entity relationship diagram (ERD)** is a graphical tool that identifies and represents the entities in an enterprise or system and the logical relationships among these entities. An ERD is very useful to capture the data elements in a system. An entity is a person, place, thing, or idea about which data is gathered. Entities in a university include teachers, students, administrators, courses, and classrooms. In a restaurant, entities include waiters, managers, customers, food items, and the kitchen. An attribute is an item of data that describes an entity. Attributes for a job include job code, wage class, job title, minimum salary, and maximum salary. Attributes for a student include the student's name, social security number, number of credits per semester, and so on. The value assigned to each attribute is called the attribute value (e.g., the student's name is Mary Joe).

Since entities are linked to each other through relationships (a relationship is the way entities interact with one another), a graphical tool that depicts the entities and their interrelationships plays a very useful role in gaining a better understanding of the "big picture." For example, an ERD can be used to show graphically how sales commission is related to salary, taxes, and take-home pay.

An ERD represents static data and is used for many modeling tasks, such as modeling an enterprise, its entities, and the relationships among them. (This is also referred to as enterprise modeling.) The ERD also plays a very important role in the design and development of information systems, since it gives a good overview of the elements in a system and their interrelationships and is hence used extensively to design information systems and capture different data elements.

There are two types of design: physical design and logical design. Physical design addresses issues related to the physical location of data; logical design addresses the logical relationships among various data items in the database and captures the essence of data interactions. The logical design presents the data from a user's perspective; the physical design presents the data from the computer's perspective. The user is not concerned about where the data is located in memory, but is concerned about the role of data in decision making (logical design). The computer, on the other hand, has no knowledge of how the data is used in decision making; it "knows" only where that data is stored in the system (physical design).

The ERD is a useful tool in the logical design of a database, because it graphically portrays the entities and their interrelationships.

ERD Symbols

Figure 6–8 shows the three primary symbols in an ERD: a rectangle to depict an entity, a diamond to depict a relationship, and lines or arrows that link different entities and express the relationships between them.

The rectangle depicts an entity (a place, person, thing, or idea). The name of the entity is written inside the rectangle. The relationship between two entities is depicted using a diamond; the relationship itself, which is usually described using a verb, is described inside the diamond.

The three possible types of relationships among entities, namely, one-to-one (1–1), one-to-many (1–M), and many-to-many (M–M), are usually shown on the lines or arrows that link different entities.

There are five steps in creating an ERD. (See Table 6–6.)

1. Identify the entities in the system that is being modeled. For example, the entities in the business school include the dean, the faculty, the students, the administrators, the courses, the scholarships, the student organizations, and so on.
2. Identify the relationships between the entities. For example, a faculty member (an entity) teaches (a relationship) students (another entity). Students (an entity) receive (a relationship) scholarships (another entity).
3. Identify the keys for each entity. A **key** is a unique way to identify each entity. For example, each faculty member has a unique social security number and each class has a unique course number.
4. Identify the attributes of each entity. An attribute is a data element that describes an entity. For example, attributes of the scholarship entity may include the name of the scholarship, the awarding agency, the scholarship amount, and so on.
5. Ensure that there are no duplicates or redundancies in the data. Duplication is not only a waste of resources but can also quickly become a maintenance nightmare.

Key
A unique way to identify each record.

FIGURE 6–8

The three symbols that are used in an entity relationship diagram are shown above. They are entity name (e.g., Customer Name), relationship name (e.g., Credit Card Number), and the links between different entities and relationships, depicted as arrows.

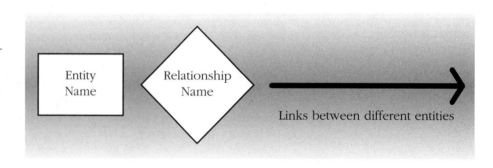

TABLE 6–6
The five steps in creating an ERD.

1. Identify the entities in the system that is being modeled.
2. Identify the relationships between the entities.
3. Identify the keys for each entity.
4. Identify the attributes of each entity.
5. Break down large data groups into smaller groups and ensure there are no data redundancies

Distributed database
Databases distributed over single- or multi-vendor hardware located in different geographic areas.

Distributed Databases

A **distributed database,** as its name implies, is a database distributed over single- or multi-vendor computer hardware located in different geographic areas. In an ideal distributed environment, a user in a given location can access any database, on any hardware, located anywhere on the network. Two variables influence the way a database is distributed: the database itself and the hardware on which the database resides. A central database can be *partitioned* so that the data relevant to each location is stored in that location. Alternatively, the central database can be replicated and stored in various remote locations. One or more databases may reside on a hardware platform from a single vendor (such as IBM) or from several vendors (such as IBM, Unisys, Digital, and so on). Databases are distributed in different ways depending on the information needs of the organization and the availability of resources. Figures 6–9a through 6–9d show different types of distributed databases.

Although the term *distributed database system* conjures up images of thousands of pieces of data being transmitted over a network, the goal of a distributed database is quite the opposite: to *localize* the data, along with the processes that operate on that data, in the location where it is most meaningful. In other words, although it may appear as if each distributed database on the network operates as a separate database with no links to any other database, from a corporate perspective, the various databases are logically tied together over the network and easily accessible to the user.

There are two primary reasons why distributed databases have become popular in recent years. First, in the early years of computing, many organizations cre-

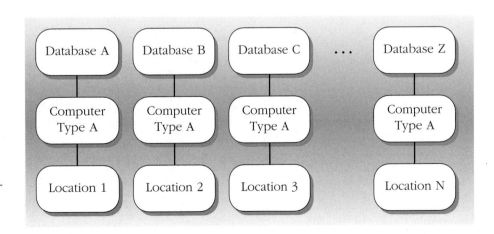

FIGURE 6–9A

Different databases reside on the same type of hardware platform in different locations.

FIGURE 6-9B

The same database resides on the same type of computer platform in different locations.

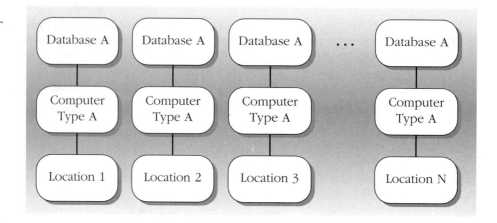

ated individual databases for different applications, such as payroll, personnel data, employee benefits, and so on. Unfortunately, many of these databases could not communicate with one another because they were created on different systems or because their architectures were very different. Distributed databases provide a way to overcome this problem. Second, the business units of an organization may be geographically dispersed and the information needs and demands of each location may be very different. Distributed databases help to store the data where it is most needed or used, and help to customize the data to meet the needs of individual business units.

Advantages of Distributed Databases

Distributed databases promote a sense of ownership, foster accountability, and provide a meaningful way to allocate the operating costs of computing to various business units in the organization. In a distributed environment, although the CIO may retain control over the enterprise data, end-users are responsible for updating and maintaining their local databases. Distributed databases also help to minimize the impact of system failures, since at least part of the network is always operational. Suppose a global credit card company does all its data processing on

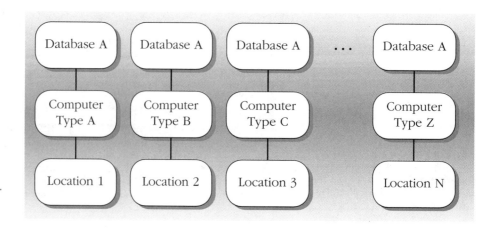

FIGURE 6-9C

The same database resides on different types of computers.

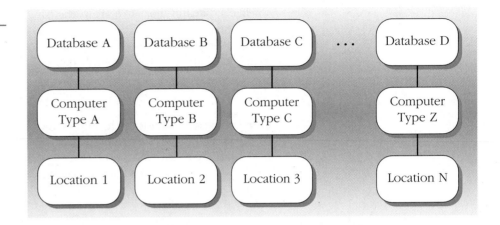

a mainframe located in Dallas. If there is a power failure, transactions cannot be processed until the power in Dallas is restored. However, if the company has a distributed database dispersed over 10 locations and there is a power failure in one location, only one tenth of the worldwide database is affected. When the power is restored, the DBMS will automatically bring that location up to date and link it immediately with the rest of the network.[13]

Disadvantages of Distributed Databases

Although distributed databases have many advantages, they are not a solution for all problems. In some cases, a distributed database may not be suitable for an organization, so IS managers must carefully assess their computing needs. For example, if a global company, such as American Express, implemented a single database in the United States to process all its credit transactions, it would be both inefficient and expensive. On the other hand, a distributed system, with separate databases in Asia, Europe, the United States, and Canada, can have a positive effect on the speed and cost of processing data. When a customer uses his or her card in another country, the transaction is sent across the network to the nearest branch.[14] For a company with branches in different places, distributed databases can provide significant advantages. On the other hand, a small company, with two branches that do not have much data in common, may not find a distributed database useful.

Distributed databases also influence the locus of control in an organization. With the spread of end-user computing, many organizations have a large number of PCs, with valuable corporate data stored on them. "Once this data has been disseminated to the users, there is no way to rein it back into a single central system. The only solution is to bring the system to the data, says one systems administrator."[15] Hence, control and security issues are big concerns in distributed databases.

Another disadvantage of distributed databases is that current tools for designing and managing distributed databases lack sophistication. Although the blueprint for a distributed computing environment (DCE) was announced in 1989, vendors have been slow in delivering products to support distributed computing. The technology necessary to build reliable distributed systems for intense and complex commercial computing is not yet fully available, although in recent years significant progress has been made in the area of updating distributed databases.

Finally, backup measures are particularly critical for distributed systems (see box on the World Trade Center). Distributed systems must be backed up frequently; otherwise companies can be in serious jeopardy. Backups are discussed in detail in Chapter 16 (Computer Security).

Principles of Database Management

Database technology has revolutionized the way organizations store, process, and disseminate data by providing instantaneous access to large volumes of information. As databases have evolved, experts have identified several principles for managing data and utilizing the full power of databases.

Principle 1: Data Resources Are Critical to an Organization and Must Be Fully Utilized and Protected.

Good data is the cornerstone of all good decisions. Unfortunately, although companies invest huge amounts of money to collect data, they are not always good at applying the data in decision making. Let us look at some steps that organizations can take to utilize this resource.

First, organizations should be selective and collect only data that is used in decision making. Often data is collected for the sake of collecting, resulting in volumes of data that are never used and perpetuating the problem of "information overload." Few organizations today believe they are fully exploiting the data they have gathered; in most cases, only a small part of the data moves outside the application that first captured it. This means that to understand or analyze the information, the user must go back to that application's database. Further, names, formats, and data structures almost always differ from one application to another. This makes data synthesis and analysis across different applications very difficult; frequently, end-users are limited to using the data as it was originally envisioned

---

BUSINESS REALITIES
World Trade Center

When the World Trade Center was bombed in February 1993, the entire nation was shocked. Many IS managers were horrified, both at a personal and a professional level, since the bombing destroyed many critical applications residing on distributed systems and local area networks in the Center. The importance of protecting mission-critical applications on distributed systems was driven home even more strongly by the incident.

Although many large companies had sound disaster recovery plans in place, many smaller firms with no prior experience were hard hit by this event. The New York Clearing House Association (NYCH), which clears roughly $1 trillion in international transactions for member banks each day, had 10 member banks in the World Trade Center when the explosion occurred. Four of those banks had to use the NYCH backup facilities in Manhattan to complete $90 billion in transactions on the day of the bombing.

Most of the organizations that suffered data losses or disruptions of distributed systems backed up data on a weekly or monthly basis, instead of on a daily basis.[16]

when the application was first automated. Clearly, this process does not recognize the dynamics of a business.

Many organizations are beginning to switch to the concept of an "information factory" with four functional components: the enterprise information base, the enterprise information directory, the data conditioning system, and the information presentation system.

- **The enterprise information base** contains all the company's data in a relational DBMS.
- **The enterprise information directory** defines the data stored in the enterprise information base, including the names, edit rules, and formats for data.
- **The data conditioning system** is a collection of procedures and control statements for extracting or unloading data from sources outside the information factory.
- **The information presentation system** is a collection of user interface products that lets authorized users access information in the enterprise information base.[17]

First, this framework allows data to be readily available across the enterprise and, further, allows users to exploit data as they see fit for decision making. Second, once the data is collected, its accuracy, timeliness, and reliability must be carefully verified. Operating on the blind faith that all data that is collected is accurate can have serious repercussions. Third, organizations should strive to get the right data to the right people at the right time. The major questions facing users are still "Where?" and "What?" and "How do I get at it?" It is important for employees to see the relationships among data, information, and action. Such learning is best effected by adding context to traditional data elements, such as spreadsheet cells or database fields. Context, in this case, means that workers receive not just facts, but the meanings and points of view that will help them make decisions. Data should be disseminated on a need-to-know basis and not simply on the basis of the organizational hierarchy. Finally, it is important to *use* the data to make better decisions.

James Cash, professor of business administration at the Harvard Business School, explains how British Airways used its databases to better serve its customers.[18] British Airways, once dubbed "Bloody Awful," is today one of the most profitable and respected airlines in the world, thanks to the company's new ability to extract and process data related to customer complaints, along with its outstanding training for service representatives and its renewed corporation-wide emphasis on customer satisfaction. In the early 1980s, service representatives consulted a 2-inch-thick manual and followed a 13-step investigation process to respond to customer complaints, normally taking close to 12 weeks simply to respond to the customer. The company estimates that poor customer service resulted in more than $600 million in lost revenue. The company realized that it had to stop the "bleeding."

Along with new performance and reward measures and extensive training, the company invested in a database that helped bring customer complaints to the surface and provided the information necessary to make immediate decisions. The original 13-step process was reduced to 5 meaningful steps: listen, apologize, express concern, make amends, and record the event.

For example, data are transmitted to the right people at the right time so that lost luggage can be found quickly, thereby saving passengers time and minimizing frustration. British Airways also keeps accurate data on passenger seat and meal preferences. The data is made available to reservation clerks, so that when a passenger calls to make a reservation, that passenger's travel preferences are available to the clerk. Cash points out that "a gold mine of useful data is hidden in any company's complaint iceberg" and that by carefully analyzing this data and taking appropriate action, a company can win and keep customers.

Principle 2: Database Technology Must Be Aligned with Business Strategy.

In Chapter 1, we emphasized that technology by itself has little or no value and that only when technology is meaningfully aligned with organizational goals can the true potential of technology be achieved.

For example, Mercedes-Benz uses it's customer databases to achieve its organizational goal of providing better customer service. When the company started to lose business to its Japanese competitors who were much better at providing superior customer service, the company quickly realized the importance of databases. Today, the company uses databases not only to provide customers with superior service but also to identify new market opportunities and fix problems before they become detrimental to the company's high quality image (see box).

Database technology, like any other technology, must be aligned with the overall goals and mission of the organization. This can be accomplished by studying the strategic information plan. The strategic information plan should indicate what data should be collected, what information is necessary to make effective decisions, who should receive it, and how it should be controlled, monitored, and managed. For example, Motorola, based in Schaumburg, Illinois, has created databases to help it achieve its business goal of becoming the market leader for electronic devices and semiconductors. Several important databases are integrated in the company so that managers can obtain instant feedback about manufacturing problems and product rejection rates.

When the strategic information plan is not used as the driving force for technology, it creates several problems. Organizations create databases simply for the sake of collecting data, large numbers of useless reports are produced, managers suffer information overload, and the right information will not be available to the right people at the right time. For example, marketing managers often must digest large volumes of data to make sound marketing decisions. Unfortunately, the volume of data that they must digest increases as the product moves closer to the marketplace. Table 6–7 shows the time that different marketing managers spend analyzing data and the volume of data they must process to make different marketing decisions. If the technology is not aligned with the goals, managers will not know how to use the data to make better decisions.

Principle 3: Control and Security Are Important Issues in Databases, Particularly Distributed Databases.

Distributed databases are becoming widespread as more and more organizations realize the benefit of distributed technology. Although distributed databases have many significant benefits, there are also some drawbacks to distributed technology.

BUSINESS REALITIES
Mercedes-Benz

When Steve Liebhoff, the owner of a Mercedes-Benz 560 SEL, got a flat tire in midtown Manhattan, he used his car phone to call Mercedes' nationwide 800 help number. They seemed to know who he was and provided courteous and timely service. Liebhoff's call went to Mercedes-Benz of North America Inc.'s customer assistance center in Montvale, NJ, where the service representative called up Liebhoff's file on an IBM PS/2 Model 77. (Incidentally, the service rep noticed that Liebhoff owned two Mercedes and had bought several others in the past!) The rep paged the closest Mercedes dealership to send assistance, and a service truck arrived within 20 minutes. "It's like having a big brother," says Liebhoff.

Delivering assistance and customer satisfaction is one of the primary goals of the integrated customer database, which replaced a number of disparate marketing and customer service databases. Customer service and marketing, says Mercedes-Benz VP Mark Juron, "are simply two ends of the same string." The company should know because in 1991, the $3.5 billion automotive arm of Germany's Daimler-Benz AG, found its sales volume was down by more than 40 percent from five years earlier. The company's strongest competitor was Toyota and its Lexus line and much of Toyota's success came from unprecedented levels of customer service.

Mercedes, led by Vice President Juron, felt that an integrated customer service system that would allow customers to interact with a single Mercedes employee, instead of being handed off from one to another, was important. Mercedes, working with consultants and Sage, a development language from Brock Control Systems Inc. in Atlanta, spent 19 months building a call center and customer information file. The system runs on an IBM 6000 and an Informix relational database management system (RDBMS). The company spent close to $5-million on the 24-hour center, and expects that the effort will save the company more than $10 million over 10 years.

The single and centralized database has played an important role in helping the company turn around. Before the new system was installed, the company had 82 different 800 numbers, 11 customer information databases, and a wide variety of disparate hardware platforms, from IBM 3090 mainframes and VAX machines to technologies that are now defunct. Reps stored customer information on whatever system they happened to own, with the result that different pieces of information about the same customer were stored on so many different systems it was impossible to get a clear and accurate picture of a given customer. Today, the company enters all relevant data when a car is sold.

This is how the center operates. A customer, using a single toll-free access number, calls the center. Callers choose the department they wish to contact through a menu prompt, and the call is routed to one of the 100 customer representatives through an automatic call distributor that is connected directly to an IBM RS/6000 Model 580 and a backup RS/6000 Model 570. When an owner calls from home, the system detects the caller's phone number, then sends his or her automobile and service records automatically to the representative, before the phone is even answered. When calls come in from the road, a representative can access a record from the Informix RDBMS by last name, home phone number, or vehicle identification number. Mercedes has provided free roadside assistance to owners for over 12 years. In a typical month, the center handles 15,000 calls for roadside assistance, 10,000 requests for printed material, and 7,000 inquiries for general assistance.

Customer information is also available to the 175 field representatives who work with the 360 Mercedes dealerships in the United States. These reps use the Procomm Plus telecommunications package from Datastorm Technologies Inc. in Columbia, Missouri, over 14.4-Kbps internal modems in their IBM 750CS ThinkPad notebook PCs to access the Informix RDBMS. Field representatives can view customer complaints as soon as they come in, review the customer's entire file, and help the dealership to resolve the issue even before the customer picks up his or her car. This builds credibility and in fact, building credibility is the primary reason to develop an in-house database, explains Daniel Soloman, president of MorCom Inc., a direct-marketing firm in Carlstadt, NJ.

Besides improving customer service, the center also helps the company to identify and fix problems quickly. For example, reps noticed that a particular model seemed to be giving trouble in the snowy winter of 1993–94. The vehicle identification numbers revealed that the cars were built around the same time. Engineers quickly took care of the problem on all affected cars.[19]

TABLE 6-7
This table shows the amount of time and the huge volumes of data that marketing managers often have to process.

Percentage of time spent working with numbers		Data volume by type of data *(in individual pieces)*	
80%	Assistant brand manager (tracks promotions)	1M	Store audit data of sample products
40%	Associate brand manager	10M	Warehouse withdrawal data as a means of tracking product demand activity
20%	Brand manager (set strategies)	300M	Market-level scanner data to track sales by region
		500M	Chain-level scanner data to track sales for an entire chain
		10,000M	Store-level scanner data to track sales at each store in the chain

Source: Blattberg, Robert, et al, eds. "The Marketing Information Revolution." *Harvard Business School Press,* 1994.

In order to truly achieve the potential of distributed databases, organizations must address the issues of control and security before developing and implementing these databases. Control and security must not be an afterthought, but instead must be the driving force in design and development of databases. (See Chapter 16.)

Principle 4: It Should Be Easy to Access and Process Data Residing in Different Databases.

More and more managers are feeling the pressure to develop open, or "seamless," systems, in which information can freely flow between different systems, regardless of the platforms on which these systems were developed or the application packages that access them. As new databases are created, it is important to ensure that data can be freely exchanged between different databases, regardless of the platform or the software on which the database was developed. If integration issues are not carefully addressed, the result is data incompatibility, data redundancies, and data corruption, which lead to serious information bottlenecks. However, easy and ready access to data must be balanced against the need for security, since easy access may result in lax security.

For example, PepsiCo International (see box) sales and marketing database provides round-the-clock access to marketing personnel on critical market data.

Principle 5: Database Tools Must Be Carefully Selected.

Today there is a wide variety of computer tools on the market and the same holds true for database tools. A large number of database packages and tools can sup-

A GLOBAL PERSPECTIVE
PepsiCo International

Roberto Waddington, manager of financial analysis in the Latin American division of PepsiCo International, has grappled with preparing short- and long-term forecasts of sales and profitability for various sales and marketing units. Those units embrace 25 products, 15 package sizes, and 72 geographical markets in 35 countries that comprise a $12.5 billion soft drink market. A member of the planning division, Waddington oversees the collection of information from the 35 countries as well as consolidating and routing it to international headquarters in Somers, New York.

Although the company uses spreadsheets for a number of applications, because spreadsheets are of limited value they give only a two-dimensional view. Further, given the number of products, package sizes, and markets that Pepsi has, it would require about five to six thousand spreadsheets to analyze all the data. Not only is this impractical but, more importantly, the numbers become unreliable and difficult to check when one is dealing with so many spreadsheets.

In the highly competitive soft-drink business, knowledge about markets is critical and has a direct bearing on the bottom line. For example, marketing managers must know which product-package size combination is the best and worst profit generator and adjust shipments accordingly. Information about products based on geography, product, brand, package, and pricing can make or break the company.

PepsiCo International uses a multidimensional database that allows individual users or workgroups to analyze sales, marketing, and other corporate data through seven dimensions: time, geography, products, package sizes/types, legal entities, accounts, and categories. The software, which costs approximately $100,000, has multidimensional capability that allows multiple users to get in-depth perspectives into local markets, round the clock. The system requires no special training because it is an extension of existing databases and spreadsheets.

PepsiCo's database is powerful and penetrates the Babel-like wall surrounding the different information systems in different countries. It consolidates such data sources as product case sales, marketing expenses, and invoices, and supports 354 data elements. Analysts can now calculate sales to specific markets by product and by container, such as a twelve-ounce Pepsi can versus twenty-six-ounce Diet Pepsi bottle and can do extensive what-if analysis, such as impact of a price change or a competitor's price change on a given product or the likely impact of a promotion on sales volume.[20]

plement the features of standard databases. IS managers often face the daunting challenge of carefully reading the product literature and selecting the best products for their companies. For example, query tools are vital to databases and a number of query tools are available; some criteria that can be used to evaluate query tools are outlined below.

- **Understand the resources required:**
  Identify the hardware and input/output requirements for the package. Many database environments require the sharing of resources, such as I/O devices, so the efficient management of these resources is a critical issue.
- **Understand database utilities:**
  Utilities such as import and export procedures, backup and recovery tools, and data tables are important. These factors should be carefully evaluated.
- **Understand SQL optimization:**
  SQL is an integral part of the DBMS. The SQL must be user-friendly and easy to edit. The DDL and DML commands in the SQL must be easy to work with and should have import and export capabilities.

♦ **Understand connectivity issues:**

PC databases are often linked to corporate databases, which tend to reside on mainframes. A good understanding of how to connect a PC database to a mainframe database is therefore essential. Also, it is important for users to know how to integrate databases with other applications, such as spreadsheets, graphics packages, or report writers.

♦ **Speed:**

How much time does it take to generate a simple report? a complex report? How much time does it take to answer a query?

♦ **Installation and configuration:**

How easy is it to install and configure the product? Can it be shared by several users on the network? Can the user interface be configured to meet the needs of the company? Can reports be deployed as runtime applications?

♦ **Database Administration:**

What steps are necessary to link the query package to the database?

♦ **Querying capabilities:**

What capabilities does the product have to query the database and filter the necessary information? Does the package protect the user from having to learn complicated SQL commands? Can the product edit the SQL code that it generates?

♦ **Event Alerts:**

Is the program capable of triggering alarms when data is corrupted? Are there multiple ways of alerting the user?

♦ **Simple reports:**

What are the features in the program that generate simple reports? Can the package generate presentation-quality output? Can the data in a summary report be easily edited and modified?

♦ **Complex reports:**

Is the product capable of generating complex reports using data or tables from multiple sources? Can data from multiple sources be brought together easily and effectively? Can the product export the database to a spreadsheet or another database?

♦ **Documentation and technical support:**

Is the documentation well written and easy to follow? Does the vendor provide unlimited technical support?

These are some issues that must be carefully addressed before buying a database package or a query tool.[21]

 ─── **Summary** ───────────────────────────────

♦ **Understand the role of data in a business and the importance of being able to quickly retrieve and process data**

Databases are the lifeline of many businesses since data resources are a valuable and critical resource, without which companies may simply not be able to function. Poorly managed and maintained data can affect the very well-being of an organization while well-managed data systems that are used creatively can provide a significant edge in the marketplace. Accurate and timely data are the backbone of good decisions, regardless of the business. Data that are well managed can save the organization time and money, increase market share, capture new markets, improve customer service, increase productivity, and enhance decision making. For data to be useful in decision making, it must meet the following three criteria: data must be accessible to the people who need it; it must be well-organized, cross referenced, and efficiently managed; it must be easy to create, update, and maintain.

♦ **Describe a data hierarchy and its elements**

The data in a computer system is organized in a hierarchy, referred to as the data hierarchy chain. The hierarchy, in ascending order, is bits, bytes, fields, records, files, and databases. A bit, as you may recall, is a boolean value that represents the presence or absence of an electronic signal and is represented as 1–0, or an on-off switch. Eight bits represents a byte and a byte is required to represent a character. A meaningful grouping of characters or bytes is referred to as a field and a group of inter-related fields is called a record. Each record must contain at least one field that uniquely identifies the entity, referred to as a key. A collection of records of the same type that are grouped together is called a file and a collection of inter-related files is a database.

♦ **Describe different methods to represent data in files**

There are different methods to organize data in files and the choice of the method depends on factors, such as storage medium, access methods, processing techniques, and so on. There are three ways to organize files: sequential file organization, direct file organization, and indexed-sequential file organization. In sequential file organization, records are written and stored on a secondary storage device (such as a magnetic tape or magnetic disk) in the same sequence in which they are collected. The records are arranged in some sort of an order using a unique key and are physically adjacent to one another. In direct file organization, data can be quickly retrieved in a random manner, without regard to the way in which the data were originally stored. In this method, the unique key that is used to organize files is converted directly to a memory address using a mathematical formula called the hashing algorithm. In indexed-sequential file organization, data are stored in a sequence (similar to the sequential method) but in addition an index is created that shows the memory address of each piece of data.

♦ **Describe and discuss the importance and functions of a DBMS**

A database is an integrated repository of logically related data organized in such a way so as to facilitate easy accessing and processing of data by users. Database systems require the use of direct access storage devices. Database Management System (DBMS) refers to support software that works in conjunction with the operating system to create, process, store, retrieve, control, and manage data. The DBMS act as an interface between the application program and the data in the database. The DBMS locates the data, displays it to the user, and performs the necessary operations on the data. Compare this with traditional file processing where the user must specify both the data and the location of the data!

♦ **Describe the components of a DBMS**

There are three main components in a DBMS. They are: data definition language (DDL), data manipulation language (DML), and the data dictionary. The contents of a database are created and modified using the data definition language (DDL). It defines the relationships between different data elements and serves as an interface for application programs that use the data. Data are processed and updated using a language called the data manipulation language (DML), which has specific commands to process, update, and retrieve data. It allows a user to query a database and receive summary reports and/or customized reports. The DML is usually integrated with other programming languages, such as 3 GLs and 4GLs in order to implement sophisticated database functions. The third component in a DBMS is the data dictionary, which is an electronic document of data definitions and data usage for each and every piece of data in an organization. All organizations, both small and large, need a tool to describe, identify, locate, control, and manage each and every piece of data in the organization and ensure consistency and standardization in the usage of data throughout the organization. A data dictionary describes data and its characteristics, such as location, size, and type; it identifies the origin, usage, ownership and methods for accessing and securing data.

Review Questions

1. Describe the elements of a data hierarchy in ascending order. The registrar's office of a local university has three student files in a database: personal data for the students, financial data (such as scholarships and financial aid), and classes in which each student has registered in the last three semesters, including the current semester. Develop a data hierarchy (files, records, fields, bytes, bits) for this example.

2. There are three ways to organize data in a file-oriented environment: sequential, indexed-sequential, and direct. Describe the three methods. Which method is the most efficient, and why?

3. What are some limitations of files and how can they be overcome using databases?

4. Explain how Readers Digest uses its database to better target its customers.

5. What is a DBMS and what are some of its primary functions?

6. Define a schema, a subschema, and a DDL. What are the relationships among the three?

7. Suppose we have two records, PERSONAL DATA and CLASSES, in a schema called STUDENT, residing in a database called UNIVERSITY. The fields in each record are shown below:
Schema STUDENT
PERSONAL DATA:
   Name:
   Address:
   Telephone Number:
   Sex:
   Age:
   Social Security Number:
CLASSES:
   Number of classes in which student is registered this semester:
   Classes taken last semester:
   Current GPA:
   Overall GPA:

Identify the fields that would be included in a sub-schema of every female student whose overall GPA is greater than 3.5.

8. Define SQL and explain its role in decision making.

9. What are the four basic operations in SQL? Refer to our schema STUDENT, which is present in a database called UNIVERSITY. The registrar would like to retrieve the name of every female student whose GPA is greater than 3.0 and who is currently registered in at least three classes. Identify the SQL operators necessary to retrieve this information.

10. What is a data model? What are the three popular data models and what is the nature of the relationship (1–1, 1–M, M–M) of the data elements in these models?

11. Compare and contrast the advantages and disadvantages of hierarchical, network, and relational models.

12. The owner of a video store would like you to develop a data model of her store. The model should reflect the relationships between movies (name of movie and videotape number of the movie) and customers (customer name, address, phone number, and account number). Develop a hierarchical model and a network model for this problem.

13. For Problem 12, develop a relational model. Of the three models, which model do you think is best suited for this problem? Explain.

14. What is an entity relationship diagram? What is the primary purpose of an ERD?

15. Draw an ERD for the example in Problem 12.

16. What is a data dictionary and what are its primary functions? Why is the data dictionary a vital tool for the IS manager?

17. What is a distributed database? Identify any four types of distributed databases.

18. Identify any two principles of database management.

 Discussion Questions

1. An important problem in information systems development and operations is poor quality of data. The amount of time spent checking or correcting spotty data can take its toll on productivity. Some organizations spend 30% to 40% of IS time on data correction and revision. QDB Solutions, a data-quality

management software maker and consultancy, based in Cambridge, Massachusetts, suggests that chief information officers (CIOs) take the initiative, concentrating on a "continuous process of data improvement" that tracks data integrity throughout a project's life cycle. The CIO must also help develop technical specifications for data quality and should call for periodic reports on data quality that should be shared with end-users. The best thing a CIO can do to promote data quality, says QDB, is to sponsor an across-the-board education effort to let everyone know just how deep a bite bad data takes from the bottom line and how severely it impedes the progress of key projects. A presentation to senior management in which these problems are clearly spelled out can overcome many of the formidable obstacles to implementing a data-quality management program.[22]

Identify what measures your university is taking to achieve "continuous process of data improvement."

2. The Jockey Club is a worldwide supplier of data for almost 2 million thoroughbred horses for the breeding and racing industries. Recently, the Club decided to merge the information buried in its mainframe with the information that resides in its many smaller, independent databases that have been developed over the years to meet the needs of individual departments. The seven-figure effort to modernize the information system uses relational databases and is the second largest expenditure in the Club's history, which spans nearly 100 years. (The first was the purchase of its headquarters.)

A few years ago, the Club realized that individuals and organizations that subscribed to its databases were often frustrated by the inflexibility of those databases. Information residing in different databases could not easily be pulled together without a major programming effort. As one manager put it, "So far, the businesses are integrated; the systems are not."

The goal of the new project venture was to achieve program-data independence so that any application, from any functional area, could access, and process data from the necessary database. The Club is creating a single database, directed by one data model, that will span organizational boundaries to replace its hierarchical mainframe database.[23]

a. Identify the data model most suitable for this application. Identify some advantages and disadvantages of this approach.

b. What do we mean by program-data independence and why is it important?

3. "Data should be used as a primary resource for enhancing customer satisfaction." Identify an organization that has used data to provide better customer service.

4. "Blob technology" is Binary Large Object technology, which allows users to create, store, retrieve, and process images, video, voice, and other digitized information from a database. Blob technology is being adopted actively by insurance companies and financial institutions that use large volumes of multimedia data. Cleveland-based Capitol American Financial Corp. is using Blob in an effort to reduce paperwork, which has the added benefit of increasing the productive time of knowledge workers. Further, one of the significant contributions of Blob technology to Capitol American is that it has voice capabilities. "In the future we expect to be able to talk into the system, to put in all the information that goes into [an insurance] policy," says the vice president and director of MIS at Capitol American.[24]

Discuss the role of object-oriented and multimedia databases in enhancing the productivity of knowledge workers.

5. Oracle, a leading vendor of database software, predicts that in the near future, multimedia databases will become the norm. These databases will contain not only different forms of media and promote electronic commerce.

What impact can a global multimedia database have on education? Develop a scenario for a global multimedia database and describe its implications for an introductory course in information systems.

6. How often do we go to an automobile repair shop, although we are unsure of the quality or the reliability of the service? CarPro Auto Advisors is designed to take the worrying out of car repairs. Car owners pay a nominal annual membership fee to access CarPro Auto Advisors, a database on car maintenance and repair data. The database contains information on more than 100,000 repair shops, automobile warranty and recall information, new and used car prices, and average repair costs gleaned over four decades by a leading lessor of corporate fleets. Besides maintenance data, CarPro also contains automobile-related data gathered from auto manufacturers and part distributors. Data such as technical service bulletins, wiring diagrams, and images of automotive components and systems are also made

available on CD-ROM for those who like to do the repairs themselves. The initial 2,000 subscribers to the service reported an average saving of $191 per repair.[25]

a. What type of data model (hierarchical, network, relational) would be best suited for this kind of an application? Explain your answer.

b. Set up a relational database for this problem using five variables that you think would be most relevant to a user trying to locate a good repair shop.

c. Give an example of a file, a field, and a record for this database.

ETHICAL ISSUES

Case 1: Sucker Databases

The most common reason for a company to buy database lists is to target potential customers for a variety of products and services. However, some unscrupulous organizations can use mailing lists to target those who are vulnerable or financially desperate. "An opportunity seeker is merely a euphemism for *sucker," says* Mary J. Culnan, an associate professor at the School of Business at Georgetown University in Washington, DC.

Scam artists are going high-tech and using "sucker" databases that contain the mailing addresses and/or phone numbers of potential victims. These databases are listed in *Direct Mail List Rates and Data,* the bible of direct marketing organizations, under names such as "Opportunity Seekers," "Sweep-Nos," and "Game, Contest and Puzzle Participants."

For example, in June 1991, a direct mail campaign initiated by evangelist Oral Roberts used databases to target consumers with heavy financial obligations and asked these consumers for charitable donations to aid in the "war against debt." In his personalized appeals, Roberts asked for $100 in exchange for prayers to be said on behalf of the consumer and "the war against debt." In another case, salespeople at the Tampa, Florida, office of Metropolitan Life Insurance used databases to identify senior citizens and push life insurance policies in the guise of high-interest-yielding retirement accounts. An internal audit by the Florida Insurance Commissioner's Office is under way.[26]

On the other hand, even databases that appear to be legal can cause problems. For example, integrated electronic medical records will allow a number of health care providers ready access to a patient's medical records, and this has the potential to violate the privacy of an individual. Consider the case where an employer learned that an employee who carried the gene for cystic fibrosis was pregnant. The employee was informed that she would no longer have insurance unless she had an abortion! In another case, the U.S. Supreme Court upheld the right of a self-insured employer to retroactively deny benefits to employees who contract AIDS. Many experts are advocating that privacy is a crucial issue and that there is pressing need for legislation that protects confidential information.[27]

1. What are some measures that consumers can take to protect themselves against "sucker databases"?
2. What are some of the sources of data for such databases?
3. What measures can consumers take to protect their privacy?

Case 2: Ad Hoc Reporting May Not Be So Ad Hoc After All!

One of the primary benefits of databases is their ability to support ad hoc reporting. In other words, managers can query the database to obtain customized information to support decision-making. However, this can lead to ethical violations. Who monitors the kind of queries a user poses to the database, particularly if it contains personal data? "If a company creates a database precisely so that users can do ad hoc reporting against a relational database, how would you know what's been extracted or what it's being used for?" asks a vice president of systems and technology at Paramount

Publishing. The real problem is the lack of standards governing the ways data can be used in an organization. While many organizations establish policies and procedures to ensure that only authorized people access the database, few organizations have any policies to monitor the way those people use the data. Though ad hoc reporting has many benefits and many organizations use it with caution, the ability to query a database is a threat of invasion of privacy.[28]

1. What measures can an organization take to ensure that free access to the organization's database does not result in abuse of this access?
2. How can schemas and subschemas help to ensure that users can view only that part of the database to which they have authorized access?

Case 3: Database Fraud

In July 1992, a federal grand jury indicted the owner of ListWorld, in Huntsville, Alabama, and nine other defendants on more than 140 counts of fraud. The defendants had contacted consumers by telephone, using a database of individuals with poor credit histories, offering them low-interest credit cards. Respondents were charged up to $200 in "processing fees," then were merely sent lists of banks that offered such cards. Such information is readily available from public sources.

There are countless such unscrupulous marketers who prey on vulnerable customers. Today, although there is considerable debate and legislative efforts about how to ensure privacy of information, the onslaught of information abuse continues.[29]

1. Although this case involves individuals who were defrauded, quite frequently even organizations are defrauded. If your organization needed data about potential customers, how would an IS manager ensure that the source was reliable and accurate?
2. In this case, should the consumer be held liable for not reading the "fine print" or should the organization be held liable?

Case 4: No More Fraud

As misuse of databases continues unabated, the IS community is somewhat divided as to the role it should play in monitoring and preventing the misuse and abuse of privileged information. Some IS managers feel that the IS community should be held responsible for abuse of information. This group advocates that IS managers be proactive in preventing abuse of privileged data and IS professionals should lead the way by establishing policies and procedures to monitor and prevent inappropriate use of the database. They argue that organizations should be held liable for inappropriate use of consumer databases. "We always consider the economic, operational or technical feasibility of an IS project, but nobody ever sits back and asks, 'Is this ethically feasible?' It's not enough to just follow orders from above if those orders are unethical." A simple "sniff test" to use when it comes to ethics is: "If you would be embarrassed to go home and tell your spouse, significant other, children, or parents what you're doing, don't do it," says Robert M. Rubin, vice president of information services at Elf Autochem North America, Inc. in Philadelphia.

Some IS managers, on the other hand, believe that developing and exercising moral standards and limits is truly not part of their job. They argue that the higher the standard, the higher the price for the consumer. And in tough economic times, when jobs are scarce and the pressure to produce more for less is on the increase, such standards can harm the organization. "We are the providers and processors of information. We can't be censors," says Ivan Brass, vice president of information systems and technology at Paramount Publishing.[30]

1. Which school of thought do you advocate?
2. If your boss required you to do something that may be viewed as unethical, what would be a tactful response?
3. If one of your coworkers were using organizational data for unethical purposes, how would you respond?

Case 5: Data Privacy

Congress is seriously considering privacy legislation to curb the sale of drivers' records by state motor vehicle departments. The legislation addresses the little-known fact that 34 states sell drivers' records—name, address, height, weight, age, vision, social security number, type

(Continued on next page)

of car,—to anyone for a small fee. Buyers include private investigators, who pay a few dollars for an individual "lookup," and direct marketers, who get complete magnetic tapes to build targeted mailing lists.

The driving force behind the bill is that stalkers can use the records to track down their victims, such as celebrities and estranged spouses. In Iowa, for example, teenagers have recorded the license plate numbers of expensive cars, obtained the names and addresses of the owners, and robbed their homes. Accessing government records is the most common way in which abusers and stalkers find their victims once they've moved in an attempt to escape.

The bill generally makes it a federal crime to disclose personal data from motor vehicle records, but carves out exceptions for government bodies, insurance companies, automobile recalls, and other business purposes. Others can choose to "opt out", i.e., specifically request that the data should not be sold or shared without the owner's permission. But there is also a long list of opponents to this bill, including marketers, private investigators and the news media, who fear their access to now-public records will be closed while investigators argue that they need to locate witnesses, missing persons, and debtors using these databases.

The Direct Marketing Association says it is concerned that the "opt-out" provision will be such a costly administrative burden that state agencies will stop selling data to commercial users. Mary J. Culnan, an associate professor of business administration at Georgetown University in Washington, DC, says that state agencies with relational databases could easily "tweak" their systems to flag names of people who want more privacy.

Other states would have to match their records to a list of "opt-out" names.

Case 6: Business as Usual??

Beverly Goodman, head of the ethics committee of the American Prospect Research Association, is increasingly concerned about the ethical issues raised by information systems and technologies. She describes a scenario in which a fundraiser for a medical facility has access to a number of databases. One database contains information on families that have lost a member to cancer, heart attack, or any other disease. These families have asked family members and friends to send donations to the appropriate medical research foundations; this information is recorded in the database. The fundraiser can access this database and solicit donations from the bereaved families. Is this ethical?

In another case, political action committees lobbying for Medicare and Social Security increases did a mass mailing to senior citizens in the Washington area asking for funds, although there are laws that protect populations perceived as especially vulnerable from unscrupulous marketers. The letter was worded so strongly that it scared many of the senior citizens into contributing funds to the PACs.[31]

1. Do you consider the behavior of the fundraisers in the above two situations to be ethical?
2. Was the PAC ethical in targeting senior citizens, or was it unethical to send senior citizens letters that scared them into believing that contributions must be made?

PROBLEM SOLVING IN THE REAL WORLD

Case 1: Pacific Gas and Electric

Pacific Gas and Electric (PG&E) is the nation's largest investor-owned utility. Its service area covers 94,000 square miles and its customers number more than 7.5 million. It has about 4.5 million customer service employees in about 100 offices all over the country. The ability to store, process, and retrieve accurate and timely information about customers is vital to the continued growth of PG&E. However, until recently the utility used a 1960s-vintage customer information system (CIS): a flat file consisting of more than 100 gigabytes of customer data. "After 4,000 changes and several generations of hardware, the flat file doesn't really support today's business organization, which consists of local work groups, divisions, regions, and general offices that frequently interact with one another."

The old CIS was built in pieces over the course of almost 25 years. As each piece of the puzzle was developed, new interfaces had to be designed so that the new application could interact with the master data file. This led to lack of flexibility and connectivity among different applications, creating constant frustration for system users and for the professionals charged with supporting and maintaining the system. Another major handicap of the old CIS was a design flaw in the way that the data was organized. The CIS centered around a single account number, rather than around the customer, who may have multiple dealings with the company. This caused information bottlenecks and resulted in a system that was incapable of meeting customer needs.

The year 1989 brought deregulation and increased competition for the utility industry. Amid increased pressure to cut costs and improve productivity, PG&E embarked on a 6-year project, involving more than 125 professionals. The goal was to redesign and rebuild a new CIS using a relational DBMS that focused on flexibility and maximizing the customer service representative's ability to handle all a customer's problems in a single call.

The new system uses IBM's DB2 database package and includes mainframes that process more than 200 million instructions per second (MIPS); a high-speed microwave- and fiber-based wide area network (WAN); satellite, voice, and data communications; 400 local area networks (LANs), internetworked over the WAN; and some 20,000 PCs and workstations.

The new database will shift its focus from the account number to the customer. As simple as it sounds, this idea was not part of the original system design. The system will also provide customer service representatives with a graphical user interface (GUI). When the system is fully functional, it will be well integrated, spanning multiple platforms, files, and databases. The utility plans to achieve this goal by "emphasizing process, partnerships, and selection of a limited number of development solutions."[32]

1. What are some problems that PG&E may encounter as it moves from a flat-file system to a relational database?

(Continued on next page)

2. A CIS that is centered around the account number is an inherently flawed system. Discuss some of the problems and limitations of such a design flaw.

Case 2: Becton Dickinson

Four years ago, the information technology (IT) organization within Becton Dickinson began implementing a vision of enterprise-wide information. The goal was to enable this international medical supplies company to work more intelligently and faster. "We want to reduce data collection time and increase information analysis time by providing the tools and information which will both improve our operating efficiencies and help us get products to market faster," says a company spokesman. The company manufactures and sells a broad range of medical supplies, devices, and diagnostic systems used by health care professionals, medical research institutions, and the general public. Working closely with users, IT is defining and implementing new systems for worldwide logistics, hospital sales, supplier and procurement information, customer service, and human resource development.

The heart of these systems is a repository of company-wide and external data and data definitions drawn from Becton Dickinson's distributed transaction systems in the United States, Canada, Latin America, Europe, the Far East, and Australia. Building the data repository is an ongoing process that involves deciding which data (masses of raw transactions), from multiple sources, are used most frequently, where they are needed and how to sort, subtotal, analyze or otherwise consolidate them. The repository receives information from the transaction systems and it organizes information into "smart files" to service the internal customer's need. The frequency of updates to the repository varies with different kinds of data. For example, order status is updated daily; transportation status updates are performed more often.

In preparing for enterprise-wide use of the data repository, IT has implemented a common set of accounting, order management, sales reporting, and human resources systems to replace the company's diverse systems throughout the world. The most difficult task in implementing the global database system has been building the data definitions. "Agreeing on formal definitions that are understandable to all parts of the world is critical and time-consuming. "We have to maintain different definitions and state the differences. An example is differing customer segmentation categories among businesses and different regions of the world," says a system developer. Another labor-intensive part of this process of building the database is figuring out how to structure data with varying definitions in the most useful way for all the business units.

The company is reaping many strategic benefits from the database. Information previously conveyed by transoceanic phone calls and fax transmissions is now available online. As a result, a traffic coordinator can act sooner to divert an international shipment to another port or change the method of transportation from surface to air, avoiding unnecessary additional shipments. The ability to access order and shipment status data sooner has also raised inventory planners' confidence in the supply chain, reducing the need to inflate stock to guard against crises, such as sales exceeding those forecasted for a given site.[33]

1. What are some steps that an organization can take to reduce data collection time and increase information analysis time for its managers?

2. What are some challenges that the company is facing in building this huge database?

Case 3: Harper's Freight Is Data

Harper Group, a $430-million shipping company based in San Francisco, was founded in 1898 as a brokerage firm. Today, it distributes, ships, and tracks goods for customers including The Limited, Procter & Gamble, and Digital Equipment, and also forwards air and ocean freight and warehouse goods. The company operates in an industry where profit margins are thin and information is one of the most critical resources for staying competitive.

Recently, the company has dedicated all its programmers to the task of designing and developing a unified database that will help Harper's customers buy, ship, and track merchandise worldwide. Other information systems in the company will be managed and maintained by outside consultants and vendors. Why is Harper paying so much attention to databases? Because up-to-date information is crucial for Harper; it can make or break the company. Further, the shipping industry's reliance on information has reached a level matched in few other industries.

Harper's business is information-intensive, making data a very valuable resource for the company. If, for example, a customer needs a shipment to be moved from a factory in Singapore to an assembly plant in Frankfurt, Harper arranges air transport, ocean carriers, and truckers and ensures that the shipment arrives on time and within budget. The success of the entire process depends on access to timely and reliable data. Harper tracks shipments by attaching to each container a bundle composed of duty and tariff forms, reams of customs documentation (electronic and paper-based), and a host of accounting papers required by each nation. Further, customers must be kept fully informed about each step of the process; this too requires access to timely information.

The new and unified database is designed to gather information on every transaction generated worldwide and to produce the kind of reports, tracking, and visibility that customers demand. Although all of this information already resides somewhere in Harper's systems, the problem is that each of Harper's worldwide subsidiaries in 45 countries has its own set of information systems. Each has a different account code for the same customer, and follows different national rules governing the customer account. Customer representatives tracking shipment from, say, Bombay to Saõ Paulo would have to delve into their particular systems and reconcile disparate representations of the same customer. That data would then be electronically transmitted to the customer.

Further, the company must function not just as a transporter of goods but also as a firm that helps its customers to reduce costs. Helping a customer choose the most suitable transportation method is the easiest part of achieving this goal. The challenge lies in helping customers to be more efficient. For example, if a clothing chain knew that the cost of blouses in Taiwan has suddenly increased, then turning to a factory in Bombay, despite higher transportation costs, might prove more profitable in the long run. Harper's database would allow the clothier to do just that.

Harper's IBM AS/400 system integrates information on freight, customs brokerage, and receiving and provides online ocean freight information, including

(Continued on next page)

the preparation of commercial invoices, packing lists, dock receipts, insurance certificates, and bills of lading. "It's also where we record specific information about a customer's shipping patterns. The goal is to get a competitive edge in information," says CIO Morrison. "We're determined to be an information company. We don't own ships or trucks, but we've always had information. That's the asset we have to market."[34]

1. In Chapter 5, we cited Harper as an innovative user of telecommunications. One of Harper's goals is to develop distributed databases. Explain if this is appropriate goal for this application.
2. Why is it important to present a uniform face for company data? What measures can an organization take to achieve this goal?

References

Andren, Emily. "Breaking and Making the Rules," *Network Computing,* September 1993, pp. 108–112.

Date, C. J. *An Introduction to Database Systems,* 5th ed. Reading, MA: Addison-Wesley, 1990.

Goldstein, R. C. and J. B. McCririck. "What Do Data Administrators Really Do?" *Datamation* 26 (August 1980).

Goodhue, Dale L, Judith A. Quillard, and John F. Rockart. "Managing the Data Resource: A Contingency Perspective," *MIS Quarterly* (September 1988).

Grover, Varun, and James Teng. "How Effective Is Data Resource Management?" *Journal of Information Systems Management* (Summer 1991).

Hayes, Mary. "The Travelers' New Direction," *Information Week,* May 8, 1995, pp. 56–57.

Kahn, Beverly and Linda Garceau. "The Database Administration Function," *Journal of Management Information Systems* 1 (Spring 1985).

Leinfuss, Emily. "One Database at a Time," *Cleint/Server Computing,* April 1995, pp. 63–66.

Martin, James. *Managing the Data-Base Environment,* Englewood Cliffs, NJ: Prentice-Hall, 1983.

Oz, Effy. "Ethical Standards for Computer Professionals: A comparative Analysis of Four Major Codes", Journal of Business Ethics, Vol. 12, pp. 709–726, 1993.

Ricciuti, Mike. "Distributed DBMSs move into the trenches," *Datamation,* April 15, 1993, pp. 59–62.

"Database Marketing: New Rules for Policy and Practice," *Sloan Management Review,* Summer 1993, pp. 7–22.

"PC Databases Grow Up," *Computerworld,* October 18, 1993, pp. 117–124.

Notes

1. Kenneth Nelson, Vice President of MIS, Readers Digest.
2. Ambrosio, Johanna. "Honing in on Target Customers," *Computerworld,* February 10, 1992, pp. 97–98.

3. Ambrosio, Johanna. "Food Banks Automate to Feed the Hungry," *Computerworld,* December 20, 1993, pp. 1, 12.
4. LaPlante, Alice. "Systems in the Slammer," *Computerworld,* April 17, 1995, pp. 89–97.
5. Betts, Mitch. "Start Paying Invoices Once, Not Twice," *Computerworld,* April 5, 1993, p. 59.
6. McPartlin, John P. "No Silk Purses From Sow's Data," *InformationWeek,* Jan. 18, 1993, p. 50.
7. McCann, Stephanie. "You're Fingered," *Computerworld,* June 7, 1993, p. 89.
8. Brandel, William. "Houston Astros Score with System that Tracks Ballplayers' Injuries," *Computerworld,* May 15, 1995, p. 41.
9. Hoffman, Thomas. "EDA/SQL Helps Ciba Decentralize Data," *Computerworld,* August 23, 1993, p. 102.
10. Fitzgerald, Michael. "Indy 500 Merges Technologies to Improve Racing," *Computerworld,* May 30, 1994 p. 42.
11. Caldwell, Bruce. "In Search of the New Dictionary," *InformationWeek,* April 25, 1994, pp. 51–56.
12. Bozman, Jean S. "Grappling with Huge Databases," *Computerworld,* May 31, 1993, p. 57.
13. Ullrich, Charles R. "Dispersion Therapy," *Chief Information Officer,* October 15, 1992, pp. 26, 28.
14. Ibid.
15. Scheier, Robert. "Not Ready for Prime Time," *PC Week,* March 7, 1994, p. 16.
16. Hoffman, Thomas. "Explosion Spotlights LAN Vulnerability," *Computerworld,* March 15, 1993, p. 67.
17. Sloan, Ken. "All Your Assets on Line," *Computerworld,* July 11, 1988, pp. 55–58.
18. Cash, James I. "British Air Gets on Course," *InformationWeek,* May 1, 1995, p. 140.
19. Groenfeldt, Tom. "The Luxury-Class Database," *InformationWeek,* April 3, 1995, pp. 100–101.
20. Taylor, Thayer C. "The Right Platform, Uh-Huh," *Sales & Marketing Management,* December 1994, pp. 41–42.
21. *InfoWorld,* November 8, 1993, pp. 76–79.
22. McPartlin, John P. "No Silk Purses From Sow's Data," *InformationWeek,* Jan. 18, 1993, p. 63.
23. Wexler, Joanie M. "Horse Club Races for Payoff From Database Overhaul," *Computerworld,* Aug. 30, 1993, p. 65.
24. Bucken, Mike. "Blobs Curb Paper Chase at Capitol America," *Software Magazine,* October 1993, pp. 82–84.
25. "Car Repair Goes High Tech," *InformationWeek,* August 3, 1992, p. 35.
26. LaPlante, Alice. "Wanna Buy a Sucker?" *Computerworld,* November 22, 1993, pp. 77–81.
27. Friedman, Emily. "Making Choices," *Healthcare Forum Journal,* January/February 1995, pp. 8–11.
28. LaPlante, Alice. "Wanna Buy a Sucker?" *Computerworld,* November 22, 1993, pp. 77–81.
29. Ibid.
30. Ibid.
31. David Beatty, spokesman for the National Victim Center in Arlington, Va.
32. Rinaldi, Damian. "PG&E Plans to Extend World-Class Customer Service," *Software Magazine,* November 1993, pp. 76–78.
33. Andren, Emily. "Breaking & Making the Rules," *Network Computing,* September 1993, pp. 108–109, 112.

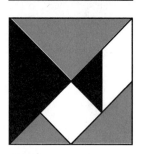

7

Client-
Server
Computing

Contents

Learning Objectives
Technology Payoff: United Behavioral Systems
Introduction
What Is Client-Server Computing?
    Difference Between a LAN Environment and a C/S Environment
Developing Client-Server Systems
    Identify the Type of Application
    Determine Network Requirements
    Select the Client-Server Architecture
    Develop the Logical and Physical Design
    Test, Implement, and Maintain the System
Organizational Implications of Client-Server Systems
    Advantages of C/S Systems
    Disadvantages of C/S Systems
Client-Server Security
    Guarding Access Privileges
    Preserving the Integrity of Applications
Summary
Review Questions
Discussion Questions
Ethical Issues
    Case 1: Ethics of Pricing
    Case 2: Beware of Employees!
Problem Solving in the Real World
    Case 1: Art and High Tech Go Hand-in-Hand
    Case 2: United Airlines Takes Off
References
Notes

Learning Objectives

In the last few years, client-server (C/S) computing has captured the attention of CEOs and CIOs all over the world. Decisions regarding investments in C/S technology have become critical for many organizations. Several major technological and social forces, such as advances in telecommunications, declining prices of computer hardware, and the downsizing trend, have made the client-server movement one of the hottest topics in the computer industry.

This chapter provides a broad overview of C/S computing and its role in corporate decision making. Because the trend toward C/S systems is somewhat recent, the material covered in this chapter is likely to change considerably in the coming years. This chapter provides some recommendations for companies making the transition to the C/S environment and is tempered with the cautionary note that C/S technologies are not a solution for all problems. A number of examples of C/S applications are given to enhance the student's understanding of this new and powerful technology. After reading and studying this chapter, you should be able to

- Describe client-server computing
- Understand development issues in C/S systems
- Identify some critical issues in C/S security
- Understand why computing C/S costs is a challenging task
- Identify some of the advantages and disadvantages of C/S systems

TECHNOLOGY PAYOFF

United Behavioral Systems

"Heal thyself" is the motto of the IS department at United Behavioral Systems (UBS), which manages many health maintenance organizations (HMOs). One way in which the company plans to do this is by cutting down on unproductive paperwork related to insurance reimbursement and health care. UBS is using client-server technology to achieve this goal.

The company's C/S system, Statistical Tracking and Evaluation of Patient Services, or STEPS, which replaces standalone DOS applications in each clinic, registers new patients, schedules patient meetings with doctors, and maintains records of these meetings. The system also allows managers to closely monitor patient programs, assess the amount of business generated by each of more than 14,000 doctors in 32 clinics around the country, instantly verify insurance coverage for each new patient, and provide centralized online reporting facilities for all health professionals in the organization.

Another C/S system, called ProvNet, is used to store and retrieve data on 14,000 doctors and other health care providers. The system allows the company to verify the certification and medical credentials of its doctors and even to provide referrals to patients.

STEPS and ProvNet can be accessed through Windows, running on PCs that are networked to two IBM RS/6000 servers in Minneapolis. UBS uses a relational DBMS running on one of the RS/6000 servers in Minneapolis to manage both

ProvNet and STEPS. The applications were developed using Powersoft's PowerBuilder, a 4GL. Both applications can access United HealthCare's Unisys mainframe applications, which contain extensive health care data on the company's clients.

Before the C/S system was installed, managers had to sift through paper printouts and manually check each claimant's data against mainframe data. Managers had to manually look up the eligibility status of a customer, because all the systems at the 32 clinics were standalone systems. This caused major delays in claim processing, which frustrated both managers and customers. The new system has eliminated many bottlenecks by providing managers with instantaneous access to timely and consistent information on patients and doctors.[1]

Client-server architectures have little to do with technology and everything to do with competitive business processes.[2]

—Charles Pelton

Introduction

Today, organizations are taking a close, hard look at ways to cut costs, increase efficiency, and trim waste. Organizations are becoming leaner, management layers are being eliminated or becoming flatter, and employees are being pressured to do more with less. All indications are that these approaches are not just short-term fads, but long-term strategies that will continue to be used in the coming years.

Computers and information systems—in particular, C/S systems—are helping organizations to achieve these goals and to become more competitive in the changing global marketplace. Fortunately, unlike many other industries, the computer industry is able to deliver better and faster products at lower and lower prices, thus making them more and more affordable to medium- and small-sized companies. Further, knowledge workers are confident and comfortable with computers, and are using them to achieve organizational goals. These workers believe "the currency of modern business is the flow of electrons within computers."[3]

The growth of C/S technologies has been rapid and widespread; computer-related trade journals and magazines are filled with articles that reiterate the criticality of C/S technologies to business competitiveness. Figure 7–1 shows the growing popularity of C/S systems, particularly for new applications. According to a recent Business Research Group (BRG) survey of medium and large U.S. and European companies, 78% of the companies surveyed indicated that they had implemented C/S systems or would do so within 12 months.[4] In fact, C/S technology is growing at such a rapid rate that many organizations are finding it difficult to recruit enough knowledgeable and skilled graduates to fill C/S-related jobs. A whopping 70% of the Fortune 100 corporations indicated that one of the primary bottlenecks in the implementation of C/S technologies is the lack of experienced IS personnel.

The rapid growth of C/S computing is attributed to three powerful forces: the

F I G U R E 7 – 1

Client-server technologies are growing at a rapid pace. Almost one out of two companies have implemented client-server systems and almost one in two client-server applications are new.

Source: Business Research Group, special advertising section *Datamation*, March 1, 1994, p. S-3.

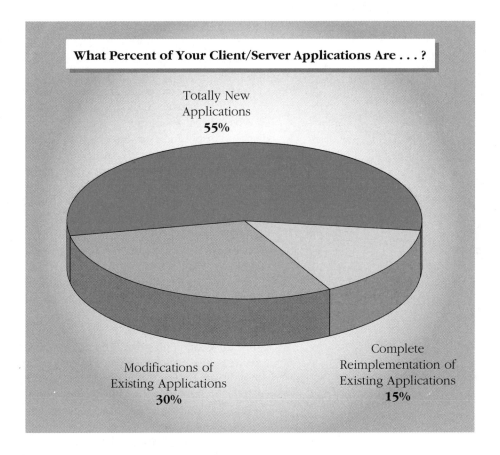

What Percent of Your Client/Server Applications Are . . . ?

Totally New
Applications
55%

Modifications of
Existing Applications
30%

Complete
Reimplementation of
Existing Applications
15%

of running and maintaining mainframes, particularly for smaller organizations.[5] PCs allow end-users to build sophisticated applications; this breakthrough has created a new breed of knowledge workers. End users are now often employees with the technical skills and the business acumen necessary to build sophisticated applications and, therefore, no longer rely on the IS department to develop new applications. The impact of these end-users on corporate America is discussed in Chapter 12 (Systems Analysis and Design Methodologies and Implications). Client-server systems further enhance the power of end-users.

Moreover, increasing competitiveness in the global marketplace has compelled many organizations to re-engineer and streamline their business processes. Re-engineering requires companies to analyze what they do and ask themselves the question "Why do we do what we do?" In many instances, companies implement a certain process or processes simply because "that's how it has always been done," creating waste and underutilization of existing resources. Client-server systems play an important role in trimming waste, although in some cases, companies downsize not so much to cut costs as to increase profits.

For example, CS Boston switched to C/S computing in order to increase sales and enhance the productivity of its salesforce. CPTrade, a C/S system developed for the bank's multi-billion-dollar short-term securities business, cuts the time used to create a portfolio of financial products for each client from half an hour to just a few minutes, thereby allowing traders to be considerably more productive and earn more profits for the company. The old mainframe application was so outdated that it took up to half an hour simply to identify a list of products that would match the needs of the client, and to make matters worse, the list could not be saved for future reference. The new system, written in C++ and based on Sybase's relational database (RDBMS), allows traders to readily access CPTrade through GUI-based Sun workstations that are connected to a Sun server. Some common data and application code resides on a central server; everything else resides on client workstations.

CPTrade presents users with a scrollable list of financial products that can be used to quickly identify the specific products that meet the financial needs of a given client. Information about investors and their buying preferences is stored on the database for future use; and a central fax server can immediately fax the information to the investor. "In half a second, the computer has gone off and picked 50 offerings that are of interest to an investor out of a list of thousands. The financial analyst makes a report, hits the fax button, and off it goes to an investor says a company spokesperson." When the new system was installed, a salesperson was able to handle seven investors in the time it had taken to handle one investor under the old system.[6]

Yet another factor that has propelled C/S computing forward is the emergence of technologies that are capable of replacing the mainframe, which until a few years ago, was, and even today to a large extent still is, the computing environment of choice for many large organizations. As we have pointed out in Chapter 3, today many smaller computers are as powerful as the mainframes of a decade ago and they are, obviously, much more affordable and easier to maintain than mainframes. Operating and maintaining mainframes is expensive, so they are out of reach for small organizations. An attractive solution to this problem is the C/S system.

By making a wide variety of information readily accessible to users, C/S systems have helped many companies improve productivity, enhance customer service, and shorten the time necessary to bring products to market. Before the emergence of C/S technology, information was often isolated and compartmentalized, leading to data redundancies and information bottlenecks. Client/server technology can provide significant benefits to organizations that make a long-term commitment to it and use it to build new infrastructures. For example, the opening story of United Behavioral Systems shows how it uses C/S technology to reduce unproductive paperwork and enhance the efficiency of its HMOs. The company's C/S system, STEPS, enables hospital administrators to take a hands-on approach to managing doctor-patient relationships; its second C/S system, ProvNet, retrieves data on 14,000 doctors and other health care providers and allows hospital administrators to monitor certification requirements and perform other legal and administrative tasks.

Another example of C/S technology is the hotel reservation system at Hyatt Hotels, which allows agents to check room availability at 156 hotels, quote rates to customers, and book any one of 80,000 rooms worldwide, all within seconds. Before the system was installed, each hotel kept a giant, hand-written diary of all room bookings and reserving a room required phone calls and faxes between hotels located in different parts of the country. For example, if a customer called Hyatt headquarters in Chicago to book a function room in San Francisco, employees in Chicago would call the manger of the San Francisco hotel to find an open date. Phone tag and mail delays took so long that customers had to wait hours, sometimes even days, to receive a response. Often, customers grew tired of waiting and took their business elsewhere.

Hyatt's C/S system was developed using PowerBuilder, a 4GL. A hotel typically has about six PCs on a local area network (LAN), which are linked to a local 486-based server that houses local business applications. The local server is linked to a server in Chicago through a wide area network (WAN). Users access data through a Windows application in order to determine status of room bookings. The application prompts users for appropriate data, verifies the data, and then exchanges the data with a central database in Chicago. The booking system has been so successful that the system alone is estimated to generate an additional $20 million per year in revenues and reduce the cost of booking rooms by over $4 million a year. That's an impressive return on a system that cost a little over $500,000 to build.[7]

What is Client-Server Computing?

Although client-server computing has been a hot topic in the computer industry in recent years, the idea itself is almost 20 years old. It is simply another name for the age-old concept of distributed processing. A **client-server system** is a distributed system that consists of a server (or host computer, such as a mainframe or a minicomputer) and one or more clients (smaller computers, usually PCs or workstations), all of which share tasks and processes. The **server** stores data and programs commonly accessed and used by a number of users. A **client** is a smaller, networked computer, such as a PC, that asks the server (or the host) to supply the data and programs that it needs. A server is usually larger than a client; it resides on a LAN or a WAN, or in some cases is a mainframe. This arrangement allows organizations to better utilize their information systems, since information can be accessed from one or many databases and distributed to users in dispersed locations. Figure 7–2 shows a graphical view of this arrangement.

Newton's *Telecom Dictionary* defines C/S technology as follows:

> "A form of shared, or distributed, computing in which tasks and computing power are split between servers and clients. Servers store and process data common to users across the enterprise; these data can then be accessed by client systems for individual processing requirements."

In addition to server and client hardware, the C/S architecture includes front-end (client) software and back-end (server) software. The front-end software provides the user interface (what the user sends and receives), communication with at least one server, and data manipulation. The back-end software primarily controls data acquisition and integrity, supports transaction management, and recovers lost transactions, in cases of system failure. Figure 7–3 identifies different types of front-end and back-end software. Other elements of client software are tools for developing user interfaces, applications, communications software to communicate with the server, document management systems (systems that manage different forms of written information, such as memos, manuals, documents, invoices, and so on), and relational database management systems (RDBMS).

Client-server system

A distributed system in which a server, such as a mainframe, stores commonly used data and programs. The client, usually a PC or a workstation, asks the server for data and programs.

Server

A large central computer that serves as a repository of data and programs commonly accessed by a number of users.

Client

A smaller computer, usually a PC or a workstation, that is on a network, shares some of its tasks and computing power with the server; both the client and the server share tasks and processes.

Client-server systems are based on
the concept of distributed computing. A mainframe or minicomputer
(the server) is connected through
a network to a number of PCs
(the clients).

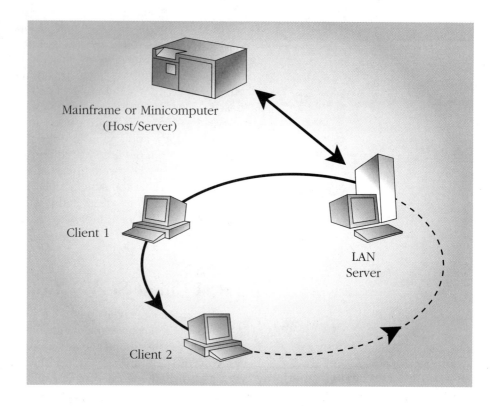

Mainframe or Minicomputer
(Host/Server)

Client 1

LAN
Server

Client 2

As you can see, the structure of C/S systems is similar to that of distributed
DBMS. In fact, distributed DMBS are also referred to as C/S systems when the data
and the database software reside on the server and clients access the server.

Judith Hurwitz, a consultant, points out that the primary difference between
C/S technology and other technologies is its remarkable flexibility and adaptabil-
ity to different environments.

"Business technologists want the same flexibility with new hardware and
software that other executives have with, for instance, the corporate car-rental
company, the stationery supplier, or the janitorial contractor. Client/server is just
another way of defining business freedom. Today, virtually all computing fits the
client/server model in one form or another."[8]

Several things should be noted about a C/S system. First, the server influences the way the client responds to a user request. For example, if a client asks
the server for data from a specific database, and if the server cannot find the data
or the client does not have access privileges for that data, the server sends an
appropriate message to the client. The client, in turn, gives the appropriate message to the user. Second, a number of clients can access the server at the same
time. Third, client processes and server processes are independent of each other.
For example, the client may be processing a database package while the server
is processing a decision support package for another client. This independence is
one of the biggest advantages of the C/S environment, because clients can be
added to or deleted from the network without affecting the server or other clients.
This arrangement overcomes some of the performance bottlenecks of traditional
LAN applications.

FIGURE 7-3

Most client-server systems have front-end and back-end software. Front-end software is designed to make the systemeasy for the end-users; back-end software is designed to help programmers and network administrators.

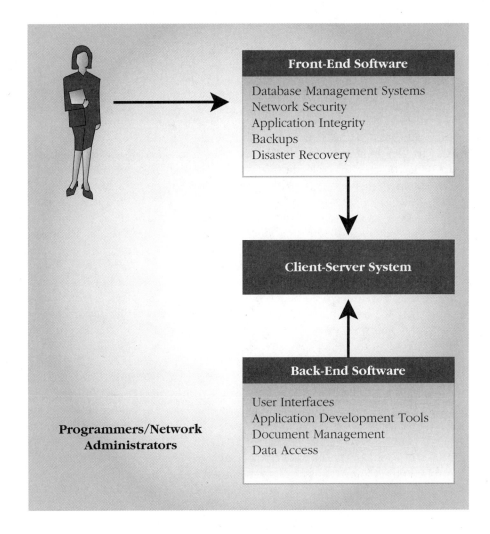

Difference Between a LAN Environment and a C/S Environment

In a LAN environment, as in a C/S environment, a number of desktop PCs are linked to one or more servers. However, each PC treats the server as nothing more than a storehouse of data and programs. In other words, to the PC, the server is just another hard drive. Therefore, in a LAN environment, when the client requests data or programs from the server, the entire file, whether it is a word processor, a database, or any other program, has to be transmitted across the network and then processed on the PC. This can cause major bottlenecks on the network. Especially at peak hours, when a number of users are on the network, this approach slows down the response time of the network.

In a C/S environment, on the other hand, when the client requests data or programs from the server, the server *processes* the data and sends the resulting information to the client—unlike the LAN structure in which the application package is sent to the client and the client processes the data. This logical separation of client processes from server processes is a significant advantage of the C/S environment.

A GLOBAL PERSPECTIVE
Leo Burnett
Worldwide Inc.

Leo Burnett Worldwide, Inc., one of the largest advertising agencies in the world, has increasingly felt the need to step up its information systems in order to keep up with younger, more technically savvy companies. The company's latest information system, called the Spot Television and Radio System, or Stars, is a client/server application that was built on Sybase, Inc. databases to track advertising methods, media, and resulting sales for Burnett's 34 global clients.

When the preliminary design for the information system was drawn, developers realized that the resulting 40G-byte system would be too big and expensive to deploy at each of Burnett's 60 offices worldwide. So the company brainstormed a novel solution to a client/-server problem that often plagues other companies trying to switch to distributed computing. The company created a thinned-to-the-bone version of Stars that cut out some of the more sophisticated analysis functions, making the system more lean and more portable.

Thus, a skinny, 20M-byte, LAN-based companion to Stars, called Coordination of Media and Expenditure Tracking (Comet), was installed at major offices in Europe and Asia and, in essence, Comet acted as a global sidekick to Stars. Comet also implied that the company did not have to hire and train 60 database administrators on the intricacies of Stars nor did they have to buy the required IBM RS/6000 Unix-based hardware and Sybase software for each location. This greatly minimized the cost of developing and implementing Stars.

A key goal of Stars and Comet is to give users an idea of which advertising methods pay off and which methods flop. This is very valuable information for clients such as Philip Morris, Inc., McDonald's Corp., and Protor & Gamble Co., who invest large sums of money in advertising. For example, if Procter & Gamble buys commercial time on Korean TV stations to sell dish soap and runs a coupon promotion in Costa Rica's *Tico Times* newspaper, advertising account managers can use Stars and Comet to show the client which advertising method was more effective and why. The new system provides this information in a timely and accurate manner.

Before the system was installed, managers tracked this information using PCs and word of mouth. Queries about advertising effectiveness often took anywhere from a few hours to two weeks. Using the new system, most queries are answered in one to two seconds, although the system may take as long as "several minutes" to respond to some of the more complicated questions. The system can also be used to clear and approve payments on-line, rather than via overnight processing, and even to negotiate better rates from media outlets, such as MTV or CNN.[9]

Developing Client-Server Systems

Organizations must carefully plan their IS development strategy before investing in C/S systems, because ad hoc growth of C/S applications can be harmful to the company. At many companies, investments in C/S systems begin as pilot projects and quickly grow into an ad hoc collection of systems. This approach can cause many problems, particularly in the area of system integration.

For example, American Airlines embraced C/S computing almost 5 years ago and has about 50 C/S applications, some of which are already obsolete. In order to maximize benefits from its investment in C/S, the company has recently initiated efforts to develop a growth plan for its C/S systems that clearly identifies their role in achieving the strategic goals of the company. The plan identifies hardware issues, such as hardware platforms and the nature and type of networking; operating systems; and broader issues, such as data management, development tools, system security, and access methods. Establishing the plan long before development begins allows the reuse of existing system components and increases the chances of achieving system integration.

BUSINESS REALITIES
Nordstrom

C/S technology is helping Nordstrom, a Seattle-based clothing retailer, to achieve its goals of delivering high-quality goods, paying attention to detail, and, above all, maintaining and exceeding its industry-wide reputation for superior customer service.

Nordstrom's operations are decentralized, so C/S systems fit right in when the company decided to invest in an end-user merchandising system. Nordstrom deals with 12,000 to 15,000 vendors each year, and purchasing agents play a very critical role in studying products from these vendors and identifying what is hot and what is not. The merchandising system identifies a stock item's style, color, size, and vendor, and keeps track of how many units of each item were sold. By knowing precisely which items are selling and which are not, purchasing agents can stock those that customers want and can also more efficiently manage the inventory of each store.

Currently, 50 store locations and corporate offices nationwide use a local NT server, which is linked to database servers at corporate headquarters. Buyers at each store use Windows for Workgroups to access information about that store, which resides in a database on the local server. The local servers function basically as application, file, and print servers, providing security authentication for the sales system. Company-wide information is stored on the database at corporate headquarters.

Since retail buyers are not generally technologically sophisticated, ease of use was a major design criterion for the front end of the system. "Rather than forcing users to change to suit the technology, as was the case in the mainframe applications of the past, we were able to change the technology to meet their needs," says a company spokesperson. Performance was another design goal; the new system answers almost 80% of all user queries in under 10 seconds. That is fairly impressive performance, considering that the main database is very large and already holds 60GB to 70GB of data.[10]

For example, Nordstrom, known for its superior customer service (see box), switched to C/S technology after recognizing that the technology fitted in with the company's decentralized management style. This is another reason for establishing the plan before development begins. Not only does following a C/S implementation plan result in robust and reliable systems, but it also forces users and developers to answer the fundamental question, "Is there a good match between this technology and our business style and needs?"

The plan for investment in C/S technology should closely follow the strategic business plan and the strategic information plan, because, clearly, one of the reasons for investing in C/S technology is to help the firm achieve its long-term goals. For example, Leo Burnett Worldwide, Inc., a multinational global company carefully aligned its business goals with client-server technology in order to hold on to its market share (see box).

Without long-term planning, C/S technology cannot deliver the goods. In the words of a CIO who emphasized the importance of planning, "It's up to you [the CEO] to provide the vision of where you want the business to go, and it's up to me to help you get there [with enabling technology]. If you don't know where you're going, I can get you there, too, like the pilot who says 'We're lost, but we're making good time.'"[11]

The Patricia Seybold Group recommends taking the following five steps before developing a client-server system. These are not very different from the guidelines used for other systems.[12]

1. Carefully identify and define the type of application (problem definition).
2. Determine network requirements.
3. Select the architecture (hardware, software, and network capabilities).

4. Develop the logical and physical design of the system.
5. Test, implement, and maintain the system.

Identify the Type of Application

As with other systems, the first step in C/S development is to carefully define the problem and identify the nature of the development application: transaction processing, general ledger systems, human resource applications, decision support, communications, and so on. When companies move from the mainframe environment to client-server systems, they appear to follow one of two approaches: Either they follow a gradual evolution from one computing environment (such as a mainframe) to another (such as a C/S system) or they take a giant leap into the new environment and hope users will learn to adjust to it eventually.

One reason why the evolution strategy is gentle and smooth is that developers often use a GUI (graphical user interface) to hide the complexities of the mainframe environment and to make users feel comfortable with the new system. In most cases, applications are driven by one or more of the following three elements: routine transactions, knowledge and experience, and business processes. Routine transactions include transaction processing systems; knowledge and experience come from knowledge workers, as in the case of decision support systems; businesses processes drive systems that deal with total quality. An analysis of the type of application also helps developers to make better decisions about the hardware architecture of the C/S system.

For example, Holiday Inn's reservation system is primarily a transaction processing system that stores and processes hotel reservations. This was clearly a driving factor in the kind of hardware platform that the hotel selected for the application. The reservations system has 10 servers (SunSparc stations) that run a Sybase relational database that can be accessed by Mac users who are linked over an Ethernet network. The Sun workstations are connected through gateways to a mainframe in Atlanta. Database processing occurs both on the Sun servers and on the mainframe server. The mainframe and its proprietary flat-file DBMS contain room rates, availability, and currency exchange rates—data that changes frequently. Data that are more stable, such as hotel locations, available parking, and proximity to local attractions, are stored on local servers.[13]

Determine Network Requirements

The next step is to carefully determine the amount of traffic that the chosen application is likely to produce on the network. If an application has only a few users or is used only occasionally, traffic over the network is likely to be light. If the company is planning an enterprise-wide C/S application that will be used by many employees, it is important to select a network that can handle heavy traffic. Determining network requirements early in the development process is important because it is very difficult, if not impossible, to change them after system development begins. Companies should also carefully assess their future growth and needs and provide for later network expansion.

Select the Client-Server Architecture

The next step is to identify and recommend other technical requirements for the system, including the hardware, software, technical staff, and other resources required to build it. In this phase, the issues to be addressed include development tools for building the system, data management strategies, and access methods for different clients. The importance of selecting the right IS development tools are discussed in Chapter 13 (Tools for Information Systems Development).

Another important part of this phase is the design of system interfaces, a critical component in C/S systems, since a number of different components and deliverables come together at the interface. This is particularly true in multivendor environments, in which integration of disparate systems is a necessity.

Develop the Logical and Physical Design

The next step is to address the physical and logical design of the system. As we discussed in the chapter on databases, the physical design of the system determines the physical location of data, programs, and related system components, in order to achieve quick response time and optimal utilization of resources, whereas the logical design addresses the relationships among data elements in the system. The logical design is a vital element in the design and development of all information systems, but it is even more important in C/S systems, because these systems are more oriented toward business needs.

Test, Implement, and Maintain the System

Finally, the system should be carefully and rigorously tested before being implemented in its operating environment. The testing should establish that the system works properly and that its interrelationships with other systems in the environment will meet users' expectations. Once the system is implemented, it should be updated, as necessary, and properly maintained. Some of these steps are discussed in greater detail in Chapter 12 (System Analysis and Design: Methodologies and Implications).

Organizational Implications of Client Servers

One of the reasons for the tremendous growth in C/S systems is that they allow corporations to re-engineer their business processes, enhance productivity and profits, reduce the time it takes to process business transactions, and increase responsiveness. They enable knowledge workers to do their jobs effectively and support a variety of business operations. Often, C/S systems can deliver new system applications in a fraction of the time it would take in a mainframe environment. In this section, we look at some advantages and disadvantages of C/S systems.

Advantages of C/S Systems

Make Data Readily Accessible to Decision Makers One of the greatest advantages of C/S systems is that they make information readily available to decision makers. As we mentioned in the preceding chapter, a major problem in corporate America today is not a lack of data but an overabundance of data. In spite of this, decision makers often don't know where or how to get the data they need to make good decisions. Client-server systems address this problem by bringing the data to the person or institution that needs the data.

For example, Lutheran General Systems in Chicago, a 6,275-employee company with $682 million in annual revenue, is an integrated health-care firm that believes technology and good patient care go hand-in-hand. In 1990, CEO Stephen Ummel decided to develop what the industry calls a "continuum-of-care strategy," under which patients will get high-quality care throughout the hospital, regardless of the unit or the person they visit for their care.

Lutheran General believed that one way to achieve this goal was to have health-care providers receive all patient data from a single, centrally managed system.

In 1991, Lutheran General launched a $21 million C/S initiative program, switching from an Amdahl 5950 mainframe to a C/S system based on Sun Microsystems Sparc 2 servers running a Sybase relational database. The system will run on a fiber-optics-based WAN in the Chicago area and it is expected to serve about 4,000 nurses, physicians, and administrators.

The primary advantage of this system is that all health care providers have access to uniform and complete data on each patient, such as medical history, current medications, other specialists the patient has visited, and diagnoses of existing or past illnesses. Medical insurance information about the patient is also made available to the health care providers so that they can find the best combination of treatments that will suit the patient. This approach has not only improved the quality of health care, but has also won patient approval, since now the patient does not have to repeat the same information to a series of different health care providers.[14]

Reduce Operating Costs   In the long run, the cost of processing information using C/S systems is less than that of mainframes, since the cost per MIPS (million instructions per second) on a C/S system is significantly less than on its mainframe counterpart. Also, C/S software is cheaper than customized mainframe software, so it costs less to process data. This is a primary reason why it is expected that in the next few years the number of mainframe applications will decrease, while the number of C/S applications will increase considerably. Figure 7–4 illustrates the accelerating shift from mainframe to C/S environments.

Client-server systems also reduce operating costs. Toyota was so successful with its C/S project in one plant that it introduced C/S technology in a second factory in March 1994. The first plant, Toyota's Camry division, based in Georgetown, Kentucky, replaced the propriety system provided by Toyota headquarters in Japan with a graphical C/S-based information system that links the Camry facility's manufacturing, finance, and administrative departments. The $500,000 system (whose cost is half that of the proprietary system) links 175 of the division's biggest parts suppliers, both here and abroad, using network technology, an IBM mainframe, and PCs. This technology has created marked improvements in operations by getting the right parts to the right place at the right time, and has also significantly reduced transportation costs. In the future, the company also plans to use C/S technology for car design, communications, and work-flow design and analysis.[15]

Increase Resource Utilization   Client-server systems help to increase resource utilization significantly because data, programs, and communication software can be shared among users. For example, a C/S system allows fund-raisers at Harvard University (see box) to access a large database of potential donors that contains detailed financial, professional, and biographical information about them. The

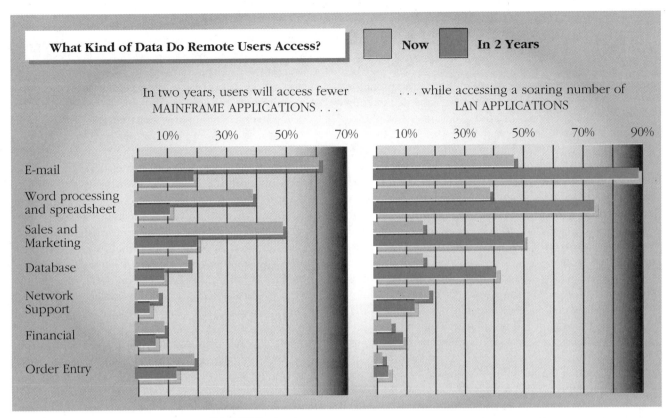

What Kind of Data Do Remote Users Access?   ☐ Now   ■ In 2 Years

In two years, users will access fewer MAINFRAME APPLICATIONS . . .

. . . while accessing a soaring number of LAN APPLICATIONS

10%   30%   50%   70%   10%   30%   50%   70%   90%

- E-mail
- Word processing and spreadsheet
- Sales and Marketing
- Database
- Network Support
- Financial
- Order Entry

FIGURE 7–4

It is estimated that in the coming years, LAN-based applications will see a steep increase and the number of mainframe applications will drop.

Source: Garcia, Mary Ryan, "Remote Control," *Information Week,* January 24, 1994, p. 52.

ability to share valuable data among users, some of whom may be in different locations, helps companies to make better use of their information systems.

Reduce Application Development Time   Some organizations have found that applications can be developed quickly and efficiently on C/S systems; this fact has attracted some organizations to C/S systems. In a C/S environment, changes or additions to existing systems can be made quickly, since applications on the server are independent of applications on the client. This also simplifies the tasks of system updates and maintenance. However, it must be emphasized that application development time is not always reduced. Companies that have some experience in moving from one computing environment to another and those with highly experienced and skilled IS staff are successful at reducing application development time. For those who are new to making a technology changeover, the reverse may be true.

Increase Organizational Responsiveness   One of the most significant benefits of C/S technology is that it acts as an agent for change, encouraging managers to be flexible and responsive to market forces. It increases individual and group productivity and enhances customer satisfaction.

A GLOBAL PERSPECTIVE
Bow Valley Industries

Bow Valley Industries is a $242-million oil exploration and production company in Calgary, Alberta. As competitive pressures increased, the company, headed by a new management team, was forced to look at new ways to reduce costs and improve efficiency. One item on the cost-cutting agenda was the company's mainframe system. Some of the applications on the mainframe were outdated, resulting in massive data redundancies, incompatibility with existing systems, and high maintenance costs. Further, licensing fees on mainframe software alone were costing the company more than $1 million per year.

Poor systems resulted in poor information, which was seriously affecting the quality of decision making. The systems were so outdated and incompatible that whenever a question required factual reports, the CEO got three different answers from three different systems, "each accurate and defensible within its own [system], but incompatible nonetheless." Decision makers were spending roughly 70% of their time simply trying to locate the data and the remaining time trying to make sense of the numbers and use them in the decision-making process.

The CEO established three goals that he felt were vital to turn things around: integration, cost reduction, and greater efficiency. He assembled a small team from each business group and asked them to identify and describe not only their business functions and data needs, but also the data that were common to all the business processes. The team was also asked to identify the processes in which data were transferred from one department to the other.

When this information became available, the company began to integrate the data from different business units and functions using C/S technology and packaged software. Using large, powerful workstations as servers, the company's PC users, including two hundred in the Calgary headquarters and two regional offices throughout western Canada, are now connected to a wide variety of databases at company headquarters by a Novell token-ring network.

The move to C/S technology has dramatically improved both efficiency and turnaround time. For instance, under the old system, when Bow Valley wanted to conduct an evaluation of any parcel of land within its more than 5 million acres of land, managers had to gather marketing and contract information, reserve data, and production data from a multitude of databases spread throughout the company. "Each question not only required talking to someone different and having them try to get the data, but the estimates could all be different depending on the source," says a company spokesperson.

Now anyone in the company can receive data on any business activity or decision by simply using a few SQL commands. What once took 3 months or more can now be done is less than 2 weeks. More important, the numbers that decision makers receive are consistent, complete, and reliable.

Another advantage of the new system is improved mapping. Before the new system was installed, when researchers required a map of a piece of land, they had to seek the services of the drafting department. Today, using application software, employees can access the database, identify the data they need, and automatically generate a map of the region in question using that data. The ready availability of information has helped decision makers not only to make timely decisions but also to make better decisions, since they can now analyze more data in a shorter time span.[16]

For example, a C/S system helped AT&T Universal Card Services to find a profitable niche in the highly competitive credit card industry by allowing sales representatives to respond to customer needs by accessing and consolidating information from different databases. In 1990, AT&T Universal Card Services (UC/S), in Jacksonville, Florida, launched the AT&T Universal Card, an all-in-one, calling, and ATM card. However, once the card was launched, the company found that its existing information system was not capable of handling the quarter of a million calls that were coming in each day—a big difference from the estimated 25,000 calls. The company switched to a C/S, GUI-based system,

BUSINESS REALITIES
Harvard University

In August 1994, Harvard University launched one of the largest fund-raising campaigns in collegiate history. Client-server technology will help the university achieve its ambitious goal of raising $2 billion in 5 years. The system will provide 250 fund-raisers with personal and financial information and detailed biographies of half a million prospects "that will help [fund-raisers] get chummy with the university's would-be benefactors who have money to burn."[17] In addition to providing basic personal information, such as addresses and phone numbers, the system will provide other personal information, such as the subject's favorite drink, names of spouse and children, hobbies and activities, golfing buddies, and favorite vacation spots. Why is this information important? Because half the battle in telephone fund-raising is to keep the conversation going! The system also provides information on Harvard alumni with whom fund-raisers are likely to have initial contact. The C/S technology ensures that "once you're a Harvard alum, it's very hard to get lost."[18]

---

appropriately titled UWIN, that allows service representatives to provide prompt and high-quality customer service by accessing and consolidating information from various AT&T customer databases. The system presents the information to the sales associate through a standardized user-friendly graphical interface. The response of customers to the high-quality service that UWIN provides has been exceptional: in just 3 years AT&T's Universal Card has attracted more than 12 million customers and AT&T has become the second largest card issuer in the country, making its investment of nearly $9.9 million in UWIN well worthwhile.[19]

Many companies are realizing that cutting down on unproductive paperwork is a way to improve profits and enhance productivity, and that C/S systems can help them do so. (See box on Hasboro).

BUSINESS REALITIES
Hasboro

Another firm that has benefited from C/S is Hasboro, the maker of the popular Cabbage Patch dolls. Most of the dolls are made outside the U.S. and U.S. companies are required to track goods and services from their countries of origin to the U.S. to comply with U.S. customs laws.

Over the last few years, the company has switched from an unwieldy paper-based system to a mainframe, and eventually to a C/S system, to track goods and services. Before the C/S system was installed, the company relied on faxes for receiving and sending information about products and materials traveling between Hong Kong and the U.S. "The same piece of paper could be faxed back and forth three or four times before we could be sure the merchandise had reached the destination and [know] the amount that we owed the government," says a company spokesperson.

The C/S system duplicated the multitude of forms that are used to meet regulatory requirements and used knowledge base management system (KMBS) software to incorporate critical data, such as pricing factors, import duties, shipping and handling regulations, and so on, into a database residing on an IBM 3090 mainframe (the server). Today, with the help of their PCs, employees can receive online updates about the locations of shipments and about customs charges. When the merchandise arrives in Seattle, customs payments are coordinated using EDI links to the federal government. Reports that once took 4 hours to print after the request was initiated are done today in 4 minutes or less. This has had a significant impact on the ability of the organization to respond to suppliers, distributors, and retailers.[20]

Disadvantages of C/S Systems

Although vendors often praise their own new technologies, it is important to remember that C/S systems cannot solve all problems. Many organizations that venture into C/S environments are finding a number of hidden costs and unpleasant surprises. Hence, although C/S systems provide many benefits, it is important that companies approach this technology with caution.

Difficult Transition for Many Companies   The transition from a mainframe to a C/S environment is fraught with challenges and obstacles. Users liken the problems of moving from a mainframe to a C/S environment to those of two people who speak different languages trying to discuss the inner workings of a lawn sprinkler.[21] The knowledge and experience gained in the mainframe environment cannot be directly transferred to the C/S environment. Some companies have gone back to the mainframe environment because they were unable to meet the challenges of changing over.

Massive Retraining Is Required   When a firm moves from a mainframe to a C/S environment, one element that greatly increases the cost of the transition is retraining employees and IS personnel. Unfortunately, since much mainframe expertise is inapplicable to C/S environments, often in-depth training is required for all employees. The C/S environment also requires a new mindset; hence, companies are finding that it is not enough to train people in the technology alone, but that they must also train people to adopt and implement new processes. Such training can be very expensive.

Forrester, a consulting group, estimates that it costs a company $25,000 to $40,000 per employee in out-of-pocket expenses and lost productivity for an initial round of training in technologies, such as relational databases, applications integration, and data access. Companies then must anticipate another $5,000 or so per employee, every 18 months, for refresher courses and training in the use of new tools.[22]

Lack of Standards   Probably because of the evolving nature of C/S systems, there is much confusion as to which standards should be followed in their design and development. Standards and procedures available in a mainframe environment, such as security, are totally lacking or minimal in the PC environment. For example, one of the issues that developers must contend with is whether to use middleware or to connect the mainframe directly to the PC network. (*Middleware* is software that connect end-users to various mainframe and minicomputer databases.) Middleware is usually housed on a server on a LAN and can access data no matter where it resides, whether it is in a flat file or is accessible through SQL.

Technical decisions such as "middleware or no middleware" are important, but without standards or clear history showing the advantages and disadvantages of each approach, companies often have to play a guessing game. Unfortunately, the losses in this game can be high and may include lost customers.

Balancing Act Between Centralization and Decentralization   Although C/S technology is based on the idea of decentralization, successful implementation of this technology often requires a balancing act between centralization and decentralization. Some aspects of C/S management must be centralized; others must be decentralized. This is difficult for most companies.

For example, in an effort to reduce data redundancies and duplication of design and development effort, many companies are centralizing hardware acquisition, coordination of various business units, and business process implementation. However, the question of exactly what should be centralized is still open to debate. The generation, creation, storage, and processing of local data are often decentralized. Further, wrong decisions as to what to centralize and what to decentralize often take a long time to rectify.

Lower Costs May Be Deceptive   Although the cost per MIPS for C/S systems is often lower than that for mainframes, the long-term cost advantages of C/S systems over other kinds of information systems appear to be minimal. This is because when all the costs of developing, implementing, and maintaining C/S systems are taken into account, they can sometimes be as costly as mainframe environments.

According to recent studies conducted by the Research Board, a New York–based IS research consultancy that works only with Fortune 100 firms,[23] the costs of mainframe, minicomputer, and C/S computing will be roughly the same in another 3 years. This is because over a 5-year period, 60% to 80% of the actual cost of C/S computing is accounted for by end-user support costs, administrative costs, and other factors. A mainframe environment requires only a few experts to support several thousand users; in a C/S environment, one support person is required for every 35 users, and support personnel can sometimes cost 3 to 5 times as much as the hardware and software. The Gartner Group estimates that in the past 10 years, users have spent close to $1.6 trillion on support and administration for C/S systems. Another significant disadvantage of such high support costs is that unlike equipment costs, which can be written off over the course of the item's lifespan, support costs do not decrease over time and cannot be depreciated. Figure 7–5 gives a breakdown of average costs for C/S projects.

Client-Server Security

One of the major problems confronting developers and managers of C/S applications is their high security risks. (System security is covered in detail in Chapter 16.) Ironically, the very same features that make the C/S system flexible, modular, and responsive also make it risky and vulnerable.

"Client/server computing is a double-edged sword. You get great productivity, but all of a sudden everybody is a systems developer and administrator, tinkering with their own applications. Without any point of centralized tracking and control, companies will end up with worse chaos than [that which arose] from the proliferation of minicomputers in the early 1980s."[24]

There are two areas that are critical to the security C/S systems: access privileges and application integrity.

Guarding Access Privileges

The first step in building system security is to ensure that only authorized users have access to the system, based on the integrity requirements of the system and

FIGURE 7-5

Although hardware and software costs for client-server systems are considerably lower than those for their mainframe counterparts, user support is expensive in a client-server environment.

Source: Maglitta, Joseph, "Large Shops Rethink PC Focus," *Computerworld*, February 2, 1994, p. 8.

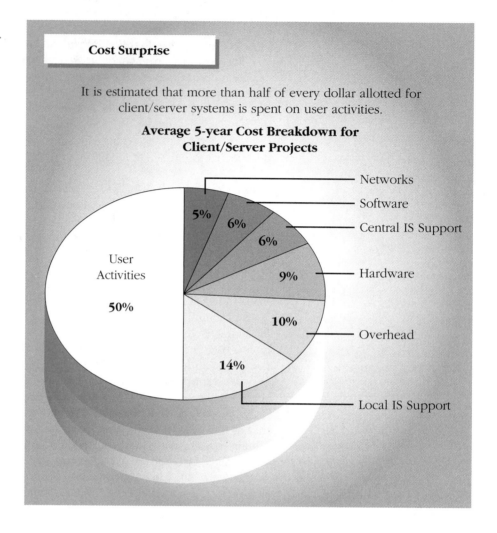

confidentiality of data residing on the system. Says one C/S system administrator, "Let's say I have a phone book for sale. I will let just about everyone look at it, but only a couple of people will be allowed to put anything into it. Here integrity is a high-level issue and confidentiality is low. You don't necessarily let one issue drive the other."[25]

Some organizations use customized interfaces that allow users to access only data fields on the interface, thus preventing users from putting "muddy, curious paws on restricted data." In other words, these interfaces are write-protected so that users can only read the data, not change it.[26]

Preserving the Integrity of Applications

Some approaches to maintaining application integrity include automatically updating copies of application software that are stored on one or more servers (some of which may be in remote locations) and monitoring the number of working copies of a given application. Many companies let employees know that their network activities will be audited; this practice may deter inappropriate activities such as sharing passwords, copying programs, and releasing proprietary information. Encryption is another way to ensure system integrity. It can be hardware- or software-based. It uses coding "keys" to create encrypted files that are later decoded. Clearly, the keys themselves should be securely guarded and should be destroyed after an encrypted file is decoded.

Summary

♦ **Describe client-server computing**
A client-server system is a kind of distributed system in which the processing power of the computer is distributed among a number of locations that are networked together. The server is usually a large central computer, such as a mainframe, that serves as a repository for data and programs commonly accessed by users. The clients are usually smaller, networked computers, such as PCs, that are linked together through networks. Distributed database systems are also referred to as C/S systems; in these systems, the data and the database software reside on the server and different clients access the server to fulfill their data needs.

There is no one universally acceptable definition of C/S computing. Often it means different things to different people. However, the common theme among most definitions is that a C/S system is a technology enabler in corporate re-engineering efforts and often induces profound changes in the organization that uses it.

♦ **Development issues connected with client-server systems**
The development of C/S applications is based on the following six components: communication services, distribution services, application services, company-specific applications, industry-specific applications, and system management and security. The Patricia Seybold Group recommends that organizations take the following five steps before launching a C/S system: carefully identify and define the type of application, determine the network requirements, select the C/S architecture, develop the logical and physical design of the system, and, finally, implement the system. The first step is to define the type of application and determine whether the application is driven by routine transactions, by the knowledge and experience of knowledge workers, or by business processes. The type of application will influence the amount of traffic on the network. Developers should be technically prepared to meet additional traffic flow on the network if it becomes necessary. The third step is to define the architecture of the system. By architecture, we mean the basic ingredients of an information system: hardware, software, and networking components. The fourth step is to develop the logical and physical design of the system. Finally, developers should address implementation issues so that the application can be successfully implemented within the organization's existing information infrastructure.

♦ **Some critical issues in client-server security**
The security of C/S environments is a critical issue for network administrators. Access privileges and application security are two issues that must be carefully addressed in order to ensure that C/S environments are well secured. Network administrators should know at all times who is on the network and what each user is doing. Clearly, network security is a balancing act between control and access and there are no easy answers. Another issue in C/S environments is preserving the integrity of system applications.

♦ **Computing client-server costs: a challenging task**
C/S technology is suited only to organizations that have a long-term commitment to it and are willing to make a large financial investment in it. Estimating the cost of C/S computing is one of the most challenging tasks confronting IS managers. Some of the elements that must be taken into account when computing C/S costs are hardware, software, peripherals, accessories, training for end-users, managers, and network administrators, contract negotiations, outside consultants, and various unexpected costs.

♦ **Advantages and disadvantages of client-server environments**
Organizations that use C/S systems become responsive, proactive, and flexible in meeting the needs of their customers as they reorganize and refocus the functions and responsibilities of knowledge workers. A

C/S system reduces operating costs, increases resource utilization, reduces application development, increases organizational responsiveness, fosters lateral communications, and changes the emphasis from control to trust and teamwork.

Like any other technology, client-server also has some disadvantages. First, companies often find it difficult to make the transition from a mainframe environment to a C/S system. Often, this transition requires major training for employees and this can very quickly become a costly and time-consuming affair. Also, there is a lack of standardization among client-server tools, making it difficult for companies to import their applications from one system to another. Finally, although the literature is filled with examples of how client-servers have helped to bring down the cost of computing, there are several cases when costs have actually increased. Hence, a cautionary approach is recommended.

 Review Questions

1. What are some factors that led to the evolution of client-server technology?
2. Explain what is meant by *client-server technology.* What is a server? What is a client?
3. Why are C/S systems similar to distributed databases? Explain.
4. What are front-end software and back-end software? Are both essential for a C/S system to function?
5. What is the difference between C/S systems and LANs?
6. Why is it important to have a plan before investing in C/S applications?
7. What are some advantages of C/S systems?
8. What are some disadvantages of C/S systems? What are some hidden costs associated with this technology?
9. What measures can IS managers take to ensure the security of their C/S systems?
10. What are some approaches to controlling the access privileges of system users?

 Discussion Questions

1. Client-server technology is viewed as vital to the growth of a business. In spite of its growing importance in the business world, colleges and universities seem to lag behind in offering courses, and even the courses that are offered appear to be too elementary to be useful. "Academia must work harder to keep up with rapidly changing trends in corporate computing. Otherwise, colleges will continue to turn out graduates unschooled in the latest technologies—and corporate retraining costs will continue to climb past the point of affordability," stated Steve Maloney, associate vice president of Data Processing and Information Services at Boise State University in Idaho.
   a. Suppose you are assigned the task of convincing the chair of the information systems department in your university that knowledge of C/S systems is critical for future graduates. Develop a presentation explaining what C/S systems are and how they are changing the American business landscape. Explain how C/S courses will help future graduates land better-paying jobs.[27]
2. One of the hidden costs in client-server computing is that of users supporting users. In other words, instead of going to the IS department for help, an end user may decide to seek the help of another user to solve his or her technical problems. Although the costs of users supporting users ranges anywhere between $6,000 to $15,000 per workstation, these costs are often difficult to monitor and control. What are some other hidden costs that come to mind?

ETHICAL ISSUES

Case 1: Ethics of Pricing

One of the thorniest issues facing managers of C/S systems is software licensing, which often places vendors and users at loggerheads. In particular, managers have to contend with the pros and cons of user-based pricing versus host-based pricing. Some companies charge their customers for a basic set of programs and software services, based on the number of users who concurrently access a given server. Other companies charge a company for each user who accesses any given server at any time. Hence, negotiating a software pricing contract is a tricky issue for IS managers. If contract negotiations are not properly executed, the vendor or the company can be cheated out of millions of dollars.[28]

a. Explain what is meant by user-based pricing versus host-based pricing. What are the advantages and disadvantages of each approach?
b. Identify three steps that managers can take to ensure that the organization gets the best software licensing deal.

Case 2: Beware of Employees!

An IS director relates an incident in which a large bank made its retail bankers responsible for maintaining the files for its C/S based Visa credit card system. Retail bankers who were clearly not well versed in the intricacies of file maintenance inadvertently set the credit limit to zero on all the cards. "All customers trying to charge items to their Visa accounts that day were turned down, including the CEO's daughter, [who] went out to buy her wedding dress [and] was rejected." Not only did the bank incur millions of dollars in losses, but it generated ill will and suffered serious damage to its reputation.

a. Is this an example of a security breach? Why or why not?
b. Whom do you think should be held liable in this case: the CIO or the employees who made the error?

PROBLEM SOLVING IN THE REAL WORLD

Case 1: Art and High Tech Go Hand-in-Hand

The National Gallery of Art (NGA) is second only to the Smithsonian's Air and Space Museum as the most popular tourist attraction in Washington, DC. It houses and displays a collection of approximately 80,000 items and performs a number of other activities, such as educating and informing the public, holding local, national, and international exhibitions, and running a national lending program to share works of art with major government departments, including the White House, the Supreme Court, and U.S. embassies and consulates all over the world.

In 1978, the NGA was one of the first organizations to create a computerized catalog and since then has stayed abreast of the technology. The computerized catalog, called the Art Information System, was an efficient way for the NGA to collect and store data about every item in its collection. However, by the late 1980s, the world of information technology had changed so much that the catalog had become relatively inflexible and difficult to use. Today, the com-

(Continued on next page)

pany has a state-of-the-art C/S system, called the Collection Management System (CMS), designed to meet a wide variety of organization needs.

The CMS supports many functions, including administration, operations, and general information for a wide variety of departments: those of the curator and the registrar, exhibitions, insurance, education and information. All departments have access to common information and also to information related to their specific functions. For example, curators maintain information about each work of art; sometimes one work of art requires more than 600 distinct pieces of information.

Two key museum responsibilities became subsystems of the CMS: movement and acquisition. The Movement subsystem helps the museum's registrar to plan, monitor, and coordinate shipments of loaned or borrowed art, both inside and outside the gallery, and to address the special shipping and handling directions that often accompany art packages, such as special containers and deliveries by couriers. The Acquisitions subsystem catalogs hundreds of new lots every year, each containing one or more art objects, with such basic information as the donor, the source, appropriate acknowledgment of the funding, and the official date of approval by the museum board. This subsystem is also responsible for managing the art exhibitions. Since art shows are sometimes planned as many as 10 years in advance and involve hundreds or even thousands of art objects, it is a slow and detail-oriented task. The Acquisitions subsystem tracks the permission necessary to move an art object, insurance or indemnity arrangements, shipping, and other factors. One of the significant advantages of this system is that it helps administrators to use the data to manage their fiduciary responsibilities, such as insurance costs for borrowed items.[29]

a. Identify some of the benefits to NGA from its C/S system.
b. Why is a C/S system appropriate for this application?

Case 2: United Airlines Takes Off

Providing snacks and meals to flight passengers is no small task. United Airlines' Catering Division, for example, handles 75 million in-flight meals per year, with 17 kitchens and 250 food contractors worldwide. Until June 1993, United's food inventory management system relied on standalone PCs; the system was slow and grossly inefficient. For example, each time there was a menu change, it had to be manually entered in each system located at each site. Service level guides, which consisted of several hundred pages providing specific details on everything from brownie ingredients to number of servings per plate, had to be printed and mailed four or five times a year to each location, since these locations did not have online access to this information.

A year ago, United developed the Integrated Tactical Plan for Distributed Systems, an integrated C/S environment. This is an online tracking and monitoring system that manages United's food inventory and related issues. An extensive database focused on food items and food preparation is stored on the server and about 13 remote kitchen sites can access this database for information on changes or guidelines for preparing a certain item. The system is expected to generate millions of dollars in savings.[30]

a. Why is C/S technology suitable for this application?
b. Would a LAN suffice for this application? Why or why not?

Notes

1. Ricciuti, Mike. "The Best In Client/Server Computing," *Datamation*, March 1, 1994, pp. 26–35.
2. Pelton, Charles. "Let's not get caught up in semantics," *Informationweek*, January 31, 1994, p. 50.
3. Ibid.
4. "Building Blocks for the New Information Technology Infrastructure," *Datamation*, March 1, 1994, special advertising section, pp. S2–S8.
5. Pelton, Charles. "Let's not get caught up in semantics," *Informationweek*, January 31, 1994, p. 50.
6. Ricciuti, Mike. "CS First Boston Corp.," *Datamation*, March 1, 1994, pp. 28–29.
7. Ricciuti, Mike. "Hyatt Hotels Corp.," *Datamation*, March 1, 1994, pp. 29–33.
8. Lile, Edward A. "Client/server architecture: A brief overview," *Journal of Systems Management*, December 1993, pp. 26–29.
9. Nash, Kim S. "Burnett's Stars and Comet Fill Traditional IS 'Black Hole,'" *Computerworld*, November 28, 1994, p. 29.
10. Johnston, Stuart J. "A good deal for Nordstrom's buyers," May 23, 1994, pp. 61–65.
11. *Computerworld*, June 28, 1993. Speech at the Lattane Center's CEO/CIO Roundtable, Towson, Md., June 28, 1993.
12. Cafasso, Rosemary. "Client/server faces up to enterprise," *Computerworld*, May 2, 1994, p. 1, 26.
13. Greenbaum, Joshua and Peter L. Francis. "Mac Answers Holiday Inn's Call." *InformationWeek*, May 23, 1994, pp. 44–47.
14. Appleyby, Chuck. "Rx for HealthCare," *InformationWeek*, June 6, 1994, pp. 64–72.
15. Nash, Kim S. "Carnmaker takes client/server road," *Computerworld*, February 28, 1994, pp. 81–82.
16. Pepper, Jon. "Bow Valley's IT Reorganization, Oil's Well That Ends Well" *InformationWeek*, July 12, 1993, pp. 28–30.
17. Halper, Mark. "Client/server setup targets big bucks," *Computerworld*, March 28, 1994, p. 47.
18. Ibid.
19. Sullivan, Deidre. "Supporting A House Of Cards," *CIO*, January 15, 1994, pp. 58–62.
20. Ballou, Melinda-Carol. "Client/server turns to kids' stuff," *Computerworld*, May 30, 1994, pp. 73–77.
21. Ambrosio, Johanna. "Walk, Don't Run With It," *Computerworld*, March 15, 1993, p. 65.
22. Ambrosio, Johanna. "Client Server costs more than expected," *Computerworld*, October 18, 1993, p. 28.
23. Anonymous. "True Value of Client Server," *Computerworld*, November 22, 1993, p. 84.
24. Freedman, David H. "To Our Clients, With Best Wishes, From The Servers," *CIO*, February 15, 1994, pp. 56–64.
25. Cassidy, Peter. "Lines of Defense," CIO, February 15, 1994, pp. 46–54.
26. Ibid.
27. Maloney, Stephen. "Colleges don't make the grade," *InformationWeek*, March 21, 1994, p. 58.
28. Horwitt, Elizabeth. "Client/Server Complicates Licensing," *Computerworld*, May 1993, pp. 57–59.
29. Gerritsen, Rob and Estelle G. Brand. "State of the Art Client/Server," *DBMS*, February 1993, pp. 54–60.
30. Booker, Ellis. "United Airlines Adds Client/Server to Menu," *Computerworld*, January 17, 1994, p. 51.

Business Applications of Information Systems

Chapter 8
Decision Support Systems and Executive Information Systems

Chapter 9
Artificial Intelligence, Expert Systems, and Neural Networks

Chapter 10
Office Automation

Chapter 11
Business Information Systems

Decision Support Systems and Executive Information Systems

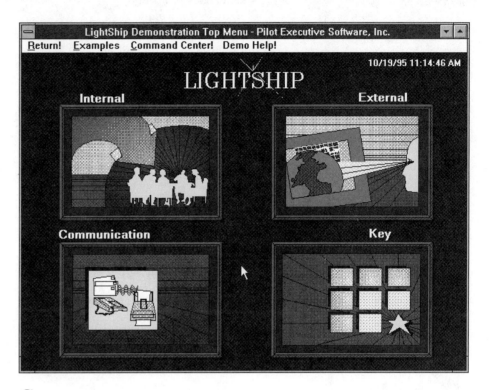

Contents

Learning Objectives
Technology Payoff: The Nebraska State Patrol's Investigative Services Division
Introduction
Steps in Problem Solving
What Is a Decision Support System?
Applications of a DSS
Components of a DSS
    Database Management Systems
    Model Management Systems
Functions of a DSS
    Model Building
    "What-If" Analysis
    Goal Seeking
    Risk Analysis
    Graphical Analysis
Tools for Developing a DSS
    DSS Generators
    DSS Shells
    Custom-Made Software
Group Decision Support Systems
    Single-Computer Systems
    Keypad-Response Systems
    Full-Keyboard Workstation Systems
    Advantages of GDSS

Executive Information Systems
Characteristics of an EIS
    Derived Information
    Drill-Down
Critical Success Factors for DSS/EIS
    Commitment from Top Management
    Availability of Accurate and Reliable Data
    Careful Problem Selection
    Integration of DSS and EIS with Existing Technologies
    Costs Versus Benefits
TPS, MIS, DSS, and EIS
Summary
Review Questions
Discussion Questions
Ethical Issues
    Case 1: Manipulating Decisions
    Case 2: Limited Access to Data
Problem Solving in the Real World
    Case 1: Amnesty International USA
    Case 2: Georgia Power Gains Power Through DSS
    Case 3: Catch the Criminal
References
Notes

Learning Objectives

Decision support systems (DSS) and executive information systems (EIS) are two types of systems that facilitate tactical and strategic decision making. A DSS helps middle managers retrieve and process large volumes of data and integrate the data with various decision-making models to generate alternative solutions to problems. An EIS is a system that presents top managers with large amounts of information in an easy-to-understand format. This chapter presents a discussion of DSS and EIS, their primary functions, and their applications. After reading and studying this chapter, you will be able to

* Identify and describe the characteristics of DSS and EIS.
* Describe a GDSS and its role in improving group decision making.
* Understand the differences among TPS, MIS, DSS, and EIS.

TECHNOLOGY PAYOFF

The Nebraska State Patrol's Investigative Services Division

The increase in criminal activity, along with budget reductions, has made the job of law enforcement agencies difficult. Many law enforcement agencies struggle to find a fair method to distribute limited resources among the cases that they must solve. One such state agency that was eager to improve the overall quality and efficiency of its criminal investigation program is the Nebraska State Patrol's Investigative Services Division.

The department developed a new DSS, called the Case Progression DSS (CPDSS), to improve tracking of cases and to allocate resources among different cases based on their probability of success. Case tracking is a semistructured problem that requires both the application of standard rules and procedures and the exercise of intuition and judgment. An investigator must use his or her judgment to determine whether it is worthwhile to allocate more resources to a case by taking into account the chance of solving that case. Investigators must also carefully track cases to that they can take the necessary actions at the appropriate times and assess what remains to be done to close each case.

Many investigators at state agencies have large workloads, so keeping track of all cases is a difficult and time-consuming task. CPDSS helps sergeants to track cases, make decisions about case assignments and case terminations, and identify the actions pending on each case. The DSS also allows investigators to estimate the amount of time they are likely to spend on each activity and evaluate the productivity of their investigative units. Besides this kind of operational support, the system provides tactical support in tasks, such as quarterly case reviews of investigators and resource allocation. The information provided by the system is used to determine how the limited resources of the department should be distributed among different investigators and even among different cases within the purview of each investigator.[1]

In today's business environment, making the best decision, right now, can be your strongest competitive advantage.

[Symbol Technologies, manufacturers of networking products in management systems]

Introduction

In Chapter 1, we identified four major types of information systems: transaction processing systems (TPS), management information systems(MIS), intelligent support systems (ISS), and office automation systems (OAS). This chapter focuses on two types of ISS: decision support systems (DSS) and executive information systems (EIS). Artificial intelligence (AI) and expert systems (ES) are discussed in the next chapter.

ISS help a manager to make sound decisions by integrating data with various decision-making models. For example, the Nebraska State Patrol's Investigative Services Division uses an ISS (a DSS, to be specific) for case assignments, case tracking, and case reviewing. Problems such as these, which require both data and decision-making models are handled well by ISS.

ISS evolved in the late 1970s and early 1980s to meet the needs of middle and top managers; several compelling factors led to this evolution. First, increasing global competition and the exponential growth of corporate data made it imperative for managers to be able to process large volumes of data quickly. Second, though the summary and exception reports generated by MIS were useful for making operational decisions, they were not sufficient for solving tactical and strategic problems.

Several significant changes in the computer industry also propelled the development of ISS. The costs of computer hardware were plummeting, end-users were becoming more sophisticated, and user-friendly software was becoming commonplace. The computer that had once been relegated to the back room was finding its way to the manager's desktop and becoming an integral part of the manager's "tool kit." User-friendly software, particularly software that went beyond simply automating tasks to facilitating intelligent activities, was becoming more readily available. The new software ran under graphical user interfaces (GUIs), making it easier for nonprogrammers to create applications. The combination of inexpensive hardware and user-friendly software led to the rapid evolution of a class of systems called ISS that were tremendously useful to middle and top managers. Before we take a detailed look at DSS and EIS, let us look at the steps involved in problem solving.

Steps in Problem Solving

Structured decisions

Decisions that are routine and straightforward. By following a set of pre-established steps, a solution to the problem can be found. Such a problem does not require intuition or judgment, so the system returns the same solution every time.

Unstructured decisions

Decisions that are unique and non-repetitive. Because they require intuition, experience, and judgment, there may be no one "best" solution and solutions may differ from one decision maker to the next.

Semistructured decisions

These decision fall somewhere between structured decisions, which are routine and repetitive, and unstructured decisions, which are unique and nonrepetitive.

Recall that managers make three types of decisions: structured, semistructured, and unstructured. **Structured decisions** are routine and repetitive and follow a set of predetermined steps. Solutions to such problems do not rely on the intuition or judgment of the decision maker. For example, calculating the compound interest on a loan is a structured decision; it follows a standard procedure and requires no intuition or judgment.

Unstructured decisions are made to solve problems that are nonrepetitive in nature. They rely heavily on the intuition, judgment, and experience of the decision maker; therefore, unstructured decisions about the same problem may vary significantly from one decisionmaker to the next. For example, developing a strategy to remain competitive in an ever-changing marketplace is an unstructured decision.

Semistructured decisions fall somewhere between structured and unstructured ones. Some parts of the problem are routine and can be approached with standard problem-solving procedures; others require intuition and judgment. For example, selecting a college or university is a semistructured decision. Some parts of this decision rely on facts and figures, such as tuition fees; other parts rely on intuition.

Intelligent support systems, such as DSS, EIS, and ES, are sets of tools that help managers with semistructured and unstructured decisions. Figure 8–1 summarizes the steps involved in this kind of problem solving. Here is a set of steps for solving such problems:

- Define the problem.
- Gather the data necessary to solve the problem.
- Integrate the data with decision-making models.
- Generate alternative solutions.
- Select the optimal alternative or the most satisfactory, given the circumstances.
- Implement the chosen alternative.

Although defining the problem and its boundaries is one of the most critical steps in making good decisions, many organizations tend to rush through this step. In defining the problem, decision makers should carefully identify the source of the problem, not just the symptoms. For example, a manager concerned with declining sales of Product A may think that the market is shrinking when the real problem is the poor quality of the product. Problems should be defined in simple terms and clearly communicated to all parties affected by them.

The next step is to identify the data necessary to solve the problem and the cost of acquiring the data. This is not always as simple as it may sound, particularly for unstructured problems. Sometimes, in the process of gathering data, new problems or new perspectives on the existing problem may emerge and the problem may have to be redefined. But if data are not available or if the data are inconsistent, the quality of the solution will be compromised. Remember, the slogan "Garbage in, Garbage Out" was coined to describe data processing. A solution to a problem can only be as good as the data that go into solving that problem.

In the next step, the data are integrated with various decision-making models. For example, a stockbroker may use data about the financial performance of a company in a forecasting model to predict future company performance. A teacher may use the class-participation points acquired by students in a model that calculates overall course grade. Different problems require different models, and sometimes different decision makers may use different models for the same problem.

Next, based on the processing described above, alternatives are generated and the best alternative is selected and implemented. Clearly, *best* is a relative term that depends on predetermined goals or criteria (such as the desire to increase profits, cut costs, or improve employee morale) and constraints that the decision maker faces (such as limited money, personnel, and time). Sometimes there is no one best alternative to a problem, particularly an unstructured problem, and the decision maker must simply select the most satisfactory solution.

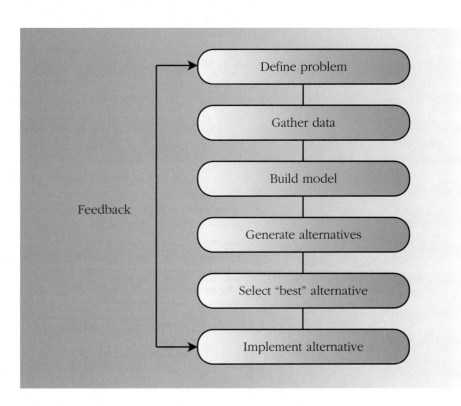

FIGURE 8-1

The steps involved in problem solving.

Although we have shown problem solving as a sequence of steps, in the real world it is not always compartmentalized into such a neat sequence. Quite often, the steps are performed iteratively and their sequence may not be as shown above. Solving problems in the real world is challenging for two primary reasons: an overabundance of data and a complex and dynamic business environment. Though advances in computer hardware and software have made instantaneous access to large volumes of data a reality, the overabundance of data can be overwhelming. Another problem-solving challenge is today's highly competitive business environment, in which business conditions and situations change rapidly, making unexpected and challenging problems an everyday occurrence in the lives of many top managers. This dynamic environment often forces managers to make quick decisions, even though they lack the necessary data. Information systems, such as DSS and EIS, can alleviate these problems somewhat.

What Is a Decision Support System?

Decision support system (DSS)
A set of well integrated, user-friendly, computer-based tools that combine internal and external data with various decision-making models to solve semistructured and unstructured problems. Among the functions of a DSS are "what-if" analysis, model building, goal seeking, and graphical analysis.

A**decision support system (DSS)** is a set of well-integrated, user-friendly, computer-based tools that combine data with various decision-making models (both quantitative and qualitative) to solve semistructured and unstructured problems. Such systems solve a specific problem or a class of problems, such as scheduling, planning, resource allocation, and forecasting. They allow managers to ask ad hoc (nonroutine) queries and receive customized responses. Although DSS were initially targeted for top managers and middle managers, today these systems are being deployed at all levels of the organization.

A DSS can be standalone or integrated with existing systems, such as TPS or MIS. They can support individual decision making or group decision making. Systems that support group decision making, called group decision support systems (GDSS), are covered later in this chapter.

An information system can be used for problem finding, problem solving, or both. In *problem finding,* the goal is simply to identify the source of the problem and carefully define it. In *problem solving,* the goal is to solve a problem using data, models, knowledge, and judgment. A DSS is primarily a problem-solving system.

A DSS has the following characteristics:

+ It facilitates semistructured and unstructured decision making by bringing together data, models, and human judgment.
+ It can provide decision support for several interdependent decisions.
+ It supports a wide variety of decision-making processes and styles.
+ It assists the decision maker to make decisions under dynamic business conditions.
+ It helps the decision maker address ad hoc queries.[2]

Table 8–1 summarizes the characteristics of a DSS.

Applications of a DSS

Problems can be classified into three categories: independent, interrelated, and organizational. Table 8–2 shows the three categories of problems and their definitions. Independent problems are "standalone problems" that

TABLE 8–1
The characteristics of a decision support system.

- ◆ Solves semistructured and unstructured problems
- ◆ Integrates data with decision-making models
- ◆ Supports a wide variety of decision-making processes and styles
- ◆ Facilitates decision making under dynamic conditions
- ◆ Helps provide answers to ad hoc queries

TABLE 8–2
The three common types of problems and their definitions.

Independent Problems	Problems whose solutions are independent of other problems. The goal is simply to find the best solution to the given problem.
Interrelated Problems	Problems whose solutions are interrelated. The goal is to find the best solution to the entire set, and not just to individual problems. Usually require team effort.
Organizational Problems	Problems that span a number of departments and units in an organization and affect the entire organization. Such problems require team effort.

have minimal influence on other problems, so that the goal is simply to find the most effective solution to the problem at hand. Truly independent problems are rare in the business world.

Interrelated problems influence, and are influenced, by each other, so that the goal is to find the most effective solution to the *group* of interrelated problems. Such problems often require a team of experts from different areas within an organization to work together to solve the problem. Suppose Pepsi's goal is to increase sales of Diet Pepsi by 5% this summer. This requires the coordination of a set of interrelated tasks, such as developing an effective advertising campaign, motivating the sales force, developing pricing strategies, and offering incentives to distributors. Accomplishing this task would require the talents of a group of experts.

Finally, organizational problems involve entire departments within an organization. An example of an organizational problem is introducing a new product into the market. Experts from design, production, manufacturing, marketing, finance, human resources, and quality control must come together to develop and market a new product. Total quality management is another good example of an organizational effort, because for it to be effective, it requires a joint effort from all units in the organization. The primary difference between independent problems and organizational problems is that the former often require multiple experts from a specific area, such as marketing in the above example. Organizational problems require multiple experts from different areas, such as marketing, finance, production, and so on.

A DSS is an ideal candidate for interrelated and inter-organizational problems. For example, in a manufacturing environment, production managers make semistructured and unstructured decisions, such as the number of machines to be operated, the amount of materials required to fill a new order, production scheduling, and labor scheduling. A DSS can help a production manager answer such complex and data-intensive questions. For example, a DSS was implemented at the Dairymen's Cooperative Creamery Association to solve the problem of production scheduling and inventory management. The system determines which machine should do what task and for how long in order to meet daily production quotas, relieving plant supervisors of about 4 hours of tedious hand calculations every day.

In our story of the Nebraska Police Department, we showed an application of DSS that helps the agency better coordinate and manage the task of allocating limited resources. Resource allocation is a critical task that confronts managers regularly; a DSS is an ideal tool for such problems. It can address questions such as these: "What quantities of manpower, money, machines, and materials should be allocated to this project to successfully complete it in time?" "What quantities of extra resources do we require to complete this project in 5 fewer days than planned?" "How should limited resources be distributed between critical and non-critical projects?"

Another application of DSS is forecasting, demand management, and supplier evaluation. A DSS can consolidate data from different sources to forecast demand, determine the appropriate quantity and mix of resources necessary to meet the demand, and balance supply and demand for a wide variety of products. It can also present managers with comprehensive data about different company projects, programs, and products so that they can make sound decisions. For example, Abbott Labs, which produces and markets some 2,000 products, uses a DSS for sales forecasting, pricing analysis, tracking of promotion results, and new product analysis. Intel uses a DSS to evaluate prospective suppliers against specific company criteria and select suppliers based on their credentials. A manager can change the criteria, check the effect of the change on supplier rankings, and monitor a supplier's performance.

Another company that uses a DSS to enhance organizational decision making is Information Resources, Inc. (see box). It integrates sales data from its invoicing system and alerts marketing managers to potential problems and trends by providing sales information arranged by client, product, and units.

An international firm, one of the largest retailers of jewelry merchandise, uses DSS to determine the best locations for its stores. A DSS compares the demo-

---

BUSINESS REALITIES
Information Resources, Inc.

Information Resources, Inc. (IRI), based in Chicago, uses a DSS to provide managers with access to a wide variety of information from many sources, so that they can see the "big picture" and make informed decisions. The system has a wide variety of modeling and analytical capabilities that can be matched to each manager's decision-making style and job responsibilities.

For example, at the end of each accounting period, the DSS gathers data from the company's invoicing system and presents marketing managers with sales figures arranged by client, product, time, and units, thus allowing managers to identify their major clients and quickly detect any sales trends or patterns. The system also allows managers to trace the source of a problem; its built-in "triggers," or early warning systems, alert executives to trouble spots (numbers on the screen change color to indicate that there is a problem) and help them to be proactive in their decision making. For example, one store may sell 50% more than another store in the same geographical area, but since overall sales for the region are fine, a manager may overlook a potential problem at the store with the lower sales. The DSS, on the other hand, alerts the manager to such hidden problems.[3]

A GLOBAL PERSPECTIVE
A DSS Application in India

The task of planning for regional development and elimination of poverty in a developing country, such as India, is a complex and challenging task, affected by bureaucracy, politics, and good intentions. Planning requires the use of large volumes of internal and external data, combined with many complex quantitative and qualitative models. Since planning is an unstructured task, the Center for Applied Systems Analysis in Development (CASAD) in India developed a DSS to facilitate regional planning and health care. The DSS has a number of models that generate alternative scenarios for different socioeconomic and environmental conditions, so decision makers can evaluate the effects of various development plans in achieving regional development goals.

In India, there are four levels of administrative hierarchy. India is a federation of states; each state is divided into a number of districts; each district is made up of a number of blocks, or *talukas;* and each block is made up of about 100 villages, whose populations range from 50,000 to 100,000 people. Data from all four levels have to be analyzed in the development plan and integrated with different planning models that decision makers use at the different levels.

Let us take a look at the DSS for health care planning. It consists of two submodules: the facility submodule and the location submodule. The *facility submodule* identifies different types of health facilities that are suitable for a given region and the number of facilities of each type that can be opened in a given period, given budget limitations. This module, therefore, generates different health care alternatives by combining data such as population, number of physicians, medical facilities, and existing diseases, with existing health care models.

The *location submodule* uses the output of the facility submodule to determine the exact location of each health facility. A large number of factors, such as the population of the region, transportation facilities, nearest medical emergency centers, and access to utilities (telephone, nearest airport, and so on), must be taken into account when health facilities are planned. The model analyzes large volumes of data and integrates them with location models of successful medical facilities.

The task of regional planning is well handled by a DSS. This system has freed administrators from the time-consuming tasks of digesting large volumes of data and generating alternatives. Further, the system has provided uniformity in developing health care plans for different regions in India.[4]

graphics of a potential location with the demographics of other company-owned stores. When the system finds a close demographic match between the future location and that of an existing store, it analyses the financial performance of the existing store and uses this information to help determine whether the new location will be profitable.

Other applications of DSS include corporate planning, developing effective advertising strategies and pricing policies, determining an optimal product mix, and handling investment portfolios.

DSS are used all over the world by companies and government agencies to solve complex and data-intensive problems. For example, India uses a DSS to develop regional health care plans (see Global Perspective box). The DSS allows managers to determine the types of health care facilities that are suitable for a given region and the number of facilities of each type that must be opened during a given period to meet the overall goals of the government. The DSS also helps managers identify the location of each facility for optimal utilization.

Components of a DSS

Figure 8–2 shows the three main software components of a DSS. They are a database management system (DBMS), a model management system, and support tools.

Database Management Systems

The data necessary to solve a problem may come from internal or external databases. Within the organization, internal data are generated by systems such as TPS and MIS; external data come from a variety of sources such as periodicals, databases, newspapers, and online data services. Some examples of external data are government regulations, tax codes, census figures, competitors', market shares, economic indicators, interest rates, and inflation. The data in the DSS database are managed by the DBMS. (All the features and functions of a DBMS were covered

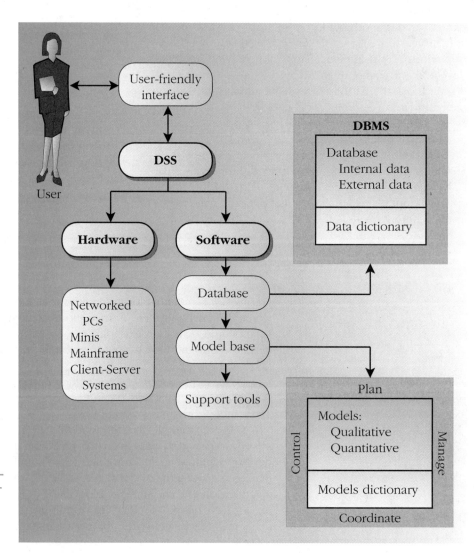

FIGURE 8 – 2

The hardware and software components of a DSS. The three main software elements are the database, the model base, and the support tools.

in the chapter on databases, including the ability to ensure data accessibility, integrity, and maintainability.) Figure 8–3 shows a DSS database as a storehouse of internal and external data and lists some of the functions of a DBMS.

Model Management Systems

Model management system
A component of a DSS that stores and accesses models that managers use to make decisions.

Model
An abstract representation of reality. Models are an integral part of decision making.

The second component of a DSS is the **model management system,** which stores and accesses models that managers use to make decisions. **Models** are an integral part of most decision making and are used for many tasks, such as designing a manufacturing facility, analyzing the financial health of an organization, forecasting demand for a product or service, and determining the quality of a particular batch of products. Although most models are quantitative—such as statistical models, financial models, forecasting models, and optimization models—decision makers also use qualitative models to make decisions. One example is a motivational model that provides recommendations for motivating employees.

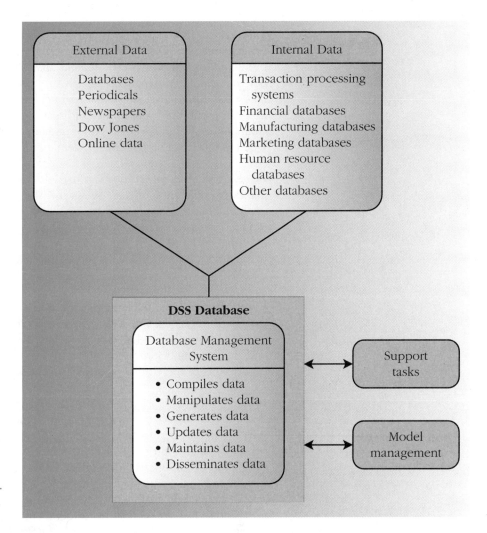

FIGURE 8–3

A DSS database utilizes both internal and external data.

Many model bases also have a component called the *model builder,* which, like a database, allows users to create, modify, maintain, and manage models. A model builder provides a structured framework for developing models by helping decision makers identify the variables and the interrelationships among the variables in the model. A model builder creates, identifies, processes, stores, updates, and maintains different decision-making models and ensures that these models are consistently applied when decisions are made. The model builder also contains a model dictionary, which, like a data dictionary, ensures consistency in the definitions and uses of models.

Let us take a brief look at some models that decision makers use to make decisions.

Statistical Models   Statistical models are used to perform a wide range of statistical functions, such as average, standard deviation, graphical analysis, regression analysis, analysis of variance, exploring and establishing relationships between different variables (e.g., the price and the number of units sold), and forecasting. They are used in finance, marketing, accounting, human resources, quality control, and management.

Financial and Accounting Models   Financial models allow decision makers to measure and assess the financial implications of various alternatives, and include profit-and-loss analysis, cost-benefit analysis, investment analysis, and capital budgeting models. Financial models are also used to calculate various financial ratios and other measures of financial health and performance. They are also used to assess optimistic, pessimistic, and realistic scenarios in a financial decision. For example, in an optimistic scenario, demand may exceed estimated sales by 25%, whereas in a pessimistic scenario, demand may be 50% lower than estimated sales.

Production Models   Production models are mostly used on the shop floor to make manufacturing-related decisions. They include models such as estimating the number of machines to be operated, calculating the amount of materials required to meet predetermined demands, scheduling, logistics, and evaluating the impact of different inventory policies. Machine scheduling, manpower planning, inventory modeling, and supply-and-demand analysis are all production models.

Marketing Models   Marketing models help marketing managers make a wide variety of decisions, including those concerning product pricing, store location, and advertising strategies. Others include product design, business intelligence, and forecasting. Some of these models help managers assess customers' perceptions of the company and its products.

Human Resource Models   Human resource models help managers make decisions that involve company personnel and job related issues. Human resource models include manpower planning, benefits analysis, assessment of training needs, skills inventory, projecting future personnel needs, labor negotiations, evaluation of hiring and firing policies, and assessment of the implementation of government rules and regulations.

Thus, models are extensively used in the different functional areas of a business. Figure 8–4 shows that the model management system is a storehouse of different models; it also manages and maintains these models.

FIGURE 8-4

A number of models are stored in the model management system.

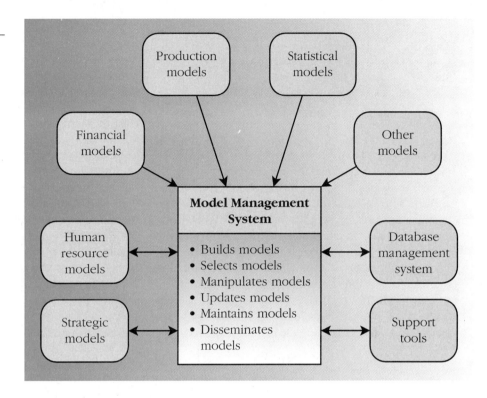

Support Tools Finally, the third component in a DSS consists of support tools, such as pull-down menus, online help, user interfaces, graphical analysis, and error-correction mechanisms, all of which facilitate users' interactions with the system. Interfaces are an important support tool. Although they are important in almost all information systems, they assume even greater significance in the case of a DSS. This is because middle and top managers have neither the time nor the inclination to learn difficult and complicated procedures in order to run a system. The better the interface, the greater the chances that users will accept the system. For example, in Hong Kong (see box), although managers recognize the power and potential of DSS, one of the obstacles to its adoption is a lack of people with training in computer technologies. In such an environment, good interfaces can make or break the system.

Functions of a DSS

A DSS has five main functions, which facilitate managerial decision making. They are model building, "what-if" analysis, goal-seeking, risk analysis, and graphical analysis.

Table 8–3 provides a brief description of the five functions of a DSS.

Model Building

Model building
A function found in DSS and EIS that identifies and develops decision-making models to solve a given problem.

Model building helps managers identify and develop decision-making models by taking into account input variables and their interrelationships, model assumptions, and constraints. For example, suppose the marketing manager for Sony is charged with the responsibility of developing a sales forecasting model for TV

A GLOBAL PERSPECTIVE

Use of DSS in Hong Kong Manufacturing Industries

The Hong Kong manufacturing industry is heavily export-oriented. However, in recent years, a number of competitive forces has made it imperative for manufacturers to produce goods and services as efficiently and effectively as possible. One way to accomplish this goal is by using information systems and technologies. Hong Kong companies, in particular, use decision support systems to help them with decisions at various levels of the entire manufacturing cycle, including preproduction planning, production planning, production execution, and post-production activities. Some of the decisions supported by DSS include product design changes, routing and plant layout, scheduling of material requirements, deliveries and purchases, stock replenishment, sales plans, forecasting, preventive maintenance, and budgets and invoicing.

Although employers recognize the usefulness of DSS, there are some hindrances to the rapid dissemination of DSS technology. These include lack of technical know-how, lack of people trained in the use and application of computer methodologies, and the incompatibility of new technologies with existing manufacturing methods. Furthermore, most companies consider only those projects that require limited resources (less than $50,000) to implement but which yield impressive results in a short span of time (less than 6 months). Most Hong Kong managers usually require a project to demonstrate immediate benefits or improvements to existing processes, so they often shy away from risky ventures.[5]

sets. A model builder uses a structured framework to identify all the variables in this forecasting model (such as demand, cost, and profit), analyze the relationships among these variables (e.g., the relationship between the cost and the selling price), identify the assumptions, if any (e.g., assume the prices of raw materials will increase by 5% over the forecasting period), and identify constraints (e.g., production capacity in Plant A is limited to 50,000 units). The system then integrates all this information into a decision-making model, which can be updated and modified whenever necessary.

TABLE 8-3
The five functions of a DSS.

Function	Description
Model building	Allows decision makers to identify the most appropriate models for solving the problem at hand. Takes into account input variables, interrelationships among the variables, problem assumptions and constraints.
"What-if" analysis	Allows decision makers to assess the impacts of changes—to model variables, variable values, and variable interrelationships—on the problem solution.
Goal seeking	Allows decision makers to determine the input values necessary to achieve a certain goal.
Risk analysis	Allows decision makers to assess the risks and uncertainties associated with different alternatives. Uses statistics and probabilistic measures to evaluate and assess risk factors.
Graphical analysis	Allows decision makers to view data and information in different formats such as graphs, charts, and figures.

"What-If" Analysis

"What-if" analysis is the process of assessing the impact of changes made to model variables, to their values and interrelationships, or to any combination of these. In our example, the Sony marketing manager might ask, "What would be the impact of a 12% increase in the cost of raw materials on future demand?" "By how much will demand increase if we give a discount of 25% during the Christmas season?" and similar questions. A bank manager might ask, "What would be the impact of an increase in interest rates on loan approvals?" A small business owner might ask, "What would be the impact on payroll expenses if we were required to provide health care for our employees?" Thus, the "what-if" func-

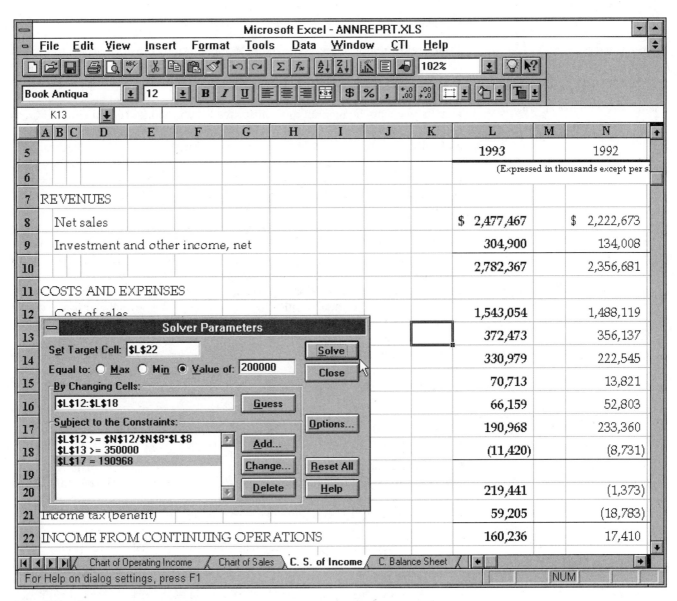

What-If Analysis

tion helps managers to assess the impacts of different scenarios on the bottom line. This helps managers to be proactive, rather than reactive, in their decision-making.

"What-if" analysis is critical for semistructured and unstructured problems because the data necessary to make such decisions are often unavailable, incomplete, or even inconsistent. Hence, managers must often use their intuition and judgment in predicting the long-term implications of their decisions. By developing a group of scenarios (best-case scenario, worst-case scenario, and realistic scenario), managers can prepare themselves to face a dynamic business environment. Many popular spreadsheet packages, such as Excel and Lotus 1-2-3, have "what-if" capabilities.

Goal Seeking

Goal seeking
The process of determining the input values necessary to achieve a certain goal. This process can be viewed as the reverse of "what-if" analysis.

Goal seeking allows decision makers to identify the course of action to take in order to achieve a certain goal. It can be viewed as the opposite of "what-if" analysis. Most of us perform goal analysis in our everyday lives. For example, students calculate the grade they must get on the final exam to get an A in the class; parents calculate the amount they must save each month to send their children to college; car buyers determine the monthly payment they can afford (say, $400) and calculate the number of such payments required to buy the desired car.

In goal seeking, the system addresses the question, "What should the values of the input variables be if a certain goal or objective is to be achieved?" For example, suppose the goal of Sony, which makes, say, 15 different TV models in 10 manufacturing facilities in seven different countries, is to achieve a gross profit of $100 million from its TV division in the coming year. The question, then, is, "How should the products be priced to achieve this goal?" The prices of the products depend on a number of factors, such as costs of raw materials, labor costs, local and national taxes, environmental regulations, costs of utilities, overhead expenses, advertising costs, and other marketing expenses. The goal-seeking function in a DSS takes all these variables into account and provides several alternative courses of action that a manager can take to achieve the goal. Many spreadsheet packages have goal-seeking capabilities.

For example, Mark, a system that helps retailers set discount prices, allows decision makers to do goal-seeking. Mark helps managers determine what the discount price of an item should be for the company to obtain a certain profit margin (see box).

Risk Analysis

Risk analysis
A function of DSS and EIS that allows managers to asses the risks associated with various alternatives.

One of the challenges that managers face frequently in decision making is evaluating the risks and uncertainties associated with different decisions; this task is referred to as **risk analysis.** Decisions can be classified as low-risk, medium-risk, and high-risk; a DSS is particularly useful in medium-risk and high-risk environments.

A DSS can help a manager calculate the risks associated with various alternatives through the use of probabilities and other statistical techniques. Based on the decision maker's preference for risk (some decision makers may be high risk takers while others may avoid risk), a DSS calculates the risk associated with each alternative. It is important to note that the risk analysis is driven completely by the

BUSINESS REALITIES
A DSS for Retailers

Until recently, clothing store retailers used some combination of rule of thumb and educated guess to determine how much they should discount the price of an item. Today, with the help of a University of Florida researcher, retailers can use a sophisticated DSS, which relies on optimization algorithms, to decide when and how much they should mark down the prices of different products and still reach the retailer's profit or inventory goals.

The system, called Mark, relies on historical sales data, sales forecasts and even the retailer's intuition to determine the price of the product in a given week and subsequent weeks (such as 20% off the first week, 25%

off the next week and so on). The model is very useful for retailers because it presents a wide variety of scenarios for different pricing strategies. The system also allows the retailer to adjust the markdown strategy based on the latest actual sales data and retail conditions. In other words, the software will recompute the prices based on any significant changes in the environment. This is important because timing is critical in the retail industry and has a significant impact on overall profitability. It takes the system only a few seconds to recommend a price strategy, although data entry can take up to 10 to 15 minutes. The goal eventually is to integrate Mark with transaction processing systems, thus eliminating the need to re-enter market-related data. The software, written in 5,000 lines of C++ code, runs on an Intel Corp. 80386-compatible PC with a math co-processor.[6]

---

input of the decision maker. If a decision maker prefers high risks, the recommendations of the system are likely to be high-risk-oriented.

Graphical Analysis

Graphical analysis

A graphical depiction of data using charts, figures, and graphs. It is particularly useful in helping managers digest large volumes of data.

Graphical analysis is the display of data in an easy-to-understand format, using graphs, charts, tables, and figures. It helps managers to quickly digest large volumes of data and visualize the impacts of various courses of action. A large number of applications lend themselves well to graphical analysis. For example, a marketing manager may look at a graph to study the sales growth of Product A; a finance manager may use a graph to look at the relationship between increase in interest rates and long-term debt; a production manager may use a graph to see the failure pattern of Machine A over the last 3 years. Since managers must often assimilate large volumes of cross-functional data, distinguish between the important and trivial, and quickly draw conclusions, graphical analysis is a very useful function in a DSS.

Many DSS packages have sophisticated graphics capabilities. For example, dbExpress, a DSS package developed by Computer Corp., has a point-and-click interface that provides different views of data selected by the user. By simply clicking on the graph, the user can get more detailed information about the data that are represented. Even spreadsheets have sophisticated graphical analysis capabilities. For example, Microsoft Excel gives the user a wide choice of graphs and charts, in many colors and patterns.

Tools for Developing a DSS

In general, there are three methods for developing a DSS: DSS generators, DSS shells, and custom-made software.

DSS Generators

DSS generator
Comprised of programs such as data management tools, electronic spreadsheets, report generators, and statistical packages to facilitate system development.

A **DSS generator** refers to tools, such as data management tools, spreadsheets, report generators (user-friendly programs that allow decision makers to produce customized reports), statistical packages, graphical packages, query languages, and model-building tools, that help in the development of a DSS. Some popular DSS generators are Symphony, FOCUS, NOMAD, Excel, and Lotus 1-2-3.

DSS Shells

DSS shell
A program that is used to build a customized DSS. Has a skeletal version of a database, a model base, and an interface.

A **DSS shell** is a program that is used to build a customized DSS. Shells eliminate the need for developing the DBMS, model management system, and user interfaces, because skeleton versions of these modules are already available in the shell. A user can simply connect the shell with the appropriate external and internal databases and input the appropriate models in order to have a fully functional DSS.

Shells have many benefits. First, since the basic versions of the DBMS, the model management system, and the set of interfaces are already in the shell, system development can proceed at a rapid pace. Second, in recent years, shells have become very user-friendly, allowing even users with little or no programming background to develop fairly sophisticated systems. The primary disadvantage of a shell is that it may have to be customized to meet the needs of the decision maker or the user may have to adapt the problem to the tool.

Example of a DSS Shell   A recent survey of 500 small businesses with sales of under $20 million found that 59 percent of the companies that had expanded in the last 2 years had a business plan, while only 38 percent of those with declining revenues had one. Although most entrepreneurs realize the importance of business plans, many of them do not have the time or manpower to develop one. Advia is a DSS that assists entrepreneurs in developing a plan, analyzing the marketing and financial aspects of their business, and implementing it. This DSS has two components: Manage and Decide.

Advia Manage is a financial model that allows managers to forecast income statements, project operating cash flow, automatically create forecasted balance sheets, and analyze key financial data and ratios. Advia Decide is designed to analyze market issues, such as "Where is our organization now?" "Where do we want to be in the next 5 years?" and "How do we get there?" It provides a methodology for creating a strategic business plan and related action plans for reaching longer-range goals. Advia Decide has two components: Situation Analysis and Vision. Situation Analysis asks users to analyze a range of items such as customers, products, marketing and sales activities, operations, and business trends. Vision analyzes the current mission of the business, the barriers to its success, and strategic actions that the company should take to overcome those barriers. Some questions that the system asks the user are structured; others are open-ended, allowing the user to provide input in a variety of ways. Depending on the size of the company and the amount of information available, a single session with Advia can last 5 to 6 hours. The output of this DSS is a first draft of a business plan, along with some interesting and useful insights about the company's market position and strategy.

Advia Manage, the second module, is designed to assist users through complex financial decision-making processes and has two components: Forecast, which helps the user develop a financial forecast and budget, and Tracking, which allows the user to enter financial results and manage a budget. Forecast is a menu-driven set of blank financial statements and other templates that are tied to the proposed marketing program. The user provides information in five general categories: assumptions, marketing templates, income statement forecast, cash flow management, and balance sheet. The Tracking module provides reports, such as income statement, operating cash flow, and balance sheet, based on the business's performance for the month and for the year to date. It also helps entrepreneurs to set up and manage a standard income statement, balance sheets, and cash flow statement accounts, and to evaluate the company's performance according to the business plan. Many CEOs of small companies struggle to assess the performance of their companies; Advia provides an objective framework to help each of them evaluate his or her firm and its performance.[7]

Custom-Made Software

An organization that is committed to DSS/EIS technology but cannot find a suitable generator or shell may choose to design and develop a customized DSS, using a procedural language, such as C, or a 4GL, such as FOCUS. In this case, the system may be developed in-house or the company may hire consultants to do the job. Organizations may also choose to combine shells and customized software. In other words, some parts of the system may be developed using a shell; others may be customized. The primary disadvantage of this approach is that the system may be expensive and time-consuming to develop and organizations may run into unexpected bottlenecks and cost overruns.

Earlier, we identified a number of applications of DSS; some of them require individual decision making while others require group decision making. In the next section, we take a closer look at group decision support systems (GDSS).

Group Decision Support Systems

Important decisions in an organization frequently require the input and participation of more than one individual; they require group thinking. Although meetings continue to be one of the most popular techniques for group decision making, Table 8–4 lists some of the common problems associated with meetings.

Group Decision Support Systems (GDSS) are computer-based information systems that enhance group decision making by facilitating the exchange and use of information by group members, and interactions between the group and the computer, to formulate and solve unstructured problems (Huber, 1984, p. 186). It allows people separated by time and space to interact with each other in a structured way.

Group decision support systems bring together a wide variety of versatile and user-friendly software tools, such as

♦ *Electronic questionnaires* (questionnaires that people can respond to using a computer)
♦ *Electronic brainstorming tools* (tools that allow people to express, share, and analyze ideas anonymously)

Group decision support systems (GDSS)
Information systems that facilitate the free flow and exchange of ideas and information among group members while maintaining their anonymity. One type of DSS.

TABLE 8-4
Some statistics about the high cost and the ineffectiveness of traditional meetings. GDSS technology helps overcome some of the problems and weaknesses of traditional meetings.

Problems with Meetings

According to a study by the University of Southern California, Los Angeles:

- The average meeting takes place in the company conference room at 11 a.m. and lasts 1 hour and 30 minutes.
- It is attended by nine people: two managers, four coworkers, two subordinates, and one outsider, who have received 2-hour prior notification.
- It has no written agenda, and its purported goal is achieved only 50% of the time.
- One-fourth of meeting participants complain that they waste between 11% and 25 % of the time discussing irrelevant issues.
- A full third of them feel pressured to publicly espouse opinions with which they privately disagree.
- Another third feel they have minimal or no influence on the discussion.
- Although 36% of meetings result in a "complete" resolution of the topic at hand, participants consider only 1% of these conclusions to be particularly "creative."
- A whopping 63% of meeting attendees feel that underlying issues outside the scope of the official agenda are the real subjects under discussion.
- Senior executives spend 53% of their time in meetings, at an average pay rate of $320 per person per hour.

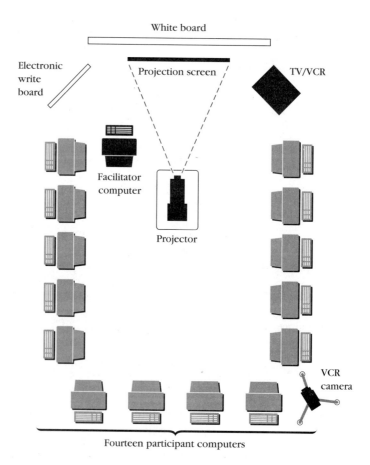

A Decision Room

♦ *Idea organizers* (tools that facilitate the coordination, compilation, and prioritization of ideas)

♦ *Voting tools* (tools that allow people to indicate their preference for an idea)

For example, the office of Emergency Preparedness, uses EMISARI, a GDSS, to support planning and decision making during national emergencies (see box). EMISARI, has many of the above tools.

There are three different kinds of GDSS: single-computer systems, keypad-response systems, and full-keyboard workstation systems.[8]

Single-Computer Systems

Single-computer system
The simplest type of GDSS, designed primarily for single users. Uses a video display system through which each group member can communicate with the others.

The simplest type of GDSS is a **single-computer system** designed primarily for single users. It uses a video display system through which each group member can communicate with other members of the group. Members can observe how other group members are approaching the problem and participate in the process by presenting their individual ideas. These systems are portable and relatively inexpensive; they are well suited to problems in which confidentiality is *not* important.

A problem that is well suited to a single-user system is making investment decisions based on standard criteria, such as return on investment, rate of return, and risk tolerance. In a single-user system, each group member can assign individual weights to these criteria. The system then ranks the different alternatives based on weights assigned by the group members. Each group member can see

BUSINESS REALITIES
Office of Emergency Preparedness

EMISARI is a GDSS that was developed at the Office of Emergency Preparedness in the Executive Offices of the President of the United States in 1971 to support data reporting, crisis planning, and decision making during declared national emergencies. Over the last decade, the system has been used in a number of crisis situations, such as oil shortages and major strikes.

EMISARI can link from 100 to 200 people, located anywhere in the country, and allow them to track, interpret, and reorganize qualitative and quantitative information associated with rapidly changing, unpredictable environments. It has many features for group decision processes that even today are not available in any commercial system. Here are some of the features of EMISARI:

♦ It can generate a wide variety of electronic data forms or questionnaires that participants can fill in on their computers. The system also automatically updates the

relevant database with the responses of the participants.

♦ People can also append detailed messages to their questionnaire responses. Further, a group member can retrieve these messages and respond to them.

♦ Electronic bulletin boards are also a part of this GDSS. These can be used to announce new policies and interpret existing ones.

♦ Another specialized data-tracking facility allows decision makers to establish the sequence of steps that must be implemented in a crisis and designate the people responsible for implementing those steps. As each step is completed, the system alerts those involved in the next step, so they can take over.

EMISARI also provides tracking and feedback so that decision makers can respond effectively to rapidly changing information in a crisis environment. Though this system was initially classified as one that supports planning, it turned out to be much more than a planning system: it has become a vital tool for monitoring the execution of plans and policies. The fact that the system has been in use for over a decade bears witness to its robustness and versatility.[9]

how other members in the group ranked the various criteria and suggest changes or modifications to the weights. The process of assigning, reassigning, and prioritizing the weights continues until the group arrives at a consensus.

Keypad-Response Systems

Keypad-response system
A type of GDSS in which group members use hand-held keypads to communicate with each other. Group members are connected by a network of PCs that are located in a single room.

Decision room
Group members linked by a network of PCs that are located in a single room.

The second type of GDSS is the **keypad-response system,** in which group members use hand-held keypads to communicate with each other. Unlike a single-computer-system GDSS, in which group members may be geographically dispersed, in a keypad-response system, group members are linked by a network of PCs that are usually located in a single room, referred to as the **decision room.**

A projector screen at the front of the room displays the inputs of different group members and each member uses his or her keypad to communicate and coordinate ideas with other members of the group. The keypad provides a wide variety of responses, such as predefined rating scales (e.g., yes/no), multiple choice, and customized rating scales. The computer receives the input of the group members from each keypad, processes, analyzes and ranks the input, and displays the output, in graphical or text form, to the group.

The biggest advantage of keypad systems is that they analyze and summarize the input of group members almost instantaneously. In other words, there is little, if any, delay between the time when input is received and the time when the output is displayed. Further, the responses of individual members are anonymous, so members feel free to share their views without fear of political repercussions. The anonymity of the responses also helps members stay focused on the issue, avoiding hostility and personality clashes. Keypad systems, like single-user systems, are portable and relatively inexpensive.

Full-keyboard Workstation Systems

Full-keyboard workstation system
A GDSS that is set up in a room with group members at networked PCs. A group facilitator coordinates the responses of group members. A projector screen at the front of the room displays the inputs of group members.

The third type of GDSS is the **full-keyboard workstation,** which, like a keypad-response system, is set up in a room with networked PCs arranged around a U-shaped table. A PC at the front of the room allows the group facilitator to coordinate the responses of group members. A projector screen at the front of the room displays the inputs of the group members, who can then make suggestions or modifications to a proposed solution. This process continues until the group arrives at a consensus.

For example, IBM-SEMEA (see box) uses GROUPS, a GDSS, to facilitate group decision making in the area of production planning. The system brings together a group of production-planning experts, each of whom individually develops a production plan. The system then evaluates each plan and designates individuals in the organization who will be responsible for implementing the plan. At the heart of GROUPS is the communication module, which records, stores, aggregates, ranks, and displays the alternatives developed by individual group members.

Full-keyboard systems allow participants to communicate while maintaining full anonymity. They are used for managerial tasks that require evaluation, rating, voting, brainstorming, idea organization, and strategic planning. For example, managers at the headquarters of Marriott Hotels, in Bethesda, Maryland, used GDSS to generate a large number of innovative ideas on how to increase customer satisfaction in their hotels. Anonymity was maintained, a large number of

A GLOBAL PERSPECTIVE
IBM-SEMEA

The IBM-SEMEA (South Europe, Middle East, and Africa) plant in Vimercate, Italy, assembles approximately 4,000 different module types for IBM's European computer market. One of the tasks confronting executives in these departments is developing a production plan for these modules. Production planning is a dynamic process, with a large number of variables that must frequently be adjusted to reflect internal changes, such as machine breakdowns, and external changes, such as variations in product demand.

IBM-SEMEA uses a *rolling* master production plan, based on demand forecasts, to accommodate dynamic business conditions. The plan is adjusted on either a weekly or a daily basis to satisfy actual market demand and to respond to special customer requests, unexpected events on the shop floor, full-capacity utilization, and problems in inventory control. A change in any one of these factors can affect the entire production schedule; any discrepancies or loopholes in the production plan can increase manufacturing costs and decrease profits. Hence, the ability to revise the production plan at short notice is of critical importance.

Before the GDSS was installed, executives addressed the problem of production planning from three levels. At level 1, a team consisting of representatives from three departments and from the production control office met weekly to define the production mix. At level 2, smaller groups met informally every day to solve departmental production problems. At level 3,

executives and suppliers communicated over a network to work on last-minute changes based on demand and supply constraints.

Although IBM-SEMEA has may IT-based tools, including databases, networks, and computer models, these tools could not support the group decision making that was central to developing a solid, rigorous production plan for the IBM plant. A GDSS would enhance communications between executives in the various departments and promote teamwork and cooperation. Toward this goal, GROUPS, a GDSS-based production planning and scheduling system, was developed.

GROUPS facilitates group decision making in the following ways: A group can select a team of experts to make decisions on a step-by-step basis, evaluate each of the alternatives generated by the experts, identify the exact point in the organizational hierarchy where those decisions can be made, and present the results to the entire group. At the heart of GROUPS is the communication module, a set of applications that record, store, aggregate, and display the alternatives identified by the group members, rank those alternatives, keep a record of the votes for each alternative, and even help in organizing meetings and updating the minutes of each meeting. In particular, for the production planning problem, GROUPS has been an invaluable tool.

Clearly, assigning an economic value to the benefits of a system such as GROUPS is difficult. However, the contribution in terms of reduced meeting times, better communication and coordination among top executives, and an improved and timely production plan has been widely felt throughout the organization.[10]

---

alternatives were quickly generated and evaluated, and members quickly arrived at a consensus.[11] Figure 8–5 shows a GDSS in which a group of networked users participate in group decision making with help from a group facilitator.

Advantages of GDSS

The primary advantage of GDSS is that it fosters an environment that is conducive to decision making. In one case, an organization suddenly had to initiate Chapter 11 bankruptcy proceedings and was concerned that the reorganization might adversely affect price of the company's stock. Managers used groupware to generate ideas for addressing this critical situation. "Within 10 minutes, we had 47 excellent ideas. By the end of the hour, we had discussed them, voted on them, ranked them in order of priority, and walked out with printed documentation in

F I G U R E 8 – 5

A GDSS supports group decision making. A group of networked users participate in group decision making with the help of a facilitator.

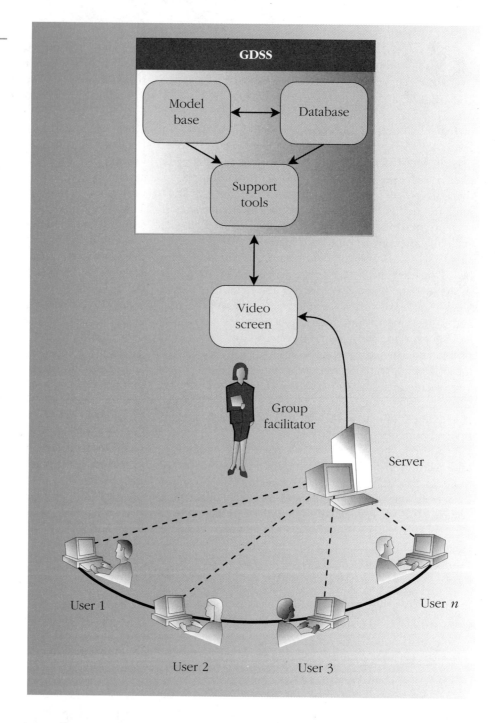

hand."[12] One of the reasons why managers in this case were able to quickly address a rather complex problem is that GDSS facilitated the free flow of ideas, encouraged consensus-building, and maintained anonymity.

A second advantage of GDSS is that whereas in traditional meetings, extroverts or politically powerful people can dominate the shy and the introverted, GDSS allows all members of the group to participate. In a decision room, any participant can express his or her ideas without fear. Anonymity gives all participants the freedom to be open, creative, and innovative. This is particularly critical when addressing sensitive problems, such as sexual discrimination cases. However, anonymity also has its weaknesses: it is difficult to reward anonymous members for new ideas, so some people may feel unappreciated. Further, sometimes anonymous input may lead to "electronic shouting," in which participants get stuck on an issue and refuse to let go.[13] For some of the above reasons, extroverts tend to drop out of electronic meetings. Hence, anonymity must be used only when the situation fully warrants it.

Another advantage of a GDSS is that it greatly enhances the efficiency of group meetings, since the system generates and processes ideas in parallel and there is no cross talk among group members. No one has to wait to be heard because everyone "talks" at the same time. Further, the system has good "organizational memory": it instantaneously captures all ideas, which reduces the need for documentation and the risk of losing or misinterpreting ideas.

Executive Information Systems

*J*ust *as executives have always had to cope with operations, strategy, financial planning and people, now they are going to have to deal with information technology.*

> —John F. Rockart, professor at MIT's Sloan School of Management

Top management, which some years ago was shielded from information technology, cannot afford to be so any longer. One type of system that helps top managers with strategic, unstructured decision making is an **executive information system (EIS).** An EIS is a set of computer-based tools with features such as color graphics, touch screens, voice-activated commands, and natural-language interfaces, that help managers to quickly retrieve, analyze, navigate, summarize, and disseminate large volumes of data. An EIS is frequently connected with online information services so that top managers can quickly access external data as well. The primary goal of an EIS is, therefore, the delivery and display of information, rather than the analysis or diagnosis of problems and possible solutions. This is one of the primary differences between an EIS and a DSS, which focuses primarily on problem solving. Figure 8–6 shows some of the features commonly found in an EIS.

In a recent article in *Harvard Business Review,* management guru, Peter Drucker, identifies the different kinds of information top managers need to make good decisions. He points out that the primary goal of an enterprise is to create wealth, not merely control costs, and this requires four sets of diagnostic tools that provide decision makers with the right information to make sound decisions:

- ◆ Foundation information (such as cash flow, liquidity, and so on)
- ◆ Productivity information

   Economic value-added analysis (EVA) measures the value added over all costs, including the cost of capital. It, therefore, measures the productivity of all factors of production and shows which product, service, operation, or activity has unusually high productivity and adds unusually high value.

- ◆ Competence information

   This tracks a company's competencies and those of its competitors. It identifies unexpected successes and failures and helps managers learn important managerial lessons. It also tracks innovations in an entire field (such as defense, auto-

Executive information system (EIS)

A program that allows top managers to quickly retrieve, analyze, and disseminate data and information. Its functions include drill-down and derived information in addition to those found in most DSS.

FIGURE 8–6

Some of the features commonly
found in an EIS.

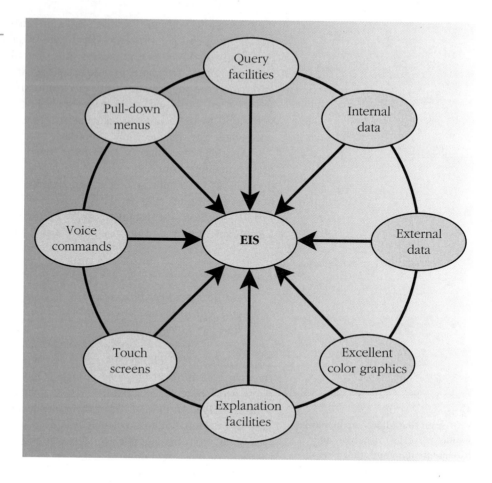

mobiles, electronic manufacturing, and so on) in a given period. "It raises rather
than answers questions, but it raises the right questions," says Peter Drucker.

♦   Resource-related information

This monitors and measures the different kinds of resources an organization
uses, such as capital and manpower. A company should look at all four financial
measures, namely return on investment, payback period, cash flow, or discounted present value in order to assess financial performance. Although many organizations spend a lot of time assessing the performance of their capital, Drucker
points out that it is people, not capital, that is one of the scarcest resources in any
organization.

The four kinds of information above allow managers to assess current business, while information related to the environment—such as markets, customers,
non-customers, technology applications, and worldwide finance—provide information necessary to operate in the marketplace.

So what kind of information should a system provide top management? "It
must lead them to ask the right questions, not just feed them the information they
expect," says Drucker. "What we need are services that make specific suggestions
about how to use the information, ask specific questions regarding the users' business and its practices, and perhaps provide interactive consultation. That is a new

and radically different view of the meaning and purpose of information: as a measurement on which to base future action rather than as a post-mortem and a record of what has already happened."[14]

EIS are used in many ways in the business world. For example, a few years ago, top officials of the U.S. Air Force were looking for a tool that would help them analyze large volumes of data related to base closings around the country. Managers had to process more than a gigabyte of data to identify the naval bases that should be closed. The Air Force selected an EIS that graphically depicted large volumes of data. It allowed decision makers to arrive at a decision quickly and saved the Air Force a great deal of time and money.

Beaver Lumber Co., in Markham, Ontario, needed a way for store managers at its 165 stores to examine sales information for approximately 30,000 items. The company selected an EIS package that allows managers to quickly and easily retrieve and process data in a number of ways, such as examining sales by department, by salesperson, or even by time of day. The company has made the EIS part of its long-term information strategy; it plans eventually to provide all managers with access to EIS tools that will allow them to generate customized reports.

Virginia Polytechnic Institute, in Blacksburg, Virginia, uses an EIS package developed by SAS Institute, to help university administrators scan through large volumes of student, faculty, and administrative data and generate reports. Once the system was installed, users could generate necessary reports immediately instead of waiting days or weeks for the MIS department to act.

Another company that relies on an EIS for quality information is Sundstrand (see box). This company uses its EIS not only to disseminate timely and valuable information to decision makers, but also as a business intelligence tool that provides the firm with critical information about competitors and their strategies so it can position itself competitively in the marketplace.

BUSINESS REALITIES
Sundstrand

For managers of Sundstrand's aerospace operations, the quantity of data that they had to process was not as much of a problem as the lack of high-quality information. The problem was so serious that it threatened to ground this $1-billion international manufacturer of aerospace and defense systems. Sundstrand's data were scattered through 600 decentralized departments that used a hodgepodge of systems, ranging from IBM mainframes to Windows-based PCs. Decision makers often had to spend large amounts of time simply to locate essential data, which often resulted in delayed decisions or poor decisions. To resolve this serious problem, the company turned to an EIS.

Before the EIS was installed, the company's monthly quality assurance reports, typically several inches thick, reached managers as much as 3 months late. Now the reports arrive in as little as a day, online, through colorful, easy-to-use GUIs on the managers' desktops. Sundstrand's Quality Group executives can now quickly determine the sources of delays in a project, assess the reasons for any cost increases, and project the future quality of products and services.

The company views the EIS as more than an information display tool. It uses its EIS to gather business intelligence about competitors and their market strategies in order to strengthen its competitive position. The EIS also does interactive budgeting, sales forecasting, and inventory analysis, and communicates these decisions to all employees.

At Sundstrand, the EIS is in demand not because of its "pretty face," but because it addresses complex, mission-critical needs. "Our EIS is of strategic importance and it allows us to penetrate new markets and provide value-added information to executives."[15]

Because of their versatility, the market for DSS and EIS is expected to more than double, to $7.5 billion, in 1997. Banks and other financial institutions, in particular, are enthusiastic users of EIS and, according to an Ernst & Young survey published in 1993, nearly one-third of the discretionary technology budgets of banks (approximately $840 million per year) is spent on systems that improve decision making. It is estimated that roughly one in four banks uses an EIS system and another 40% of banks are in the process of installing EIS.[16] In fact, EIS is considered such an important technology that some universities in the U.S. devote a considerable portion of their research money to EIS research. The University of Texas at Austin, and MIT are major centers for DSS and EIS research.[17]

EIS have also become liaison tools that link operational data (accounting ledgers, payroll, production control, and so on) with other tools, such as spreadsheets, wordprocessors, and accounting packages. This helps managers assess the who, what, where, and why of data. EIS also help to increase the productivity of knowledge workers. For example, Data General, a manufacturer of computers and peripherals, once had all its data stored in a minicomputer. At the end of each business day, managers were responsible for compiling, printing, and disseminating all daily business transactions to top managers. Today, the company uses an EIS that provides instantaneous access to all managers about company-wide information.

Finally, as corporations around the world try to "achieve more with less," managers are searching for tools that reduce bureaucratic waste and operating costs. For example, Serfin Financial Group in Mexico relies on an EIS to track past-due loans (see box).

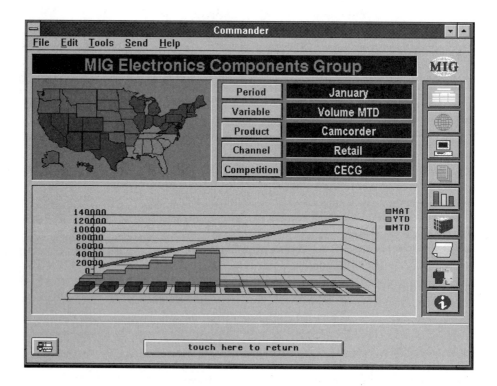

EIS/Commander

A GLOBAL PERSPECTIVE
Serfin Financial Group, Mexico

As Mexico struggles under the pressures of triple-digit inflation and double-digit interest rates, Mexican banks find themselves saddled with mounting loan obligations. One bank, Serfin Financial Group in Mexico City, the country's third-largest bank with $2 billion in assets and 800 branches, is using a leading-edge technological approach to track its past-due customer loans. The bank is using a client-server-based Executive Information System to enable its top officers to do a daily review of outstanding customer loans on a branch-by-branch basis. The graphical EIS has helped decision makers keep track of outstanding loans and monitor the daily growth of liabilities.

Prior to the EIS, bank managers could look only at daily customer data using graphical spreadsheet software. The EIS allows them to view a month's worth of data, which helps executives do better budgeting and forecasting. The EIS also extracts, loads and summarizes customer data into a database and this has decreased the time it takes to do forecasting from two hours to 30 seconds. EIS "is a very exciting piece of software that I've seen at a number of banks, but this is a first for a Mexican bank," says Raphael Benabou, a former consultant for Nolan, Norton & Co.[18]

Managers at Classicomm Cable TV, which supplies cable TV service to almost 100,000 subscribers in the northern portion of the Greater Toronto area, found it difficult to acquire market information, because they had to study and analyze a large number of reports. An EIS has eliminated the need for many reports and reduced many layers of bureaucracy, whose primary function had been to gather and disseminate data.[19]

The Manitoba Public Insurance Corporation reduced its operating costs by using an EIS. Before the system was installed, the company used a mainframe to determine automobile insurance rates. Unfortunately, each time there was a rate change, considerable portions of the software had to be rewritten. Today, the company relies on an EIS to make these changes automatically and provide managers with current information; this has resulted in significant cost savings. The EIS also does "what-if" analysis, helping managers to be proactive in their decision making.[20]

Sherwin Williams, manufacturer and retailer of paint supplies, uses an EIS to assist its workforce. Before the EIS was installed, each Monday morning managers had to telephone 20 to 25 stores in their districts to get sales figures for the previous week. Each manager then drafted a sales report for his or her district and sent it up the chain of command to each of the 14 area vice presidents! Today, an EIS provides instantaneous access to detailed sales information to managers throughout the company, allowing them to focus on more productive tasks, such as increasing sales.[21]

Some popular EIS packages are Commander-EIS, SAS/EIS-Express, IRI Software, Lightship, and EIS ToolKit. Table 8–5 lists some popular EIS packages.

Characteristics of an EIS

DSS and EIS have many functions in common, including "what-if" analysis, goal seeking, risk analysis, and graphical analysis. In addition to these, an EIS has two special functions: the derived-information function and the drill-down function.

TABLE 8-5
Some popular EIS packages and their operating systems.

Package	Vendor	Operating System
Commander EIS	Comshare	Windows, OS/2, UNIX
SAS/EIS Package	SAS Institute	OS/2, UNIX
IRI Software	Information Resources, Inc.	MS-DOS
Lightship	Pilot Software	Windows, OS/2
EIS ToolKit	MicroStrategy	Windows

Derived Information

Derived information is gleaned from existing data with the primary purpose of identifying the cause or the source of a given problem. For example, when a manager is informed that sales in Region A have fallen by 30%, the information simply identifies the presence of a problem; it does not indicate the cause of the problem. The derived-information function in an EIS identifies the what and the why of information and assists managers with further data analysis so that the cause of a drop in sales can be determined.

Drill-Down

Drill-down is the location and retrieval of data at whatever level of detail is desired by the user. For example, a human resource manager may want to know the total number of employees working in Division A (summary data) and a breakdown of employees in production, sales, and administration (more detailed data) in that division. For example, managers in the state of Wisconsin's health insurance office can drill down for specific information about a health claim or even about the doctor treating a specific patient (see box). The drill-down function in an EIS allows a manager to obtain summary or detailed data through a few simple keystrokes.

Another recent feature found in DSS and EIS that increases the usefulness of drill down and derived information is a software agent. Agents are small software programs that perform specific background tasks and filter information so it reaches decision makers in a ready-to-use format. Software agents can also alert users to exceptional or unusual data.[22] Agents are very good at identifying specific data and are highly suitable for repetitive tasks. Comshare is one of the leading producers of agents for DSS.

Many spreadsheets have some simple EIS-like capabilities. For example, Improv for Windows is a Lotus 1-2-3 package that allows users to manipulate information in 12 different ways. Microsoft Excel also has many EIS features.

Critical Success Factors for DSS/EIS

Although DSS/EIS technology has existed for almost three decades, not all organizations have been successful in adapting DSS/EIS technology. Critical success factors (CSFs) for DSS/EIS are those that significantly increase the chances of successfully using and implementing these technologies. Table 8–6 presents a brief summary of these factors. Although some of the factors listed below (such as commitment from top management) are in fact critical

---

Derived information
A function of an EIS that allows managers to find the cause or source of a certain problem through detailed data analysis.

Drill-down
A function of an EIS that can precisely locate and retrieve necessary information at any desired level of detail.

BUSINESS REALITIES
The State of Wisconsin

Wisconsin pays almost $2.3 billion each year in health insurance claims: No questions asked, until recently. A new $5.8 million information system will, for the first time in the state's history, help state officials analyze large volumes of Medicaid data, identify questionable claims and detect fraud. The federal government is paying for 90% of the new system.

Many states often focus all their efforts on the most cost-efficient way to process claims. They pay little or no attention to analyzing the data for trends or fraud. But Wisconsin is taking a more aggressive and comprehensive approach to Medicaid claims, directing its efforts at cost reduction and fraud detection.

Wisconsin has contracted with Unisys to develop a system that will run primarily on a Hewlett-Packard HP 9000 system and Oracle's Version 7.1 relational database management system. Layered on top of the Oracle database is an Executive Information System that provides managers with summary data and vital statistics on a number of important variables. The system will allow all authorized state employees, not just top managers, to drill down and obtain detailed information for detailed investigation on individual claims; whereas, under the old system, data was often fragmented, incompatible and incomplete. The new system also reviews payments for prescriptions, while an expert system contained in the information system, can detect fraud and abuse.

One of the primary benefits the new system provides managers is the opportunity to act on data rather than merely collect it. Under the old system, managers spent an enormous amount of time collecting the data and very little time processing or acting on it. Managers also had to write customized programs simply to extract a specific piece of data or generate a data report from the mainframe. The new system allows managers to be action-oriented. "We're sitting on top of a $2.3 billion gorilla—the most complicated social welfare program ever created—and the politics of the situation require that we find answers in minutes, not weeks."[23]

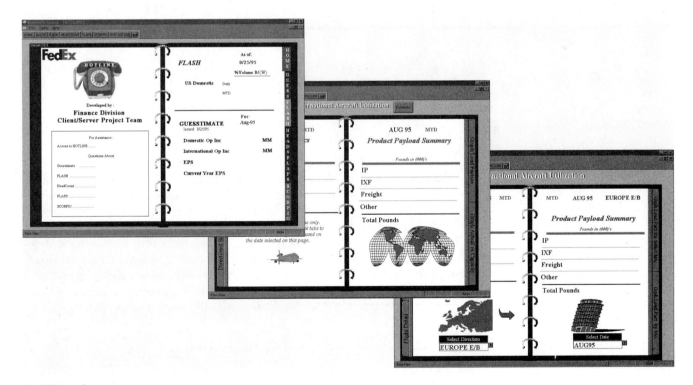

Drill-Down Screens

BUSINESS REALITIES

Internal Revenue Service

The Internal Revenue Service (IRS) has implemented an EIS that will, for the first time, enable hundreds of IRS executives to electronically access and manipulate nationwide tax data. Though the completion of an EIS project may not seem like a technological milestone, it is a major breakthrough for the IRS. Until recently, regional commissioners and other agency executives were restricted in their ability to compare and contrast tax data. They either had to plow through stacks of paper-based records themselves or had to enlist the aid of IRS analysts to crunch the numbers. Although the IRS has never been short of data, finding specific items was quite another matter.

Thanks to the new EIS, executives will now be able to quickly identify tax-return trends and pinpoint geographic pockets of "deadbeat filers." IRS executives can view national and regional tax data and will eventually be able to conduct preprogrammed, automated analyses on tax-return data and even identify trends, such as bankruptcy filings. The IRS system is composed of 10 core applications that cover every operational function within the U.S. Treasury Department, including manage-

ment and administration, information systems, financial management, and taxpayer services. The data, which were once spread across disparate systems, now reside in a single database.

"The value of this system is in the multidimensional models that are used," says David Goldstein, an assistant professor of information at Boston University's School of Management. Goldstein, who recently viewed the system, says other EIS systems he has seen generally have simpler graphics, which are not automatically updated on a nightly or weekly basis. The IRS "has developed a much more robust method of mining through the data," he says. Goldstein has evaluated a number of EIS systems during the past few years, including those used by Frito-Lay, J. C. Penney, and the U.S. Department of Defense. He found the IRS system to be one of the best.

Even more impressive, the agency completed the project within 3½ years for less than $2.5 million. In fact, the project has gone so smoothly that the project group returned $100,000 in funding last year to the national office in Washington! Though government agencies have historically been viewed as technological laggards, EIS experts describe the IRS project as one of the most innovative in either the private or the public sector today.[24]

---

to the success of almost any type of information system, these factors have even greater importance in the success of DSS and EIS because these systems are used mostly by top and middle managers.

Commitment from Top Management

A critical factor in the successful adoption of any technology is commitment from top management. Since DSS and EIS are targeted primarily toward top and middle managers, this factor becomes even more important. Further, since these systems evolve over time in terms of breadth, depth, and functionality, the continued support of top management is vital to their success.

One way to get commitment from top management is to build organization-wide systems, rather than systems that solve a specific problem in a given department or business unit. For example, although a DSS/EIS quality control application may ensure that the system gains visibility, an application that is linked to management compensation is more likely to sustain the interest of top managers.[25]

Availability of Accurate and Reliable Data

Because intelligent support systems are data-driven, the quality of the decisions produced by the system can only be as high as that of the data input into the sys-

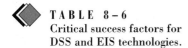

TABLE 8–6
Critical success factors for DSS and EIS technologies.

- Commitment from top management
- Availability of accurate and reliable data
- Careful problem selection
- Integration of DSS and EIS with existing technologies
- Meaningful analysis of costs versus benefits

tem. If the data necessary to make decisions are not readily available, accessible, or reliable, users may be unwilling to use the system; eventually, confidence in the technology itself will be eroded.

Careful Problem Selection

Problems to be solved using an ISS should be carefully selected to be neither too easy nor too difficult. Though there is no method to determine objectively whether a problem is too easy or too complex, the people who make the decisions are often good at judging the level of difficulty of a problem. A subjective definition of an easy problem is that it can be solved in a short period of time and does not require complex analysis of a large number of variables. If the problem is too easy, the cost of developing the system will far outweigh its benefits; further, decision makers may not use the system if they can solve the problem easily without any help from the system; if, on the other hand, the problem is too complex, it may be too difficult and time-consuming to model it. Even if the problem can be modeled, the cost of developing a system for highly complex problems may be prohibitive. This is not to say that a DSS or EIS cannot be applied to solve complex problems, but the organization should be fully aware of the challenges of doing so.

Another consideration in problem selection is the way managers view the problem. If the system is to be successful, managers should believe the problem is critical to the well-being of the organization and affects the bottom line. Finally, an ISS should be built around the problem and not around the cognitive style of the decision maker. In other words, the intent should be to capture the problem and its characteristics, not just the decision-making style of the manager.

Integration of DSS and EIS with Existing Technologies

ISS should be integrated with existing systems and technologies in the organization, because this is the only way to ensure the free flow of information. Without integration, it is difficult to achieve the full potential of systems and to deliver the full power of technology. However, integration is not easy to achieve; it requires vision, long-range planning, standardization, and teamwork between the MIS department and other business units in the organization. Unfortunately, some organizations treat integration as an afterthought; such an ad hoc approach is often disastrous. This is not to say that all standalone systems are bad; but even standalone systems should be part of a well-thought-out plan.

Costs Versus Benefits

As with any information system, the cost of a DSS or EIS depends on factors such as the information needs of managers, the impact of the changeover on the organization, the nature and criticality of the application, the number of users, and the hardware and software resources of the organization. Issues such as technology sophistication, technology use in the organization, existing network capabilities, the cost of training, and system maintenance also affect the cost of the system. In particular, ISS continues to evolve over time; the costs of these changes should also be factored into the analysis. "The development of an EIS can be thought of as an ongoing journey rather than as a destination. The system continues to evolve over time in response to market, industry, and organizational changes that affect executives' information needs."[26]

In many cases a simple cost-benefit analysis may not be sufficient to make the investment decision. Instead, a company may have to ask a two-sided question: Can we afford it, and can we afford not to have it?[27]

These are only some of the factors that influence the success of ISS in an organization. Further, not all the factors identified above may be relevant to an organization. However, each organization must carefully identify the success factors that are relevant to its managerial style and culture before embarking on system development.

TPS, MIS, DSS, and EIS

The different types of systems, including TPS, MIS, DSS, EIS, ES, and OAS, can together help an organization to meet its information needs. Although there are similarities and differences among these systems, it is important to recognize that no one system is superior to another and that each system is designed to serve a specific purpose.

A transaction processing system (TPS) is designed to capture data related to various transactions within the organization and is well suited to highly structured and routine tasks that support operational decision making. The output of the TPS becomes the input to the MIS, which produces summary and exception reports to facilitate tactical, or semistructured, decision making. While TPS and MIS provide lower-level management with the information necessary to make operational decisions, middle and upper management need systems that support tactical and strategic decision making, which is most often semistructured or unstructured. By integrating data with decision-making models and providing instantaneous access to relevant information, DSS and EIS improve the quality of decision-making.

The differences among TPS, MIS, DSS, and EIS are shown in Table 8–7.

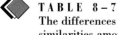

TABLE 8–7
The differences and similarities among TPS, MIS, DSS, and EIS.

	TPS	**MIS**	**DSS**	**EIS**
Targeted Audience	Operational management	Operational management	Middle management	Top management
Primary Purpose	Capture transaction data	Generate summary and exception reports	Facilitate decision making	Generate clear, concise, enterprise-wide information
Nature of Tasks	Highly structured	Highly structured	Semi- or unstructured	Semi- or unstructured
Kind of Data	Internal	Internal	Internal and external	Internal and external

Summary

♦ **The characteristics of a DSS and those of an EIS.**
A DSS is a set of well integrated, user-friendly, computer-based tools that use internal and external data and decision models to solve semistructured and unstructured problems. A DSS supports problem solving by identifying, analyzing, and selecting the best alternative.

A DSS has five main functions: model building, "what-if" analysis, goal seeking, risk analysis, and graphical analysis. Model building is the process of identifying and developing the most appropriate model to solve the problem at hand. "What-if" analysis assesses the impact of modeled changes on the solution. Goal seeking is the process of determining the input values necessary to achieve a certain goal. Risk analysis allows managers to assess the risks and uncertainties associated with changing business conditions. Finally, graphical analysis is the graphical representation of data and information.

In addition to these functions, an EIS has two more: derived information and drill-down. The derived-information function allows managers to determine the "why" of information by looking at the causes of the behavior of data. The drill-down function allows managers to access data at any chosen level of detail.

♦ **The GDSS and its role in improving group meetings.**
A GDSS is a computer-based information system that facilitates the free flow and exchange of ideas and information among group members, in some cases maintaining their anonymity. The three different kinds of GDSS are the single-computer GDSS, the keypad-response GDSS, and the full-keyboard-workstation system.

Research has shown that a GDSS improves the quality and effectiveness of meetings by keeping group members focused on the task at hand and promoting an environment that is conducive to decision making. Anonymity allows GDSS participants to air their ideas without fear of being judged or penalized. Finally, the efficiency of meetings is improved manyfold by a GDSS, since ideas are generated and processed in parallel and there is no cross talk among group members.

♦ **The differences among TPS, MIS, DSS, and EIS.**
TPS and MIS primarily support operational decision making; DSS and EIS support tactical and strategic decision making. A few years ago, the lines separating DSS and EIS were clear and rigid. Today, DSS and EIS are used at all levels in the organization. The overall goal, however, is to integrate the different systems to meet the overall needs of the business.

 Review Questions

1. Identify and describe the different steps in problem solving. How does a DSS help in the problem-solving process?
2. Describe a DSS; identify any three characteristics of a DSS.
3. What are the differences among structured, semistructured, and unstructured decision making? Give an example of each.
4. Business problems can be classified into three types: independent, interrelated, and organizational. Describe each problem type and give an example of each.
5. Describe any three applications of DSS.
6. Name and describe the five functions of a DSS.
7. What is a GDSS and how does it facilitate group decision making?
8. What is an EIS and how does it support unstructured decision making?
9. Describe the drill-down function through an example.
10. What are the critical success factors for EIS technology? Why is selecting the right problem a critical step?
11. What are the differences among TPS, MIS, DSS, and EIS?

Discussion Questions

1. Selecting the right software package is a difficult and challenging task. Some criteria that can be used to evaluate EIS software are identified below.[28]

   User Requirements

   The functions of an EIS package, such as ad hoc query capabilities, exception reporting, "what-if" analysis, goal seeking, drill-down, derived information, quick response time, and high-quality displays, should closely match the requirements of the user, if the system is to gain acceptance.

   Pricing

   The cost of software, hardware, network configuration, training, consulting fees, upgrades, and documentation.

   Security and Control

   Features that ensure system security and data integrity, and other measures that are built into the system to protect the software.

   Developer Productivity

   Features that may affect the productivity of system developers, such as graphic capabilities, ease of creating and editing files, screens, menus, and the ability to generate reports.

   Vendor Information

   The vendor must be reliable and have a good reputation. Product ratings, company history and size, and consumer reports are considered in the evaluation of a vendor.

   Maintenance

   Since an EIS must frequently be updated and maintained, the maintenance requirements of the system should also be evaluated.

   Based on the information provided above, identify and evaluate any PC-based EIS package. Popular trade journals, such as *Computerworld* and *PC World,* often perform evaluations of various software packages. They provide a good starting point.

2. Commander FDC is a software package that produces monthly, quarterly, or annual financial closing statements and merges information from various accounting and management databases in a company. Reports of the closing process are generated in two stages: First, the system reviews the data at the point of origin for any inconsistencies. If any are found, they are brought to the attention of the user for resolution. Second, the system merges data from different business units and makes the necessary journal entry adjustments, or foreign currency translations, when necessary. Based on the consolidated data, a user can prepare customized management reports in a variety of formats.

   The system has proved useful to many companies. Before installing Commander FDC, one company had to obtain financial data from 80 operating units, re-enter the data into a Lotus spreadsheet, and then upload the data to its mainframe so that the necessary reports could be generated for decision makers. After moving to Commander FDC, the company experienced a 50% reduction in its quarterly reporting cycle time and significantly fewer errors in its reports.

   Identify some of the characteristics of this system. Would you classify Commander FDC as a DSS, an EIS, or both?

3. Some experts indicate that an EIS should be viewed as a high-risk system. A 1991 study found that of 50 EIS that were investigated, "21 of them had experienced an EIS failure *prior* to development of a successful system." One of the major problems that the development team faced was deciding what information to include in the system. Many developers indicated that their primary concern was getting executives to specify what they want in the system. Executives often cannot describe in detail what they do and how they do it; hence, developers find it extremely difficult to determine their information needs.[29]

   Identify any top executive in an organization of your choice. Discuss with that executive the nature and scope of his or her responsibilities and develop the requirements for any one of his or her job functions.

4. Carl DiPietro, a consultant specializing in computer-assisted meetings, indicates that one of the strengths of groupware is its ability to avoid what is called the "Abilene paradox." He explains the paradox as follows:

   "A Texas family gathers one Sunday morning to decide what to do for the day. No one has any ideas—or if they do, they are afraid to speak up. Finally, the patriarch of the family suggests going to Abilene, which is 100 miles away, on the hottest day of a Texas summer. Everyone agrees, with relief, and they take a long, hot, joyless trip there and back. At the end of the day it turns out that no one wanted to go to Abilene, not even the person who suggested it. But everyone just fell in line with the suggestion. We make decisions based on other people's behaviors rather than . . . on our own ideas or beliefs."[30]

How can a GDSS help organizations avoid the "Abilene paradox"?

E T H I C A L   I S S U E S

Case 1: Manipulating Decisions

Proprietors of Places to Live, an East Meadow, N.Y. apartment referral service, were sued in February, 1994, by the New York state attorney general for allegedly manipulating computer programs to deny information to minorities about housing in white neighborhoods. Places to Live owner John McDermott was accused of programming his company's computer to indicate the ethnic background of prospective tenants and landlords, along with biases of the landlords.

Many decision support tools can be programmed to incorporate the prejudices and biases of the decision maker. For example, banks can use racial or ethnic data to avoid giving loans to certain groups, schools can use data to avoid admitting certain groups of students, and so on.[31]

1. Do you think it is morally wrong to incorporate the biases and prejudices of a decision maker into a system or do you feel that they form an integral part of decision making, either explicitly or implicitly?

Case 2: Limited Access to Data

Many companies have reservations about allowing decision-support queries to tap into their production data-bases. "We don't want our business analysts making strategic decisions off operational data," says Robert Typanski, manager of emerging information systems technologies at Miles, a chemical and pharmaceutical manufacturer in Pittsburgh. The goal is to get users to stop and think whether their problem is operational or informational and this goal can be achieved only when users don't have free access to all data. Some IS officials also worry that decision-support queries could bog down the performance of their databases.

But others argue that holding and hoarding data without giving access to decision makers defeats the very purpose of data. The quality of decisions is directly tied to the quality of data and following a broad policy that denies data access to decision support queries takes a limited view of an organization.[32]

1. "We don't want our business analysts making strategic decisions off operational data." Do you agree with this view? Why or why not?
2. Do you believe that giving access to "all data" may have ethical implications for decision makers? Discuss.

PROBLEM SOLVING IN THE REAL WORLD

Case 1: Amnesty International USA

Amnesty International USA has a network, called Urgent Action Network (UAN), in Nederland, Colorado, whose primary function is to send telegrams to government officials anywhere in the world to draw their attention to alleged human rights violations. The network is supported by members of Amnesty International, who make pledges to a Telegram Pledge Program (TPP) to reimburse UAN for operating the telegram program. The TPP requires decision makers to match pledges with human rights violations. Decision makers operating the TPP must perform a cost-benefit analysis of each telegram, maintain detailed in-house records, and ensure that the individual preferences of pledging members are honored.

Although the TPP looks like a simple task of sending telegrams, it involves critical decisions that require analytical skills, intuition, and judgment. The task of sending telegrams involves the following decision points:

Decision Point 1—Number of Telegrams

The decision maker must first decide how many telegrams to send to officials around the world. This decision depends on factors such as the specific nature of the case, the number of available pledges, and the number of estimated cases in that given month that may require the agency's intervention. Hence, this task is unstructured.

Decision Point 2—Pledge Selection

The decision maker must determine the most suitable pledge for the case at hand. This decision may depend on factors such as the nature of the case, any special requests by the individual or organization making the pledge, and the number of available pledges. This task varies between being semistructured and unstructured.

Decision Point 3—Telegram Text and Telegram Addresses

The text of the telegram must be worded carefully and sent to the billing office and the office that transmits the telegram. This is a semistructured task.

Decision Point 4—Billing

The agency must manage the cost associated with sending telegrams, although this task is fairly routine. The billing office must then inform the pledging member about the telegram, its cost, and the method of payment. This is a structured task.

Decision Point 5—Receipt of Funds

Receiving and managing funds requires intuition and judgment on the part of the decision maker. For example, the account may not be balanced, funds for telegrams may be exhausted, or the agency may be burdened with a negative balance, and all of these problems require managers to take action. The decision maker must take into account many factors before making decisions about delinquent members and account balances.

Clearly, the task of sending telegrams involves a number of decisions that can be structured, semistructured, or unstructured, and involves the use of data, models, and the decision maker's intuition and judgment.

A DSS was developed to automate the TPP system. The DSS performs a number of tasks: it facilitates creating and sending telegrams, manages TPP funds, actively seeks and promotes membership, and maintains up-to-date membership databases.[33]

1. Describe the decision points involved in the process of sending telegrams.
2. Why would a DSS be appropriate for this problem?

Case 2: Georgia Power Gains Power Through DSS

Georgia Power, based in Atlanta, is one of the largest utilities in Georgia. It generates, buys, distributes, and sells energy to 153 of the 159 counties in the state. It has residential and industrial customers and also sells power to cooperatives and municipally owned electric distribution systems. Utilities are information-intensive organizations, governed by a large number of internal and external regulations and guidelines.

Executives at Georgia Power were overwhelmed by a large number of internally generated computer reports; however, these reports were not providing managers with the information necessary to make timely and effective decisions. The company had a pressing need for tools that would provide executives with instantaneous access to reliable information.

A system known as CADET (Computer Aided Decision Tool) was developed on a PC-based network to provide executives with access to current information in easy-to-use and easy-to-understand formats. When the system was fully functional, CADET provided more than 100 corporate performance indicators and 300 department performance indicators to executives at corporate headquarters and to others in selected divisions and plant locations. CADET, in its initial years, far exceeded the initial expectations of system developers and yielded significant organizational benefits.

However, over the years the system began to deteriorate, because it was unable to keep up with the dynamic environment in which utilities operate and the changing financial information needs of its executives. The system also became cumbersome to use; there were too many complex menus, which made system use time-consuming. The status of the system deteriorated from that of an executive decision-making tool to that of a report generator. The overhead costs of the system burgeoned as the utility dedicated four people simply to maintain the system and "a small army of data entry clerks" to re-enter data from various sources.

The system also had other serious drawbacks. CADET did not have drill-down capabilities, so executives had to use the phone each time they needed more detailed information, thus defeating the very purpose of an EIS. Another major problem was that CADET was not integrated with the existing mainframe, so information from mainframe-based reports had to be re-entered by hand into PCs. After much deliberation, the utility decided that the problems associated with CADET were serious enough to completely abandon the system and build a new EIS.[34]

1. Recall some of the critical success factors identified in this chapter and show how these factors were relevant to the initial success of CADET.
2. What are some of the factors that led to the deterioration of CADET? What

measures can an organization take to ensure that its system will not die a slow death?

Case 3: Catch the Criminal

The Atlanta Police Department (APD) uses CATCH (Computer-Assisted Tracking of Criminal Histories), a DSS for investigating homicide, rape, and aggravated assault cases. The system helps investigators find and link common criminal patterns, such as geographical and temporal patterns, by searching a database that contains records of past and current criminal cases. Investigators can also query the database for additional information through queries such as these: "Did the perpetrator belong to a gang?" "Was he drunk or drugged?" Based on user queries, the system retrieves cases that are similar.

Recently, CATCH was used in an aggravated assault case to determine the identity of a suspect. The investigator had incomplete information about the suspect and searched the database for a physical description and nickname matching those of the suspect. CATCH cross-referenced the known information to three previous assault cases. The suspect in all four assault cases was also an alcoholic. In another case, the system matched the physical characteristics of a suspect (whose name was missing) to those of a suspect in a murder case that was still under investigation. The records for the earlier case included the suspect's full name, which led to his arrest.

CATCH also lightens the managerial and administrative burdens of supervisors by facilitating case assignments, balancing case loads, tracking cases, and ensuring that all the reporting requirements of the government are met. Supervisors use the system to improve operational performance and to develop and control strategic plans for the department. Plans are also under way to integrate CATCH with related databases, such as prison population databases, that may further help to catch criminals. The use of CATCH is voluntary; this fact has been cited as one of the reasons for high user involvement in the development and implementation of the system.[35]

1. What are some features of CATCH that make it a decision support system?
2. How does it facilitate decision making in the Atlanta Police Department?

References

Alavi, Maryam and Erich A. Joachimsthaler. "Revisiting DSS Implementation Research: A Meta-Analysis of the Literature and Suggestions for Researchers." *MIS Quarterly* 16, no. 1 (March 1992).

Chidambaram, Laku, Robert P. Bostrom, and Bayard E. Wynne. "A Longitudinal Study of the Impact of Group Decision Support Systems on Group Development." *Journal of Management Information Systems* 7, no. 3 (Winter 1990/1991).

Dennis, Alan R., Joey F. George, Len M. Jessup, Jay F. Nunamaker, and Douglas R. Vogel. "Information Technology to Support Electronic Meetings." *MIS Quarterly* 12, no. 4 (December 1988).

DeSanctis, Geraldine and R. Brent Gallupe. "A Foundation of the Study of Group Decision Support Systems." *Management Science* 33, no. 5 (May 1987).

Drucker, Peter F. "The Information Executives Truly Need," *Harvard Business Review,* Jan.-Feb. 1995, pp. 54–62.

El Sherif, Hisham, and Omar A. El Sawy. "Issue-Based Decision Support Systems for the Egyptian Cabinet." *MIA Quarterly* 12, no. 4 (December 1988).

Ginzberg, Michael J., W. R. Reitman, and E. A. Stohr (eds.). *Decision Support Systems.* New York: North Holland, 1982.

Grobowski, Ron, Chris McGoff, Doug Vogel, Ben Martz, and Jay Nunamaker. "Implementing Electronic Meeting Systems at IBM: Lessons Learned and Success Factors." *MIS Quarterly* 14, no. 4 (December 1990).

Ho, T. H. and K. S. Raman. "The Effect of GDSS on Small Group Meetings." *Journal of Management Information Systems* 8, no. 2 (Fall 1991).

Houdeshel, George and Hugh L. Watson. "The Management Information and Decision Support (MIDS) System at Lockheed, Georgia." *MIS Quarterly* 11, no. 2 (March 1987).

Huber, G.P. "Cognitive Style as a Basis for MIS and DSS Design: Much ado about nothing?" *Management Science,* (1983) vol. 29, no: 5, pp. 567–579.

King, John. "Successful Implementation of Large-Scale Decision Support Systems: Computerized Models in U.S. Economic Policy Making." *Systems, Objectives, Solutions* (November 1983).

Meador, Charles L. and Peter G. W. Keen. "Setting Priorities for DSS Development." *MIA Quarterly* (June 1984).

Sanders, G. Lawrence and James F. Courtney. "A Field Study of Organizational Factors Influencing DSS Success." *MIS Quarterly* (March 1985).

Turban, Efraim. *Decision Support and Expert Systems,* 2d ed. New York: Macmillan, 1990.

Watson, Hugh J., R. Kelly Rainer, Jr., and Chang E. Koh. "Executive Information Systems: A Framework for Development and a Survey of Current Practices." *MIS Quarterly* 15, no. 1 (March 1991).

Notes

1. Kendall, Kenneth E. and Barbara A. Schuldt, "Decentralizing Decision Support Systems," *Decision Support Systems,* vol. 9, 1993, pp. 259–268.

2. Bielecki, Witold Tomasz, "DSS Manager: Turning Business Simulation into a Decision Support System," *Journal of Management Development,* vol. 12 (3), 1993, pp. 60–64.

3. Blears, James, "Software for Busy CEOs," *Business Mexico,* June 1994, pp. 28–29.

4. Datta, S. and R. Bandyopadhya, "An Application of O.R. in Micro-Level Planning in India," *Computers and Operations Research,* April 1992, vol. 20, no. 2, pp. 121–132.

5. Chung, Walter W.C., Migar M. C. Tam, K.B.C. Saxena, and K.L. Yung, "Evaluation of DSS Use in Hong Kong Manufacturing Industries," *Computers in Industry,* vol. 21, 1993, pp. 307–324.

6. Betts, Mitch, "Program Takes Guesswork Out of Discount Decisions," *Computerworld,* December 1994, pp. 77, 81.

7. Sterling, John W. and Angela Stubblefield, "Advia: Planning and Decision Support for Smaller Businesses," *Planning Review,* January/February 1994, pp. 50–53.

8. Turoff, Mary, Roxanne Starr Hiltz, N. F. Ahmed, and Ajaz R. Rana Bahgat, "Distribution Group Support Systems," *MIS Quarterly,* December 1993, pp. 399–405.

9. Donelan, Joseph, "Using Electronic Tools to Improve Meetings," *Management Accounting,* March 1993, pp. 42–44.

10. Migiliarese, Piero and Emilio Paolucci, "A System for Group Production Planning in Manufacturing," *Interfaces,* 23(3) May–June 1993, pp. 29–40.

11. Donelan, Joseph, "Using Electronic Tools to Improve Meetings," *Management Accounting,* March 1993, pp. 42–44.

12. LaPlante, Alice, "Brainstorming," *Forbes* ASAP, March, 1993, p. 46.

13. Donelan, Joseph, "Using Electronic Tools to Improve Meetings," *Management Accounting,* March 1993, pp. 42–44.

14. Drucker, Peter F., "The Information Executives Truly Need," *Harvard Business Review,* Jan.-Feb. 1995, pp. 54–62.

15. Klein, Paula, "Make That 'Easy Info System,'" *InformationWeek,* February 22, 1993, pp. 58,62.

16. Borsook, Paulina, "And the Twain Shall Meet," *InformationWeek,* January 31, 1994, p. 39.

17. Eom, Sean B. and Sang M. Lee, "Leading U.S. Universities and Most Influential Contributors in Decision Support Systems Research (1971–1989)," *Decision Support Systems,* 9, 1993, pp. 237–244.

18. Hoffman, Thomas, "Mexican Bank Finds Crisis Control," *Computerworld,* June 6, 1995, p. 79.

19. Barber, Paul and Katherine Gay, "EIS: A Strategic Resource That Can Help Organizations Gain a Clear Competitive Advantage," *CMA Magazine,* March 1993, pp. 23–28.

20. Ibid.

21. Booker, Ellis, "Pushing Decision Support Beyond Executive Suite," *Computerworld,* December 20, 1993, p. 65.

22. Hoffman, Thomas, "Tax Man Finds Better Way to Reach Data Trove," *Computerworld,* April 11, 1994, pp. 65–67.

23. Betts, Mitch, "Wisconsin System to Scrutinize Medicaid Bills," *Computerworld,* December 5, 1994, p. 75.

24. Cafasso, Rosemary, "Comshare Agents Aid With Database Searches," *Computerworld,* April 10, 1995, p. 73.

25. Harris, Jeanne, "Is Your EIS Too Stupid To Be Useful?" *Chief Information Officer Journal,* May/June 1993, pp. 52–56.

26. Watson, Hugh J. and M. M. Frolick, "Determining Information Requirements for an EIS," *MIS Quarterly,* September 1993, pp. 255–269.

27. Barber, Paul, and Katherine Gay, "EIS: A Strategic Resource That Can Help Organizations Gain a Clear Competitive Advantage," *CMA Magazine,* March 1993, pp. 23–28.

28. Frolick, Mark N. and Seavy Jennings, "EIS Software Selection at Georgia Power: A Structured Approach," *Information Strategy: The Executive's Journal,* Spring 1993, pp. 47–52.

29. Watson, Hugh J. and M. M. Frolick, "Determining Information Requirements for an EIS," *MIS Quarterly,* September 1993, pp. 255–269.

30. LaPlante, Alice, "Brainstorming," *Forbes ASAP,* September 13, 1993, pp. 45–61.

31. Bozman, Jean S., "Computing for the Gold," *Computerworld,* Feb 21, 1994, p. 10.

32. Stedman, Craig, "Data Warehouse Access in Question," *Computerworld,* Feb 28, 1994, p. 73.

33. Farwell, David C., "Decision Support for Human Rights: A Case Study," *Journal of Applied Business Research,* vol. 9 no. 2, 1993, pp. 92–96.

34. Frolick, Mark N. and Seavy Jennings, "EIS Software Selection at Georgia Power: A Structured Approach," *Information Strategy: The Executive's Journal,* Spring 1993, pp. 47–49.

35. Fazlollahi, Bijan and Jonathan S. Gordon, "CATCH: Computer-Assisted Tracking of Criminal Histories System," *Interfaces,* 23(2) March–April 1993, pp. 51–62.

9

Artificial Intelligence Expert Systems, and Neural Networks

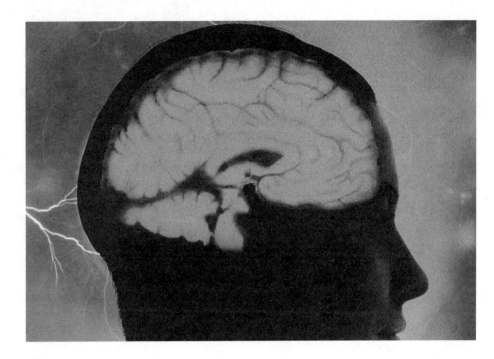

Contents

Learning Objectives
Technology Payoff: The Federal Aviation Administration
Introduction
What is Artificial Intelligence?
Appropriate Areas for an Expert System
Applications of Expert Systems
Components of an Expert System
    Knowledge Base
    Inference Engine
    User Interface
    Working Memory
    Explanation Module
Knowledge Representation
    IF-THEN Rules
Inferencing Techniques
DSS, EIS, and ES: A Comparison
Neural Networks
    How Neural Networks Work
    Applications of Neural Networks
Summary
Review Questions
Discussion Questions
Ethical Issues
    Case 1: Fighting Fire with Fire
    Case 2: Hidden Knowledge

325

Case 3: Who's to Blame?
Problem Solving in the Real World
    Case 1: Doctors Fight Infections with Artificial Intelligence
    Case 2: Moopi Scheduler: The Real Expert
References
Notes

Learning Objectives

Artificial intelligence (AI) is the study of using computers to emulate human intelligence and expertise. *Artificial intelligence* is also a broad term that covers a number of fields, such as expert systems, neural networks, vision, speech recognition, and robotics. In this chapter, we provide a broad overview of the contributions of AI to business and identify some AI applications that have revolutionized the way knowledge workers learn, process, and disseminate knowledge. The contributions of expert systems to organizational productivity are also discussed.

After reading and studying this chapter, you should be able to

* Define and describe artificial intelligence and its various branches
* Identify the attributes of intelligence
* Define an expert system, its components, and its characteristics
* Understand the role of neural networks in information processing

TECHNOLOGY PAYOFF

The Federal Aviation Administration

Some 40 traffic management specialists in a national air command center are responsible for the safety and the timely arrival of many thousands of air travelers in the United States. Each day, air traffic controllers must determine the routing landscape of the entire national airspace system and be prepared for contingencies, such as snowstorms and accidents. The task is not an easy one. Today, U.S. air space is crossed by approximately 50,000 flights a day from 300 major airports. Air traffic control is so challenging and complex that an FAA official described it as "the equivalent of fighting a Desert Storm every day. The air traffic wizards in the FAA's Central Flow command center must understand situations spanning thousands of miles, keeping in mind such details as [these:] Fog in San Francisco usually lifts by 10 a.m. and a certain runway at Boston's Logan International cannot be used after sunset because it is not lighted."

In spite of their best judgment, air traffic controllers sometimes make poor decisions. During a recent thunderstorm, a Chicago airport official diverted approaching airplanes to other airports. The next day, one airline found that a large number of its aircraft had to be retrieved from many different places, resulting in a loss of millions of dollars.

To minimize these types of mistakes, the Federal Aviation Administration (FAA) now relies on an expert system called Smartflow Traffic Management System to guide the decisions of airport personnel in tricky situations. Smartflow holds the knowledge, experience, and intuition that air traffic experts have accumulated over many decades. The system monitors a database that contains information about airports, runway status, weather, flight schedules, and aircraft positions around the clock. It recognizes impending problems and provides recommendations, such as rerouting flights and increasing the space between aircraft.

Smartflow presents color-coded maps at three levels: level 1, all of U.S. airspace, including 20 regional FAA air traffic centers; level 2, individual regions, including individual airports; and level 3, individual airports, including showing the locations of runways, towers, and terminals. Smartflow has about 15,000 expert rules, collected over the years from 10 FAA air traffic experts. "A few [experts] have been there 10 to 20 years, and we're trying to pick their brains bigtime." With the help of user-friendly interfaces and rapid prototyping methodologies, the entire system is being developed by one person.[1]

Artificial Intelligence continues to be a possible dream worthy of dreaming.
—Ray Reddy at his acceptance speech of the 1994 A. M. Turing Award
from the Association for Computing Machinery.

Introduction

Every firm, regardless of the industry in which it operates, relies on the knowledge and skills of its employees. Knowledge workers make up a critical resource because it is knowledge that is at the heart of a successful organization. For instance, the Federal Aviation Administration relies on the knowledge of its air traffic controllers to ensure the safe and timely arrival of air passengers. Their knowledge bears directly on the safety and quality of air travel for thousands of passengers every day.

The output of knowledge is reflected in many ways: an innovative idea for a product, a new approach to a procedure, or an elegant solution to a nagging problem. Clearly, knowledge must be preserved, protected, enhanced, consolidated, and coordinated. Knowledge must be *preserved* so that it is not lost when an employee leaves the organization. It must be *protected* from competitors if an organization is to succeed in the long run. The organization must make all attempts to *enhance* its knowledge in order to compete in the marketplace.

Knowledge *consolidation* is the integration of knowledge from a variety of experts. It lies at the heart of many large-scale, complex intelligent systems. For example, US West consolidates the knowledge of its telemarketers, who sell services over the telephone. The system analyzes the responses of customers to a series of questions and infers their product needs.

Knowledge from different sources must also be *coordinated;* as companies become global, this task becomes more and more challenging. For example, Ford Motors, in Dearborn, Michigan, coordinates the design knowledge for circuit boards from electrical engineers in seven manufacturing plants all over the world to ensure that its designs conform to established manufacturing standards. Coordination has significantly reduced the number of design revisions. Today, fewer than 5% of the designs are returned; the reject rate was once 55%. Ford also coordinates knowledge in developing manufacturing schedules for the entire plant. Today, a number of schedulers can log onto a computerized scheduling system and work on a schedule in interactive mode. This improvement has reduced the task of scheduling production to an hour or so per day; it once took the better part of every week.

The technologies that assist in the handling of knowledge are broadly referred to as artificial intelligence. In this chapter, we give a broad overview of artificial intelligence and a more detailed view of two of its branches, expert systems and neural networks.

What Is Artificial Intelligence?

Let us first take a look at what we mean by intelligence, and then define artificial intelligence. Although the word *intelligence* is used frequently, there is no single, universally accepted definition of intelligence. Some attributes frequently associated with intelligence are shown in Table 9–1.

If we view intelligence as consisting of this set of attributes, artificial intelligence can be viewed as the study of these attributes. (The term *artificial intelligence* was first coined by an MIT professor, John McCarthy, at a 1956 conference held at Dartmouth that laid the foundation for this field of study.)

The field of **artificial intelligence (AI)** includes the design and development of machines capable of performing tasks that, if performed by a human being, would require intelligence (Rich, 1987). A machine that can reason, learn, understand, recall, and explain its behavior and actions can be viewed as an intelligent machine. However, even today, three to four decades after AI was conceived, the creation of truly intelligent machines is still not quite a reality.

A more formal definition of AI, from Barr and Feigenbaum (1981), is as follows:

"Artificial intelligence (AI) is a branch of computer science concerned with designing intelligent computer systems; that is, systems that exhibit the characteristics we associate with intelligence in human behavior—understanding, language, learning, reasoning, solving problems, and so on."

AI is an interdisciplinary field. It is influenced and shaped by disciplines such as psychology, mathematics, cognitive science, computational linguistics, data processing, decision support systems, and computational modeling. AI is made up of various branches of study, such as expert systems, computer vision, speech synthesis and recognition, natural language interfaces, neural networks, and robotics. Let us take a brief look at the various branches of AI. Figure 9–1 shows the areas that influence AI and the branches of AI.

Expert systems—programs designed to emulate the knowledge and expertise of human beings in a specialized area—are the focus of this chapter. An

Artificial intelligence
A field of study that designs and develops machines capable of performing tasks that would require intelligence if performed by a human being. AI is a branch of computer science that includes areas such as expert systems, robotics, natural language, speech recognition, and neural networks.

Expert systems
Programs designed to model the expertise of human beings in a specialized area. The knowledge, intuition, and problem-solving capabilities of the human expert are modeled by the system.

TABLE 9–1
Although we use the word *intelligence* frequently, there is no universally accepted definition of intelligence. Instead, intelligence is best thought of as a set of attributes such as those shown in this table.

- Ability to think, process, reason, and solve complex problems.
- Ability to use knowledge, intuition, judgment, and rules of thumb to solve problems.
- Ability to quickly and efficiently identify all possible solutions to a problem and narrow the array of solutions to a few good alternatives that have a high probability of success.
- Ability to reason using conflicting, inaccurate, or uncertain information.
- Ability to learn from experience and modify one's behavior accordingly.
- Ability to distinguish the trivial from the important when dealing with complex situations.

FIGURE 9-1

Artificial intelligence is an umbrella term that covers a number of areas, such as expert systems and neural networks. The field of AI itself is influenced by other disciplines, such as psychology, mathematics, and computer science.

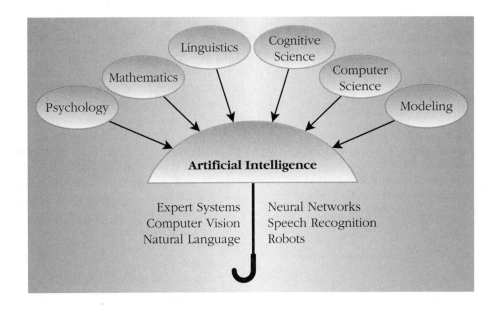

expert system stores the knowledge of an expert in a specific area of study, such as internal medicine, genetic engineering, and production engineering. The system applies various reasoning methods to the information stored in it, in order to solve complex problems that require both knowledge and intuition. This requires both knowledge and some intuition because some answers may not always be right or wrong. Sometimes, the problem-solving capabilities of such systems are as good as, or even better than, those of human experts.

Computer vision is a field of study whose goal is to endow computers with the ability to recognize and identify objects and the context to which they belong. An attribute of intelligence is the ability to visualize objects, based on partial or complete information, and to use that ability to fully recognize the object. Vision capabilities enhance the ability of computers to emulate human intelligence.

Speech recognition is a field of study whose goal is to enable computers to recognize and respond to human speech. Although researchers have worked on speech recognition systems for almost 30 years, the hardware to support this technology was not available until recently. For example, Janus is a speech recognition system that allows people to communicate in several languages. Imagine this: At your Boston office, you speak English into your workstation and your Tokyo-based colleague hears the Japanese translation. She responds in Japanese, and you hear her answer in English. Janus allows people to communicate, under some limiting conditions, in Japanese, German, or English. At present, Janus has a vocabulary of only 400 words, but research is underway to apply other AI-based technologies to recognize sound patterns other than voice to increase the speed of the recognition process and to improve the system's vocabulary.[2]

A computer with a **natural-language interface** allows human beings to communicate with the computer in the same way as they communicate with each other. A natural-language interface eliminates the need to use special programming languages to communicate with the computer; instead, users can simply speak to the computer. Janus has natural-language capabilities.

Computer vision
A field of study that endows computers with the ability to recognize objects.

Speech recognition
Computer recognition of the human voice. The goal of speech recognition technology is to allow users to communicate with machines just as they do with other human beings.

Natural-language interface
A technology that enables computers to recognize and respond to the language in which human beings communicate with one another.

Neural networks
Programs that model the capabilities of the human brain. They have excellent pattern-recognition capabilities and can also learn new information and behavior.

Robots
Machines that are capable of human-like tactile perception and motor activities. Robots can perform routine tasks and more challenging ones. Robotics, the study of robots, is a branch of AI.

Neural networks are intelligent programs that are modeled on the human brain. They can process large volumes of information, even if the information is inaccurate or incomplete, and recognize problem-solving patterns that the human eye may be unable to discern. Neural networks are covered later in this chapter.

Finally, **robots** are reprogrammable machines with human-like tactile and motor capabilities. Their ability to "see" and "hear" make them useful in environments that are too complex or dangerous for human beings. They mostly perform repetitive tasks, but can be programmed to do a wide variety of things. Robots have three main components: a controller (hardware and software) to guide the robot; a manipulator, a device with a movable arm that allows the robot to perform "hand" movements; and a device that performs the task at hand, such as painting or welding.

Robots are used in a wide variety of situations. Many hospitals across the U.S. have installed robotic couriers for routine deliveries. For example, there is D. T., which delivers intravenous drug solutions to nursing stations at the University of California at San Diego (UCSD) Medical Center. The 5-foot-tall robots operate on 12-hour batteries and move 2 feet per second. These robots use a digital map of the building to find their way around the hospital, plan the best route from Point A to Point B, and use feedback from optical vision and ultrasonic sensors to detect walls and corners and to avoid dangerous collisions. The robot's controller is a microprocessor containing proprietary software that guides the robot. It also uses a radio transmitter to call an elevator using a synthesized speech system with a vocabulary of about 16 phrases, such as "My path is blocked; please move."[3] Hospitals and similar organizations are actively installing robots because they make great employees. They never call in sick or come late for work and do precisely what is expected of them!

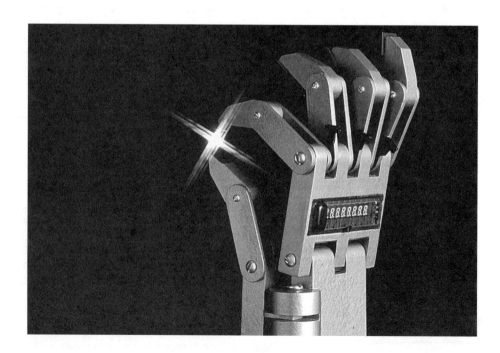

Robotics

Appropriate Areas for an Expert System

An expert system, as you may recall, is a system that records the knowledge and expertise of human experts in a specific area and uses this knowledge and expertise to solve complex problems. One of the most critical steps to be taken before developing an expert system is to make sure the chosen subject area is appropriate, because expert system technology is not useful in all areas. More often than not, expert systems fail because the wrong area was selected. What types of problems can be successfully solved using expert systems? Table 9–2 identifies some criteria to be applied to an area under consideration.

1. Is expertise in the given area rare and expensive? If the expertise is readily available and is cheap to acquire, then it is not worthwhile to invest a great deal of resources in capturing it.
2. Is the knowledge that is to be modeled likely to be inconsistent and incomplete? If the knowledge is always accurate and complete, there is no need for an expert system, because in such cases, problems can usually be solved using other types of systems.
3. Will the problem-solving process involve judgment and heuristics (trial-and-error methods)? If-not, the problems are structured. Expert systems are better suited to semistructured and unstructured problems.
4. Is it possible to specify objectively what the system should accomplish? Because heuristic problems involve the use of intuition and judgment, it is sometimes difficult to specify system goals. However, without specifications, it is impossible to build a system.
5. Can significant benefits be derived by capturing and disseminating this knowledge? An expert system is expensive and time-consuming to develop, so it should provide significant long-term benefits.

These are some issues that must be addressed before selecting the set of problems and solutions that is to be modeled using expert system technology.

TABLE 9–2
Although expert system technology is versatile, not all problems should be addressed by expert systems. There are seven key questions that must be answered to determine whether expert systems should be used.

- Is domain expertise rare and expensive?
- Is the knowledge likely to be inconsistent and incomplete?
- Does the problem-solving process involve judgment, heuristics, and rules of thumb?
- Is it possible to state precisely what the system should do?
- Is common sense required to solve the problem?
- Can significant benefits be derived by distributing the solutions to this class of problems?
- Is top management committed to solving this problem?

BUSINESS REALITIES
Kaiser Foundation Health Plan

An expert system-based application helped Kaiser Foundation Health Plan, of Oakland, California, move "from the 19th century to the 21st century." Kaiser evaluates applications to determine if an individual qualifies medically for membership. Before the expert system was installed, the qualifying process was entirely manual. Employees wrote information on scratch pads and index cards and transferred it to other employees until the process was complete, with almost 15 handoffs from start to finish. The process was so tedious and time consuming that it took four to six weeks to process a single application.

Kaiser realized the need to automate this process because it affected its reputation as a customer-oriented company. In particular, the company was trying to move away from a paper-based system and prepare itself for the coming century when most business transactions are likely to be electronic. Kaiser purchased Trinzic Aion Development System's rules-based expert system. This system contains all the rules employees and medical practitioners use to process applications. Dubbed System for Individual Marketing and Review, the system cut in half the time a doctor needs to review applications. Furthermore, the system also allows users to input rules that reflect their individual judgment and experiences. Today, the new system handles about 80% of individual applications to Kaiser. By accepting 28% and rejecting 12% immediately, 40% of applications do not require medical review. Processing costs have decreased significantly and customer satisfaction has increased.[4]

Applications of Expert Systems

There are many applications of expert systems all over the world. Some of these are described below. For example, Kaiser Foundation Health Plan (see box) developed an expert system to automate the process of qualifying applicants for the company's health plan. The expertise required for this process often takes people years to achieve and involves judgment and intuition. The company achieved significant benefits from the system because it carefully addressed the problem characteristics of the process before development began. Federal Express is another example of a company that uses expert systems to support and facilitate cooperative decision-making (see box).

One of the earliest computer systems was XCON (Expert VAX System Configuration), developed by Digital Equipment Corporation (DEC) and Carnegie Mellon University in the early 1980s. The primary purpose of XCON was to help computer technicians and engineers to successfully install computers and their peripherals. DEC made a large variety of computers that were customized for its customers. Thus, configuring a system often required extensive knowledge about the client's products, years of experience and training in configuration, and outstanding problem-solving abilities. When an experienced technician left the organization or died, DEC often found it hard to replace him or her. DEC decided that the valuable knowledge of configuration technicians should be stored in a system, and thus XCON was born.

XCON modeled the knowledge, experience, and intuition of hundreds of DEC computer technicians and engineers, so DEC was able to automate a process that had been labor-intensive and error-prone. The combined knowledge of DEC's technicians created a configuration system whose performance often exceeded that of some of the best human experts. XCON was so successful, and proved to be so beneficial for DEC, that it spurred the commercialization of expert system technology and encouraged other companies to explore the use of expert systems for business applications.

BUSINESS REALITIES
Federal Express

Federal Express (FedEx) uses expert systems to support and facilitate cooperative decision-making in a highly charged and competitive industry where good decisions translate into many thousands of dollars in savings and poor decisions have a serious impact on the company's competitive position. FedEx has always been an innovative and enthusiastic user of information technology. One ambitious and closely guarded project is an expert system that facilitates cooperative decision making by closely and extensively controlling, monitoring, and assessing the impacts of the organization's decisions.

One of the key goals of this system is ensuring that decision makers have carefully evaluated all possible scenarios before making their decisions. For example, the decision to reroute a FedEx plane is not a simple one. It can affect a number of outcomes, some of which may have been overlooked. FedEx can be fined if a rerouting causes one of its planes to miss a scheduled maintenance check. On the other hand, even a 1% increase in the efficiency of FedEx's fleet of 450 aircrafts and 34,000 vehicles can produce significant savings.

The cooperative AI-based decision-making system alerts decision makers to *all* factors that are affected by a decision and even recommends an appropriate course of action. Expert systems not only capture the knowledge and expertise of experienced decision makers but also help to spread the art of making good decisions throughout the organization.[5]

Today, DEC is a firm believer in expert systems. It saves more than $200 million annually with the help of some 50 AI applications that help it to run its worldwide business. These AI systems are used throughout a product's life cycle, from design and development to delivery and support.

Another popular application of expert systems is computer help desks, which provide telephone support to users who have computer hardware, software, or network problems. By modeling the expertise of troubleshooters in an expert system, Color Tile, in Fort Worth, Texas, supports 1,600 technicians at 800 locations, who handle about 13,000 calls per month from users with a wide variety of computer problems. The company has reduced the average call time from 10 minutes to less than 2 minutes. Further, the system provides consistency in solutions to computer problems: every caller gets the same response to the same problem. Also, when a help desk expert leaves the company the knowledge is not lost and can be updated easily as new solutions emerge.

Mrs. Field's, Inc., headquartered in Park City, Utah, relies on a number of expert system applications to manage its large chain of stores. Expert systems do everything from running back-office accounting operations and scheduling part-time and full-time employees to assuring the consistency and quality of the company's cookies. In fact, Mrs. Field's has been so successful with its use and application of expert systems that in 1990 the company started a new division, called Park City Software, that consults and sells expert system products to other companies, such as Woolworth and the Disney Store.

Xerox is another company that is known for its investments in expert systems. Worldwide, there are more than 30,000 Xerox copiers; the company uses an expert system to increase the performance and reduce the downtime of these machines. Sensors located in each copier are linked to an expert system at company headquarters. The expert system analyzes the data and anticipates repairs and performance failures, guiding technicians so they can prevent problems before they occur. The system has earned Xerox a reputation for superior customer service.

Baltimore Gas & Electric, a utility that serves 1.2 million customers, uses expert systems to schedule and route service calls for customers moving into and

BUSINESS REALITIES
Tax Expert Systems

One of the most fruitful applications of expert systems has been in the area of tax law, primarily because taxation is highly knowledge-intensive and an individual must undergo many years of training to become an expert. Further, knowledge about taxes is critical to an organization, since they can have a significant impact on its profits and the value of its stock.

Public accounting firms use expert systems to solve tax problems. The IRS has developed several expert systems for various tax-related areas, such as identifying items on individual tax returns with high audit potential,

selecting estate tax returns for possible audit, and finding out whether a pension plan meets all the appropriate regulations.

There are many tax-related expert systems. TAX-MAN I and II are expert systems that analyze the tax consequences of corporate reorganizations. TAXADVISOR provides expertise on income and transfer tax planning. ExpertTAX is a highly successful tax expert system, developed by Coopers and Lybrand for corporate tax accrual and planning. Besides capturing and disseminating valuable knowledge, expert systems have helped companies and government agencies, such as the IRS, increase productivity and provide consistent performance.[6]

out of their residences. Scheduling was formerly a complicated manual process requiring 26 clerks and 2 or 3 dispatchers to process as many as 2,000 work orders per day. Today an expert system performs the same task in less than a day—often in just a few hours. Now in operation for over a year, the scheduler has allowed a 42 percent reduction in the scheduling workforce, greater efficiency in scheduling of routes, a 48-percent reduction in overtime, and a 25-percent reduction in back orders. The system paid for itself in 6 months and the utility is actively exploring other areas that can be improved through AI technology.

Expert systems are also widely used in the area of taxation (see box on Tax Expert Systems). Taxation is an ideal problem for expert systems because tax problems require extensive knowledge and years of experience and training. The IRS

```
EXSYS EL ══════ RULE NUMBER: 25 ══════════════════════════     RULE TRUE
IF:
        (1) Driving on unimproved or dirt roads will be frequently done

THEN:
            Saab 900 Turbo - Confidence=7/10
    AND     Toyota Camry w. All-trac - Confidence=9/10
    AND     Subaru 4WD Wagon - Confidence=9/10
    AND     Mercedes-Benz 300SE - Confidence=3/10
    AND     Ford Escort - Confidence=1/10
    AND     Cadillac Eldorado - Confidence=3/10
    AND     Hyundai Excel - Confidence=1/10
    AND     Lincoln Continental - Confidence=3/10
    AND     Isuzu Impulse - Confidence=1/10
    AND     Honda Prelude - Confidence=2/10



IF line # for derivation, <K>-known data, <C>-choices
↑ or ↓ - prev. or next rule, <J>-jump, <H>-help or <ENTER> to continue:
```

Expert System

A GLOBAL PERSPECTIVE
Canada Trust

Canada Trust relies on an expert system to detect credit card fraud, estimated at $450 billion in 1993 alone. The $163 billion savings and loan company uses an expert system with more than 250 rules to calculate and analyze credit card transaction patterns. Since the system went into production in July, 1993, Canada Trust has eliminated using reports from credit card companies, such as MasterCard International. More importantly, the bank has saved more than $1.2 million in MasterCard losses since the software was installed.

The expert system extracts data from its IBM ES/9000 mainframe-based credit card authorization records every two hours during the business day and once nightly. It then automates the search for deviations from a customer's profile, such as big-ticket purchases outside the customer's normal purchasing patterns, and unusual transactions, such as cash advances or jewelry or electronic purchases, frequent targets of fraud. The expert system then assigns an overall score to each suspicious transaction based on the likelihood of fraud. This data is then routed to the bank's fraud department for analysis. For example, the system identified a Canada Trust MasterCard customer who had not used his credit card for three months but whose account suddenly showed a large jewelry purchase. The purchase turned out to be fraudulent.

Prior to the development of the expert system, Canada Trust relied on "velocity reports," or credit card usage reports, from MasterCard to analyze suspected fraudulent activity. But the data was two to three days old before Canada Trust fraud experts could begin analyzing it, and the bank wanted to be able to detect fraudulent activity before customer statements were produced.

The bank received a return on its investment in its expert system after 15 days! While credit card fraud rose 46.4% in Canada in 1993 alone, Canada Trust's expert system helped the bank reduce its credit card fraud to an annual rate slightly less than 25%.[7]

and many major accounting firms rely on expert systems for solving a wide variety of tax problems. Many companies are also investing in tax-based expert systems, since tax policies and procedures have a direct bearing on the bottom line.

The U.S. Customs Service at Washington, D.C., has deployed an expert system, called the Cargo Container Targeting Information System (CCTIS), that monitors all imports to the U.S. via sea for illegal cargo. Given the magnitude of the task, Customs often finds that its force of more than 1,600 seaport inspectors cannot inspect every cargo shipment. The object of the new system is not to replace the inspectors, but instead to assist them to prioritize shipments that should be inspected. When the system was initially tested at Newark and Los Angeles, the two largest ports in the U.S., the number of seizures and the total number of shipments inspected increased. Eventually, Customs plans to deploy the system in every U.S. port.[8]

Expert systems are used not only in the U.S. but throughout the world. For example, Canada Trust (see box) uses expert systems to detect credit fraud. Another global example of expert systems is the crew tracking and scheduling system of Singapore Airlines (see box).

Although there are many applications of expert systems, for competitive reasons most companies are reluctant to discuss their systems and the benefits derived from them. For example, one of the largest manufacturers in the United States declines to go on the record about its 50 or so expert system applications, which do everything from payroll to scheduling. It is estimated that expert systems save this company more than $1 million each month. Pacific Bell is also reluctant to discuss its successful AI applications because they provide the company with a significant competitive advantage. "AI may be only 15 percent of the

A GLOBAL PERSPECTIVE
Singapore Airlines

Singapore Airlines is turning to an artificial-intelligence-based system to manage its flight crew scheduling and handle disruptions to crew rosters. The project, called the Integrated Crew Management System (ICMS), is scheduled to be implemented in stages during the next two years. ICMS consists of three modules: a roster assignment module for cockpit crew, one for the cabin crew, and a crew tracking module. The first two modules are designed to automate the tracking and scheduling of flight crew timetables, while the crew tracking module will allow schedulers to access a powerful graphical user interface to manage crew rosters more effectively than the existing system does. For example, often crews need to be rearranged if a member falls ill, especially in a foreign port. The intelligence system will check the crew roster to determine the best way to reschedule the different crew members' rosters to accommodate the sick person. Should the need arise, another person can be flown in from the base port to replace the absent crew, until he or she recovers. The crew disruption handling module will be integrated with the crew tracking system and will provide decision-support capabilities in real time. This system has captured the expertise of experienced professionals who handle flight crew scheduling disruptions and hence can often come up with very good solutions. The core components of the system are written in C with an interface to Oracle database.[9]

code, but this 15 percent may bring 80 percent of the value added of the entire system," says a company spokesman. Harvey Newquist, author of *The Brain Makers* and editor of the newsletter *Critical Technology Trends,* estimates that today at least 10,000 applications all over the world include AI components.

Components of an Expert System

An expert system has five main components. They are the knowledge base, the inference engine, the user interface, the working memory, and the explanation module.

Figure 9–2 shows these five components and their interrelationships. Each component is described below.

Knowledge Base

The knowledge base is a repository of knowledge that human experts might apply to solve problems in a subject area, such as medicine, engineering, or

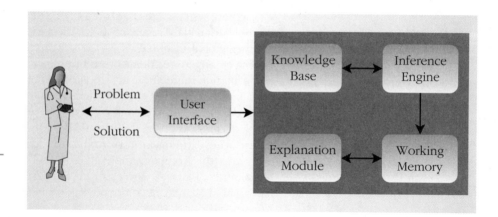

Deep knowledge
Includes general theories, principles, and axioms derived from books.

Surface knowledge
Knowledge that comes from experience and consists of heuristics and rules of thumb.

Knowledge acquisition
The process of acquiring knowledge from a variety of sources, such as human experts, books, journals, databases, and electronic media. Acquiring knowledge from experts is a major challenge in the development of expert systems.

Knowledge engineers
Professionals responsible for acquiring knowledge and representing it in the system. Besides good communication skills, knowledge engineers must have a good understanding of system development.

finance. Knowledge includes facts, theorems, principles, rules, heuristics, and rules of thumb that experts use to solve a problem. Heuristics are based on experience, intuition, and judgment, and hence vary from one expert to another. Knowledge can be divided into two broad categories: deep knowledge and surface knowledge. **Deep knowledge** includes general theories, first principles, and axioms; it is mostly acquired from textbooks and in school. This type of knowledge can be applied to a variety of fields of study because its principles are generic to a number of areas. **Surface knowledge,** on the other hand, is knowledge that comes from experience and consists mostly of heuristics and rules of thumb. Such knowledge is not acquired from books, but from experience and from other experienced people. Surface knowledge is related to a specific field of study, such as medicine, engineering, genetics, or music. Figure 9–3 shows the two types of knowledge.

The knowledge in the knowledge base is gathered from a variety of sources, including human experts, books, journals, databases, and electronic media; this process is known as **knowledge acquisition (KA).** Knowledge may also be acquired through study and observation, formal and informal interviews, questionnaires, prototypes, and face-to-face contact. Several automated tools for knowledge acquisition are also available. The professionals responsible for acquiring knowledge are known as **knowledge engineers (KE).** They are trained professionals with excellent oral and written communication skills and a solid technical background in computer science and AI.

Knowledge acquisition is an extremely challenging and time-consuming process; it is often viewed as a bottleneck in the design, development, and implementation of expert systems. One of the reasons for the difficulty of KA is that the knowledge of experts is not necessarily structured or well defined, so that experts

F I G U R E   9 – 3

Knowledge is made up of both surface knowledge and deep knowledge. Most experts rely on both types of knowledge for solving problems.

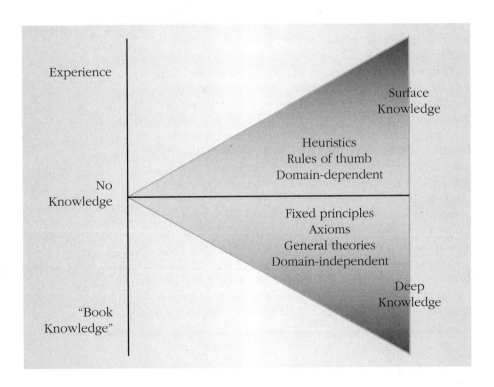

often find it difficult to articulate *what* knowledge they use and *why* they use that knowledge to solve a specific problem.

Consider the NYNEX example (see box below), in which an expert system is used to automatically draft a wide range of legal documents. The process of KA entails gathering the knowledge and experience of a number of legal experts, including not only factual knowledge of the law and its ramifications but also knowledge gained from experience in drafting legal documents. Gathering the experiential knowledge of domain experts is a major KA challenge for system developers.

When the knowledge has been acquired from the expert(s), it must be converted into machine-readable form. This process, known as *knowledge representation,* is discussed in the next section. (See Figure 9–4).

BUSINESS REALITIES
New York's NYNEX

Spending a million dollars is no big deal for Harry Bolton. As a buyer of wire cable for the $13.4 billion New York telecommunications giant NYNEX, he places dozens of orders of that size annually. Despite the amount of money at stake, when Bolton bargains with suppliers, the powerfully built "bulldog" negotiator drafts his own custom purchase agreements without even consulting an attorney. After selecting the type of legal document he wishes to create from a menu with more than 20 choices, the screen begins to ask him questions: What is the name of the supplier? How long will the contract last? Will there be an option to extend the agreement? Will NYNEX receive "most favored customer" pricing?

A half hour and 25 to 35 questions later (depending on the complexity of the deal), Bolton can print out a comprehensive 14-page agreement tailored to the transaction. Before NYNEX installed the contract engine in January, 1992, it would have taken at least 4 hours of Bolton's time, 4 hours of word processing and 2 attorney hours to produce an equally sophisticated document. The approximate cost of all that effort: more than $500.

Nynex's Contract Drafting System belongs to a new breed of expert systems that enable non-attorneys to create legal documents, once prepared exclusively by attorneys. The software gathers the factual information from the user. The pre-programmed expertise of these systems then plugs it into a highly developed decision tree that can include hundreds of variations on the document being created. Commercial packages are now available that produce wills, trusts, simple employment contracts, incorporation documents and regulatory compliance forms.

By cutting the time needed to create some routine legal documents by more than 90 percent, these expert systems promise to slash corporate legal costs—and ultimately lawyer income. At NYNEX, the contract system is used by approximately 70 buyers in the purchasing unit of the Telecommunications Group's corporate services organization. It has saved $200,000 annually by eliminating the need for the six-person word processing staff that once cranked out purchase agreements. By boosting productivity, expert systems will also indirectly help NYNEX move forward with plans to reduce the number of lawyers and buyers it employs. Over the next 3 years, NYNEX plans to trim 22 percent of its 76,200-person workforce.

Bolton estimates the contract system saves him one day a week. "I can just go bing, bam, boom, and it's done," he says. "My manager can feel confident that we've got all of the bases covered with each of the clauses."[10]

By 1999, more than 75 percent of all legal documents will be written with the assistance of expert systems, according to Jon E. Klemens, a principal at Altman Weil Pensa, a Newtown Square, Pennsylvania, consulting firm specializing in legal work.

FIGURE 9-4

Knowledge is acquired from different sources and is then represented in the knowledge base.

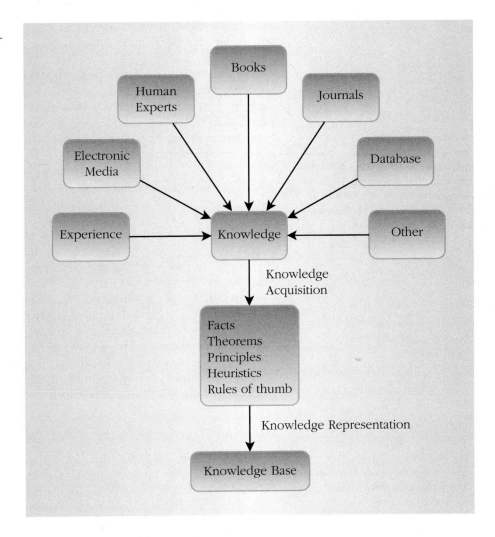

Inference Engine

Inference engine

The inference engine is a component of an expert system. It is the control mechanism that applies reasoning to the knowledge in the knowledge base and decides what knowledge to apply and when and where to apply it.

Deductive reasoning

Reasoning that arrives at a specific conclusion based on a set of general principles and facts. Moves from the general to the specific.

The second component of an expert system is the **inference engine,** a piece of software that determines what knowledge to apply, and when and how to apply it, to solve a given problem; it controls and guides the problem-solving process and arrives at conclusions by applying reasoning to the knowledge in the knowledge base. Although the term *inference engine* may suggest a piece of hardware, an inference engine is in fact a program that has the ability to reason and draw inferences.

There are two types of reasoning: deductive and inductive reasoning. **Deductive reasoning** arrives at a specific conclusion based on a set of general principles and facts. For example,

General Principle: All human beings are intelligent.
Fact: Elizabeth is a human being.
Conclusion: Elizabeth is intelligent.

In this case, based on the general principle that all human beings are intelligent and the fact that Elizabeth is a human being, the system concludes that Elizabeth is intelligent.

Another example of deductive reasoning is as follows:

General Principle: Every business has employees.
Fact: IBM is a business.
Conclusion: IBM has employees.

Inductive reasoning, on the other hand, uses specific facts to arrive at general principles. For example,

Fact: Lassie is warm and affectionate.
Fact   Fluffy is warm and affectionate.
Fact: Both Lassie and Fluffy are dogs.
General Conclusion: Dogs, in general, are warm and affectionate.

Another example of inductive reasoning is as follows:

Fact: IBM has a profit-and-loss statement.
Fact: Microsoft has a profit-and-loss statement.
Fact: Both IBM and Microsoft are businesses.
General Conclusion: Businesses, in general, have profit-and-loss statements.

Of the two types of reasoning, inductive reasoning is more challenging, because as new facts are discovered, general conclusions may have to be revised. In some cases, general principles may even be proven wrong after a large number of facts are considered. For example, margarine was once considered to be a good substitute for butter, but this is no longer the case. New facts show that more research is required before any conclusions can be drawn.

User Interface

A **user interface** is software that helps a user to interact with the computer by accepting input from the user and displaying different kinds of output. The physical components of an interface are input devices, such as keyboards, mice, sound cards, and voice recognition systems, and output devices, such as terminals and printers. The software component includes pull-down menus, graphs, charts, icons, touch screens, and natural language interfaces. The quality of an interface depends on what the user can see or sense (output), what the user must know in order to comprehend and act on based on system output, and actions that a user must or can take to accomplish a given task (Turban, 1993). The more user-friendly the interface, the higher are the chances of system acceptance.

Working Memory

Working memory, also referred to as the "blackboard," is the fourth component of an expert system. It provides temporary storage for data related to the problem at hand. During the problem-solving process, working memory holds the intermediate and final values assumed by the problem variables and maintains a record of three things:[11]

* The plan of action for solving the problem
* The actions that need to be implemented to solve the problem
* The alternative courses of action that can be taken to solve the problem

This information helps the user to trace the steps taken by the system to solve the problem. Hence, the output of working memory can also be used as a training tool for novices to help them better understand the problem-solving process.

Inductive reasoning
Uses specific facts to arrive at general principles. It is more difficult than deductive reasoning, because a large number of facts have to be gathered and analyzed before generalizations can be made.

User interface
Software that helps a user to interact with the computer.

Working memory
A component of an expert system. It is a temporary storage area where the initial data, the intermediate results, and the problem-solving steps are stored.

Explanation Module

Expert systems are designed to solve complex problems. For such problems, it is not enough if the system simply gives a solution; it must also be able to explain *how* it arrived at that solution by describing the knowledge and the reasoning principles it used. This is precisely what the **explanation module** does, by answering questions such as these: "How was the solution reached?" "What were some of the intermediate steps in the problem-solving process?" "Why were certain alternatives rejected?" "What pieces of knowledge were used to solve the problem?"

The explanation module can provide either "canned" or customized explanations to user queries. "Canned" explanations are standard explanations to predetermined queries; if they are used, all users will receive the same explanation. Customized explanations, on the other hand, are those whose nature, scope, breadth, and depth are tailored to match the profile of the user; therefore, sophisticated and experienced users may get explanations at a different level than novices.

Take, for example, the expert system used by NYNEX to create legal purchase documents (see box). If an attorney has a question about a legal document generated by the system, the explanation module can provide the facts of the case and the reasons that the contract was drafted in a specific manner. It can identify and explain the data that were taken into account when the contract was prepared, such as the name and financial status of the client, his or her legal history, regulations governing the client, and so on; it can explain how this data was analyzed, and identify the precise steps that the system took to draft the contract. The explanation module also provides details showing why the system rejected other alternative ways for drawing the contract. Hence, an explanation module is like a teacher who explains the how and why of the problem-solving process.

Knowledge Representation

Knowledge representation is the process of converting the expert's knowledge into a form that can be used by the system. The role of the knowledge engineer in acquiring and representing knowledge is shown in Figure 9–5.

In general, any piece of knowledge can be viewed as an **Object-Attribute-Value (OAV)** triplet. An *object* can be a physical object, such as a table, a building, or a machine, or a conceptual object, such as an idea, an opinion, or a strategy. An *attribute* is a characteristic of the object. For example, a car is an object that can be defined by its attributes, such as its make, model, color, year, and price. Finally, the *value* is the specific quality assumed by the attributes. In the above example, the value of the attribute *make* may be *Honda;* the value of the attribute *model* may be *Accord,* and so on. Knowledge can be represented using the OAV triplet. Figure 9–6 shows a graphical view of the OAV.

IF-THEN Rules

One of the most popular ways of representing the object, attribute, and value in an expert system is the use of IF-THEN rules. IF-THEN rules work as follows: IF a certain condition, also referred to as the **antecedent,** is true, THEN perform the following action, or **consequent.** Rules are sometimes referred to as *production*

Explanation module
A module in an expert system that explains the problem-solving process in detail. Explanations can be either "canned" or customized to the user's level of sophistication.

Knowledge representation
The conversion of the knowledge and judgment of the expert into a form the system can use. There are a number of ways to represent knowledge in the system, including IF-THEN rules.

Object-attribute-value (OAV)
Any piece of knowledge can be represented as an object-attribute-value triplet. The object can be a place, thing, person, or object. An attribute is a characteristic of the object; a value is the specific quality assumed by the attribute.

Antecedent
The IF part of an IF-THEN rule. If the conditions in the IF part are fully satisfied, the system executes the actions identified in the THEN part.

Consequent
The THEN part of an IF-THEN rule. If the conditions in the antecedent are satisfied, the actions in the THEN part of the rule are executed.

FIGURE 9–5

How the process of knowledge acquisition and knowledge representation fits into the development and maintenance of an expert system. The role of the knowledge engineer is also shown.

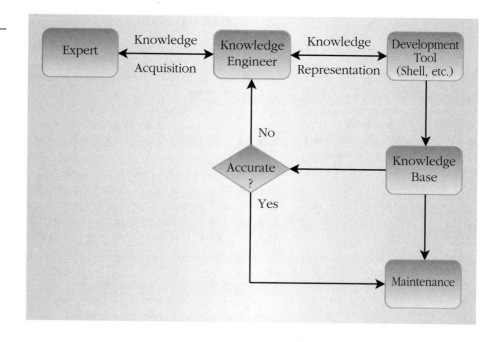

Rule-based systems
One way to represent the knowledge and judgment of an expert within a computer system is by using IF-THEN rules. Systems that use IF-THEN rules are called rule-based systems.

rules, so systems that use IF-THEN rules are called *production systems* or **rule-based systems.**

For example, Merced County, one of California's poorest counties, uses a rule-based expert system to process welfare applicants. Before it implemented an expert system, the county had a manual screening system for recipients of entitlement programs that had a high (and costly) error rate of almost 11%. Applicants had to fill out 30-page forms and wait up to 3 weeks to get an appointment. In 1992, Merced's human services agency implemented a client-server-based/rule-based expert system, called MAGIC, that has more than 6,000 eligibility IF-THEN rules in its knowledge base. Applicants go through interactive interviews with the system to determine eligibility status, freeing workers to focus on other tasks. Applicants fill out a one-page form and get an appointment within 48 hours. The

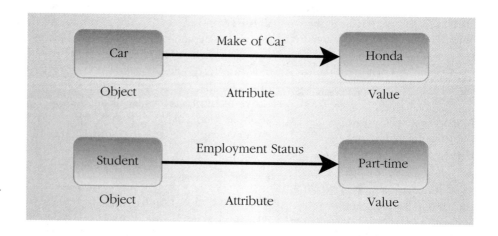

FIGURE 9–6

Two examples of object-attribute-value (OAV) triplets.

average interview time, which was once four to six hours, has dropped to 1½ hours; the processing time for applicants has dropped by more than 50%, from between 3 and 5 days to between 1 and 2 days. A check is mailed to an applicant one day after approval. Staff turnover rates have fallen by two thirds, to about 11%. The average caseworker handles about 225 cases as compared to the former caseload of 175. The staff has been cut by 30%; the number of cases the agency handles has increased by 40%, and overall productivity has increased another 40%.[12]

IF-THEN rules are also used in other systems, such as TPS, MIS, and DSS, to represent different kinds of knowledge. However, unlike other systems, which can function only if their information is complete and consistent, an expert system can function even if its information is not.

IF-THEN rules have the following basic form:

IF: **A** and/or **B**,
THEN: **D** and **E**.

The antecedents in a rule can be linked by AND or by OR. If they are linked by AND, **all** the antecedents in the rule must be satisfied before the actions in the THEN part are implemented. If the antecedents are linked by OR, if at least one of the antecedents in the rule is true, the THEN part of the rule will be executed. Of course, some rules may have only one antecedent or one action.

Although each rule in the knowledge base can be viewed as an independent piece of knowledge, in reality rules are interrelated because the actions of one rule may trigger another rule. However, the sequence in which facts are stored in the knowledge base is irrelevant and does not affect the way in which they are processed. Although IF-THEN rules may appear simple, as the number of rules increase, the complexity of interactions between the rules also increases significantly. In other words, it becomes difficult to trace which rule triggered which and to follow the sequence of actions triggered by a rule.

Examples of several IF-THEN rules are shown below.

IF   a student's overall grade is greater than 89% AND the student has actively participated in class
THEN   overall class grade is A.

IF   the car lights were left on AND the car does not start
THEN   the battery is dead.

IF   actual sales are 10% less than estimated sales OR product returns are 1% greater than sales
THEN   send express report to regional marketing manager.

IF   number of defective parts per lot is $\geq$ 0.1% OR Machine A fails 2 times in an 8-hour shift
THEN   change Valve A from high to medium.

IF   car is less than 3 years old AND driver of car is more than 25 years old AND driver has never been arrested for DUI
THEN   give insurance discount of 2%.

Fuzzy logic

A set of mathematical and logical principles that make it possible to use incomplete, inconsistent, and imprecise knowledge in an expert system.

As you may know, expert systems are designed to solve problems that require intuition and judgment. But how can we capture intuition and judgment in a system? One way is to do this by using **fuzzy logic,** which is based on a set of mathematical and logical concepts designed to capture knowledge that is imprecise, uncertain, and incomplete. For example, a weather expert may indicate that when it is very hot, it is likely to rain, although the estimation of the likelihood of rain may vary from one expert to another depending on the intuition, judgment, and experience of each expert. For example, likelihood can be represented as a number between 0 and 1 or a number between 0% and 100%, or any other appropriate scale can be used. If a weather expert indicates there is a 75% likelihood of rain, this estimate can be represented in the system as 0.75 or as 75%. These numbers, sometimes called *certainty factors,* play an important role in acquiring and representing expert knowledge.

Inferencing Techniques

As we have seen, the inference engine plays a leading role in the problem-solving process. There are two popular reasoning methods: forward chaining and backward chaining.

In **forward chaining,** the system begins with a set of known facts (data or initial conditions connected with a given problem), analyzes them, and looks for rules that match the given facts. If a match is found, then the system executes the actions given in the THEN part of the rule. Since in this approach data are the starting point for solving a problem, forward chaining is sometimes referred to as data-driven reasoning.

Forward chaining

The system begins by analyzing a set of data to solve a problem. Since data are the driving force behind this process, it is sometimes referred to as data-driven reasoning.

Let us look at an example of forward chaining. Suppose we classify individuals as tall or short. If John's height is say, 5'9", this value is input into the system and stored in working memory. Next, the inference engine searches for rules that show how to classify a person whose height is greater than 5'9". Suppose there is a rule in the knowledge base that states

> IF   Height $\geq$ 5'8"
> THEN   Person = tall.

When the expert system finds this rule, it recognizes a match between the problem data and the antecedent of the rule and *fires,* or activates, the rule. In other words, the system executes the THEN part of the rule, which in this case, indicates that the individual should be classified as tall.

As another example, consider the following rule:

> IF   number of defects per lot $\geq$ 3 AND shipment is in import category
> THEN   reject entire lot as defective.

The expert system searches the data it receives to see whether the number of defects in the lot is 3 or more. If so, the system takes the action of rejecting the entire lot.

As another example, consider this rule:

> IF   number of hours worked by part-time employee > 20 OR number of
>   hours worked by full-time employee > 40
> THEN   Overtime rate = Yes

Backward chaining
The inference engine begins with a goal, or hypothesis, and searches for data to support this goal. This method of reasoning is also referred to as goal-driven reasoning.

Hence, if a part-time employee works more than 20 hours, the system recognizes that an overtime rate must be paid.

The second type of reasoning is **backward chaining,** in which the inference engine begins with a goal, or hypothesis, and searches for data that support it. Since it is the goal that initiates the problem-solving process, backward chaining is sometimes referred to as goal-driven reasoning. In this approach, the inference engine searches for a match between the *consequent* (the THEN part of the rule) and the system goal; when a match is found, it searches for data that support the goal. If no match is found, the system continues to search the knowledge base until it finds evidence either to support or to reject the goal.

For example, suppose we begin with the goal "car = does not start." The system searches for a rule whose *consequent* is "car = does not start," and then looks for evidence that supports this goal, such as "bad engine," "weak battery," "transmission problem," or the like. For example, the rule may state

IF   battery = dead
THEN   car = does not start

Since the consequent of the rule matches the initial goal, the system next determines whether the IF condition of the above rule matches the facts stored in working memory. In this case, the system examines the working memory to see whether the battery is in fact dead. If a match is found, the problem is solved. If not, the system continues to search for evidence that does support the goal that the car does not start.

Another example of backward chaining, in a factory-floor setting, may be as follows:

IF   absenteeism rate is > 18% for the night shift
THEN   regulatory requirements are violated AND notify shift manager

In this case, given that regulatory requirements were violated, the system searches the problem database to see whether the absenteeism rate for the night shift was greater than 18%. (Figure 9–7 graphically shows the difference between forward chaining and backward chaining.)

In summary, forward chaining and backward chaining are two reasoning approaches commonly used to solve problems. Neither approach is better than the other. The type of reasoning technique to use depends on the nature and scope of the problem. For example, if the goal is to draw some conclusions based on a given set of facts, forward chaining is preferred. If, on the other hand, the goal is to find the facts that led to a given conclusion, backward chaining is appropriate. In fact, most systems use both forward and backward chaining in a given problem-solving session; this approach is referred to as **mixed chaining.**

Mixed chaining
The use of both forward and backward chaining to solve problems. Most expert systems are equipped to use both.

DSS, EIS, and ES: A Comparison

DSS, EIS, and ES are three types of intelligent support systems that have some common characteristics and some differences. DSS, EIS, and ES are all designed to solve semistructured and unstructured problems—that is,

FIGURE 9-7

The difference between forward
chaining and backward chaining.

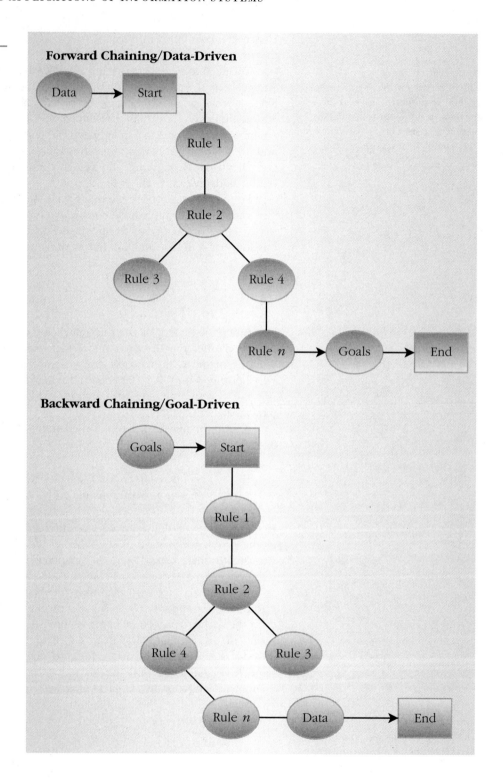

FIGURE 9-7

The difference between forward
chaining and backward chaining.

problems that require intuition and judgment. DSS is designed to help managers analyze data, integrate data with decision-making models, and arrive at alternative solutions to a problem. An EIS is designed primarily to display internal and external data in a wide variety of formats that facilitate understanding the data and acting on it. An ES, on the other hand, is a tool designed to model and disseminate knowledge and use it to solve complex problems in a specific area of study. DSS and EIS almost never replace the decision maker, but ES can do so. DSS and EIS use internal and external data, whereas expert systems use human expertise, which consists of knowledge, intuition, and judgment. Note, however, that ES knowledge may come from both internal and external sources. Finally, while all three systems are interactive, user-friendly, and menu-driven, and DSS and EIS are designed for middle and top managers, who are responsible for tactical and strategic decisions, ES are designed for knowledge workers throughout the organization.

Neural Networks

Another growing branch of artificial intelligence is neural networks (NNs), computer systems that model the pattern-recognition capabilities of the human brain, thereby endowing machines with the ability to identify and classify faces, voices, pictures, and written characters. Neural networks are programs that model the interconnections of human brain cells.

The power of NNs lies in their ability to recognize patterns that are difficult for the human eye to see, and in their ability to detect and perceive correlations among hundreds of variables, unlike human beings, who can assimilate only two or three variables at a time. While most computer programs process and digest data in small chunks, a neural network digests and processes large chunks of information and this is one of the primary reasons why neural nets are excellent at pattern recognition. NNs are ideal for applications that require pattern matching, performing multiple operations simultaneously, making associations, making generalizations, and addressing situations that require learning from experience. An application where neural networks can be highly beneficial is customer surveys. While many companies may identify the preferences of their customers using surveys, few companies understand why their customers prefer certain products or services over others. Philadelphia-based Pattern Discovery, uses AI and fuzzy logic to find the "halo effect" on customers' overall perceptions and preferences. For example, in a large fast-food company, restroom cleanliness was shown to have a halo effect on diners' perception of overall food quality. In another case involving Public Service Gas & Electric in Newark, N.J., fuzzy logic showed a direct relationship between billing accuracy and how customers rated the reliability of electric service. "In other words, if you get your billing right, customers think you're providing better electric service, even though you haven't spent a cent."[13]

Other popular applications of neural nets include fraud detection, financial analysis, character recognition, and text retrieval.

A major difference between more familiar computer programs and NNs is that while other systems mechanically obey a precise set of instructions and have limited ability, if any, to learn new skills, NNs carefully select the instructions to be implemented and learn from their own experiences. Users can train an NN to recognize patterns by exposing it to a large number of examples and teaching it the difference between a desirable and an undesirable response. For example, a neural network can be taught to speak by giving it sample words, sentences, and desired pronunciations, then correcting it each time it makes a mistake. Although NNs can learn from new information, they still require human intervention because they can only do what they are taught to do.

How Neural Networks Work

A neural network is made up of interconnected processing elements (PEs), which are self-adjusting units that are tightly connected with other PEs in the system. A PE receives inputs from the user; each input has a certain weight assigned to it. The weights influence the way the input is processed by the PE, and the PE is capable of autonomously and automatically adjusting the weights of the inputs based on its past experiences. Each PE processes the input and generates a *single* output signal to other PEs in the network. The system observes the overall *pattern* of outputs generated by the PEs; this pattern forms the basis for information analysis and retrieval. Thus, unlike other computers, which are *programmed* to perform a task, neural computers are *trained* to perform a task. By controlling and fine-tuning the type and flow of information among PEs, the software gradually changes the connections between them, and in this way new information is "learned." For example, one neural network learned overnight to pronounce 20,000 words; although it spoke like a child at first, it gradually picked up speed and can now speak in full sentences.[14]

Applications of Neural Networks

In a recent survey, *Electronic Engineering Times* found that 85% of engineers surveyed in the U.S., Europe, and Japan ranked NNs as one of the hottest emerging computer technologies. Initially, NNs were slow to take off because many managers had difficulty in selling the technology to top management. "How are you going to sell a brain to your average CIO?" quips one IS manager.[15] But as the applications of neural nets have grown in nature and scope, many organizations are beginning to invest in this technology and today, attitudes toward NNs are changing. "It will become irresponsible *not* to use this technology because it provides a way to recognize complex patterns," says one user of neural nets.[16]

The applications of NNs include detection of credit card fraud. In one case, an NN helped Mellon Bank notify a customer that her credit card was stolen even before she had missed it. "This technology is making finding that needle in the haystack a lot easier," says one bank official. Another NN is a diagnostic tool called Neuroscope, developed by researchers at IBM, France, which runs on a PC and provides early warnings of failure in industrial machinery such as motors, cleaning tools, and pneumatic robots, thus making "predictive maintenance" a reality.

NNs are also used extensively in financial forecasting. By studying factors such as changing patterns in debt level, cash flow, earnings estimates, and other financial variables that measure the health of an organization, NNs are proving to be excellent forecasting tools. In many cases, they have consistently beaten the

BUSINESS REALITIES
U.S. Department of Defense

The U.S. Department of Defense stores, retrieves, and processes many gigabytes of important data on a daily basis. To increase the productivity of the knowledge workers in the agency, analysts in the employ of the Joint Chiefs of Staff were asked to develop an intelligent data retrieval system. The system had to display intelligence because "in data retrieval, a miss is as good as a mile." Non-AI data retrieval systems were found to be inadequate because even a simple data entry error would result in a failed search. NNs seemed to provide the solution.

The agency bought a neural network, called Excalibur, that "greatly reduced the odds that sloppy queries or dirty data will lead to the heartbreak of an empty screen." For example, a user typed in "Ask not what," in seconds, out of 14,000 stored documents, would come the response "Ask not what your country can do for you; ask what you can do for your country,"

from President John F. Kennedy's 1960 inaugural address.

This is possible because NNs support "fuzzy searching": the ability to search for and locate data even when not all the information relevant to the search is available or when the information is inconsistent. Another advantage of a neural network is that, like its human counterpart, the network grows smarter with use. It also recognizes search patterns that may not be so obvious to the human mind.

The network is particularly appropriate for defense databases, in which data are input through optical character recognition (OCR). Although OCR scanning can cause some errors in the data, the neural network can automatically edit and correct these errors. The agency scans approximately 3 million microfilm images and 750,000 paper pages per year by OCR into databases. Simply eliminating the need to have humans edit the errors caused by scanners has resulted in significant savings of time and money for the agency. An NN can also handle images, and the FBI plans to use NNs for fingerprint recognition.[17]

Standard and Poor 500 at forecasting stock prices and have advised clients to sell stocks weeks before their prices began to fall.

Neural networks also perform real estate appraisals by taking into account variables such as location, interior layout, and building materials. The appraisals of the NN are more consistent and accurate than those of human appraisers, because the system also compares and studies data on similar houses in similar markets. While human beings are capable of taking into account only a few factors and analyzing their correlations, NNs take into account a large number of factors and perform a detailed analysis of the correlation among hundreds of variables. This is why they often outperform human experts.

Airlines in the U.S., Great Britain, and Australia are beginning to use NNs to forecast load factors and revenues; this technique has proven to be 20% more accurate than conventional forecasting methods. The NN predicts the estimated number of passengers on a plane and the fare that each passenger is likely to pay. It can even anticipate demand based on time of day, day of the week, and season, thus helping airlines to better meet fluctuating demand. The U.S. Department of Defense uses a neural network for data retrieval (see box).

One of the biggest advantages of NNs is that they do not require any special hardware and can easily be integrated with existing applications and technologies, such as spreadsheets and expert systems.[18] Successful use of NNs requires only a good understanding of the organization, its data, the business processes that generate the data, and the business implications of the data.

Summary

- **Artificial intelligence and its various branches.**
  Artificial intelligence is a field of study that designs and develops machines capable of performing tasks that would require intelligence if performed by a human being. The goal of AI is to create "intelligent machines" by modeling human intelligence in computers. A machine that can reason, learn, understand, recall, and explain its behavior and actions can be viewed as an intelligent machine. *Artificial intelligence* is a broad term that covers many branches of study, such as expert systems, computer vision, speech synthesis, speech recognition, natural language, neural networks, and robotics.

- **The attributes of intelligence.**
  Intelligence can be defined as a set of attributes that are frequently associated with intelligence, such as the abilities to think, process, reason, and solve complex problems, to apply knowledge, intuition, and judgment in problem solving, to reason with conflicting, inaccurate, or uncertain information, and to learn from past experiences and modify one's behavior accordingly.

- **An expert system and its components.**
  An expert system is a program designed to model the expertise of a human expert in a specialized field of study, where expertise is defined as the product of judgment, knowledge, and experience. An expert system has five main components: the knowledge base, the inference engine, the user interface, the working memory, and the explanation module. The knowledge base is a repository of knowledge; the inference engine is the reasoning mechanism of the system; the user interface facilitates user interaction with the system; the working memory keeps track of the problem-solving process and its results; and the explanation module addresses queries regarding the problem-solving process.

- **The role of neural networks in information processing.**
  A neural network is a program that models the capabilities of the human brain; it consists of a network of processors that are connected, and behave, like neurons. Neural networks can find patterns that may not be obvious to the human eye and can detect and perceive correlations among hundreds of variables, whereas humans can consider only two or three variables at a time.

Review Questions

1. Why is knowledge a critical organizational resource? How can an expert system help in the collection, coordination, and dissemination of knowledge?
2. Describe artificial intelligence. Identify some of the fields of study that have influenced artificial intelligence.
3. Name the different branches of AI and briefly describe them.
4. Describe each of the following in a sentence or two: robots, natural language processing, and computer vision.
5. Describe an expert system and give some reasons why it has continued to be one of the most successful applications of AI.
6. What are some characteristics of applications that are well suited to the use of expert systems? Is tax analysis a good application for expert systems? If so, why?
7. What are the differences among knowledge acquisition, knowledge representation, and knowledge engineering? Why is knowledge acquisition a challenging task?
8. What are the five components of an expert system? Briefly describe each one.
9. What is the difference between deductive reasoning and inductive reasoning? Backward chaining and forward chaining? Give an example of each.
10. Why is object-attribute-value a good way to represent knowledge? Can you give an example of OAV?

11. Describe the role of the knowledge base and the inference engine in problem solving.

12. What is a neural network and how does it differ from more familiar software? Give two examples of neural networks.

 Discussion Questions

1. Computer help desks handle hardware, software, and network queries or problems. With the spread of PCs, the number of computer users has multiplied many-fold, increasing the challenge for help desk personnel. Kaiser Permanente, of northern California, which serves nearly 2.4 million patients at its various medical centers, realized that its help facility was lacking in many ways. Its data center received almost 2,000 calls per day from employees requiring technical assistance with their computers and the phone lines were frequently jammed. When callers did get through to the help desk, the personnel did not always have the answers to their questions.

   Kaiser decided to build an expert-system-based help desk that uses voice response systems to assist help desk personnel with callers. The voice response system answers simple and straightforward queries without human intervention; the expert system helps solve complex cases that might otherwise have required the intervention of a human expert.[19]

   Explain why an expert system is suitable for modeling a help desk.

   Would "canned" explanations, customized explanations, or both be useful for this application? Discuss.

2. Carnegie Group, one of the leading developers of expert system technology, has developed an expert system called the Service Bay Diagnostic System (SBDS) for the Ford Motor Company to solve problems related to dealer servicing of automobiles. Ford was facing a unique problem in its servicing department: As the complexity of its cars increased, auto mechanics felt it was easier to throw away a subassembly rather than to fix a defective component in the subassembly, with the result that warranty costs were skyrocketing at Ford. The company realized that part of the problem was lack of training for its auto mechanics and invested in an expert system.

   The 20,000 rule, user-friendly diagnostic system guides mechanics through the process of diagnosing and repairing defective parts. The system provides detailed instructions on repairing and replacing a part in a subassembly and walks the auto mechanic through the process in a step-by-step fashion. The immediate result has been a significant decline in the number of subassemblies discarded. This has not only lowered warranty costs, but has also resulted in faster service delivery, which subsequently led to improvements in the J. D. Power satisfaction ratings. The system has also become an excellent training tool for hundreds of mechanics in dealerships all over the country.[20]

   One of the primary goals of an expert system is to gather and disseminate knowledge. What knowledge did this system help to disseminate and how did this benefit Ford?

   Explain why an expert system is suitable for solving this problem.

3. Identify some business applications in which an association between neural nets and spreadsheets would be beneficial.

4. Carefully define a problem in any area of interest to you (finance, marketing, accounting, and so on), then identify an expert in that area. Interview the expert and try to determine the knowledge and judgment that the expert would use to solve your problem. Identify some of the challenges that you faced in the process of acquiring knowledge from the expert.

ETHICAL ISSUES

Case 1: Fighting Fire with Fire

Sometimes computers are part of the solution; at other times, they are part of the problem. In the 1980s, a man and his sons stole $16 million from Medicaid by programming their medical clinic's computer to generate phony claims for nearly 400,000 phantom patient visits. But computers are also part of the solution to the nation's $84 billion problem with medical billing fraud and abuse.

Many insurance firms are using expert systems to screen thousands of incoming claims for overcharges. Using the expertise of eminent physicians, the claims-auditing expert systems look for evidence of "code gaming," or manipulation of the five-digit codes for medical diagnoses and procedures to increase a doctor's reimbursements. Most medical fraud involves billing for work never done, but overpayments are also very common in the industry.[21]

1. Explain how a computer can be both a problem and solution in the health care industry.
2. Could the father and son in this case use an expert system to steal money? What measures, if any, should developers take to ensure that their systems are not used for wrongful purposes?

Case 2: Hidden Knowledge

An expert system is only as good as the knowledge that is modeled in the system. However, knowledge acquisi-tion is not an easy task. Sometimes experts are reluctant to share their knowledge out of fear that they may lose their jobs or that their perceived value to the company may diminish. In fact, the development of some expert systems has had to be abandoned because experts were reluctant to share their knowledge.

1. If you were an expert, what are some reasons why you might be unwilling to share your knowledge?
2. Is unwillingness to share knowledge unethical or understandable? What steps can be organization take to win the cooperation of the expert?

Case 3: Who's to Blame?

Expert systems are sometimes used in life-threatening situations. For example, many expert systems are used in medicine to diagnose and even to treat patients. Suppose that a physician prescribes a certain drug based on an incorrect recommendation by an expert system and causes serious harm to a patient.

1. Who, if anyone, should be held responsible for the actions of the physician: the physician, the expert, or the knowledge engineer? Explain your answer.
2. Do you think that the system should be treated like a human expert and held to the same professional standards? Should the liability of expert systems be limited?

PROBLEM SOLVING IN THE REAL WORLD

Case 1: Doctors Fight Infections with Artificial Intelligence

At LDS Hospital, in Salt Lake City, Utah, an expert system helps doctors select the best antibiotic for a given patient. For example, when a critically ill hospital patient has a severe cough, the doctor may suspect a lung infection. However, deciding on the proper antibiotic treatment is exceedingly complex, especially because the doctor must often decide on the antibiotic even before test results are available. Factors that should be taken into account before prescribing antibiotics include the patient's medical history, the most likely bacterial culprits, the most inexpensive drug that is effective against all of the bacteria in that class, the proper dosage, and possible drug interactions.

Since this is a complex and knowledge-intensive problem, an expert system is well suited to this application. The expert system developed by LDS Hospital is considered to be "the most complex artificial intelligence system ever created for clinical decision-making." Termed the "antibiotic computer consultant," the system runs on a fault-tolerant mainframe and is part of a hospital-wide information system called Health Evaluation through Logical Processing (HELP).

It has been found that physicians who use the expert system make better decisions and make them faster. The computer has suggested the best antibiotic regimen for 94% of the cases studied, whereas unaided physicians have had only a 77% success rate. Because doctors are notorious for disliking computers, the best measure of the system is its popularity with the doctors, who in fact use it an average of three times per day. 85% of the physicians agreed that the program improved their antibiotic selection and 81% said that it even improved patient care. Today, use of the expert system has expanded to include all cases involving antibiotics, including those prescribed to prevent infection during surgery, in outpatient clinics, and in five other hospitals within the Intermountain Health Care conglomerate.

The system accesses the electronic medical records of a patient and carefully examines several variables in that patient's health history. It then looks for similar cases nationwide over the last 10 years to gain a better understanding of the disease. Only after it has analyzed the disease and the history of the patient does the system make a recommendation.[22]

1. Give at least two reasons why the system outperforms the physician in its ability to prescribe the appropriate antibiotic.
2. Why is this problem well suited for modeling in an expert system? Are knowledge collaboration and coordination important for this problem? Explain.

Case 2: Moopi Scheduler: The Real Expert

Today, custom ordering of goods and services is becoming more and more common and is gradually replacing mass merchandising for many manufactur-

(Continued on next page)

ers. As the trend toward custom ordering of goods and services grows, software that allows managers to make instant adjustments in their production schedules is becoming vital for many companies.

Cobe Laboratories, in Lakewood, Colorado, is one such company. It uses an automated production scheduling system called Moopi (an acronym for the French translation of *Industrial Production Sequencing Optimizing Method*). Cobe manufactures about 3,750 kidney dialysis machines per year. Its ability to schedule work and, even more important, to have the flexibility to reschedule work at short notice is important to the growth and success of the company.

Before Moopi, Cobe scheduled its production the old-fashioned way: Using paper and pencil, production managers manually developed a schedule. Each time there was a change in existing orders or new orders arrived, the entire schedule had to be manually redone. Since schedulers based their decisions on sales projections, which were uncertain to begin with, any changes in the sales projections meant redoing the schedule. Hence, scheduling was a time-consuming, labor-intensive process (sometimes taking days). This also meant that the medical equipment manufacturer lacked the flexibility to respond to changing customer demands or to handle unforeseen events on the plant floor. A bottleneck here, a late delivery of parts there, or a change in a custom order threw the schedule out of line. These were compelling reasons for Cobe to look for new solutions to the scheduling problem.

The company developed Moopi, which is based in part on a rule-based system that models the decision-making capabilities of scheduling experts. The product is designed specifically to address the issue of how to schedule new orders or custom orders without disrupting the existing schedule. Moopi allows schedulers to simulate, almost instantly, the impact of any new order on orders already in the queue, or on the rest of the plant, or even on suppliers. If Moopi uncovers a potential bottleneck, it also provides solutions for overcoming the bottleneck by using a trial-and-error approach that is similar to the thought processes that a human scheduler would go through.

The benefits of such a system are enormous. First, it has helped Cobe to become much more responsive to customers' needs. As new orders come in, the schedule can easily be modified to accommodate the orders. Second, plant efficiency has increased significantly, because the machines are now better utilized. Finally, it relieves managers to address problems on the shop floor instead of spending days drawing up a schedule that may have to be revised many times before it is actually implemented.[23]

1. Describe Moopi and identify some of its benefits.
2. Is forward chaining, backward chaining, or mixed chaining appropriate for this application?

References

Barker, Virginia E. and Dennis E. O'Conner. "Expert Systems for Configuration at Digital: XCON and Beyond." *Communications of the ACM* (March 1989).

Byrd, Terry Anthony. "Implementation and Use of Expert Systems in Organizations: Perceptions of Knowledge Engineers." *Journal of Management Information Systems* 8, no. 4 (Spring 1992).

Cox, Carl. "Solving Problems with Fuzzy Logic." *AI Expert* (March 1992).

Feigenbaum, Edward A. "The Art of Artificial Intelligence: Themes and Case Studies in Knowledge Engineering." *Proceeding of the IJCAI* 5 (1977).

Hinton, Gregory. "How Neural Networks Learn from Experience." *Scientific American* (September 1992).

Leonard-Barton, Dorothy and John J. Sviokla. "Putting Expert Systems to Work." *Harvard Business Review* (March–April 1988).

Meador, C. Lawrence and Ed. G. Mahler. "Choosing an Expert System Game Plan." *Datamation* (August 1, 1990).

Michaelson, Robert and Donald Michie. "Expert Systems in Business." *Datamation* (November 1983).

Motiwalla, Luvia and Jay F. Nunamaker, Jr. "Mail-Man: A Knowledge-Based MAIL Assistant for Managers." *Journal for Organizational Computing* 2, no. 2, 1992.

Mykytyn, Kathleen, Peter P. Mykytyn, Jr., and Craig W. Sinkman. "Expert Systems: A Question of Liability." *MIS Quarterly* 14, no. 1 (March 1990).

Rich, Elaine. *Artificial Intelligence*. New York: McGraw-Hill, 1983.

Stylianou, Anthony C., Gregory R. Madey, and Robert D. Smith. "Selection Criteria for Expert System Shells: A Socio-Technical Framework." *Communications of the ACM* 35, no. 10 (October 1992).

Sviokla, John J. "Expert Systems and Their Impact on the Firm: The Effects of PlanPower Use on the Information Processing Capacity of the Financial Collaborative." *Journal of Management Information Systems* 6, no. 3 (Winter 1989–90).

Trippi, Robert and Efraim Turban. "The Impact of Parallel and Neural Computing on Managerial Decision Making." *Journal of Management Information Systems* 6, no. 3 (Winter 1989–90).

Turban, Efraim and Paul R. Watkins. "Integrating Expert Systems and Decision Support Systems." *MIS Quarterly* (June 1986).

Apte, Uday, Chetan S. Sankar, Meru Thakur, and Joel E. Turner. "Reusability-Based Strategy for Development of Information Systems: Implementation Experience of a Bank." *MIS Quarterly* 14, no. 4 (September 1988).

Haavind, Robert. "Software's New Object Lesson." *Technology Review* (February–March 1992).

Joyce, Edward J. "Reusable Software: Passage to Productivity." *Datamation* (September 15, 1988).

Korson, Timothy D. and Vijay K. Vaishnavi. "Managing Emerging Software Technologies: A Technology Transfer Framework." *Communications of the ACM* 35, no. 9 (September 1992).

Korson, Tim and John D. McGregor. "Understanding Object-Oriented: A Unifying Paradigm." *Communications of the ACM* 33, no. 9 (September 1990).

Lauriston, Robert. "OS/2 Versus Windows NT." *PC World* (February 1993).

Littlewood, Bev and Lorenzo Strigini. "The Risks of Software." *Scientific American* 267, no. 5 (November 1992).

Nerson, Jean-Marc. "Applying Object-Oriented Analysis and Design." *Communications of the ACM* 35, no. 9 (September 1992).

Notes

1. Anthes, Gary H. "FAA Expert System Aims Sky High," *Computerworld,* March 7, 1994, pp. 73–75.
2. Ballou, Melinda-Carol. "Guten Tag! Bonjour! Good Day!" *Computerworld,* September 21, p. 28.
3. Betts, Mitch. "Robots Deliver Medicines, Savings to Hospitals," *Computerworld,* April 11, 1994, p. 66.
4. Caldwell, Bruce. "Survival of the Fastest: FedEx's 20th Birthday Present: A Blank Check for IS," *InformationWeek,* April 5, 1993, pp. 40–41.
5. Ballou, Melinda-Carol. "Expert System Modernizes Kaiser," *Computerworld,* November 14, 1994, p. 121.
6. McDuffie, R. Steve. "Tax Expert Systems and Benefits from Using Them," *The National Public Accountant,* October 1992, pp. 16, 54.
7. Hoffman, Thomas. "Security Demands Fuel Growing Industry," *Computerworld,* April 24, 1995, p. 82.
8. "Customs Service Tracks Down Illegal Cargo," *OR/MS Today,* December 1994, p. 10.
9. Ying, Tong. "Singapore Airlines Moves into Intelligent Systems," *Computerworld,* June 5, 1995, p. 81.
10. France, Mike. "Smart Contracts," *Forbes ASAP,* August 29, 1994, pp. 117–118.
11. Turban, E. *Decision Support and Expert Systems,* Macmillan Publishing Company, 1993, p. 433.
12. "Merced County's MAGIC Act," *CIO,* January 1993, p. 104.
13. King, Julia. "AI Determines Customer Preference," *Computerworld,* November 14, 1994, p. 120.
14. Bylinsky, Gene. "Computers That Learn," *Fortune,* September 6, 1993, pp. 96–102.
15. Ibid.
16. Mayor, T. "Neural Net Gains," *CIO,* April 15, 1994, pp. 68–74.
17. Anthes, Gary H. "How the Feds Find Data," *Computerworld,* August 30, 1993, pp. 47, 50.
18. Vizard, Michael. "Neural Net Program Gives Excel Users Added Power," *Computerworld,* January 24, 1994 p. 39.
19. Bartholomew, Doug. "Kaiser's Help Desk Gets a Transplant: New System Uses Voice Response, Expert Systems to Free Staff," *InformationWeek,* August 17, 1992, p. 18.
20. Newquist, H. P. "AI Burnout," *Computerworld,* April 18, 1994, pp. 134–135.
21. Betts, Mitch. "Health Fraud: Computer at War," *Computerworld,* September 13, 1993, pp. 1, 14.
22. Betts, Mitch. "Doctors Get Help to Fight Infections," *Computerworld,* June 6, 1994, p. 67.
23. Bartholomew, Doug. "The Schedule's the Thing," *InformationWeek,* May 23, 1994, p. 48.

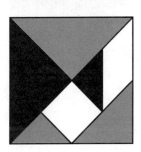

10

Office Automation

Contents

Learning Objectives
Technology Payoff: International Foundation for Art Research
Introduction
The Virtual Corporation
Types of Office Automation Systems
 Electronic Publishing and Processing Systems
  Document Management Systems
  Multimedia
  Imaging
 Communication Systems
  E-Mail
  Fax
  Voice Mail
 Electronic Meeting Systems
  Audio Conferencing
  Video Conferencing
  Groupware
Summary
Review Questions
Discussion Questions
Ethical Issues
 Case 1: Videoconferencing for Prisoners: An Ethical Dilemma
 Case 2: Shredding E-mail: The Iran-Contra Affair
 Case 3: The Wrath of a Fired Employee
 Case 4: Mind Your Own Affairs!
 Case 5: Computerized Performance Monitoring

Problem Solving in the Real World
    Case 1: A Leading Jeweler Buys into Office Automation
    Case 2: Quintiles Transnational
References
Notes

Learning Objectives

This chapter provides a broad overview of office automation, which encompasses the techniques and systems that facilitate oral and written communications in the workplace. Some office automation tools are word processing, desktop publishing, multimedia, imaging, electronic mail, voice mail, fax machines, groupware, and videoconferencing. In this chapter, we identify the broad categories of office automation tools and discuss their impact on office productivity. After reading and studying this chapter, you should be able to

* Discuss the role of office automation in enhancing the productivity of knowledge workers
* Identify broad categories of office automation tools
* Describe office automation tools that facilitate written communications and their contribution to productivity
* Describe office automation tools that facilitate oral communications and their contribution to productivity

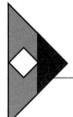

TECHNOLOGY PAYOFF

International Foundation for Art Research

Even in New York, the phone call might have seemed extraordinary. An FBI agent was describing a wild-eyed man in a dark outfit, riding a horse, pursued by two naked women—two naked, flying women. But to Constance Lowenthal, the executive director of the International Foundation for Art Research (IFAR), "it clicked automatically" as she realized that the detective was fumbling to describe an oil painting by the French artist Eugene Delacroix, "Tam O'Shanter Pursued by Witches." The detective was pursuing an art thief who was trying to sell the stolen masterpiece. With a few keystrokes, Lowenthal confirmed the agent's suspicions.

Art theft has been going on for centuries, but its pace has accelerated recently. In the last two decades or so, more than 60,000 works of art, valued at more than $3 billion, have been stolen. Until recently, once a famous or valuable piece of art disappeared, chances of recovery were slim. That's changing, partly because of the Art Loss Register (ALR).

ALR was set up in 1991, as a collaborative venture by the IFAR, major auction houses such as Sotheby's and Christie's, and several London insurance brokerages, in an effort to coordinate art-theft investigations. With fewer than two dozen staffers and offices in New York and London, it has been instrumental in recovering hundreds of treasures, valued at nearly $20 million, including Pablo Picasso's "Head of a Woman with Golden Earrings," Edgar Degas' "Dancer Fixing

Her Shoe," and a Roman sculpture of Jupiter Capitolinus. One of the secrets of ALR's success is an information technology called multimedia.

This is how it works: From a townhouse office near Fifth Avenue, ALR's New York staffers compare their list of stolen art with multimedia database that contains descriptions and images of the hundreds of items that appear on the international auction block every month. Items appearing in both databases are flagged and investigated. If a Jan Vermeer painting is to be auctioned in southern France next week, ALR investigators in New York and London can tap into an OS/2-based LAN and call up a full-color image of the work, along with the details of its dimensions and conditions.

The database is divided into seven groups: Fine Arts, Decorative Arts, Antiques, Enthographic Objects, Asian Art, Islamic Art, and Miscellaneous Objects. These categories are further subdivided by object, type, and school, along with a brief description of each work, its IFAR catalog number, and the date and place of its theft. Each night, ALR's New York and London offices update each other's files using modems. By 1996, ALR expects its database to contain 65,000 images and to be able to identify up to 150,000 items offered in auction-house sales.[1]

Many IS professionals who excel at providing work group computing solutions will end up running their organizations before this decade is over.

—John Denovan, senior consultant[2]

Introduction

Office automation systems (OAS)
Computer-based information systems whose primary purpose is to facilitate oral and written communication between individuals and groups.

Office automation systems (OAS), also referred to as office information systems, are systems whose primary goal is to facilitate communications. Such a system is a set of tools that gather, process, store, retrieve, and disseminate information between individual workers, team of workers, and business entities, both inside and outside the organization. Figure 10–1 shows some office automation tools, such as word processing, desktop publishing, image processing, groupware, E-mail, voice mail, fax machines, multimedia, computer conferencing, and videoconferencing. Table 10–1 summarizes the various kinds of office automation tools and provides a brief description of each.

For many years, office communication was considered to be a clerical function. However, today, systems that support workplace communications are viewed as important systems that must be actively managed. This new approach has placed OAS in the same league as TPS, MIS, and ISS. For example, Japan (see box), which is a world leader in high-quality products and business efficiency, is lagging behind other nations in office automation and is making a serious effort to upgrade its office communications.

The electronic office of today looks dramatically different from the mechanized office of just a few years ago, when typewriters, mechanical devices, and the postal system were the primary means of communication. But even more dramatic changes are in store. We are beginning to witness the *virtual corporation,* which gives people the ability to work from anyplace without being confined by physical boundaries. Virtual corporations and their implications for organizations are discussed in the next section.

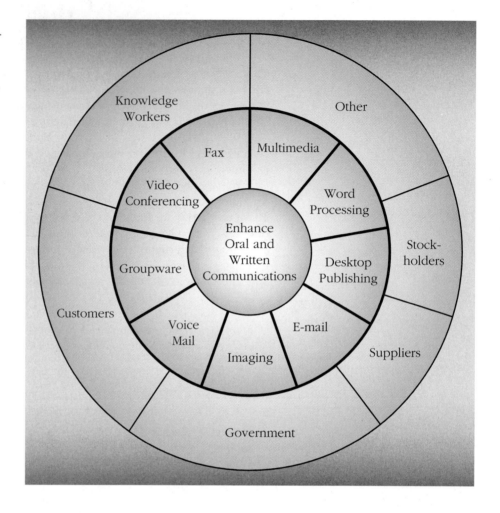

The Virtual Corporation

Virtual corporation
A firm whose employers and employees are not limited by a physical work environment, but instead use communications technology to work from anywhere and at anytime.

Experts predict that the trend toward an electronic virtual workplace will continue unabated in the coming years. The **virtual corporation** is a revolutionary idea that was popularized by consultant William Davidow a few years ago. It is a group of employers and employees who are not bound by a physical work environment, but instead use technology to come together temporarily and communicate to achieve a shared business goal. In a virtual corporation, employees don't come to a place called work; instead, they can work from anywhere, at any time; thus businesses need not invest in office space, furniture, and other amenities.

Although today there are only a few virtual corporations, their number is expected to increase significantly in the coming years as mobile computing technologies become commonplace. Mobile computing allows workers at remote locations to dial up the office, retrieve messages and urgent documents via touchtone phones or voice recognition systems, and give directions to their coworkers in the organization as easily as if they were in the same building. Clearly, the virtual office will create a different kind of knowledge worker and pose new challenges for management.

Tool	Type of Data	Computer	Description	Technology
Word Processing	Written	Yes	Programs that make it easy to create and alter documents.	Computer, printer
Desktop Publishing	Written	Yes	Programs with extensive word processing and graphic capabilities.	High-resolution computer, printer
Imaging	Written, graphic	Yes	Imaging converts paper, microfilm, microfiche, and electronic data into digital images that can be printed, faxed, or viewed on a computer screen.	Scanner, optical disks, workstation
E-mail	Written	Yes	Programs that allow individuals, who are linked through a network, to electronically communicate with each other, any time, anywhere in the world.	Computer, network
Fax	Written	No	Uses telephone lines to transmit documents.	Fax machine, telephone
Groupware	Oral, written, visual	Yes	A broad term given to communication tools such as E-mail, voice, fax, and videoconferencing, that foster group decision making.	A multitude of tools are used in groupware. The nature of the tool depends on the kind of application
Multimedia	Written, audio, visual	Yes	A computer-based tool that uses a graphical and interactive interface and combines two or more media types, such as text, graphics, animation, audio, and video. Today, many computers have multimedia capabilities which include a sound card and a video card.	Multimedia computer and printer
Voice Mail	Oral	Yes	The sender's voice message is processed by a modem and stored in a server at the receiver's end. When the receiver is ready to receive the message, the digitized message is retrieved from the server and reconverted into analog signals.	Telephone, server, network
Videoconfer-encing	Oral, visual	No	A type of electronic meeting system that uses telephone, television, computers and communication links to allow geographically separated decision makers to hear and see each other.	Telephone, television, network

T A B L E 1 0 – 1
The various kinds of office automation tools and the equipment needed to support these tools.

"Successful managers will know how to differentiate when it is appropriate to use technology to share resources and when a face-to-face meeting is called for. Managers will 'roll with the punches' in responding quickly to electronic needs. Managers who can't cope with a feeling of losing control over unseen employees are heading for trouble. They will be recycled into a different function."[3]

Perhaps the greatest challenges will be the culture shock and the lack of control that managers may feel when they face quiet corridors and invisible employees. The personal lives of employees will also be affected, because the virtual

A GLOBAL PERSPECTIVE
Japan

For the past two decades, Japanese factories have won worldwide admiration and praise for their ability to churn out high-quality products, using high-tech production methods. However, when it comes to office automation, they are still in the stone age. Most senior managers still have a serious allergy to computers that prevents them from touching a keyboard.

A quick tour of an office of Nikko Securities, one of Japan's largest brokerages, provides a snapshot of the typical Japanese workplace. In big, open, smoke-filled rooms, long rows of gray desks face each other. Standard office equipment includes the latest fax machines and copiers, but a computer on a desktop is extremely rare. Usually a group of employees shares one word processor, and E-mail is still a rarity in Japan.

Leading the way in IT advancement and office automation is Shiseido, Japan's oldest and largest cosmetics company, which has long been incorporating Western technology and management concepts into its otherwise traditionally Japanese operation. However, today, even Shiseido is struggling to find a balance that will work for the 1990s.

Founded in 1872 as Japan's first Western-style pharmacy, the company is located in the posh Ginza district of Tokyo. Now a household word in Japan, Shiseido boasts annual worldwide sales of about $4.9 billion. The company attributes much of its success to its relatively early embrace of computers and networks. Shiseido started using IBM computers in 1957—well ahead of other Japanese companies—to track orders, plan products, and handle logistic operations. During the 1960s and 1970s, the company computerized the distribution network for its core products. "Our corporate culture has always been a mix of modern science with Japanese business practices," says a company spokesperson.

Today, one of the most challenging tasks facing the company is to raise office productivity and efficiency without blindly embracing technology. "Efficiency alone would make us a cold company. Heart-to-heart communication is so important." Further, in Japan, productivity at the expense of layoffs often runs counter to the tradition of lifetime employment that has been a part of the tradition of Shiseido and most large Japanese companies.

However, the younger generation of Shiseido managers is growing impatient for change and is pressing for greater use of office automation and for reducing the number of workers.[4]

office guarantees around-the-clock electronic access to any employee, any time, anywhere in the world, thus increasing the potential for employee burnout. Also since the success of the virtual office depends to a large extent on technology and its applications, technology decisions and failures will be critical to organizational success. Finally, in a virtual office, communicating with employees assumes new importance. Avon Products, the New York–based beauty products manufacturer, with a worldwide staff of 1.7 million mobile salespeople, manages its virtual office through continuous communications with its employees. "The motivation of people is emotional, [so] we have to get together every couple of weeks in person because people support each other and share experiences. You can't do that over the phone or with a conference call."[5]

In summary, any discussion of office automation must be based on the understanding that tremendous change is on the way and that new approaches to information sharing will fundamentally change the way knowledge workers receive, process, and disseminate information.

Types of Office Automation Systems

Office automation systems can be broadly divided into two categories: Electronic publishing and processing systems, and electronic meeting systems. Figure 10–2 classifies office automation systems into electronic publishing and processing systems, which facilitate written and voice communi-

The two broad categories of office automation systems and the different types of systems under each category.

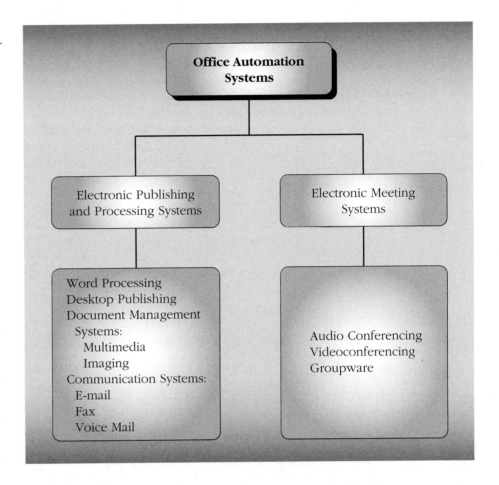

Office Automation Systems

Electronic Publishing and Processing Systems

Electronic Meeting Systems

Word Processing
Desktop Publishing
Document Management
    Systems:
        Multimedia
        Imaging
Communication Systems:
    E-mail
    Fax
    Voice Mail

Audio Conferencing
Videoconferencing
Groupware

cation, and electronic meeting systems, which focus primarily on communications within groups.

Electronic Publishing and Processing Systems

Electronic publishing and processing systems include word processing and desktop publishing (covered in chapter 4), document management systems (multimedia and imaging), and communication systems (E-mail, fax, and voice mail).

Document Management Systems **Document management systems (DMS)** are computer-based tools that provide access to repositories of data, regardless of their form (text, graphics, or images) or location. The retrieved documents can be displayed in a wide variety of formats, edited, distributed, and integrated using other communication systems, such as word processing and desktop publishing. Such systems allow knowledge workers to better control, coordinate, and manage the myriad electronic documents used in decision making.

For example, the Douglas Aircraft division of McDonnell Douglas developed a text retrieval system that replaced its paper-based technical guides and procedure manuals and is saving the division about $500,000 each year. Encyclopaedia Britannica, in Chicago, uses document management systems to allow users to create new products by mixing and matching various documents, thus promoting the idea of "reusable text."[6]

Document management systems Computer-based tools that allow users to access text and graphics, regardless of where they are located and in what form the data are stored.

Two popular types of document management systems are multimedia and imaging.

Multimedia

An interactive system that combines several types of media, such as text, graphics, animation, audio, and video. Most multimedia applications require a sound card, a video card, and a CD-ROM drive.

Multimedia   **Multimedia** encompasses a group of computer-based technologies that integrate different types of media, such as text, graphics, animation, audio, and video, to generate information. Multimedia is made possible by integrating audio and video capabilities into personal computers. Besides the usual CPU and peripherals, for a computer to have multimedia capabilities it should also have a CD-ROM drive, stereo speakers, a microphone for voice input, a sound card, a video card, and a video compression card. (Some of these elements were discussed in Chapter 3.)

Multimedia was used to track 1,700 athletes—and to create images of players on badges—for the 1994 World Cup soccer tournament.[7] It is used to teach languages to 1,200 foreign students at the Air Force Academy, to "walk" potential homeowners through remote properties, and to use images of athletes to promote sales of Reebok running shoes at retail sales meetings. Multimedia kiosks were

---

A GLOBAL PERSPECTIVE

Elections in South Africa

No one doubts that the 1994 elections in the Republic of South Africa were a historic event. But one aspect of this drama that has received little recognition is the critical role multimedia applications played in educating voters. In a country plagued by poor communications, an inadequate infrastructure, violence, and literacy problems, a small company called Sandenbergh Pavon undertook the Herculean task of providing information to first-time voters using multimedia kiosks.

When an election involves about 16 million first-time voters, 39 million people who have never dealt with a computer, and 19 political parties, the task of voter education is a daunting one. But the historic election in South Africa had some help from advanced multimedia kiosks throughout the country.

Each kiosk consisted of a 14-inch color monitor and a 486-based PC featuring color photos, digitized one-minute video messages from the candidates, and the mission statements of their political parties. The kiosks used interactive touch screens that looked the same as the actual election ballot and provided voters with all the information necessary to make an informed choice.

The kiosk application was created using IconAuthor, a multimedia application development system that allows

developers to combine text, graphics, animation, full-motion video, and sound for interactive presentations. The kiosk project required about 3 months of development work with the European Economic Community and UNESCO (United Nations Economic, Scientific, and Cultural Organization). However, most of the actual authoring, construction, and installation was done in the 3 weeks prior to the election by Sandenbergh Pavon's 13-person company. The total cost to UNESCO was $15,000 per kiosk, which covered the hardware and software as well as the development work.

The system was designed to be very flexible, making it easy to update information as the political landscape changed. "The design is very friendly. They hear the kiosk saying 'Come touch me,' and when they touch it, a crowd forms very quickly," says Sandenbergh. The only drawback is that the kiosks are not networked. "I would like to have been able to network them all," he adds. "But that's South Africa heaven."

A total of 30 kiosks were rotated around the country to 70 different sites. "We tried to make the kiosks as graphical and simple as possible, since many illiterate people were voting for the first time." Over 1 million people have used the kiosks since they were rolled out in February 1994. The project has been so successful that UNESCO is lobbying to create similar projects in Europe and Africa.[8]

used during the recent elections in Africa (see box), which involved almost 16 million voters. Any problem that requires the integration of text, graphics, sound, and video can be approached by using multimedia.

In particular, multimedia is very useful in corporate training and business presentations. For example, the transportation company CSX uses a multimedia training network to train its 30,000 employees, in 19 states and Canada, in a number of procedures ranging from conducting train inspections to handling hazardous materials. The integration of different forms of media often helps to capture and retain the attention of trainees. Further, the company has found that a multimedia system sometimes costs less than a single traditional training program. Besides, multimedia is interactive (allows two-way communication) and provides consistency in the content and the delivery of training material. Another advantage of using multimedia for training is that the material can be accessed by trainees at their convenience and can be viewed at any desired pace.[9]

Imaging　Most organizations have a large number of paper documents to be processed and preserved for future use. For example, a human resources department often has to keep copies of educational degrees, certifications, birth certificates, social security numbers, and so on. Other functional units keep paper-based documents such as invoices, credit and debit slips, return items, memos, and so on. **Imaging** digitizes documents—that is, it converts paper, microfilm, microfiche, and electronic documents into digital form so that the original documents can be discarded. Thus, instead of taking up space in cabinets and storehouses, all the necessary information is stored in digital form. Once digitized, documents can be readily accessed, regardless of their physical location, and can be edited, printed, faxed, or viewed on a computer screen.

An imaging system consists of scanners that digitize the images, workstations or PCs for processing the images, imaging software, and high-capacity storage devices, such as optical disks. For example, one kind of imaging software that is essential for most applications is the index server, which keeps an index of all documents in the system for easy retrieval. Therefore, when a document is digitized, it is immediately indexed according to its name, its date, and any other relevant criteria.

The greatest benefit of imaging systems is the decrease in storage costs. In cities such as New York, where space is at a premium, this can be vital. Imaging also increases worker productivity because it allows instantaneous access to documents. In many organizations, considerable time is spent looking for documents. Knowledge workers also spend a great deal of time filing documents. Imaging eliminates the need for such unproductive tasks. Another significant benefit of imaging is that it allows more than one person to view or analyze a document at the same time. In the absence of an imaging system, only one person can work on a document; this creates a sequential work flow system in which one person works on a document, then passes it on to the next. Imaging changes the work flow from sequential to parallel, increasing productivity.

At Caterpillar, Inc., in Peoria, Illinois, 43,000 images of the company's products, their components, and the people who use the equipment are stored in an imaging system called C-Quest. The marketing staff uses these digital images (which contain product names, model numbers, and machine types) to produce advertising pamphlets, dealer brochures, training literature, and specification documents. In less than 10 seconds, the system can retrieve up to 18 images that

Imaging systems

A type of document management system that converts paper, microfilm, microfiche, and electronic data into digitized images that can be printed, faxed, or viewed on a computer screen.

match a given criterion and even provide information as to where the originals are filed. "We estimate savings of at least $250 every time somebody uses the system to find an image they need instead of spending money to shoot the same thing." The system can also be accessed by manufacturing and production and any other unit at the same time, further increasing productivity.[10]

Another imaging program, called K.I.D.S. (Kid Identification Digital System), in California, creates digitized photos and fingerprints of missing children, stores them on a CD-ROM, and makes them accessible to law enforcement agencies all over the country.[11]

The IRS uses digital imaging to scan incoming tax forms, digitize them, and record taxpayer data. An OCR reads the taxpayer data and converts any hand-written numbers on the form into computer data for further processing. The imaging system is expected to result in faster tax refunds.[12]

Connecticut Mutual credits imaging systems for its increased responsiveness to customer claims and requests (see box). After an imaging system was installed, the processing of death claims was cut from 3 weeks to 3 days; the processing of title and beneficiary changes, which once took days, now takes seconds; and printed statements listing a client's entire policy holdings are also produced online in seconds, instead of hours or days. This has not only increased customer satisfaction but has also helped the company to attract new customers.[13]

Norfolk Southern, in Atlanta, is a 166-year-old railroad whose tracks cover 14,500 miles in 20 states and Canada. The company is using an advanced imaging system to digitize paper records such as maps and deeds; some of these pre-date the company and some even survived the Civil War. About 250 users, with 486 PCs running Windows, access the images over Norfolk Southern's WAN to make decisions. The railroad plans to digitize all the documents in its archives, a total of 6 million pages.[14]

Imaging is also helping New York City's Board of Elections process nearly 3.4 million registered voters. A mayoral task force propelled the $9-million, 3-year

BUSINESS REALITIES
Connecticut Mutual Life Insurance

Until a few years ago, Connecticut Mutual Life Insurance was a paper-intensive company. It had 48 internal groups clamoring for the paper files of policy holders, almost 45% of which were stored off-site. The company changed this ineffective arrangement by using office automation to re-engineer its entire policy-issuing process. At the heart of this effort was an imaging and automated work-flow system. The office automation system was so powerful, effective, and innovative that the company was recently named a cowinner of *Network World's* Ninth Annual User Excellence Award.

The system, which cost $6.5 million, became operational in 1991. Since then, productivity has increased by 35%, operating costs have been reduced by $4 million,

and ten different job functions have been collapsed into two. All of this happened in less than 18 months, 6 months short of the estimated 2-year payback period. The company has also reduced its backlog from 6 weeks to zero and has reduced the number of employees in the Customer Services Division from 250 to 184.

Before the system became operational, the company had separate applications for different products, resulting in data redundancy and other gross inefficiencies. The new imaging system digitized more than 300,000 policy-holder files in under 3 months. Regardless of the product or the policy holder, the data are all in one place, easily accessible to all who need them. Says a company spokesperson, "We look at [the networked imaging system] as the cockpit of a 747 jet. It is a very powerful workstation that is the integration point of data for knowledge workers."[15]

project, which has automated the city's voter verification process. Before the Hewlett-Packard imaging system was installed, voter verification was done using a manual ledger system, which was labor-intensive and error-prone. Under the new system, voters register by filling out and signing a card with personal information, such as age, party, and citizenship. The imaging system located at the board's Manhattan headquarters, scans the signatures into a database; the personal data are keyed in by hand. The imaging system retrieves and prints the original signature during verification, thus eliminating the need to lug 35-pound looseleaf binders containing the signed cards to the polling place for ID verification.

Communication Systems

In this section, we will discuss communication systems, which include E-mail, fax, and voice mail.

E-mail   In the last decade or so, E-mail has changed from an esoteric technology to one that is considered essential to workplace communication. Knowledge workers have grown to depend on E-mail for quick and reliable communications with people and organizations around the world.

Electronic mail, or **E-mail,** as it is popularly called, is a system that allows a person or a group to electronically communicate with others through a network. Figure 10–3 shows how E-mail works. A user sends an electronic message over a network; the message is stored in the electronic mailbox of the receiver. The electronic mailbox is usually a file on a server; the messages in it can be retrieved when the recipient is ready to receive them. Users can also edit, sort, save, and classify messages and forward them to other individuals on the network. If two users are logged onto the network at the same time, then they can converse through E-mail. Some E-mail systems have multimedia capabilities allowing E-mail users to send not only text, but also voice and still pictures.

There are many kinds of E-mail software; depending on the characteristics of each type used, mail can be sent between different computers or may be restricted to users on one computer. If an organization has different types of systems, say IBM, Digital, and so on, these systems must be linked together for E-mail to be successful.

E-mail
A system that allows people who are linked through a network to electronically communicate with each other, in written form, at any time, from anywhere in the world.

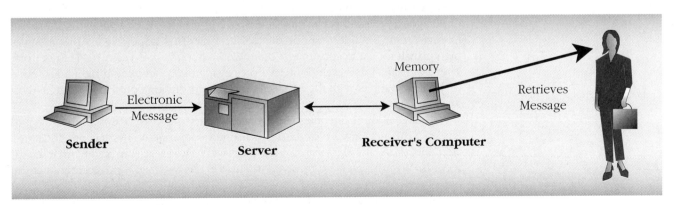

Sender — Electronic Message — Server — Receiver's Computer — Memory — Retrieves Message

FIGURE 10–3

In E-mail, the message of the sender is stored by a computer (usually a server). The receiver can access the message any time, modify it, and forward it to others.

E-mail screen

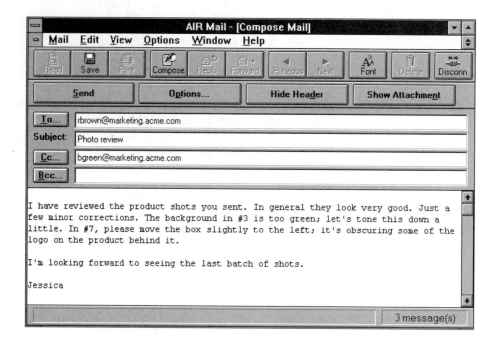

E-mail has many benefits. First, it allows organizations to be responsive to customer needs. For example, when Freddie Mercury died, his fans around the world sent E-mail messages to his music company, EMI Records, to order his music. As a tribute to his memory, radio stations around the world began to play his once-neglected songs. The box-office blockbuster film *Wayne's World* featured one of Freddie's old hits and MTV began showing his music videos. The dead star was suddenly hot. EMI subsidiaries around the world were flooded with E-mail orders for the star's music. The Queen albums in EMI's catalog were particularly popular with the E-mail users. The result: EMI sold 3 million Queen albums in 1 month, generating $30 million to $50 million in revenue and accounting for $10 million to $15 million of the year's profits for the $2-billion company.[16]

The "big 3" credit reporting agencies—TRW, Equifax, and Trans Union, use E-mail to respond quickly to customers' concerns and queries. Before the system was installed, consumers who were trying to rectify errors in their credit reports often felt harassed by the credit agencies. Consumers were forced to write to all three agencies about any errors in their credit reports. Each agency had to write to retailers and lenders about the corrections. This paper-driven process was nightmarish for some consumers; there were enormous delays in rectifying errors. There were mail delays and internal processing delays in getting the paper forms to the right people, with the result that dispute resolution could take from 30 days to 8 months.

Today, all three agencies use E-mail systems to correspond with retailers and lenders. This not only saves the agencies time and money, but has greatly alleviated the problems that consumers face when there are errors in their credit records. Most disputes are resolved in under 5 days—a big improvement over the old system.[17]

Another advantage of E-mail is that it provides instantaneous access to and dissemination of information, thereby eliminating the time lag involved in using the postal service. E-mail messages do not get lost or reach the wrong party.

In spite of its many benefits, E-mail should be used carefully. John Beamish, senior systems analyst at the Ministry of Education in Toronto, tells this E-mail story: "At my last place of employment, the unwritten rule was: If you drink the last of the coffee, make a fresh pot. Unfortunately, not many people did. In response, an angry coffee drinker sent a raging five-page E-mail message regarding his dissatisfaction. The message was so long and went to so many people, it used all the memory of at least one disk, and no one could access their E-mail messages."

E-mail also raises many ethical issues; some of these are covered in the ethical cases at the end of this chapter.

Finally, E-mail systems must be carefully selected, since a poor package may not only deter users from using E-mail but can also result in poor communications. Some factors to consider before selecting an E-mail package are: What hardware and operating system platforms must the mail system support? How many users do we currently have? How many users will we have in 2 years? In 5 years? Will remote users at multiple sites need to use the system? Must users access external services, such as Compuserve? Can messages be sent between different platforms (say, from a UNIX machine to a Macintosh or an IBM PC)? Is the package capable of meeting the growing needs of the organization? Will the vendor provide training and technical support if necessary? These and other related questions must be carefully addressed.[18]

Fax   **Fax,** or facsimile transmission, is another type of electronic publishing and processing system. Fax technology uses telephones, modems, and scanners to transmit text and graphics to individuals and organizations all over the world who have access to telephones. Note that a computer is not required to send a fax; all that is needed is a fax machine at either end of a telephone connection. The idea itself is very simple and elegant. A scanner in the fax machine scans the document at one end and a built-in modem sends it; in the fax machine at the other end, a build-in modem receives the message, a scanner scans the document, and a printer prints it.

In a short time, the fax, sometimes viewed as a "long-distance copier," has become part of the home office, the work office, and even of war zones! Journalists reporting the war in Bosnia used fax machines to transmit war stories because editors preferred to see the stories in hard-copy form.[19] It is estimated that there are 24.5 million fax machines in the world today.[20] The Japanese, in particular, rely heavily on fax communication because their language, with its thousands of ideographs, is easier to write in longhand than to type on cumbersome Japanese word processors.

Fax machines can send the same document to multiple users. They can also be integrated with applications such as word processors, so that faxes can be edited without being rekeyed into the computer. Fax machines can be programmed to send faxes when telephone rates are lowest. A portable fax machine allows users to retrieve documents using a touch-tone phone's keypad. An interesting development is the fax modem, which allows users to send or receive faxes using their PCs.

At Southern Pacific Railroad (SP), the sixth largest railroad in the United States, roughly 50% of purchase orders and a substantial proportion of the company's internal communications are sent by fax. As part of its total quality management effort, SP implemented a mainframe-connected fax system in 1993 that

Fax

A technology that uses telephones, modems, and scanners to transmit text and graphics to an individual or organization anywhere in the world. The scanner in the fax machine scans the document at one end and at the other end, a built-in modem receives the message.

Fax machine

enables the company to prioritize faxes so the most critical are immediately delivered. Senders are notified of transmission problems, and a confirmed copy of every fax is stored in the hard disk archival system.

The new system also allows users of the railroad's WAN to send and receive faxes directly from PC applications, so they can be highly customized and can include graphics. Automated fax-on-demand allows customers and others to request standard documents via touch-tone phone. In addition to saving the cost of an outside service, the new fax system saves the railroad $8,500 a month by eliminating the need to print and mail purchase orders.[21]

Another new feature is fax-on-demand (FOD), which uses touch-tone phones and prerecorded instructions to provide users with customized information by treating the keypad of the touch-tone phone as a data terminal and the fax machine as a printer. Companies are actively embracing FOD technology because it can reduce operating costs. For example, some companies are replacing telemarketers at 800- and 900-number call centers with FODs so that customers can receive information without human intervention.

The Interep Radio Store in New York City, a company that sells radio advertising and other marketing services to advertising agencies, has increased its market share by using a fax-on-demand system to give customers market information on major product categories. A salesperson can dial the network's 800-number and retrieve, within 2 minutes, a detailed outline of the key characteristics of a typical buyer for a particular product, using data gathered from several sources. The report includes information about demographics, the top 50 markets, suggestions for advertising media, and even successful case studies. The ability to give media planners at ad agencies detailed information on a product is vital for successful radio advertising and the fax system allows Interep to do that. In 1993, the company's sales increased $22 million.[22]

Another new development is LAN-based fax systems, also called enterprise-wide fax systems. Such systems are becoming increasingly popular because they help to centralize the receiving and sending of faxes and thereby better monitor and control the cost of fax traffic. (Incote, a communications software vendor in New York, estimates that its LAN-based fax system, which cost $75,000, saves the company $260,000 annually.) Although more than 36% of the telephone costs of many large corporations is fax-related, very few organizations monitor and control the costs of faxing. A recent survey of middle managers showed that 78% did not know how much it cost to send a fax; 70% of the polled organizations do not have any fax policies; and an astounding 63% of these organizations were not tracking fax expenditures.[23]

Rosenbluth International, a $1.7-billion travel services company, has a network operations center that it uses as a kind of "global traffic helicopter" to track storms and other events that could affect travelers, so that customers can avoid airport delays, flight cancellations, and other inconveniences. The company monitors CNN and the Weather Channel for travel-related information, which is immediately broadcast, via fax machines and E-mail, to corporate clients and other travel offices. Although the idea is quite simple, the network center gives Rosenbluth a competitive edge. Since travelers appreciate any information that makes their travel a little more pleasant.[24]

Voice Mail   **Voice mail** facilitates oral communication. The way it works is illustrated in Figure 10–4. The sender dictates a message over the telephone. A special device, called a *codec,* converts the analog signal of the sender's voice into a digitized message. (Unlike a modem, which transmits over analog lines, a codec converts analog video images and sound waves into digital signals, compresses them, and transmits them over digital lines.) The message is transmitted over the network and stored in a server at the receiver's end. A blinking light on the receiver's phone indicates that he or she has a voice message. When the receiver chooses, the digitized message is retrieved from the server, reconverted into analog form, using a codec at the receiver's end, and the receiver receives it over the phone.

Although voice mail is a simple idea, it eliminates a number of problems, such as "phone tag;" it also ensures that a message reaches the right party even when that party is not available. Some voice mail systems can send the same message to several people, reroute a message to another phone (say, your home

Voice mail

The transmission, storage, and retrieval of spoken messages using computers. Eliminates many problems associated with telephones.

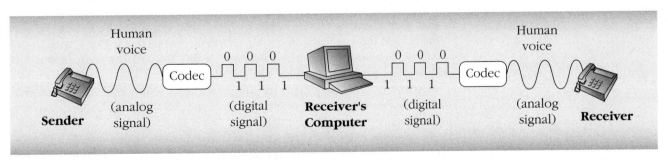

FIGURE 10–4

Voice mail uses telephones, computers, and codecs. The analog signal of the human voice is converted into digital signals and stored in the receiver's computer until the receiver is ready to retrieve the message.

phone), save messages for future reference, and retrieve messages from any telephone, anywhere in the world. In some systems, users need a password to access voice messages, making voice mail a secure medium for confidential messages.

Electronic Meeting Systems

In this section, we will discuss electronic meeting systems, which include audio conferencing, videoconferencing, and groupware.

Electronic meeting systems consist of tools and techniques (both computer-based and non-computer-based) that allow a group of people, separated by time and distance, to exchange ideas using audio, video, and other electronic media. One of the primary benefits of electronic meeting systems is that they reduce operating costs and increase productivity because decision makers do not have to travel to attend face-to-face meetings. One type of electronic meeting system is the group decision support systems (GDSS), which was discussed in Chapter 8. In this section, we discuss three other types of electronic meeting systems: audio conferencing, video conferencing, and groupware.

Audio Conferencing **Audio conferencing** allows two or more people who are geographically separated to communicate over the phone. Telephone conversations usually are one-to-one; this can be a limitation when more than one person has to participate in the conversation. For example, if a design manager in Los Angeles wanted to communicate with a group of production managers in New York, it would not be possible to do this over the telephone; however, it can be done using audio conferencing. Audio conferencing is ideal for managing small- to medium-sized projects. It is most useful with groups of 5 to 15 people.

Videoconferencing **Videoconferencing** is another type of electronic meeting system that uses telephones, TV monitors, computers, and networks to link geographically separated decision makers. Sophisticated large-scale videoconferencing may require specially equipped video conference rooms with facilities for computers, video cameras, microphones, and monitors. In confidential meetings that involve sensitive information, the information can be encrypted before it is sent over the public telephone network. In audio conferencing, the participants can only hear each other; in videoconferencing, they can both see and hear each other.

This is how videoconferencing works: A computer digitizes sound and video images, then converts them to analog signals and transmits them over the telephone lines to the receiver's computer, which reconverts the analog signals to digital signals. These are then translated into audio and video messages and presented on the television monitor and sound system.

There are three basic types of videoconferencing (Mcleod, 1993): one-way video with one-way audio; one-way video with two-way audio; and two-way video with two-way audio.

In one-way video with one-way audio, the signals are sent in only one direction. This type of system is adequate in situations that require only the dissemination of information, without any response from the recipients. For example, if the CEO of a company wants to introduce the new human resources manager to all the employees in the organization, a one-way system is adequate.

Electronic meeting systems
Tools and techniques that allow groups of people, separated by time and distance, to exchange ideas, using audio, video, and other electronic media. Includes audioconferencing, videoconferencing, and groupware.

Audio conferencing
Allows a group of people who are geographically separated to exchange verbal communications.

Videoconferencing
A type of electronic meeting system that uses telephone, video, computer, and communication links to enable geographically separated decision makers to hear and see each other.

In one-way video with two-way audio, members who are geographically separated can hear each other, but only one party can be seen by the others. A good example is a televised course. Both the teacher and the students can hear each other, but the teacher cannot see the students, although all the students can see the teacher.

In two-way video with two-way audio, all the parties can see and hear each other. A top-management group that is planning a downsizing strategy might use this type of system.

Although today nearly half of all Fortune 1000 corporations use videoconferencing, "Meet me onscreen" is not yet as common an invitation as "Let's do lunch."[25] One of the primary reasons that videoconferencing has been slow to catch on is that it requires that the same long-distance carrier be used for every site on the system. Since often different sites have different carriers, this has been a problem.

Also, until recently, videoconferencing equipment was very expensive, and thus out of reach for most companies. In recent years, the price of desktop videoconferencing equipment (using PCs) has dropped from $10,000 to about $2,000 per user (and in some cases even less), making it a very attractive investment.[26] Desktop videoconferencing systems are based on the same components as large videoconferencing systems, except that they are housed in PCs and a caller's image may appear in a corner of the PC monitor instead of on a TV monitor.

Leasing videoconferencing capabilities from carriers such as AT&T is an attractive alternative. For example, Kinko's, the nation's largest retail document reproduction chain, leases videoconferencing capabilities. The company has private cubicles in some of its stores, where customers can set up a video conference by simply dialing an 800 number. Thus, through videoconferencing, a traveling executive can attend a meeting in Los Angeles, followed immediately by a meeting in New York. The cost of Kinko's videoconferencing is estimated to be about $150 per hour, much less than it would be if the company bought its own system. Kinko's also plans to employ videoconferencing for internal meetings.[27]

Groupware
Communication tools, such as E-mail, voice mail, fax, and videoconferencing that foster electronic communication and collaboration among groups.

Groupware   In Chapter 8, we discussed that a large number of decisions in organizations are made by teams. Only rarely, if ever, are important decisions made by one person. Hence, it is important to provide an environment that supports group decision making. In Chapter 8, we discussed the use of GDSS to facilitate group decision making. In this section, we discuss another type of group decision-making tool known as **groupware**. *Groupware* is a broad term for communication tools that foster electronic communication and collaboration in groups. Some examples of groupware tools are

- Electronic calendars and schedulers
- E-mail
- Voice mail
- Fax
- Electronic bulletin board systems
- Videoconferencing
- Project management
- Group decision support systems

Figure 10–5 shows some electronic tools that are classified as groupware.

Groupware is sometimes referred to as work-group computing, because it allows groups to work together. It is important not to confuse work-group computing and work-flow software. Here is the difference between the two terms: Work-group computing products are designed to let work groups or individuals transfer information and share it. The key element here is information. In a work-flow application, the business process itself is managed and analyzed. The key element, therefore, is not the information but the process. (See Figure 10–6.) Work-flow products are discussed in greater detail in Chapter 13 (Tools for Information System Development).

Although there is no standard definition of groupware, it is generally agreed that an electronic tool that helps groups to communicate, collaborate, and exchange ideas, information, and knowledge may be considered groupware. Linking group members who are geographically separated requires networks, which are among the essential components of groupware. Recall our discussion of task-oriented organizations versus pyramid organizations in Chapter 1. Task-

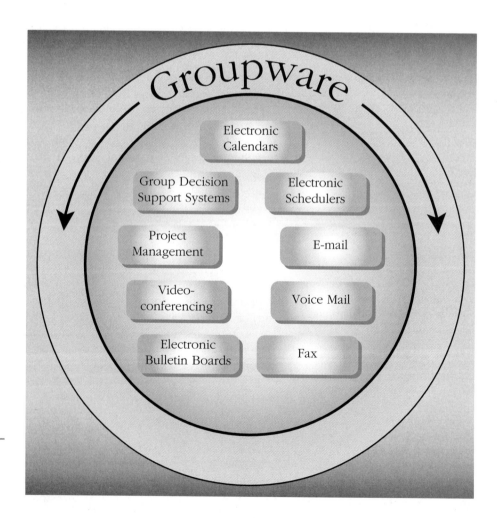

FIGURE 10–5

Groupware is a broad term covering a variety of electronic tools. This figure shows some of the tools in this category.

FIGURE 10-6

The difference between work-group computing and work-flow computing.

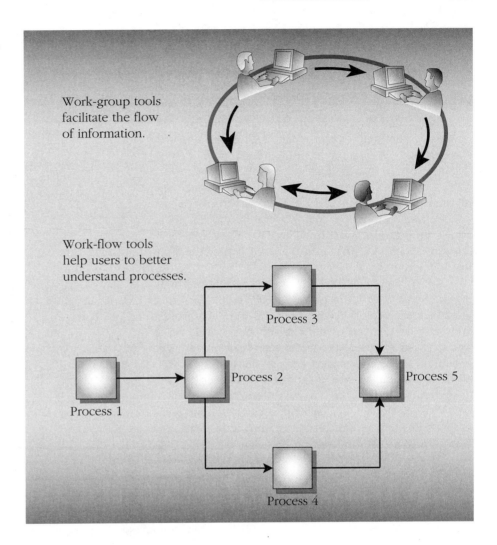

Work-group tools facilitate the flow of information.

Work-flow tools help users to better understand processes.

Process 3

Process 1   Process 2   Process 5

Process 4

oriented organizations are highly group-oriented; bringing groups together in a fluid and dynamic way to complete specific projects or tasks. Such organizations may find groupware particularly useful.

Why is groupware effective? Groupware allows people to freely exchange, analyze, edit, store, and retrieve documents and messages. It eliminates the barriers of time and space and allows different group members to work on the same document at the same time. Electronic bulletin boards allow members to post their ideas and elicit responses from other group members. Primary benefits are increased responsiveness to market forces and significant improvement in the quality of business processes, such as product development, account management, and customer service.[28] For example, KPMG Peat Marwick (see box) uses groupware to achieve some or all of the above goals.

Organizations can take several steps to utilize the full potential of groupware. First, since groupware can be used for a number of applications, IS managers must make sure that the various applications can be integrated to facilitate the free

BUSINESS REALITIES
KPMG Peat Marwick

KPMG Peat Marwick relies on groupware to help its professionals share their expertise and talent throughout the corporation. "We want to deliver to every individual in the firm the combined intellectual global assets of the firm." says Michael Donahue, a management consulting partner at the firm. FirstClass, a client-server groupware system from SoftArc, is a critical component of the company's information tools, providing a unified front end for various information sources to the company, both internal and external.

The system, dubbed Knowledge Manager, will eventually be used by more than 17,000 employees and is accessible both on Macintoshes and PCs. The tool is fairly easy to use and is menu-driven. By clicking on a few icons, employees can access remote databases that contain valuable information, such as successful proposals, business intelligence, competitors' strategies, advertising options and so on.

Michael Donahue, a management consulting partner, narrates how a pilot version of Knowledge Manager helped KPMG win a bid at a Northeast insurance concern. "At 3 p.m. on a Friday afternoon in August, the insurer asked KPMG for a proposal for a major technology overhaul. Four partners working in different cities collaborated over the weekend using Knowledge Manager to gather background information, access graphics libraries and communicate with one another. By noon Monday, they delivered a thick proposal to the insurer, complete with graphics and diagrams." In this case, KPMG won the account, beating Electronic Data Systems, IBM and Coopers & Lybrand. "Without Knowledge Manager, putting together such a proposal would have taken three to five business days, even pulling out all stops," he added.

Although KPMG recommends Notes to many clients, it was not suitable for KPMG's application, in part because of the proprietary database structure of Notes. For instance, much of the company's information is contained in Microsoft Word, Excel and PowerPoint files. To use Notes, the firm would have had to move the information in all those documents into Notes' proprietary databases. Since the FirstClass groupware system did not have this requirement, the company preferred it over Notes.[29]

---

flow of information among them. Second, since most groupware applications are networked, security issues must be carefully addressed in the early stages of groupware development so that valuable information will not be lost or fall in the wrong hands. Third, groupware reduces bureaucracy and requires people to work in teams; in some organizations, this may require fostering a new mindset. "Command, control and communications are no longer the driving forces in companies. Coordination, cooperation and collaboration are what's in store for the future."[30]

One of the most popular groupware packages is Notes, from Lotus. Basically, Notes is a distributed database that allows users to share a wide variety of documents in different forms and from different sources, such as text, spreadsheet data, graphics, and images. With some hardware and software enhancements, this application can even support sound and video. It is menu-driven and icon-based, so that even people with little or no programming background can use it effectively.

Notes is form-driven in the sense that it has a number of predefined forms that can be used to enter and store data in the database. For example, data on customer complaints can be entered on a form. The forms can also be customized to meet the unique needs of the organization if necessary. Once a form has been created, Notes puts a date and time stamp on it, along with the name of the per-

Lotus Notes

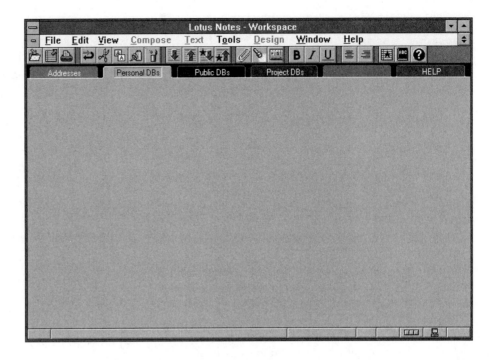

son who created or modified the document. By keeping a log of group members who have viewed or modified a document, the system can maintain an up-to-date history of events that affect the group and its task. Members of the group can access any form in the database, respond to the form, and disseminate their views to all the other members.

Notes operates on IBM-compatible microcomputers and workstations and on Macintosh computers. It runs under a number of operating systems, including Windows, OS/2, and UNIX, and can be loaded on both LANs and WANs. It can also be integrated with a number of popular word processing, spreadsheet, graphics, and database packages, which further increases its usefulness and versatility.

Mary Kay, one of the world's leading cosmetics suppliers, uses Notes groupware to facilitate office communications and support collaborative efforts in task-oriented groups that manage specific projects.[31]Frito-Lay uses Notes to monitor its sales in different stores. When a store runs low on, say, nacho cheese seasoning for Doritos chips, the company's trading partner, McCormick & Co., already has a purchase order in hand. Using Notes, the two companies can instantaneously trade inventory information and purchase-order forms, thus reducing operating costs and increasing organizational productivity.[32]

Another company that uses Notes to enhance enterprise-wide communications is Asea Brown Boveri, a multinational engineering consulting firm (see box). Notes has helped the company provide a uniform face to data on a global basis, while at the same time capturing the information needs and preferences of its local business units.

A GLOBAL PERSPECTIVE
Asea Brown Boveri Ltd.

The world's largest electrical engineering firm, Asea Brown Boveri (ABB), has a reputation for attacking problems head on. Global computing is a problem ABB appears to be tackling rather well. Formed in 1987 by the merger of engineering giants Asea AB of Sweden and BBC Brown Boveri Ltd. of Switzerland, ABB challenged its information systems personnel to create, within months, a single financial reporting application for 1,300 companies employing more than 20,000 people in 140 countries.

This was no small task because the $28 billion giant continues to balance the paradoxes facing an international, multi-domestic organization. Although global, the company has deep local roots; the overall company is very large but individually it is made up of close to 5,000 small profit centers. Decentralized in many of its business functions, it has centralized reporting. The company's current challenge is to balance a diverse, decentralized structure while leveraging centralized efficiencies in purchasing and other operations.

An IS steering committee, consisting of top IS managers, financial officers, and board members, serves major geographic and business entities and meets several times a year to approve budgets and ensure that technology plans fit the overall company direction. The company has three geographic regions, five business segments and 45 business areas. Although each business chooses its own applications, ABB has standardized its office automation infrastructure.

Recently, the company adopted groupware technology, subscribing to Lotus Development Notes. All of ABB's business units use it and this standardization has helped enhance communications. Today, more than 13,000 employees use Notes worldwide. Groupware has helped the company break all communication barriers and build a global information infrastructure.[33]

Summary

* **The role of office automation in enhancing productivity of knowledge workers.**

  In order to make effective decisions, information must be disseminated to the right people at the right time. Office automation systems facilitate oral and written communication and eliminate the barriers of time and space. These systems help to reduce operating costs, increase the productivity of knowledge workers, and increase the responsiveness of organizations to their customers.

* **Office automation tools.**

  Office automation tools include electronic publishing and processing systems and group communication systems. These systems include word processing, desktop publishing, electronic mail, voice mail, fax, audioconferencing, videoconferencing, and imaging. Electronic publishing and processing systems facilitate written and voice communication, while electronic meeting systems focus primarily on communication within groups.

* **Office automation tools that enhance written communications and their contribution to productivity.**

  Some office automation tools are designed specifically to enhance written communications. These include word processing, desktop publishing, document management systems (imaging and multimedia), E-mail, and fax. Imaging converts paper, microfilm, and microfiche images into digitized images that can be edited, printed, faxed, or viewed on a computer screen. Multimedia includes computer-based technologies that integrate different types of media, such as text, graphics, animation, audio, and video. E-mail is a system that allows people to communicate with one another electronically. Fax machines use telephones, modems, and scanners to transmit text and graphics to individuals and organizations anywhere in the world.

* **Office automation tools that facilitate oral communications and their contribution to productivity.**

  Tools that facilitate oral communications include voice mail, electronic meeting systems, such as audioconferencing, videoconferencing, and groupware. Voice mail allows users to send and retrieve messages at their convenience. Audio conferencing allows more than two people to communicate over the phone at the same time. Videoconferencing uses telephones, TV monitors, computers, and telecommunications to link people who are geographically separated. Group-ware includes group decision support systems (GDSS), elec-tronic bulletin boards, and electronic calendars and schedulers, all of which foster electronic communica-tion and collaboration among the members of a team.

Review Questions

1. What is the primary goal of office automation sys-tems? What are some tools that can be classified as OAS?
2. What is a virtual office and what are some reasons for its increasing popularity?
3. What are some managerial implications of the vir-tual office?
4. What specific tools can be categorized as electron-ic publishing and processing systems?
5. Describe a multimedia system and its components. What are some uses of multimedia?
6. What is E-mail? Explain how it works. What are some of its advantages? Disadvantages?
7. What is groupware? How does it facilitate group decision-making?
8. Why are fax machines sometimes referred to as long-distance copiers? What is the difference, if any, between stand-alone fax and fax-on-demand?
9. What is the difference between audio conferencing and videoconferencing? Explain how they work.
10. What is an imaging system? What are some of its components? Identify some advantages and disad-vantages of imaging systems.

Discussion Questions

1. When Nannerl O. Kohane, a 53-year-old information systems enthusiast and former president of Wellesley College, became the president of Duke University, she was in for an unpleasant surprise: Duke did not have E-mail. "I felt like I had my hand cut off," she said. "I can't function without E-mail." Today, Duke has undertaken a major E-mail project, named Project Hermes after the Greek messenger god, that links 22,000 students, faculty, and staff into a shared communication environment.[34]

   Assume that you have been given the respon-sibility of convincing a team of top-level Duke University officials of the importance of E-mail. Develop a presentation that emphasizes the benefits of E-mail in a university environment.
2. Organizations using Notes sometimes run into prob-lems while assimilating Notes into the existing infor-mation systems environment. On the technical side, Notes requires an administrator at every site where there is a Notes server. This makes it a very expen-sive proposition to introduce groupware in the com-pany. Second, Notes is so complex that the learning curve for users is steep. On the organization side, Notes promotes a highly democratic application environment, which in turn makes control difficult. Striking a balance between controlling end-users and giving them the freedom to move at their own pace is a challenge for IS managers.
   a. Identify some steps that an organization can take to eliminate some of these problems.
   b. Identify a company in your local area that uses Notes. Interview the IS manager of the compa-ny and find out some of the benefits and chal-lenges of groupware.
3. What are some of the advantages and disadvantages of a "virtual office"? Explore why some people may prefer the traditional workplace over a virtual office.

ETHICAL ISSUES

Case 1: Videoconferencing for Prisoners: An Ethical Dilemma

Several state judicial systems use videoconferencing to significantly reduce the cost of transporting inmates from jails to courthouses where judges decide on bail and other related issues. (Although the visit itself lasts only a few minutes, "live" visits entail strip-searching inmates at the beginning and at the end of the trip, providing security as they are transported between the jail and the courthouse, and confining them to a supervised holding room for 3 to 6 hours before taking them before the judge.) Even though 17 U.S. counties are using videoconferencing, it has stirred a debate about the constitutionality of using videoconferences to replace live courtroom appearances.

In particular, using videoconferencing for arraignments (an accused person's first court appearance after arrest, during which the judge sets bail and a court date) has inspired heated debate over an individual's legal right to be physically present before a judge. Some public defenders even require the defendant to waive his or her right to a live appearance. Opponents argue that videoconferencing discriminates against an individual based on financial status and hence is a violation of due process, and that some inmates may look "guiltier" on video because many of them are not technology-savvy.[35]

1. Do you agree that videoconferencing for prisoners may be a violation of due process? Discuss.
2. What other communication tool would be suited to this problem?

Case 2: Shredding E-mail: The Iran-Contra Affair

The Executive Office of the President and the National Security Council (NSC) were ordered by a U.S. district judge not to destroy E-mail records relevant to the Iran-contra scandal and other infractions of the law committed by the Bush administration. Although the Executive Office and the NSC agree in principle with the judge's request, they argue that retaining original records would "interfere" with their use of E-mail, since it would require much more memory than the system can handle. The judge, on the other hand, found those arguments to be "incomprehensible" and is holding these agencies to the law. However, a technology consultant agrees with the Executive Office that maintaining E-mail records is not an easy task, because given the massive amounts of E-mail that the two agencies receive, it is difficult, if not impossible, to sort the public records from the private ones. "The technology is a couple years behind the law," says the consultant.[36]

Research your local library and identify some ethical and legal issues that are raised by E-mail.

Case 3: The Wrath of a Fired Employee

A court in California recently addressed the issue of whether ex-employees have the right to use a company's E-mail system to stay in touch with former colleagues, particularly when the company does not want them to. A former employee of the Santa Cruz Operation (SCO) argues against this restriction, stating that there is no difference between communicating by post or through E-mail. The defendant argues that if he has the right to correspond with his friends by mail, he must also have the right to correspond through E-mail. This precedent-setting case will determine the extent to which a company has control over the information that is sent and received on its E-mail system.

Michael Taht was a programmer at SCO, in Santa Cruz, California. In 1991, he was fired because of a dispute. The company claims that when Taht started to send a "series of threatening and distracting" E-mail messages, they sought and won a restraining order against him from the Santa Cruz County Superior Court, prohibiting Taht from using SCO's E-mail system to contact company employees. Taht argues that paper and electronic mail are equal, and hence that the restraining order violates his rights.

Unfortunately, SCO isn't sure whether Taht used the company network, his own private Internet account, or a commercial online service to send E-mail messages, a question that is crucial in this case. If Taht used a private service, SCO's case becomes weak; if, on the other hand, he used the company's network, Taht may not have a strong case. In the last few months, the messages from Taht have stopped. Why? Because his computer was stolen![37]

1. Do you agree with Taht that the right to correspond by E-mail is similar to the right to correspond by post?
2. Should ex-employees be allowed to correspond with employees over the company's network?

Case 4: Mind Your Own Affairs!

One of the hot debates currently raging in the computer industry is whether it is legal to surreptitiously monitor the on-line activities of employees. Since there are no laws that provide clear guidance and direction regarding this issue, experts on employee privacy laws say that notifying employees in advance that their on-line activities will be monitored is the only way to avoid lawsuits.

One such suit now pending against fast-food giant McDonald's of Oak Brook, Ill., is likely to be a groundbreaking case. It may even result in an amendment to the Federal Electronic Communications and Privacy Act, which allows employers to monitor electronic conversations of employees. The American Civil Liberties Union (ACLU) takes strong exception to this act and is actively pursuing increases in the right to privacy of employees in the workplace.

The McDonald's lawsuit was filed in January, 1995, by Michael Huffcut, a former McDonald's franchisee manager. He alleges that his former co-manager recorded personal voice-mail messages Huffcut had left for a woman, also a McDonald's employee, with whom he was having an affair. His co-manager then played these messages back to Huffcut's wife!

Had McDonald's notified employees in writing that electronic communications were subject to surveillance, "[the company] would certainly be in a better position than it is right now," and wouldn't have left itself so open to legal scrutiny, says Milind Shah, a research fellow on ACLU's National Task Force on Civil Liberties in the Workplace. "Companies should be upfront and hon-

est with employees about surveillance. Besides, it would create good faith between the employer and employee," says Shah.[38]

1. Do you think it is unethical to tap voice mail messages of employees? Why or why not?
2. Would you be willing to work for a company that monitors your voice mail messages? Discuss.

Case 5: Computerized Performance Monitoring

Computerized Performance Monitoring (CPM) has generated a number of heated discussions in the IS community. CPM refers to the "computerized collection, storage, analysis and reporting of information about employees' productive activities. . .[obtained]. . . directly through their use of computer and telecommunication equipment." CPM devices capture data describing specific worker behaviors and work measurement, such as the number of work units completed per time period, the number and length of times the terminal is left idle, error rates, the number of keystrokes and telephone calls, and so on. The Office of Technology Assessment estimates that approximately 6 million workers in the United states have some or all of their work evaluated through computerized performance reports.

Those in favor of CPM devices argue that it provides managers with valuable data to assess worker productivity and evaluate worker performance, although there is very limited evidence that CPM does in fact enhance worker productivity. Opponents are concerned that such data may be grossly misused against an employee. They argue that it invades worker privacy, creates a dehumanizing and unsatisfying work environment, creates unnecessary stress and opens the door for unfair performance evaluation.[39]

1. As a manager of an IS department, would you have any hesitation using CPM tools and devices? Discuss.
2. What are some potential abuses of CPM?

PROBLEM SOLVING IN THE REAL WORLD

Case 1: A Leading Jeweler Buys into Office Automation

Zale Corporation, the world's largest jewelry retailer, has a jewelry processing center in its world headquarters in Irving, Texas. Each year, the center receives about 300,000 unsalable pieces of damaged, discontinued, or repossessed jewelry from the company's 1,500 stores. In the past, the center did not have sufficient processing capacity and hence was forced to ship these goods to a local smelter, who would write a check to Zale for the value of the recovered gold along with glass bottles containing the diamonds and other precious gemstones that were recovered from the melting process. Since the value of melted jewelry is far below its original cost, disposing of unsalable jewelry in this manner resulted in significant losses for Zale, particularly because much of the damage to the jewelry was slight: for example, a loose prong or a scratch. The diamonds and gems recovered from the smelting process were sold through brokers in large batches; their individual size and quality were not adequately monitored.

Zale was having a difficult time keeping an accurate inventory of the loose gemstones that were recovered when large quantities of jewelry were melted. Poor inventory management was causing losses of tens of thousands of dollars each month. The consequences of these practices were clearly illustrated when a broker was handed a bottle of loose diamonds and was told that their total value was probably about 1 million dollars. An appraisal determined that their value was closer to 2 million dollars.

The company actively explored other ways to dispose of the jewelry, but found them to be expensive and complex. These alternatives required experienced gemologists to perform a detailed appraisal of each piece of jewelry to determine its value; this often involved scientific measuring devices, complex calculations, and subjective analysis. They also had to look up current commodity prices for gold and gemstones to determine the true salvage value of the jewelry. Since a gem expert can evaluate only about 25 pieces of jewelry per day, traditional methods were not found to be cost-effective.

To address this problem and increase the productivity of its gem experts, Zale considered the possibility of automating the entire process. At first glance, appraising jewelry appeared to be incompatible with automation, but when the company closely examined jewelry salvage processes by gemologists, it came up with a creative application of modern technology.

An automated system to receive and appraise the jewelry was proposed. (See Figure 10–7.) The end result was an intelligent multimedia system called MEDUSA, which was designed to run on a LAN, using voice recognition as the primary method of capturing data. The system recorded voice input from gem experts, describing their analyses, and also captured data directly from their calipers and diamond scales. Bar codes were used to track items as they made their way through a multitude of possible places. This system allowed the gemologists to increase their productivity by 600%, and Zale's recovery of money from damaged merchandise increased by millions of dollars.

To build the system, three criteria were identified that in combination would have a great impact on productivity: The system must allow the gemolo-

F I G U R E   1 0 – 7

An overview of the MEDUSA
appraisal system.

Source: Newman, Julie and Kenneth A.
Kozar, "A Multimedia Solution to
Productivity Gridlock: A Re-engineered
Jewelry Appraisal System at Zale
Corporation," *MIS Quarterly*, March
1994, p. 25.

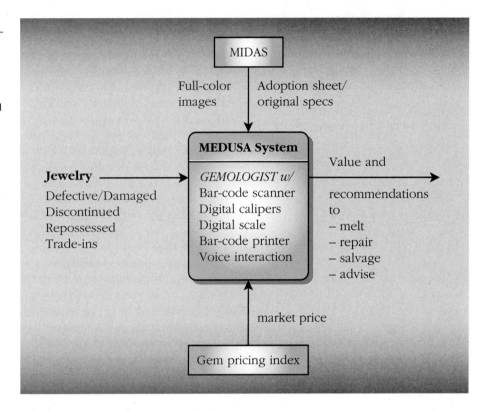

gist's hands and eyes to be used solely for evaluating jewelry, not for completing forms or performing data entry; eliminate as much as possible the need to
evaluate every item; and provide decision support for the gemologist throughout the entire appraisal process. Each objective was met by integrating new techniques with leading-edge systems already in place at Zale.

The first objective was realized to be of pivotal importance after the system
designers conducted simulated evaluations and observed that the gemologists'
hands and eyes were continually occupied with instruments and of course, with
the jewelry itself. Voice recognition technology was obviously a good choice. To
activate the voice processor, the gemologist uses a lightweight microphone
headset plugged directly into a voice processing card in a 386-class workstation.
Digital calipers and a highly sensitive digital scale, which are used to measure
and weigh the jewelry, are connected to the workstation through serial ports.
Positive identification of each item is ensured by its bar-code label. When an
expert is ready to evaluate an item, he or she scans the bar code with a fixed
laser bar-code scanner. If a repair is prescribed, a repair label is created and, if
necessary, a bar-code label is created for a "diamond paper," in which the dia-
mond(s) will be stored in inventory.

The second criterion—the elimination of the need to evaluate every item—
was met by a LAN environment that allows access to databases on various
servers. The expert first scans the item's bar code into MEDUSA and checks to
see if the item is Zale-owned inventory. If so, MEDUSA queries a database called
MIDAS, on another LAN, and retrieves a file containing the jewelry's original
manufacturing specifications. Adaptation sheet data include the type and weight

(Continued on next page)

of the mounting metal, the cut, color, and clarity of the diamond(s), and any other information that the expert needs during an appraisal.

An expert can confirm the stored evaluation by retrieving an image of the item from MIDAS and displaying it on a workstation monitor. This allows the expert to quickly determine whether the item being evaluated is the item described on the adaptation sheet and to make the necessary corrections if an identification error has been made. After the values of all the item's components have been established, the system computes the total salvage value of the item and displays the amount for the gemologist's approval.

Since the first phase of MEDUSA implementation, in November 1991, the system has been accumulating data about the company's inventory of unsalable jewelry. The system is now yielding strategic information that is being used for much more sophisticated management of this valuable corporate asset. Executives now know the exact value of each commodity (gold, diamonds, and so on) in each of the disposition categories, and they can shift the categories in response to changing business demands.

For instance, it is possible to ascertain exactly how much cash can be generated quickly by melting all items currently designated for repair as well as the loss that will be incurred by doing so. Zale can now verify that it is paid by the smelter for the correct amount of gold and that the correct number of diamonds is returned after a melt. Prior to the implementation of MEDUSA, Zale had to trust the smelters to perform these calculations accurately.

Another example of better asset management was described by one of the gemologists. Zale's National Diamond Bond Replacement Center, a service center that satisfies insurance claims by replacing lost or broken diamonds, was running short of 0.25-carat diamonds. Using MEDUSA, the gemologist was able to locate quickly all the diamonds of this size that were mounted in jewelry that was destined to be melted. These stones were removed from their mountings, transferred to the replacement center, and used as replacements. Over $100,000 worth of diamonds were supplied immediately.

In addition to financial control and increased revenues, MEDUSA also produces information that can be used to provide better-quality merchandise to Zale's customers. The company's merchandisers now have the ability to identify chronically defective merchandise and advise manufacturers about defects. The MEDUSA gemologists are alerting the merchandisers to manufacturing techniques that should be avoided and are using information from MEDUSA to support their advice. In one instance, the same defect was found repeatedly in a flexible tennis bracelet (it snapped in two instead of flexing). The item was recalled from all stores.

MEDUSA also makes it possible to monitor shipments from the stores to the surplus processing center and ascertain whether abuse of corporate return and trade-in policies is occurring. Some stores grant excessive trade-in allowances in order to disguise unauthorized merchandise discounts. Now, when a trade-in is evaluated by MEDUSA, its appraisal value is compared to the trade-in allowance granted to the customer, and significant discrepancies are reported to store management. Stores had also been returning "damaged" merchandise to headquarters to relieve their inventories of admittedly undesirable, but definitely undamaged, merchandise. These practices can now be identified and prevented.

The MEDUSA system has positively influenced the morale and productivity of its users. The gemologists believe that they could not accomplish their job without the system, because of the magnitude of the work to be done. Without MEDUSA, they would either be faced with an impossible task or, more likely, be forced to do work that was far below their personal standards. MEDUSA provides the user with the means to increase productivity while meeting high standards of quality.[40]

1. What are some of the problems that Zale was facing before it implemented MEDUSA?
2. Explain how MEDUSA works. What are its primary functions?
3. What are some of the primary benefits that Zale derived from MEDUSA?

Case 2: Quintiles Transnational

Employees at Quintiles Transnational, in Morrisville, North Carolina, are attending a slide presentation by Dennis Gillings, CEO of the 11-year-old company. It's nothing out of the ordinary, except for one small detail: Gillings is nowhere in sight. Gillings is in Quintiles' office in Reading, England; his narrative arrives via a speakerphone.

The company, which administers and analyzes drug-testing studies that pharmaceutical companies prepare for government agencies, has grown rapidly while remaining consistently profitable. Although Quintiles opened its first overseas location only in 1987, today it has offices in 5 countries and 35 percent of its business is now done outside the United States.

However, opening successful offices is only one of the challenges of running a global business; implementing the company's vision is another matter. Gillings envisioned an international company connected by the free and timely flow of information among its offices all over the world. For example, a client could collect data in Europe and have it processed in North Carolina for submission to the U.S. government, a task that requires all offices to communicate seamlessly.

But as the company grew and new offices opened all over the world, Gillings found that these offices were deeply separated by culture and language, and often developed their own way of doing things. For example, the British office began using a different data entry method from that used in the U.S. and the two offices used different software for critical applications; such differences could derail the company's pursuit of international projects.

Gillings and his top managers made a key decision: Each office should add the other's software to its existing system. The result would be that each office would be able to run software packages used by the other offices. That would force them to learn from each other. In other words, Quintiles Transnational had to become truly transnational.

But what is a transnational company? Christopher Bartlett and Sumantra Ghoshal, authors of *Managing Across Borders: The Transnational Solution* (Harvard Business School Press, 1989), argue for a new model of international management. Instead of either a headquarters that dominates overseas offices or independent subsidiaries that have little to do with one another, they advocate a *transnational* corporation. In such a company, offices all over the world work together and learn from one another. They do report to an international headquarters, but an overseas office can have its own special areas of expertise.

(Continued on next page)

The decision to build a seamless environment proved to be a good one for Quintiles Transnational. The company also set up a WAN that links many of its offices; today, a U.S. office can send data directly to the British office without using a modem, which both speeds delivery and improves accuracy. Everyone in the company can communicate through the E-mail system. Employees can also communicate by videoconferencing, voice mail, and fax, and often fax information directly from one computer to another.

Drew Zinck, director of U.S. operations, knows from experience that communications has been vital to improving organizational decision making. He tells of a phone meeting in which he explained to his British counterpart why he could not divulge the details of a marketing alliance that the company had recently completed. When the meeting's minutes were routinely sent by E-mail, he was bombarded with messages from both sides of the Atlantic. Why was he withholding information from his colleague? Didn't he understand the importance of transnational cooperation? When he explained that it was a confidentiality agreement that enforced his silence, a way was quickly found for him to get around this problem and share vital information with his colleagues.[41]

1. What is a transnational company? Does Quintiles fit the description of a transnational company? Discuss.
2. What are some steps that the organization took to improve its communication? Discuss.

References

Bikson, Tora K., J. D. Eveland, and Barbara A. Gutek. *Flexible Interactive Technologies for Multi-Person Tasks: Current Problems and Future Prospects.* Rand Corporation, December 1988.

Busch, Elizabeth, Matti Hamalainen, Clyde W. Holsapple, Yongmoo Suh, and Andrew B. Whinston. "Issues and Obstacles in the Development of Team Support Systems." *Journal of Organizational Computing* 1, no. 2 (April–June 1991).

Johansen, Robert. "Groupware: Future Directions and Wild Cards." *Journal of Organizational Computing* 1, no. 2 (April–June 1991).

Kling, Rob and Charles Dunlop. "Controversies about Computerization and the Character of White-Collar Worklife." *The Information Society* 9, no. 1 (January–March 1993).

Press, Lawrence. "Lotus Notes (Groupware) in Context." *Journal of Organizational Computing,* 2, nos. 3 and 4 (1992).

Sproull, Lee and Sara Kiesler. "A Two-Level Perspective on Electronic Mail in Organizations." *Journal of Organizational Computing* 1, no. 2 (April–June 1991).

Sproull, Lee and Sara Kiesler. *Connections: New Ways of Working in the Networked Organization.* Cambridge, MA: MIT Press, 1992.

Notes

1. Daly, James. "Tracers of the Lost Art," *Forbes ASAP,* October 10, 1994 pp. 21–25.
2. Donovan, Joseph. "Groupware," *Computerworld,* December 27, 1993/January 3, 1994, pp. 73–75.
3. Wexler, Joanie M. "Ties Bind," *Computerworld,* June 28, 1993, pp. 97–98.
4. Graven, Kathryn. "The Eastern Front," *CIO,* October 1, 1994.
5. Ibid.
6. Booker, Ellis. "Users Gain Flexibility with Document Management," *Computerworld,* March 7, 1994, pp. 47, 50.
7. Perey, Christine. "Business Takes a Harder Look," *Information Week,* October 31, 1994, pp. 52–56.
8. Betts, Mitch. "Multimedia Kiosks Provide Voter Education in South Africa Election," *Computerworld,* May 9, 1994, p. 75.
9. Livingston, Dennis. "Information Alchemy," *CIO,* November 1, 1992, pp. 34–36.
10. Ibid.
11. Booker, Ellis. "Digital Photo Bank Aids Missing-Kid Search," *Computerworld,* February 28, 1994, p. 41.
12. Betts, Mitch. "IRS Goes Digital to Speed Returns," *Computerworld,* March 7, 1994, p. 8.
13. Messmer, Ellen. "Insurer Rebuilds Net in its Own Image," *Network World,* November 22, 1993, pp. 42–46.
14. Appleby, Chuck. "Norfolk Southern Speeds Up Service," *Information Week,* September 26, 1994, p. 54.
15. Messmer, Ellen. "Insurer Rebuilds Net in its Own Image," *Network World,* November 22, 1993, pp. 42–46.
16. Thyfault, Mary E. "E-Mail: EMI's Latest Hit," *Information Week,* August 3, 1992, p. 43.
17. ;Betts, Mitch. "Credit Industry Employees E-mail to Address Dispute Resolution Woes," *Computerworld,* April 4, 1993, p. 61.
18. Fryer, Bronwyn. "E-mail: Practical Tips for Finding the E-mail Package That's Right for You," *Computerworld,* December 13, 1993, p. 128.
19. Fitzgerald, M. "High-Tech Tools Help Report on Low-Tech War," *Computerworld,* October 4, 1993, p. 38.
20. Radosevich, Lynda. "Fax-on-Demand Grows," *Computerworld,* January 17, 1994, p. 63.
21. Auer, Katherine. "Fax on the Tracks," *CIO,* May 1, 1994, p, 80.
22. Stambler, Sarah. "A Matter of Fax," *CIO,* Jan. 15, 1994, pp. 78, 82, 84.
23. Gallup Organization, "Ignorant the Fax," *Business Week,* May 9, 1994, p. 8.
24. Alter, Allen E. and Mitch Betts. "Tracking System Aids Travelers," *Computerworld,* March 21, 1994, p. 42.
25. Thyfault, Mary E. "Low Prices Hit the Big Screen," *Information Week,* January 25, 1993, p. 51.
26. Korzeniowski, Paul. "Video Closer to Desktops," *Information Week,* July 11, 1994, pp. 61–62.
27. Stahl, Stephanie. "Convening at Kinko's," *Information Week,* September 20, 1993, p. 56.
28. Radosevich, Lynda. "Groupware Piques Business Interest," *Computerworld,* March 7, 1994, pp. 19, 20.
29. Radosevich, Lynda. "KPMG Turns to FirstClass Groupware," *Computerworld,* November 21, 1994, p. 58.
30. Ibid.
31. Radosevich, Lynda. "Groupware Piques Business Interest," *Computerworld,* March, 7, 1994, pp. 19, 20.

32. Radosevich, Lynda. "Frito, McCormick Trade Data," *Computerworld,* May 9, 1994, p. 59.

33. Ferranti, Marc. "ABB Asea Brown Boveri," *Computerworld The Global 100,* May 1, 1995. p. 17.

34. Anthes, Gary H. "College Puts Up E-mail Dukes," *Computerworld,* January 17, 1994, p. 63.

35. Wexler, Joanie M. "Tune In the Prisoner," *Computerworld,* April 5, 1993, pp. 51, 54.

36. Thyfault, Mary E. "Is E-mail Above the Law?" *InformationWeek,* January 18, 1993, p. 14.

37. Stromoski, Rick. "A Case for the E-Mail Police," *InformationWeek,* January 31, 1994, p. 55.

38. "Big Mac or Big Brother?" *InformationWeek,* May 1, 1995, p. 49.

39. Hawk, Stephen R. "The Effects of Computerized Performance Monitoring: An Ethical Perspective," *Journal of Business Ethics* (Netherlands: Kluwer Academic Publishers, 1994), pp. 949–957.

40. Newman, Julie, and Kenneth A. Kozar. "A Multimedia Solution to Productivity Gridlock: A Re-engineering Jewelry Appraisal System at Zale Corporation," *MIS Quarterly,* March 1994, pp. 21–30.

41. Mangelsdorf, Martha E. "Building a Transnational Company," *Inc.,* March 1993, pp. 92–93.

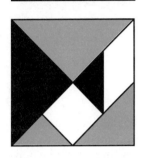

11

Business Information Systems

Contents

Learning Objectives
Technology Payoff: Information Systems and Organizational Productivity: Myth Versus Reality
Introduction
Functional Information Systems
Marketing Information Systems
    What Is a Marketing Information System?
    Developing Marketing Information Systems
    Benefits of Marketing Information Systems
Manufacturing Information Systems
    Developing a Manufacturing Information System
    Agile Manufacturing
    Benefits of Manufacturing Information Systems
Quality Information Systems
    Benefits of Quality Information Systems
Financial and Accounting Information Systems
    Types of Financial and Accounting Information Systems
    Integrated Financial and Accounting Systems
Human Resource Information Systems
    The HRIS and the Competitive Strategy of the Firm
    Developing an HRIS
Geographical Information Systems
Developing Cross-functional Systems

Summary
Review Questions
Discussion Questions
Ethical Issues
 Case 1: Vendor-Managed Inventory
 Case 2: The Dangers of Sharing Information
 Case 3: False Job Security
Problem Solving in the Real World
 Case 1: An All-Star Team: The Tambrands Case
 Case 2: Viacom International
 Case 3: Boulevard Bancorp
References
Notes

Learning Objectives

The purpose of this chapter is to present a broad overview of the role of information systems in the various functional areas of business: marketing, finance and accounting, manufacturing, quality control, and human resources. Although stand-alone information systems were developed some years ago to meet the functional needs of the organization, today the emphasis has shifted from functional systems to highly integrated, cross-functional, customer-focused information systems. The primary emphasis of this chapter is to show the student the versatility and persuasiveness of information systems in corporate America through the use of real-world case studies. After reading and studying this chapter, you should be able to

- Discuss why measuring the productivity of information systems is challenging
- Describe the role of information systems in functional areas such as finance, marketing, manufacturing, quality control, and human resources
- Provide real-world examples of the use of information systems in the various functional areas of an organization

TECHNOLOGY PAYOFF

Information Systems and Organizational Productivity: Myth Versus Reality

The following is an excerpt from an article on IS productivity.
The U.S. service sector's huge investment in information technology during the 1980s produced virtually no gain in productivity. However, those data leave out the real information technology payoff, which came in the form of business benefits such as higher market share and better customer service. The traditional pro-

ductivity measure (output per labor-hour) is fine for wheat and steel, but this way of studying productivity is not adequate for the information age. Unless the IS investment triggers worker layoffs, it does not show up in macroeconomic productivity figures. Missing from those calculations is the role IS plays in improving customer service, inventory management, financial analysis, and other business functions, as well as creating new services. The difference in perceptions is rooted in the fact that U.S. service industries spent more than $750 billion on IS hardware alone in the 1980s, yet the sector managed a tiny 0.7% average yearly growth in productivity during that time. Possible explanations include wasteful or mismanaged IS investments, faulty statistical measurement, and the possibility that IS-generated productivity gains are offset by other factors or take more time to show up.

After interviewing business and IS executives and citing well-known IS success stories, the research committee concluded that information technology has produced positive benefits for the service sector. That anecdotal evidence is not likely to end the productivity debate. But the report does show that it is misleading to rely solely on productivity as a measure of IS impact.

An example of hard-to-measure data that do not appear in national productivity figures is the deployment of ATM networks in the 1970s. Early adopters, such as Citicorp, won more market share and profits as a direct result, but showed no productivity gain because the companies did not reduce costs or labor. The recent wave of layoffs spawned by technology–enabled business re-engineering projects may boost productivity figures in the next few years.[1]

"In the quality process, IS is a facilitator."
—Bruce Speckhals, Vice President, Information Systems, Ritz-Carlton

Introduction

The traditional idea that companies can boost profits and increase market share by expanding their operations is no longer valid. Though expansion is certainly an alternative, it is no longer the primary means for remaining competitive in the marketplace. Instead, the emphasis has shifted to achieving operational excellence at minimum cost. Although this idea of being the best at what one does goes by different names, such as re-engineering, business process engineering, and total quality management, the theme is always the same: Deliver high-quality goods, at the best possible price, quickly and efficiently to the customer, while achieving higher and higher levels of organizational productivity.

Although many of us are aware of the significant contribution made by computers to corporate America, the opening vignette describes the difficulty of *measuring* the contribution of information systems to organizational productivity. The productivity debate, which started in the late 1980s, continues even today. Some argue that there is no clear relationship between technology and business productivity; others argue that the impact of technology on productivity is so profound, pervasive, and intangible that it defies traditional productivity measures.

Measuring productivity is difficult because traditional measures of productivity do not necessarily apply to information systems. Quite frequently, information systems provide long-term, intangible benefits, such as improved customer service, ready availability of timely and accurate data, competitive advantage, leadership in the global marketplace, and high-quality decision making. However, none of these factors can be evaluated using traditional productivity measures.

Any measure of productivity, if it is to be truly meaningful, must be broad, not narrow. Some new productivity measures, such as "slash cycle times," "delighting the customer," and innovative partnerships are beginning to emerge. "Slash cycle times" is a term for reduction of the amount of time between product conception and product delivery. For example, automobile manufactures have reduced product cycle times from 48 to 50 months to 24 to 36 months.[2] Instead of pursuing the traditional "zero defects" goal in quality control, organizations are now measuring quality by how well they can "delight the customer." Traditional, sometimes adversarial, relationships between customers and suppliers are now changing into strong, cooperative alliances that emphasize partnership over competition. These new measures of productivity, which bring together advanced information technologies, brilliant minds, and caring organizations, all focus on the customer.

However, even these new measures do not completely resolve the productivity dilemma. Ironically, it is more difficult to measure productivity gains in organizations that have been successful in using information systems than in those that have not.

"When a person reinvents a process or a whole business, you interrupt the continuity that makes aggregate measurement possible. The more successful you are, the more problems you are going to have trying to measure it."[3]

The primary objective of this chapter is to present real-world information systems and their contribution to the evolving concept of organizational productivity. Although quantitative measures of productivity gains may be hard to come by, the cases shown in this chapter provide strong evidence that information systems help companies to increase profits, decrease costs, enhance customer satisfaction, sustain competitive advantage in the marketplace, reduce product life cycles, achieve increased efficiencies, hire and retain outstanding people, and develop strategic alliances between retailers and suppliers.

Functional Information Systems

Information systems (IS) are pervasive, versatile, and instrumental in helping organizations achieve their strategic, tactical, and operational goals. One way of assessing the contribution of IS to organizational productivity and market growth is to study the impact of IS on each of the five functional areas in an organization:

- Marketing
- Manufacturing
- Accounting and finance
- Quality control
- Human resources

Although for ease of discussion we classify systems into these five functional areas, truly successful systems that have a lasting impact on the organization are those that are cross-functional—that is, systems that are not narrowly defined by functional boundaries, but instead address the broad information needs of managers, regardless of their functional specifications. Figure 11–1 shows how all these systems are interrelated and share the common goal of satisfying the customer.

Recall that there are many different types of information systems: transaction processing systems, management information systems, and intelligent support systems, consisting of decision support systems, executive information systems, expert systems, and office automation systems. All of these play a vital and supportive role in a business function and functional information systems often consist of one or more of the above-mentioned systems. Figure 11–2 shows how the different types of systems form the foundation for functional information systems.

Marketing Information Systems

Marketing systems have evolved through different phases, from a focus on information on key market indicators from a *single* source, on a *periodic* basis (say, weekly, monthly, or biannually), to systems designed to

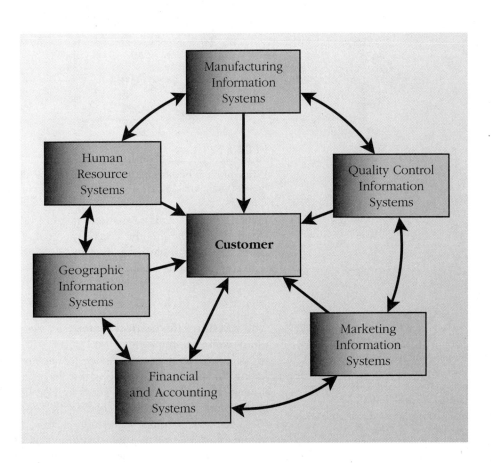

FIGURE 11–1

In today's environment, every functional system should be customer-oriented. Also, each system should be open and integrated with other existing systems to facilitate the free flow of information.

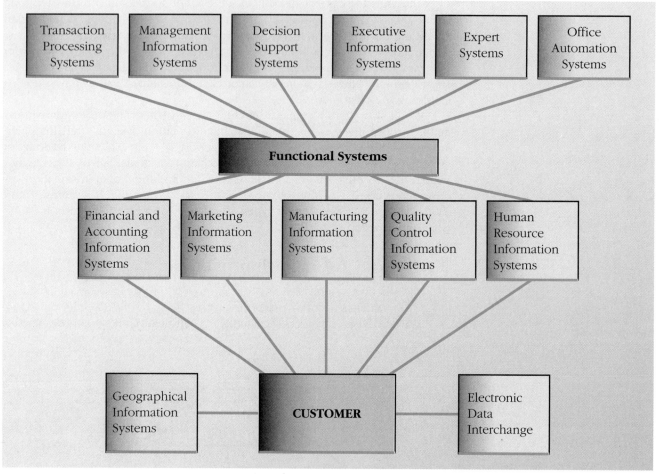

FIGURE 11-2

Different types of information systems, such as TPS, MIS, ISS, and OAS, form the backbone of functional information systems, all of which should be customer-oriented.

gather different kinds of marketing data from *multiple* sources, both internal and external, more frequently. Today, the goal of marketing systems is to gain *instantaneous* access to global market information, from internal and external sources, with the primary goal of retaining existing customers and attracting new ones.

What Is a Marketing Information System?

Marketing information system
A system that meets the marketing information needs of an organization. These are primarily customer-oriented and work toward achieving the strategic sales and marketing plan of the organization.

A **marketing information system** is a system that meets the information needs of an organization in sales, distribution, advertising, market analysis, market intelligence, product research, service management, customer profile, and other marketing functions. Organizations that have customer-oriented marketing information systems are inevitably leaders in their fields: L. L. Bean, Federal Express, and MCI are all companies that rose to the top because of their relentless customer focus and their ability to gather, access, analyze, and disseminate up-to-the-minute, customer-related information. This gives marketing managers the ability to be flexible and responsive to evolving market forces.

Market information systems are primarily customer-oriented information systems that work toward realizing the strategic sales plan and the marketing plan of an organization. A system that is dedicated exclusively to the marketing functions of an organization is called a **dedicated marketing information system.** However, not all organizations have dedicated marketing information systems and small businesses frequently rely on reports from their transaction processing systems for marketing information.

Marketing systems, unlike other functional systems, cannot be standardized for all companies. Every company has its own way in which it generates leads and prospects, prepares bids, fills orders, and delivers goods to its customers. Therefore, marketing systems must be tailored to match the marketing policies, procedures, and practices of each company. However, every marketing system is guided by, and in turn guides, the strategic marketing plan of the organization, and hence should be developed based on the mission, goals, and objectives stated in the strategic marketing plan. Figure 11–3 shows the close relationship between the strategic plan and the marketing plan.

A very popular marketing information system is one that automates the sales and marketing function. Such systems capture valuable customer information, and hence can improve productivity, enhance customer service, and create better sales and marketing strategies. Campbell Soup, for example, has maintained a leadership position in the highly competitive soup market because it gathers extensive market data and uses it to respond quickly to changing market forces and customer needs. The marketing system helps the company closely monitor and quickly respond to marketing information—such as stock on hand, merchandising opportunities, effectiveness of latest promotion, advertising strategies and so on—that its 900 retail sales reps and 300 account sales reps gather from grocery stores, distribution centers, and customer headquarters. Campbell's representatives gather detailed information through hand-held terminals. The information is then transmitted to the mainframe located at corporate headquarters where the data is then used in sophisticated market analysis and forecasting models. The results are then transmitted back to laptop computers that each sales rep carries. Before the new system was installed, it took the company 6 to 8 weeks to respond to market dynamics. Today, it can do so in less than a day.

In fact, these systems are so powerful that frequently companies that use them realize a 10% to 20% increase in sales each year and a relatively quick return on their investment in software and services. So for a sales center with $8 million annual sales, a sales automation system is likely to increase sales to about $8.8 million.[4]

Another company that has been highly successful in automating its sales function is ITT Sheraton (see box). Although sales automation provides significant benefits, it is not enough. What is necessary is sales *augmentation:* tools that augment the abilities of salespeople by helping them to sell more and serve the customer better. Augmentation can be achieved by integrating marketing information systems with other systems in the company, helping the salesperson see the "big picture."

Paul Selden, president of the Sales Automation Association, a nonprofit group in Dearborn, Michigan, believes that integrated marketing systems are capable of even enhancing the total quality management (TQM) efforts of the organization. He argues that the principles of TQM should be vigorously applied to marketing by rewarding both quality and quantity, including quality of leads, reduction of product cycle time for closing a deal, and decreases in the rejection rate of proposals.

Marketing information systems are influenced by, and influence, the strategic business plan and the strategic marketing plan. Some of the subsystems of a marketing information system are shown here.

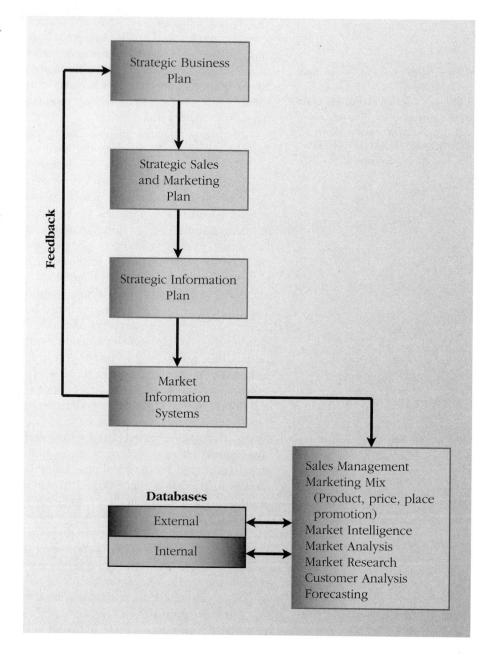

A company that has successfully applied TQM principles to marketing is Telogy of Redwood Shores, California, which leases, rents, and refurbishes electronics testing and measuring equipment. Before a new marketing system was installed, Telogy's sales department was divided into three distinct areas: an outside sales group that called on customers and established relationships with high-potential prospects; inside sales reps who provided customers calling in with configuration information; and telesales, which qualified leads and tracked low-potential prospects. Unfortunately, since the systems were not integrated, information could not be shared; thus, major bottlenecks were created in the sales

BUSINESS REALITIES
ITT Sheraton Corp.

When ITT Sheraton checked into sales force automation, the company discovered that technology can play an important role in attracting customers. Sheraton began automating its sales force on the corporate level primarily to give salespeople better information on room availability for corporate conferences, a primary source of revenue for hotels. Side benefits included establishing a sales presence in new markets and increasing employee job satisfaction. "This addresses one of my pet peeves in this industry. We are the only industry that puts its salespeople in the factory and hopes customers come to us." says Yale Feldman, general manager of the Washington City Center.

Today, salespeople are equipped with notebooks that tie into the company's data network and customized software system. The notebooks have boosted sales. One salesman indicated the notebook "gives me something with pizzazz." Salespeople can also work out quotes in the customer's office itself. Interestingly, Sheraton invested in notebooks to keep its employees happy. When four members of the Sheraton sales force became pregnant at roughly the same time and wanted to work from home, notebooks seemed the ideal choice. However, the experiment of equipping the women with notebooks worked so well that Sheraton explored the possibility of equipping the entire sales force with mobile technology. Another significant advantage of notebooks is that they have allowed Sheraton to expand into secondary markets where establishing an entire office was not cost effective. Salespeople are also provided with a modem and a cellular phone to further facilitate communications.[5]

cycle. For example, to get a price quote for a customer, an outside rep would call an inside rep, who would call the customer with the information. Many reps spent half their time gathering and rekeying data.

To increase customer responsiveness, Telogy provided each salesperson with all of the information necessary to handle every step of the sales process, from identifying and tracking leads to preparing price quotes and filling orders. Telogy's client-server-based information system centralized customer, inventory, pricing, and manufacturing information in a relational database. Desktop applications provide each salesperson with access to customer-contact information, giving every salesperson the ability to manage a deal through the entire process, from initial contact to final sale. The system has changed the way people relate to each other and communicate with their customers. Salespeople talk to more customers, do less paperwork, and devote more time to selling. "We can now process an order in record time. We can take an order at 5 p.m. and guarantee delivery of the equipment by 10 a.m. the next day," says a company spokesperson. Simply speaking, the ability to "slice and dice" information has changed the way salespeople at Telogy work.[6]

Developing Marketing Information Systems

The first step in developing a marketing system is creating a database of internal and external marketing data, a time-consuming process that requires creative thinking. The database should go beyond simply providing information about customers to providing information about noncustomers and the reasons why they have stayed away from the organization. The database should also measure customers' willingness to use new technologies in the process of dealing with the company so that the IS department can use this information when considering the introduction of new marketing technologies. Safeway Stores, a 1,100-store super-market chain, introduced an automated point-of-sale system that would allow shoppers to check out their own groceries. When a six-month trial at one of Safeway's busiest stores showed that only 15% of the store's customers used the technology, further investment in the technology was abandoned, thus saving the company hundreds of thousands of dollars.[7]

The database should also provide answers to the following queries:

♦ What is the best way to capture data at the point of sale?
♦ How can we ensure that marketing operations are run smoothly and efficiently?
♦ What are the goods and services that our customers want?
♦ How do customers define customer service?
♦ What kinds of services are important to customers?
♦ Are customers interested in and willing to use information technology?
♦ How much are customers willing to pay for higher-quality service?
♦ What impact would higher-quality customer service have on the profits of the company?
♦ How can we attract and retain customers?

Benefits of Marketing Information Systems

A good marketing system provides employees with information that helps companies capture niche markets in highly competitive industries. For example, MusicWriter, a company that sells music-related products, captured the market in sheet music through the innovative use of CD-ROM. Its market analysis showed that there was a fairly good market for sheet music, a market that retailers and publishers had chosen to ignore. MusicWriter set up a kiosk called NoteStation in 165 music stores throughout the U.S., Canada, and the United Kingdom. Each NoteStation is equipped with CD-ROMs that store sheet music for 4,000 compositions in all 12 keys. Customers make their choices using touchscreen PCs located in the kiosk. As soon as a credit card payment is approved, a printer in the kiosk prints the music.[8]

Another company that benefited from its superior marketing system is the retail chain Ikea North America. The company's market data showed that customers preferred self-service and lower prices over customized service and higher prices. The company found a niche in the highly competitive grocery industry and continues to reap the benefits of its good market analysis.[9]

Marketing information systems have a deep and direct influence on the quality of customer service. In fact, poor customer service can often be traced to poor information systems. Take a look at these facts:[10]

♦ A whopping 90% of a customer's contact with a company is through the customer service department.
♦ A dissatisfied customer generally tells three or four people about a bad experience that he or she has had with a company.
♦ A satisfied customer tells at most one other person about a good experience.
♦ Recruiting customers costs five times as much as retaining customers.

In spite of these facts, companies are 60% more likely to focus on winning new customers than on keeping existing ones. Hence, marketing information systems play a critical role in helping an organization achieve its goals.

Manufacturing Information Systems

The world of manufacturing is undergoing significant and rapid changes; today's manufacturing environment looks quite different from the shop floor of a decade ago. In the last few years, mechanical manufacturing has given way to automation, and in the coming years computers and information technologies are expected to play an even bigger role in changing the manufacturing landscape.

Manufacturing information system
A system that supports the manufacturing functions of purchasing, receiving, quality control, inventory management, material requirements planning, capacity planning, production scheduling, and plant design. Applies to both manufacturing and service environments.

Production systems
A subset of manufacturing information systems pertaining to the production of goods and services. Specifically addresses information needs relating to raw materials, equipment, manpower, and other issues related to production of goods and services.

A **manufacturing information system** is a system that supports the manufacturing functions of purchasing, receiving, quality control, inventory management, material requirements planning, capacity planning, production scheduling, and plant design. The term *manufacturing information system* actually applies to both manufacturing and service environments. Hence the term *manufacturing* should be viewed within the broad context of delivering both goods and services, since a manufacturer of automobile parts and a travel agency are both likely to have manufacturing information systems. **Production systems,** a subset of manufacturing information systems, are directly associated with the production of goods and services. While *manufacturing systems* is an umbrella term that covers all activities related to manufacturing and services, production systems specifically address information needs related to acquiring and managing raw materials, scheduling equipment, manpower planning, repair and maintenance, and other activities directly related to production.

Figure 11–4 shows how the strategic business plan forms the basis for the strategic manufacturing plan and the strategic information plan, which, in turn, provides the foundation for the manufacturing information system.

Developing a Manufacturing Information System

It is difficult to discuss manufacturing information systems without discussing MRP and MRP II. MRP stands for material requirements planning, a category of software that achieved prominence in the 1970s, which automates the process of production planning. MRP II (manufacturing resource planning) is the next generation of MRP systems; it integrates all the resources required to make a product: personnel, machines and equipment, plant capacity, pricing, distribution, and cost accounting. Some examples of popular MRP and MRP II products and their vendors are shown in Table 11–1. MRP and MRP II are central to manufacturing information systems. Yearly sales of these systems are estimated to be about $2.8 billion and are continuing to increase.

One of the primary problems with such systems is that companies that use them often fail to look at the big picture. George Stalk, Jr., the time-management guru at the Boston Consulting Group, says that many companies use MRP and MRP II software on a piece-meal basis with the goal of reducing costs or achieving incremental improvements in efficiency. But the true power and potential of MRP and MRP II can be utilized only if they are integrated with other non-manufacturing systems in an organization. This is the only way decision makers can get different views of the same customer: a marketing view, a production view, a finance view, and so on. Unfortunately, although MRP and MRP II systems provide a wealth of information that can be used by decision makers throughout the organization, they continue to be used in a limited way as manufacturing systems. However, a new and evolving concept, agile manufacturing, is intensifying the need to develop integrated systems.

FIGURE 11–4

The term *manufacturing information systems* actually applies to both manufacturing and service industries. These systems provide information on all aspects of producing and delivering goods and services. Some subsystems of manufacturing information systems are shown here.

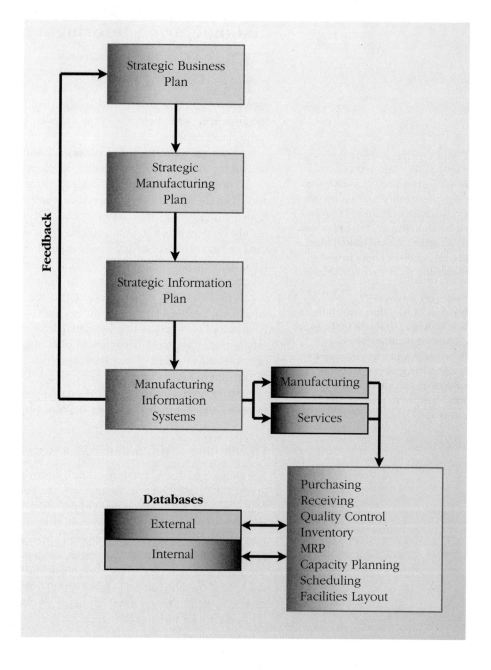

Agile manufacturing
The activities of manufacturing environments that are dynamic and flexible enough to instantaneously produce customized goods and services in different quantities and effortlessly switch the manufacturing process from one product to another.

Agile Manufacturing

Agile manufacturing is a term that refers to manufacturing environments that are dynamic and flexible enough to instantaneously produce customized goods and services in varying quantities and to effortlessly switch the manufacturing process from one product to another. Agile organizations have four key characteristics:[11]

♦ The ability to thrive on constant change
♦ Recognition by the organization that people are its main asset

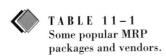

TABLE 11-1
Some popular MRP packages and vendors.

Package	Vendor
Avalon CIIM	Avalon Software
MRG/PRO	Qad Inc.
Oracle	Oracle Manufacturing
R/3 System	SAP America
Symix Advanced Manufacturing	Symix Computer Systems
Triton	Baan

- Incorporation of the virtual-company idea through the use of telecommunications
- A focus on creating products and services with real added value

Steven L. Goldman, technical director of the Agile Manufacturing Enterprise Forum, at the Iacocca Institute at Leigh University in Bethlehem, Pennsylvania, draws an analogy between agile manufacturing and the emergency room at a hospital. Hospital emergency rooms have special equipment and highly skilled staff that provide services to patients at a very short notice. When the idea is transferred to a manufacturing environment, we have an agile organization: one that can respond quickly and effectively to a wide variety of customer needs.

Textile/Clothing Technology (TC^2), a federally funded textile industry research and development group based in Cary, North Carolina, has an agile prototype. This prototype uses the data captured at POS terminals at retail outlets to give manufacturing instructions to computerized sewing machines in remote loca-

---

BUSINESS REALITIES
Spartan Stores Inc.

Spartan Stores, a wholesale food distributorship located in Grand Rapids, Michigan, with annual business in excess of $2.1 billion, recently revamped its manufacturing information systems. The company faces stiff competition from companies, such as Walmart and Kmart, which are becoming "alternative format" grocers that often can sell goods cheaper and faster. They do so by bypassing Spartan and other middlemen on the supply chain between producers and retailers.

In order to survive and grow in a tough and competitive market environment, Spartan recently focused on revamping its order-fulfillment and billing system. "We had basically been patching up a bunch of old legacy systems on an IBM 3090," says a company spokesperson.[12] It quickly became clear that modernizing the order system

alone would only temporarily fix a nagging problem. The company made a crucial decision to reinvent itself from a grocery wholesaler to a full-service distributor.

A team of eight Spartan executives, including representatives from IS, operations and procurements, worked three months to hammer out a plan. Hundreds of interviews were conducted with truck drivers, distribution workers and inventory control supervisors with the goal of reducing the 321 processes by two-thirds. The result was a system called Business Automation Support Environment (BASE) that capitalizes on a simple and elegant idea: Apply just-in-time (JIT) principles to food delivery. BASE involved nine key areas including distribution, logistics, inventory, order management, financial systems, and procurement. The system is based on client-server technology and object-oriented principles and several parts of the system are still under development. The multi-million dollar system expected to yield annual saving of $20 million.[13]

tions. For instance, suppose that POS data reveals that 100 units of Product A were sold at retail outlet B. The prototype immediately places an order for another 100 units of Product A to be delivered at the outlet. The system is so efficient that an order for one-of-a-kind monogrammed garments are usually ready 4 hours after the order is placed, a feat that would be impossible in traditional manufacturing environments, where it takes more than a year to deliver the goods.[14]

Agile manufacturing is likely to change the face of many industries in the U.S. and all over the world. For example, the $200-billion textile industry in the U.S., which is now struggling to survive, is hoping that agile manufacturing will bring back the glory days of the industry. Textile industry experts view agile manufacturing as the "great equalizer" that will help textile manufacturers counteract low foreign labor costs, which have so far cost the U.S. more than 420,000 jobs.[15]

Agile manufacturing will also help companies to better integrate their information systems. Erik Keller, of the Gartner Groups, speaks of "the networked manufacturing company": a multicelled organism that will link suppliers, manufacturers, distributors, and customers and monitor them on a real-time basis, providing instantaneous information to decision makers on manufacturing, sales, marketing, finance, quality, regulations, customer satisfaction, performance, and profitability. Managers will receive "triggered" information when something happens on the shop floor that affects their particular functions, such as human resources or accounting.

Benefits of Manufacturing Information Systems

Clearly, manufacturing goods and services is the primary function of a business. The information generated from the shop floor (or service floor) drives the rest of the organization, so companies that have well-integrated manufacturing information systems are bound to reap significant benefits. For example, the quality of its manufacturing information systems helped Red Devil, supplier to stores such as Home Depot and Ace Hardware, reduce operating costs and inventory levels. When Red Devil changed over from its mainframe to an NCR 3455 UNIX server running manufacturing software in client-server mode, software costs immediately dropped by 80% and hardware costs by 70%. MIS costs, which were 2.2% of sales, fell to 1.37% of sales, and MIS personnel were reduced by 27%. A whopping $2 million in inventory was slashed when users began to trust the output of the system and stopped "padding" inventory. Red Devil's ultimate goal? "Software that anticipates when Home Depot is likely to generate the order, so we can start production ahead of time."[16]

Another company that uses its manufacturing information systems to achieve its strategic goals is SynOptics Communications, in Santa Clara, California. The company manufactures leading-edge networking products and management systems. In a few short years, the company has grown from 300 people and $120 million in annual revenues to 1,700 employees and $183 million in *quarterly* revenues. It attributes much of its growth and success to information systems and technologies.

In late 1990, the company began replacing its PC-based manufacturing system with a new manufacturing information system called Integrated Information Systems Architecture. The primary objective was reducing manufacturing costs and cutting down-cycle times. The new system, which uses databases, networks,

GUIs, and off-the-shelf software, allows 1,500 employees distributed throughout the company to easily access enterprise-wide manufacturing data by integrating a number of core business systems (such as general ledger, accounts payable, and manufacturing). Embedded with decision support capabilities, the system allows managers to be decision-makers instead of data-gatherers. "We used to spend two days gathering information and an hour analyzing it. We're now able to reverse that axiom." says a company spokesperson. The system is expected to save the company $3.5 million by reducing operating expenses and increasing employee productivity. Overhead costs have decreased by 30 to 60 percent and lead time has decreased from 21 to 6 days. "One day of inventory is worth $1 million; so cutting out 15 days means we can put a lot of money to other uses."[17]

Quality Information Systems

Total Quality Management (TQM) has been embraced, with religious fervor, by some organizations and discarded by others as a passing fad. Some use TQM to achieve and hold leadership positions in the marketplace; others have been frustrated by their limited success with it. Regardless of the rate of success or failure of TQM, this simple and elegant idea continues to haunt corporations all over the world. In a recent survey of 455 senior managers, 87% of them viewed quality as the key factor for achieving competitive success.[18] **Quality information systems** are standalone systems or embedded systems that help an organization to achieve its quality goals.

Figure 11–5 shows how the strategic quality plan is derived from the strategic information plan. In some cases, a company has no separate quality plan, but instead makes quality a component of other plans, such as marketing, manufacturing, and so on. Table 11–2 provides some dos and don'ts for CIOs involved in TQM efforts.

The IS department plays a major role in ensuring the success of TQM efforts in an organization. An information system can promote quality and provide tools and techniques to help the company achieve its quality goals. Information systems also help companies achieve quality certification. There are many institutions and agencies that certify the quality efforts of an organization and provide guidelines to companies that plan to instill quality in all aspects of their operations. The most popular quality certification programs are the Malcolm Baldrige National Quality Award and the ISO 9000, both administered by the Office of Quality Programs at the National Institute of Standards and Technology. A 1993 survey of 455 top executives by the American Electronics Association (AEA) revealed that 92% of the companies surveyed were using either the Baldrige Award or the ISO 9000 standards to measure the effectiveness of their quality programs.[19]

The role of IS may vary from one organization to the next, or even from one program to the next, but there are four major areas where IS plays an important role in the certification process.[20] They are partial systems overhaul, full systems overhaul, training, and oversight.

In a *partial systems overhaul,* existing systems are partially revamped in order to update them and make them more responsive to the changing needs of decision makers. Partial systems overhaul may include providing users with better interfaces, better end-user support, or better integration of existing systems. The

Quality information system
Stand-alone or embedded systems that help an organization to achieve its quality goals. The quality plan is derived from the strategic information plan.

FIGURE 11-5

Quality control information systems support and facilitate an organization's TQM efforts.

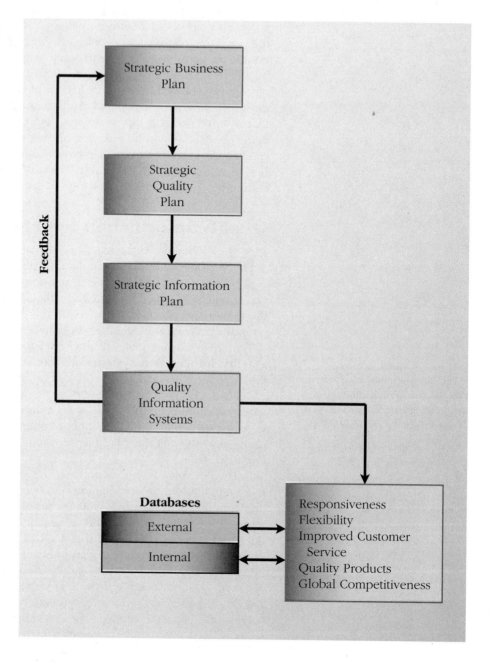

IS department at DuPont Merck Pharmaceutical Company, in Delaware, in a partial systems overhaul, developed interfaces to link its corporate information system with its manufacturing information systems in order to reduce inventory, enhance customer support, and increase overall productivity.[21]

In a *full systems overhaul,* the old system is replaced with a new system. This may sometimes be necessitated by outdated equipment or systems that can no longer be updated or maintained. For example, ICI Films, a $1-billion manufacturer of film for the packaging industry, implemented and installed new materials

TABLE 11-2
CIOs play an important role in helping organizations achieve its quality goals. This table provides some do's and don'ts for the CIO and IS personnel involved in an enterprise-wide quality effort.

Lessons for IS Executives

Here's some advice from two CIOs who have lived through a TQM effort:

Good Moves

✔ Help provide an enterprise-wide perspective to the TQM effort.

✔ Volunteer at the outset. Don't wait for someone to ask you to be involved.

✔ Be a consensus builder in the corporate effort, a catalyst rather than a driver.

✔ Be a leader for the IS staff. They will be watching to see if you really support the process or just give it lip service.

✔ Become a resource for the quality teams in resolving cross-functional conflicts.

✔ Get the IS staff [your people] trained in the quality process. Many of the skills used in systems analysis will translate well.

✔ Be realistic with the time frames that you set. People will lose interest if a task can't be accomplished in 6 months or less.

Bad Moves

☒ Don't try to control information production and use. Encourage end-user access to information, off-the-shelf software, etc.

☒ Don't allow IS to be a bottleneck at the implementation phase. Anticipate recommendations to re-engineer systems or support streamlining efforts.

☒ Don't be an obstacle to the TQM effort. Look for opportunities to change "can't be done" to "can do."

☒ Don't promise more than you can deliver.

☒ Don't permit the overinvolvement of just one or two individuals in the IS department.

Source: David Loebig, CIO, Owen Healthcare, Inc. Houston: Charles M. Jones, CIO, Charleston Area Medical Center, Charleston, W. VA; College of Healthcare Information Systems Executives, Ann Arbor, Mich.

requirement planning software in order to achieve quality certification. Its existing systems were beyond revamping, so the company decided to replace them with new systems.

Training is another area where IS can play an important role in quality certification. Users must be well trained in systems that are partially or fully overhauled, because this has a direct impact both on quality and on productivity. More important, good data come from well-trained users and good data form the basis of good decisions.

Finally, IS should oversee the entire quality certification process; this is often a time-consuming task. It requires coordination and cooperation among departments; IS can play a facilitating role by ensuring the free flow of information between decision makers. Often, company data and information have to be sent to external agencies and IS plays a critical role in getting the right data to the right people at the right time. Cross-functional teams, such as those formed at Nypro (discussed below), are vital to the certification process. For example, the city of Dallas uses cross-functional teams to provide high-quality city services (see box).

BUSINESS REALITIES
City of Dallas

There are very few IS departments in the country that have made quality teams a part of their everyday routine operations and achieved quantifiable benefits in the process. The IS Quality Team for the City of Dallas stands out in this regard, winning the 1994 "Best of the Best Award" in the IS category from the Quality Assurance Institute. At the Dallas department of information services, which supports city services—such as police, fire protection, water service, housing, parks and recreation, health services and building inspections—quality assurance is fully documented and the quality circle, called the Production Control Committee, meets weekly to discuss all problems reported the previous week and brainstorm solutions.

The committee is highly cross-functional and consists of a representative from each of the three application programming divisions: systems programming, database administration, quality assurance—plus the operations manager, data control manager, and security administrator. Front-line IS personnel log all production problems, including abends or abnormal terminations that require manual intervention in order to complete a job, missing reports, and incorrect data. The committee holds a one-hour meeting to identify the biggest problem areas and then asks subcommittees to find solutions. The team approach has cut abends by 66%, with the city saving roughly $1,000 for each abend that is fixed. Also, the data generated by the committee is highly useful for budget justification since high-problem areas are likely to get immediate attention. The data helps the committee spot trends and track progress toward solving problems.[22]

Benefits of Quality Information Systems

The goal of many corporations all over the world is to produce high-quality goods and services; information is essential to achieve this goal—accurate, timely, and reliable information. For example, a few years ago, the $100 million structural products division of Coors Ceramics, Golden, Colorado, was in trouble because its 15-year-old information system was outdated. The system took as long as 2 days to process an order and salespeople couldn't track the status of customer orders. Managers often fudged numbers so that goods could be delivered on time, often resulting in higher finished-goods inventories and an increase in overhead costs. The system also tracked shipping only on a weekly basis. Therefore if a customer wanted an order Monday and Coors shipped it Saturday, the system logged that order as "on time." When customers called to complain, the salesperson got no valid data from the system other than a cheerful "on time" report.

Coors realized that lack of information was one of the primary reasons why its quality was slipping and identified three goals for the new information system: increase customer satisfaction, reduce lead times, and reduce operating costs. The new client-server system runs on a UNIX-based IBM RS/6000, which provides integrated manufacturing, distribution, field service and financial applications. The system tracks inventory and shipments and provides managers with detailed information on the status of customer orders. The system provides managers with complete and comprehensive information on customers, including order placement, production or shipment status, and payment reports. The new system has helped the company to reduce the product cycle from 10 to 14 weeks to 6 to 10 weeks. On-time shipments have improved to more than 95% and Coors salespeople can be confident that "on time" means that it was delivered on time, not just within a week.[23]

Achieving quality also involves being able to develop strategic alliances with suppliers and customers, and information is again essential to this process. Nypro, a precision injection molder in Clinton, Massachusetts, tripled its sales to $200 million in just 6 years by using information systems to build strategic alliances with its suppliers by sharing company-related information with them. This has led to the creation of management teams, comprising members from both Nypro and its suppliers, who freely exchange the information necessary to produce high-quality goods.[24]

Auto Alliance International (see box) believes that information is essential to building high-quality automobiles and developed a quality information management system (QIMS) to achieve its quality goals. The system tightly integrates information generated on the shop floor, for instance about defective automobiles, so that decision makers can take immediate action to correct the situation. Managers have changed from data gatherers to quality enforcers, since now they can take proactive action to keep the company on the quality track.

Financial and accounting information system (FAIS)
A system that provides information related to the accounting and financial activities of an organization. Includes a large number of subsystems that address the operational, tactical, and strategic information needs of the business.

Financial and Accounting Information Systems

AFinancial and accounting information system (FAIS) is a system that provides information related to the accounting and financial activities in an organization. The FAIS includes a number of subsystems, such as budgeting, cash and asset management, capital budgeting, portfolio analysis, general ledger, accounts receivable, inventory control, and payroll systems. Other systems

---

B U S I N E S S   R E A L I T I E S
Auto Alliance International

Auto Alliance International (AAI), a joint venture of Mazda and Ford, produces the Ford Probe, the Mazda 626, and the Mazda MX-6. The Alliance has implemented a quality information management system (QIMS) to ensure the delivery of high-quality automobiles.

QIMS provides managers and senior executives with instantaneous information on any defective car. Inspectors on the plant floor inspect each automobile and record any problems or defects on a ticket that accompanies the vehicle to the end of the production line. Inspectors at the end of the production line use a 600-word vocabulary to describe what is wrong with the vehicle by reading the information on the ticket into headsets that have voice recognition software. The information is then transmitted, using radio waves, to a workstation 70 feet away that is connected to a LAN. Managers can view the data in their offices. For those who are away traveling, the information is sent every 2 hours by modem. "The way we are disseminating information is changing how people look at data. They don't

have to seek out a PC; the data comes to them, and that keeps people focused on quality," says a spokesperson.

Why is information the driving force behind building quality automobiles? Says one IS manager, "There are some people that say, 'You aren't going to change manufacturing or make an improvement with just the data.' That is correct. But you also aren't going to make any changes unless you have the information, so this is just one step in being able to improve the quality of the vehicles." Before the system was implemented, it took about two and a half days before managers could respond to the data collected on the shop floor. Also, there was no way to detect patterns, since the paper-based reports were highly rigid and inflexible.

Today, the ability to respond to information quickly and effectively has contributed significantly to building quality automobiles. AAI has become a more responsive organization and has significantly reduced the number of defective parts and automobiles. Administrative and personnel costs have come down because fewer people are needed to collect and distribute the data. The half-million-dollar investment in hardware, software, and programming hours had a payback period of less than 8 months.[25]

include recordkeeping, account analysis, cash management, financial analysis, leasing options, insurance underwriting, insurance claims processing, and investment management. Financial institutions, such as banks, use specialized FAIS, such as commercial loan analyzers, credit approval systems, commercial account rating systems, credit application systems, automated teller control, and securities trading. Other institutions and companies may have their own specialized FAIS subsystems. Regardless of the type and number of subsystems, financial and accounting subsystems work together to create, record, generate, and disseminate financial and accounting information vital to good decision making. For example, UCLA medical school relies on its financial system to provide decision makers with timely financial data (see box).

Figure 11–6 shows how the financial information plan is derived from the strategic information plan and the strategic business plan. Although most financial and accounting managers operate under the "tyranny of the urgent," a strategic financial plan and an integrated set of information systems that support the plan are a necessity for the survival and growth of any organization.[26]

Types of Financial and Accounting Information Systems

An FAIS is a collection of subsystems that perform different functions, including general ledger, asset management, order entry, accounts receivable, accounts payable, inventory control, and payroll systems. Since most of these terms are fairly self-explanatory, this section provides only a brief description of each system.

General ledger systems generate the company's income statements and balance sheets and are responsible for managing new and old accounts in the company. *Asset management systems* maintain an inventory of the company's long-term assets and ensure that accounting practices for company assets comply with regulatory standards. The output of this system often becomes input to the general ledger system. *Order entry systems* capture and manage different kinds of data relating to a transaction, such as number of units sold, customer billing, credit history, sales tax, and inventory levels. The output of this system is input to a num-

---

 BUSINESS REALITIES
UCLA Medical School

The one good thing to come out of a devastating fire two years ago at UCLA's department of medicine was a chance to redesign the department's cumbersome financial system," says the IS director at UCLA Medical School. His sentiments are shared by other users of the old financial system, which was tedious and cumbersome to use and did not provide the information decision makers needed to make sound decisions.

Under the old system, users had to download financial data from the university's mainframe to "dumb" terminals in the department. The data then had to be

retyped into the department's database. Reports were generated only on a monthly basis; hence, decision makers did not know on a day-to-day basis the amount of funds already committed. All that changed when the system and the application software went up in flames.

Today, UCLA boasts a sophisticated client-server system that links 250 PCs and Macintoshes to a single database that contains information on clinical income, payroll, general ledger, and personnel applications. The system has front-end software that allows accountants with little or no programming background to easily access and manipulate the database. One of the primary benefits of the system is the timeliness of reports, which can now be customized and generated on a real-time basis.[27]

FIGURE 11-6

Like other functional systems, the FAIS is driven by the strategic business plan and the strategic information plan. The subsystems of FAIS are shown in the box.

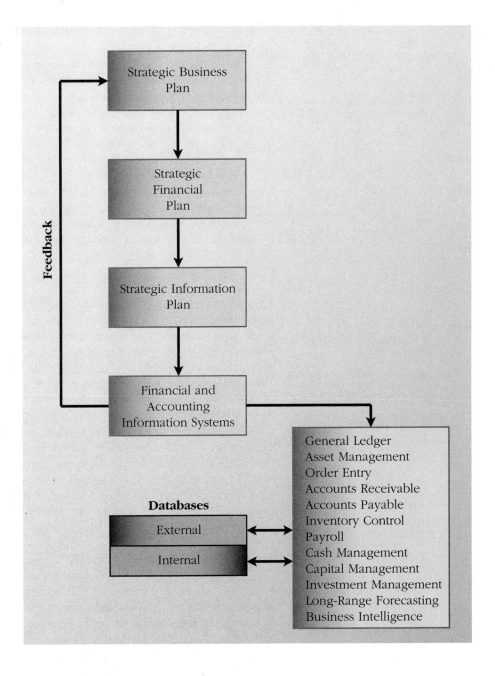

ber of other systems, such as accounts receivable and inventory management. *Accounts receivable* and *accounts payable* capture and process data, such as creditor and customer billing information, payments received and owed, credit terms, account balances, and payment schedules. The *inventory control system* captures, processes, and manages all data related to the company's inventory, such as items in inventory, inventory levels and costs, accounting practices related to inventory maintenance, stock balance, and data on lost, damaged, or returned goods. Finally, *payroll systems* capture and process data related to wages and salaries, including federal and state taxes, other payroll deductions, employee benefits, overtime, and related data.

These systems are designed to support mostly operational decisions. There are other kinds of FAIS to support tactical and strategic decision making in the organization, such as the following:

♦ *Cash management systems:* systems that ensure that the organization has enough cash to conduct normal business, to receive the best possible return on its short-term cash deposits, and to leverage its cash flow to achieve good ratings in financial markets
♦ *Capital budgeting systems:* systems that ensure the acquisition and disposal of capital assets, such as land, buildings, and so on
♦ *Investment management systems:* systems that ensure that the organization gets the best possible returns on its long-term investments

Integrated Financial and Accounting Systems

FAIS are often integrated with other functional systems in the organization to facilitate data sharing and team decision making. After all, financial decisions are not made in a vacuum; they often involve marketing, manufacturing, and human resources, so a free flow of information among these functional units is vital for good decision making. For example, Air Touch Communications (see box) achieved significant benefits when it opened its financial system for use by other departments. A radically different form of accounting, called ABC accounting (see box) is helping companies integrate financial information with other systems.

For global and multinational companies, integrated financial and accounting systems are simply a necessity. For example, a multinational corporation with operations in the U.S., Canada, Europe, and Asia relies on its integrated financial system to monitor the overall financial health of the organization and keep managers abreast of important financial events. Although each overseas business unit operates as a separate company with its own policies, procedures, and systems, a common financial reporting system links the company's domestic offices with its international offices. The system ensures that every application, regardless of where it originated, complies with the accounting rules and principles of the U.S.[28]

Another example of an integrated financial system is that of Allergan's. A few years ago, Allergan, a maker of pharmaceuticals and ophthalmic products, had two nonintegrated, cumbersome, financial reporting systems: one for international operations and one for domestic operations. Financial data from Allergan's 40 international subsidiaries had to be re-entered manually into different systems: the company's general-ledger system for currency translation and consolidation, and the company's domestic accounting system for generating financial reports for the entire company.

In early 1992, the company installed a PC-based financial software package that allows data to be sent electronically from the international subsidiaries to the domestic general-ledger system; from there, it is uploaded to the company's central database. Users can now produce customized reports faster and with fewer inconsistencies, thus enhancing organizational decision making. "Information is now transmitted with the speed of a phone call; everyone can pull up the system and see the same set of numbers with just a few keystrokes."[29]

BUSINESS REALITIES
Air Touch Communications, Inc.

Air Touch Communications, a wireless communications firm, standardized 11 sets of books into four processes and opened its financial system for use by other departments to cut costs and improve bottom line. Before the new system was installed, generating monthly financial reports was a nightmare since most financial data was in disparate ledgers and accounting systems. Getting the 10 business units (which offer cellular, paging and vehicle-locator systems and services) to report numbers in a uniform manner was difficult, and it took 9 days just to close the books.

The new financial system maintains 150 general ledgers, 60 in foreign currencies. About 150 users have access to all corporate financial data and the level of access depends on users' security profiles. The system created a uniform chart of accounts and standardized each division into four uniform processes: accounts payable and receivable, fixed assets, billing/cost recovery and purchasing. The system has paid dividends: shorter closing times, reduced training costs, and fewer personnel in the accounting department. Corporate accounting now closes its books in two to three days, the cellular group in four, and the international group in six. Although the number of employees at headquarters has increased fourfold since 1991, the accounting staff has remained relatively static.[30]

Another example of a global company that has benefitted by integrating its financial systems is Russell Reynolds (see box).

Human Resource Information Systems

Human resource information system (HRIS)
A system that supports the planning, control, coordination, administration, and management of an organization's human resources. Includes a large number of subsystems that address the information needs of various human resource functions.

Human resource information systems (HRIS) support the planning, control, coordination, administration, and management of the human resource assets in an organization. They provide managers with information, policies, and procedures concerning recruiting, layoffs, employee evaluation, promotion, termination, transfer, salary equity monitoring, job descriptions and responsibilities, training, affirmative action, and equal employment opportunities. Since they also provide vital information on matters such as payroll, federal and state taxes, health benefits, child care, grievance procedures, and other

BUSINESS REALITIES
ABC Accounting

In spite of the inadequacy of the practice, many accounting systems even today assign overhead somewhat arbitrarily across the board, making it difficult to determine the true cost of a product. But companies such as Procter & Gamble, National Semiconductor, Boeing, Harley-Davidson, Valvoline, and Clorox are experimenting with a radically different, controversial form of accounting that assigns overhead costs based on actual consumption of resources, known as activity-based costing (ABC). A key benefit of ABC is that it allows a company to determine the true cost of a product and the cost of serving a customer.

The ABC system is simple but highly information-intensive. Instead of viewing the business as a collection of salaries and machines, ABC views it as a collection of processes or activities, and calculates the cost of each process or activity. These calculations are made by integrating information from different sources, such as the company's general ledger and time-keeping systems. Determining the true cost of a product is the first step toward increasing profits and a FAIS can help a company achieve this goal.[31]

A GLOBAL PERSPECTIVE
Russell Reynolds Associates

Russell Reynolds Associates, an executive search firm, has no alternative but to deal with the vagaries of international accounting practices. As the company grew globally throughout the 1980s, opening 22 offices in countries from France to Singapore, its financial and accounting systems grew correspondingly complex. Eventually, the company had full accounting departments at its U.S. headquarters and eight international locations simply to keep up with its world-wide accounting requirements. "It was inefficient, to say the least," says Roger S. Pierce, Jr., director of international finance at the New York-based firm. So his unit embarked on a two-part project to ensure that all locations spoke the same accounting language and cut the company's finance-operations overhead by almost 20 percent.

The toughest problem the company faced was conforming to the different regulatory climates in each country. Taxation and other legal requirements varied widely among the company's different locations and was different even among European Union nations. To complicate matters further, each international location reported its monthly data in the local currency and in whatever form it found most convenient. While some business units used their own accounting package, in less sophisticated environments the accounting was done on "a piece of paper covered with figures." In addition, international offices reported financial information only in summary form, making it difficult for analysts at headquarters to use.

Starting in 1990, the company realized it was imperative to compare the performance of different profit-centers on an apples-to-apples basis using universal definitions and standards. So they designed standard accounting procedures that conformed to both international and U.S. regulations. Once this was accomplished, the company began standardizing its accounting departments using software from Sun Systems. (So far, all European and Asia Pacific offices have been converted to the same package.)

Pierce also has all company divisions using the same chart of accounts, which meets U.S. accounting principles. "Everybody pigeonholes expenses, income, assets and liabilities the same way," he says. This uniformity allows top managers to get detailed information on any item, such as how much an individual recruiter spends on rental cars.

Once all the international accounting departments implemented and followed the same procedures, the company began examining each process and procedure in an effort to eliminate inefficiencies and enhance the productivity of knowledge workers. Today, a number of processes have been greatly simplified. For example, previously an international expense report went through eight different steps between from submission to payment. An automated billing system cut that time in half.

The standardized procedures also helped the company consolidate some of its activities and centers. Five accounting departments in Europe were consolidated into one in London, enabling Russell Reynolds to cut personnel costs and benefit from economies of scale. The company is also planning to switch to activity-based accounting (see box), in which a company bases its financial decisions on business processes rather than geographic districts.[32]

---

personal information that affects employees' personal and professional lives, it is imperative that these systems be highly responsive to employee needs.

Human resource systems, unlike accounting and financial information systems, were slow to be computerized. In the 1960s, HRIS were primarily record-keeping systems that were developed, managed, and maintained by IS professionals with little or no input from the personnel department. But by the early 1980s, many organizations began to realize the importance of HRIS. In the early 1980s, almost 60% of the nation's largest 150 banks and nearly 40% of the Fortune 500 firms invested in some kind of personnel information system, largely because of the Johnson and Nixon administrations' legislation on equal employment, benefits, and workplace conditions. It is estimated that by the year 2000, HRIS will be a necessity for major corporations if they are to keep up with increasing government regulations and respond to personal information queries about employees.[33] Table 11–3 provides some guidelines on selecting an HRIS.

Although many people believe that HRIS systems can be used only to enhance HR decisions, in fact they can be used to cut costs, increase efficiency, and achieve a competitive edge in the marketplace. For example, finance and human resource managers at NCR jointly developed a HRIS that determines how hiring and training decisions made by the personnel department can increase sales revenues. Also, the system links the performance of an individual to items such as past training, educational background, and work history, so that managers can be better equipped to make such decisions.

To keep the cost of employee relocation down and ensure smooth transfers, Mobil Oil uses an HRIS to select the best relocation site. Armstrong World's HRIS enabled the company to self-insure and to better control health care costs. The human resources department at Apple Computer developed a system for effec-

---

TABLE 11–3
Some guidelines for selecting an HRIS.

	How to Pick an HR System
Get advice	Help from a reputable HR consulting firm minimizes the risk. These specialists have been through the process before.
Test the payroll	High-volume transaction processing is the toughest job for client-server systems. Ask prospective human resources vendors to run your payroll for you.
Play the numbers	Don't ignore the benefits of outside service bureaus—especially in the area of payroll. Tax, retirement, and other legal conditions change. If you've got more than 500 employees, run a cost-benefits analysis.
Get it in writing	Don't be afraid to ask your vendor for a guarantee. At least two HR suppliers, Ross Systems and ADP, offer "Statements of Commitment."
Train, train, train	Provide plenty of project staffing and technology education for your HR staff on the new system.
Be prepared	A merger or acquisition can affect your business at any time. A firm might need to add 5,000 employees to benefits and payroll systems within 30 days.
Act like traditional IS	Today's human resources departments must worry about security and data integrity, taking over that responsibility in some cases from information systems departments.

Source: Winkler, Connie, "The New Line On Managing People." *InformationWeek,* May 23, 1994, p. 68.

tively sorting through the thousands of resumes that the company receives each day (see box).

The HRIS and the Competitive Strategy of the Firm

HRIS are powerful systems that can shape, and be shaped by, the competitive strategies of a firm. Broderick and Boudreau (1987)[34] identify three competitive firm-based strategies that influence the objectives and design of the HRIS: cost leadership, customer satisfaction, and innovation.

Cost leadership strategy focuses on economies of scale; customer satisfaction strategy focuses on enhancing customer services to gain market share; innovation strategy emphasizes differentiation through new products, services, and technologies. Table 11–4 shows how the human resource function can be tied directly to the competitive strategy of the business.

Regardless of the strategy that drives the firm, HRIS must be integrated with other systems in the organization. For example, when an HRIS is integrated with a FAIS, it helps accountants to measure employment-related cost factors and to understand the relationship between performance and productivity, such as assessing the financial implications of productivity differences between full-time, temporary, and part-time workers. This helps the entire organization to better plan its workforce and to explore employee-related cost-benefit relationships.

Some companies use HRIS to publicize job openings over the network and encourage employees to submit computerized resumes. Resumes are then matched with existing online skill inventories, or "competency libraries," of employees to identify relevant skills, work experience, qualifications, and educational background. This greatly increases the efficiency of finding good employees who are suited to the job at hand.

Developing an HRIS

Figure 11–7 shows how the HRIS is derived from the strategic business plan, the strategic human resources plan, and the strategic information plan. Some subsystems within the HRIS are personnel data, payroll, benefits administration,

---

BUSINESS REALITIES
Apple Computer

Gone are the days when human resource managers carefully sorted through piles of resumes to identify potential candidates. Today, information technology sorts out the "good apples" from the bad ones. At least, that's the way it works at Apple Computer, which uses resume scanners equipped with artificial intelligence to take the first look at applicants.

Optical scanners read about 900 pages of resumes per day and feed the data into a resume database, where a computer searches through the data using descriptors such as job titles, technical expertise, education, geographic location, and employment history. Each scanned resume is ranked and filed based on job categories and then matched with available openings. If a match is not found, the system automatically prints a rejection letter, signs it, and mails it off to the candidate!

The system also helps managers schedule interviews for applicants and generate offer letters. Once the applicant comes on board, salary increases, performance reviews, personnel history, benefits, transfers, training levels, hazardous-materials exposure, and other information pertinent to the employee is stored in the database for future use.[35]

TABLE 11-4
This table shows how the competitive strategies of a firm can directly influence the objectives of the human resource information system (HRIS).

	Firm-Level Competitive Strategies		
HR Competitive Objectives	**Cost Leadersip** **People Working** **Harder**	Quality/Customer **Satisfaction** **People Working** **Smarter**	**Innovation** **People Working** **with Vision**
HR Decisions and Actions	• Streamline • Standardize • Decrease production time/head count • Reduce costs (e.g., increase accuracy)	• Educate line managers and other "clients" • Delegate/share decisions • Use customer-driven performance criteria • Increase flexibility	• Define vision • Attract creative talent • Reward risk • Provide opportunities/ tools for exploration

Source: Broderick, Renae, and John W. Boudreau. "Human Resources Management Information Technology and the Competitive Edge," *Academy of Management Executives,* 1992, vol. 6, no. 2, p. 10.

equity monitoring, processing job applications, monitoring positions, training and development, safety, workers' compensation, union negotiations, and collective bargaining.

The core of an HRIS is a database that contains detailed personal and professional information about each employee in the organization. Personal data include name, age, gender, address, and social security number; professional data include educational level, job title, job description, department code, years of employment, number of promotions, performance evaluations, and so on. All other human resource subsystems derive their information from this core database.

An important subsystem of the HRIS is the compliance system, which closely tracks and monitors the organization's record of compliance with government laws and regulations, such as affirmative action, equal employment opportunities, the health and safety codes of the Occupational Safety and Health Administration (OSHA), and others. In the last two decades, the amount of regulatory paperwork has increased manyfold and organizations are actively looking for ways to cut down the time and money they spend on these activities. One way to achieve this objective is through compliance subsystems.

Another vital HRIS subsystem manages records and generates information regarding recruitment, transfer, promotion, layoff, and termination of employees. Often, when any of the above situations occur, a large amount of information is generated and the organization needs a system that processes it. As the number of lawsuits for improper hiring, promotion, and firing policies increases, accurate and timely recordkeeping becomes even more important.

Other subsystems of the HRIS include systems that develop and maintain job titles and job descriptions for all jobs in the company, compensation and benefits information systems, and manpower planning systems. A performance appraisal

Like other systems, the HRIS is driven by the strategic business plan and the strategic information plan. The subsystems of a HRIS are shown.

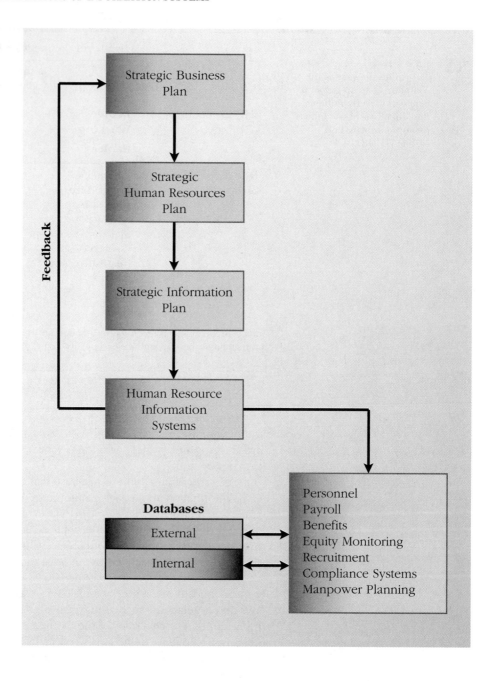

system that provides employees with real-time information on corporate performance measurements, thus making continuous performance improvement a way of corporate life rather than an annual chore, is another important subsystem in an HRIS. Pretesting compensation policies, ensuring that employees meet certification requirements, identifying problem areas in employee turnover, administering drug and alcohol policies, and providing training and employee empowerment programs are some other functions of an HRIS.[36]

Today many organizations are using PC-based kiosks to share vital HR information with employees (see box).

Geographical Information Systems

Several years ago, telecommunications carrier GTE tracked the progress of its fiber-optic network by poking pins into maps handed out by a car rental agency.[37] Today, Geographical Information Systems (GIS) provide a much more sophisticated way for companies such as GTE to gather a wide range of information and display it on computer-generated maps. Geography plays an important role in many business decisions, since 85% of corporate data involve geographical elements, such as customer addresses and supplier locations. Also, a number of business decisions, such as store locations, sales territories, sales promotions, and regulatory compliance rely heavily on geographical data. Awareness of this has led many software vendors, such as Lotus, to embed mapping technology in their products so that users can produce maps easily.

Although the term *Geographical Information Systems* may conjure up images of software tools for geography majors, they are in fact among the most powerful and versatile tools for the business community and can be used in many different ways in the various functional areas of a business. A **geographical information system** is a computer-based system that stores and manipulates data that are viewed from a geographical point of reference. A GIS has four main capabilities: data input, data storage and retrieval, data manipulation and analysis, and data output. (Although there are many manual geographical information systems, this section focuses on computer-based systems.) Note that a GIS should not be confused with cartographic systems, which merely store and generate computer-based maps. A GIS is much more versatile and powerful than a cartographic system, since it can create information by integrating different data, sometimes from different sources, and display the data in different ways to the end-user.[38]

The number of business applications of GIS has grown significantly in the last few years. For example, Mobil Oil uses a GIS product called MapInfo for crisis management in the event of an oil spill or tank explosion; Levi Strauss uses GIS to match a store's product mix with customer demographics; the *Chicago*

Geographical information system Powerful and versatile tools that allow users to generate and process information with a geographical point of reference. Data input, storage and retrieval, manipulation and analysis, and data output are its four main capabilities.

BUSINESS REALITIES
Kiosks and Human Resources

Today's human resource departments are squeezed between the need to cut soaring administrative costs and administer increasingly complex benefits plans, regulations, and training programs. So HR departments are deploying information technology, such as PC-based kiosks and interactive telephone systems, to handle routine tasks, such as explaining HR programs to employees, and free staff for more strategic matters. A new concept, referred to as "virtual HR," or the use of technology to give employees direct contact with the organization's

HR information systems, is now evolving in many organizations.

For example, employees at Apple Computer use "Mac 401(k)" desktop software to enroll and invest in their 401(k) plan and "MacLoan" software to process loans. Bell Atlantic employees use an interactive telephone system to enroll in benefits programs and change the information about dependents. At Becton Dickinson, based in Franklin Lakes, N.J., employees can monitor the performance of their 401(k) investments using PC kiosks/touch-screen PCs. Merck, for example, uses kiosks to administer a flexible benefits program. The system even allows the employees to do "what-if" modeling to see how their selections will affect their return on investments.[39]

Tribune uses GIS for developing new sales territories based on demographics; and Arby's uses GIS for site selection.

The banking industry uses GIS to respond to regulatory pressures and to comply with the Community Redevelopment Act, which requires banks to demonstrate to regulators that their lending practices are nondiscriminatory. A GIS allows a bank to compare deposits with loan approvals in a given area and show that loan approvals meet regulatory standards in areas with high deposits, especially in parts of the country that have heavy minority populations. Essential Information, a Washington-based public-interest group founded by Ralph Nader, recently used a GIS to illustrate its charges that mortgage lenders in some parts of the country are violating the Fair Housing and Equal Credit Opportunity acts. Automobile insurers use GIS to estimate the distance traveled between home and work for potential clients, because this is an important factor in determining insurance rates. A recent study by the Industry Research Council showed that many Americans believe it is acceptable to lie about the distance they drive between home and work in order to lower their insurance rates![40]

For example, the city of Shanghai in China is using GIS to increase the efficiency of the city's basic infrastructure (see box).

In summary, a geographical information system is an excellent decision-making tool that integrates geographical data with other business data. For companies with a customer focus, a GIS provides clear profiles of customers and their needs; hence, these tools can be integrated with any of the functional systems discussed above, such as marketing information systems, production information systems, and so on. The ability to integrate different data, analyze their impact on the customer, and integrate the findings in organizational decision making is one of the key factors that separates winners from losers.

Developing Cross-functional Systems

Clearly, today the emphasis is on building cross-functional systems that facilitate the flow of information among all units in an organization. Decision-making should not be compartmentalized in functional areas, but should instead be viewed in the context of the entire organization. The close link between information systems and the various functional units in the organization emphasizes the fact that students, regardless of their area of specialization, should be well grounded in information systems and technologies. In the coming years, computer skills will be grouped with the basic skills of reading, writing, and arithmetic, and computer-literate individuals with a good understanding of information systems will be eagerly sought after by employers.

What is the relationship between the functional systems and the different *types* of information systems that were covered in Chapter 2, namely, TPS, MIS, DSS, EIS, ES, and OAS? Look at Figure 11–2. As you can see, the various types of information systems form the backbone of the functional information systems. The type of functional system depends on the nature, scope, and complexity of the task. If the task is routine, structured, involves transactional data, and is related to operational decisions, whether in finance, accounting, marketing, manufacturing, or human resources, the system is likely to be a transaction processing system. Summary and exception reports for different functional areas are likely to be generated by a management information system. For example, a report of the number of people who worked overtime last month (human resources) or the

A GLOBAL PERSPECTIVE
Shanghai's GIS

Shanghai is bursting at the seams. Population growth and unruly property development in recent years have made urban planning in the city a nightmarish task. Now, with help from abroad and computer technology, city officials are trying to get a handle on the problem.

In Shanghai's pre-1949 glory days, the city boasted the most highly developed urban amenities in Asia outside Tokyo. The foreign officials who managed the city's International Settlement and the French Concession built electricity networks, sewage lines, and tramways that were the equal of those in most European cities.

But just as political affairs in the city's foreign sectors were administered separately, so were their municipal services. Buses and sewage lines stopped at concession boundaries. Even today, these disparate systems are not fully linked. Residents often complain about the numerous places along the city's former boundary lines where raw sewage oozes to the surface, according to Shanghai native Lynn Pan, author of several books about the city.

An Ottawa-based urban planning company, Chreod Development Planning Consultants, is helping the Shanghai Construction Commission draw up a GIS. Such systems, which link infrastructure databases with computerized maps, are a relatively new idea. They allow more efficient operation and better planning of water and gas lines, sewage systems, transport networks, and electrical grids.

The World Bank is designing the Shanghai Environmental Project. The project could eventually entail the expenditure of up to $300 million on developing an environmental master plan for the city, as well as modernizing the city's solid-waste management and its sewage- and water-treatment facilities.

Shanghai's most urgent task is to learn the dimensions of its problem; this is where the GIS comes in. It will plot the locations of water lines, along with their carrying capacity and other technical features, making it possible to spot weak points.

The GIS will enable planners to call up the infrastructure of a whole city or of a district on a computer screen. A particular system, for example, can be analyzed in more detail to find an explanation for an unplanned loss of pressure in gas lines. In the case of a break in a power line in a certain district, a GIS can quickly locate the most convenient route on which to bring in backup power.

The system will also be used in forecasting. Because of the huge amount of stored data, it will be relatively easy for planners to alter assumptions on which development is based and to predict the consequences for other aspects of the infrastructure.

For Shanghai, help cannot come too soon. The city was crowded in the 1930s, when its population was 3 million. Today, the city proper has 8 million residents, with another 7 million in the surrounding area.

It is not simply a matter of numbers, either. Some problems result from an uneasy relationship with the central government in Peking. In 1979, Shanghai set out to devise a master plan to guide development in such areas as population, land use, and transport. By the time Peking approved the blueprint in 1986, Shanghai's population had overshot the plan's target by 1.5 million, rendering most recommendations obsolete.

Chreod began work in October 1992 on the initial design of the GIS, but it will take an estimated 6 years to get the system fully operational, because it takes time to digitize a city.

The first phase of the Chreod project is being funded by a grant from the Canadian International Development Agency. The city's construction commission had originally asked Chreod to focus more narrowly on water, sewage, and gas lines, but the effort has been broadened to include such urban planning issues as land use and density, property values, and transportation.

Shanghai's willingness to take a broader view reflects the changes that have taken place throughout China in the past few years. When Chreod emissaries began talking to Shanghai officials about urban development issues in 1987, they shared little common ground. At the time, the elementary principle that land use should be linked to property values was deemed "inappropriate for Chinese conditions." But city officials have become receptive to the notion that land can be used to generate revenue to finance Shanghai's development objectives.

But officials realize now that there is no excuse for not improving Shanghai's basic services. And with the help of such international lending agencies as the World Bank and the Asian Development Bank, as well as companies such as Chreod, they are beginning to get their city into shape.[41]

number of machines that operated during the night shift last month (manufacturing) are often the output of an MIS.

If a problem is semistructured or unstructured, requires internal and external data, and is related to tactical decisions, the system is likely to be a decision support system. For example, decisions involving large capital outlays (finance) or the location of a new retail store (marketing) can be facilitated with the help of a DSS. Strategic decisions made by top managers that require data and information to be presented in a succinct manner are likely to be supported by an EIS.

Capturing and disseminating knowledge in the various functional areas of a business often requires an expert system. For example, experience associated with loan approvals in a bank can be modeled by an expert system. Finally, office automation systems facilitate the flow of oral and written communications throughout the organization, and hence are used by all the functional areas.

Summary

♦ **Measuring the productivity of information systems.**

Measuring the contribution of information systems to organizational productivity has been extremely challenging. This is partially because the benefits of information systems are often intangible, manifesting themselves in areas such as improved customer service and greater organizational responsiveness. Hence, organizations are developing new measures, such as "slash cycle times" and "delighting the customer," to better measure the impact of information systems on organizational productivity. Though some argue that information systems have contributed very little to productivity, most experts believe that their contribution cannot be measured using conventional measures. Whether we can objectively measure IS productivity or not, it is obvious that information systems play an important role in corporate America.

♦ **The role of information systems in functional areas such as finance, marketing, manufacturing, quality control, and human resources.**

This chapter has provided a number of real-world illustrations of the innovative use of information systems.

The various functional areas in a business, including marketing, manufacturing, quality control, finance, accounting, and human resources, have all been influenced by IS. Although a few years ago the emphasis was on developing standalone functional systems, today the goal is to integrate the various functional areas and to create customer-oriented systems. Without integrated systems, companies would be burdened with "islands of information" and decision makers would be unable to share data and information.

♦ **Real-world examples of the use of information systems in the various functional areas of an organization.**

In this chapter, we have described several companies that have successfully used IS to capture new markets, achieve a competitive edge in existing markets, and provide exceptional customer service. We gave examples in each of the functional areas of a business; marketing, finance, accounting, manufacturing and production, quality control, and human resources. We also gave examples of several cross-functional systems. Today, most companies are planning to develop such systems.

Review Questions

1. Why is it difficult to measure the contribution of information systems to organizational productivity? What are some new measures of organizational productivity? Describe "slash cycle times."

2. What are some of the benefits of information systems to an organization? Identify at least three intangible benefits of IS.

3. Briefly describe the five types of functional information systems. Is any one system more important than the other? Discuss.

4. What do we mean by a dedicated marketing information system? What are some of its subsystems? Do all organizations have dedicated marketing systems?

5. Why should manufacturing information systems be integrated with other systems in the organization? Describe MRP and MRP II.

6. Describe agile manufacturing. What are the four key characteristics of agile manufacturing? Why is agile manufacturing sometimes called the "great equalizer"?

7. What is the difference between manufacturing information systems and production systems? Can you give an example of a production system?

8. What is meant by vendor-managed inventory? Identify two advantages and two disadvantages of vendor-managed inventory.

9. How can information systems help an organization achieve its quality goals? What are some kinds of information that decision makers may collect in the process of monitoring and assessing the overall quality of goods and services?

10. What are some subsystems of financial and accounting information systems? Describe any one subsystem of financial and accounting information systems.

11. What are the three competitive strategies of a firm? Why should a firm's competitive strategies be taken into account before designing a HRIS?

12. Describe a GIS; identify some uses of a GIS. What are some types of decisions that rely on geographical data?

 Discussion Questions

1. Music Writer was cited as an organization using information technology to capture new markets (see box). Identify another example, in any industry, where a firm can attract new customers through the use of information technologies.

2. Why should a marketing information system capture information about noncustomers? Would IBM benefit from such an approach? Discuss.

3. Can the idea of agile manufacturing be applied to a service industry? How might the travel industry benefit from the ideas of agile manufacturing?

4. Although experts emphasize the importance of developing integrated, customer-oriented systems, many organizations seem to have difficulty in developing such systems. Identify any three reasons why organizations may not be successful at developing integrated, customer-oriented systems.

 E T H I C A L   I S S U E S

Case 1: Vendor-Managed Inventory

Vendor-managed inventory, a fairly new practice, shifts the burden of managing inventory from the retailer to the supplier. The supplier is held responsible for ensuring that no stock-outs occur.[42] Many retailers penalize suppliers if a stock-out occurs. The table below is an example of what a retailer can do.

OFFENSE	PENALTY
FIRST STRIKE	10% cut in payment for the order
SECOND STRIKE	50% cut in payment
THIRD STRIKE	You're Out!

1. As a supplier, do you approve of the concept of vendor-managed inventory? Do you think that the retailer passes on the savings to the consumer?

2. Is it ethical to penalize a supplier for stock-outs? Or should inventory management be the joint responsibility of both the supplier and the retailer?

Case 2: The Dangers of Sharing Information

A fundamental requirement for building integrated, customer-oriented information systems is that managers and employees be willing to share and disseminate information. However, in many organizations, information is viewed as a currency that can be used

(Continued on next page)

to achieve job security, promotions, and power. Some employees feel that giving away information may reduce their value and power in the organization, and may therefore resist change and even provide inaccurate information in an effort to stall the process of building integrated systems.

1. Would you, as a manager, be sympathetic toward an employee who hoards information in an effort to protect his or her job?

Case 3: False Job Security

Before embarking on integrated information system projects, top managers often know which employees are likely to be laid off. However, in an effort to win the cooperation of employees during system development, managers often provide verbal assurances of job security to employees who will be laid off a few months after the system becomes operational.

1. Managers often find themselves in a dilemma: Being truthful about coming layoffs may interfere with employee cooperation. How would you, as a manager, handle this situation?

PROBLEM SOLVING IN THE REAL WORLD

Case 1: An All-Star Team: The Tambrands Case

The trick to achieving growth in business is extending your reach without losing your grip. The challenge for Tambrands, based in White Plains, New York, which controls 45% of the world's tampon market, was to extend its reach by creating a kind of "corporate Esperanto" that would allow a plant in Auburn, Maine, to perform the same processes in the same manner as a plant in Kiev, Ukraine. Developing uniform manufacturing, marketing, and financial processes based on the best practices in the company allows the company to freely exchange information among all its divisions and units and thus to facilitate more consistent decision making. "Our vision was that when it was all over, it was going to be like we were all in one building," explains Dianne Forrest, Vice President of Information Technology. "The first floor would be North America, the second floor would be Europe, the third floor would be our other international locations, and the top floor would be corporate."

The company has manufacturing plants in seven countries, including France, Brazil, China, Ukraine, Ireland, and the United Kingdom. The differences between practices at these locations, which operated largely independently throughout the 1980s, was hurting the manageability of an organization that was already suffering from high operating costs. That's how things stood in 1989, and the IS department was in no position to improve matters. Stashed away on the ground floor, across from the cafeteria and next to the computer room, "we were segregated from the rest of the organization, and it was a real struggle to participate in business conversations," says one IS staffer.

Slowly, the CEO and the CIO began putting into place a long-range strategy for using IT to support a shift from independent, country-centered groups to an integrated global organization. They had to work with a patchwork of geographic divisions that used largely the same hardware but different software and operating procedures. The plan was to pool the company's technical and knowledge resources worldwide, and over 3 or 4 years to implement standard business systems in all locations, including common coding structures, performance metrics, and business definitions. The task was simplified by the fact that Tambrands has only one product line, which is packaged almost identically worldwide.

The company decided to begin the restructuring with its financial systems, running on AS/400s, which were antiquated and were strained because of a rising volume of financial activity. Although these systems were able to churn out the reports required by regulatory bodies, they failed to provide the basic information that management needed for decision making, such as financial performance of products and markets all over the world. In addition, reporting procedures for the different locations were so many and so varied that corporate staff had to personally visit sites in China and Brazil to understand the processes and procedures. "We didn't know what our cost structures were or how best to maximize return for the owners." Fixing financial systems "was our top priority and was done on a whatever-it-takes-to-get-it-done-quickly basis."

Beginning in 1990, Tambrands implemented a system that streamlined cost and profit-center reporting. This system allowed employees to look at key performance measures worldwide and use comparative information to allocate resources. The new system has cut the company's worldwide book-closing time by more than half and enhanced the role of finance employees, transforming them from number crunchers into analysts. "Systems helped financial people refocus such that they are no longer simply adding up numbers but rather are providing perspective on business issues."

The company improved its manufacturing operations through internal benchmarking. Since it had operated in a decentralized way for so long, things such as product specifications had evolved differently in different locations. The company, once again, sought uniformity in its standards. "It's very easy to build systems around these differences, but it's much sounder and much smarter to ask why those differences exist, make them go away, and then put the system in place."

Teams consisting of IS staff and users began setting standards for everything: inventory systems, productivity per employee, number of duplicate items, purchase prices, and cost of production. With the help of the newly integrated financial systems, they gathered data from plants worldwide and evaluated all the manufacturing plants. Less formally, employees at different plants shared information on practices in their own locations to determine which plants were producing the best result. At the time of these efforts, Tambrands lacked an E-mail system, so employees communicated by fax, telephone, and written reports. Members at some locations even made videotapes, showing how they had successfully changed processes on the line, for their fellow benchmarkers.

Once the best practices and processes had been identified, the units that had the best processes were asked to lead the world-wide effort to develop uniform practices throughout the company. The company told the units, "You're the center of excellence for a specific business process. You are responsible for

(Continued on next page)

showing how this process is going to work at all units. You will bring the new system and processes over to other locations, and they will take ownership."

The company decided to begin its efforts in Europe and the United States, and then to roll out the new systems and procedures in other locations. It decided to focus on manufacturing in its European markets and on its marketing operations in the U.S., and U.S. and European teams would work closely with each other. "When we get something up and running here in North America, for example, the people in Europe already know what it is and when it's coming because they've participated along the way." Though the objective is to make U.S. and European operations as close to identical as possible, Wright warns against a "cookie-cutter approach to globalization." Room for variation must be allowed if, for example, a preferred product is not available in all locations or a vendor in one country charges exorbitant fees.

Allowances are also made in countries where human-resources and technological limitations make them necessary. When the company decided that sites in China and the former Soviet Union were not large enough to warrant the use of AS/400s, for example, Tambrands compromised with PC LANs. In Kiev, where most people are trained in local accounting practices that bear little resemblance to U.S. and European models, the company installed a software package that allows employees to use local methods and then translates their results into the language of Western accounting. But these are interim solutions; Tambrands has deployed experienced people in these countries to bring local workers up to speed with the rest of the organization as quickly as possible.[43]

1. What was the goal of Tambrands in restructuring its information systems? Explain the sequence of steps that the company took to achieve this goal.
2. Why did the financial systems of the company need restructuring? What are some benefits that the company realized when it rebuilt its financial systems?
3. What are some of the challenges in developing integrated information systems for a global organization?

Case 2: Viacom International

Recent surveys by Gartner Group and Forrester Research show that CIOs overwhelmingly favor finance as their top priority for business process re-engineering and that financial information systems can become invaluable decision support systems. There are many reasons for the growing interest in developing financial information systems and using them to achieve business goals. First, many financial systems are aging because finance was one of the first functions to be automated in companies. Hence, many venerable accounting and financial systems are now in desperate need of redesign and rebuilding. Second, more and more managers need financial information to make decisions concerning every aspect of the business, from choosing a marketing campaign to developing new products. But that information is not always readily available or complete and many financial reports are in summary form, insufficient to meet management's need for detailed information.

At Viacom International, the New York-based parent of MTV, Nickelodeon and other entertainment interests, the CFO teamed with executives from sales, marketing and contracting to lead the company in new directions. Because financial processes are so intertwined with the processes of other departments, top managers felt that redesigning finance should ideally be part of a company-wide, comprehensive reengineering project. Although some turf wars were inevitable, executives involved in this large-scale effort to reorganize the company were persuaded to support cross-departmental process change. Viacom targeted its financial systems to find a better way to handle the financial reporting of its wholly owned subsidiaries, which it is acquiring at the rate of about three every year. Another goal in rebuilding the financial application was to eliminate the company's dependence on paper, particularly the financial transactions which often involve re-keying, rechecking, and doing accruals. The company plans to develop a system which reduces paper pushing and facilitates the electronic transmission of transactions from one decision maker to the next. Another goal of the company is to build financial systems that give decision makers time to analyze data rather than spending their time collecting it.[44]

1. Identify two reasons why financial information systems are excellent tools for facilitating decision making.
2. Explain why financial information systems were at the center of initiating change at Viacom.

Case 3: Boulevard Bancorp

When Boulevard Bancorp (BBC) was adversely affected by the real estate woes of the late 1980s, it focused on its financial systems to streamline business processes and eliminate waste. BBC had acquired a number of banks at different times but had not standardized their accounting procedures or systems. As a result, two banks processed their accounting books in-house, using customized versions of the same software, while smaller banks had their books processed by service bureaus. Moreover, since each bank's chart of accounts was different, an accountant moving from one bank to another would have to learn different names for the same type of account.

The company realized it had a serious problem must standardize its accounting and financial systems to capitalize on the economies of scale available to a centralized organization. The company moved toward standard processes by converting all banks to a common software. At the same time, the company began standardizing its accounting processes. Second, the bank focused on increasing the productivity of each knowledge worker by ensuring that their expertise was fully utilized. This helped cut the closing cycle from 20 days to 6 days. However, managers still lacked the information they needed to make good decisions. "A mainframe makes a great debit/credit machine, but it had significant shortcomings in its financial- and management-reporting capabilities." The bank switched to a client-server platform and installed software that allowed employees to generate reports without entering data. "My people now get the opportunity to do financial writing and analysis rather than just crunching numbers."[45]

1. What are some steps that the company took to standardize its business processes?
2. What are some benefits of this approach?

References

Beer, Michael, R. A. Eisenstate, and B. Specter. "Why Change Programs Don't Produce Change," *Harvard Business Review,* Nov.-Dec. 1990, pp. 64–73.

Boynton, A. C., R. W. Zmud, and G. C. Jacob. "The Influence of IT Management Practice on IT Use in Large Organizations" *MIS Quarterly,* September 1994, pp. 299–319.

Caron, J. R., S. L. Jarvenpapp, and D. B. Stoddard. "Business Reengineering at CIGNA Corporation: Experiences and Lessons From the First Five Years," *MIS Quarterly,* September 1994, pp. 233–251.

Dennis, A. R, A. R. Hemminger, J. F. Nunamaker, Jr., and D. R. Vogel. "Bringing Automated Support to Large Groups: The Burr Brown Experiences," *Information and Management,* Vol. 18, No. 3, March 1990, pp. 111–121.

DeSanctis, G., M. S. Poole, H. Lewis, and G. DeSharnais. "Using Computing in Quality Team Meetings: Initial Observations from the IRS-Minnesota Project," *Journal of Management Information Systems,* Vol. 8, No. 3, Winter 1991–2, pp. 7–26.

Gallupe, R. B., G. DeSanctis, and G. W. Dickson. "Computer-based Support for Group Problem Finding: An Experimental Investigation," *MIS Quarterly,* Vol. 12, No. 2, June 1988, pp. 277–296.

Gurbaxani, V. and S. Whang. "The Impact of Information Systems on Organizations and Markets," *Communications of the ACM,* Vol. 34, No. 1, Jan. 1991.

Ives, B., and S. Jarvenpaa. "Applications of Global Information Technology: Key Issues for Management," *MIS Quarterly,* Vol. 15, No. 1, March 1991.

Leifer, R. "Matching Computer-based Information Systems with Organizational Structures," *MIS Quarterly,* Vol. 12, No. 1, March 1988.

Malone, T. W. Yates, J., and Benjamin, R. I., "Electronic Markets and Electronic Hierarchies," *Communications of the ACM,* June 1987.

Milliman, Z., and J. Hartwick. "The Impact of Automated Office Systems on Middle Managers and Their Work," *MIS Quarterly,* Vol. 11, No. 4, Dec. 1987.

Pine II, J., D. Peppers, and M. Rogers. "Do you want to keep your customers forever?", *Harvard Business Review,* March-April 1995, pp. 103–114.

Vitale, M. R. "The Growing Risks of Information System Success," MIS Quarterly, Dec. 1986.

Notes

1. Betts, Mitch. "Real IS payoff lies in Business Benefits," *Computerworld,* Dec. 27 1993–Jan. 1, 1994, p. 10.
2. Ray, Gary. "The Productivity Chase," *Computerworld,* Dec. 27 1993–Jan. 1, 1994, p. 56.
3. Ibid.
4. DePompa, Barbara. "The Electronic Sales Call," *InformationWeek,* August 17, 1992, pp. 21–22.
5. Fitzgerald, Michael. "Hotel Automation is Booking Bonanza," *ComputerWorld,* Jan. 16, 1995, p. 41.
6. Santosus, Megan. "Pursuing the Perfect Pitch," *CIO,* June 1, 1994, pp. 30–34.
7. King, Julia. "Are You Being Served?" *Computerworld,* October 18, 1993, pp. 107–114.

8. Wilson, Linda. "Sheet Music Suppliers Play a Different Tune," *InformationWeek,* January 31, 1994, p. 25.
9. King, Julia. "Are You Being Served?" *Computerworld,* October 18, 1993, pp. 107–114.
10. Ibid.
11. Earls, Alan. "Manufacturing Finds Firmer Ground," *Computerworld,* February 28, 1994, pp. 92–93.
12. Vink, Ken. A senior business analyst, Spartan Stores, Inc.
13. Maglita, Joseph. "Best Face Forward," *Computerworld,* May 16, 1994, p. 107.
14. King, Julia. "Can America Win the Wardrobe Wars?" *Computerworld,* January 24, 1994, pp. 67–68, 72.
15. Ibid.
16. LaPlante, Alice. "Faster Factories," *Forbes ASAP,* October 10, 1994, pp. 37–41.
17. Santosus, Megan. "The Critical Link," *CIO,* January 15, 1994, pp. 40–42.
18. King, Julia. "Quality Conscious," *Computerworld,* July 19, 1993, p. 89.
19. Ibid.
20. Ibid.
21. Ibid.
22. Betts, Mitch. "Dallas' Qualitative Edge," *Computerworld,* April 18, 1994, p. 22.
23. "Coors Ceramics: Figuring Out Customer Needs First, Faster Factories," *Forbes ASAP,* Oct. 10, 1994, p. 38.
24. Earls, Alan R. "Keeping the Customer Ecstatic," *Computerworld,* February 21, 1994, p. 80.
25. Radosevich, Lynda. "Ford, Mazda Put Car Quality On-line," *Computerworld,* March 1, 1993, pp. 51–52.
26. Reiff, Stephen D. and Matt, Nelson. "Financial Planning: A Necessity for the 90s," *Computers in Healthcare,* May 1993, pp. 20–25.
27. Anonymous. "UCLA Medical School Finds Tight Elixir," *Computerworld,* November 1, 1993, p. 114.
28. Ricciardi, Lucy R. "Is Your Data Integrated and Under Your Control?," *Financial Executive,* July/August, 1993, pp. 30–33.
29. Hildebrand, Carol. "Financial Affairs," *CIO,* March 15, 1994, pp. 62–67.
30. Hildebrand, Carol. "Closing Encounters," *CIO,* September 1, 1994, p. 88.
31. Betts, Mitch. "As Easy as ABC?" *Computerworld,* May 23, 1994, pp. 107–108.
32. Auer, Katherine. "A Farsighted System," *CIO,* January 15, 1994, p. 90.
33. Broderick, Renae, and John W. Boudreau. "Human Resource Management, Information Technology, and the Competitive Edge," *Academy of Management Executive,* 1992, vol. 6, no. 2, pp. 7–17.
34. Broderick, Renae and Bourdeau, John W. "Human Resource Management, Information Technology and the Competitive Edge," *Academy of Management Executive,* Vol. 6, No: 2, 1992, pp. 7–17.
35. Ibid.
36. DeSanctis, Geraldine. "Human Resource Information Systems: A Current Assessment," *MIS Quarterly,* Vol. 10, March 1986, pp. 15–27.
37. Leibs, Scott. "Throw out the Push Pins," *InformationWeek,* June 6, 1994, p. 33.
38. Aronoff, Stan. "Geographic Information Systems," *WDL Publications,* Ottawa, Canada, 1994, p. 39.
39. Betts, Mitch. "The Kiosks are Coming," *Computerworld,* Jan. 24, 1994, p. 40.
40. Betts, Mitch. "Mapping Tools Reach Mainstream Market," *Computerworld,* April 25, 1994, p. 20.
41. Goldstein, Carl. "Taming Shanghai," *Far Eastern Economic Review,* November 26, 1992, p. 74.
42. Betts, Mitch. "Manage My Inventory or Else!" *Computerworld,* January 31, 1994, pp. 93–95.
43. Buchanan, Leigh. "A Process-Change All-Star Team," *CIO,* March 15, 1994, pp. 46–52.
44. Hildebrand, Carol. "Financial Affairs," *CIO,* March 15, 1994, pp. 62–68.
45. Ibid.

Managing the Development and Maintenance of Information Systems

Chapter 12
System Analysis and Design: Methodologies and Implications

Chapter 13
Tools for Information Systems Development

12

System Analysis and Design: Methodologies and Implications

Contents

Learning Objectives
Technology Payoff: California's Department of Motor Vehicles
Introduction
System Development Life Cycle (SDLC)
    System Definition
    System Analysis
      Understanding the Problem
      Feasibility Analysis
      Establishing Functional Requirements
    System Design and Programming
      System Development
    System Testing and Implementation
    System Maintenance
    Limitations of the SDLC
Prototyping
End-User Development
Managing End-User Computing
    Coordination
    Support
    Evaluation
    Approaches to Managing End-Users
      Sink or Swim
      The Stick

             The Carrot
             Support
      Principles for Managing PCs
      Off-the-Shelf Software
             Advantages of Off-the-Shelf Software
             Disadvantages of Off-the-Shelf Software
      Outsourcing
             Strategic Focus
             Economic Reasons
             Market Forces
             Technical Considerations
             Advantages and Disadvantages of Outsourcing
      Comparison of Different Methodologies
      Challenges in Developing Information Systems
      IS Development in a Global Environment
      Summary
      Review Questions
      Discussion Questions
      Ethical Issues
             Case 1: Blue Cross Fails to Take Care of Displaced Employees
             Case 2: Minolta Runs into Outsourcing Snag
             Case 3: Trouble at California's Office of Information Technology
             Case 4: Moral Minority
      Problem Solving in the Real World
             Case 1: Doomsday Date
             Case 2: Crash at Denver International
             Case 3: Falconbridge Ltd. Soars to New Heights
      References
      Notes

Learning Objectives

Knowledge workers, regardless of their functional specialization (marketing, finance, manufacturing, and so on), are likely to be influenced by, and to influence, the design, development, and maintenance of information systems. Knowledge workers, therefore, have the responsibility of being proactive in the development of high-quality systems. Also, many of today's students will be end-users charged with the responsibility of developing information systems that will meet their own information needs. Thus they must have a solid education in system design and development. Further, system development should be viewed not just within the context of a business, but in the larger context of a sociotechnical society. This has implications for all students, regardless of their majors.

There are several different approaches to building information systems; this chapter explores some popular and emerging development methodologies. Since no one methodology is applicable to all systems, knowledge of different methodologies and of their strengths and weaknesses is essential for anyone who wishes to be a good steward of information systems.

End-users are users who assume responsibility for developing, managing, and maintaining their information systems. The increase in the number of end-users, spurred by the rapid spread of PCs, is becoming one of the key managerial issues of the 1990s. In this chapter, we explore the nature and scope of end-user computing, its managerial and organizational implications, and its contribution to the productivity of knowledge workers.

The purpose of this chapter is to identify and describe various development methodologies and to explore the strengths and weaknesses of each. The consequences of selecting an inappropriate methodology are also discussed.

After reading and studying this chapter, you should be able to

- Understand the importance of selecting the right methodology
- Identify and describe different system development methodologies
- Understand the challenges faced by developers of information systems
- Identify resources and strategies necessary for managing end-users
- Define and explore the implications of end-user computing

TECHNOLOGY PAYOFF (or Lack Thereof):
California's Department of Motor Vehicles

In May 1994, the state legislature of California cut off funding for an information systems project in which the state had already invested more than $44 million over 7 years. The information system was being developed to replace the aging computer system at the state's department of motor vehicles. Something had seriously gone wrong with the development effort. In an effort to determine the cause of the problem, the state hired a private consultant (at an additional expense of $500,000) to review the project. Said one spokesman, "We tried to throw the long bomb from the backfield up to the front, and that kind of strategy is fraught with peril."

Meanwhile, the DMV, which yearly tracks 50 million vehicle registrations and drivers' licenses and collects approximately $5.2 billion in taxes and fees, is continuing to use its archaic technology. The current technology is so obsolete that it took the agency 18 programmer-years to add a social security number to the driver's license file! The system is written in assembly language, which was state-of-the-art in the mid-1960s. A number of reasons have been cited for the project failure, including poor project management, developing information systems without understanding the business processes, and a steep learning curve for newly introduced development tools.[1]

There is no sense being exact about something if you don't even know what you're talking about.

—John von Neumann

Introduction

Developing information systems is an enormously challenging and complex task. As you can see from the opening vignette, when IS projects are not properly managed, they can run into serious trouble and result in losses in the millions of dollars. Though there is no one easy way to develop systems successfully, over the years, researchers and practitioners have developed models and methodologies that can significantly contribute toward the building of high-quality information systems. Table 12–1 identifies five "C's"—capability, control, communication, cost, and competitive advantage—as possible reasons for system development. In this chapter, we look at some methodologies, their strengths and weaknesses, and the role they play in system development.

Recall from Chapter 2 that a system is a collection of interrelated parts that work together to achieve one or more common goals; in particular, an information system is a set of processes and procedures that transform data into information and knowledge. A system has five basic components—input, processes, output, feedback, and control—as shown in Figure 12–1. These five elements are central to any information system. For example, consider a newspaper delivery system. The name and address of a subscriber and the number of newspapers delivered to that subscriber become system input; various processes are used to determine total payments; the system output is an invoice; feedback may come in the form of complaints about missing newspapers, requests to stop deliveries during vacations, or reports of delinquent accounts. The feedback enters the system and control mechanisms ensure that the actual performance of the system meets expected levels.

Developing successful systems is the joint responsibility of the IS department and the end-users. The traditional and outdated view that information systems are the exclusive responsibility of the IS department no longer works for pragmatic and proactive companies. Successful companies understand that information systems are core systems that provide a strategic edge in the marketplace and that therefore every employee is in some way influenced by IS quality.

What can knowledge workers do to ensure the development of high-quality systems? First, they should be knowledgeable about the various development methodologies and their strengths and weaknesses so that they can actively participate in the chosen methodology. Second, they must recognize that system development breeds organizational change, and that change, by its very nature, is complex.[2] Information systems can change job functions or even eliminate jobs, demand new skills from employees while eliminating traditional ways of doing business, and cause fear, resistance, feelings of inadequacy, and morale problems. This is why all students, regardless of their functional specialization, should have some basic knowledge of methodologies and other aspects of system development.

There are five different (and complementary) IS development methodologies:

- System development life cycle (SDLC)
- Prototyping or rapid application development (RAD)
- End-user development
- Off-the-shelf software packages
- Outsourcing

TABLE 12-1
Some reasons why
organizations develop
information systems.

Five C's: Reasons for Initiating Information Systems Projects

Reason	Explanation
Capability	
Great processing speed	Using the computer's ability to calculate, sort, and retrieve data when greater-than-human speed is desired.
Increased volume	Providing the capacity to process a greater amount of activity, perhaps to take advantage of new business opportunities. Often a result of growth that causes business to exceed the capacities and procedures underlying the achievements to date.
Faster information retrieval	Locating and retrieving information from storage. Conducting complex searches.
Control	
Greater accuracy and improved consistency	Carrying out computing steps, including arithmetic, correctly and in the same way each time.
Better security	Safeguarding sensitive data in a form that makes them accessible only to authorized personnel.
Communication	
Enhanced communication	Speeding the flow of information between remote locations as well as within offices.
Integration of business areas	Coordinating business activities taking place in separate areas of an organization, through distribution of information.
Cost	
Cost monitoring	Tracking the costs of labor, goods, and facilities to determine how actual costs compare with expected ones.
Cost reduction	Using computing capability to process data at a lower cost than would be possible with other methods, while maintaining accuracy.
Competitive Advantage	
Lock in customers	Changing the relationship with, and the services provided to, customers in such a way that they will not choose to change suppliers.
Lock out competitors	Reducing the likelihood that competitors will be able to enter the same market.
Improve arrangements with suppliers	Changing the pricing, service, delivery arrangements, or relationship between suppliers and the organization to benefit the firm.
New product development	Introducing new products that are influenced by information technology.

James A. Senn, *Analysis and Design of Information Systems* (New York: McGraw-Hill, 1989), p. 53.

FIGURE 12-1

The components of a system.

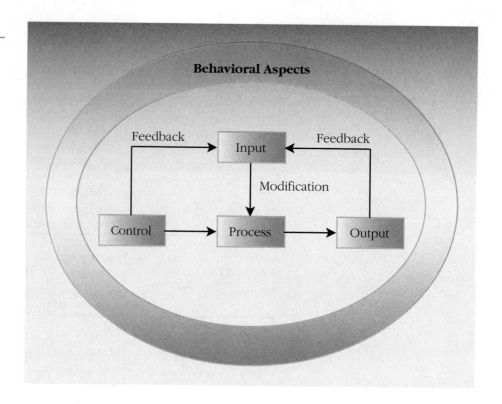

System Development Life Cycle (SDLC)

The system development life cycle (SDLC) is based on the systems approach, which divides problem solving into a set of interrelated activities:

Problem Definition
1. Identify the problem.
2. Gather the data and information necessary to solve the problem.

Problem Analysis
3. Identify alternative solutions.
4. Analyze the solutions and select the best.

Design and Implementation
5. Design, test and implement the solution.

Evaluation and Maintenance.
6. Evaluate the solution. If it is not successful, go back to step 1.

Figure 12–2 presents the activities involved in the systems approach and shows how this approach can be applied to the task of buying a car.

The **system development life cycle (SDLC)** is one of the oldest and most traditional development methodologies. For humans and other living beings, life consists of several phases: birth, childhood, adulthood, old age, and death. Similarly, the development of an information system follows a life cycle, from the conception of the system to the delivery of that system; hence the term *systems development life cycle*. The SDLC is broadly divided into five phases: system definition, system analysis, system design and programming, system testing and

System development life cycle (SDLC)

A traditional and popular development methodology for information systems. It consists of 5 phases: problem definition, system analysis, system design, system development and programming, and system testing and implementation.

FIGURE 12–2

The steps involved in the systems approach to problem solving. This approach is applicable to a large number of problems, such as buying a car.

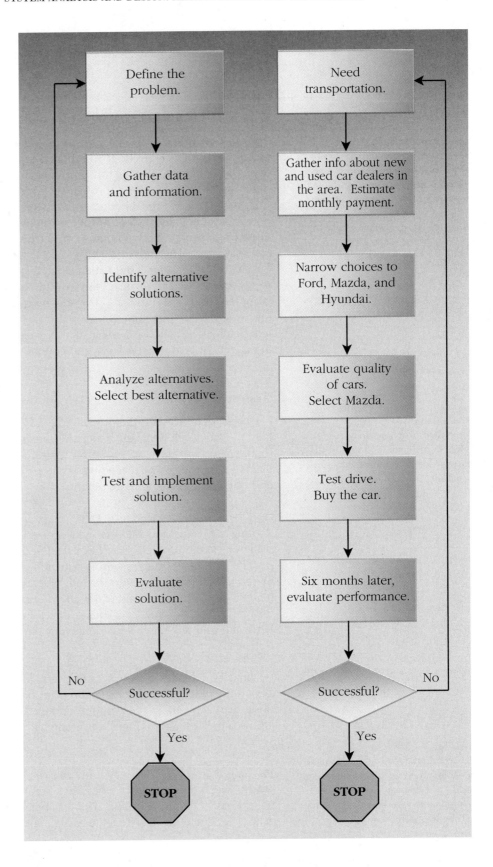

implementation, and system maintenance. Although these phases are usually implemented in sequence, sometimes, depending on the nature and scope of the system, some phases may be repeated and others may be executed concurrently.

System Definition

System definition

The process of defining the existing problem, determining why a new system is needed, and identifying the objectives of the proposed system.

System definition is the process of defining the existing problem, establishing that a new system is needed, and identifying the objectives of the proposed system. Unfortunately, though this is a critical phase in system development, it is often overlooked or rushed through by system developers.

In this phase, the primary goal is to answer the questions "Why do we need a system?" and "What are the objectives of the new system?" Both questions are critical and must be answered from an organizational perspective, not just that of IS. The question "Why do we need a system?" identifies the inadequacies of the existing system and elaborates on how these problems can be eliminated by developing a new system. This discussion can be used as a starting point for cost-benefit analysis. The second question—"What are the objectives of the new system?"—identifies the primary goal(s) of the system and establishes system boundaries, which are essential to prevent the project from becoming a "moving target" or growing too large and complex to be successfully completed.

System Analysis

System analysis

A detailed problem analysis undertaken in order to understand the nature, scope, requirements, and feasibility of the new system.

System analysis is the process of developing a detailed analysis of the problem so that developers can better understand the nature, scope, feasibility, and requirements of the new system. There are three main activities in this phase: gaining a thorough understanding of the problem, conducting a feasibility study, and establishing system requirements.

Understanding the Problem　Developers and users should fully understand the existing problems and the strengths and weaknesses of the existing system. In some cases, the problem may be that there is no system; in others, the problem may be that the existing system is outdated or incapable of meeting users' needs. Other activities in this step include identifying the overall implications and benefits of the new system for the entire organization (not just the department or unit for which the system is being developed), taking an inventory of existing hardware and software, and identifying the information needs of existing and potential users.

This information is gathered from a variety of sources—including corporate documents, interviews with system users, and other internal and external entities—and sometimes by observation. The output of this phase is a system proposal that summarizes the way the current system works, identifies its strengths and weaknesses, and outlines the strengths, weaknesses, and benefits of the new system.

Feasibility study

A careful analysis of the technical, economic, operational, scheduling, legal, and strategic factors of a system to make sure that the system can be successfully developed.

Feasibility Analysis　The system analysis phase also involves a **feasibility study,** which determines whether the system is feasible within the sociotechnical framework of the organization. The feasibility study carefully examines technical, economic, operational, scheduling, legal, and strategic factors.

Technical feasibility analysis determines whether the proposed system can be developed and implemented using existing technologies or whether new technologies are required. Hardware, software, and network requirements for the new system are also determined in this step.

Economic feasibility analysis evaluates the financial aspects of the project by performing a cost-benefit analysis and assessing both the tangible and the intangible benefits of the system. If an organization does not have the resources to develop a new system, then regardless of how useful or innovative the system is, it cannot be done. Establishing economic feasibility is such a difficult task, and is often so badly done, that poor project estimates are cited as one of the top reasons for system failures. (See Figure 12–3.)

Operational feasibility analysis determines whether there will be any problems in implementing the system in its operational environment, looks at issues such as integrating the new system with existing systems in the organization, and assesses how the system fits with the strategic business plan and the strategic information plan of the organization. For example, Honda uses a committee-based approach to decide which IS projects to approve (see box).

Trouble from the Start

At the outset, the cost estimate for an IS project may be as much as 80% too high or too low, because so little is known about the ultimate scope of the project.

Work Completed	IS Project Steps	Estimating Accuracy
2%	1.1 Project proposal	± 80%
	1.2 User requirements	
	1.3 System definition	
	1.4 Advisability	
15%	2.1 Preliminary design	± 40%
30%		± 20%
	2.2 Detailed design	
	2.3 Program design	
60%	2.4 Program and test	± 10%
	3.1 Implementation and test	
80%		± 10%
	3.2 System test	
	3.3 Operations turnover	
	3.4 Training/startup	
	3.5 Acceptance/wrapup	

FIGURE 12–3

Many organizations have a difficult time estimating the cost of an IS project.

Source: Betts, Mitch. "How to Get 'Runaway Projects' on Track," *Computerworld*, March 15, 1993, p. 95.

BUSINESS REALITIES
Honda of America

Honda of America's Anna Engine Plant, in Anna, Ohio, is staffed by 5,000 engineers and office personnel. It produces 500,000 engines and related parts each year. This huge (690,000-square-foot) facility houses the engine group and the suspension group, which handles everything from aluminum casting in a foundry to steel machining and parts assembly.

In spite of its tremendous success in producing high-quality engines, the company was not very successful in helping plant managers and IS personnel see eye-to-eye. To end the disruption caused by conflicts between the two groups, the company formed a committee that would address these conflicts.

The committee, called the Computer Integration Vision Information Committee (CIVIC), identified its primary goal as helping each side see the other's viewpoint, to find common ground in situations where the two groups had conflicting goals, and to embark only on those projects that benefited the entire organization. The committee meets weekly; plant representatives view it as an aid to seeing the "global picture" (the needs of the entire organization and not just of their individual units.)"One of the very big successes [of CIVIC] is you can articulate to your customers why their project isn't being done and let customers know that sometimes their projects were actually in direct conflict with the strategic information systems plan of the organization." The biggest contribution of the committee is the streamlining of the processes whereby resources are allocated to projects. This is a far cry from the old situation, in which "squeaky wheel" projects were approved.[3]

Schedule feasibility studies address the time it will take to complete the project. In this step, decision makers must take into account available resources, such as manpower, time, money, and equipment. It also helps to identify any additional resources that may be required to complete the project on time. Although this may sound like a simple task, determining project completion time is often very difficult. This is one of the primary reasons why so many software projects are behind schedule.

Legal feasibility studies take into account factors such as copyrights, patents, and federal regulations, if any. As the number of lawsuits in the computer industry increases, organizations are being more cautious about the legal implications of system development. In the case of life-threatening systems, legal feasibility can become a deciding factor.

Finally, *strategic feasibility* analysis looks into factors such as the ability of the system to increase market share, give the company a competitive edge in the marketplace, enhance the productivity of knowledge workers, and achieve other strategic goals of the company. "Will the system make the organization more competitive?" "Can competitors easily imitate the system and diminish its long-term benefits?" "Will the organization be at a competitive *disadvantage* if it does *not* develop this system?" These are some issues addressed during this phase.

Table 12–2 summarizes some of these issues and outlines some guidelines that companies use in project feasibility analysis.

Establishing Functional Requirements   The third and final activity in the system analysis phase is establishing the **functional requirements** for the new system; the who, where, when, and what the system must do. Some questions addressed during this phase are

Functional requirements
Systems specifications identified by asking who, what, where, when, and how: Who are the users? What are their needs? Where, when, and how do they want the information?

♦ Who needs the system and for what purposes?
♦ What, exactly, are the needs of the user?
♦ Who will receive system output?

TABLE 12-2
Feasibility analysis is done in the system analysis phase. This table summarizes the different areas of feasibility analysis and the issues to be addressed. Some guidelines that companies use during this phase are also shown.

Build Knowledge

Process: Define technology and business issues

Goal: Formulate preliminary goals

Timetable: Can take months

Players: Affected business unit and its IS liaison

Determine Feasibility

Technology: Are current products sufficient?

Skills: Does present staff have them?

Time and cost: Are projections workable?

Risk factor: Is the potential downside acceptable?

Players: Affected business unit and its IS liaison

Test Practicality

Pilot: Build a prototype of the system

Experiments: Test various tools and technologies

Involvement: Make development interactive

Reviews: Keep business users abreast of progress

Players: Application developers, affected business unit and its IS liaison, central IS

Prove Profitability

Analysis: Do a traditional cost-benefit analysis

Benefits: Predict intangible benefits

Players: Affected business unit and its IS liaison, central IS

Commercialization

Deployment: Utilize the finished application or system

Source: "Gateways to Innovation," *Computerworld,* October 31, 1994, p. 81.

* When should the system be delivered?
* How, or in what format, should the output be delivered?
* Who are the users? What training will they require to become proficient in the use of the system?
* What are the maintenance requirements of this system?

System requirements, therefore, establish the various functions of the new system so that it can achieve the objectives established in the system definition phase. For example, if one of the system objectives is to gain easy access to external databases; then in the system requirements phase, developers identify exactly what needs to be done to accomplish this objective. Developing functional requirements may appear to be a simple task, but it is complex, time-consuming, and challenging, and many systems have failed because of poor functional requirements.

For example, the Meredith Corporation abandoned an IS project that had been delayed by almost a decade and had cost three times its original budget. The problem was later traced to lack of well-defined system requirements. "The scope [of the project] kept creeping and creeping, and by the time the system neared completion, it was such a godawful mess [that] it really didn't do what it was sup-

Creeping requirements
New requirements that keep emerging throughout the development life cycle. These can seriously jeopardize system development.

posed to do." Capers Jones, chairman of Software Productivity Research, in Burlington, Massachusetts, estimates that requirements "creep" at an average rate of 1% per month. For a 2-year development project, this implies that about one fourth of what is delivered is not anticipated or defined at the outset.[4] The problem of changing or shifting requirements is referred to as **creeping requirements**—requirements that are not finalized during the system analysis phase but continue to evolve throughout the development life cycle. Some reasons for creeping requirements are shown in Figure 12–4.

Config, an artificial intelligence system designed to configure computer systems, is another example of the curse of creeping requirements. In Config's case, creeping requirements became an excuse to avoid using the system. "Rather than saying they don't want it, they say, 'I think I would use it if it just had this feature or that feature.'" Config was designed to help computer salespeople configure complex computer systems at order time. Unfortunately, the existing system rewarded sales volume, not sales quality, and since salespeople were never

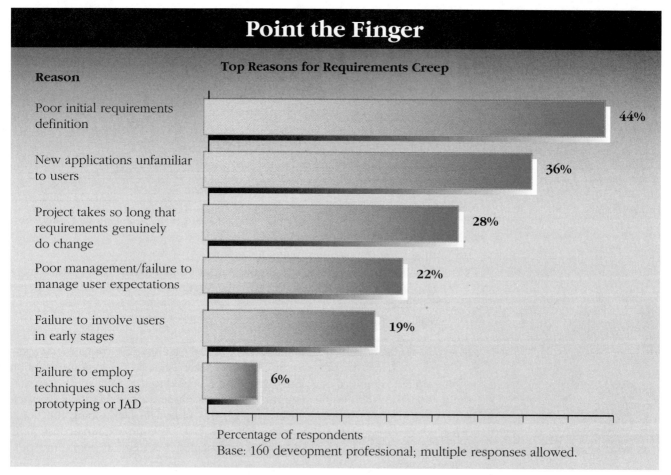

FIGURE 12–4

Some of the major reasons for creeping requirements.

Source: Anthes, Gary H. "Function Points to the Rescue," *Computerworld*, May 2, 1994, pp. 108, 110.

rewarded for their configuration skills, they had no interest in the success of the system. This was evident in a memo written almost 11 years *before* development began: "-Config's [developer] is concerned that the company's [intended users] are not showing enough interest in the project."[5]

System Design and Programming

System design
A roadmap that shows system developers how to convert system requirements into system features.

System design is the creation of a roadmap that shows system developers how to convert system requirements into a workable, operational system by exploring different designs and identifying the best design for the project. A number of technical, organizational, and managerial considerations, along with user preferences and resource constraints, should be taken into account before designing a system.

System design involves carefully scrutinizing each system requirement and converting it into a sequence of detailed procedural steps and system specifications. For example, an architect looks at the blueprint of a house (the requirements) and identifies the specifications—the amount of concrete, wood, wiring, and so on, that are required to convert the blueprint into a reality. Similarly, the system developer must analyze each requirement and determine how to make the system meet it.

There are two types of design: *logical* and *physical* design. Logical design identifies the records and relationships to be handled by the system. It focuses on

System Design Software

the logic, or the reasoning, behind the system by breaking down the system into subsystems, and each subsystem into smaller subsystems, until the process cannot be repeated any further. The logical design establishes the relationships among the various subsystems, the records and variables in the subsystems, and the interrelationships among variables and subsystems. The logical design defines the database as seen by end-users and programmers.

Physical design, on the other hand, addresses the physical aspects of the system: input and output devices, hardware configurations for the network, memory and storage, physical security, and so on. The physical design also defines data structures, access methods, file organization, indexes, blocking, pointers, and other attributes of the system.[6] In particular, system design involves three main activities:

1. ***Identify the technology required to implement the system.***
    System designers and developers must identify the hardware, software, and network requirements of the new system. In some cases, the required technologies may already be present; in others, new technologies may have to be acquired.

2. ***Ensure that the design is rigorous and reliable.***
    System design is not an isolated activity, but is interwoven with other activities in the development cycle. Hence, activities in the design phase must be coordinated with other phases in the development life cycle.

    A key factor in ensuring a robust and reliable design is to involve users from the early stages of system development. Although the role of the user appears to be obvious, many organizations fail to involve users; this failure leads not only to resentment and frustration, but also to system abandonment. IBM, for example, lost its market share in the minicomputer market primarily because of a company policy that prohibited any user involvement in the design of new products. The company, however, has recently reversed its policy and users were actively involved in the design of IBM's AS/400.[7]

3. ***Provide detailed specifications and a one-to-one mapping of the specifications and system objectives.***
    The system designer should map system specifications against system objectives so that all people involved in the project clearly understand their contributions to the overall system. By linking each specification to a specific system objective, developers can better understand how the specification will contribute to overall system goals.

    Lederer and Nath (1990)[8] argue that good system design entails designing both the "technological subsystem" and the "human subsystem," something that many organizations fail to do. Technology design addresses the issues covered earlier; human design addresses issues such as organizational climate and culture, training and motivation level of users, job satisfaction, and work environment. When human design issues are not taken into account, designers may become dogmatic and users may resist the system.

System Development   Although most students associate system development with computer programming, programming is only one phase in the system development life cycle. Programming is a very time-consuming and labor-intensive task; in some projects, programming alone may take many years. Large- to medium-sized systems usually involve a team of programmers.

System Testing and Implementation

Testing involves thoroughly probing the system to ensure that its performance matches system requirements and meets the expectations of end-users. Testing is one of the most difficult tasks in system development; it requires creativity, persistence, and a thorough understanding of the system and the principles of computer science. Good testers find creative ways to make the system fail, because this will arduously test the boundaries of the system and make it less likely to fail in the future.

Organizations find it extremely difficult to estimate the resources required for testing, simply because it is difficult to estimate how many "bugs" (problems) will be found in the system. Some software manufacturers are reluctant to commit resources to testing because they are eager to get the product "out the door" as quickly as possible. This is one reason why many programs already on sale are riddled with errors and why software companies often bring out several versions of a given program before major errors are eliminated.

There are three types of testing: unit testing, system testing, and acceptance testing. If a system is viewed as a collection of programs (units), in **unit testing,** each program is individually tested. However, this does not guarantee that the system is free of errors. The second type of testing is **system testing,** in which the system is tested in its entirety to ensure that its component units will function effectively when brought together as a system. System testing also involves testing other system-related issues, such as performance time, memory requirements, backup functions, and security controls. Finally, in **acceptance testing,** developers and actual users test the system under actual or simulated operating conditions to determine whether the system is ready for its operational environment and whether its performance is acceptable to users.

Many empirical studies show that it is relatively inexpensive to rectify errors in the early phases of system development and that costs escalate by a factor of 10 for each phase in the SDLC. In other words, it would cost 10 cents to fix a mistake in the analysis phase, $1 to fix the same mistake in the design phase, $10 to fix it in the programming phase, and $100 to fix it in the implementation phase. If major errors are detected during testing, the cost of the system quickly escalates.

After testing is completed, the next step is to implement the system in its operational environment. Systems should be implemented without disrupting the daily operations of the company; this requires careful planning and coordination. If the system is new, and not a replacement system, implementation is fairly straightforward. If the system is replacing an existing one, implementation becomes critical.

When a new system replaces an existing system, there are four types of conversion strategies: parallel conversion, direct cutover, a pilot study, and a phased conversion. Table 12–3 summarizes these methods.

In **parallel conversion,** the old system and the new one run in parallel until all the bugs in the new system have been identified and eliminated. Clearly, for mission-critical applications, in which failures can have disastrous effects, parallel conversion is the safest. For example, a computer system for air traffic control is a highly critical system, in which failures can have disastrous consequences; in such a case, therefore, parallel conversion would be the most appropriate implementation method. The disadvantage of this approach, however, is that it is expensive for two systems to be running in parallel.

Unit testing
The individual testing of each module of the system preparatory to testing of the entire system.

System testing
Testing the performance of the entire system, after unit testing has been successfully completed.

Acceptance Testing
Developers and users test the system under actual or simulated operating conditions to make sure that it is acceptable to users.

Parallel conversion
The new system and the existing system continue to operate until all bugs in the new system are identified and eliminated. Most critical systems are implemented using this approach.

TABLE 12–3
The four approaches to introducing a new system into its operational environment when it is replacing an existing system.

Method	Description
Parallel conversion	• Old and new system run in parallel till new system becomes reliable • Costly but safe approach • Best suited to critical applications
Direct cutover	• Old system is replaced with new system • Less costly but more risky than parallel approach • Best suited to noncritical applications
Pilot study	• One department or unit is testing ground. • Good for systems that are moderately critical.
Phased conversion	• New system is slowly phased into the operational environment • Safe and conservative approach • Well suited to critical systems

Direct cutover
During system implementation, the old system is removed and the new system is installed.

Pilot study
Uses one department or business unit to test a system before installing it throughout the organization.

Phased conversion
The new system is slowly phased into its operational environment by replacing parts of the old system with parts of the new system.

The second approach to implementing new systems is the **direct cutover,** in which the old system is removed and the new system is installed. This usually works for small, noncritical systems that will not seriously affect everyday operations. However, this approach, although less costly than the parallel approach, is not recommended, because it has no "safety net." Further, if the new system has high visibility in the organization, system failures can embarrass system developers.

The **pilot study** approach uses one department, or unit, as a testing ground before installing the system throughout the organization. When the pilot version is free of errors, the system is installed throughout the organization, either simultaneously or in stages. A marketing system that keeps track of damaged goods is a good example of a system that would work well in a pilot study.

Finally, in a **phased conversion,** the new system is slowly phased into its operational environment by replacing parts of the old system with parts of the new one. This is a safe, conservative approach to introducing a new system; it is by far the most popular method of system conversion.

A post-implementation review, or post-implementation audit, helps developers and users to analyze and highlight the successful and not-so-successful parts of a system. The purpose of such a review is to perform a systematic search for better ways to develop and implement systems. It helps the organization to recap the important lessons that it gained from developing the system and use them in its next development project. Such an audit is usually conducted after the system is fully operational and its performance can be evaluated. The audit should not be delayed, because developers may forget some aspects of their development experience.

System Maintenance

Since businesses operate in a dynamic environment, the needs of system users are also dynamic, so good systems must continuously evolve. System maintenance is one way of ensuring that the system continues to meet the growing and changing needs of users through system additions, deletions, and enhancements. Clearly, as the system ages, the extent and criticality of system maintenance increase.

The IEEE defines maintenance as "modification of a software product after delivery to correct faults, to improve performance or other attributes, or to adapt the product to a changed environment."

System maintenance begins after the system becomes operational, and should last as long as the system is in use. Although it lacks the glamor of development, maintenance is the key to continuing to derive the maximum benefits from a system. User requests for new features or for enhancement of existing features, a changing business climate, new technologies, or new information needs within the organization can accelerate system maintenance. Maintenance costs usually increase with time and at some point it becomes more expensive to maintain the system than it is to develop a new one. At that point, the company may make the decision to abandon the existing system and build a new one.

Although maintenance continues to be a neglected topic, it constitutes about half of the information systems activity in most companies and is a vital process. "[Maintenance] is not as sexy as development. Everyone wants to be the artist, but very few want to be curator of the museum. To present the artwork well, however, you have to be a very good curator."[9]

In summary, the SDLC is one of the most common and traditional system development methodologies. It is based on a systems approach to problem solving. Although it lends itself well to large projects, it has certain inherent limitations, which are covered in the next section. Table 12–4 summarizes the various phases of the SDLC.

Limitations of the SDLC

The SDLC is well suited to systems that are highly structured and routine, such as TPS and MIS. In recent years, however, the SDLC has come under a lot of criticism for its inflexible, sequential processes.

TABLE 12-4
The activities in the five phases of the SDLC. Sometimes activities in one phase may overlap with activities in others.

System definition and planning	Address the questions: • Why do we need a new system? • What are the objectives of the new system?
System analysis	• Gain thorough understanding of the problem • Conduct feasibility study • Determine and establish system requirements
System design and development	• Explore different designs and select best design • Provide a detailed roadmap for converting requirements into actual performance • Create logical and physical design specifications • Plan, coordinate, control, and manage technical aspects of the system • Convert design specifications into program code
Testing and implementation	• Perform unit, system, and acceptance testing • Decide on implementation strategy: parallel conversion, direct cutover, or phased conversion • Evaluate system performance
Maintenance	• Make modifications and enhancements to ensure that system continues to meet user needs

"Structured methods just don't work. None of that bears any relation to the way things are done today. The way things are done today is fast, cheap, and [involves] the maximum amount of reality checking along the way."[10]

Hence the step-by-step approach of the SDLC, in which each phase is completed before the next begins, often works well for highly structured and low-risk projects, but not necessarily for PC-based systems.

The SDLC assumes that system requirements can be frozen during the system analysis phase. However, this is rarely the case in the dynamic real world, where user requirements change frequently. The SDLC works better in stable environments, where hardware and software changes are gradual and contained, an environment that existed a decade ago: slow, steady, and predictable. But today, the world of IS is in turmoil and the number and complexity of operating systems, user interfaces, network choices, software languages, and development tools has grown manyfold. The SDLC can support such an environment in only a very limited way.[11]

The SDLC is also inflexible because all its activities take place sequentially; this sometimes increases the money and time required for system development. Further, any major changes or modifications to system requirements may entail redesigning the entire system, thereby increasing the cost of development.

In spite of its limitations, the SDLC continues to be widely used for developing large, monolithic systems. However, other approaches, such as prototyping and end-user computing, which are better suited for PC-based systems, are increasing in popularity.

Prototyping

Prototyping, also referred to as rapid application development (RAD), is a development methodology in which a system is developed by constructing a prototype, which is a working or an experimental model of the proposed system or parts of it. It is an iterative methodology, in which different development phases take place in parallel, rather than in sequence, as in the SDLC. (See Figure 12–5.)

There are two types of prototypes: throwaway prototypes and evolutionary prototypes (Alter, 1990). A **throwaway prototype** is discarded after several iterations and system development begins with a clean slate. Throwaway prototypes are used primarily as experimental models and not as development models; consequently, they are useful for projects that involve state-of-the art technologies. An **evolutionary prototype,** on the other hand, evolves into a full-fledged system as expansions and enhancements are made to the initial prototype. It is useful for projects in which system requirements are unstable and users do not have a clear understanding of system deliverables.

As in the SDLC, the first step in prototyping is to develop system requirements, but unlike the SDLC, which conducts system analysis, design, and development in sequence, prototyping conducts these phases in parallel. After the initial prototype is developed, it is carefully studied so that it can be improved. Then the processes of analysis, design, and development start all over again, and an enhanced version of the earlier model is developed. This is why prototyping is referred to as an iterative method. The cycle of problem definition, analysis, design, development, and testing is iterated until the system becomes fully functional.

Prototyping

A system development methodology in which the system is iteratively developed using prototypes (models of the system). Also referred to as rapid application development (RAD).

Throwaway prototype

A prototype that is discarded after several iterations. This is a useful approach when state-of-the-art technologies are involved. System development begins with a clean slate based on the lessons learned during prototyping.

Evolutionary prototype

A prototype that eventually evolves into a full-fledged system. Each iteration of the prototype builds on the previous version.

FIGURE 12-5

Prototyping is an iterative methodology in which the above four steps are repeated until the system is completed. The prototype is continually refined and modified until it meets the requirements of end-users.

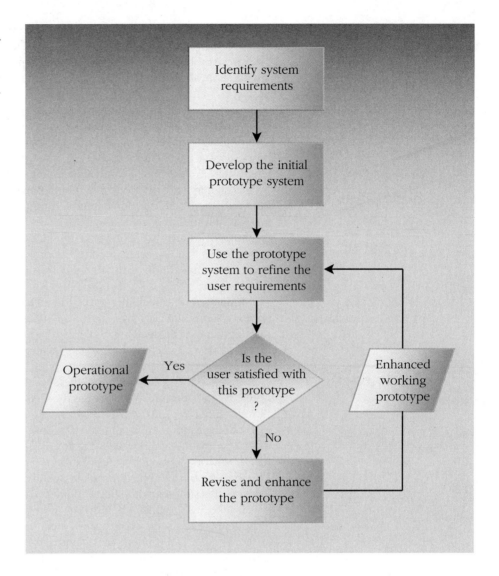

Each iteration can be divided into four phases:

1. Define the problem and identify system requirements.
2. Build the initial prototype.
3. Use the prototype to refine existing requirements.
4. Revise and enhance the prototype.

   Prototyping is an effective way to design and develop systems, since each prototype is a small, highly manageable piece of a larger system. It allows users to interact with a preliminary working model of the system and to gain an understanding of how the system will work when it is completed. Unlike the SDLC, RAD devotes less time to the early phases of development, such as problem definition, analysis, and design, and places greater emphasis on developing, testing, and refining the system.

Prototyping is beneficial for both users and system developers. At the heart of the success of prototyping lies the ability to get immediate and detailed feedback from system users, which leads to changes in existing requirements and to the addition of new requirements. Unlike the SDLC, in which user involvement is desirable, but not mandatory, the prototype methodology is highly user-oriented and cannot be successfully completed without the full cooperation and participation of users. In fact, many users become so actively involved in prototyping the system that they feel a personal responsibility to ensure its success; often simply by observing the RAD methodology, users become aware of some of the challenges that IS personnel face in developing information systems.

Designers and developers can also benefit from this methodology, because often new and better designs emerge during iteration; this helps to build reliable systems. Prototyping gives developers the ability to experiment with different technologies (hardware, software, interfaces, and so on) and finally to select the technologies that are best suited to the project. It creates a learning environment, encourages innovation, and fosters collaboration among system developers and system users.

RAD methods are so powerful and effective that some experts claim they can speed systems delivery by almost 1,300% as productivity increases and system development costs decrease.[12] This is because RAD is based on four powerful ideas: teamwork, achievable goals, incremental system delivery, and reduced waste.

Teamwork is a key factor in the success of RAD, because developers work in teams, and these teams work with users. At Travelers Insurance, for example, IS was "under the gun" to deliver business applications. Traditional development methodologies took an average of 18 months to deliver the goods; end-users were dissatisfied with such long delivery times. The company turned to RAD and found that teamwork among business partners and system developers was essential. This in turn promoted healthy risk taking and team-based decision making, resulting in better systems with shorter delivery dates.

Unlike SDLC, which allows goals to be set by management, RAD allows goals to be set by end users, which makes them more likely to be achieved. Developers at the Virginia Department of Taxation, for example, successfully designed and developed a large and complex tax accounting system, which integrated 1,500 programs and 40 databases. Developers attribute the success of the project to "aggressive but achievable goals".[13]

In RAD, the system is delivered in modules, not all at once. The first component may be delivered in 3 to 4 months, with no delivery date more than 6 months after the last one. This leads to less waste, because even if there is a serious error in the system, only one portion of it has to be rebuilt. A Houston energy company found that prototyping reduced development time from an estimated 1 year to 7 months. The system was delivered in two parts: the first after 4 months; the second, 3 months later.[14]

Chubb's Health, which provides health insurance for small companies, noticed it was losing business fast as clients abandoned traditional medical plans for health maintenance organizations (HMOs). At the heart of the problem was an aging computer system and an outmoded way of working: One sales rep handled claims adjudication, another supplied basic policy information, yet another checked the customer's account status, and so on, and each rep tapped into separate mainframe databases that could not share information. Says Vince Mace, V.P.

of employee benefits at Chubb Health: "We had two [bad] choices: continue business as usual, or lose hundreds of millions in revenue."

Chubb realized that traditional application development methods would not deliver the product in a hurry and, therefore, launched a RAD project to build a GUI-based, customer service workstation in 6 to 9 months that would allow any customer service rep to answer any request on the spot. The company got help from the IBM Open Systems Center in Dallas, which built a prototype in Powersoft Corp.'s Powerbuilder tool. In just three weeks, IBM was able to create a working prototype that could access DB2 and the data residing on Chubb's IBM mainframes.[15]

How can organizations ensure that their prototyping efforts are successful? Experts recommend that developers who are experimenting with prototyping start with a simple set of requirements and have a good understanding of the firm and its basic data requirements.[16] Although many IS managers initially find it difficult to adapt to the prototyping methodology, they quickly become converts, convinced that prototyping produces better systems and eliminates the bias and rigidity that are otherwise inherent in the development process.

On the other hand, RAD is an intense development methodology that can easily result in employee burnout. The average IS professional spends 60% of his or her day on creative activities; this proportion increases to more than 80% with RAD methodology. Hence, IS managers should make specific efforts to reduce stress and reward creative efforts when developers are using RAD.

Managers must also ensure that workers are given adequate training in RAD and that it is not used as an excuse for poorly designed and developed systems. Documentation, in particular, can sometimes be completely overlooked in prototyped systems. This can cause serious problems if key developers or users leave the project. IS managers must both capitalize on the strengths of RAD and take the necessary steps to overcome some of its potential weaknesses.

End-User Development

End-user computing (EUC)
The design, development, and maintenance of information systems by system users, rather than by the IS department.

End-user computing (EUC) is the design, development, and maintenance of information systems by system users, rather than by the IS department. EUC has been an important item on the IS manager's agenda since the late 1970s, and even today it continues to be a major concern.

Several compelling factors spurred the EUC movement. In the 1980s, an exponential growth in the volume of information that managers had to retrieve and process increased the demand for computing resources. At the same time, hardware prices were plummeting and GUIs were evolving that required users to have little or no programming background. End-user development was further accelerated by fourth-generation computer languages (4GLs). (These languages were covered in Chapter 4, Software.) Further, many IS departments found themselves backlogged and unable to meet the information needs of their users. These factors encouraged end-users to explore the idea of developing their own applications, and the end-user movement was born.

In order to gain a full understanding of EUC, it is important to ask "End-user computing versus what?" In other words, what are we comparing EUC against? How is an end-user different from other users of information technology? The answer can be found by comparing mainframe users with PC users, or corporate computing with end-user computing.

In the early 1970s, corporate computing focused on traditional data processing projects and structured decision making and gradually expanded to include semistructured and unstructured decision processes. Early EUC applications, on the other hand, began by focusing on unstructured processes and today are moving toward more structured applications, such as TPS, MIS, manufacturing systems, and expert systems, including departmental, corporate, and sometimes even interorganizational systems.

Though the phases of end-user development may differ somewhat from one application to another, or from one company to another, in general the phases of end-user development are those of the SDLC: problem definition, analysis, design, development, testing and implementation, and maintenance. The primary difference between end-user development and other development methodologies is that in this approach, the end-user is solely responsible for the success of the system. The end-user is the designer, the developer, and the maintenance programmer, all rolled into one. Thus, in general, the phases of end-user development are less structured and more flexible than those of SDLC.

This movement has many benefits, the most impressive of which are shorter lead time for system development, greater control and flexibility over system development, and lower development costs.[17] There are other benefits. EUC removes some of the burden from backlogged IS departments and allows systems development personnel to work on larger and more complex technical projects. Also, the responsibility of system maintenance shifts from the IS department to the end-users who develop the system; this improves the utilization of IS resources. Finally, extracting functional requirements is easier and more controlled than in the SDLC, since the user can add, delete, or change requirements as the system is being developed.

On the other hand, end-users may develop systems in a hurry, with minimal regard to their quality. Since such systems are rarely tested by an independent panel of experts, sometimes they can cause problems rather than solve them. Second, without formal education or training in developing information systems, end-users may not be aware of all the design and development issues that must be addressed in order to build good systems, such as proper design procedures, development methodologies, resource consumption, standardization, documentation, and so on. Thus, even with good intentions, they may create systems with information bottlenecks or poor utilization of limited computing resources. End-user systems also suffer from data redundancies, because two end-users developing different systems may use the same data. Companies that do not enforce data policies may find themselves burdened with data duplication and inconsistencies. Finally, in some cases, end-user systems may lead to "turf protection." An end-user may not be willing to share the data residing on his or her system; this could lead to information ownership rather than information stewardship. (We discussed the difference between these two concepts in Chapter 2.) Thus, the advantages of end-user computing must be carefully balanced against its disadvantages before a decision is made.

Despite some of its disadvantages, the end-user movement has completely revolutionized the way organizations develop information systems. It is estimated that there are about 6 million end-users in the U.S. today. This number is expected to grow by at least 12% each year as computer-literate high school graduates enter the job market.[18] Given the importance of the end-user movement to organizational productivity, it is important to carefully manage end-users; this is the focus of our next section.

Managing End-User Computing

The task of managing end-users can be broadly divided into three activities: coordination, support, and evaluation. Although the lines separating these categories are not strict or obvious, all three are essential.

Coordination

Hardware, software, networks, applications, personnel, and other resources associated with end-user computing must be carefully coordinated, controlled, and managed. Coordination is vital to developing an integrated information environment within the organization and to ensuring that all end-users follow standard development policies and procedures.

Support

Supporting end-users involves providing all the resources that they need to develop, manage, implement, and maintain information systems. This includes a wide range of activities such as advising them on problems and system selection, providing backup for applications and systems, helping with system development, ensuring that all systems are properly documented, facilitating error resolution, providing information on resources available within the organization, ensuring that systems are properly maintained and secured, and providing necessary training. Some of the questions that must be addressed for end-user support are shown in Table 12–5.

Evaluation

The third component in end-user management is evaluation, which provides both management and end-users with feedback so that they can resolve existing problems and identify potential problems before they arise. Evaluation provides managers with the information needed to resolve the paradox inherent in simultaneously supporting and controlling, facilitating and restricting, enabling and disciplining, nurturing and regulating, and fostering and restraining end-users. Clearly, no one evaluation mechanism works for all organizations, but all evaluation mechanisms must take into account the nature of the organization, its man-

TABLE 12–5
Some issues that must be considered when assessing the level of end-user support required in an organization.

Hardware Decisions
1. What department will purchase or lease the equipment?
2. Will the hardware be formally registered with the MIS department?
3. Will the hardware be compatible with the MIS department's computing environment?

Software Decisions
1. What department will purchase or develop the software?
2. Will the software be formally reviewed by the MIS department?
3. Will the software be formally registered by the MIS department?
4. Will the software be compatible with the MIS department's computing environment?

Data Decisions
1. What department will provide the data?
2. What will be the support level of the software that processes the data? (See above.)
3. Will the data be formally registered with the MIS department?

agerial style, the profile of its end-users, and the extent of the end-user movement in the organization.

There are four approaches to bringing together the elements of coordination, support, and evaluation.

Approaches to Managing End-Users

Sink or swim　This is basically a no-action approach in which the responsibility of managing end-users rests with the users themselves. Management takes no initiative to increase or accelerate development or to address any related issues; therefore, any benefits derived from EUC are attributable solely to the initiative of the end-users.

The Stick　This approach establishes strict policies and procedures to control end-user computing with the goal of minimizing any risk that may arise from user-developed systems. It may curb the creativity of end-users and may cause problems such as increased lead times, higher development costs, and reduced flexibility.

The Carrot　This approach treats the end-user as a responsible employee who understands the risks, rewards, and implications of developing systems. A reward system is in place that encourages end-users to be creative in designing and developing applications; they are also cautioned against engaging in high-risk ventures.

Support　In this approach, the organization plays a supportive role: IS managers and end-users cooperate and collaborate. The end-user is given the freedom to select the type and level of application; the IS department provides the support necessary to enhance the success of these applications.

Which approach should an organization use? Clearly, no one approach will work for all organizations; even within one organization, different approaches may be required to meet the profiles and needs of different end-users. However, there are some guidelines that promote responsible end-user computing. They divide end-user applications into three categories: high-impact, medium-impact, and low-impact.[19]

- High-impact applications affect a significant group of people in the organization. They must run correctly and reliably, because the consequences of failure can be severe. Such systems should be thoroughly tested and fully documented. High-impact applications must be approved at the corporate or divisional level.
- Moderate-impact applications affect only a small workgroup and are not very critical systems. Testing and documentation are necessary simply to ensure that the applications are easy to operate and maintain; procedures must be backed up to ensure minimum data loss. Moderate-impact applications must be approved at the supervisory or business-unit level.
- Low-impact applications are limited to a single individual and require little support or supervision. IS managers must simply make sure that such applications do not in any way compromise the integrity, reliability, or security of the organization's information systems.

Finally, a key factor in successfully managing end-users is to foster a partnership of shared responsibility and authority between end-users and IS professionals. But the gap separating end-users from system developers is becoming narrower. In the 1980s, end-users and IS professionals had skills that complemented one another; end-users were knowledgeable about the business and its functional activities, while IS professionals had the technical expertise to develop systems that met the users' needs. Today, end-users have a broad range of technical skills and many IS manages have a good understanding of the business.

"Gradually end-users and IS professionals are becoming more aware of one another, and in some ways, even more alike. Nevertheless, it remains the responsibility of end-users to advance the business and information needs of their respective functional domains. Notwithstanding, it remains the responsibility of IS professionals to advance the organization-wide viewpoint, and to provide the technical expertise required, for the effective and integrated management of the information assets of their respective organizations."[20]

As we stated earlier, one of the most compelling reasons for the spread of end-user computing is personal computers. Hence, no discussion of end-user computing would be complete without addressing the issue of managing personal computers.

Principles for Managing PCs

Although it has been only a decade or so since PCs were introduced to corporate America, they have completely transformed the landscape of organizational information systems and technologies. Until a few years ago, very little attention was paid to the task of managing PCs. Many organizations regarded PCs as "little machines that did big work" and felt that PCs required little or no managing at all. But a decade into PCs, organizations are highly aware of the costs associated with PCs and the tremendous gains that can be achieved through effective management of PCs and their users. Several managerial principles have emerged for managing PCs and related technologies; some of these are discussed below.

Principle 1: Managing the inventory of PC hardware and software is important.

As PCs spread rapidly, many managers are not aware of the different kinds of hardware and software that are used in their organizations. It is estimated that today there are more than 60 million PCs and 80,000 individual components required to run and maintain these systems.

Some of the principles of inventory management should be applied to PCs and their peripherals. Managers should be aware of licensing agreements and warranty clauses for the various PC products used in the company. Simply stated, a manager who is not aware of the hardware and software that the organization uses, cannot effectively manage the use of these resources.

In many organizations, the IS department is a big black hole. A recent survey of 2,000 IS managers revealed that less than 1 in 5 companies knows the size of its application portfolio; not even 1 in 30 companies knows its "portfolio flux," the amount by which systems assets change during a set period of time; and only

1 in 100 companies tracks IS defect levels, technical quality, or functional quality.[21] But poor management of computer assets has a number of serious implications. Andrew Dailey, a London-based analyst in the software asset management service of Gartner Group, Stamford, Conn., states, "I would not be surprised if over the next five years there are some shareholder suits due to the fact that there are assets greater than what is shown on companies' balance sheets."

Systems that track and record an organization's assets are referred to as asset management systems. In the case of computer asset management systems, they not only track the quantity of each item, but also identify who is using what, what they're using it for, and the extent of their usage. Experts estimate that by tracking the latter two items alone, companies could reduce overall software purchase costs by as much as 30%, simply by reallocating software licenses that may be unused in one department to other department and business units.

It is therefore imperative that companies conduct a "cradle-to-grave" analysis of how PC assets are managed, starting with forecasting the needs of the technology through purchase and disposal of equipment. Service contracts, licenses and vendor reports must also be tracked and managed.[22]

The negative impact of poor asset management is enormous. The Personal Computer Assets Management Institute, Rochester, N.Y., and the Software Publishers Association, Washington, D.C., estimate that users lose almost $20 billion annually from misallocated resources, ineffective support, unused equipment warranties, misapplied maintenance and lease contracts, and unrealized volume purchase agreements.[23]

Principle 2: Plan, monitor, control, and manage the costs of supporting PCs.

One of the major challenges facing PC managers is the hidden costs associated with providing technical support to PC users. Most organizations do cost-benefit analyses before they invest in the technology. However, very few organizations monitor the costs of supporting it after it is implemented. In the case of PCs, support costs have been estimated to be $12,000 to $16,000 per year. The cost of PC ownership over a five-year cycle, including equipment, training, usage and maintenance, has mushroomed from $19,000 in 1987 to more than $41,500 today. Even though the cost of hardware and software has decreased, the complexity of hardware and software has increased significantly, resulting in significantly higher costs for support, training and maintenance.[24] The first step toward reducing computing costs in an organization is to track and monitor the costs associated with computer technologies, including those of PCs. For example, some organizations require IS managers to buy from the lowest bidder. However, this policy can backfire and cause major headaches, and even litigation, for the company.

Help desk
A computer support facility that consists of a group of highly trained employees who are knowledgeable about hardware and software.

Many organizations use computer help desks to provide technical support to PC users. A **help desk** is a support facility that consists of a group of highly trained employees who are knowledgeable about computer hardware and software. The help desk staff support PC users with hardware and software problems by answering questions over the phone. When a problem cannot be solved over the phone, the help desk staff may direct the user to other sources of help. Help desks, along with proper hands-on training for end-users, can go a long way toward reducing support costs.

Another effective way to decrease computing costs is to issue some guidelines for PC maintenance and repair. PC repair technicians often charge by the hour, so if repair costs are not closely monitored and controlled, repair bills can add up very quickly. Some simple procedures, such as determining whether the problem is hardware- or software-related, taking detailed notes about the problem before calling for repairs, replicating the problem so that the repair person can look at it when he or she visits the premises, noting the exact language of the error message, and keeping a log of erratic failures, can go a long way toward reducing maintenance costs.[25]

Principle 3: Standardization is the key to effective PC management.

Standardization is an important issue that IS managers face regularly. In the case of PCs, standardization assumes even greater importance, since without it an organization will be confronted with islands of incompatible information, which can result in spiraling costs. PC hardware and software should be compatible, and upgrades of hardware and software should be uniform and consistent throughout the organization. For example, Aetna Life & Casualty, of Hartford, Connecticut, has 27,000 PCs, of which about one third are standardized. In such a large computing environment, standardization is the key to realizing the full potential of PCs.[26]

The national director of information and technology for Price Waterhouse, at the company's Technology Center in Menlo Park, California, is responsible for managing approximately 15,000 PCs, spread over 100 geographical locations in the U.S. Price Waterhouse, one of the leading accounting firms in the country, is a global organization that has decentralized its purchasing of PCs and related technologies. Clearly, the requirements for PCs in Taiwan may be different from those in England. However, though decentralized purchasing is the most effective strategy, the company has set minimum standards for hardware, to be adhered to by its units throughout the world. In an effort to standardize PC software, the company acquires global licenses for core applications, such as word processors and spreadsheets, and then distributes the software to its business units all over the world. For example, the company's version of WordPerfect has customized fonts and macros that are used uniformly in all its units.[27] (Standardization is covered in greater detail in Chapter 15, Information Resources Management.)

Principle 4: Ensure that proper and effective performance measures are put in place to assess the productivity gains from PCs.

Performance measures are "vital signs" that indicate the health of an organization. Organizations have performance measures for sales, inventory levels, financial performance, and so on; often these measures are used not only to indicate the health of the organization but, more important, to bring potential problems to the attention of managers. Performance measures for PCs should be well thought out and applied throughout the organization. For example, suppose an organization determines the effective use of its PCs by measuring the amount of time each user spends on his or her PC. This may not actually be an effective measure of performance, because some of the heavy users may be spending time on the PC playing computer games! "Do you measure the value of the phone by how long people are on it? When someone says they use the computer an hour a day, that's probably plenty. Ultimately, the best computer may only require a user to spend about 10 minutes with it."[28] There are no set ways to measure the value of PC usage. It depends on the information needs of the organization, the nature of the applications, and the criticality of those applications. Each organization must customize its performance measures to reflect both the organizational culture and the profile of its users.

Principle 5: Backup of PC files is critical and can affect the very life of an organization.

With the spread of PCs, vital corporate data and information are created, processed, and stored on PCs. However, quite frequently managers fail to monitor and control backup procedures for PCs; this can put the organization in serious jeopardy. Some simple backup measures are to ensure that files, new and altered, are backed up every day, except on Friday, when a full system backup should be done. Further, there should be at least two sets of backups for critical data, and one set must be kept in an offsite location. These are some very simple measures that a PC manager can take to ensure that critical data are not lost.

Off-the-Shelf Software

Another way to develop information systems is to use off-the-shelf software packages that are designed for specific tasks. Off-the-shelf packages are well suited to noncritical applications such as word processing, financial analysis, inventory control, scheduling, project management, and employee benefits. They eliminate the need to "reinvent the wheel" and provide developers with an effective tool to quickly develop systems. If some tasks or functions are common to many departments or units in the business, it makes good economic sense to buy off-the-shelf software that will meet user needs immediately. They are also a good choice when companies have a shortage of IS talent or when systems have to be developed very quickly.

Buying off-the-shelf packages has in recent years become a very attractive alternative to developing systems. These packages range in complexity from very simple to highly sophisticated systems. For example, Kaneb Services, a $200-million pipeline management and repair company, in Richardson, Texas, uses off-the-shelf software. The company has no IS staff and uses a commercially available database package to perform a variety of complex and sophisticated tasks, such as compiling and analyzing financial information from 40 different offices using six national currencies.[29]

Many off-the-shelf packages and vendor options are available today. In fact, the choices are so numerous that many IS managers feel overwhelmed when it comes to selecting the right software. However, in spite of the wide choices, sometimes a program still has to be customized. Customizing allows companies to overcome some of the bottlenecks inherent to in-house development, while reaping all the benefits of tailor-made software. However, changing the source code of the program may invalidate the warranty provided by the vendor, so companies must carefully look into this issue.

Advantages of Off-the-Shelf Software

One advantage of ready-made software is that it greatly reduces system development cost, time, and manpower. PACE (see box), an information system that the Phoenix Department of Police uses to catch criminals, was developed using off-the-shelf software. The entire system was built in less than 18 months, primarily because of the benefits of packaged software. Small businesses, in particular, are heavy users of off-the-shelf software, since a small company may not have an IS department large enough to develop its own software.

In the discussion of the SDLC, we saw some of its problems and limitations. It is time-consuming because the phases of development are sequential. Off-the-shelf software eliminates some of the problems and limitations of the SDLC. Reputable software packages are most often free of major errors, reducing the need for extensive testing. Reputable vendors often provide training (at a price) for their software, and sometimes even toll-free technical support; this can reduce some of the overhead associated with system development. Maintenance of packaged systems is also a lot lower than that for customized systems; given the high costs of maintenance in the long term, this is a significant advantage.

Disadvantages of Off-the-Shelf Software

The major disadvantage of packaged software is that it is not customized to meet the needs of the organization and this may require the company to fit the problem to the tool, rather than finding a tool that fits the problem. On the other hand, extensive customization may greatly increase the cost of the program and sometimes make it even more expensive than software developed in-house. Also, under pressure to get their software to market early, some vendors ship defective products. Sometimes they leave the burden of product testing to the consumer by adopting this attitude: "If you find it, we'll fix it." Even if a vendor corrects the error, the company often loses valuable time in the process. Finally, software vendors tend to produce products with a large number of advanced features, many of which users never use. Thus, the firm often ends up paying for features that are not used.

BUSINESS REALITIES

The Phoenix Police Department

In 1990, the City of Phoenix Police Department was eagerly looking for a break in the case of the elusive Yogurt Bandit, who had robbed 15 yogurt shops, convenience stores, and banks over a 3-month period. Using a system called PACE (Police Automated Computer Entry), a detective matched the vehicle license plate of a suspect with a partial license plate number given by a witness. This system has eliminated the need for officers to file handwritten reports; the department's 2,100 officers can now telephone their information to data entry clerks, who enter the information directly into PACE. The system can even prompt an officer for additional information.

One of the primary components of PACE is a database that stores information filed by patrol officers based on interviews with suspects; this database was developed using off-the-shelf packages.[30]

Outsourcing

To outsource or not to outsource?" is a question that many CIOs are grappling with today. **Outsourcing** is the hiring of outside professional services to meet the needs of an organization in areas as diverse as human resources, taxes, facilities management, or inventory management. In IS, outsourcing means using external agencies to create, process, manage, and maintain information systems and to provide the company with a wide range of information-related services, such as data processing, accessing external databases, systems integration, global networking, and gathering business intelligence.

Outsourcing is somewhat like the time-sharing concept that was popular during the 1960s and 1970s. In time-sharing, organizations purchased computer time to process data, but assumed the full responsibility for designing, developing, and maintaining their systems. In outsourcing, on the other hand, organizations can simply outsource the tasks of managing, updating, and maintaining information systems while assuming full responsibility for system design and development, or they can outsource the entire job of designing, developing, and maintaining information systems. (Such projects are referred to as turnkey projects.)

However, quite often organizations outsource only basic data processing operations (such as data entry and data verification), general business functions (such as accounting, marketing, and production), and systems that are not in their direct line of business. Rarely do companies outsource their strategic systems.

Organizations outsource for reasons that can be classified into four broad categories: strategic focus, economies of scale, market forces, and technical considerations (Gupta, 1992).

Strategic Focus

An organization may outsource so that it can better focus on its primary line of business and channel its limited resources to meet its strategic goals and achieve its mission. The question "What do we do best and how can we do it better?" may lead to a decision to outsource information systems. In 1989, Kodak outsourced its data centers to IBM, its communications systems to DEC, and its microcomputer-based networks to BusinessLand, and indicated that it was doing so because these functions were not in its direct line of business.

Economic Reasons

Companies may also outsource for economic reasons. Since most outsourcing agreements are fixed-price contracts, this eliminates the escalating costs that are often associated with system design and development. When outsourcing contracts are carefully designed, it can decrease the overall cost of IS operations because firms whose primary business is information systems and services can often deliver the goods more efficiently than organizations in which IS is a staff function.

Market Forces

Sometimes market forces compel organizations to consider outsourcing. If an outside vendor can provide a support function more efficiently, outsourcing that function can reduce operating costs and give the company a competitive advantage. For example, Esprit de Corp.'s decision to outsource (see box) was based partially on its inability to meet its own information needs efficiently. Mergers, acquisitions, leveraged buyouts, and downsizing are some of the other market dynamics that can force an organization to outsource its IS function.

Technical Considerations

Finally, technical considerations, such as a lack of qualified technical personnel, may make outsourcing an attractive alternative. Companies on the leading edge of technology often face a shortage of skilled personnel. For example, Greyhound Lines of Canada was recently trying to attract IS talent so that it could expand more aggressively into new markets. The company found that its location in Calgary made it difficult to attract IS professionals; hence, it decided to outsource its information systems.[32]

One of the primary concerns that managers face when it comes to outsourcing is legacy systems, which are large systems (usually on mainframes) that handle the company's payroll, inventory management, and so on. There are three primary outsourcing options with regard to legacy systems:

BUSINESS REALITIES
Esprit de Corp.

Esprit de Corp.'s old 3090 Model 200 was obsolete, inflexible, and incapable of running most current software. It was causing major headaches for company executives. The company solved its problem through a multi-million-dollar outsourcing contract with Software Maintenance Specialists (SMS) in Santa Ana, California, which transferred the burden of meeting the information needs of the company to SMS. When choosing the outsourcing vendor, the company had several firm requirements. Most important was that the cost of outsourcing should not be greater than the cost of performing the IS function in-house. "We weren't willing to pay a premium for relief," says the IS chief. "The bottom line had to make sense."

The CIO included every conceivable factor in his calculation of current costs, down to the amount of power consumed by computers. Esprit spent roughly 18 months evaluating outsourcing vendors. After narrowing down the field from nine to six, it sent to those six vendors tapes of systems-measurement facility files provided by the mainframe operating system. These log files gave the vendors a full accounting of what Esprit

demanded of its system and how the system responded. The vendors were told that their systems must at least match Esprit's in performance. For example, 1-second response time was a minimum requirement. In addition, overnight batch processing results from Esprit's San Francisco office and 17 retail outlets had to be completed before the company's New York showroom opened the following day, at which time control was turned over to online transaction processing systems.

The company solicited proposals from outsourcers ranging in size from EDS, with more than 70,000 employees, down to the 100-person SMS. The company favored SMS on the basis of several recommendations from people in the outsourcing field, including a competing vendor that had been eliminated from consideration and a former employee of another outsourcer.

Over some 10 weeks, SMS committed between 3 and 5 work-months to making sure its employees understood the Esprit operation, documenting the company's procedures, run books, and system-dependency charts more thoroughly than the IS staff itself had done. Before taking control of Esprit's mainframe operations, the outsourcer ran one of the company's daily cycles repeatedly, testing applications one at a time until they ran flawlessly. Despite minor glitches, the new system was available to users in New York 4 hours ahead of schedule.[31]

1. Outsource the maintenance of legacy systems and use in-house staff to build new systems.
2. Outsource the development of new systems and keep in-house staff to run and maintain legacy systems.
3. Use insourcing for both legacy systems and new systems.

For example, two of PepsiCo's best-known business units, Pepsi-Cola North America, in Somers, New York, and KFC, in Louisville, Kentucky, have adopted different postures for outsourcing. In an effort to replace its legacy platforms, Pepsi-Cola North America is outsourcing both maintenance of existing systems and development of new systems. The company is developing a distributed environment, including 270 LAN servers that connect 4,000 PCs and numerous database servers and application servers. The massive project was too great a burden for IS staff.

"Contractors have been deployed mostly to keep the legacy systems running since they're dealing with the systems that will go away anyway. In-house staff focus mostly on new systems development since they're the folks who will have to support it," says a company spokesperson.

The department of worldwide information services at KFC has taken the opposite approach. The company has outsourced the development of an innovative new point-of-sale (POS) system that employs UNIX, C++, object-oriented development, and code reuse. "We're a food company, not a technology company," says a company spokesperson. In a contract with many condition clauses, the company is protecting itself from any failures on the part of the contractor.

The third alternative is to pursue the option of "insourcing," which involves treating the IS department as a "business within the business" and training the systems development staff to meet present and future development needs. Merrill Lynch has launched a sizable insourcing effort to consolidate its legacy systems support into a focused service-providing core group that provides economies of scale for many IS resources, such as systems, tools, and training.[33] Table 12–6 presents a summary of these three options.

Advantages and Disadvantages of Outsourcing

Like other development methodologies, outsourcing has both advantages and disadvantages. The primary advantage of outsourcing is that the burden of developing and delivering high-quality information systems is on the outsourcing vendor, not on the organization. Outsourcing, when carefully implemented, can reduce the cost of IS functions and services, decrease overhead, and reduce problems associated with technological obsolescence. The organization can also concentrate on its strategic or primary business and thus put its resources to better use. Good, reputable outsourcers provide state-of-the-art technologies, which can help a company to be responsive and competitive.

But outsourcing also has some disadvantages. It often results in job losses; when it does, fewer employees end up carrying a higher workload. This can be demoralizing and unproductive, and can result in high employee turnover. Employees may also view outsourcing as a vote against their technical skills or as a sign that troubled times are ahead for the company, prompting key IS personnel to quit the company. Finally, outsourcing to the wrong vendor may result in loss of control over the quality and reliability of the IS function. For example,

TABLE 12–6
This table shows the three different options for firms that may wish to outsource their legacy systems and/or new system development.

The Outsourcing/Insourcing Options[i]

Outsource legacy maintenance, keep new development.

+ Investment in internal staff brings state-of-the-art technical know-how in-house and keeps staff motivated.

+ IS management can tap available supply of labor well-versed in older technologies (readily available, cheaper).

− Outsiders must be entrusted with operating key legacy systems that are needed to run business today.

− Internal staff may not be malleable enough to adjust to new technologies and techniques.

Outsource new development, keep legacy maintenance.

+ Enables IS management to make quick progress on new development efforts by using the latest techniques.

+ Staff members work on what they know best (i.e., the legacy systems).

− The company may end up with new systems that cannot be supported by its own staff.

− Internal staff may feel neglected and become discontented or quit the organization.

Insource the development.

+ Insourcing promotes a "business-within-a-business" atmosphere to focus and professionalize the group.

+ Economies of scale are leveraged to provide development personnel with training and tools.

− Lack of familiarity with the approach may confuse IS staff and distract them from user needs.

− IS may be pressured to offer new services that are not within its capabilities.

[i] Eliot, Lance B. "Legacy Systems, Legacy Options," *Computerworld,* July 11, 1994, pp. 86, 88.

Texas State Bank, in McAllen, Texas, is suing Electronic Data Systems (EDS), an outsourcer, for $300 million in exemplary damages and $65.5 million in lost business opportunities. The suit alleges that in 1988, EDS misrepresented itself when it claimed that it fully understood the bank's existing information system and was technically capable of converting from existing system to a more responsive, EDS-based system within 3 months. "To the contrary, the EDS conversion and post-conversion data processing and [automated teller] service were disastrous, causing serious problems to [the bank's] daily operations and growth," the suit alleges. The bank also claims that it missed two acquisitions, worth $17.5 million, and lost another $40 million in business transactions because of the faulty information systems developed by EDS.[34] Clearly, organizations must be extremely careful when choosing an outsourcing vendor. This is a delicate partnership that can be highly beneficial or highly disastrous.

There is no easy or simple answer to the question "To outsource or not to outsource?" A company must carefully analyze and balance the pros and cons of outsourcing and take into account not only its information needs, but also the organizational culture, the managerial style, and the strengths and weaknesses of its IS personnel.

Comparison of Different Methodologies

So far, we have discussed five methodologies for developing information systems and their advantages and disadvantages. Is any one methodology superior to any other? No. Each methodology has its own strengths and weaknesses and all should be carefully weighed and assessed before one methodology is selected. The strengths and weaknesses of the five methodologies are shown in Table 12–7.

Although selecting the right methodology is a very important factor in ensuring the success of a system, it is not the only factor. If following the methodology becomes an end in itself, it can become unproductive and other innovative approaches to system development may be overlooked. "Methodologies lead you into quicksand. We once spent three years following a methodology and ended up with a diagram that we couldn't code."[35]

There is a strong movement in many organizations to shift the focus from rigid methodologies to the needs of the customer. Many CEOs argue that meeting customer needs should be the primary focus of IS projects. Larry Runge conveys this message powerfully:

"Customers . . . are a different breed. All they ask is that we do our job well and efficiently. Then, in return, they pay our mortgages, buy our groceries, help send our kids to college and give us money to buy that boat or stereo we've always

	Characteristics	**Advantages**	**Disadvantages**
SDLC	Traditional development approach Sequential step-by-step approach Five phases	Suitable for large projects Provides structure and control	Expensive Time-Consuming Inflexible Limited role of users
Prototyping	Iterative methodology Based on building a working model	High user emphasis Promotes teamwork Reduces wastage Flexible	Sometimes used as an excuse for poor development methods High levels of stress
Application Software	Off-the-shelf packages used to develop applications Can be customized	Eliminates some development problems Reduces overhead costs Speeds up development	Fitting the problem to the tool Allows only limited customization
End-User Movement	End users assume full responsibility for system development	Speeds development Reduces IS backlog Users become sponsors	Lack of control results in lax security and standards
Outsourcing	Outside vendors provide full or partial IS related services	Business can focus on strategic areas Cost-effective Reduces obsolescence	Eliminates jobs Can cause morale problems Loose control over quality of systems

TABLE 12–7
The features, the advantages, and the disadvantages of the five different IS development methodologies.

wanted. Frankly, if our customers are willing to pay for the good life we enjoy in return for a bit of programming, then they deserve our respect and our best efforts to get them what they want, when they want it. . . . Our measurements and rewards have to be based on meeting the customer's needs. Anything else will be counterproductive to our goal of serving the customer."[36]

Challenges in Developing Information Systems

Organizations face two major challenges in system development: backlogs and runaway projects. A **backlog** occurs when the development of an information system has been delayed. In many organizations, the back-log queue continues to grow at a rapid rate. In a recent survey of 101 CIOs by *Computerworld*, 34% indicated that their application backlog had grown in the past year and more than 75% indicated that end-users were asking for more and more new applications.[37] Experts cite the increasing complexity of systems, the growing demand for sophisticated systems, major overhauls of outdated systems, and the complexity of new development tools and technologies as some major reasons for this problem.

The second IS development challenge facing many organizations is **runaway projects,** projects that are behind schedule and over budget. "It may be known as the black hole, the white elephant, the Golden Fleece, the boondoggle—or it may be too painful to mention at all. Sometimes, it gets the chief information officer fired."[38]

Indeed, the statistics about runaway projects and their implications are staggering:

- 50% of finished projects are over budget by 60% to 190% and contain less than 70% of originally promised functionality.
- 25% of projects are canceled due to scope increase.
- 25% of projects are completed on time, within budget and to a client's satisfaction.
- Less than 15% of IS project managers have created a change-management plan to deal with scope changes.
- Less than 11% of IS project managers know the critical paths of their projects.[39]

Runaway projects are a universal problem. For example, the London Stock Exchange failed miserably in its efforts to update its outdated trading system (see box on U.K. Taurus project). There are many examples in popular literature on the embarrassment and the serious consequences of runaway projects. The FAA recently canceled a project whose cost was estimated to be $2.6 billion in 1988; by 1994, nearly $7 billion had been spent and the project was nowhere near completion.[41]

The Standish Group International, in Dennis, Massachusetts, recently surveyed 365 companies that together represent more than 8,000 development projects. According to those respondents, only 16% of all projects are completed on time and within budget. Also, the bigger the company (especially if its revenues amount to more than $500 million), the bigger the problem. Large companies typically have lower-than-average success rates with development projects because the projects are too large to be completed on time.

The survey also found that the top five reasons for success were

- User involvement
- Executive management support
- Clear statement of requirements
- Proper planning
- Realistic expectations

The top five reasons for failure were

- Lack of user input
- Incomplete requirements and specifications
- Changing requirements and specifications
- Lack of executive support
- Technological incompetence[42]

Runaway projects are more often the result of poor management than of technological complexities (see box on Federal Aviation Authority). Though organizations make an effort to hire only those system developers who are technically superior, few organizations pay attention to the project management skills of system developers. Further, IS managers sometimes tend to "underquote" on the resources required for a project in order to get the approval of top management. Then, when the project has been approved, it turns out to be much more costly than the initial proposal indicated. "Then, it is almost a no-win situation. You want

A GLOBAL PERSPECTIVE
The U.K. Taurus Project

How do you recover from one of the largest, if not *the* largest, runaway systems debacle in the history of information processing? The answer, it appears, is to reassess and begin again. The Taurus project, an attempt to update an existing electronic trading system, was scrapped in March 1993 after nearly a decade of development, wasting not only the $100 million that the London Stock Exchange had poured into the project's development, but also an estimated $400 million that the London financial community had invested in preparations to link their existing systems to Taurus. The project's failure resulted in the resignation of Peter Rawlins, chief executive of the stock exchange.

The problems Taurus was intended to solve have not gone away. The exchange's existing trading system, Talisman, is by all measures outdated and inflexible; it takes 3 to 6 weeks to settle trades made on the London exchange, compared to 3 to 5 days in the United States,

and 2 days in Japan. But it is more than just efficiency that is at stake: London's jealously guarded reputation in the world of international finance is also at stake.

The Bank of England has begun the development of Crest, a project designed to update the electronic settlement system for the London Stock Exchange. It will use fault-tolerant computers to link the London exchange with other financial institutions in Europe. Crest is expected to cost only $50 million (of which only $7.5 million is allocated for development costs) and is expected to be completed in 1996. The auditing firm Price Waterhouse, however, has already voiced concerns that the cost estimate "does not include sufficient contingency." If Taurus can be used as a guide, they expect that Crest will cost the investment community four times the allocated amount. But many others are confident that Crest will be able to deliver the goods. "The reason this will work while Taurus failed is because of the strong management and the system simplicity. The Bank of England is in a strong position to ensure that the project's specifications don't snowball."[40]

BUSINESS REALITIES
The Federal Aviation Administration

The Federal Aviation Administration's (FAA's) Advanced Automation System (AAS) project is a classic example of a runaway project. Billions of dollars over budget and many years behind schedule, FAA officials admitted to a congressional panel that the best alternative might be to scrap the project in its entirety or to scale it back considerably and reassess the entire set of initial requirements. "The AAS program, if unchanged, would pose certain cost and schedule increases that are unacceptable. Software volatility is running 100%, meaning every line of code has to be rewritten at least once, compared to original expectations of a 40% rate," said an FAA spokesperson.

FAA and contract representatives indicated that technological obsolescence was a primary factor in the runaway project. The emergence of extremely powerful workstations and the greater availability of commercial off-the-shelf software may enable the project to save some hardware and software development cost. The FAA has already spent about $1.5 billion to date on the estimated $6.9-billion air traffic control system.

In retrospect, several reasons have emerged for the fact that the AAS became a runaway project. First, both the FAA and IBM grossly underestimated costs and schedules; second, the AAS project was poorly managed and FAA officials did not adequately supervise the project, particularly in the problem definition and analysis phases; third, there were very few control mechanisms, so managers were often unaware of missed deadlines and cost overruns. Finally, the FAA was somewhat ad hoc, arbitrary, and indecisive in establishing the initial set of requirements. These four problems together resulted in a runaway system.[43]

---

to revise the schedule, but that means publicly admitting that you screwed up the schedule in the first place. In the past, you would add more people to it, but there isn't enough evidence that adding more people to a late project will bring it back."[44]

What are some ways to regain control of runaway projects? Sometimes the best alternative is to cancel the project, although many organizations are reluctant to do that for fear of losing face. "Most U.S. organizations don't [cancel the project], whereas in the U.K. and Canada, they're more apt to cancel. Also, there is a certain amount of ego or face-saving among senior executives; they would rather put more money in a deep hole than cancel the project."[45] Another approach is to recruit users as system sponsors so that they have a personal stake in the success of the system. A third alternative is to hire managers with good planning and project management skills, Finally, good reporting systems and tracking systems can give early warnings of deadline slippage and cost overruns.

In summary, there are several methodologies for system development. End-users must be knowledgeable about the strengths and weaknesses of these approaches because selecting the right methodology is crucial to developing good systems.

IS Development in a Global Environment

As the trend toward globalization continues, there is a pressing need for systems that link business units around the world with their headquarters so that information can flow freely across national and international boundaries. Languages, currencies, time zones, government regulations, and technological barriers must all be overcome for a company to operate globally. For example, Procter & Gamble's expansion of sales of its Tide detergent to nearly every consumer market in the world is a prime example of the international marketing of goods and services by American firms. With globalization comes the need for information systems that can operate in a number of countries. Nestlé is another example of a company that has successfully integrated its information systems to serve a global market (see box).

American managers are discovering that information systems are not as generic or as transportable across national borders as they once thought. These systems are often very complex and must be able to cross a number of time zones, governments, languages, and currencies, and must be developed quickly if they are to provide strategic advantages for the companies that use them.

Traditional approaches to IS development are often unsatisfactory because they are designed for a specific problem at a specific site. International information systems must be developed in such a way that will allow a high degree of coordination between different and distant sites with large numbers of users. Philip Morris encountered many of these challenges, including language barriers, government regulations, poor infrastructure, shortage of vendors with global experience, and cultural barriers and biases, when it became engaged in developing international information systems.

A bottom-up approach is recommended for international systems. This involves developing a system locally and then transporting it to other units outside its original location. This runs counter to the popular approach, in which systems are developed at headquarters and then transported to business units all over the world. The bottom-up approach allows local organizations to develop

A GLOBAL PERSPECTIVE
Nestlé Inc.

Nestlé is the archetypal multinational company: top management hails from the four corners of the globe and English, French, and Spanish are the company's three official languages. But this $40 billion food and pharmaceuticals company, with close to 300 operating companies and 220,000 employees worldwide, is managed by a headquarters staff of just 1,600, thanks to the company's efficient use of information systems and technologies.

The Swiss company is a fascinating study in the use of information systems and technologies to meet global information needs. Nestlé's recipe for its technology blend looks something like this: one large measure of centralized planning, a dollop of local input, and a healthy dash of common computing standards! Mixed together, these ingredients form the essence of Nestlé's North American and European information technology strategy that is designed to ensure smooth operations in global markets. Nestlé's goal is to create information systems that will adhere to company-wide standards while satisfying the information needs of hundreds of operating companies around the world.

In the past, the company had a "one of everything" mix of computer hardware and software that would make any IS director wince. Over the past four years, Nestlé's technology team standardized both hardware and software, although the company does not impose these standards on subsidiaries or operations in far-flung countries. Usually, developers from different countries provide input to ensure that standards blend smoothly into Nestlé's different markets. The IS staff only recommends standards; the individual units can adapt them to individual markets. The company makes every attempt to foster a culture of teamwork and cooperation by soliciting the input of experts from around the world.

Here's how the Nestlé technology strategy works: Core applications are developed by teams at headquarters and other locations, often with the assistance of hardware and software experts from within Nestlé or its vendors. Consensus is reached on applications requirements, development strategies, hardware platforms, operating systems, and other specific issues. Once an application is developed, it is sent to the local unit where the application will be used after it is modified to meet local requirements and regulations.[46]

autonomous, yet cohesive, systems, and often much faster than headquarters can. Its success depends on the provision of standardization guidelines for the entire company, although actual development is delegated to local sites.

Global systems also require that critical data elements be efficiently managed. This is often done by using a global data dictionary that identifies all data elements that are common to all units around the world. The global dictionary can be expanded at local sites by adding any additional data elements required by local regulations and requirements. The format of the data in the global dictionary is then standardized so that the data will have a uniform face across national and international boundaries.[47]

In the coming years, as organizations become increasingly global, the need for international system projects will also grow. Knowledge workers and IS managers must be prepared to meet the unique challenges that these new systems will bring.

 **Summary**

* **The importance of selecting the right methodology.**

The traditional view that information systems are the sole and exclusive responsibility of the IS department no longer works for pragmatic and proactive companies. The job functions of many employees are influenced by information systems; therefore, all knowledge workers, regardless of their functional specialization, should be knowledgeable about IS development. The impact of information systems goes far beyond technical implications and productivity gains. Therefore, system development should be viewed not just within the context of a business, but in the larger context of a sociotechnical society.

* **Different system development methodologies.**

There are five different development methodologies for information systems. The system development life cycle (SDLC) methodology is a traditional development approach that divides the task of developing information systems into five phases: system definition, system analysis, system design and programming, system testing and implementation, and system maintenance. It is well suited to large systems that are highly structured and routine, such as TPS and MIS.

The second methodology is prototyping, in which different phases of system development are carried out iteratively, rather than in sequence. This methodology, also referred to as rapid application development (RAD), has four main phases: problem definition and identification of system requirements, building the initial prototype, refining the prototype, and further revising and enhancing the prototype. Prototyping is an inexpensive, yet effective, way to design and develop systems, since each prototype is a small, highly manageable piece of a larger system.

The third approach to information systems development is end-user computing, wherein end-users design, develop, and maintain information systems to meet their own needs. The proliferation of PCs and user-friendly software packages has made the end-user movement possible.

The fourth approach is using off-the-shelf software packages. Off-the-shelf packages are useful for noncritical applications, such as payroll, word processing, financial analysis, inventory control, scheduling, project management, and employee benefits. They eliminate the need to "reinvent the wheel" and provide developers with an effective tool to quickly develop systems.

The fifth approach to IS development is outsourcing, in which an organization hires an outside firm to design, develop, and maintain its information systems or some part thereof. Organizations outsource only rudimentary data processing operations, general business functions, and systems that are not in their direct line of business; rarely do companies outsource their strategic systems.

Each of these approaches has its strengths and weaknesses; no one methodology is suitable for all applications, and sometimes a combination of methodologies is used to build a given system.

* **The challenges faced by developers of information systems.**

There are two primary challenges in developing information systems: backlog and runaway projects. Backlog is a term for projects whose development has not yet begun, although these projects have been approved for development. This often occurs because IS departments have many more requests for development projects than they can handle. Runaway projects are projects that are behind schedule and over budget. Runaway projects are a major, yet common, problem in many organizations.

♦ **The implications of EUC.**

End-user computing is the design, development, and maintenance of information systems by end-users. EUC allows shorter development times, greater flexibility and control over system development, and lower development costs. It removes some of the burden from backlogged IS departments. However, an organization should carefully monitor and control EUC if it is to truly benefit the firm.

♦ **Resources and strategies necessary for managing end-users.**

EUC must be carefully managed; there are a number of strategies for doing so. Coordination, support, and evaluation are three strategies that organizations can use to effectively manage end-user computing. Coordination is management of the resources associated with EUC, such as hardware, software, networks, and people. Support is provision of help to end-users so that they can fully utilize their systems. Evaluation is the process of receiving feedback so that any weaknesses in the system can be quickly identified and rectified.

 Review Questions

1. What are the five components of an information system? Describe each component. Are these components also found in other systems? Explain.

2. What are the five different development methodologies for information systems? Why should knowledge workers be aware of these methodologies?

3. Briefly discuss the five phases of the SDLC. For what type of system is the SDLC appropriate?

4. Identify and briefly describe the three primary activities in the system analysis phase. What are some types of feasibility analysis that are conducted in this phase?

5. Define functional requirements. Explain why it is difficult to develop them.

6. What are creeping requirements and why are they common?

7. What are the two types of system design? Identify the three main activities in the system design phase.

8. Identify and describe three types of system testing. What are the three implementation methods that are used to replace existing systems with new systems? Which of the three is the safest?

9. Describe prototyping. Identify any two strengths and two weaknesses of this methodology.

10. What are some reasons why organizations choose to outsource their information systems?

11. What are some advantages and disadvantages of outsourcing?

12. Identify two major challenges that organizations face in developing information systems.

13. What are some of the challenges in developing international system projects?

14. Who is an end-user? What are some factors that have enabled the end-user movement to gather momentum?

15. Coordination, support, and evaluation are three strategies for managing EUC. Describe each of these strategies.

16. We have identified four approaches to managing EUC. Identify these approaches and explain which one, if any, is best.

 Discussion Questions

1. There are two competing views of the role of litigation in ensuring the quality of software systems.

   Viewpoint 1: Competition, not litigation, ensures quality systems. Because computers influence all aspects of our personal and professional lives, the implications of faulty systems are serious both for users and for developers. Although faulty systems may result in damaging lawsuits, such measures do not necessarily result in better systems. Instead, they simply increase the costs of developing information systems, which are passed on to the consumer. "Competition, not litigation, ensures quality systems."[48]

Viewpoint 2: Responsible lawsuits keep vendors honest. Companies incur devastating financial losses because of faulty computer systems. For example, a company in Massachusetts alleges that it became insolvent because of a financial system that caused errors in the company's integrated general ledger system, passbooks, and loan statements. The errors were so serious that dissatisfied customers withdrew more than $5 million from the bank and took their business elsewhere. Faulty systems have created undesirable—sometimes even life-threatening—situations. For example, a Boeing 747 had to make an emergency landing because of an error in the plane's autopilot system. Lawyers argue that just as professionals such as doctors, lawyers, and architects are held liable and accountable for their actions, so should programmers and system developers, particularly when the software can cause catastrophic losses.[49]

Should computer programmers, like other professionals, be held accountable and liable for their actions? Discuss.

If a structural engineer uses a program that miscalculates the stress loads in a building, thereby causing serious injuries to its residents, should the programmer be held liable? Discuss the cost implications if such liabilities are imposed on programmers.

Will higher liability standards simply increase the cost of developing information systems with little or no effect on the quality of systems? Discuss.

2. "Good project managers are those who can explain to users the cost and scheduling implications of their requests to make changes to the system and, if possible, get them to agree to defer them until after the base system is up and running."

How would you convince a rather obstinate user to postpone changing the requirements until the original system becomes operational? What policies and procedures should an organization put in place to address users' requests for requirement changes?

3. Many end-users, and even some IS chiefs, do not want to be bothered with the details of development methodologies. One IS chief recently commented, "I don't care whether we use pencil and paper or crayons and drawing tablets—whatever works."[50] Do you agree with this approach? Why or why not?

4. One of the major drawbacks of traditional development methodologies, such as the SDLC, is that the lead time from product conception to delivery is often too long, often between 3 and 5 years. In today's environment, such development times can put a company at a disadvantage as competitors beat them to the market with new, high-quality products. On the other hand, high-quality systems take time to develop and cannot be rushed.[51]

Which methodology would you recommend if a system is to be delivered quickly? Why?

ETHICAL ISSUES

Case 1: Blue Cross Fails to Take Care of Displaced Employees

There was no leniency in the ruling. For failing to give 580 former employees adequate notice of a computer outsourcing agreement with EDS, Blue Cross of Massachusetts was ordered to pay more then $7 million in compensation and was told that it may not offset these damages by using any of the benefits or severance pay its former employees may have received since their transfer to EDS.

In 1991 the insurer awarded an $800-million 10-year outsourcing contract to systems integrator EDS.

Because of a loophole in Blue Cross's own rules, workers laid off as a result of the agreement were eligible for severance pay and other payments, even though they were immediately hired by EDS. As part of the outsourcing deal, Blue Cross had transferred employees from its IS department to EDS in January 1992 with only 8 days' notice. Lawyers for Blue Cross argue that even though the notice was short, employees started receiving benefits and pay from EDS as soon as the transfer took place. Many of the transferred employees were let go by EDS 18 months after the outsourcing arrangement was made.

(Continued on next page)

Blue Cross argued that the severance package that the employees received should be used to offset some of the court payments. But the judge rejected that plea and ordered the company to pay its former employees the cash equivalent of 60 full days' notice, to which they were originally entitled. "We feel the plaintiffs' position is one of an absolute windfall," says a Blue Cross spokesman. "When they were originally transferred to EDS, they received a job and severance." The company plans to appeal.[52]

1. Do you agree that Blue Cross should be held liable for not giving employees 60 days' notice or equivalent pay?
2. What should Blue Cross have done to avoid such costly litigation?

Case 2: Minolta Runs into Outsourcing Snag

Minolta decided to outsource its data center operations to reduce costs and capital investments by 10% to 12% annually. When Minolta entered a 5-year outsourcing agreement with PKS Information Services, in Omaha, in August 1993, the Ramsey, New Jersey, business equipment supplier ran into an unexpected snag. It was hit with a six-figure surcharge from one of its software vendors, American Software, for transferring its inventory control and order processing software to the outsourcer. The hefty surcharge surprised both Minolta and industry software analysts, who said application developers rarely charge such fees. However, the reason for such an unusual charge is obvious: American Software was not among the five vendors considered for the outsourcing contract.[53]

1. Do you think that American Software was right in charging Minolta such a large surcharge for transferring its software to PKS? Discuss.

Case 3: Trouble at California's Office of Information Technology

The California legislature plans to review the state's $1.2-billion information technology budget following allegations by the legislative analyst's office that the Office of Information Technology (OIT) failed to properly manage some of its largest computer projects: "Our review of the OIT's performance over the past year indicates that the office has not fulfilled its leadership role and that this has resulted in a more costly statewide implementation of computer systems."

As a result, a California state senate subcommittee withheld 5 months of proposed funding for the OIT's 1994–95 budget and approved a state management review of the OIT. The senate hearings followed revelations that the Department of Motor Vehicles (DMV) spent $44 million for a project that failed to produce any working applications, and the DMV project is just one of several very large projects that were poorly managed. The report cited other problems, including incompatible computer systems, poor access to departmental databases, and an overall lack of standards.

On May 12, 1994, Governor Pete Wilson issued an executive order to create a task force to review the way the state manages and oversees its computer purchases. However, OIT director Steve Kolodney responded that the legislative analyst's charges were unfair. "The law itself does not give substantial authority for oversight, other than financial oversight," he said. "So we have no explicit authority to go into departments and to do management reviews or audits of the status of their projects."[54]

1. Why is the OIT under review by the California state legislature?
2. If the OIT director is not authorized to audit the status of a project, do you think it is fair to hold the office liable for failed projects?

Case 4: Moral Minority

"What changed?" Janice Devin asked. "Is it just me or does anybody else feel like this?" Devin was reflecting back on her decision 4 months earlier to join the development team for Liberty Hospital's new imaging and workflow system. Her manager, Robert Harding, did not know how to respond to her question. He began to realize that Devin had underestimated the impact the project would have on the people in the accounts payable department, and by extension, on her own feelings about her work at the teaching hospital.

In the past 12 months, the hospital's financial situation had improved significantly. Much of the credit had gone to the administration and finance team, which 2 years before had begun an aggressive effort to examine every critical business process at the hospital. A year before, the administration had begun to translate the results of their analysis into an action plan. However, though their effort had improved the hospital's bottom line, it had also caused stress for staff in different departments. There had been rumors that the union representing the maintenance staff was considering a strike over proposed changes in work rules, and several of the hospital staff had filed a protest over what they described as "interference" from nonmedical personnel.

Until she joined the new project team, Devin's interactions with staff outside her own department had been limited. As a result of another of the process changes proposed by the new administration, most members of the IS department had for the most part operated in isolation from the groups they served. Harding had been an internal advocate of the new approach to working with the IS department's internal "customers" and had encouraged Devin to participate on the project team. Harding had painted an attractive picture of the opportunity. In addition to letting Devin work with exciting new technology, it would give her visibility outside her own group. After some friendly encouragement, she volunteered for the team. But once she joined the team, things began to look different from the picture Harding had painted.

Devin found Robin Groci, the administration and finance member of the project team, difficult to work with. Robin had joined Liberty straight out of a health care management program, 3 months after the senior management team had turned over. This was her first job. Mary Trayte, the head of the accounts payable department, was pleasant enough, but seemed intimidated by Groci. Devin liked the two other IS team members, but they were focused on the technical architecture for the application, whereas she had to worry about how the application's functions matched up with the system specifications.

Things got worse when Devin discovered—relatively late in the project life cycle—that when the application was completed and phased in, more than 20 members of the accounts payable department would lose their jobs. When she inquired further, she was told by Groci that it was not her concern and that she should concentrate on getting the application completed on time. Realizing that she had to talk with someone about how she felt, Devin approached Harding and requested a private meeting. During the meeting, she expressed her discomfort with the work she was doing and asked for Harding's advice.[55]

1. How should Harding respond? Discuss.

PROBLEM SOLVING IN THE REAL WORLD

Case 1: Doomsday Date

"The information systems community is heading toward an event more devastating than a car crash. We are heading toward the year 2000. We are heading toward a failure of our standard date format: MM/DD/YY. This is a good news/bad news story. First the bad news: There is very little good news. There is no way to avoid the fact that our information systems are based on a faulty standard that will cost the worldwide computer community billions of dollars in programming efforts. The cost for programming to adjust all systems for the year 2000: $50 billion.

"The date change in the year 2000—an event that may trigger fatal errors in mission-critical systems—is fewer than 2,000 days away. Many IS people are unprepared or unconcerned. The problem is twofold: the date issue itself and, more important, our reluctance to address the problem. The cost when you add design, management, hardware, software, and support: $75 billion.

(Continued on next page)

"What exactly is the 'problem'? To save storage space and perhaps reduce the amount of keystrokes necessary to enter a year, most IS groups have allocated two digits to the year. For example, '1993' is stored as '93' in our date files, and '2000' will be stored '00'. This two-digit date affects data manipulation, primarily subtractions and comparisons. For instance, I was born in 1955. If I ask the computer to calculate how old I am today, it subtracts 55 from 93 and announces that I'm 38.

"So far, so good. But what happens in the year 2000? The computer will subtract 55 from 00 and will state that I am -55 years old. If you have some data records and want to sort them by date (e.g., 1965, 1905, 1966), the resulting sequence would be 1905, 1965, 1966. However, if you add in a date record such as 2015, the computer, which reads only the last two digits of the date, sees 05, 15, 65, 66 and sorts them incorrectly. The task facing us is to identify and correct all the date data and check the integrity of all calculations involving date information.

"We must correct the data residing in all date files or write code to handle the problem. The only choice we have is to examine each line of code and make the necessary changes. One IS person I know of performed an internal survey and came up with the following results: Of 104 systems, 18 would fail in the year 2000. These 18 million-critical systems were made up of 8,174 programs and date-entry screens as well as some 3,313 databases. With less than seven years to go, someone is going to be working overtime. By the way, this initial survey required 10 weeks of effort—ten weeks just to identify the problem areas.

"The crisis is very real. Estimate that Fortune 500 organizations will each have to spend about 35 to 40 cents per line of code to convert all their existing systems to accept the change from the year 1999 to 2000. That translates into about $50 million to $100 million for each company. The mind boggles at a maintenance problem with that price tag.

"Typically, all I get are snickers and comments such as, 'I won't be in this position or this company in the year 2000. It's not my problem.' It is very difficult for us to acknowledge that we made a 'little' error that will cost companies millions of dollars. It is also a 'pay me now or pay me later' situation. Total programming time for all systems: 1.2 million man-years.

"If software engineering managers cannot manage a change that they've had 1,000 years to prepare for, how can we expect them to manage a change that happens without notice? In other words, if this change causes a crisis in your organization, everything will cause a crisis in your organization—and often nothing will cause a crisis."[56]

1. Suppose you have been assigned the task of developing an information system to address the date-change problem in your organization. Use the SDLC development methodology and identify the tasks that you would perform in each phase of the SDLC.

2. Identify some of the challenges involved in designing an information system of this magnitude. What measures would you take to ensure that this will not become a runaway project?

3. To what phase do you attribute the cause of this problem: analysis, design, development, testing, or maintenance? How could this problem have been avoided?

Case 2: Crash at Denver International

The city of Denver put the opening of Denver International Airport, the nation's first major airport to open since Dallas–Fort Worth Airport in 1974, on hold for months as the nation's largest airfield struggled to resolve problems with a 20-mile-long computerized baggage-handling system that had mangled its cargo. The airport, which replaced Denver's Stapleton airport, opened behind schedule by many months and each day of delay added another $500,000 to the cost of the $3-billion project for Denver taxpayers.

The PC-controlled baggage system is outside the purview of the airport's IS department, because the entire airport has a decentralized computing environment. Each functional unit of the airport, such as security, heating, ventilation, facilities management, and the individual airlines, has its own computer system, operated by subcontractors in most cases. The central fiber distributed data interface (FDDI) network itself is operated by the airport's IS department, which also supports PC LANs and workstations on the network and maintains the central servers. The airport chose a client-server environment that supports specialized functions, such as security and flight management.

The automated baggage system is based on PCs, proprietary applications software, and a multiasking operating system thought to be IBM's OS/2. The systems are intended to speed turnaround time by routing bags automatically among airlines. Laser scanners route the baggage carts on underground tracks, directing each piece of baggage by reading its bar-coded label. There is only one piece of luggage per cart; as many as 60 carts per second traverse a single track.

The automatic baggage-handling system, which was once touted as the world's best, has become a classic case of project failure; power fluctuations, mechanical glitches, and software problems are cited as some of the primary reasons for this debacle. Another reason cited by experts is that Denver has pushed the technology to its limit. The project was too ambitious—it involved a number of leading-edge technologies, and integrating these technologies has been a major challenge and a primary cause of system failure. Although the baggage system is similar to the one the company installed in San Francisco's United Airlines terminal, it is 10 times larger, with PC consoles in nine control rooms tracking bags throughout the airport on some 4,000 automated carts.[57]

Recently, United Airlines was hired as the systems integrator and given the responsibility of solving the problem. However, negotiations between the city of Denver and BAE Automated Systems, which built the computerized baggage system, must be completed before the project can begin. Denver is attempting to recover more than $80 million for BAE's failure to deliver a working system. BAE has demanded $40 million in payment for additional personnel and equipment it used during the delays. BAE denies that computer problems prevented the baggage system from working; the firm alleges that last-minute changes to the original plans, made by the city, caused the delay.

Experts at United believe that the sheer size and complexity of the system is the reason for its catastrophic failure. United wants to simplify the system and reduce the workload of the individual computers that track luggage on the 4,000 one-bag carts. Denver International's baggage system was modeled on an integrated system used in Frankfurt. But the Frankfurt system uses conveyors to carry bags instead of the 4,000 PC-driven automated carts used at Denver

(Continued on next page)

International. Now United is suggesting additional tracks and fewer carts per track. "It's just like adding another lane onto a highway," says a spokesperson.[58]

1. Identify some of the problems with the automatic baggage system.
2. What should the city of Denver have done, if anything, to avoid some of these problems?

Case 3: Falconbridge Ltd. Soars to New Heights

In the dynamic commodities market, information is crucial because prices and costs change quickly and, further, they vary from place to place. Toronto-based Falconbridge Ltd. is a $1.65-billion company that sells nickel, copper, zinc, and other metals and minerals to countries all over the world. In the past, it was often hard for decision makers to know whether a specific sale was a good deal, because a large number of factors had to be taken into account before the profit per sale could be determined. For instance, if two batches of nickel were sold at exactly the same price, one in Hong Kong and the other in Norway, Falconbridge might make 25 cents per pound more on the Norwegian sale because of factors such as shipping costs. Base prices for most metals are set on the London Metal Exchange, and although Falconbridge is not primarily in the business of selling at commodity prices, it receives a premium by guaranteeing quality supplies.

In 1988, the company invested in an information system that would facilitate decisions by making valuable data quickly available to decision makers. Falconbridge's Strategic International Marketing Online Network (SIMON) now provides up-to-the-minute information for about 30 senior decision makers throughout the company and is changing the way they make decisions. It allows them to take advantage of trends and business activities that otherwise might have gone unnoticed. The system has become such a vital part of decision making that one manager said, "It's more than just useful. It's absolutely fundamental to me in my job."

This is how the company went about building the system: The first task was to acquire data from its operations worldwide and to organize the data so that decision makers all over the world would see them in the same format. The task was much more complex than it first appeared because of the many different automated, and even manual, systems that the company had in its different offices. For example, the office in Japan had an IBM System/34 and the Toronto office had an IBM System/38. Brussels had no computer system at all. Currencies, business practices, laws, and regulations also differed a great deal among countries. Further, the U.S. is the only country in the world that sells commodities by the pound; the rest of the world uses kilograms. So Falconbridge had to calculate transportation costs paid in the U.K. in pounds sterling per kilogram and report them in dollars per pound.

From the beginning, plans for the system faced "tremendous concern and resistance" from employees who worried that it would eliminate or substantially change their jobs. The company felt strongly that it should deal with its human problems before facing the technical challenges of the project. It formed both an international project team, made up of senior management from all its offices, and a user committee that included the people "in the trenches" whose jobs the system might affect. The company fully realized that the system could not succeed without the cooperation of employees; it was honest with them about possible layoffs. It emphasized that the system was a strategic tool that would give the company an edge in the marketplace, and not a performance measuring tool designed to penalize people.

Once the human resource issues had been addressed, the company tackled the task of incompatible systems. Falconbridge replaced the assortment of IBM systems in its sales and marketing offices with HP 3000-series minicomputers (since replaced with HP 900-series machines). Although this was a very expensive proposition, the company realized that it was essential in order to give data a uniform face in all its business units worldwide.

Next, the company wanted to link all its business units to facilitate the free flow of information. However, setting up the communications network proved to be an enormous challenge, primarily because of the different legislative restrictions in various countries. The company started with one office at a time; as it gained experience in setting up global networks, the task at hand became easier.

The next step involved collecting data and installing an off-the-shelf transactional software package to handle order entry, invoicing, and accounts receivable. But the company's needs were so unusual that it had to perform a good deal of customization on the software. The company obtained the source code from the vendor and added new code to handle international currencies and units of measure. The changes were so extensive that the company now supports the modified software in-house. Today, the program can easily convert currencies combined with other units of measure, for instance translating pounds per kilometer to dollars per mile. To handle currency conversions, Falconbridge programmers established an external table of exchange rates, which is updated daily. Thus if the Japanese office enters, in yen, transportation costs in September for an order to be shipped in January, managers can see what the bill will be in U.S. dollars at today's exchange rate.

As the company got further into system development, it realized that IS people were often ignorant of its business operations. In the summer of 1991, it selected four of its IS people to become part of the marketing staff in order to give IS people a hands-on approach to other business functions. While the IS staff continued developing IS, they also learned about marketing and found more meaningful ways to automate the marketing function. This integration of IS staff with other business staff proved to be one of the key success factors in system development.

The next step was to design a user-friendly interface for the system. Since the existing software could not support ad hoc queries, the company decided to invest in an executive information systems (EIS) tool that would provide managers with instantaneous access to data and customized reports. Today, the EIS continues to be fine-tuned to meet the changing needs of managers.

The system cost about $1.7 million to set up. It produced $4 million in cost savings in its first year alone. In one product group, Falconbridge cut the cost of sales by 10 percent, saving $1.3 million. More important, the system has equipped managers with the data they need to make good decisions. Employees have a better understanding of the business and are often able to look at the "big picture" simply by accessing and studying data. The company's response to

(Continued on next page)

market forces has also improved significantly, since it can detect trends long before they surface.

Another interesting result of the system is that productivity at meetings has gone up many fold. Formerly, the major order of business at quarterly world-wide marketing meetings was sharing information through reports. Today, since that information is already available, managers use meeting time to *act* on it and see how to improve business. "In the past it might have taken me 40 minutes just getting to the point of asking the right question," says one manager. "Now asking the right questions is easy."[59]

1. Identify some key steps that the company took to make this a successful project.
2. What are some of the challenges in developing a global information system?
3. Describe some of the key features of SIMON.

References

Alvi, Maryam. "An Assessment of the Prototyping Approach to Information System Development." *Communications of the ACM* 27 (June 1984).

Cerveny, Robert P. Edward J. Garrity, and G. Lawrence Sanders. "The Application of Prototyping to Systems Development: A Rationale and Model." *Journal of Management Information Systems* 3 (Fall 1986).

Clermont, Paul. "Outsourcing Without Guilt." *Computerworld* (September 9, 1991).

Gould, John D. and Clayton Lewis. "Designing for Usability: Key Principles and What Designers Think." *Communications of the ACM* 28 (March 1985).

Gupta, U.G., and A. Gupta, "Outsourcing the IS Function," *Journal of Information Systems Management,* vol. 9, no. 3, (Summer 1992), pp. 44–50.

Janson, Marius and L. Douglas Smith. "Prototyping for Systems Development: A Critical Appraisal." *MIS Quarterly* 9 (December 1985).

Lucas, Henry C., Eric J. Walton, and Michael J. Ginzberg. "Implementing Packaged Software." *MIS Quarterly* (December 1988).

Matos, Victor M. and Paul J. Jalics. "An Experimental Analysis of the Performance of Fourth-Generation Tools on PCs." *Communications of the ACM* 32, no. 11 (November 1989).

Notes

1. Bozman, Jean S. "DMV Disaster," *Computerworld,* May 9, 1994, pp. 1, 16.
2. Lederer, Albert L. and Raghu Nath. "Making Strategic Information Systems Happen," *Academy of Management Executives,* vol. 4, no. 3, 1990, pp. 76–82.
3. Booker, Ellis. "Civic Virtues," *Computerworld,* April 11, 1994, pp. 81–82.
4. Anthes, Gary H. "Function Points to the Rescue," *Computerworld,* May 2, 1994, p. 110.
5. Anthes, Gary H. "No More Creeps," *Computerworld,* May 2,1994, pp. 107–108.
6. Whitten, Jeffery L., Lonnie D. Bentley, and Victor M. Barlow. *Systems Analysis and Design Methods,* 3rd edition, 1994, pp. 607–609.
7. Lederer, Albert L., and Raghu Nath. "Making Strategic Information Systems Happen," *Academy of Management Executives,* vol. 4, no. 3, 1990, pp. 76–82.

8. Ibid.
9. Goff, Leslie. "A Vanishing Breed," *Computerworld,* April 11, 1994, p. 119.
10. Kelleher, Joanne. "Quick Isn't Dirty," *Computerworld,* July 19, 1993, p. 32.
11. Grochow, Jerrold M. "Tidal Wave Approaching" *Computerworld,* September 20, 1993, p. 41.
12. Foss, W. Burry. "Fast, Faster, Fastest Development," *Computerworld,* May 31, 1993, pp. 81,83.
13. Ibid.
14. Ibid.
15. DeJong, Jennifer. "RAD to the Rescue," *Information Week,* February 6, 1995, pp. 54–55.
16. Ibid.
17. Leltheiser, Robert L. and James C. Wetherbe. "Service Support Levels: An Organized Approach to End-User Computing," *MIS Quarterly,* December 1986, pp. 337–348.
18. Caldwell, Bruce. "Who needs programmers," *Information Week,* April 25, 1994, p. 23.
19. Gotlieb, Leo. "Information Management," *CMA Magazine,* September 1993, pp. 13–15.
20. McLean, Ephraim, R., L. A. Kappelman and John P. Thompson. "Converging End-User and Corporate Computing," *Communications of the ACM,* December 1993, Vol. 36, No: 12, pp. 79–92.
21. McPartlin, John P. (editor). "Illuminating the Black Hole," Executive Notebook, *Information Week,* November 30, 1992, p. 24.
22. King, Julia. "Minding the Store?" *Computerworld,* March 27, 1995, pp. 99, 103, 105.
23. Ibid.
24. Ibid.
25. Henschell, Todd. "A PC Technician's Advice: Do Some Legwork Before You Call," *Computerworld,* April 5, 1993, p. 106.
26. Soat, John and Mike Fillon, "PC Management," *Information Week,* January 4, 1993, p. 25.
27. Ibid., p. 30.
28. Ibid.
29. Caldwell, Bruce. "Who Needs Programmers," *Information Week,* April 25, 1994, p. 30.
30. Hoffman, Thomas. "Taking a Byte Out of Crime," *Computerworld,* August 16, 1993, pp. 81–83.
31. Bates, Peter. "Profit in Preparedness," *CIO,* September 1, 1994, pp. 58–59.
32. Fitzgerald, Michael. "Greyhound Outsources IS to Get the Best Staffing Talent," *Computerworld,* February 28, 1994, p. 74.
33. Eliot, Lance B. "Legacy Systems, Legacy Options," *Computerworld,* July 11, 1994, pp. 86, 88.
34. Halper, Mark. "Texas Bank Sues EDS," *Computerworld,* May 30, 1994, p. 8.
35. Radding, Alan. "To Methodology or Not to Methodology," *Computerworld,* June 14, 1993, p. 114.
36. Runge, Larry. "What's Wrong with Us," *Computerworld,* September 20, 1993, pp. 139–140.
37. Ballou, Melinda-Carol and Derek Slater. "Still Backlogged After All These Years," *Computerworld,* December 27, 1993/January 3, 1994, p. 58.
38. Ibid.
39. 1994 Survey of 150 IS Project Managers, Center for Project Management, San Ramon, Calif., from article by Alice LaPlante, "Scope Grope," in *Computerworld,* March 20, 1995, p. 82.
40. Tate, Paul. "City of London Tries Again," *Information Week,* May 30, 1994, pp. 85–88.
41. Anthes, Gary H. "Air Traffic Takes Another Turn," *Computerworld,* April 25, 1994, pp. 79, 82.
42. Betts, Mitch. "How to Get 'Runaway Projects' on Track," *Computerworld,* March 15, 1993, p. 95.
43. Anthes, Gary H. "Air Traffic Control System Running Aground," *Computerworld,* June 13, 1994, p. 32.

44. Cafasso, Rosemary. "Few IS Projects Come In on Time, on Budget," *Computerworld,* December 12, 1994, p. 20.

45. Betts, Mitch. "How to Get 'Runaway Projects' on Track," *Computerworld,* March 15, 1993, p. 95.

46. Greenbaum, Joshua. "Nestle's Global Mix," *InformationWeek,* April 25, 1994, pp. 44, 46.

47. Barker, Robert M. "IS Development in a Global Environment," *Business Forum,* Winter/Spring 1993, p. 57.

48. Palenski, Ronald J. "Competition, Not Litigation, Ensures Quality Systems," *Computerworld,* March 28, 1994, p. 86.

49. Bierhans, Bruce A. "Responsible Lawsuits Keep Vendors Honest," *Computerworld,* March 28, 1994, pp. 86–88.

50. Dix, Lori. "Cool Under Fire," *Computerworld,* April 11, 1994, pp. 111–113.

51. McPartlin, John P. "Crossed Up," *InformationWeek,* January 31, 1994, p. 12.

52. Hoffman Thomas. "Outsourcing Deal Proves Costly," *Computerworld,* January 10, 1994, p. 14.

53. Ibid.

54. Bozman, Jean S. "California IS Projects Mismanaged," *Computerworld,* May 23, 1994, p. 6.

55. Rinaldi, David. "Moral Minority?" *Client/Server Computing,* April 1994, pp. 33–39.

56. de Jager, Peter. "Doomsday," *Computerworld,* September 6, 1993, pp. 105, 108–109.

57. Bozman, Jean S. "Denver Airport Hits Systems Layover," *Computerworld,* May 16, 1994, p. 30.

58. Bozman, Jean S. "United to Simplify Denver's Troubled Baggage Project," *Computerworld,* October 10, 1994, p. 76.

59. Buckler, Grant. "Harnessing Global Information," *IT Magazine,* June 1993, pp. 16–20.

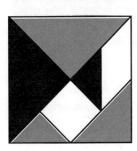

13

Tools for Information Systems Development

Contents

Learning Objectives
Technology Payoff: Computer-aided Software Engineering (CASE)
Introduction
Decision-Making Framework for Selecting IS Tools
    Envisioning Phase
    Transition Phase
Structured Tools
    Tools to Analyze and Design Systems
        Context Diagrams
        Data Flow Diagrams
    Tools to Represent System Data
        Entity Relationship Diagram
    Tools to Represent Processes in the System
        The Constructs of Structured Programming
    Tools for Structured Programming
        Structure Chart
        System Flowchart and Program Flowchart
        Decision Tables
        Decision Trees
    Tools to Convert Program Specifications into Code
        Structured English (Pseudocode)
Computer-Aided Systems/Software Engineering (CASE)
    Advantages of CASE
    Disadvantages of CASE
Summary
Review Questions
Discussion Questions
Ethical Issues
    Case 1: Andersen in Trouble

Problem Solving in the Real World
    Case 1: Amtrak Runs with CASE
    Case 2: Building Blocks for a New Age
References
Notes

Learning Objectives

Developing information systems is a challenging, complex, and labor-intensive activity. Over the last few decades, a number of tools and techniques have evolved to support and facilitate this process.

This chapter provides a broad overview of IS development tools and techniques that are essential for building reliable information systems. Since many knowledge workers will also be end-users, an understanding of system tools and techniques will help them develop such systems. After reading and studying this chapter, you should be able to

- Understand why IS tools and techniques can create organizational change
- Identify and describe tools that support system analysis, design, development and implementation
- Identify and describe tools that represent system data
- Identify and describe tools that represent system processes
- Describe the role of CASE in developing high-quality systems

TECHNOLOGY PAYOFF

Computer-aided Software Engineering (CASE)

Computer-aided software engineering (CASE) emerged in the late 1980s as a new IS development tool. It uses a graphical approach to identify user requirements and then automatically translates these requirements into system code. More important, CASE has brought discipline to a process that was largely ad hoc.

CASE has had a tremendous impact on system quality and employee productivity. For example, General Electric found that CASE increased the productivity of its development teams by 20% to 80%, even after including the learning curve and training time. GE also noticed that after a system development team completes its third project using CASE tools, its productivity doubles or even triples. Also, systems that are developed using CASE need much less maintenance than systems developed using traditional methods.

Union Gas, in Chatharm, Ontario, reports a 30% increase in productivity after it introduced CASE and indicates that the figure will be close to 100% if the learning curve is factored out. Similarly, Revenue Canada, the customs and excise agency of the Canadian government, credits CASE with helping it process more than 900 requests for system specification changes after system development began; developers were still able to meet every single product deadline.[1]

Given the dramatic change in what the IS department must deliver to the organization, it is not surprising that how it is delivered must be changed dramatically as well.

　　　　　　　　　　　　　　　　　　—John F. Rockart and J. Debra Hofman[2]

Introduction

Today, time has become a critical element that affects the competitive posture of many organizations. "Time has become a critical competitive differentiator: time to market for new products, manufacturing cycle time for existing products, and timeliness of decision making, all previously important, are now critical."[3] Information systems can help organizations to be responsive, flexible, and adaptable to fast-changing environments by reducing product development time and improving the timeliness of decision making. However, as we saw in the last chapter, developing and implementing information systems are not easy tasks. One way to address this challenge is to use tools and techniques that accelerate the system development process.

Modeling tools play three roles in system development: communication, experimentation, and prediction (Burch, 1993). *Communication* tools help end-users and developers communicate effectively with each other and are particularly useful in representing system specifications. Such tools also facilitate communication through the use of consistent terminology. *Experimentation* tools allow developers to experiment with different design and development approaches and learn by trial and error. Re-engineering tools fall in this category. They help developers find the best match between the available tools and the systems to be developed. Finally, *prediction* tools are designed to help users and developers predict the impact of a new system on a firm, including the system's financial and human resource implications and its effect on competition.

Decision-Making Framework for Selecting IS Tools

Two important factors should be taken into account when IS development tools and techniques are selected.[4] These are the future business environment of the company and the IS environment necessary to support the envisioned business environment. Organizations that do not take these two factors into account are, in effect, treating their information systems as isolated entities that have no relationship to the business environment.

The selection of IS tools should be viewed as a business decision, not just a technical decision; therefore, top management, IS managers, end-users, and key players from various functional areas should be actively involved in this decision, because IS tools and techniques often require considerable investment of time and money and can create significant organizational change.

In this section, we describe Rockart and Hofman's two-phase framework to facilitate the selection of IS tools and techniques.[5] This framework was based on discussions with senior managers at 12 companies that had invested heavily in IS.

Figure 13–1 shows the two phases (the envisioning phase and the transition phase) of the selection of IS development tools and techniques.

FIGURE 13–1

A two-phase process for selecting IS tools and techniques: the envisioning phase and the transition phase. The organization must envision its needs (business, systems, and development) before investing in IS tools. The transition phase addresses the question, "How do we get from where we are today to where we want to be in the future?"

Source: Rockart, John F. and J. Debra Hofman. "Systems Delivery: Evolving New Strategies," *Sloan Management Review,* Summer 1992, p. 22.

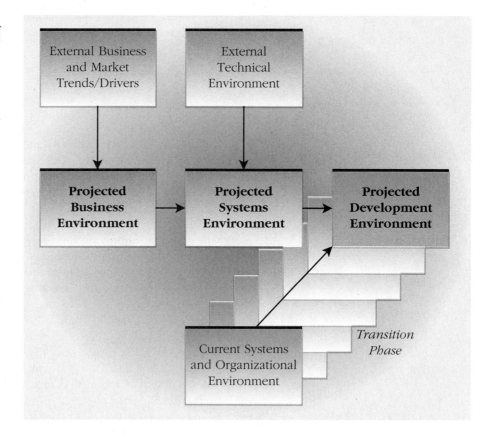

Envisioning Phase

In the envisioning phase, managers analyze three scenarios: projected business environment, projected systems environment, and projected development environment.

* *Projected business environment: Outline the overall vision, including future businesses, markets, and products.*

Major business changes, such as downsizing, employee empowerment, global competition, and increased sensitivity to the impact of time on a business, are part of the future business environment. Managers should identify factors that can shape and influence the company and the industry in which it operates.

* *Projected systems environment: Outline a vision of how IS can help the company achieve the overall business vision.*

The systems of the 1960s, 1970s, and the 1980s are not fully adequate to meet the dynamics of today's business environment; today's systems must be capable of instantaneously delivering customized information to meet the needs of the knowledge worker. Further, systems must be developed quickly for a responsive and flexible organization.

"Not only the *nature* of the systems has changed; the *speed* with which they are needed and, more important, with which they must be *changed* has increased as well. The new organization is not simply a remake of the old one with connections between its sub-units; it is a re-engineered entity that is now coordinated rather than simply connected. New systems development environment is not simply one in which bridges are built between previously unconnected systems; it is now one in which the relations and interconnections between systems are articulated and well understood before they are built so that coordinated systems can be developed, where each system is one component within an integrated framework."[6]

Given this new and changing environment, it is important to have a clear vision of the role of IS in helping the organization achieve its goals.

◆ *Projected development environment: Identify a portfolio of tools, techniques, and methods necessary to create the projected systems environment.*

The projected development environment should include an integrated set of tools that promote the reusability of system components, that are robust and flexible enough to support continuous change, and that are capable of linking different systems, such as TPS and ISS.

Transition Phase

The projected IS environment indicates what *should* be done; the current IS environment dictates what *can* be done. The transition phase addresses the question "How do we get from where we are today to where we want to be in the future?" In other words, what tools do we need to make the transition from today's business environment to the projected environment?

The move from the current environment to the projected environment implies change. Five organizational components are likely to be affected by such a transition: technology, corporate strategy, organizational structure, managerial processes, individuals, and their job functions.[7] When evaluating the merits of a development tool, managers must take into account the impact of the tool on these five factors; otherwise, the company will not be able to derive the full benefits of the tool. For example, although the automobile industry has made huge investments in technology, it has not made proportional investments in its employees (factor five) and therefore has not been able to derive the full benefits of its systems. Hence, in the transition phase, managers must carefully analyze the impact of IS tools on each of these five factors and must also analyze the ways in which the interrelationships among these factors will be affected.

Table 13–1 identifies some other factors that should be taken into account when IS tools are being selected.

Structured Tools

Top-down approach
Provides a view of the system from the highest level to the lowest. It moves from the general to the specific, and from the abstract to the concrete.

In the systems approach, a system is broken down into subsystems and each subsystem is further broken down until no subsystem can be broken down any further. A **top-down approach** is used, providing a view of the system that starts from the highest level and extends to the lowest level of detail, from the general to the specific, from the abstract to the concrete. The systems

T A B L E   1 3 – 1
Some factors that should be taken into account when selecting IS tools and techniques.

Change is critical.

If the IS organization is to keep up with the changing needs of the business, a new systems development approach is absolutely necessary. *The question is not whether, but when and how.*

Choices are strategic.

Decisions about development tools and techniques are strategic in nature, are major, and must be addressed by senior management. They require careful balancing of factors that are affected by change.

Change is ongoing.

Future environments (business, systems, and development) will continue to change and management must recognize this. Predicting future environments *is not an event; it is a process.*

Context determines the "portfolio of solutions."

Tool selection must (1) create a portfolio of development tools and techniques that are customized to meet the needs of the organization and (2) create an organizational environment in which excellence through system delivery can be achieved.

Selecting IS development tools and techniques is a major business process redesign.

If we recognize that developing and delivering information systems is one of the key business processes of the IS organization, then changing the way systems are developed is a major "business process redesign." IS often helps other functions redesign their business practices. *If the cobbler's children are not to be without shoes, the same thinking must be brought to bear on the redesign of the systems development process.*

Source: Adapted with permission. From Rockart, John F. and J. Debra Hofman. "Systems Delivery: Evolving New Strategies," *Sloan Management Review,* Summer 1992, pp. 21–31.

---

approach facilitates the development of high-quality information systems because it does the following:

* Provides a top-down view of the system so that users and developers can see the "big picture"
* Breaks down a system into smaller and more manageable units
* Helps users understand the logic of the system by specifying the processes that take place within each subsystem
* Helps users and system developers use consistent definitions when communicating with each other

Structured tools

Tools and techniques that support the various phases of traditional development methodologies, such as the SDLC. The four popular structured tools are the structure chart, the system flowchart, decision tables, and decision trees.

Structured tools are tools and techniques that support traditional development methodologies, such as the SDLC, which was covered in the preceding chapter. Recall that the SDLC is broadly divided into the following phases: problem definition, system analysis, system design and development, system testing and implementation, and system maintenance. Structured tools and techniques support these phases of the SDLC.

Figure 13–2 shows the tools used in each of these phases. We will provide a broad explanation of this figure, followed by a detailed explanation of each of the tools identified in the figure.

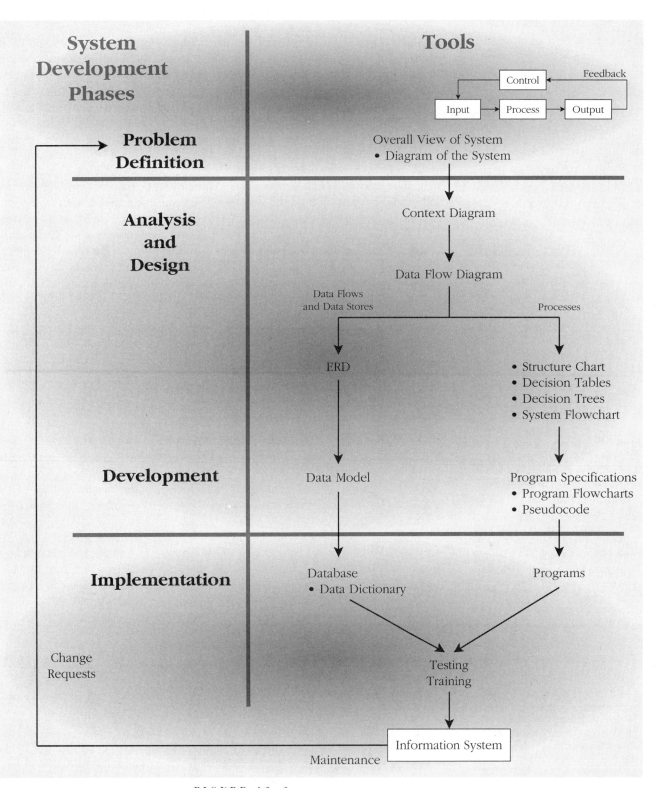

FIGURE 13–2

Structured tools and techniques that can be used during the various phases of traditional systems development. A portfolio of tools and techniques, customized to meet the information needs of the organization, is vital to successful system development.

In the problem definition phase, the goal is simply to gain an overall understanding of the system and its main components: the input, processes, output, feedback, and control. (These five components are shown in the problem definition phase of Figure 13–2.)

When the problem has been defined, the next step is to analyze and design the system. The context diagram gives a broad overview of the system and its major inputs and outputs and helps users and developers to see the "big picture." The context diagram, which depicts the overall system, can be broken down into smaller, more manageable subsystems. Each of these subsystems, in turn, can be described in detail using the data flow diagram (DFD), which depicts the flow of data (inputs and outputs), the processes that transform the data from inputs to outputs, and the data stores (the places where the data are stored in the system).

The DFD has two main elements: data and processes. System data are captured using the entity relationship diagram (ERD), a type of data model that eventually leads to the implementation of the database. The processes in the system are schematized using tools such as the structure chart, the system flowchart, decision tables, and decision trees. The output of these tools consists of the program specifications; details about program specifications are shown by using flow charts and pseudocode. In summary, the ERD models system data and flowcharts and pseudocode model system processes. When data are integrated with processes, we have an information system.

Each of the tools identified in Figure 13–2 is described below.

Tools to Analyze and Design Systems

Context Diagrams   A **context diagram** provides a broad, abstract, top-down view of a system by identifying the major inputs, outputs, processes, and entities in the system. An **entity** is a person, place, thing, event, or concept about which data are gathered. A context diagram, which depicts the overall system, can be exploded into subsystems, each of which, in turn, is depicted using a data flow diagram (DFD).

Figure 13–3 shows a context diagram for a bank processing system with two entities (shown as rectangular boxes with shadows): customers and a check clearinghouse. The input and output flows are depicted as arrows; for example, bank drafts are inputs to the processing system and transmit items are outputs.

Context diagram
Provides a broad, abstract, top-down view of an entire system by identifying its major inputs, outputs, and processes.

Entity
A person, place, thing, event, or concept about which data have to be gathered in order to build the system.

FIGURE 13–3

The context diagram for a bank. The two entities are Customer and Clearinghouse.

Source: Adapted with permission. From Burch, John G., *System Analysis, Design and Implementation*, Boyd and Fraser Publishing Co., 1992, pp. 40–41.

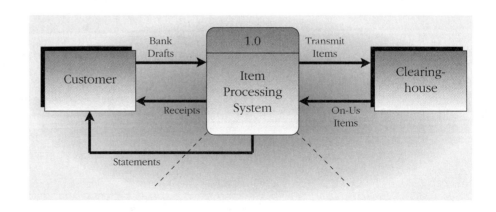

Similarly, *on-us* items (bank instruments, such as checks, drafts, and the like, that have been drawn on the sending bank) are inputs from the clearing house to the processing system, whereas receipts are outputs from the processing system to the customer. Note that the context diagram summarizes all the subprocesses in the bank processing system and depicts them as a single process. This is always the case in a context diagram.

Another context diagram is shown in Figure 13-4, which depicts a processing system for a video rental store. In this system, there are two entities, the customer and the inventory system. The inputs to the video processing system are customer data; the output data are related to rental movies. The process involved in renting a video is shown in a single box, labeled Video Processing System.

Data Flow Diagrams   Each of the subsystems of a system is described using the **data flow diagram (DFD),** a graphical tool that performs three primary tasks: the flow of data in a system (inputs and outputs), depict the processes that transform the data from inputs to outputs, and show where the data are stored in the system (data stores).

A DFD graphically shows the underlying logic of a subsystem by showing the flow of data (inputs and outputs) between different entities (or objects) and the processes that transform the data into information. Note that the single process depicted in the context diagram becomes the set of subprocesses in the DFD.

Data flow diagrams are constructed using four basic symbols, shown in Figure 13-5, and described below.

Data Flow Symbol   Data flows are depicted as arrows, where data may be manual or automated, and can flow among entities, processes, and data stores. The name of the data is usually depicted above or below the arrow.

Process Symbol   The process symbol is represented as a rounded box. Processes are described using two elements: a description of the process and a number to identify the process.

The process description consists of a verb and a noun. For example, the process of calculating the final grade in a course can be described as *calculate* (verb) *final grade* (noun). Other process descriptions include *check* (verb) *credit (noun), update* (verb) *system (noun), and send* (verb) *notice* (noun). A brief description of the process is given inside the rounded box.

A numbering system is also used to identify items in the process. The major process shown in the context diagram is given a number of 1.0; the subprocess-

The four symbols used in a data
flow diagram. Together they depict
the flow of data and the processes
that transform the data. The DFD
also shows where the data are
stored.

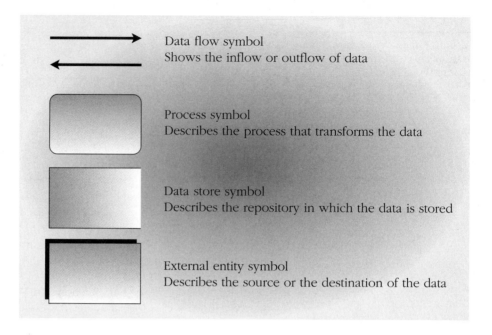

Data flow symbol
Shows the inflow or outflow of data

Process symbol
Describes the process that transforms the data

Data store symbol
Describes the repository in which the data is stored

External entity symbol
Describes the source or the destination of the data

es in the DFD are numbered 1.1, 1.2, and so on. For example, if process 1.0 has
three subprocesses, they can be numbered 1.1, 1.2, and 1.3 in the DFD. The subprocesses of 1.1 will be shown as 1.1.1 and so on. For example, process 1.3 in
Figure 13–6 is broken down into subprocesses 1.3.1, 1.3.2, 1.3.3, and 1.3.4.

Note that all processes have inputs and outputs. Without inputs, the system
cannot create anything; without outputs, it becomes a "black hole." (Burch, 1993).

Data Store Symbol   The data store symbol gives the name of the data and the
type of storage, and is depicted as an open rectangle. There are different types of
data storage, both manual and automated, such as databases, file cabinets, and
microfiche. For example, student grades may be stored in a database (type of storage) called GRADE (name of data). If a data flow (shown as an arrow) comes
from a data store, the process is *using* the data in the data store; if it enters a data
store, the process is *updating* or *changing* the data in the data store.

External Entity Symbol   An entity, as we explained earlier, is a person, place,
thing, event, or concept about which data have to be gathered in order to build
the system, and is represented by a rectangle. Although no distinction is made
between internal and external entities in the DFD, information systems include
both. Examples of internal entities are employees, products, and departments;
external entities include suppliers, customers, stockholders, and the government.

These four elements—data flow, process, data store, and external entity—
and their respective symbols can be used to depict any system, no matter how
large or complex it may be.

Figure 13–6 shows the DFD for the bank example. As you can see, the
process called Item Processing System (1.0) in the context diagram is exploded
into four subprocesses: Accept Transactions (1.1), Proof Transactions (1.2), Sort
Batch (1.3), and Generate Statement (1.4).

Second-Level DFD

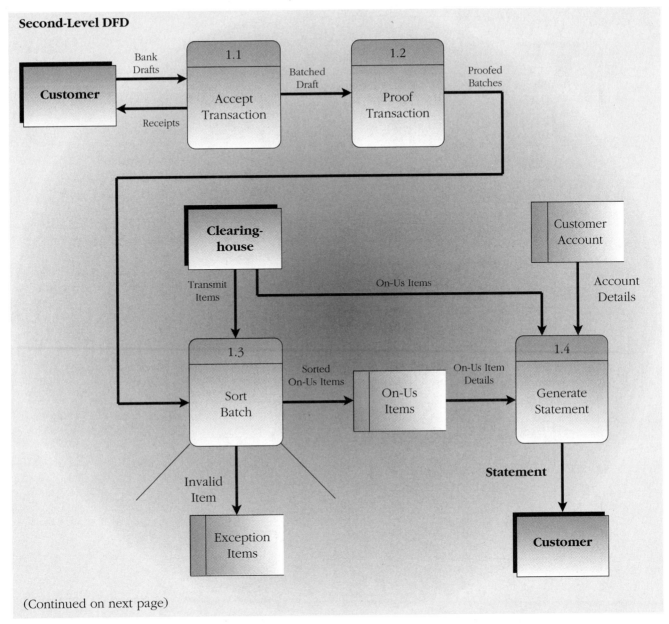

FIGURE 13-6

The DFDs for a processing system in a bank. The boxes with shadows represent the entities in the system.

The context diagram is then broken down into DFDs. In the second-level DFD, the single process in the context diagram is broken into other processes (1.1, 1.2, 1.3, 1.4).

Source: Adapted with permission. From Burch, John G., *System Analysis, Design and Implementation* Boyd and Fraser Publishing Co., 1992, pp. 40–41.

Subprocess 1.3 is further broken down into four subprocesses and is shown as a separate DFD.

The DFD for the video rental system is shown in Figure 13–7, where the single process Video Processing System, shown in the context diagram, is broken

Detailed-Level DFD

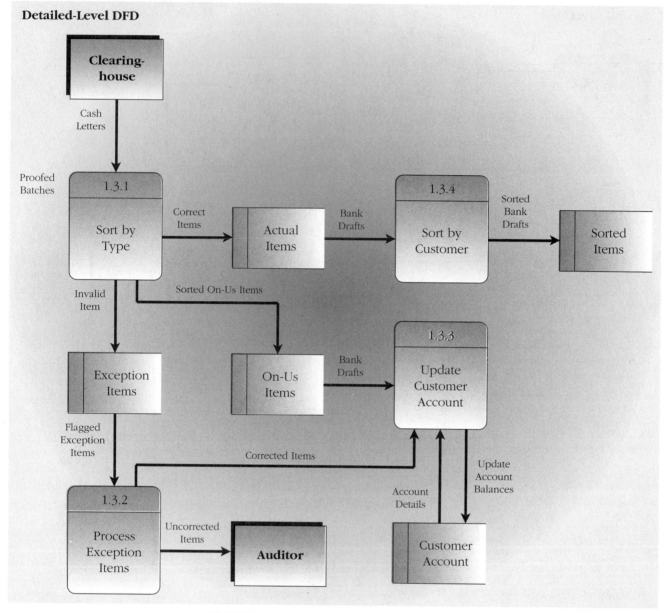

Continued

down into four subprocesses: Capture Customer Transactions (1.1), Process Transactions (1.2), Correct Errors (1.3), and Update Inventory System (1.4).

Tools to Represent System Data

Because data are vital to any information system, tools that gather and represent data are critical to system development. One popular tool for representing data is the entity relationship diagram (ERD). Unlike DFDs, which depict both data and

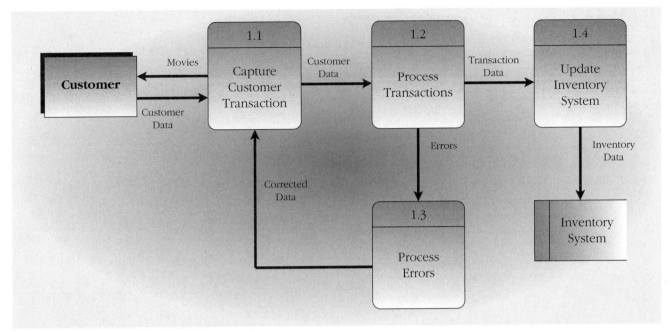

FIGURE 13–7

The first level of DFD for a video rental system. The single process Video Processing System in the content-level DFD is broken up into four processes (1.1, 1.2, 1.3, and 1.4). Inputs and outputs are also shown in greater detail.

processes, ERDs simply depict data without any regard to the processes that influence them. ERDs supplement the DFDs and are extensively used in enterprise modeling (providing a graphical overview of a system or an enterprise) and in software design.

Entity Relationships Diagram   An **entity relationship diagram (ERD)** shows the entities in a system and the relationships among them. In an ERD, an entity is represented by a rectangle; the name of the entity appears within the rectangle.

A **relationship** is an association between two or more entities in a system; it is represented by a diamond. Relationships between entities can be described using verbs, such as *order, remove, teach,* and *create.* As you may recall from Chapter 6, on databases, there are three types of relationships between entities: one-to-one (1-1), one-to-many (1-M), and many-to-many (M-M). Figure 13–8 shows the ERD for the video rental store.

Steps in Creating an ERD   There are five steps in creating an ERD:

1. Developers and users work together as a team to identify the entities in the system. In the video store example, the entities are video store, movies, and inventory system.
2. Establish the nature and scope of the relationships among the different entities identified in the previous step—that is, 1–1, 1-M, or M-M relationships. Note that an entity can have different relationships with different entities in the system. For example, entity A may have 1–1 relationship with entity B

Entity relationship diagram (ERD)
A graphical tool that models the entities in a system and the relationships among them. An ERD is used primarily to model the data stores identified in the DFD; it depicts data without regard to the processes that affect the data.

Relationship
An association between two or more entities in a system is referred to as a relationship and is represented in the ERD as a diamond.

FIGURE 13-8

An entity relationship diagram. The entities for this video store example are Video Store, Customers, Movies, and Inventory System. The relationships are represented by diamonds.

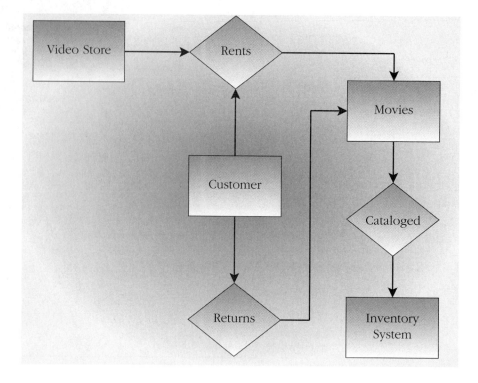

and a 1-M relationship with entity C. In our example of the video rental store, the customer entity has a 1-M relationship with the video entity because a customer can rent several movies.

3. Describe each entity using a set of data elements. For example, the entity *movie* can be uniquely defined using the data elements *movie number* and *movie name.*

4. Graphically depict the data elements in each entity and the type of relationship between each pair of entities (this is usually shown next to the diamond).

5. Make sure that no entity is missing and that the relationships between entities are all accurately portrayed. Also, at this point, a careful analysis of the data should be performed to identify and eliminate data redundancies.

In summary, an ERD supplements the DFD and provides a static view of system data. By graphically depicting the entities and their interrelationships, developers gain a better understanding of the overall system.

Tools to Represent Processes in the System

The processes that convert data into useful information are identified and represented in the system using structured programming. **Structured programming** is based on two key concepts: the top-down approach and modularization. The top-down approach, as you may recall, breaks down a system into smaller logical units. Modularization, on the other hand, breaks a *computer program* into smaller, more manageable units, called **modules.** Although the modules in a program may be interconnected, they should be independent of one another and the

Structured programming
Program development that takes a top-down view of the system and also breaks down the system into smaller, more manageable units, called modules. Structured programming is based on three simple constructs: sequence, selection, and repetition constructs.

Modules
When a large program is broken down into smaller, more manageable units, these units are called modules.

output of each module should be localized to that module. When modules are not independent of each other, the result is **spaghetti code**—code whose interconnections are so confusing that it is difficult or impossible to understand the logic behind the code. Spaghetti code is the bane of system developers; it must be avoided to build reliable systems.

The Constructs of Structured Programming   Structured programming is based on three simple constructs, or ideas: sequence, selection, and repetition.

The **sequence construct** identifies the sequence of steps that must be executed in order to implement a programming instruction. Individual instructions, such as READ, WRITE, PRINT, ADD, and SUBTRACT, are linked together to form a sequence structure. For example,

> READ X, Y
> ADD X + Y
> SET Z = X + Y
> PRINT Z

is a sequence structure that reads the values of variables X and Y, adds them together, and prints the new value, Z, that is the sum of X and Y.

In the **selection construct,** the computer selects the path it must follow in order to execute a given set of instructions. When the computer is faced with a decision, the selection structure shows it which path to take and what steps to implement.

The selection construct is based on the IF-THEN-ELSE clause. For example, suppose a scholarship of $500 is to be given to a business major whose GPA is greater than 3.9. The selection construct would look as follows:

> IF
>   Student's GPA is greater than 3.9
> THEN
>   Give award of $500 to student
> ELSE
>   Send thank-you note to applicant

In this case, the selection construct helps the computer decide whether to award a scholarship or to send a thank-you note.

The third construct is the **repetition construct,** which allows the computer to perform the same operation a number of times. In the repetition construct, the computer executes a given operation until a certain condition is met, at which point the computer terminates the operation and control passes to the next instruction in the program.

As an example, consider a short program that calculates the net monthly pay for employees:

> FOR EACH Employee
> CALCULATE Net Monthly Pay
> UPDATE Employee Benefits File
> IF Number_of_Employees = 50
> PRINT Employee Benefits File

Spaghetti code
Programming code that is so intertwined that it is difficult or impossible to follow its logic. When the modules in a program are not independent of each other, the programs that constitute the modules are likely to be written in spaghetti code.

Sequence construct
There are three constructs in structured programming: sequence, selection, and repetition. The sequence construct executes instructions one after another.

Selection construct
The computer must take a path when faced with a decision. The selection construct shows the computer how to decide the path to take.

Repetition construct
Allows the computer to perform a given operation a number of times until a certain condition is met.

When the computer first begins execution, it assigns a value of 1 to Number_of_Employees, calculates the net monthly pay for the first employee, and updates the Employee Benefits File. It then checks to see if Number_of_Employees is equal to 50. If not, it increases the value of this variable by 1 and repeats the operation. When Number_of_Employees is equal to 50, the computer terminates the current operation and executes the next instruction, PRINT Employee Benefits File.

Tools for Structured Programming

Four main tools are used to depict the logic and structure of system processes. They are the structure chart, the system flowchart and program flowchart, the decision tables, and the decision trees. Each of these is described below.

Structure Chart   A **structure chart,** somewhat like an organization chart, is a graphical tool that represents the hierarchy of software modules in a program and the relationships, or links, among modules. It is particularly useful in software design.

Figure 13–9 shows the structure chart for a program designed to calculate the average letter grade for each student. This program is divided into four submod-

Structure chart
A graphical tool that shows the hierarchy of software modules and the relationships among modules.

FIGURE 13–9

A simple structure chart that shows how the task of calculating a student's overall grade can be broken down into subtasks.

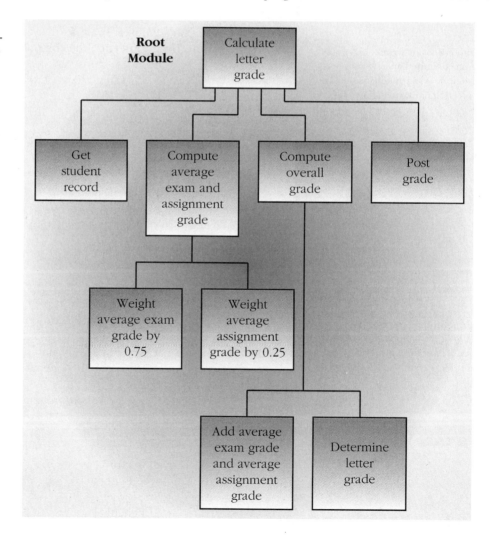

ules: *get record, compute overall course grade, compute average exam and assignment grade,* and *post grade.* The structure chart graphically portrays these modules and their interrelationships. For example, by studying the structure chart, we know that *compute average exam and assignment grade* has two modules, *weight average exam score by 75%* and *weight average assignment score by 25%.*

The topmost module in the structure chart is called the *root module (calculate letter grade).* Control passes down from the root module to other modules in the program. Some guidelines should be followed when control is passed from one module to another. First, control should always be returned to the module that originally had control. For example, if module A passes control to module B, module B must return control back to module A after executing its instructions. Second, there should be only one control relationship between two modules, failing which we get spaghetti code. Third, designers should be careful to avoid infinite loops, which occur if module A passes control to module B, module B passes control back to module A, and the process is repeated without terminating. Finally, a module cannot pass control to itself, because this too will result in an infinite loop. These guidelines help to make the flow of control between modules smooth and logical.

Figure 13–10 shows the structure chart for the video rental example. The root module is the *video processing system,* which is broken down into two submodules, *customer processing system* and *movie inventory system.* The customer processing system is, in turn, broken down into submodules.

The development of a structure chart is often followed by a **walkthrough,** in which designers and users carefully scrutinize each level of the structure chart to make sure that it accurately depicts the proposed system. The walkthrough helps developers to detect any inconsistencies or errors in the program design early in the development process, and thus to avoid costly corrections in the later stages of system development.

System Flowchart and Program Flowchart   Another popular structured programming tool is the **system flowchart,** a symbolic representation of system processes, relationships among processes, and the data required for each process. Just as the structure chart showed the relationships among the modules in the program, the system flowchart shows the relationships among the processes, as well as the process flows (from top to bottom). Figure 13–11 shows the system flowchart for the video rental system. For example, one of the processes in the video rental system is a customer's requesting a movie. If the movie is available, the customer rents it and the inventory is updated.

A **program flowchart** depicts the flow of logic in a computer program. It is built around the three software constructs of sequence, selection, and iteration, which we discussed earlier. There are two primary differences between the system flowchart and the program flowchart. First, the system flowchart portrays the flow of both data and processes in the system, whereas the program flow chart portrays only the processes, not the data. Second, the system flowchart represents system processes, whereas the program flowchart represents the logic behind the processes.

Decision Tables   Another tool that facilitates structured programming is the **decision table,** which shows the logic behind system processes and the logical relationships among system variables by using a set of conditions (IF clauses) and

FIGURE 13-10

This structure chart shows the sub-program structure for the video rental system.

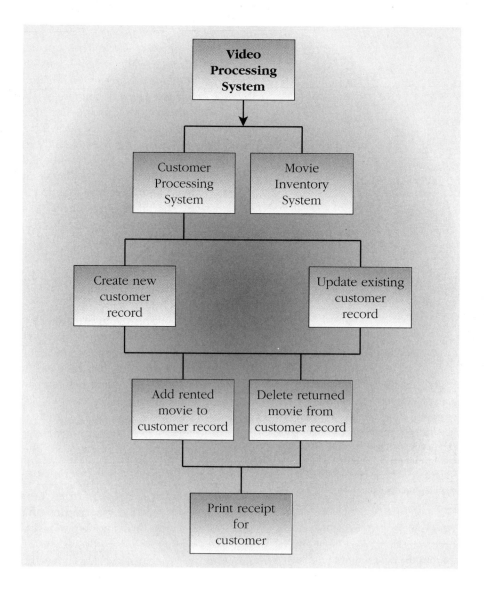

actions (tasks that must be performed if a condition is met.) Decision tables are useful for documenting the logic of situations that are highly structured and clearly understood. This may seem similar to the IF-THEN rule covered in Chapter 9, on expert systems. In fact, a decision table is a set of IF-THEN rules represented in a tabular format. The conditions and outcomes are displayed in a two-dimensional table, whose upper half includes all IF conditions, some of which may be mutually exclusive, and whose lower half shows the THEN actions that are executed if the conditions are met.

Figure 13–12 shows a decision table for selecting scholarship recipients. There are three conditions in this table: GPA, income level, and number of years before graduation. Depending on the values of these conditions, two courses of action can be taken: award the scholarship or reject the applicant. The table clearly shows the logic used to make this decision.

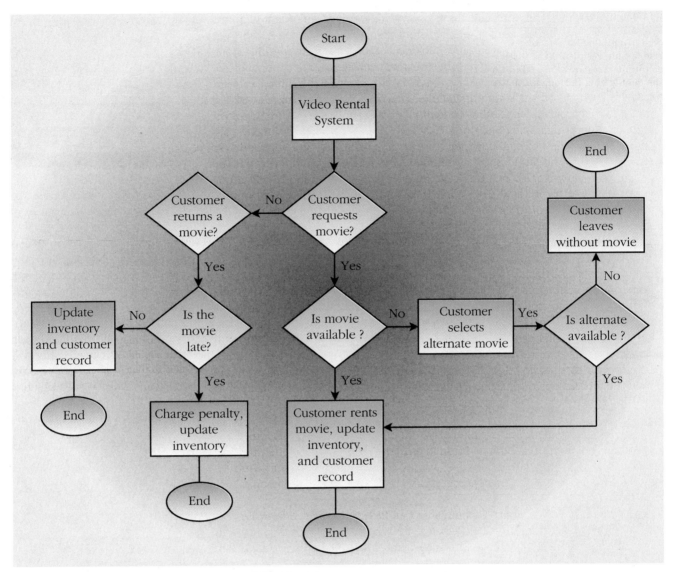

FIGURE 13–11

System flowchart for the video rental system.

Figure 13–13 shows two decision tables for the video rental system. The first shows the conditions that must be met if a customer is to be charged a late fee. The second shows the logic used to process membership applications.

Decision tree

A graphical representation of the logic in a decision-making process and the sequence of decision points that constitutes the decision.

Decision Trees   A **decision tree** is a graphical representation of the sequence of steps and decisions taken to solve a given problem—that is, decision points in the problem-solving process for that problem. The branches of the tree, whose number depends on the number of steps involved in the decision-making process, represent the alternatives available to the decision maker. Branches proceed from left to right. The values associated with each alternative are shown

FIGURE 13-12

A decision table for selecting a scholarship recipient. The three condition rules are shown above the double line; the actions, below the double line.

1. GPA ≥ 3.5	Y	Y	Y	N	Y	N	N	N
2. Income level ≤ 25,000	Y	N	Y	Y	N	N	Y	N
3. Number of years to graduate > 1	Y	Y	N	Y	N	N	N	Y
Approve $500 scholarship	X	X	X	X				
Reject application					X	X	X	X

at the end of a branch. The starting point of the decision tree is often referred to as the *root node;* all alternatives available to the decision maker branch out from the root node.

The primary difference between the decision table and the decision tree is that the decision table displays only individual units of logic; it does not show the sequence of actions related to the logic. The decision tree, on the other hand, graphically displays both the logic and the sequence of steps to be implemented.

Figure 13–14 shows an automobile buy-versus-lease decision tree. The alternatives in this problem are to buy the automobile or to lease the automobile. If the decision maker decides to buy the car, he or she has to decide between a 3-year loan and a 5-year loan. Once this decision is made, the next step in the problem-solving process is to determine the make of the car: *Honda, Concord,* or *Taurus.* Each alternative results in a different dollar value, which is

Decision Table

For Existing Customer

Customer requests movie	Y	Y	N	–			
Check if movie available	Y	N	–	–			
Movie returned late	–	–	–	Y	N	Y	
Movie damaged	–	–	–	N	Y	Y	
Rent movie	X						
Charge late penalty					X		
Charge cost of video						X	X

For New Customer

Check for valid driver's license	Y	N	Y	N
Check for major credit card	Y	Y	N	N
Approve application	X			
Reject application		X	X	X

FIGURE 13-13

Decision tables for renting a movie to an existing customer and to a new customer. The conditions are shown above the double line; the actions, below the double line.

FIGURE 13-14

A decision tree for an automobile buy-versus-lease decision. The value associated with each alternative is shown at the end of each branch.

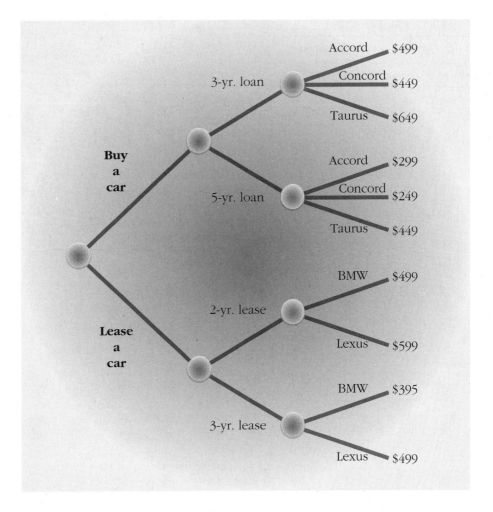

shown at the end of each branch. Note that the logic flows from left to right: first comes the decision to buy or lease, then the choice of the term of the loan, and finally the choice of the make of the car.

Figure 13–15 shows another decision tree for the video rental system. A customer can either rent a movie or return one or do both. The tree shows decision points behind each alternative and their respective values.

When we analyze and describe the output of a structured tool, we get program specifications, which are step-by-step instructions for converting system design into programs. Program specifications provide the basis for writing program code; in the next section, we look at some tools that facilitate this process.

Tools to Convert Program Specifications into Code

Structured English (Pseudocode)   Pseudocode, or structured English, is one of the most popular tools used to convert program specifications into programming code. **Structured English (pseudocode)** describes the specifications for a program using simple, unambiguous, easy-to-understand English phrases. When used in conjunction with the DFD, the pseudocode brings structure and sequence to the process of converting specifications into code. It is widely used as an efficient way to document the processes that drive a program.

Structured English (pseudocode) Describes the logic in a program using simple, easy-to-understand English phrases. It is widely used to document the processes that drive the program and is often used to supplement the DFD.

FIGURE 13-15

A decision tree for the video rental system. The outcome associated with each alternative is shown at the end of each branch.

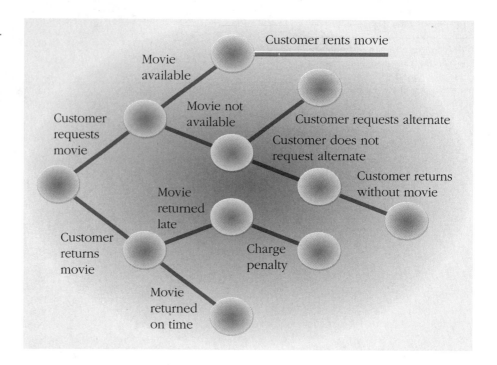

Some guidelines for writing structured English are as follows:

- Statements must be brief and should avoid adjectives (such as *good* or *quick*).
- Statements should begin with an action-oriented verb, such as *order, process,* or *send*.
- Statements must be formatted using multiple levels of indentations so that each level corresponds to a block, or a group of program statements that must be processed together to achieve a given goal, such as *calculate assignment grade*.

An example of structured English is shown in Table 13–2; pseudocode for the video rental system is shown in Table 13–3.

Recall that an information system usually consists of a database and the programs that drive and manage the database. In the implementation phase, the physical design of the database (where to store the data, how much memory the data will occupy, data processing speeds, and so on) are addressed by the database administrator (DBA), who is responsible for the technical design and development of the database. A tool that is very useful in implementing the database is the data dictionary, which was covered in the chapter on databases.

Computer-Aided Systems/Software Engineering (CASE)

CASE
CASE is a tool that automates several phases of information system development. It graphically represents system requirements and automatically converts system requirements into program code.

Computer-aided systems/software engineering (CASE) is a modern IS development approach that uses a formalized set of diagramming techniques to identify system requirements and automatically convert require-

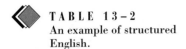

TABLE 13-2
An example of structured
English.

```
VALIDATE _ CUSTOMER
        VALIDATE CUSTOMER INFO
        IF NEW ITEM
                CHECK NAME AND ADDRESS
                CHECK FOR PAYMENT MODE
                IF ERROR
                        SET INVALID FLAG
                ELSE
                        SET VALID FLAG
                END IF
        END IF
        IF VACATION NOTICE
                SET VACATION INDICATOR
                STOP DELIVERY
        END IF
```

ments into program code. CASE emerged in the late 1980s as a development approach that could enhance the productivity of system developers and eliminate the nagging problems of backlogs and runaway systems. It was an attempt by the software engineering community to make the development of new systems more scientific and disciplined.

CASE is a graphics-oriented tool that can automatically create charts, diagrams, matrices (to show the relationships among items), data flow diagrams, structure charts, and entity relationship diagrams. It also automatically converts program specifications into program code and automates some of the tasks associated with coding, testing, and maintaining information systems. The power of CASE lies not so much in *what* it does but in *how* it can be used to build better systems. Thus, CASE by itself has little merit, but when used in conjunction with a well-thought-out development methodology, it can yield significant benefits.

The overall goals and objectives of CASE are to improve the productivity of system developers, improve the quality, reliability, and robustness of systems, reduce system maintenance, and ensure that systems meet the needs of their users.[8]

CASE tools are valuable in each phase of the development life cycle. In the problem definition phase, CASE helps to identify system specifications by using a systematic approach to identifying the information requirements of users. These requirements are then stored in an easily accessible CASE database so that any member of the development team can study them. Further, any changes to the requirements are reflected immediately in the database, which thus imposes consistency on the development process.

CASE also helps in the analysis and design phases by providing user-friendly graphical tools that depict data, processes, and input and output flows. If a piece of data or a process changes, the impact of that change is automatically entered in the system.

TABLE 13-3
An example of structured English for the video rental system.

```
VALIDATE_CUSTOMER
        VALIDATE CUSTOMER INFO
        IF NEW CUSTOMER THEN
                CHECK NAME AND ADDRESS
                CHECK FOR CREDIT HISTORY
                IF ERROR
                        SET INVALID FLAG
                ELSE
                        SET VALID FLAG
                END IF
        IF EXISTING CUSTOMER
                CHECK FOR MOVIE REQUEST
                IF REQUEST = YES THEN
                        CHECK FOR MOVIE AVAILABILITY
                        IF YES THEN
                        RENT MOVIE
                        SET FLAG IN INVENTORY TO OUT
                END IF
                ELSE
                  CHECK FOR MOVIE RETURN
                        ADD MOVIE TO INVENTORY
                        SET FLAG IN INVENTORY TO IN
                        ACCEPT PAYMENT
                END IF
        END IF
```

Many companies all over the world use CASE to build better systems. General Electric found, after it developed five projects using CASE, that the productivity of its programmers had increased by 20%. The company also found that considerably less system maintenance is required for these systems and customer satisfaction with them is greater.

Union Gas, in Chatham, Ontario, is another company that used CASE and achieved more than a 30% gain over the results of traditional methods (See Technology Payoff). The company estimates that if the learning curve were factored out of the analysis, productivity gains would be almost 100%. (The term *learning curve* refers to the period when developers are learning to use the tool, so productivity figures derived during the learning curve do not reflect the true potential of CASE tools.)

Another successful CASE story is that of Revenue Canada, a tax administration system developed by the Customs and Excise Department of the Canadian government. CASE tools were used to develop this system, in one of the largest systems development projects ever undertaken by the Canadian government. The system was built in less than a year, during which system developers processed more than 900 requests for changes to system specifications; in spite of the many changes that were made to system specifications, developers met every single project deadline because of the systematic approach that CASE provides.[9]

Advantages of CASE

Some of the advantages of CASE are as follows:

- It brings discipline to a complex and labor-intensive process. Without the proper tools in place, system development can very quickly become ad hoc and arbitrary, resulting in missed deadlines and cost overruns.
- Lack of proper system documentation is one of the most pervasive problems in system development. CASE tools facilitate and greatly simplify the creation of clear and concise documentation.
- CASE helps control and coordinate the multitude of activities that take place during system development. It provides uniformity in the use of terminology and promotes good communication among project team members.
- It enhances the quality and the reliability of the overall system by minimizing the potential for human error.
- CASE promotes reusability of system components. This allows systems to be cloned and customized to meet the needs of different users.

Disadvantages of CASE

Figure 13–16 shows some disappointing results of using CASE tools.

- The benefits of CASE have often been oversold by vendors. CASE is not a "silver bullet" that can solve all development problems. It is simply a tool to facilitate the development process.
- It takes time to reap the benefits of CASE. Only organizations that have a serious commitment to CASE over the long term can benefit from it.
- CASE is sometimes viewed as "shelfware"—a colloquial term for software that is infrequently used because it is too difficult to learn. CASE is a complex tool, so it often takes some time for developers to master its use.
- Some of the methods underlying CASE tools are very complex and inflexible. The development methods on which CASE is based do not allow for any customization. Hence, sometimes developers are forced to fit the problem to the tool rather than the tool to the problem. Also, CASE fails to take into account managerial issues such as resource allocation.
- CASE requires extensive training, which organizations are often hesitant to undertake. Some organizations try to train a few key project people on CASE and hope that these will be able to train others. However, this approach has had only limited success. Training the entire development team, on the other hand, can be prohibitively expensive.

In summary, it is important to recognize that the selection of IS development tools has repercussions beyond the IS department; consequently, top managers and knowledge workers should play an active role in the selection of IS tools and techniques.

FIGURE 13-16

Some disappointing results of CASE.

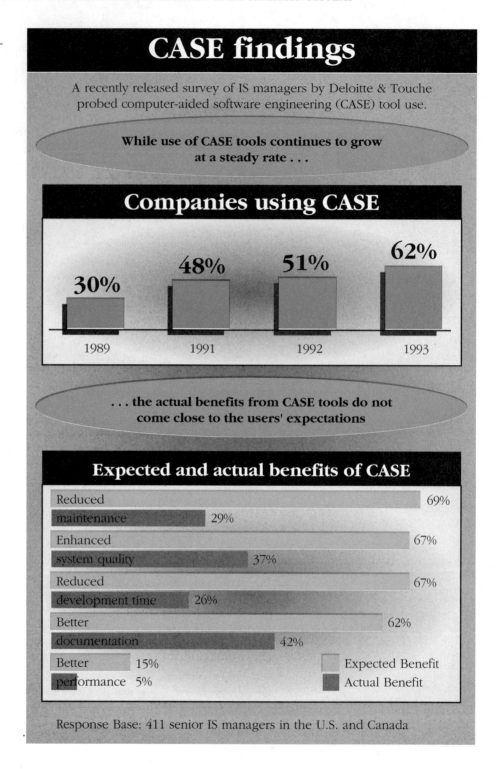

Summary

♦ **IS tools and techniques can create organizational change.**
IS tools and techniques effect organizational change of significant proportions; hence, decisions involving them should be made with the entire firm in mind. Rockart and Hofman recommend a two-phase decision process: the envisioning phase, in which managers take into account the projected business, systems, and development environment, and the transition phase, in which managers determine how the company will make the transition from its existing systems to future systems.

♦ **Tools that support system analysis and design.**
The two tools that facilitate system analysis and design are the context diagram and the data flow diagram.

The context diagram gives a broad overview of the system and identifies the major inputs, processes, and outputs in the system. It allows users and developers to see the "big picture."

The data flow diagram (DFD) identifies the inputs, outputs, processes, and data stores of subsystems within the overall system, providing a layered, or hierarchical, view of the context diagram. The DFD uses four symbols: the data flow symbol, the process symbol, the data store symbol, and the external entity symbol (an entity is a person, place, thing, or concept about which data are collected). The DFD depicts the flow of data in a system (inputs and outputs).

♦ **Tools to represent system data.**
The primary tool used to represent system data is the entity relationship diagram, which brings together, through the use of symbols, the entities in a system and the relationships among them. The entities are represented by rectangles; their relationships are represented by diamonds. There are three types of relationships between entities: 1–1, 1–M, and M–M. Unlike DFDs, which depict both data and the processes that influence the data, ERDs simply depict the data. ERDs supplement DFDs.

♦ **Tools to represent system processes.**
Four tools are used to represent system processes. The structure chart, the system flowchart and the program flowchart, the decision tables, and the decision trees. The structure chart, which resembles an organization's hierarchy chart, depicts the logic that links the different modules in a program. It is particularly useful in software design. The flowchart symbolically depicts the processes that convert input into output, the data required for each process, and the relationships among the processes. Decision tables and decision trees are tools that represent the logic behind system processes and the logical relationships among system variables. Decision tables show the condition clauses and their corresponding action clauses; decision trees show both the logic and the sequence of steps behind that logic.

♦ **The role of CASE in developing high-quality systems.**
Computer-aided systems/software engineering (CASE) is an IS development tool that automates several integral steps in the system development process. CASE brings discipline to a highly complex process by coordinating a multitude of activities that take place during system development. CASE automates the creation of data flow diagrams, structure charts, and entity relationship diagrams; it can automatically convert program specifications into program code. It enhances the quality and reliability of the overall system by minimizing the possibility of human error.

Review Questions

1. Why should selecting IS tools be viewed as a business decision as well as a technical decision? Describe the three roles that modeling tools play in system development.
2. Describe the two phases in Rockart and Hofman's model for selecting IS tools. Describe some of the issues that are analyzed in each of these two phases.
3. Give any three reasons why the systems approach facilitates the building of high-quality systems.
4. Describe structured analysis and structured tools. Identify any three structured tools and explain how these tools facilitate system development.

5. Describe the context diagram and its primary purpose. How is the context diagram related to the data flow diagram?
6. What are the three primary tasks of a DFD? What are the four symbols used in a DFD?
7. What is an entity? How are relationships represented in an entity relationship diagram? Does the ERD represent data or processes?
8. An ERD supplements the DFD. Explain.
9. Identify the steps in developing an ERD. Develop an entity relationship diagram whose entities are *teacher, students,* and *course grade.*

10. Define structured programming and the three constructs on which it is based.
11. Compare the structure chart with the system flowchart. How do these two tools represent system logic?
12. What is the difference between decision tables and decision trees? When is the decision tree preferred over the decision table?
13. Describe CASE. How does it differ from the traditional tools discussed in this chapter?
14. Identify any two advantages and two disadvantages of CASE.

 Discussion Questions

1. Explain the relationships among context diagram, a second-level DFD, and a detailed DFD.
2. Ask the director of information systems at your university how IS development tools and techniques are selected at your university. Would Rockart and Hofman's model work for a university system? Why or why not?
3. Make a presentation to your top management explaining why CASE is beneficial in the long run.

4. Experienced programmers and systems analysts don't need structured tools to develop a system. Do you agree with this viewpoint? Why or why not?
5. An end-user is using an off-the-shelf software package to develop an information system. How would you convince this end-user that using structured tools and techniques will result in a more robust and reliable system?

 ETHICAL ISSUES

Case 1: Andersen in Trouble

A ruling may be months away, but a $100 million fraud lawsuit filed recently against Andersen Consulting offers valuable lessons on how to avoid botched consulting projects. The suit against Andersen stems from work the $3.4 billion consulting giant performed at UOP, an 80-year-old, $800 million engineering company that develops technology used to build oil refineries. In 1992, UOP hired Andersen to streamline its engineering specifications and cost-estimating processes and develop a series of client-server software applications.

Three years later, UOP president and chief executive officer Michael D. Winfield claimed that "the difference between what Andersen promised us at the outset and what it actually delivered is staggering." "From the beginning we were not included in the actual development process." Eugene Schmeizer, director of support systems centers at UOP, said. Andersen insisted on using

their own staff for coding and software work. They also kept reestimating the number of man-hours it would take to complete the project."

Also problematic was Andersen's deployment of inexperienced staffers, who ultimately delivered incomplete, defective and largely unusable systems. Meanwhile, Andersen's periodic progress reports to UOP indicated all was going well. Of the half-dozen former or current Andersen clients contacted, some were not altogether surprised by the charges, especially those about Andersen consultants' alleged lack of expertise.

Other Andersen clients characterized unplanned time extensions as commonplace on their projects, and some complained about Andersen's often undisciplined approach to projects.

In September, 1994, First Union, a Charlotte, N.C. bank with $77 billion in assets, selected Andersen to head a call center project. But the bank ended its $6 million contract with the consultancy after the first phase was completed March 13, because the work "had become a struggle to complete," said Judge Fowler, senior vice president and director of systems development at First Union. Andersen did not manage the initiative "with the appropriate project disciplines," according to Fowler.

Experts say there are several important lessons to be learned form this experience.

♦ Never let contractors work exclusively on their own. Always insist that some in-house developers be part of the project.

♦ Negotiate all costs up front.
♦ Ask lots of questions early in the process and often.[10]

1. Based on the tools, techniques, and principles discussed in the last chapter (Chapter 12) and this chapter, identify some steps that a consulting firm should take to ensure the success of an IS project.
2. Given the limited information currently available on this case, what are some steps Andersen Consulting should have taken to avoid the lawsuit?

PROBLEM SOLVING IN THE REAL WORLD

Case 1: Amtrak Runs with CASE

In 1987, Amtrak, in response to a growing backlog of requests for information systems and a declining workforce, undertook an evaluation of CASE tools for enhancing its application development process in a mainframe environment. After a great deal of analysis and evaluation, Amtrak chose IEW Toolset, from Knowledge Ware, as its CASE tool. The company then conducted a series of meetings with the vendor to ensure the smooth introduction of the CASE tool. A group of IS employees were selected to become in-house experts in CASE; each was given 10 days of training. The vendor was also actively involved in training employees in the features of the tool. Today, Amtrak has used CASE tools for a number of projects and approximately 15 in-house programmers are CASE experts.

In the process of introducing and using CASE, the company learned many valuable lessons, some of which are described below.

♦ **A methodology must be in place for CASE to work.**
Amtrak realized that in order to gain the full potential of CASE, it is important to have a methodology in place. The type of methodology is not as important as having one in place and telling the staff, programmers, managers, and users what to expect and how to interpret the deliverables of the methodology. Amtrak realized that without a methodology in place, it was difficult, if not impossible, to realize the full benefits of CASE, such as reusability, reliability, and consistency.

♦ **Users should be given extensive training.**
Amtrak realized that the amount of training required to bring programmers, analysts, and users up to speed was far greater than it had anticipated. Even management had to be trained in the implications of CASE, since development tools often create organizational changes that have far-reaching

(Continued on next page)

impact. The company also realized that the timing of the training was critical and propagated the idea of "just-in-time" training. If people are trained one time in all the features of the tool, they tend to forget what they learned. Informal discussions with users of CASE tools prior to training often seemed to help trainees to learn the material faster.

♦ **Vendor support is crucial.**

Although vendors often promise that the tools are easy to use and will work smoothly on existing equipment, Amtrak found that this is not always the case. Once the goods are sold, vendor support is often difficult to come by and often getting a straight answer to a simple question is difficult. Quite often, both the customer and the vendor are responsible. Customers should be willing and prepared to pay for additional consulting support and should do so from the start of the project, not after things have gone bad. In other words, "you get what you pay for." Amtrak realized that frequent visits from vendors do not necessarily translate into substantive support.

♦ **User involvement is vital for CASE to succeed.**

User involvement is critical to the success of CASE. Amtrak found that in order to win the enthusiastic support of users, it is important to communicate the reasons for the new approach and its benefits. The role of users in system development should be clearly identified, and it is desirable to involve them in all phases of development. Users should also be provided with training on CASE tools, although to a lesser extent than programmers and system developers.

♦ **Start with a noncritical project.**

From Amtrak's experience, it appears that when a new tool, such as CASE, is introduced, it is advisable to test that tool on noncritical projects that do not have high visibility in the company. Amtrak's first CASE project was one that had been started and stopped twice before and had high visibility. Given the project's track record, its further delays owing to inexperience with CASE tools were not received well and many problems that had nothing to do with CASE were still blamed on it. A smaller project, which could quickly demonstrate its value, would have been a more effective starting point.

"There are, of course, many skeptics in the department. Most of those skeptics are people who have not yet had an opportunity to work with the tools and see their benefit. We underestimated the use of the programmers as proselytizers."

At Amtrak, although the CASE experience was sometimes painful, frustrating, and time-consuming, users are still sold on CASE and its long-term benefits. The quality of the company's information systems has been significantly improved by CASE.[11]

1. Describe any two of the important lessons that Amtrak has learned from its CASE experience.
2. Is the type of development methodology critical for the success of CASE or is it more important to have a methodology (any methodology) in place? Discuss.

Case 2: Building Blocks for a New Age

Many technology managers say that creating a piece of business software is like constructing an office building. In both cases, three elements are essential: construction methods, users' needs, and the overall success of the end product. New development tools are emerging to help developers take into account these three elements in the design of information systems.

Existing tools and techniques are often not capable of building applications that support large, complex, mission-critical tasks because the tools were originally designed to work with a limited number of clients accessing just one type of database management system (DBMS). In today's environment, applications must operate on several hardware platforms and access more than one type of database. Further, many tools lack the group programming features that allow companies to build an integrated application that performs different business functions, such as a program that links accounting, distribution, and sales systems. "Current tools are teenagers," complains one IS director. "They have moved past infancy but have not yet reached adulthood."

Many software vendors are actively building a new generation of development tools that help businesses build more complex, integrated applications spanning multiple platforms. These tools are particularly well suited to a client-server environment in which there is a client, a database server, and an applications server.

One such tool that is grabbing the attention of system developers is PowerBuilder. In early 1992, Amoco Canada Petroleum, a Calgary-based subsidiary of Amoco, decided to move a mainframe application that tracked the use of oil and gas wells to UNIX workstations using PowerBuilder, a tool that allows programmers without extensive training to create fairly complex applications. Northern Trust, a $17 billion bank holding company in Chicago, used PowerBuilder to create software for retail banking, mortgage, and other business applications in less than 9 months. The company plans to have 100 developers use PowerBuilder to write 15 more programs over the next few years.

Another tool that is gaining wide acceptance is Microsoft's Visual BASIC, which is suitable for writing applications that run under Microsoft's Windows operating system. However, Visual BASIC is not appropriate if large programming teams are involved.

Vendors are trying to make their tools more attractive to companies that want to build complex, enterprise-wide applications. One way to accomplish this is to integrate existing development tools with CASE tools, because this can eliminate some of the networking and operating-system idiosyncrasies that programmers often have to deal with. In many companies, multiple application development tools are becoming more and more popular, because these can be modified and adapted to the level of complexity of a given application.[12]

1. Why are some existing development tools not suitable for building complex and mission-critical applications?
2. Look into some popular computer magazines and write a one-page report on PowerBuilder. Explain why PowerBuilder is an advanced development tool.

References

Bacon, C. James. "The Uses of Decision Criteria in Selecting Information Systems/Technology Investments." *MIS Quarterly* 16, no. 3 (September 1992).

Boynton, A. C., C. G. Jacobs, and R. W. Zmud. "Whose Responsibility is IT Management?" *Sloan Management Review* (Summer 1992), pp. 32–38.

Buss, Martin D. J. "How to Rank Computer Projects." *Harvard Business Review,* (January 1983).

Caldwell, Bruce. "Who Needs Programmers?" *Information Week* (April 25, 1994), pp. 23–30.

Cerveny, Robert P., Edward J. Garrity, and G. Lawrence Sanders. "A Problem-Solving Perspective on Systems Development." *Journal of Management Information Systems* 6, no. 4 (Spring 1990).

Davis, Gordon B. "Strategies for Information Requirements Determination." *IBM Systems Journal* 1 (1982).

Dos Santos, Brian. "Justifying Investments in New Information Technologies." *Journal of Management Information Systems* 7, no. 4 (Spring 1991).

Franz, Charles and Daniel Robey. "An Investigation of User-Led System Design: Rational and Political Perspectives." *Communications of the ACM* 27 (December 1984).

Grudnitski, Gary. "Eliciting Decision Makers' Information Requirements." *Journal of Management Information Systems* (Summer 1984).

Kim, Chai and Stu Westin. "Software Maintainability: Perceptions of EDP Professionals." *MIS Quarterly* (June 1988).

King, William R. "Alternative Designs in Information System Development." *MIS Quarterly* (December 1982).

Konsynski, Benn R. "Advances in Information System Design." *Journal of Management Information Systems* 1 (Winter 1984–1985).

Orlikowski, W. J., "CASE Tools as Organizational Change: Investigating Incremental and Radical Changes in Systems Development." *MIS Quarterly* (September 1993), pp. 309–340.

Matlin, Gerald. "What Is the Value of Investment in Information Systems?" *MIS Quarterly* 13, no. 3 (September 1989).

Notes

1. Grant, Don. "CASE Tools in the Systems Development Environment," *CMA Magazine,* October 1993, pp. 25–28.
2. Rockart, John F. and J. Debra Hofman. "Systems Delivery: Evolving New Strategies," *Sloan Management Review,* Summer 1992, pp. 21–31.
3. Ibid.
4. Ibid.
5. Ibid.
6. Ibid.
7. Rockart, J. F. and M. S. Scott Morton. "Implications of Changes in Information Technology for Corporate Strategy," *Interfaces,* January/February 1984, pp. 84–95.
8. Grant, Don. "CASE Tools in the Systems Development Environment," *CMA Magazine,* October 1993, pp. 25–28.
9. Ibid.
10. King, Julia and Thomas Hoffman. "Lessons from a Lawsuit," *Computerworld,* April 10, 1995, p. 28.
11. McComb, Mary E. "CASE Tools Implementation at Amtrak—Lessons Almost Learned," *Journal of Systems Management,* March 1994, pp. 16–20.
12. Korzeniowski, Paul. "Building Blocks for a New Age," *Information Week,* July 25, 1994, p. 62.

Strategic and Managerial Implications of Information Systems

Chapter 14
Strategic Information Systems

Chapter 15
Information Resources Management

Chapter 16
Computer Security

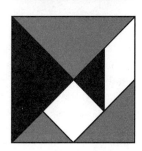

14

Strategic Information Systems

Contents

Learning Objectives
Technology Payoff: Blockbuster
Introduction
What Is a Strategic Information System (SIS)?
 Examples of Strategic Information Systems
Characteristics of Strategic Information Systems
 Telecommunications
 Multiple Vendors
 Interorganizational Systems
Strategic Information Systems Plans (SISP)
Strategies for Developing an SIS
 Is the Project Financially Feasible?
 Is the Project Technically Feasible?
 Steps to Ensure Success of a Strategic System
Potential Barriers to Developing an SIS
 Problem Definition
 Implementation
 Maintenance
A Classic Tale of a Strategic Information System: SABRE
 Seek Leverage from Existing Systems
 Use Existing Knowledge to Grasp Opportunities
 Start Early
 Delegate Authority
Summary
Review Questions

Discussion Questions
Ethical Issues
    Case 1: Credit Card Versus Debit Card
    Case 2: Airlines Use Their Muscle
    Case 3: Patenting Innovation and Creativity
Problem Solving in the Real World
    Case 1: Strategic Information Systems Planning for a Hong Kong
             Hospital
    Case 2: McKesson Water
    Case 3: J. C. Penney
References
Notes

Learning Objectives

In the last decade or so, the role of information systems has changed dramatically from that of a "back-room" support function to that of a vital part of organizational decision making. In this chapter, we describe strategic information systems—that is, systems that provide long-term strategic advantages to an organization by helping it to compete successfully in the marketplace. Strategic systems are the product of creative thinking and are often difficult to develop. A system, whether it is a TPS, a MIS, a DSS, an EIS, or an ES, becomes strategic when it is used to give the company an edge in the marketplace.

After reading and studying this chapter, you will be able to:

* Describe a strategic information system and understand its potential
* Identify some common attributes of strategic information systems
* Describe the elements of a strategic information systems plan
* Identify strategies for developing successful strategic information systems

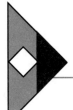

TECHNOLOGY PAYOFF

Blockbuster

Information systems have played a critical role in Blockbuster's rapid growth. The company is now using them again to achieve similar results with its burgeoning Blockbuster Music chain. "It's critical that our different organizations—music, video, and so on—be closely integrated," says a company spokesperson. "Each must be aware of what the others are doing so we don't end up going down different tracks and taking different turns."

Blockbuster's national inventory system is one of the finest in the industry. The system stores information on all store transactions in a mainframe computer, which in turn feeds the information to various applications running on PCs and other computers in different stores throughout the country. The company's information systems are easy to use and ensure that Blockbuster gets the right product to the right store at the right time.

The company is not resting on its laurels. Instead, it has some ambitious goals for its information systems:

◆ To create a national membership card that customers can use throughout the entire Blockbuster enterprise.
◆ To integrate information on Blockbuster's 40 million customers to exploit cross-marketing opportunities.
◆ To streamline back-office operations such as processing invoices and purchase orders.
◆ To improve merchandising and product information at Blockbuster's 253 music stores so that store managers are aware of products that are "hot" and need to be reordered and of those that are "not hot" and need to be removed from the shelves.

Blockbuster's information systems have been especially important in improving its purchasing operations. The store-wide system pinpoints exactly which movies are rented in which markets, allowing the company to customize its purchasing to meet the needs of individual stores. The goal is to develop an information system that can support a diversified range of entertainment businesses in the face of rapidly changing technologies. Blockbuster's information systems have played an important role in helping the company to achieve and maintain a leadership position in the video rental market.[1]

Innovation does not just happen. The sequence for integrated information technologies requires a strong push from the top so that people at all levels can contribute to the principal ingredients: vision, policy, and architecture. Mobilizing begins when people share the vision, the culture buys into it, and people believe that they can, and should, make a contribution.

—Peter Keen

Introduction

Until a few years ago, information systems and technologies were considered to be support functions for essential business functions, such as accounting, manufacturing, marketing, and human resources, and were designed primarily to help managers make operational and tactical decisions. Today, the role of information systems has grown from a support function to a strategic one, particularly as competition stiffens in the global marketplace and companies are forced to do more with less. Some key differences between support systems and strategic systems are shown in Table 14–1.

A number of factors have contributed to the changing role of IS. First, the costs of information technologies have declined significantly in the last decade, making computers and information systems affordable for many companies. Second, computer technologies have become more sophisticated and easy to use, resulting in more enlightened and aggressive end-users. Third, global competition

TABLE 14-1
A comparison of the benefits, impacts, and costs of support systems versus those of strategic information systems.

	Support System	Strategic System
Benefit	Improved efficiency Improved effectiveness	Competitive advantage
Impact	Cost improvements Higher-quality decisions	Increased market share Increased profits
Cost	Administrative/overhead	Administrative/overhead Direct business expense

Source: Moriarty, D. D., "Strategic Information Systems Planning for Health Services," *Health Care Management Review,* vol. 17, no. 1, 1992, pp. 85–90.

has increased tremendously, forcing companies to increase their efficiency and responsiveness. The recurring theme of successful companies is customer satisfaction; this goal requires finding creative ways to put existing technologies to work. Finally, the business community is witnessing the emergence of cooperative ventures among some unlikely business partners in an effort to outsmart the competition. The success of such ventures often depends on how they use information to develop new markets and maintain existing ones. Hence, the strategic use of information system is no longer a choice but a necessity for many companies.

Many companies, like Blockbuster, have used IS as a valuable strategic resource to cut costs, increase profits, improve market share, and enhance customer satisfaction. Instead of simply using its inventory system to keep records of past transactions, Blockbuster is using the system to provide new insights into the buying patterns and preferences of its customers. The company is using IS to present a uniform face to its customers, regardless of their geographical location; this can be an attractive feature for customers who are mobile. In some cases, the strategic use of IS has revolutionized an entire industry and caused a fundamental paradigm shift. We will look at some industries in which the innovative use of information systems has opened up new markets or completely changed the way business was done.

What Is a Strategic Information System (SIS)?

Researchers have classified information systems into three categories:[2]

1. Systems that support business functions, such as accounting, marketing, and manufacturing information systems (Chapter 11).
2. Systems that support strategic planning, such as DSS and EIS (Chapters 8, 9) (Note: Not all DSS and EIS support strategic planning, but they can be used to support strategic planning.)
3. Systems that are part of a firm's strategy.

Strategic information system (SIS)
A system that delivers information products and services that play a direct and prominent role in helping the firm achieve its strategic goals.

Systems in the last category are called **strategic information systems (SIS).** They deliver information products and services that play a direct and prominent role in helping a firm achieve its strategic goals. An SIS also supplies an organi-

FIGURE 14–1:

Three characteristics that are commonly found in Strategic Information Systems

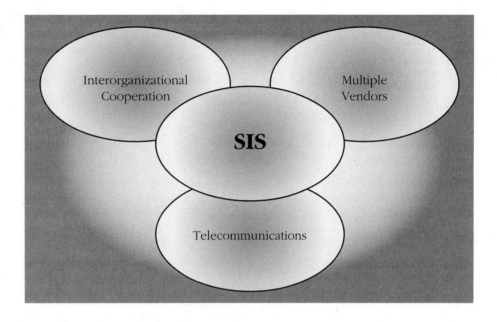

FIGURE 14–1:

Three characteristics that are commonly found in Strategic Information Systems

Business intelligence
Internal and external data that help a company assess and analyze the business environment and identify any possible opportunities or threats.

External strategic systems
Systems that are used primarily by a company's customers, clients, suppliers, or other external entities.

Internal strategic systems
Systems that are used by employees within an organization and designed primarily to enhance internal productivity.

zation with business intelligence, or competitive information. **Business intelligence** consists of internal and external data used to assess and analyze opportunities and threats in the business environment. If an information system helps a firm gain an edge over its competitors, or at the very least helps it to keep up with the competition, it can be viewed as a system of strategic importance.

It is important to recognize that an SIS is *not* a type of information system, like a TPS or an MIS. An information system is classified as a strategic system based on *how* it is used and on the benefits it provides to the organization. In other words, if an information system is used in creative ways to achieve the goals and fulfill the mission of the organization, it can be viewed as an SIS, whether it is a TPS, an MIS, or any other type of system.

Strategic information systems can be external or internal systems.[3] **External strategic systems** are used primarily by external entities in the business environment, such as customers, suppliers, and distributors, and have a value-added component that gives developers some time to reap the benefits of system innovation. Some of the benefits of external strategic systems are shown in Table 14–2.

Internal strategic systems, on the other hand, are used by employees within the organization and do not have a value-added component. Instead, they focus on issues such as improving the quality of products and services and enhancing the decision-making capabilities of managers. Such systems are often used at all levels in the organization; they have long-term implications for the firm and for the business processes within the firm. For example, PRISM, a state-of-the-art human resources system at Federal Express (see box), is an internal strategic system that provides the company with significant advantages in the marketplace.

Examples of Strategic Information Systems

Minitel, the only successful public videotex system in the world, is often cited as an international strategic system (see box). Designed and developed in France, it gave the French an unmatched competitive edge in IS by allowing users to access

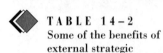

TABLE 14–2
Some of the benefits of
external strategic
information systems.

Benefits to the Customer

Increased customer satisfaction

Increased customer control

Reduction in transaction costs (such as shipping and handling costs, merchandise returns, and reordering)

Benefits to the Organization

Increased market share

Reduction of processing costs

Ability to charge higher prices because of value-added component

Increase in profit margins

large volumes of data for a variety of personal and professional tasks and to exchange E-mail messages. Although many companies tried to promote the idea of videotex before Minitel's success, they were unsuccessful until the *informatisation de la société* persuaded the French government to provide users with free terminals. These were a key factor in the success of Minitel, which today boasts approximately 6.6 million members and an average of 18 calls per month per member.[5]

The ASAP system, designed by American Hospital Supply (AHP) (see box), is a TPS that gained the stature of a strategic system because it allowed customers to order products from their offices without the help of a company salesperson. The system provides customers with detailed information on a wide variety of company products, along with their prices and delivery schedules.

Another strategic information system is the automated teller machine (ATM), first introduced by Citibank in 1977. When the company first invested in ATM technology, it did not realize that such systems would completely revolutionize the banking industry and forever change the way people conducted financial transactions. ATMs provided Citibank with such a powerful edge that many competitors found it hard to catch up with, or imitate, the firm. Many competitors got together and formed the New York Cash Exchange (NYCE) in order to diminish some of the competitive power that ATMs were giving Citibank. The effort met with only limited success.

ATMs were strategic systems because the only alternative to ATMs would require banks to open branch offices at a large number of convenient locations, such as malls and grocery stores; further, these offices would have to remain open 24 hours per day, 7 days per week, to provide the same level of service as ATMs. In one stroke, ATMs eliminated the need for such a costly alternative while greatly increasing the convenience of performing financial transactions. The ATM "brought the bank to the customer," delighting customers and creating significant entry barriers for new entrants to the market. This shows that strategic systems are the result of the *way* companies use information, and not of the *type* of system.

In general, strategic information systems can be divided into three broad areas, based on three strategies:

BUSINESS REALITIES
The PRISM System at Federal Express

Although PRISM was first implemented by Federal Express in the early 1980s to support personal functions, today it has evolved into an advanced multi-technology system that is at the heart of Federal Express's organizational effectiveness, providing managers and employees worldwide with valuable data. For example, managers can input and access all data pertaining to their subordinates, while employees can examine pertinent personnel data in real time.

Other innovative functions of PRISM include job posting and bidding, training and testing, safety and security, applications for employment, hiring employees, processing employee benefits, processing salary changes, affirmative action, verification of employment, employee assessment, training and development, leave time, employee safety, employee input to management, retirement, and a computer-based management-by-objectives (MBO) implementation. The PRISM system, one of the most advanced human resource systems in the world, provides a foundation that supports the vast Federal Express organization worldwide and has had a significant impact on most of the company's external human resource processes, including affirmative action reporting, data exchange with benefits providers, and OSHA reporting.

Many important and interesting characteristics differentiate PRISM from other human resource systems. Almost all PRISM input is provided directly by end-users at the source of the data, thus saving time and errors associated with clerical or data entry personnel. Every job application to Federal Express is entered via a scanner or online terminal into the PRISM applicant-tracking database, allowing managers to track applicants' histories worldwide. A hiring manager knows whether an applicant has applied at other Federal Express offices, whether that applicant has been identified as unsuitable for hire, and, if so, why.

When a manager decides to hire an applicant, PRISM verifies that the position has budget authorization and, if so, creates an employee record for entry into its employee database. Note that no paper is generated in the process. Each Federal Express employee maintains and updates his/her own personal data, such as address, telephone number, and benefit options, and can select and change benefit options directly through PRISM. The system walks an employee through the large selection of benefit options, records any additions, deletions, or changes, notifies benefit providers through the benefits interface, and passes the appropriate data on to the payroll system through the payroll interface. Most PRISM transactions require no paper forms, no mail, no document storage, and no additional data entry.

PRISM provides immediate verification of employment for employees seeking loans. The average verification-of-employment transaction takes a total of 15 minutes from employee request to completion by management. Federal Express employees have access to over 4,000 different training courses through a network of 1,200 PCs and more than 25,000 online terminals; training is arranged to accommodate each employee's work schedule. All aspects of course enrollment, training, and testing are coordinated by PRISM.

Any interested employee can view positions that are open within the company and apply for a position from any terminal in the worldwide Federal Express network. PRISM responds to an employee's interest by verifying that employee's qualifications for the position and providing an authorization screen for the employee's supervisor. If the employee is authorized, it adds him or her to an electronic candidate list for the hiring supervisor. PRISM provides pertinent data, such as seniority, job history, training history, test scores, and evaluations, all online, to the hiring supervisor. Complex seniority rules, which vary for different job classifications as determined by corporate policy, are automatically applied. At no point during the process is paperwork generated, transported, or stored, nor is there any additional data entry.

The investment in PRISM has been returned many times over on the basis of direct cost savings alone, besides many intangible long-term strategic benefits. While the total number of employees in the company has dramatically increased from 7,000 to 90,000 in less than 10 years, the size of the personnel department has remained fairly stable. Conservatively, without PRISM, the personnel department staff would have had to increase by at least 50 percent just to accomplish the basic personnel functions. This savings alone is worth over $28 million per annum.[4]

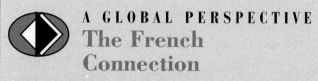

A GLOBAL PERSPECTIVE
The French Connection

France's Minitel is the only successful public videotex system in the world; it gives that country, which designed and developed the system, an unmatched competitive edge in IS. A videotex system is based on the simple idea that data have multiple uses and hence users should be allowed to manipulate data in different ways for different purposes. The idea of videotex itself has been around for many years. For example, large computers, such as mainframes, allow organizations to create centralized databases, which can then be sold to a large number of customers that use "dumb" terminals. But other countries, such as the United Kingdom and Germany, failed when they tried to promote this idea.

The key reason why France succeeded where others failed was that it provided free terminals to users. The French government took this step in order to encourage users with little or no training in computers to use videotex. However, this is only half the story.

Although free terminals were a necessary condition for Minitel's success, they were not a sufficient one. In the beginning, the use of Minitel was sluggish and many doubted that it would ever take off. What eventually attracted customers was the system's messaging capabilities, which had not been promoted in the early days. The story goes that during an experiment in Strasbourg, a local newspaper put its classified ads selection on videotex and a hacker started using Minitel to respond to the ads. This helped to establish a direct electronic dialog between advertisers and customers. It was the beginning of Minitel as a national public E-mail system, not just a system for accessing a database. At that point, the availability of free terminals turned out to be crucial to the increased use of Minitel. Almost instantaneously, Minitel created a new market, where many businesses could sell their services and customers could access the service from their homes. The system became so popular that its supporting network, Transpac, broke down and France adapted a new network infrastructure to support the growing traffic.

Today, Minitel boasts approximately 6.6 million members and an average of 18 calls per month per member. It is heavily used as an E-mail messaging system. Minitel continues to be one of the great strategic information system success stories.[5]

- Systems that focus on innovation for competitive advantage
- Systems that use information as a weapon
- Systems that increase productivity and lower the costs of goods and services.[7]

Table 14–3 shows some strategic systems that fall into each of these three categories.

Systems that support *innovation* help companies to be responsive to customer needs. These include customer-oriented systems and planning systems. For example, Merrill Lynch's Cash Management Account (CMA) system allows customers to withdraw cash, conduct credit transactions, and analyze investment options using just a single account. They can manage their financial portfolios by moving money among stocks, bonds, and other financial instruments, at their convenience, all free of charge. This has given customers the freedom to manage their portfolios, which financially astute customers have found exceptionally attractive. Merrill Lynch's competitors, which include major banks and financial institutions, were forced to offer such services in order to avoid losing customers. This is a customer-oriented system because it provides ways not only to keep and please existing customers, but also to attract new ones.

Systems that support *information services* provide managers with vital financial and statistical data that enhance internal decision making. Financial planning, executive information, logistics systems, electronic data interchange

BUSINESS REALITIES
AHP: ASAP System

ASAP is a strategic order entry information system that was developed by American Hospital Supply (AHP) in the late 1980s and was later acquired by Baxter Travenol. The system was initially designed to help customers order pharmaceutical items over the telephone. However, the system was inflexible and error-prone; customers were frustrated by mishandled orders, lack of confirmation of product availability, and late deliveries.

AHP was losing customers because of its poor order-entry system; sales people were extremely frustrated by customer complaints and lost sales. The company decided to invest in a more sophisticated order entry system, one that would link all hospitals to AHP using various technologies such as bar codes, touch-tone telephones, and PCs. Thus, a strategic information system was born.

The success of ASAP is largely attributable to the company's decision to closely scrutinize its business processes before building a system to automate those processes. The new system made it easy for hospitals to place orders and provided customers with up-to-date information on the status of their orders. Product descriptions, prices, and delivery schedules were readily available both to customers and to AHP managers, who used the information to improve the quality of their decisions.

ASAP was a groundbreaking development because it changed the rules of the game; AHP became a market leader as it continued to sign up new customers while competitors played catch-up. Sophisticated order entry systems became the industry norm. Competitors found AHP clients were reluctant to switch because they liked the company's high level of customer service. ASAP is a true strategic information system because it not only provided the company with long-term strategic benefits, but also changed the rules of the industry, increased switching costs for customers, and created entry barriers for new competitors.[6]

(EDI), external database access, and expert systems (ES) can be considered information service systems. McKesson's Economost, an order entry system for pharmacies, is such a system (see box) because it provides both McKesson's managers and its customers with valuable information that facilitates good decision making. For example, the system provides customers with reports that encourage cost-effective purchasing decisions, such as what items to order, when, and how much to order. A monthly management purchase report, provided by Economost, also shows customers the items that were ordered, the prices at which they have sold, and the profit margin broken down by item, by individual department, and by pharmacy.

Finally, *productivity systems* are support systems such as transaction processing, inventory management, centralized databases, production planning, personnel, factory floor control systems, and other systems that help to increase the overall productivity of the organization. Throughout this book, we have seen many such systems.

Characteristics of Strategic Information Systems

Three characteristics are commonly found in all strategic information systems. They are as follows:

1. Telecommunications as a central part of an SIS
2. Reliance on a number of vendors for providing information technologies
3. Cooperation among a number of organizations

TABLE 14–3
Various strategic information systems that support the three broad strategies of innovation, information services, and productivity.

Innovation

Customer Service Systems:

Order, order inquiry, service systems

Marketing Planning Systems:

Forecasting, sales analyses

Information Services

Financial Planning Systems:

Systems with mathematical models to aid financial planning

Executive Information systems:

Systems that allow top management to retrieve internal and external data and information directly from the computer

Logistics:

Vehicle routing, freight rate management, shipment tracing, performance measurement

Electronic Data Interchange (EDI):

Electronically sending bills, payments, or orders to suppliers and customers

Access to External Databases:

Compustat, Compuserve, Dow Jones, and so on.

Expert Systems:

Computerized "consultant" systems for specialized situations

Productivity

Transaction Processing:

Accounting, billing, payroll.

Inventory Management:

Raw materials, finished products, work in process

Centralized DBMS:

Software systems to facilitate access to all organizational data and information

Production Planning:

Materials and capacity requirements planning, scheduling, due-date setting

Personnel System:

Skills inventory and personnel performance tracking

Statistical Systems:

SAS, SPSS, Minitab, and so on.

Factory Floor Control:

Robotic islands, automated guided vehicle systems, automated storage and retrieval

Source: Hagmann, Constanza, and Cynthia S. McCahon, "Strategic Information Systems and Competitiveness," *Information and Management,* vol. 25 (1993), pp. 183–192.

Telecommunications

Telecommunications is often a vital part of an SIS; the most successful SIS are those that transcend traditional organizational boundaries and eliminate the barriers of time and space through the use of telecommunications.

BUSINESS REALITIES
McKesson's Economost

Economost, often cited as a prime example of a strategic information system, is a group of information systems that allows retail pharmacies to place orders for drugs and other related items by simply walking through the aisles of a McKesson store with a hand-held electronic order entry device. A description of the item, the quantity, and the total amount of the sale is transmitted to the company's data center in Rancho Cordova, California, and the items are delivered the same day or the next day to the pharmacy in cartons that match the aisle arrangement of the pharmacy.

Customer service at McKesson is exemplary: the company saves pharmacists the trouble of creating price stickers by providing these with every order; store managers get reports from McKesson that help them decide what items to order and how much to order. A monthly Management Purchase Report, provided by Economost, shows store managers and customers the items that were ordered, the prices at which the items were sold, and the profit margin broken down by item, by individual department, and by pharmacy. The system has been beneficial both to the pharmacies and to McKesson.

For pharmacies, the cost of placing orders has decreased significantly and the number of stock-outs has also fallen considerably. For McKesson, the rewards have been tremendous. The number of warehouses has been cut in half; the national purchasing staff has been reduced from 140 to 12, and the number of telephone order clerks from 700 to 15. The productivity of warehouse staff increased at a rate of 17 percent, compounded annually, between 1975 and 1985. From 1975 to 1987, McKesson's sales increased by a whopping 424%, from $922 million to over $4.8 billion.

In spite of its tremendous success, Economost started out as a simple order entry system; it was not the product of a grand strategic information plan, but was the outcome of an evolutionary, piecemeal approach that focused on utilizing the potential of existing systems. "Economost was stumbled upon almost accidentally, the outcome of what the French call *bricolage,* i.e., tinkering and serendipity."[8]

"Many of the exemplary cases of the use of information technology for competitive advantage have required telecommunications for their delivery . . . indeed, it is probably the telecommunications technology, rather than advances in computing, automation, or software, that has so far released most of the strategic gains claimed of IT in the 1980s."[9]

Our opening vignette about Blockbuster shows how the company uses telecommunications to get the latest sales information from video rental stores throughout the country so that the right video can be available to the customer at the right time. The system also allows Blockbuster to study the contribution of a given video to the store's profitability, so that when customers do not show interest in that video, the company can acquire the rights to it for a nominal sum, thereby avoiding overpurchase of overpriced videos.

However, developing and implementing information systems that rely heavily on telecommunications is an extremely challenging task and is often cited as one of the development bottlenecks in SIS.

Multiple Vendors

Since SIS often require the integration of complex technologies, in many cases several vendors are needed to develop an SIS. For example, when Merrill Lynch built its Cash Management Account (CMA) system, it had to link more than 600 brokerage firms all over the world. The telecommunications equipment for this venture was acquired from 30 different vendors! Therefore, one of the critical ingredients of an SIS is the ability to identify, coordinate, and manage transactions with a number of vendors and effectively bring together diverse technologies to achieve a goal.

Interorganizational Systems

Interorganizational Systems (IOS)
Computerized information systems that are shared by more than one company.

Interorganizational systems (IOS) are systems shared by two or more companies, in the spirit of cooperation and collaboration rather than that of blind competition. Since interorganizational systems often involve bringing together a diverse group of assets and talents, such ventures often result in powerful systems that enhance productivity, reduce operating costs, increase market share, and create new partnerships, especially for companies that conduct business transactions in global markets.

"It is a brand new world. . . . Competition today is a team sport. Alliances help you find purpose for the company. There are no longer permanent enemies."[10]

Today, interorganizational systems are proliferating; there are several reasons for this. As the trend toward globalization continues to accelerate, managers are under pressure to quickly access and disseminate large volumes of information across national and international boundaries. This often requires the cooperation of diverse business units. Second, interorganizational systems are the lifeline of multinational companies that rely on the free flow of information between business units and head offices; this too often requires collaboration among diverse units. Third, as the cost of hardware declines and advances in technology become commonplace, it is becoming less expensive to build interorganizational systems.

American Airlines' SABRE reservations system is a classic interorganizational SIS. In this case, external entities, such as travel agents, became the main users of the system. The system was initially developed when the airline industry was heavily regulated and huge investments in information systems and technologies had limited value. But when the airline industry was deregulated, SABRE became one of the most profitable elements of American Airlines. The system allowed the firm to process ticket reservations for its competitors while strongly encouraging travel agents to select American over other airlines. This capability was crucial to the remarkable growth rate of American's market share. By breaking down the traditional boundaries between the company and the customer, American built a successful IOS that made SABRE one of the classic strategic systems of its time.

Another type of IOS is Electronic Data Interchange (EDI) which was discussed in detail in Chapter 5, Telecommunications. Clearly, EDI transcends traditional organizational boundaries and establishes strategic alliances between trading partners. For example, Mapco (see box) uses EDI to link with one of its leading suppliers, BellSouth, resulting in a significant reduction in operating costs.

Another company that views EDI as a competitive necessity is Thiokol, whose $175-million Huck Manufacturing Division uses an EDI-based delivery system by integrating incoming orders with the order management system. The system has eliminated data entry, reduced order-related errors, greatly increased the speed of processing orders, and increased the number of orders without increasing staff size. The company's strong commitment to EDI is reflected in these words: "EDI is like a little piece of cheese in a sandwich. You may not see it, but without it things aren't going to work. We see EDI not as an end in itself but as a way to facilitate strategic partnerships."[12]

BUSINESS REALITIES
Mapco

In the southeastern U.S., Mapco, a $3-billion company based in Tulsa, Oklahoma, operates a chain of convenience stores and offices. BellSouth has been Mapco's communications supplier for several years. With the tremendous volume of business that Mapco did with BellSouth came a tremendous amount of paperwork. "We got reams and boxes of paper from [BellSouth] every month," says a company spokesperson. "Somebody had to go through all of that to ensure that billing and invoices were done accurately."

Recently, however, an EDI-based re-engineering project has linked Mapco's accounting system and BellSouth's billing, thus reducing unproductive work. EDI has helped Mapco to better analyze its communications costs and has enhanced its decision-making capabilities, since accounts payable clerks who once did just data entry now review invoices and proactively look for irregularities and problems.

Mapco, like many other Premier 100 companies, is discovering the benefits of an interorganizational system. EDI has helped the company reduce personnel costs and improve the decision-making of its employees. More important, EDI has reduced Mapco's operating costs and enhanced the quality of its decisions.[11]

The ASAP online ordering system, discussed earlier, is being replaced with an interorganizational EDI system, OnCall EDI. OnCall EDI is a new order entry system that links hospitals with multiple vendors and runs on PCs with Microsoft Windows as the user interface. The system has a built-in database for tracking transactions, the ability to exchange information with a company's material management system, and instantaneous access to pricing information on thousands of products from many vendors. EDI is expected to reduce the cost of placing an order from between $30 and $40 to $12 and the cost of processing an order from between $24 and $28 to 32 cents.[13] Baxter Healthcare, whose proprietary ASAP online ordering system was one of the legendary strategic information systems, is replacing ASAP with a standards-based package that will not be owned by Baxter. Like OnCall EDI, the resulting multicompany system will enable all hospital suppliers to compete for business on an equal technological footing—exactly the opposite of ASAP's original mission.

The implications of OnCall EDI, developed by TSI International, are that hospitals no longer will be burdened with running and managing different proprietary ordering systems from different suppliers. Instead, they will have one system for ordering supplies from multiple vendors. Baxter's goal is to deliver information to its customers in a more timely fashion than its competitors. OnCall EDI software, which runs on PCs with Windows, includes a built-in database for tracking transactions and interfaces to material management systems. OnCall EDI provides communications support for direct links between hospitals and suppliers, dial-up access to third-party networks, and processing purchase orders.

Strategic Information Systems Plan (SISP)

Strategic business plan
A plan that identifies a company's goals as a means of achieving the organizational mission; also includes what is popularly referred to as SWOT analysis.

The strategy that a company chooses to follow in order to capture and retain markets and to achieve its mission is described in the **strategic business plan,** wherein the company identifies and defines its strategic mission and its overall goals. The strategic business plan also includes what is popularly referred to as the SWOT analysis: strengths, weaknesses, opportunities,

Strategic information systems plan (SISP)
Identifies the information systems and technologies that are vital to support a firm's business strategy; derived from the strategic business plan.

and threats in the marketplace. For further analysis of SWOT, see any introductory management textbook.

The **strategic information systems plan (SISP),** derived from the strategic business plan, identifies the information systems and technologies required to support the business strategy identified in the strategic business plan. An SISP is like a roadmap that helps IS managers determine where to go and how to get there by identifying current and future information requirements and matching these needs with existing systems and technologies to identify any potential gaps between what *is* available and what *should* be available to promote good decision making. In the process, the SISP identifies emerging technologies and explores the ways these technologies can strengthen the competitive posture of the company.

The SISP should specifically target the following four areas:[14]

♦ Aligning IS investment with business goals
♦ Exploiting information technologies for competitive advantage
♦ Ensuring the efficient management of IS resources
♦ Developing technology policies and practices

For example, the Dallas Police Department faced the same problems as other police departments all over the country: increasing crime and dwindling budgets. To improve efficiency, the department decided to build an information system that would integrate a hodgepodge of existing systems: phone, computerized dispatch, radio, and squad car terminals. The assistant chief of police and the director of information services for the City of Dallas created a strategic alliance that proved extremely beneficial for the city. The $3-million project that resulted has operated successfully for the last 5 years and has paid for itself over and over because of the increased productivity of its officers.

Under this system, when a citizen dials 911, the address and phone number of the caller appear on the terminal of a dispatcher, who electronically dispatches the message to the nearest patrol car via its mobile data terminal. This has reduced the time it takes to respond to a call and the number of people required to do the job. The system also allows officers access to federal and state criminal databases from their patrol cars, retrieving valuable information in seconds. This information often helps prepare an officer to face the situation at hand. The director of information services for the City of Dallas and the assistant chief of police maintain that their mutual respect and understanding for each other's knowledge and skills allowed them to successfully complete this mammoth project.[15]

Some of the steps involved in developing an SISP are summarized in Table 14–4.

Strategies for Developing an SIS

Strategic systems are among the most difficult to develop. Even if a company is successful in developing a strategic system, it is extremely difficult and challenging to maintain a strategic edge over the long term as competitors relentlessly pursue new ways to improve their operations. Researchers have studied many strategic systems with the goal of determining what makes a system successful. Are there any key ideas or guidelines that can help a company to achieve and maintain a competitive edge through strategic systems? Unfortunately,

TABLE 14-4
Steps involved in
developing an SISP.

Establish the purpose of the plan and develop a broad outline describing what the plan will address.

Update the strategic business plan and the goals of the business. Reassess the current business environment.

Identify the existing information systems including hardware, software, and networking capabilities. Determine future information needs and systems.

Identify the new systems, projects, and capabilities required to meet the changing environment and changing information needs.

Identify the resources required to implement the plan and to win the support of top management for the plan.

there are no set rules or formulas for building a successful strategic system, only some guidelines that may eventually lead to one; these are discussed in this section. In most cases, innovation, risk taking, and a good deal of luck seem to be the main ingredients of a successful strategic system.

An organization should ask two important questions before investing in strategic systems. Though these are asked before developing any kind of system, they assume particular importance in the case of strategic systems:

◆ Is the project financially feasible?
◆ Is the project technically feasible?

Is the Project Financially Feasible?

Strategic systems require substantial resources over an extended period of time, often with little or no guarantee of success. For example, it is estimated that Citicorp spent close to $3.25 billion to develop its Global Transaction Network; Sears invested close to $450 million on its interactive videotex system, which provides entertainment, home shopping, and banking services; Federal Express *lost* $350 million in an unsuccessful attempt to build an SIS.

Globex, the 24-hour international futures network once heralded as the leading edge of electronic trading, a network which would allow the free flow of transaction data all over the world, is another example of a strategic system that far exceeded initial cost estimates. After 7 years of planning and roughly 2 years of operation, Globex's volume has fallen far short of projections, the system has yet to turn a profit, and its financial backers are threatening to pull the plug on the network. The crisis at Globex is a reminder of just how difficult it is to build a strategic system.

The Globex launch was delayed at least a half dozen times by systems problems. An early version was deemed too slow; later versions were plagued by software glitches. Finally, in June, 1992, Globex began operation. But the system was several years late and cost $100 million to develop—$25 million more than originally anticipated. Demand was also much less than anticipated.[16]

The primary reason why strategic systems are risky financial ventures is that they are often ground-breaking systems with few or no precursors, so they must be justified on the basis of the business strategy they support. "SIS will have to be justified as a necessary component of strategy; the system is then justified to the same extent as the strategy in which it is embedded."[17] Justifying SIS primarily by financial standards is often futile.

Is the Project Technically Feasible?

Some great ideas for strategic systems have failed simply because they were not technically viable. Strategic systems require technologies that are well established, well understood, and widely accepted by users; otherwise, they are doomed from the start. For example, some years ago, when a New York bank invested more than $10 million to develop a strategic home banking system, it attracted fewer than 10,000 customers because home PCs were still a novel (and expensive) idea.

Sometimes the complexity of the technology can hinder the success of the system. For example, the efforts of Federal Express to develop a strategic electronic document transmission service failed because the firm was unable to solve the complexities of setting up global telecommunications. After investing close to $200 million, the company decided to take its losses and run.

State-of-the-art technologies and untested technologies can add a new and unexpected twist to the development of strategic systems. In the mid-1980s, American Express invested in an expert system for credit card approvals. However, AI technology was new and expensive, and few people had experience with it. This led to the eventual failure of a good idea, which would be implemented some years later when the technology stabilized.

Technical failures of strategic systems can even place the company at a strategic disadvantage. H&R Block, the tax preparation agency, created an SIS called Rapid Refund, which promised tax refunds one day after the tax forms were filed. Customer demand for the system far outweighed the company's initial estimates, so computing resources had to be expanded quickly by more than 50%. In spite of it, the technology was inadequate and unable to deliver on its promises. Although the goal of the new system was to increase customer satisfaction, many customers were so dissatisfied with the system and its failures that they took their business elsewhere.

Steps to Ensure Success of Strategic Systems

Re-engineering
Re-evaluating and radically redesigning the way in which a company does business; driven by the question, "Why do we do what we do?"

Once a company determines that the project is both financially and technically feasible, it must take five steps to ensure the success of its strategic systems. (See Table 14–5.) First, the organization should carefully study its business processes before investing in strategic systems. Today, many American corporations are actively involved in what is known as **re-engineering,** a term coined by Michael

---

TABLE 14–5
Five factors that contribute to the success of a strategic system.

Technology decisions should be grounded in a clear understanding of the processes that drive the technology.

Strategic systems should be driven by strategic alliances between trading partners.

Continuous improvement and investment in strategic systems are essential for their long-term success.

The organizational culture should encourage some risk taking.

Users must be fully trained if the full potential of the strategic system is to be achieved.

Hammer that refers to the process of re-evaluating and radically redesigning business processes before automating them. One of the reasons why ASAP was so successful was that it was based on sound business processes.

Second, strategic systems can succeed only if there is collaboration between business entities that crosses traditional organizational boundaries. Third, a strategic system can be successful over the long run only if the company is willing to invest in updating and maintaining it. In other words, the development of a strategic system is never really complete; instead, it is an evolutionary system that must be frequently updated and enhanced if it is to continue to benefit the company.

For example, although United Airlines was one of the first airlines to have a sophisticated online reservation system, APOLLO, the company failed to invest in system improvements. The result was that United was forced to invest an estimated $1 billion between 1986 and 1991 just to catch up with its competitors. Carrier, a New York–based manufacturer of heating, ventilation, and airconditioning (HVAC) equipment, developed a system that allowed users to design their own HVAC specifications. Although the system was capable of giving the company a strategic edge, Carrier's competitor, Trane, quickly developed a more sophisticated system, reducing the advantage given by the system to Carrier.

Sustainable competitive advantage The ability of a firm to introduce a product, service, or technique that provides an ongoing benefit of competitive significance.

The ability to continue to reap the competitive benefits of a strategic system long after it is developed is referred to as **sustainable competitive advantage.** Refer to Figure 14–2. For example, Federal Express has sustained its leading position in the delivery business because it continues to invest in its strategic systems. However, its arch-rival, United Parcel Service, faithfully plays catch-up with many of the features of FedEx's strategic systems. An SIS can provide sustainable advantage to a company under any one of these conditions:

- Competitors cannot duplicate the system and its advantages.
- Competitors cannot derive the benefits of the system even if they do duplicate it.
- Competitors do not wish to duplicate the system.

ATMs show how competitors *can* eventually diminish the competitive edge of a strategic system. Although Citicorp was the first to introduce ATMs, competitors soon joined forces and formed consortiums to reduce and eventually eliminate Citicorp's advantage. Similarly, when competitors developed reservation systems similar to SABRE, American Airlines' profit margin dropped almost 50% in just 2 years (1985–1987). Hence, continuous investment in strategic systems is vital to staying ahead of the competition.

Fourth, the organizational culture should encourage top managers to be "champions" and "passionate sponsors" who are willing to play a key role in the development and implementation of the system and encourage its use and acceptance by employees and customers.

Finally, the organization should have a pool of talented people with excellent technical skills and a good understanding of the business; this is fundamental to the development of complex and sophisticated information systems. The company must also be willing to invest in training, since strategic systems often fundamentally alter the way business is done. For example, Federal Express trained 22,000 couriers over a 10-month period, then trained another 23,000 people over a 5-month period, to become knowledgeable about its computerized tracking system. This was one of the largest technical training programs ever undertaken outside the military.[18]

Other factors that influence the success of a strategic system include involvement of customers from the early stages of system development, extensive marketing of the benefits of the system, building on the strengths of existing systems, and finding ways to circumvent organizational politics and bureaucracies to win approval for strategic systems.

Potential Barriers to Developing an SIS

Even if a company were to follow some of the strategies outlined above, it might still face many barriers to developing an SIS. Some of these barriers are identified in this section.

In a report titled "Systems Development Risks in Strategic Information Systems,"[19] two researchers, Chris Kemerer and Glenn Sosa, both of the Sloan School of Management, identified 11 barriers to the successful development of SIS, which are shown in Table 14–6. These barriers fall into three categories: defining, implementing, and maintaining strategic systems.

Problem Definition

Very few companies are successful at making innovative ideas practical, technically feasible, appealing, and affordable. This process is particularly difficult in organizations that do not encourage risk taking or experimentation and that penalize their employees for failure. Also, defining a strategic idea requires that business managers communicate clearly with technical managers. If the two groups cannot communicate clearly, this can be a barrier to the development of strategic systems.

Implementation

Even if companies cross the barriers to defining an idea, they often have a difficult time implementing it (American Express, for example). As is shown by the many cases discussed in this chapter, strategic systems rely heavily on telecom-

FIGURE 14–2:

The difference between the initial impact and the sustained impact of strategic information systems.

Source: "Strategic Information Systems Revisited: A Study in Sustainability and Performance," *MIS Quarterly*, March 1994, p. 42.

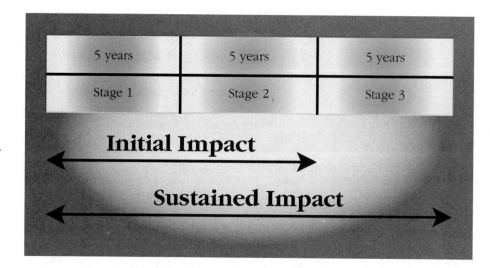

TABLE 14-6
Some of the development, implementation, and maintenance barriers to strategic information systems.

Development (Definition) Barriers

Generating workable ideas requires leadership and teamwork.

Many innovative ideas are technically infeasible.

Many innovative ideas are prohibitively expensive.

Many ideas die because they lack a sufficient market.

Implementation Barriers

Telecommunications increases the complexity of implementing SIS.

Multiple systems are difficult to integrate.

SIS systems often require interorganizational cooperation.

State-of-the-art technologies are difficult to implement.

Maintenance Barriers

Competitors can copy SIS.

Unanticipated demand can overwhelm the usefulness of an SIS.

Applications can be expensive to maintain or enhance.

High exit barriers can cause devastating losses.

munications and other leading-edge technologies; many companies lack the talent necessary to build such systems. Further, interorganizational systems require a great deal of cooperation among diverse departments; this is often hard to come by (ASAP, for example).

Maintenance

Companies that overcome the first two types of barriers are often stumped by the complexity of maintaining these systems so that they can sustain the advantages derived from them. Strategic systems are often expensive to maintain and can sometimes be an enormous drain on the corporate budget (SABRE, for example). When competitors diligently try to imitate the strategic idea, the success of a strategic system can be diminished (ATMs, for example). On the other hand, the company may be caught off guard by the unexpected success of a system and may not be prepared to meet the demand it places on corporate resources (H&R Block, for example).

Companies with limited financial resources, technological sophistication, and organizational flexibility will very likely face one or more of these barriers.

A Classic Tale of a Strategic Information System: SABRE

No discussion of strategic information systems is complete without a discussion of SABRE, the flight reservation system created by American Airlines. Since the system's introduction in 1962, American has enjoyed astronomical returns on its investment. It is estimated that between 1976 and 1986 the cumulative cash return from this system was over $900 million, producing an internal rate of return close to 70%. Less conservative estimates put the net contribution at $1.7 billion, a return of almost 130%. As of late 1991, SABRE had 85,000 terminals in 47 countries and provided fares and travel schedules for 665 airlines, accounting for almost 85% of the company's earnings.[20]

Since SABRE, many companies have ventured into developing strategic information systems, although few have been as successful as American. What are some important lessons that future developers of SIS can learn from the enormous success of SABRE? Four of these lessons are summarized in Table 14–7.[21]

Seek Leverage from Existing Systems

SABRE was not developed from scratch. It was the product of extensions and enhancements made to an existing information system that was clearly reliable. The company had in-house technological expertise that helped it to develop and operate a teleprocessing system that even today is regarded as one of the most technologically advanced information systems in the world.

Use Existing Knowledge to Grasp Opportunities

The company used data that were already available to identify new strategic opportunities in the marketplace. SABRE was not a groundbreaking idea to begin with. In fact, it emerged as a countermeasure to the reservation system APOLLO, which arch-rival United Airlines had developed. United offered its travel agents remote access to its APOLLO system. In order to counter this offer and to remain in a market that was becoming highly competitive, American made a similar offer to its travel agents. However, in the early stages of this offer, American noticed something very interesting when it analyzed the data that the reservation system was generating. Travel agents who used SABRE booked more passengers on American than they had before. In other words, simply by providing access to its

---

TABLE 14–7
Some of the lessons learned from the success of SABRE.

Seek leverage from existing systems:

SABRE was built on the strengths of an existing reservation system and emerged as a counter measure to a competitor's system. The company had in-house technological expertise that helped it to develop and operate a teleprocessing system that even today is regarded as one of the most technologically advanced information systems in the world.

Use existing knowledge to grasp opportunities:

By simply providing access to its internal information system, American Airlines increased its market share, capacity utilization, and revenues. As travel agents used the system to book passengers on *all* airlines, American realized that it had a wealth of customer information at its disposal.

Start early:

Companies that wait and watch often wait and lose. Because it started early, American had a wealth of proprietary knowledge about its travel agents, which it used to develop innovative systems.

Delegate authority:

American was highly successful in delegating authority and in ensuring excellent communications with all parties involved in the design, development, and implementation of SABRE.

internal information system, American had increased its market share, capacity utilization, and revenues. As travel agents used the system to book passengers on *all* airlines, American realized that it had access to a wealth of information. It came up with new programs and flight schedules to build customer loyalty and higher switching costs. In short, awareness of existing data led to a better understanding of the marketplace and eventually led to one of the greatest information technology success stories of our times.

"What began as a necessary competitive counter to a precipitous action on the part of a major competitor has now evolved into a project of significant financial magnitude to American Airlines. Further, it is occurring at a time when we are threatened with major regulatory changes which potentially could lead to a situation in which marketing information and even a limited control over the distribution mechanism could prove invaluable."[22]

Start Early

Companies that wait and watch often wait and lose. They lose valuable time while their competitors gain a competitive edge. Both United and American saw an opportunity and utilized its potential, with the result that today the two airlines together have more than 60% of the market share for automated travel agents. Because it started early, American gained a wealth of proprietary knowledge about the needs of travel agents, which it used for further offerings in its information system. American was an innovator and innovators are, by definition, making it up as they go along.[23]

Delegate Authority

Building an information system as huge and pervasive as SABRE is not an easy task. It cannot be accomplished by a few individuals, but demands a large group of people, with different functional skills, from all over the organization. American was highly successful in delegating authority and in ensuring excellent communications among all parties involved in the design, development, and implementation of SABRE. Table 14–7 summarizes the lessons learned by the firm.

 Summary

- **The far-reaching potential of strategic information systems.**

  Today, information systems are no longer support systems; they are strategic systems that can help a firm compete successfully in the global marketplace. A firm's strategic information systems are part of its strategy; they deliver products and services that play a prominent role in helping the company achieve its strategic goals. In this chapter, we have described information systems that gave companies a significant and sustained edge in the marketplace, attracted new customers, and increased the loyalty of existing customers.

- **Some common attributes of strategic information systems.**

  Strategic information systems have three common characteristics. Most of them rely heavily on telecommunications, they use several vendors to bring together several technologies, and they require the cooperation of several organizations. Most SIS rely heavily on telecommunications. Since SIS use several technologies, they often require the integration of products from several vendors; this can sometimes be a challenge. Finally, SIS require the cooperation of several companies and hence they often create new business partnerships.

- **The elements of a strategic information system plan.**

  A strategic information system plan (SISP) is derived from a strategic business plan and identifies the information systems and technologies required to support the strategy identified in the strategic business plan. The SISP should focus on making the most effective use of IS resources and on developing technology policies and practices that are in line with the company's overall business plan. Aligning the company's information systems plan with its business strategy is a top priority for executives who understand that such an alignment is the key to realizing the power of information systems and technologies.

- **Strategies for developing successful strategic systems.**

An organization should ask two important questions before developing a strategic information system: "Is the project financially feasible?" "Is the project technically feasible?" Although financial justification of information systems is often a challenging task, organizations should develop some cost estimates for the system. Also, the technical feasibility of strategic systems must be carefully analyzed, because strategic systems are often at the cutting edge of technology. Companies must also carefully study and improve their business processes before investing in strategic systems; they should be driven by strategic alliances with trading partners; and, finally, they must continue to invest in their strategic systems if they are to sustain their competitive advantage.

 Review Questions

1. What are some factors that have changed the role of information systems from that of support systems to that of strategic systems?
2. What is a strategic information system? "An information system is classified as a strategic system based on *how* it is used." Discuss.
3. What is the difference between external and internal strategic systems? Can you give an example of each?
4. Why is the ATM often cited as an example of an SIS?
5. What are the three characteristics of an SIS? Briefly describe each characteristic.
6. What are interorganizational systems? Give some reasons why IOS are on the increase.
7. Why is EDI viewed as an example of IOS? Describe any IOS that was discussed in this chapter.
8. What is an SISP? Why should the SISP be closely aligned with the strategic business plan?
9. Identify some strategies for developing and implementing successful strategic systems.
10. What is meant by sustained competitive advantage? What can a company do to achieve this advantage?
11. Identify some barriers to the successful development of strategic systems.

 Discussion Questions

1. CIOs who spend their time going over numerous drafts of a long-term strategic planning document are simply wasting their time, say some industry experts. Rapid changes in information technologies, particularly in software, coupled with economic constraints and fierce market competition, are making long-range planning somewhat obsolete. These experts believe that current conditions are too volatile for anyone to predict technology needs beyond the short term.

   In the past, it made a great deal of sense to try to forecast requirements and budgets well into the future. Today, IS executives will be judged not on how good the strategic plan looks, but instead on their ability to adapt quickly to unforeseen circumstances. In other words, what CIOs desperately need is contingency planning. Contingency plans create mechanisms for dealing with sudden, unexpected changes in a controlled fashion.[24]

   In this chapter we discussed some benefits of strategic planning. Are the experts right in saying that a CIO no longer needs a strategic plan? Discuss.

2. Describe McKesson's Economost and explain why it is a strategic system. Was the company able to sustain the competitive advantage provided by the system?

3. Find out whether your university has an SISP. If it does, describe the main elements of the plan. If it does not, develop a presentation for top university professionals explaining the merits of an SISP and how it should be developed.

ETHICAL ISSUES

Case 1: Credit Card Versus Debit Card

Strategic information systems can run into antitrust problems if they provide too much of a competitive advantage. Antitrust liability is one of the risks of SIS, particularly for companies that have a dominant share of the market. Antitrust suits focus on efforts to create or sustain monopolies, on unfair competition, on price fixing, or on actions that create barriers to entry into the market. In June 1989, 12 states filed suit against MasterCard and Visa, charging them with attempts to monopolize the market in an attempt to prevent debit cards from emerging as a successful alternative to the credit card industry. The companies had bought out all their competitors, thus effectively eliminating any competition to the credit card market.

Companies face the challenge of developing strategies to prevent customers from switching to their competitors. What, if any, did the credit card company do that might be construed as unethical?

Can buying out competitors be construed as unethical?

Case 2: Airlines Use Their Muscle

In August 1992, the House of Representatives passed the Airline Competition Enhancement Act of 1992, which makes it illegal for any reservation system provider to discriminate against a travel agent participating in its service. Airlines, such as American, have in the past flexed their muscles to ensure that travel agents subscribe to their reservation systems. The new law allows travel agents to choose the computer equipment that they will use to access a particular reservation system rather than being locked into equipment supplied by the reservation system's provider. The law will also make it easier for travel agents to switch from one reservation system to another. American has also been accused of biasing the displays of airline listings in such a way as to favor its own flights by failing to load data about other carriers into the database in a timely and accurate manner.

The chairman of American Airlines, however, feels that government intervention is wrong and that such "legislation is both unnecessary and completely inappropriate."

Do you agree with the chairman of American Airlines?

In the absence of such legislation, smaller companies often have a difficult time entering the market. On the other hand, big companies have invested millions of dollars in building strategic systems and should be allowed to derive the benefits of their systems. Discuss the pros and cons of legislating the airline reservation system.[25]

Case 3: Patenting Innovation and Creativity

A recent court decision gives corporations the green light to seek 17-year patents for their most innovative information systems. The July 29, 1994 ruling by the U.S. Court of Appeals for the Federal Circuit declared that a general-purpose computer controlled by a program can be patented because the program essentially creates a new machine. The potential for patents is greatest in the financial services industry, which is continually creating complex software-driven financial products. Until now there was a lot of uncertainty and debate about the possibility of patenting strategic information systems. Now they are patentable.

Despite the sometimes rough going on the patent trail, dozens of pioneering firms have already won patents for strategic information systems in hopes of locking in their competitive advantage. The most famous include Merrill Lynch, for its computer-based Cash Management Account (CMA), and Mrs. Field's, for its staff scheduling system.

The advantage of a patent is that it gives the holder 17 years of monopoly rights over the system. Competitors and even vendors have to pay royalties if they use or sell a patented system or risk a lawsuit for infringement. The patent process is costly (about $20,000) for the first application, which can be rejected, and the entire process takes about 2 years.

The increasing number of IS patents naturally leads to more litigation, too, such as the legal battle between Hallmark Cards, in Kansas City, Missouri, and arch-rival American Greetings in Cleveland. In a still-pending case, Hallmark charges that American Greetings' computer kiosks for creating custom greeting cards infringes on

(Continued on next page)

Hallmark's patent for a touch-screen greeting-card kiosk.[26] (Note: We discussed Hallmark's kiosks in Chapter 3.)

Do you think strategic information systems should be patented? Why or why not?

Competitors of firms that have successfully developed strategic systems may be completely eliminated if they are not allowed to imitate the industry leaders. Patents increase the risk of eliminating competition. Discuss.

PROBLEM SOLVING IN THE REAL WORLD

Case 1: Strategic Information Systems Planning for a Hong Kong Hospital

This case study illustrates the strategic planning process that was successfully used to develop a new market-oriented information system for the New Baltic Hospital (NBH) in Hong Kong.

Some years ago, the Hong Kong government established a private organization, the Hospital Authority, to oversee all government medical resources in the territory. NBH, consisting of nearly two dozen government or quasi-government hospitals, was affected by the policy change. Throughout its 30-year history, NBH was managed and operated by the health department of the Hong Kong government. Traditionally, some 75% of its expenses were paid by government subsidies; the remaining 25% came from private donors. The hospital's patient base of 400,000 paid only nominal amounts for "pay as-you-go" medical care. However, political leaders felt that there should be an arm's-length relationship between hospitals and the government and that cost-effectiveness would improve if subsidies were reduced. Accordingly, the government slashed public subsidies to the hospitals by 60% over a 3-year period.

NBH had to adapt quickly to drastic reductions in public funding, greater management autonomy in key areas such as financial management and marketing, growing accountability to the community, and a revised reporting relationship with the newly formed Hospital Authority. Senior management suddenly found itself facing new challenges. Dr. Leung, the hospital's chief administrator, quickly recognized that the new government policy would require NBH to adopt a market orientation. Thinking about patient needs and about the profitability of various hospital services had, until now, been low priorities for NBH administrators. But overnight, it became crucial for the hospital to create an image of care, dedication, efficiency, and value if NBH was to compete effectively against other facilities in the area. Success as a market-oriented organization would require a greater focus on efficiency and cost-consciousness.

NBH had two target markets: its patients and its donors. Patients would have to be persuaded that NBH best met their needs by offering the best services at a reasonable price and by helping them in their time of need. Donors would have to be convinced that their money would be well spent, that the hospital was worthy of their donations, and that their donations would be suitably recognized.

Administrators realized that in a market-oriented environment an information system that provided up-to-date information must be designed around these two primary groups: patients in the immediate community and potential donors in Hong Kong and throughout the world. However, explicitly identifying the information required to make good decisions and the ways in which this information should be tied to the business needs of the organization proved difficult and resulted in considerable discussion among managers and other hospital entities.

The hospital's mission was loosely defined as being a medical diagnostic and treatment center that delivered quality health care services to the neighboring population. Before developing a new information system, senior managers felt it was important to map their information needs to the following goals, which they felt were critical to fulfill the mission and meet the overall objectives of the hospital:

♦ Providing high-quality service by creating a caring environment and encouraging positive personnel attitudes
♦ Facilitating an efficient flow of patients through the referral, admission, treatment, and discharge processes
♦ Delivering clinical cures by increasing the efficiency of its treatment program
♦ Integrating and coordinating services and information within the hospital and between the hospital and related institutions
♦ Creating empathy with patients' families by providing custodial care and emotional support[27]

Hospital administrators were charged with the responsibility of developing an SISP that would link the hospital's mission and objectives with those of the IS department.

1. What are some factors that caused NBH to become a market-oriented company?
2. Develop an initial draft of an SISP to help NBH align its business goals with those of the IS department.

Case 2: McKesson Water

When an earthquake shook southern California in February 1994, it shut down many businesses, but provided McKesson Water Products, a $235-million division of Pasadena drug distributor McKesson, with a unique opportunity to test its newly renovated information system. The system passed with flying colors when it fielded hundreds of rush orders for bottled water after the region's public water system failed.

A few years ago, McKesson Water noticed that almost 87% of the tasks in just one area were nonvalue activities; just eliminating those activities would save the company $1 million. The firm realized that better business processes were critical if it was to retain its number one position in the U.S. market for noncarbonated bottled water delivery. Therefore, it embarked on a $5-million overhaul of its business, using information systems and technologies to re-engineer

(Continued on next page)

many of the new processes. Today, the company has a 20% market share, with four water brands in Arizona, California, Nevada, and Texas.

In particular, the company invested $1 million in a telecommunications switching and call processing system, which became the backbone of the company's teleservices center. The new system helped McKesson Water track missing inventory, which was often traced to inadequate route accounting controls. Under the old system, drivers, who acted as the sales force, would record on paper the number of bottles they took out with them. When they returned at the end of their shift, they would record both the number of bottles delivered and the number of bottles remaining in the truck and give the written record to their manager. All too often, the figures did not add up correctly, and the company had no way to account for the discrepancies. Today, McKesson Water has equipped workers with hand-held radio-frequency devices that are linked both to branch office PCs and to an IBM AS/400 minicomputer in the company's home office. Drivers can count the loads on their way in and out of the yard and the information is immediately updated in the database.

The next challenge was McKesson's customer service function, which one top manager defined as "torturous and labyrinthine." When a customer service rep was faced with a customer's problem, he or she often passed it off to a company specialist, who then looked into the matter and responded to the customer service rep, who would then call the customer back. The system was so inefficient that it would cost as much as $60 to settle a $5 service dispute.

McKesson's goal was to improve customer service. To do so, it consolidated telephone sales and customer-related operations from seven regional offices into a new teleservices center in Pasadena. The telecommunications switch directs calls to the service reps; each customer has an identification number, which allows the sales rep to pull up the customer's background on the screen. By having online access to a customer's account and updated product information, service reps can take appropriate and immediate action while the customer is still on the phone.

In a business where customer attrition is often high, McKesson Water has boosted its customer "save rate" (i.e., how often reps are able to retain customers who call to cancel their bottled water deliveries) from 3% to 24% between April and October of 1993; the "close rate" (measure of the number of inquiries that are converted to orders) increased from 30% to nearly 70%.

Signing up new customers is also much easier under the redesigned system. Under the old procedure, up to 100,000 addresses had to be looked up each year in guidebooks before they could be added to drivers' routes. Now an IBM RS/6000 workstation uses a geographic information system to instantly add new customers to the correct routes.

In the field, drivers formerly received new orders by calling their branch office daily. It was a time-consuming project whereby the drivers had to stop somewhere and call in, and someone at a terminal at the office had to read them their messages about new customers on their routes. Now the drivers receive customers' names, addresses, and orders instantly on pagers they wear on their belts. These and other changes helped McKesson Water cut somewhere between $6 million to $7 million in fixed costs while profits have continued to increase even in a highly competitive market.[28]

1. The new call processing system and customer service system are viewed as strategic systems that have helped McKesson Water improve profits, cut costs, and attract new customers. Explain how these systems can be viewed as strategic systems.
2. What are some measures that McKesson Water can take to ensure that competitors do not reduce or eliminate the competitive advantage provided by these systems?

Case 3: J. C. Penney

In recent years, J. C. Penney has not placed an order for Lee Jeans, because when the stock level for jeans becomes low, more jeans will automatically be shipped to the store. Buyers for J. C. Penney don't even have to make a telephone call to order the merchandise, thanks to an automated inventory management system developed by the manufacturer of Lee Jeans.

In the late 1980s, as VF, the manufacturer of Lee Jeans, became "big, sloppy, and arrogant," it faced a number of daunting problems: The company lost touch with its customers and was losing them to competitors; managers lacked the data to make good and timely decisions; production cycles were long and sales were declining. When profits dropped from $176 million to $81 million, the company took notice. One of the first steps it took to enhance productivity and improve profits was to develop a state-of-the-art inventory system.

The inventory management system, called *flow replenishment,* feeds up-to-date point-of-sale (POS) data to managers so that they can detect changes in customers' buying patterns and immediately modify production quotas. The system also monitors the level of jeans inventory for each customer and when a retailer's inventory reaches a predetermined level, the company automatically ships more jeans to that retailer. Flow replenishment also allows the company to be responsive to market changes, to monitor the quality of jeans, and to eliminate any customer-related problems.

The new system has played a significant role in turning things around for VF. Sales have steadily increased and the product life cycle (the time it takes from the time an idea is conceived till the product enters the store), which once used to be between 18 months and 2 years, has dropped to a few weeks. The system has also created strategic alliances between VF and its retailers. Industry analysts are giving the company high marks for its responsiveness to the needs of its customers and managers. "We can't pass price increases the way we did in the '80s. In order for us to reduce our costs, we had to fundamentally change the way we manufacture our products."[29]

1. Is flow replenishment an example of an interorganizational system? Discuss.
2. How did the inventory system help VF to improve its operations?

—— **References** ——

Bakos, J. Yannis. "A Strategic Analysis of Electronic Marketplaces." *MIS Quarterly* 15, no. 3 (September 1991).

Barrett, Stephanie S. "Strategic Alternatives and Interorganizational System Implementations: An Overview." *Journal of Management Information Systems* (Winter 1986–1987).

Barua, Anitesh, Charles H. Kriebel, and Tridas Mukhopadhyay. "An Economic Analysis of Strategic Information Technology Investments." *MIS Quarterly* 15, no. 5 (September 1991).

Clemons, Eric K. "Evaluation of Strategic Investments in Information Technology." *Communications of the ACM* (January 1991).

Feeny, David F. and Blake Ives. "In Search of Sustainability: Reaping Long-Term Advantage from Investments in Information Technology." *Journal of Management Information Systems* (Summer 1990).

Ives, Blake and Gerald P. Learmonth. "The Information System as a Competitive Weapon." *Communications of the ACM* (December 1984).

Johnston, H. Russell and Shelley R. Carrico. "Developing Capabilities to Use Information Strategically." *MIS Quarterly* 12, no. 1 (March 1988).

Keen, Peter G. W. *Shaping the Future: Business Design Through Information Technology.* Cambridge, MA: Harvard Business School Press, 1991.

Rackoff, Nick, Charles Wiseman, and Walter A. Ullrich. "Information Systems for Competitive Advantage: Implementation of a Planning Process." *MIS Quarterly* (December 1985).

—— **Notes** ——

1. Govoni, Stephen J. "Hot Ticket," *InformationWeek,* August 30, 1993, p. 28.
2. Lucas, H. C. and J. Turner. "A Corporate Strategy for the Control of Information Processing," *Sloan Management Review,* Spring 1982, pp. 25–36.
3. Clemons, E. K. "Information Systems for Sustainable Competitive Advantage," *Information & Management,* November 1986, pp. 131–136.
4. Palvia, Prashant C., James A. Perkins, and Steven M. Zeltman. "The PRISM System: A Key to Organizational Effectiveness at Federal Express Corporation," *MIS Quarterly,* September 1992, pp. 227–292.
5. Ciborra, C. U. "From Thinking to Tinkering: The Grassroots of Strategic Information Systems," *The Information Society,* March 23, 1992, volume 8, pp. 297–309.
6. Moriarty, D. D. "Strategic Information Systems Planning for Health Service Providers," *Health Care Management Review,* 1992, Vol. 17, No. 1, pp. 85–90.
7. Ciborra, C. U. "From Thinking to Tinkering: The Grassroots of Strategic Information Systems," *The Information Society,* March 23, 1992, volume 8, pp. 297–309.
8. Hagmann, Constanza and Cynthia S. McCahon. "Strategic Information Systems and Competitiveness," *Information and Management,* vol. 25 (1993), pp. 183–192.
9. Clemons, E. K., and M. Row. "A Strategic Information System: McKesson Drug Company's Economost," *Planning Review,* September-October, 1988, pp. 14–19.
10. Ciborra, C. U. "From Thinking to Tinkering: The Grassroots of Strategic Information Systems," *The Information Society,* March 23, 1992, volume 8, pp. 297–309.
11. Runge, D., and M. Earl. "Gaining Competitive Advantage from Telecommunications." In M. Earl ed., *Information Management: The Strategic Dimension* (Oxford: Clarendon Press 1993), pp. 125–146.
12. Jenkins, Mary. "Get Connected," *Computerworld Premier 100,* September 19, 1994 pp. 26–32.

13. Betts, Mitch. "EDI Cures Ills of Hospital Supply Procurement," *Computerworld,* May 16, 1994, pp. 63, 66.
14. Earl, Michael J. "Experiences in Strategic Information Systems Planning," *MIS Quarterly,* March 1993, pp. 1–20.
15. Santosus, M. "Strategic Pairings," *CIO,* October 1990, pp. 106–108.
16. Wilson, Linda. "Future Bleak for Globex: Trader Losing Long-Fought Automation Struggle," *InformationWeek,* March 7, 1994, pp. 131–32.
17. Lucas, H. C. and J. Turner. "A Corporate Strategy for the Control of Information Processing," *Sloan Management Review,* Spring 1982, pp. 25–36.
18. Margolis, N. "High Tech Gets It There on Time," *Computerworld,* July 2, 1990, p. 77.
19. Eckerson, Wayne. "Study Identifies Pitfalls to Strategic IS Net Projects," *Network World,* July 2, 1990, pp. 17–18.
20. Copeland, D. G. "So You Want to Build the Next SABRE System?" *Business Quarterly,* Winter 1991, pp. 56–60.
21. Ibid.
22. Ibid.
23. United States District Court, Central District of California, American Airlines Document AA080717.
24. Yosri, Akram. "Say Goodbye to Strategic Planning," *Computerworld,* August 30, 1993, p. 33.
25. McPartlin, John P. "Reservation Systems are Up in the Air," *InformationWeek,* August 17, 1992, p. 14.
26. Betts, Mitch. "Ruling Opens Door to Software Patents," *Computerworld,* September 5, 1994, p. 73.
27. Martinsons, Maris G. and Suzanne Hosley. "Planning a Strategic Information System for a Market-Oriented Non-Profit Organization," *Journal of Systems Management,* vol. 44, no. 2, February 1993, pp. 14–19.
28. Bartholomew, Doug. "Keeping Water Flowing in L.A.," *InformationWeek,* February 14, 1994, pp. 41–42.
29. Cafasso, Rosemary. "Jean Genies," *Computerworld,* June 14, 1993, pp. 101–102.

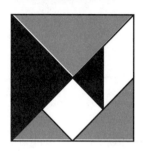

15

Managing Information Resources

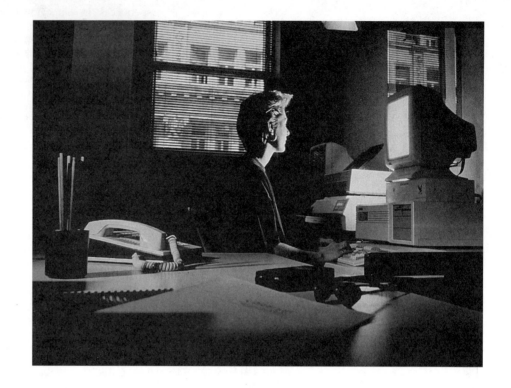

Contents

Learning Objectives
Technology Payoff: The Department of the Treasury
Introduction
What Is IRM?
Principles of Managing Information Resources
Objectives of IRM
IRM Functions
    Technology Management
    Data Management
    Distributed Management
    Functional Management
    Strategic Management
    End-User Management
Summary
Review Questions
Discussion Questions
Ethical Issues
    Case 1: Fear the FBI
    Case 2: Inflation Is Not Welcome
Problem Solving in the Real World

Case 1: TIAA-CREF Uses Systems to Delight Customers
Case 2: Coopers Embraces the Age of Technology
References
Notes

Learning Objectives

Earlier chapters of this book have emphasized the importance of information to the growth and success of an organization. Information must be managed and protected like any other corporate resource, such as manpower, machines, materials, and money. In this chapter, we discuss some basic principles for managing both information and the resources that create, process, and disseminate it. The study of managing information resources is referred to as information resource management (IRM) and is the focus of this chapter.

After reading and studying this chapter, you should be able to:

- Describe IRM and how it helps an organization
- Identify the four principles of managing information resources
- Understand the objectives of IRM
- Identify and describe the six functions of IRM

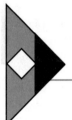

TECHNOLOGY PAYOFF

The Department of the Treasury

The U.S. Department of the Treasury, which has spent close to $3 billion in the last few years on IS services, is now undertaking a 10-year, $850-million project to revamp the department-wide communications systems for its 14 treasury bureaus, including the Internal Revenue Service (IRS), Customs, and the Secret Service.

The new communications project, called the Treasury Communications System (TCS), will analyze the technology required to meet the information needs of three very different classes of users: top executives, system managers, and end-users. This implies identifying and analyzing all aspects of information technology, such as hardware, software, databases, networking, and development applications, that are necessary to meet the changing information needs of this organization.

Developing such a large-scale system often requires the collaboration of a large number of vendors. In the past, the agency provided vendors with a set of predetermined specifications and the vendors would bid based on these specifications. Unfortunately, many of these specifications became obsolete even before the system was built. Today, the U.S. Treasury is adopting a pragmatic procurement policy that will help it to stay ahead of the technology game. In this proactive approach, the federal government will describe its information needs to the vendors, and it will be the responsibility of the vendors to develop viable technical solutions to meet those needs. Vendors who develop specifications that become outdated even before the system is installed are likely to be penalized. This new procurement policy will greatly reduce technological obsolescence and will allow the government to stay on the leading edge of technology.

This is what IRM is all about: ensuring that the information needs of the end-user are met in the most effective manner possible; developing policies and principles that will protect the information resources of an organization and will put existing resources to the best possible use.[1]

Information is a valuable national resource no less essential to the survival of government, industry, and the individual citizen than are human, material, or natural resources. Information is a resource that is in need of conservation, recycling, and protection.

—Commission on Federal Paperwork (1977)

Introduction

Many companies have succeeded through the innovative use of information systems and technologies. Thus, information, information systems, and information technologies should be treated as strategic resources and should be managed like other corporate resources, such as people, machines, materials, and money. The study of managing information and its associated components is referred to as information resource management (IRM).

Managing information resources requires a broad perspective on information, its uses, and its impact on the goals and the mission of the organization. Various entities that influence, and are influenced by, information, such as people, policies, procedures, products, and internal and external business entities, must collaborate for IRM to be effective. The story of the U.S. Treasury Department (see opening vignette) shows that the government invests large sums of money in information systems and technologies; in order to get good returns on these investments, it is essential to manage and monitor information-related resources. The Treasury Department is ensuring that it gets the best possible returns by establishing policies that require vendors to provide state-of-the-art technology at the best possible price, while protecting the agency from the risk of technological obsolescence.

Earlier chapters have emphasized the importance of promoting information stewardship rather than information ownership. Understanding the objectives, principles, processes, and philosophy of IRM is the first step toward being a good steward of information. Table 15–1 identifies some forces that are shaping the way IRM is viewed by the organization.

What Is IRM?

In broad terms, **information resource management (IRM)** refers to policies, principles, and processes that effectively manage all components of an organization that collect, store, process, retrieve, and disseminate information. As seen in Figure 15–1, these components include hardware, software, databases, telecommunications, different types of information systems, such as TPS, MIS, ISS,

Information resource management (IRM)
The process of managing all the components of an information system that collect, store, process, retrieve, and disseminate information. These resources include hardware, software, networks, systems, and personnel.

TABLE 15–1
Forces that are shaping management's views of IRM.

♦ Information technology is growing and changing rapidly. Expectations as to what information systems can do for an organization have increased greatly in the last few years.

♦ Increasingly, top management is dissatisfied with the poor returns and inadequate performance of information systems. As corporate resources become tighter, there is increased pressure to put existing resources to better use.

♦ Information systems are no longer regarded as just an operational tool. More and more managers realize that if utilized creatively, IS can provide a strategic advantage that competitors find hard to overcome.

and OAS, management structures, strategic information systems (SIS), IS personnel, and end-users. According to the Office of Management and Budget (OMB), IRM can be defined as "the planning, budgeting, organizing, directing, training, and controlling of information systems and its associated elements. The term encompasses both information and its resources, such as personnel, equipment, funds, and technology." IRM is a multidisciplinary approach that is closely linked to the overall mission and objectives of the organization and permeates all aspects of the organization's culture.

The Paperwork Reduction Act of 1980 was the first major legislation that recognized information as a valuable resource. Under this act, agencies that managed information for the government were required to comply with the information

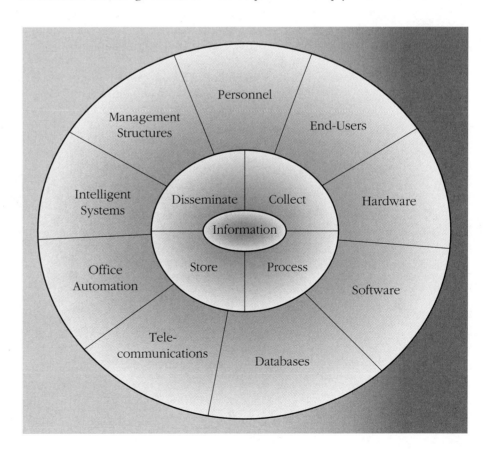

FIGURE 15–1

Some of the information-related resources that must be managed in an organization.

policies, principles, standards, and guidelines prescribed by OMB. Today, all government agencies are required by law to report their IRM policies, plans, and procedures to Congress. This makes good sense, because information is the end product of many government agencies, so they should be evaluated according to how well they manage their information resources. The act also made many organizations take a good look at how they manage their information resources. Today, IRM is considered a vital part of good decision making.

Principles of Managing Information Resources

Companies that are successful users of information, information systems, and information technologies follow well-established IRM policies and principles, and in particular, they share the four principles described below.

Principle 1: The IS department should be managed like any other unit or division of the business.   Basic principles of management, such as planning, organizing, staffing, directing, and controlling, that are applied to the various disciplines in an organization, (e.g., finance, production, marketing, and human resources) should also be applied to information systems and management. The argument that the IS department and its technical personnel *cannot* be managed using classic management principles is weak and disruptive and often leads to gross inefficiencies and mismanaged growth. This is not to say that the IS department does not have certain unique characteristics that separate it from other departments; only that those differences should not be used as excuses for managing the IS department poorly.

Principle 2: The sole purpose of information systems is to help the organization meet its goals and objectives.   A common complaint of CEOs and other top

IRM is the responsibility of all managers.

managers is that the CIO and the IS personnel have a limited understanding of the business and the industry in which it operates. Top management often complains that IS personnel are more interested in acquiring the latest technology than in fully utilizing existing technologies. Technology for the sake of technology often results in a poor return on IT investments and leads to disillusionment about the power of technology in achieving the goals of the organization.

Good IRM policies emphasize and promote aligning technology investments with business goals. In other words, IS personnel in organizations with good IRM practices often have a sound understanding of the business and its details and therefore strive continuously to find technologies that will enhance the strength of the company. When the IS department understands that its primary role is to support the rest of the organization in achieving its overall mission and goals, the CEO and the CIO become partners, rather than adversaries.

Principle 3: IRM is the responsibility of all managers, regardless of their discipline or function. IRM is the responsibility of all functional managers who are involved, directly or indirectly, in the creation, collection, storage, use, manipulation, and dissemination of information. Treating IRM as a function of the IS department reflects a narrow and limited view, one that often results in gross inefficiencies and poor management of information and information-related resources. In Chapter 11, Business Information Systems, we looked at the effects of information systems on the various functional areas in an organization; many examples showed the positive impact of information systems on profits, productivity, and people, emphasizing the active participation of all employees.

Most organizations that utilize the power and potential of information systems to achieve their goals firmly believe in and practice IRM policies and principles. In such organizations, IRM is an enterprise-wide effort. Therefore, it is not surprising that there is a tendency today to hold functional managers, regardless of their specialization, responsible not only for their own job functions but also for managing the information generated by their units. The efforts to build integrated, cross-functional, customer-oriented systems can be successful only if IRM becomes central to corporate life.

Principle 4: The commitment of top management is the key to realizing the full potential of information resources. Throughout this book, we have emphasized that the success of information systems and information technologies depends to a great extend on the commitment of top management to using technology in new ways to achieve the goals of the organization. A short-term commitment to some technologies will not do; neither will technology investments for the sole purpose of immediate gains help the organization. If top management is lukewarm in its commitment to IRM and in the implementation of IRM policies, employees will treat IRM as a "buzzword" that will eventually be forgotten. What is required is a long-term commitment to technology; and this often demands vision, some risk taking, and the ability to apply technology in new ways. Often this requires that top management be well versed in the *management* of information systems and technology, though not necessarily in possession of detailed *technical* knowledge about information systems. Good IRM policies will shift technical responsibilities and decisions to the IS department, while providing top managers with good technology management skills.

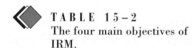

TABLE 15–2
The four main objectives of IRM.

- ◆ **To effectively utilize information resources** in order to achieve the overall goals and mission of the organization.
- ◆ **To inventory, document, and control all resources** that create, process, store, and disseminate information.
- ◆ **To create a model of the enterprise** from an information point of view in order to improve communications, both within and outside the organization.
- ◆ **To emphasize the reusability of information,** eliminate or reduce data redundancy, and ensure that all internal systems are developed within a common framework so that systems developed on different platforms can communicate with each other.

Objectives of IRM

Why does an organization need IRM and what are the objectives of IRM? Organizations need IRM so that they can be effective in managing their data, information, knowledge, information systems, and information technology. The four main objectives of IRM are presented in Table 15–2. The first objective of IRM is to use information in the most effective manner possible. This requires that the right information, in the right format, be made available to the right decision maker at the right time. Simply collecting data and generating reports is not enough; it is important to closely monitor the way those reports are used by decision makers and the additional information they need to increase the quality of their decisions.

Second, as an organization grows and expands, it is easy to lose track of its information resources such as hardware, software, telecommunications, databases, and the like. When managers do not have a clear idea and a detailed accounting of existing resources, the result is often haphazard growth and incompatible systems. This can have a negative impact on the overall productivity of the organization by creating major information-flow bottlenecks. Keeping an inventory of existing information resources is therefore more than just an accounting function. It can make all the difference in an organization's ability to build integrated systems rather than being burdened with incompatible systems.

One way to address this problem is through standardization, which requires the company to establish a set of plans and policies that guide the purchase of hardware, software, and other information-related items. For example, a company may establish a standardization policy for word processing packages that requires all employees to use only Microsoft Word or only WordPerfect; it may have a standardization policy for its PCs that requires them all to be IBM-compatible; and so on.

There are other benefits of standardization. It provides an ethical framework for managers in the purchasing department of an organization and limits opportunities for favoritism or nepotism. Other benefits include lowering the costs of hardware and software, simplifying IS training needs, reducing maintenance costs, and increasing productivity. Unfortunately, despite the many benefits of standardization, only one in four Fortune 500 companies currently has standards for hardware and software.

Let us look at some companies that have benefited from standardization. Inland Steel Industries, a $4-billion company, found that although its computers were churning out about 84 million pages of data, employees were often complaining that they did not get the right information at the right time. When the company investigated the problem, it found that its systems were highly compartmentalized and therefore decision makers could rarely get the information that would let them see the "big picture." Further, there was no strategic information plan detailing what the company should do to meet its current and future information needs, so individual departments within the organization were making their own technology decisions. In order to resolve this problem, the company formed an information technology council, made up of managers from all over the company, to coordinate investments in IT and ensure standardization of the company's information systems. The move increased productivity, reduced employee frustration, and led to increased utilization of information systems.[2]

Another example of the benefits of standardization is provided by Grumman Data Systems, an aerospace and electronics defense contractor in Bethpage, New York. Some years ago, each business unit in the company made its own technology decisions without any concern for compatibility with existing systems in the organization. The company found that its 10 divisions had about 30 PC brands, making it increasingly difficult to monitor and approve new purchases, perform system maintenance, and provide technical training to employees. In 1987, in response to an urgent need to better manage its growing networks and to control costs, the company formed a standards committee, which standardized about 1,300 information-related products and reduced the number of PC brands from 30 to 6. This standardization effort greatly reduced the cost of buying and managing information technologies and providing training. Productivity improved and the flow of information within the organization was greatly accelerated.[3]

The third objective of IRM is to build a good understanding of the information inflow and outflow in an organization. Only when managers know the information inflow and outflow can they be successful at managing them. Managers should also be aware of who uses the information, when, how, and for what purpose. This is essential for employees to avoid becoming "paper pushers" and being overwhelmed by the number of reports generated in the organization. A good knowledge of data inflow and outflow is essential to an understanding of issues such as where to acquire information, how to use that information, who are the other decision makers in the organization who use that information, and so on.

Finally, IRM aims to eliminate redundancy of information and increase the reusability of information that is already present within the organization. Recall our discussion of reusability in Chapter 4, Software, where we outlined the many benefits of reusability. Today, reusability is an important consideration for IS managers as they search for ways to derive the maximum return from their investments in information systems and technologies. Reusability can be achieved only if the three objectives described above are achieved.

Why are IRM objectives so important to a company? Without IRM objectives and policies, decisions are of poor quality because decision makers do not get the right information at the right time or because information is undervalued in the company. Employees may have a very narrow view of information, seeing it as the responsibility of the IS department, and top managers may have little or no commitment to promoting the use of information systems and technologies to achieve the overall goals of the organization. Without clear objectives, organizations will be burdened with incompatible systems that create major information bottlenecks within the organization. Other problems include information mismanagement, acquiring technology for technology's sake, obsolescence, hostile relations between the IS department and end-users, and projects with cost over-runs and missed deadlines. Figure 15–2 illustrates some of these problems.

For example, when HFSI, a subsidiary of Bull HN, in McLean, Virginia, changed its business focus from selling hardware to providing system integration services, it first had to overhaul the company's 22 internal standalone business systems. The company realized that in order for it to be successful with its new line of services, it first had to establish sound IRM policies and principles. Based on interviews with 200 upper-level employees, IS planners prescribed specific technologies that would effectively support and integrate different business functions. Today, HFSI has a set of well-integrated information systems that are well synchronized with the goals of the business.[4]

IRM Functions

IRM can be broadly divided into six functions:

- Technology management
- Data management
- Distributed systems management
- Functional management
- Strategic management
- End-user management

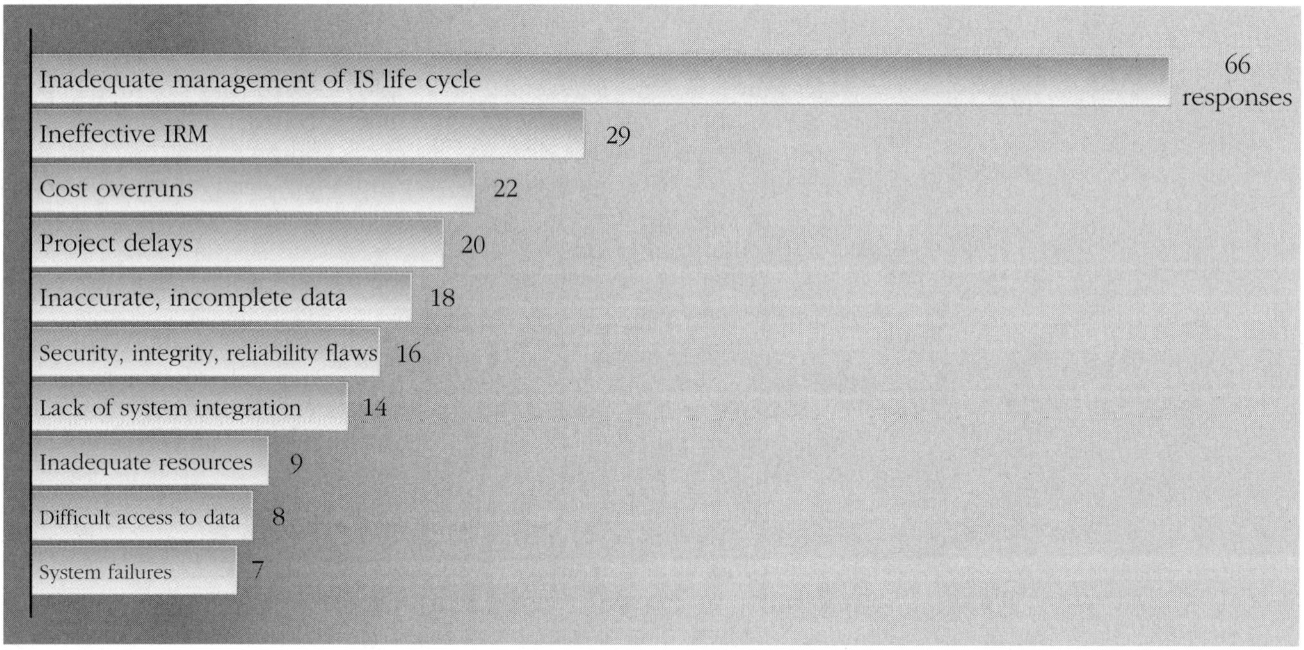

FIGURE 15–2

The top 10 IS headaches faced by managers. Many of these problems are attributable to poor or nonexistent IRM plans and policies.

Source: General Administrative Office, *Computerworld*, May 18, 1992, p. 20.

Figure 15–3 illustrates these functions visually. Note that many of these IRM functions were covered in earlier chapters, so that this section will summarize concepts that were introduced earlier in the book.

Technology Management

Technology management is the process of managing the information technologies that an organization uses to meet its information needs, including hardware, software, telecommunications, and different types of information systems, such as TPS, MIS, ISS, OAS, and strategic information systems. As an organization grows in size and complexity, the task of technology management becomes more challenging. IT managers must develop policies and procedures to ensure that existing technologies are put to the best possible use and closely monitor emerging technologies to make sure there is a good fit between new technologies and the information needs of the business. Technology inventory management and standardization, as discussed earlier, are also important aspects of technology management.

Parson's model of the impact of IT on industry, firm, and strategy is shown in Table 15–3. Managing information technologies requires a good understanding of three factors:

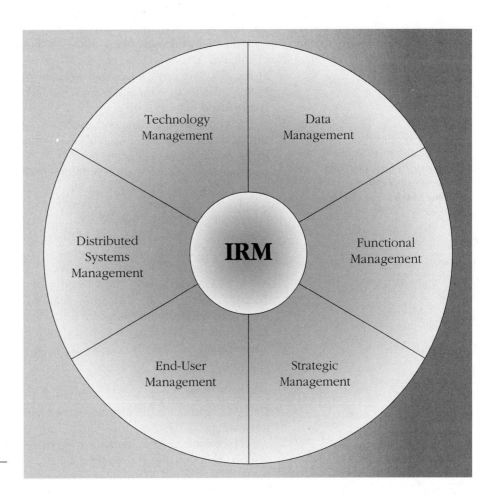

FIGURE 15–3

The six functions of IRM.

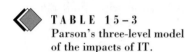

TABLE 15–3
Parson's three-level model
of the impacts of IT.

Industry	IT changes an industry's: ♦ Product and services ♦ Markets ♦ Production economics
Firm	IT affects competitive forces: ♦ Buyers ♦ Suppliers ♦ Substitution ♦ New Entrants ♦ Rivalry
Strategy	IT affects strategy: ♦ Low-cost leadership ♦ Production differentiation ♦ Concentration on product or market niche

♦ The strategic orientation of the organization
♦ The competitive elements of the firm
♦ The characteristics of the industry in which the firm operates

Several chapters of this book have emphasized the importance of integrating technologies with these three themes. The main challenge of technology management is not so much the technology itself as it is the planning, controlling, coordinating, and monitoring the acquisition, implementation, and maintenance of different technologies. Imagine the challenges of managing the technologies at the U.S. Treasury Department (our opening example), which spends several billion dollars on information systems and technologies located in geographically dispersed units and offices.

Technology management also lays the foundation for building **open systems,** which allow the free exchange of files, programs, and databases among multivendor hardware platforms (such as systems from IBM, DEC, Hewlett-Packard, and so on) or between different types of computers, such as mainframes, minicomputers, and microcomputers.

For example, the United States Department of Agriculture (USDA) has made a concentrated effort to move to open systems (see box) by initiating the Info Share Project. The primary goal of this project is to facilitate the flow of information between farmers and the different subagencies of the USDA. Before the open systems architecture was implemented, it took many days, a long paper trail, and many bureaucratic procedures to provide farmers with necessary information. Today, farmers can link their individual PCs to the agency's network and directly retrieve the necessary information from various databases residing on USDA's different systems. This has eliminated data redundancy and promoted a better relationship between the agency and the customers that it serves.

Open system

A group of systems that communicate with each other. In such a system, files, programs, and databases can readily be transferred from one system to another.

Data Management

Data management is the process of managing data and all resources that are used to create, process, store, disseminate, and maintain organizational data. Data may be in electronic or document form (up to 90% of information still takes the form of documents); data can be created manually or automatically. Regardless of the

USDA's Info Share Project

The United States Department of Agriculture (USDA) is one of the largest federal agencies in the country. It supervises more than 40 agencies and employs more than 124,000 people in 15,000 locations all over the world, with a budget of $60 billion and assets worth $140 billion.

To facilitate both internal and external communications, this mammoth organization has created the Info Share Project, a collection of projects whose aim is to provide the agency with significant operating efficiencies and decision-making abilities. In particular, the goal of the USDA project is to promote the free flow of information among different systems in the organization. Many large organizations find that although they have invested millions, or even billions, of dollars on information systems, many systems in the organization cannot communicate with one another. This often leads to data redundancy, gross operating inefficiencies, and information mismanagement. The agency is therefore focusing its efforts on building systems that can freely communicate with each other—that is, open systems.

For example, one of the systems proposed under the Info Share Project will affect about 45,000 farmers who can access a repository of government data from their own PCs. This replaces a manual system that often involved exchanges of papers between the farmers and the agency; often farmers had to drive long distances simply to get the information they needed.

The new system is expected to change all that. Farmers can link their individual PCs to the USDA's network. This will provide them with access to agricultural databases that the agency maintains on different systems. Before the new system was installed, it was difficult to retrieve the relevant information because the databases resided on different systems that did not communicate with each other. Today, at least some of the major databases are part of an open system architecture; this promotes the free flow of information between the agency and the many farmers that it serves.[5]

form or the medium used to create and maintain data, data are valuable organizational resources that must be actively managed, carefully protected, and efficiently utilized. The problems of managing data was covered in Chapter 6, Databases.

Kaiser Permanente of Northern California is a chain of 30 hospitals and medical clinics, a $2.5-million member health maintenance organization (HMO), and an insurance company. As the company diversified into different markets, hospital data was often stored in diverse, incompatible systems, making the task of data management time-consuming and error-prone. The hospital integrated the data residing in different locations and provided users with a uniform and a single logical view of relevant data. It allows doctors to monitor the cost-effectiveness of different medical treatments and even to select the best combination of treatments for the patient.[6]

Distributed Management

Computer-based information systems are usually centralized, decentralized, distributed, or some combination thereof. Figures 15–4a, 15–4b, and 15–4c show the differences among these three forms of technology management.

In a **centralized environment,** all computer facilities, systems, and resources are installed in a central location and are then linked to other business units through telecommunications networks. A centralized environment provides users with access to large systems and resources that might otherwise be unaffordable. Further, since all resources are in one central location, it is often easier

Centralized environment

All computer facilities, systems, and resources are in one central location and other parts of the organization are linked to this central facility through telecommunication networks.

FIGURE 15-4a

A distributed environment. Distributed systems are systems in different locations that are linked through a network.

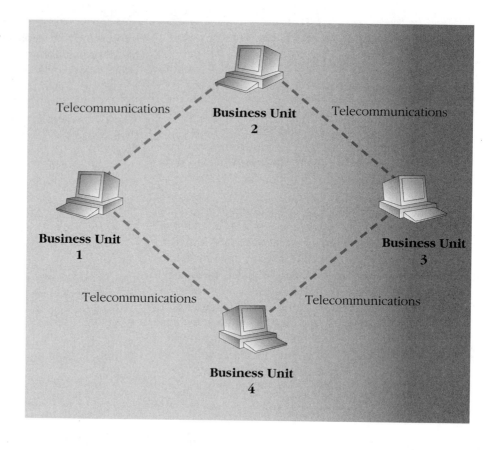

to manage and monitor them. Today, however, there are only a few organizations that still operate under a fully centralized environment, primarily because of significant advances in building small yet powerful machines, declining prices of computer hardware, the increasing sophistication of end-users, and continuous re-engineering efforts.

Decentralized environment
Each individual site designs, develops, acquires, and maintains systems that meet its local needs.

In a **decentralized environment,** each individual site or business unit is free to acquire and develop systems that meet its local information needs; therefore, each business unit is responsible for the acquisition, development, and maintenance of its own systems. The greatest advantage of a decentralized approach to information systems is that end-users have greater control over their systems and the information they generate. Users can customize their systems to meet their own needs and often have easy and timely access to information.

The debate over centralization versus decentralization is an ongoing one; the pendulum swings from one environment to the other every few years. Both types of environments have their advantages and disadvantages and are influenced by a number of factors such as organizational structure, management style, corporate culture, resource availability, and the information needs of decision makers. In order to possess the best of both worlds, some organizations centralize some IS functions and decentralize others. (For example, the payroll function may be centralized and marketing may be decentralized.)

Distributed systems
Multi-vendor systems that reside on different types of computers, such as PCs and mainframes, that are linked by networks.

Distributed systems are collections of systems developed by different vendors (such as IBM, Apple, DEC, Hewlett-Packard, and so on) on different types

FIGURE 15–4b

In a centralized IS environment, all computer facilities, systems, and resources are in one central location and other parts of the organization are connected to this central facility through telecommunications networks.

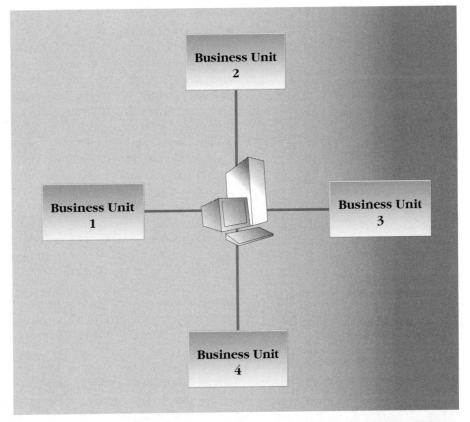

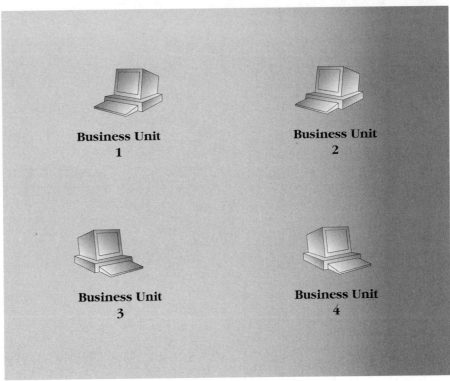

FIGURE 15–4c

In a decentralized IS environment, each business unit designs, develops, and maintains its own information systems.

of computers (such as PCs, minicomputers, and mainframes) and linked together through telecommunications.

For example, Snapple, the manufacturer of a very popular juice drink, uses the distributed systems to stay ahead in the highly competitive beverage market. Although the company's sales had doubled every year starting in 1988, in 1993, the company found itself facing stiff competition as giants such as Coca-Cola, Pepsi, Nestle SA, and Lipton entered the fruit juice market through strategic partnerships. Snapple recognized that one way to stay ahead of the competition was to stay on the cutting edge of information systems and technologies, and made the decision to switch to a distributed environment. Now the company has electronic links with its suppliers and distributors; these links are essential if the company is to maintain its leadership.

Today, distributed computing has become the norm as more and more companies have realized its potential to effectively delegate authority and responsibility throughout the organization and thus to support remote decision making. Figure 15–5 shows that 60% of the companies surveyed have implemented distributed computing and another 25% (17% + 8%) are planning to implement it or are considering implementing it.

Companies frequently decentralize before they become distributed. Each user may get a PC as a first step toward decentralization, then after decentralization is achieved, companies may address the problems of linking these units. Clearly, this approach has its problems, since linking decentralized systems to build a distributed environment is not always as easy as starting from scratch.

Some advantages of distributed computing include lower operating costs, better customer service, and better information flow because of easier access to data. The disadvantages of distributed computing are that as employees gain

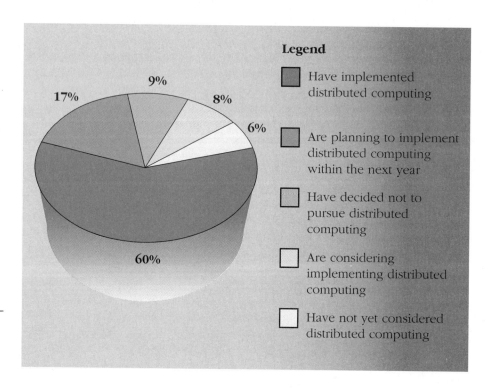

FIGURE 15–5

Statistics on the use of distributed computing. Note that distributed computing is increasing in popularity.

access to information residing on multiple systems, problems such as data redundancy and security violations are likely to increase.

Distributed management is the task of managing information resources in a distributed environment, which includes network administration, database administration, systems integration, system security, system maintenance, and end-user support.

Distributed management
Policies and procedures designed to manage the distributed systems in an organization.

Functional Management

See Figure 15–6. This book has emphasized the importance of integrating the various functional units in a business through cross-functional customer-oriented information systems. This is the only way to gain a total and uniform view of the customer. Although a number of systems, in the early days, were built as compartmentalized units, today the goal is to understand and manage the different functions and integrate them into a unified whole. This, as we have pointed out earlier, is not an easy task. Functional management is the task of integrating the information flows among the various functional units in a business.

Strategic Management

Strategic information systems (SIS) were covered in detail in the preceding chapter. Strategic management is the task of managing strategic systems and all resources that are strategic for the success of the company (see Table 15–4.) In particular, strategic information systems should be updated and maintained if they are to provide sustained benefits to the organization.

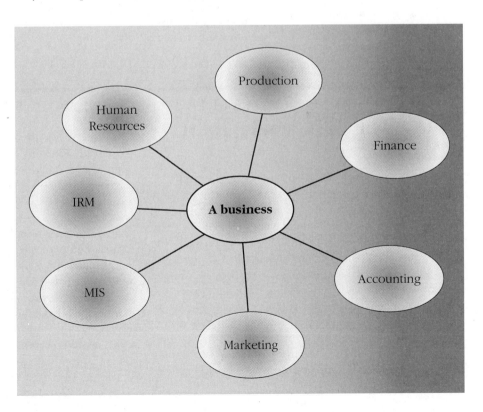

FIGURE 15–6

The IS department must be treated like any other functional unit in the organization.

TABLE 15-4
Facts that can help a
company to develop
strategic information
systems.

Strategic systems need a sponsor at the highest level.

Strategic systems have to be effectively marketed.

Strategic systems should be built on an existing infrastructure.

Strategic systems should be customer-oriented.

Sometimes strategic systems result from collaboration between allies; and in such cases, managing such systems becomes even more challenging. For example, the Electronic Joint Venture (see box) is a strategic system that was initiated through the cooperative efforts of six Wall Street firms, which led to significant advantages that each firm operating individually could not have attained. However, the continued success of such systems requires careful management and monitoring by all parties involved.

End-User Management

End-user management
Managing end-users, who are vital
links in an organization's
information chain, to properly
manage and maintain their
information systems.

End-user management was covered in detail in Chapter 12, System Analysis and Design. As you may recall, in the 1960s and 1970s, the task of managing the information resources of an organization was strictly the job of the IS department. However, by the mid-1980s, end-users had become active participants in developing and managing information systems, thus changing IRM from an IS function to a management function.

Although there are many advantages to sophisticated end-users and end-user computing, end-user computing is a double-edged sword. If the end-users are not properly managed, the results can include ad hoc development of informa-

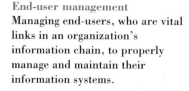

BUSINESS REALITIES
The Electronic Joint Venture

Using IS as a strategic weapon is more easily said than done. Strategic information systems require not only vision and foresight but also huge investments. Further, strategic systems require many years of development before they become fully operational and yield the desired results. Today, several leaders in the computer industry feel that computerizing for strategic advantage may be an expensive proposition with high risks and sometimes insignificant returns. So what should a company do to achieve a strategic advantage using IS? A new approach recommends that businesses form strategic partnerships by pooling their resources and developing systems that not only enhance the way they do business but also make it difficult for competitors to enter the arena.

That is exactly what a group of six major Wall Street firms did. Citibank, First Boston, Goldman Sachs, Morgan Stanley, Salomon Brothers, and Shearson Lehman Brothers formed the Electronic Joint Venture (EJV). The primary goal of EJV is to design and develop information systems that will provide the six firms with critical information for their bond-trading businesses. This gives these firms a competitive edge, tends to ward off new entrants, and reduces the costs of providing their services. What is even more attractive is that the joint venture is selling its information services at a premium to competitors. Such partnerships have the power to change not just the way a company does business but the way an entire industry operates. EJV shows the power that the insight and expertise of a group of experts can bring to running a business.[7]

tion systems, lack of system standardization, data redundancy, poor system maintenance, and security violations.

IRM policies must ensure that end-users are equipped with the hardware and software necessary to effectively perform their job functions, keep them abreast of new technologies, and provide necessary job training and education on issues such as system maintenance, system security, and system integration.

 # Summary

♦ **How IRM helps an organization.**

Information is a vital resource in any organization; therefore, resources that create, process, store, and disseminate information should be effectively managed. IRM is the process of managing the components of an information system. It requires employees at all levels to value information as a critical resource. The Paperwork Reduction Act of 1980 was the first major legislation that recognized information as a valuable resource. By establishing sound IRM policies and principles, organizations can achieve the full potential of their information systems.

♦ **The objectives of IRM**

The four main objectives of IRM are (1) to effectively utilize information resources to achieve the overall goals and the mission of the organization; (2) to inventory, document, and control all resources that create, process, store, and disseminate information in the most efficient and cost-effective manner; (3) to create a model of the enterprise from an information point of view in order to improve communications, both within and outside the organization; and (4) to emphasize the reusability of data and information, eliminate or reduce data redundancy, and ensure that all systems are well integrated so that they can easily communicate with each other. The pursuit of these four objectives will help an organization manage the information resources that are so vital to good decision making.

Corporations that lack clear IRM objectives and policies often face crippling information bottlenecks. In such companies, information is frequently mismanaged, system personnel have little understanding of the needs of the business, systems cannot communicate with each other, and system development is often out of control.

♦ **The six functions of IRM**

The six functions of IRM are (1) technology manage-ment, (2) data management, (3) distributed systems management, (4) strategic management, (5) functional management, and (6) end-user management. Technology management involves information technologies and systems. An important part of technology management is standardization of hardware and software. Data management involves all resources connected with creating, processing, storing, disseminating, and maintaining data and information. Distributed management is the task of managing information resources in a distributed environment. Functional management includes planning, organizing, directing, and controlling all information resources in a company and, in particular, helping functional managers put information resources to good use. Finally, end-user management includes making sure that end-users have the information resources they need to function effectively and that they are given proper training in IS tools and techniques.

♦ **The four principles of managing information resources.**

The four principles of IRM are as follows: (1) The IS department should be managed like any other unit or division of the business. (2) The sole purpose of information systems is to meet the goals of the organization. (3) IRM is the responsibility of all managers, regardless of their discipline or function. (4) The commitment of top management is the key to realizing the full potential of information resources.

When IRM is simplistically viewed as just an IS function, it can have only a very limited effect on the enterprise. Without the full and long-term commitment of top management, IRM will simply be a set of policies and procedures that have minimal impact. Hence, top management should be fully educated in the benefits of IRM and its ability to help an organization achieve its goals.

Review Questions

1. Define IRM and explain how it can help an organization to better manage its information resources. What are some of the components of IRM?
2. What is the Paperwork Reduction Act and how did the act promote IRM?
3. What are four objectives of IRM? What happens when a company does not have clearly stated IRM objectives?
4. What are some problems that manifest in companies that do not have well-established IRM policies and procedures?
5. Identify and describe the six functions of IRM. Why is end-user management an important IRM function?
6. Why is standardization of hardware and software an important part of technology management? What are some of the benefits of standardization?
7. What are distributed systems? What are some special issues that arise in managing these systems?
8. Define the terms *centralized, decentralized,* and *distributed systems.* Which approach, if any, is best?
9. What are the four principles of managing information resources? Discuss any one principle.
10. Who is the main advocate of IRM in an organization? Why?

 Discussion Questions

1. The federal government is held back by entrenched bureaucracies, so improvements and progress come rather slowly. A number of problems plague the IS departments of federal agencies. Federal IS projects are often out of date by the time they are completed. The bidding process for projects is too long and complicated. For example, companies that are not awarded a contract may appeal the decision to a number of groups and agencies. The appeals process is so lengthy that by the time it is completed, the contract specifications have often become obsolete. Finally, good IS personnel are hard to find. Low salaries and a high turnover rate cause talented people to seek nongovernment jobs.[8]

    What are some IRM policies that might help to streamline the government's IS functions?

2. A 1993 survey by *Computerworld* found that on the average, women in IS earn 15% less than men for the same job with the same title.[9] However, as more women continue to work in the IS field, the pay gap between men and women is narrowing. Another survey, in 1992, found that only 7 out of 100 CIOs were women. One of the reasons cited for this "glass ceiling" is that top management is simply not ready for a woman CIO!

    But there is good news. A survey conducted by Korn/Ferry International and the University of California at Los Angeles (UCLA) found that in the past 10 years the average annual salary of women executives has nearly doubled to $187,000, as shown in the following table:

Position	1992 Gender Gap*	1993 Gender Gap*
Chief Information Officer/ Vice President	21%	6%
IS Director/Manager	18%	15%
Average of all IS jobs	21%	5%

*Percentage difference between the annual salaries of women and those of men.

    a. One of the responsibilities of the IRM manager is to provide training to its employees to keep them current with the changes in technology. What special measures, if any, would you take to ensure that women get equal job opportunities and equal pay for equal work?
    b. What should women in the IS field do to protect themselves against wage discrimination?

3. In the four years since its inception in 1981, People's Express had become the fifth largest airline in the world, with 150 planes and $2 billion in revenues. But on January 15, 1985, People's Express declared bankruptcy and was sold to its arch-rival, Texas Air. The CEO of People's Express cited the sophisticated

information systems of its competitors as the primary cause of the demise of his airline.

People's Express, in order to cut costs, had opted for a low-cost "dumb" reservation system instead of a sophisticated reservation system, such as American Airlines' SABRE. People's Express simply failed to see that IS was not simply an administrative tool, but a strategic weapon in the airline industry.

If you were the CIO of People's Express, what arguments would you present to the CEO in favor of a more expensive and sophisticated reservation system, rather than a low-cost, home-made one? How are such technology decisions related to effective IRM policies?

4. The Farmers Home Administration provides a textbook example of how *not* to manage large development projects. After 9 years and $26 million in investments, the U.S. General Accounting Office (GAO) is disillusioned with its efforts to revamp its IS operations. For example, the Commerce Department National Weather Service had set the goal of improving the nation's weather forecasting service and believed that sophisticated information systems could

help the agency achieve its goal. The government approved the development of information systems at a cost of $1.4 billion. Today, the system carries a price tag of $4.2 billion—a 200% increase. By the time the system is complete, it is estimated that it will be 7 years late and 335% over budget, according to GAO.

Fed up with such horror stories, the Department of Commerce has started a new program called "Trail Boss," sponsored by the U.S. General Services Administration (GSA). Under this program, a senior program manager, with solid technical and managerial skills, is appointed "Trail Boss" and is held responsible for the successful completion of IS projects.

a. Suppose you were hired as a "Trail Boss" by the federal government. Identify five measures that you would take to ensure the success of an IS project.

b. Ineffective IRM seems to be the second major cause of project failure. (See Figure 15–2). What are some steps you would take to design an effective IRM policy to ensure the successful development of IS projects?

ETHICAL ISSUES

Managing the information resources of a company is a challenging task. There are no set rules or guidelines for all the situations that a manager may encounter during the day-to-day operations of the company. More often than not, a manager is called upon to use his or her intuition, character, and judgment. Although the culture of the organization plays an important role in setting explicit and implicit behavior guidelines, the ethics of the individual play an important role in decision making. There are no easy answers, only difficult questions. We present below some situations that can create ethical dilemmas.

Case 1: Fear the FBI

New telecommunications technology is sophisticated enough to make wiretapping difficult. Guess who is unhappy about this? The FBI would like to ensure that all communications equipment sold in the U.S. *can* be tapped. The FBI's proposal for building equipment that

can be tapped raises difficult ethical issues for individuals in the computer profession.

1. Should the interests of the FBI and national security take precedence over an individual's right to privacy?
2. If security of information systems is one of the objectives of IRM, would you support the government's stand?

Case 2: Inflation Is Not Welcome

Litton Industries was rocked when a federal judge ruled that it may be liable for $500 million in damages and penalties stemming from a long-standing lawsuit accusing its commercial data processing division of inflating the costs of government contracts. Litton is accused of adding onto federal contract costs that should have been paid by commercial users. The extra costs incurred by

(Continued on next page)

commercial users were allegedly added on to bills for work done for the government.

1. If you were responsible for establishing the IRM policies for Litton, what measures would you take to ensure that such violations are not committed?
2. In recent years, several companies have taken a "free ride" on the coattails of the government. Their attitude has been "Catch me if you can." If you could make a large profit by inflating invoices to the government, would you do it? Assume that the chances of getting caught are pretty slim, that nobody is getting hurt in the process, and that your company really needs the money to avoid layoffs.

PROBLEM SOLVING IN THE REAL WORLD

Case 1: TIAA-CREF Uses Systems to Delight Customers

TIAA-CREF is a mammoth nonprofit institution, based in New York, which has close to $113 billion in assets and owns almost 90% of the retirement-funds market for private colleges in the U.S. In the 1980s, the world's largest pension fund created and introduced a number of financial products to meet the various needs of its customers. But new products also made the task of providing customers with information more complex, and often customers found it confusing to understand and select from the wide array of product offerings. When newer and smaller companies started to chip away at the customer base of TIAA-CREF, the company decided to do something about it.

In 1991, former CIO Cliff Wharton decided to assess the quality of the organization's customer service. A task force interviewed 100 employees and received 1,000 suggestions, which were translated into a plan of action. The result was a decision to build an IT-based customer service system. The new system consists of two parts. The first is an information system that will help telephone representatives deal with customers over the phone; the second is a tracking system that helps the company to keep tabs on work requests in order to ensure that customer requests are promptly handled.

The customer support system gives phone reps detailed information about each policyholder, such as maiden name, power of attorney, and so on. By not asking redundant questions, the sales rep can provide the customer with better service while simultaneously recording their discussions. The manager can look at these notes at his or her convenience and gain a better understanding of the customer and his or her needs. The system allows the staff to track the status of a customer's request. It allows the rep to find out how long the request has been in the system and who is handling it.

Although the project is still under development, it is estimated that when it is completed, more customer requests will be handled without hiring more staff. The goal of the company in developing this system is not just to save money but also to improve the quality of customer service. The company is eager to get to know its customers better so that it can provide better products and services.[10]

1. Can systems such as the one developed by TIAA-CREF reduce the effects of competition and increase customer loyalty? Can such effective systems be developed in companies with poor IRM policies?

Case 2: Coopers Embraces the Age of Technology

Within 2 months of being named vice chairman of technology at New York-based Coopers & Lybrand in December 1992, Ellen M. (Lin) Knapp laid out the company's technology status for top executives at the company. She was not bearing good tidings and top management was jolted by what she had to say. "I told the partners that if I had known what the situation was, I would never have taken this job," says Knapp.

The situation, it turned out, was a nightmare. Cooper's culture, a decentralized web of independent local offices, had created an incoherent muddle of technologies, which was creating a dysfunctional organization for the $5.2-billion accounting firm. Although U.S. operations alone had spent upward of $100 million annually on technology for almost a decade, no one had a clue as to what the money had bought. In trying to get a handle on the preceding 5 years of computer purchases, Knapp discovered that technology spending was included in no fewer than 125 different budget items. "It was accounted for radically differently office by office, and in most budgets it was thrown into capital accounting, which also includes furniture, carpeting, facilities upgrades, and the like."

Standards were nonexistent in the company. The hundreds of geographically dispersed pockets of technology had become isolated islands. Each unit had *carte blanche* to buy whatever computers and software it wanted. Not only did partners buy virtually anything they wanted, but they bought items one at a time. There was no volume purchasing to make use of Coopers's enormous buying power, not even of Lotus 1-2-3, the spreadsheet that, as it happened, came as close to a standard as anything at Coopers. No one had ever taken an inventory of company computers or programs.

Isolated Islands   Most damaging, there was no technology chief, at this multinational firm with 67,000 employees, to build a cohesive company-wide information network. But when Eugene Freedman had become the chairman in 1991, things had begun to change. He was a true leader, in an organization where collegial bantering and countless committees of managing partners were the norm. In less than 3 years, Freedman replaced as much as 35% of the consulting staff, slimmed 130 individual profit centers down to 30, cut as much as $30 million from the company's annual operating costs, and invested $100 million in technology, marketing, and development costs to support the overhaul of the firm. Freedman also understood a fundamental truth that had eluded Coopers management for a decade: Information technology is vital to a prosperous future.

Freedman championed Knapp even though a woman had never before reached the vice-chairman level in any of the big accounting firms. In the men's-club atmosphere of Coopers, where just 7% of the partners are women, the move was tantamount to anarchy. But Knapp soon won the support of even her staunchest critics. "She had the ability to explain in English what we needed to know. And she had the determination to make [things] happen."

(Continued on next page)

Setting, Meeting Goals   Knapp single-handledly began to transform the firm's technology profile, instituting desperately needed standards and bringing together new technology with the right people to implement it. Says Knapp, "Can [Coopers] change? They have no choice. If not, they'll be out of business. There's no law that says we must have *six* big accounting firms."

Among the objectives of Knapp's technology strategy are these:

- Tie nearly all of the Coopers' 67,000 worldwide partners and staff together over an electronic information network, using Notes as the worldwide standard.
- Provide the Coopers & Lybrand Audit Support System, CLASS, to the firm's 6,000 U.S. auditors, and eventually to all 15,000 auditors worldwide. CLASS automates and facilitates every aspect of an audit, from the initial planning to the final report. It allows members of an engagement team, no matter where they are, to simultaneously view and update audit files. Coopers estimates that CLASS will cut up to 20% of the time and cost of an audit while significantly enhancing quality.
- Incorporate the Knowledge Network, an innovative in-house information network, which is a repository of timely broadcast information on various subjects, internal presentations, newsletters, and other outside data.
- Build a multimedia online information service for all Coopers partners and staff worldwide. The network will include news articles, courseware, team development tools, and video setpieces sharing individual partners' expertise. It is designed to keep Cooper's professionals a step ahead of clients and reduce the amount—as much as $5,000 per year per employee—that Coopers now spends on education and training.

Knapp's grand plan aims to turn the staid 96-year-old accounting firm into a massive collaborative information effort that will link its 67,000 employees in 750 offices in 140 countries, not only to each other but also to the company's clients, such as Allied Signal, AT&T, 3M, Johnson & Johnson, and DEC. Knapp is also, for the very first time, creating a set of worldwide technology standards for Coopers in an effort to sharpen the firm's competitive edge, increase gross margins, and bring in new business in an increasingly tough accounting and consulting market.

Like its competitors, Coopers faces the stark reality that "business as usual" won't fly any more. Revenues grew just 4% for all of the Big Six accounting firms in both 1992 and 1993; smaller local accounting firms, with leaner staffs and lower costs, are grabbing business at a much higher rate. Coopers is now fighting back with information technology.

Coopers' auditors, armed with Compaq and DEC 486 laptop computers and the firm's new CLASS auditing software, have greatly improved the audit process; this is having a significant impact on profits. Coopers' profits were up 7% in 1993. The firm is acquiring more new clients now than any other accounting firm. It garnered more than 12% of all new business in 1993, compared to 10% for Arthur Anderson and Ernst & Young. In the first half of 1994, Coopers and Arthur Anderson were the only two of the Big Six that brought in enough new business to offset their loss of clients. Technology has finally hit home with Coopers. "I've never seen a collective light bulb go on like it has here," says Knapp.[11]

1. What were some information-related problems at Coopers & Lybrand before Knapp took over as vice chairman of technology? Were these problems indicative of inadequate IRM policies and procedures?
2. How did lack of standardization affect the flow of information within and outside the company?
3. What are some measures that Knapp took in order to bring Coopers up to speed on the IT frontier?

References

Alter, S., and M. Ginzberg. "Managing Uncertainty in MIS Implementation," *Sloan Management Review,* vol. 20, Fall, 1978.

Applegate, L. "Technology Support for Cooperative Work: A Framework for Studying Assimilation in Organizations," *Journal of Organizational Computing,* vol. 1, no. 1, Jan.–March, 1991.

Barki, H., and J. Hartwick. "Rethinking the Concept of User Involvement," *MIS Quarterly,* vol. 13, no. 1, March 1989.

Best, J. D. "The MIS Executive As Change Agent," *Journal of Information Systems Management,* Fall, 1985.

Nelson, R. R., I. R. Nelson and K. Yamazaki. "Information Resource Management Within Multinational Corporations: A Gross-Cultural Comparison of the U.S. and Japan," *International Information Systems,* vol. 1, no. 4, October, 1992.

Roach S. S. "Services Under Siege—The Restructuring Imperative," *Harvard Business Review,* Sept.–Oct. 1991.

Notes

1. Anthes, Gary H. "Treasury Department's Wild Ride," *Computerworld,* July 27, 1992, pp. 81–82.
2. *InformationWeek,* April 29, 1991, p. 68.
3. McPartlin, John P. (editor). "Illuminating The Black Hole," Executive Notebook, *InformationWeek,* November 30, 1992, p. 24.
4. Anonymous. "HFSI Overhaul," *CIO,* June 1, 1992, p. 23.
5. Anthes, G. H. and J. S. Bozman. "USDA Sows Plan to Overhaul Systems," *Computerworld,* September 6, 1993, pp. 28.
6. Bozman, Jean S. "Kaiser Knits Together Diverse Systems," *Computerworld,* May 18, 1992, pp. 87–88.
7. McPartlin, John P. "Electronic Joint Venture: A Strategic Partnership," *InformationWeek,* July 1993, p. 64.
8. Gillin, Paul. "Editorial: Federal Case," *Computerworld,* May 25, 1992, p. 32.
9. Betts, Mitch. "Women Cheer Salary Gap News," *Computerworld,* September 13, 1993, p. 6.
10. Appleby, Chuck. "Fixed Pensions," *InformationWeek,* July 26, 1993, pp. 28–30.
11. Rifkin, Glenn. "Powering the Comeback at Coopers," *Forbes ASAP,* 1994, pp. 118–121.

16

Computer Security

Contents

Learning Objectives
Technology Payoff: Newark Airport's Blackout
Introduction
What Is Computer Security?
Why Are Computer Systems Vulnerable?
    Intentional Breaches by Employees
    Increased System Complexity
    Choices of System Components
    Network Vulnerabilities
    Sophisticated Hackers
    Complacent Management
Types of Computer Security Breaches
    Accidental or Unintentional Errors
    Intentional Errors
    Natural Disasters
Security Controls
    Application Controls
    Development Controls
    Physical Facilities Control
    Personnel Controls
Disaster Recovery Plan
    Developing a Disaster Recovery Plan
Summary
Review Questions
Discussion Questions
Ethical Issues

      Case 1: Monitoring Employees
      Case 2: Worker Privacy
  Problem Solving in the Real World
      Case 1: Is It an Angel or SATAN in Disguise?
      Case 2: The Clipper Chip
  References
  Notes

Learning Objectives

Because information is a critical strategic resource for organizations, information systems must be closely guarded and protected from accidents, intentional mischief, and natural disasters. This chapter provides a broad overview of the types of computer security breaches and of the measures that an organization can take to protect itself from them. Many students will be working closely with information systems and will be responsible for protecting these resources, so it is important for them to be knowledgeable about computer security.

After reading and studying this chapter, you should be able to

- ◆ Understand why computer security is vital to the survival of a firm
- ◆ Identify the weak links in information systems that make them vulnerable to security breaches
- ◆ Identify different types of security breaches
- ◆ Describe security controls that organizations can implement
- ◆ Discuss the importance and the elements of a disaster recovery plan

TECHNOLOGY PAYOFF

Newark Airport's Blackout

Newark International Airport and its tenants were victimized twice in a single week: a construction gaffe cut power cables feeding the airport's main terminals and poor disaster-recovery planning caught airport administrators with their pants down. A construction crew driving 60-foot steel beams into the ground for a new parking deck inadvertently cut three 27kVA power cables, knocking out power to the airport's three main terminals. The blackout, which occurred at 8:30 A.M., forced the airport to shut down at 5 P.M. Power was restored to the airport 12 hours later. During the blackout, airline and rental car computerized reservation systems in the terminals went down, forcing airlines to divert passengers to other East Coast airports and costing the airport and the airlines millions of dollars in lost sales.

    The incident raised several questions about the airport's tenuous infrastructure, including why the hub's primary and auxiliary power sources are laid side by side in the same conduit. "If you run cables in the same conduit, it's less expensive, but IS people learned years ago that if you have a primary telecommunications path and a backup path, you don't put them in the same physical location." In addition, the power configuration at Newark was put in place 25 years ago, long before diversified power and telecommunications feeds had become *de rigueur*. Ironically, the cost to fix this problem is minimal and airport authorities could have easily avoided it.

Along with its infrastructure problem, the airport seemed to have inadequate backup power supplies, such as uninterruptible power supplies and diesel generators, to keep the entire facility humming. During the crisis, airline agents whose computer reservation terminals went black after the power outage were left scrambling to direct passengers to New York's La Guardia Airport, John F. Kennedy International Airport, and Philadelphia International Airport.[1]

There are two kinds of customers: those who have been the victims of computer fraud, and those who will be.[2]

Introduction

Computer security violation is likely to be the leading white-collar crime of the 1990s. It is one of the thorniest, most neglected, and most dangerous problems facing organizations all over the world. It is estimated that 70% of U.S. organizations have suffered some kind of security breach and, ironically, 80% of those breaches have been caused by company employees.[3] Security experts indicate that these figures are probably too low, since many security breaches go unreported because companies are embarrassed, or afraid that the news might turn away customers—or even worse, because some companies may be too technically ignorant to recognize that a breach has occurred!

In spite of these alarming statistics, most companies, particularly small businesses, are lax when it comes to computer security, treating it as a waste of time and money. As our opening vignette about Newark Airport shows, sometimes simple, common sense measures are all it takes to provide better system security. A recent book, titled *Secrets of a Super Hacker,* by an author using the name Knightmare, drives home the point that security policies in many organizations are lax or nonexistent. Many organizations hold everyone responsible for computer security, but few hold anyone *accountable* for security breaches! Security is made the responsibility of professionals, such as systems software specialists, internal auditors, chiefs of data management, network administrators, and systems analysts,[4] and in some companies no special skills are required to be a security expert. Good intentions will do!

Good security measures are an important way of protecting the financial stability of a company. In the fall of 1985, a computer system in the Bank of New York was breached. Although the problem was corrected 26 hours later, the bank incurred a short-term loss of more than $34 million and was forced to borrow several billion dollars overnight in order to complete financial transactions from the previous day. The story of the Masters of Deception (see box) shows how a group of individuals broke into the computer systems of several major U.S. corporations and caused significant losses for these companies.

The Masters of Deception were five New York hackers who gained illegal access to computers at many major corporations. Companies such as Southwestern Bell, British Telecom, New York Telephone, Martin Marietta, New York University, and TRW were all victims of this group. A two-year surveillance operation by 150 Secret Service agents, called Operation Sundevil, culminated in 28 search warrants and indictments on 11 charges of security breaches in 14 cities. The damage caused by the group had resulted in almost $50 million in losses. The influence of the group was so widespread that 42 computers and 23,000 disks were confiscated in New York, Chicago, Los Angeles, and 10 other cities.[5]

Today there are laws and regulations that mandate computer security. The 1991 federal sentencing guidelines, in fact, require organizations to be vigilant, failing which knowledge workers, such as yourself, and senior management (including MIS and telecommunications managers) can be held liable for security-related losses.[6]

What Is Computer Security?

Computer security
A set of policies, procedures, tools, and techniques, to protect computer assets from accidental, intentional, or natural disasters. It covers all components of a company's computing environment: hardware, software, networks, physical facilities, data and information, and personnel.

Computer security includes the policies, procedures, tools, and techniques designed to protect a company's computer assets from accidental, intentional, or natural disasters, including accidental input or output errors, theft, breakins, physical damage, and illegal access or manipulation.

Computer security is a complex and pervasive problem that often stumps many organizations, which struggle to balance proper security against the cost and inconvenience of providing it. It cannot be achieved through automation or sophisticated equipment alone; it also requires the active participation of employees with common sense, good judgment, and high moral values, because security is ultimately the responsibility of the individual using the computer. Therefore, it is not surprising that organizations that promote creativity, innovation, trust, and high ethical standards appear to be more successful in enforcing computer security than organizations with stifling cultures.

Why Are Computer Systems Vulnerable?

There are a number of reasons why computer systems are vulnerable to security breaches.

Intentional Breaches by Employees

Unfortunately, among the primary sources of security breaches are employees who are either callous or forgetful about security standards. In some cases, employees intentionally cause breaches, either for financial gain or for the fun of it. One of the best ways to reduce security breaches is to educate employees about security policies and to clearly communicate the penalties for violations.

Increased System Complexity

Today, with the spread of end-user computing, the number of computer systems in the workplace has increased manyfold. Moreover, information systems have gone from being support systems to being the lifelines of many businesses, so the number of mission-critical systems has also increased significantly. Technological advances in computers have made many systems extremely complex and difficult to manage. As networked systems become the norm, the task of securing computer systems is becoming more and more challenging. Finally, users working on such systems have technical sophistication that can be misdirected.

Choices of System Components

In recent years, the number of hardware, software, and network options available to managers has increased manyfold. As IS mangers attempt to integrate this wide variety of tools and techniques, providing system security is often a daunting task. Further, many systems run on different operating systems, and security considerations are often different for different systems. Network components and configurations have also increased, creating the opportunity to "mix and match" or "plug 'n play." It is even more difficult to provide security for a diverse set of systems.

Network Vulnerabilities

As we saw in Chapter 5, Telecommunications, advances in networks and telecommunications have profoundly affected organizational productivity and decision making. The way companies do business has been completely revolutionized by telecommunications. Unfortunately, networks are also among the most vulnerable links in the security chain for computer systems—in fact, in a recent survey of CIOs, more than 90% of the respondents indicated that network security was a *strategic* concern for their organizations.[7]

"Networks are essentially sieves to anyone with minor technical skills and the desire to retrieve other people's information."[8]

The Internet (see Chapter 5) is a vital link that connects people and organizations all over the world. However, in recent years it has been plagued with security problems (see box) and, as Figure 16–1 shows, as the number of Internet users has increased, the number of security breaches has also increased.

BUSINESS REALITIES
Internet Security Breaches

Security breaches on the Internet have increased dramatically in recent years and are causing national concern. (See Figure 16–1.) The Internet connects 2 million host computers and provides access to a rich and extensive array of data and information to millions of users, whose numbers increase by more than 15% every month. The Internet transmits more than 100 billion bytes of data every day; every country in the world has an Internet connection. It is easy to understand why the Internet is considered an ideal target for "cyberterrorists."

In February 1994, hackers stole thousands of passwords over the Internet, allowing them illegal access to government, financial, research, scientific, and defense computers around the country. "This large-scale digital robbery is in a class by itself for scope, audacity, and potential damage." The chief of the FBI's Financial Crimes Section testified that in more than 80% of the FBI's computer-crime investigations, the Internet had been used to gain illegal access to systems.[9]

F I G U R E   1 6 – 1

As the number of users on the Internet has increased, the number of security violations on the Internet has also increased.

Source: Panettieri, Joseph C. "Guardian of the NET," *Information Week,* May 23, 1994, p. 32.

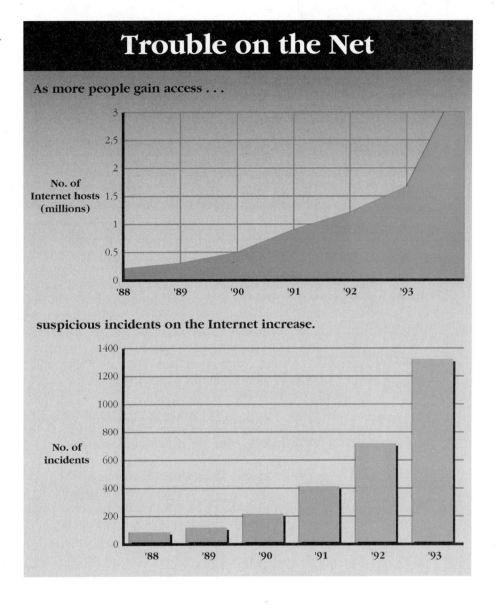

Trouble on the Net

As more people gain access . . .

No. of Internet hosts (millions)

suspicious incidents on the Internet increase.

No. of incidents

There are many reasons why networks are so prone to security violations. The arrival of cellular phones, radio modems, and sky pagers has created new points of vulnerability in the electronic exchange of information, since many unauthorized parties can tune into a company's voice or data transmissions. Second, in a distributed environment, there are innumerable opportunities for security breaches. "In contrast to the fortress-like architecture of the mainframe, security exposures in client-server computing almost defy identification."[10] Third, networks transmit large amounts of data and information around the world and it is difficult to continuously keep track of who is doing what, where, when, and how. Fourth, in many organizations network administrators are rewarded for providing easy access to the network, but not for tight security, and obviously the two do not go hand-in-hand. Fifth, many network users are ignorant of network security measures and, intentionally or unintentionally, can cause considerable damage. Users often view security policies and procedures as cumbersome and counterproductive, so they try to find short cuts or even to completely bypass security controls.

Sophisticated Hackers

Hacker
An individual who has the knowledge to illegally break into a computer system or facility, although he or she does not cause any harm to the system or the organization.

Cracker
A computer thief who breaks into a system with the intent of stealing passwords, files, and programs, either for fun or for profit.

They are given different names—hackers, crackers, information warriors, cyberpunks, cyberterrorists, and phone freaks—but they are all people who violate computer security. A **hacker** is an individual who is knowledgeable enough to break into a computer system or facility, although he or she does not cause any harm to the system or the organization. A **cracker,** on the other hand, is a computer thief who breaks into a system with the intent of stealing passwords (sets of characters that allow users to log onto a system or to access a program), mail messages, files, programs, and so on, for fun or for profit. For example, in 1991, Pierre Marion, the former head of French intelligence, admitted that France had been spying on IBM, Corning, and Texas Instruments for almost a decade, causing IBM alone losses of billions of dollars. And why not? Marion asked. After all, "in economics, we are competitors, not allies."[11]

Crackers can cause financial damages and injure the competitiveness of a firm. For example, in 1991, when a security breach occurred at the research facility of a major U.S. automobile manufacturer, the company lost $500 million worth of designs for future cars and suffered in the marketplace because its designs fell into the hands of competitors.[12]

Complacent Management

In spite of the many highly publicized cases of security violations, top management in many organizations is oblivious to security violations and their ability to bring a corporation to its knees. They are often reluctant to invest in security because they do not believe it has a direct impact on profits. But unless management takes a vigilant and proactive approach to computer security, security breaches are like time bombs waiting to explode.

The challenges of securing computer systems in an organization are summarized in Table 16–1.

TABLE 16–1
The six primary reasons why computer systems are vulnerable to security breaches.

- **Intentional breach by employees:** A primary source of security breaches is the intentional or unintentional actions of employees.
- **Increased system complexity:** Open, integrated, mission-critical, and real-time systems are highly complex and difficult to monitor and manage.
- **Too many choices in system components:** The number of hardware, software, and network configurations has increased tremendously.
- **Increased network vulnerabilities:** Networks have become increasingly complex and difficult to manage.
- **More skilled crackers:** Crackers are better educated and more technically skilled, making it easier for them to break into computer systems.
- **Complacent top management:** Top managers often feel that security violations happen at other companies, not at theirs.

Types of Computer Security Breaches

The different types of computer breaches can be broadly classified into three categories: accidental or unintentional errors, intentional errors, and natural disasters. The most common security breaches are shown in Figure 16–2.

Accidental or Unintentional Errors

Accidents in the workplace can cause security breaches; it is often said that the cost of unintentional damage exceeds the cost of computer crime. Accidental security violations can be reduced by education and training, and by establishing and communicating security policies and procedures. Let us look at some types of accidental security violations.

Sometimes hardware components accidentally fail—the memory, keyboards, terminal emulators, LAN connection cards, network cabling, network servers, routers or bridges in networks, WANs, mainframe front-end processors, and a multitude of peripherals and accessories—causing a security breach. Cables, modems, fax machines, and cellular phones are particularly prone to failure. Countless cables installed underground or on building roofs link and support corporate networks; since they are not visible, they are often forgotten during development of security plans. However, cables can be accidentally cut or destroyed during building repairs and maintenance, so measures should be taken to protect them. Software errors—in input, processing, output, or storage—can also cause security violations.

FIGURE 16–2

The frequencies of some of the most common security breaches that affect computer systems.

Sources: Edwards, John. "Be Prepared," CIO, March 15, 1994, p. 72; Contingency Planning Research Inc., Jericho, N.Y. A 1993 study of 533 U.S. information executives.
* Includes hardware error, hurricane, network problems, terrorism, and software error.

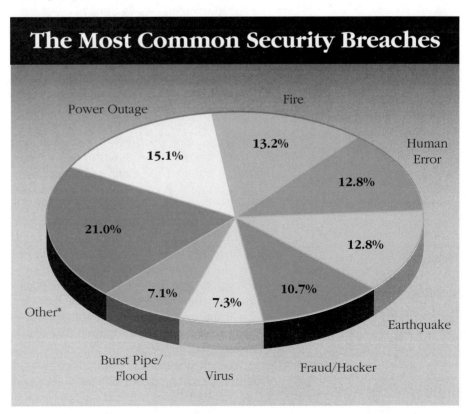

Intentional Errors

Intentional damage to systems is also common. It is widely believed that IS personnel are the greatest threat to system security, because they have intimate knowledge of the workings and the critical elements of a system. Intentional errors may take the form of illicit entry to a system, access to valuable proprietary corporate data, stealing passwords in order to snoop around, reading E-mail, or destroying important files. Regardless of the motives behind such acts, they are serious violations. They may go undetected for days, weeks, or even months, particularly if the violator is good at what he or she does. Let us look at some types of intentional security violations.

Cracking Passwords   Cracking, or decoding, passwords, which are the Achilles' heel of computer security, is one of the most common security violations, since hackers and crackers can easily guess passwords or capture them as they travel over the network. Once the *super-user* (the user, such as a system administrator, who has access to all passwords) password is cracked, the perpetrator has full control of the system and can set up accounts, use the system to uncover more passwords, and gain access to vital information, all without even being detected.

Breaking into Computer Hardware   Another type of intentional security breach is breaking into and damaging computer hardware. Modems, fax machines, and cellular phones are particularly vulnerable to this type of damage.

Millions of modems all over the country give employees and other legal entities access to a company's computer system. Unfortunately, modems are also highly vulnerable to security breaches. For example, "demon dialers" are programs that first identify all the phone numbers connected to a modem and then break down passwords to gain illegal access to the system. Two hackers in Seattle used "demon dialers" to break into a federal court computer, decoded user passwords, and gained access to several files of national importance.[13] Even worse, hackers often share phone numbers and passwords with other hackers for a price, further spreading the results of the crime.

Fax machines, the "long-distance copiers" of corporate America, are a weak link in computer security. Information sent through fax machines can be intercepted, copied, or rerouted to another machine. Although users rarely hesitate to give out their fax numbers, this practice can be a security threat. A risk management consultant tells the story of two U.S. companies that were negotiating merger terms through their law firms, located in Chicago and in New York. When clerks at the New York firm faxed sensitive contracts to Chicago, they misdialed the Chicago firm's fax number by one digit. The documents, instead of arriving at the Chicago law office, arrived at the office of *The Wall Street Journal,* which made the negotiations public. The merger fell through and one misdialed digit cost the company millions of dollars and irreparable damage to its competitive position.[14]

Experts recommend that you *never* send anything confidential or proprietary by fax. "Assume that everything that you fax could go to the local newspaper," says one security expert. Also, documents received by fax should not be treated as original documents. Using a pair of scissors, a little bit of Scotch tape, and a falsified signature, a hacker persuaded a London bank to transfer $600 million into his account! Banks learned an important lesson in the process; today, the U.S.

Uniform Commercial Code requires phone-call verification for any fax-based fund transfers.[15]

Cellular phones are the weakest links in communication networks, because they are essentially shortwave devices that can easily be accessed with a $100 scanner. Experts recommend that you should not discuss proprietary information over cellular phones and strongly urge callers to use code words when discussing confidential matters.

Software Viruses   There are two primary sources of intentional software security breaches: computer viruses and "sniffer" programs.

The greatest threat to software is a **computer virus,** a program that causes a computer system to behave in unexpected and undesirable ways. Some signs of a virus include unexplainable loss of free memory, unusually long times for program loading or execution, changes in file or program size, print routines that stop working, computers "freezing up," strange beeps or messages, computer reboots in the middle of a process, and corrupted files. It is estimated that there are more than 2,100 computer viruses and that about 50 new ones are created each month.[16] When a virus is executed, it makes copies of itself and spreads from one system or application to another through networks and diskettes. It is precisely for this reason that many companies strongly discourage the sharing of diskettes between systems.

Figure 16–3 shows the detrimental effects of viruses on organizational productivity. Damages from computer viruses for a single organization can range between $100,000 and $100 million; cleaning up alone costs U.S. businesses almost $2 billion dollars each year.[17]

Computer virus

A program that causes systems to behave in unexpected and undesirable ways. When the virus program is executed, it makes copies of itself and spreads from one system or application to another, either through networks or through shared diskettes.

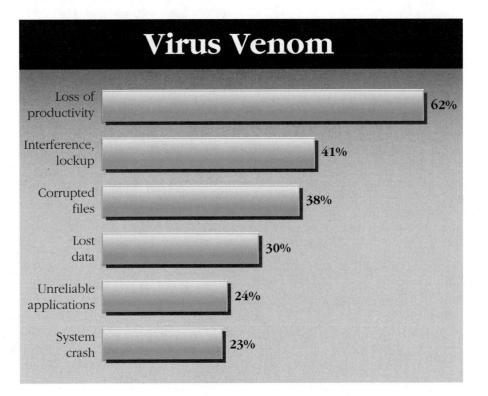

FIGURE 16–3

The dire consequences that computer viruses can have on an organization. Note, in particular, the negative effect on worker productivity.

Sources: Dataquest, San Jose, California; Anthes, Gary H. "Viruses Continue to Wreak Havoc at Many U.S. Companies," *Computerworld*, June 28, 1993, p. 52.

TABLE 16-2
The cost of eliminating even a single virus can be quite high. This table shows how it cost Rockwell International nearly $44,000 to eliminate a 4-day "Hi" virus.

Hi Costs	
Approximate cost breakdown for the Hi virus	
Length of infection:	
Four days (April 29–May 2, 1993)	
Contractor support (200 hours at $40/hr)	$ 8,000
PC network support (160 hours at $45/hr)	7,200
Server downtime (8 hours × 100 users at $45/hr; avg. computing downtime per day: 25%)	9,000
Additional antivirus software required ($800/server, $20/PC)	19,800
Total:	$44,000

Source: Daly, James. "Virus Vagaries Foil Feds," *Computerworld,* July 12, 1993, p. 1.

Viruses are not easy to isolate and cure. A security manager at Nynex's New York headquarters recalls when a PC on his company's network became infected with the Jerusalem B virus. Every machine on the company's network, and all machines that shared portable disks, had to be examined. Four LAN administrators worked 2 full days plus overtime to isolate and clear the virus; a technician had to spend 9 hours clearing "trouble tickets;" a security specialist spent 5 hours on followups and reports; 200 users on the LAN each suffered at least 15 minutes of downtime.[18] Table 16–2 shows how just a 4-day infection with the "Hi" virus cost Rockwell International $44,000.

Legal Implications of Spreading a Virus   Believe it or not, it is still legal in the United States to create a virus and inject it into any computer system, because the writing of software is protected by the First Amendment, although federal regulatory agencies are working hard to change this situation. There are other reasons why it is difficult to make viruses illegal. Researchers often use viruses for scholarly study, such as testing system security; this makes it difficult to ban them. Also, a law that makes it illegal to delete information, would make the popular delete function, DEL *.*, illegal! Further, with no uniform definition of a "malicious virus," it is difficult to prosecute those who create them. Every state except Vermont has its own definition of what constitutes a computer crime, so catching perpetrators is a legal battle that few are willing to wage.[19]

To further aggravate the problem, when someone is convicted of infecting a system with a virus, the punishment is often light. For example, in 1988, Robert Morris actually brought down the Internet and other major networks around the country by injecting a virus into the network. Although this resulted in losses in the millions of dollars and loss of productivity for thousands of workers, he was given only 3 years' probation, a $10,000 fine, and 400 hours of community service. This is because the Computer Fraud and Absue Act of 1986 uses the victims' dollar loss to determine the severity of the crime, rather than considering the larger consequences of the crime. However, a strong and concentrated effort is being made to make the writing of a virus illegal by focusing on the intent of the virus, not just the financial result.

The second type of intentional software security breach is using "sniffer" programs, which explore the system to gather data about network users, their passwords, their access codes, and the nature of their work. These programs, which are very useful for network administrators, can be dangerous in the hands of a hacker who stealthily monitors data transmissions.

Natural Disasters

The third type of security breach is caused by natural disasters, such as hurricanes, earthquakes, tornadoes, and floods. These can be so devastating that companies, and even entire cities, take a long time to recover from them. In 1992 alone, insurers in the U.S. handled a record $18 billion in natural-disaster claims.[20] Table 16–3 shows the financial implications of natural disasters.

Some less damaging natural disasters include those that affect power supplies, cooling systems, communication networks, alarm systems, lightning protectors, building structures, and other facilities that support computer systems.

Lightning is one form of natural disaster. Keven L. Erwin Consulting Ecologists, a Fort Myers, Florida, firm, lost about $40,000 worth of personal computer and network equipment when its installed lightning surge protectors failed. It took the firm 2 days to recover from the calamity and more than 6 months to recover from the problems of corrupted data.[21]

Power outages are another common cause of computer downtime and lost productivity. They should not be taken lightly, because a power failure of just 50 milliseconds can result in at least 10 minutes of computer downtime, which can translate into losses of millions per minute for large financial institutions.[22] The average company loses 2% to 3% of its gross sales within 8 days of a sustained power failure; if the outage lasts longer than 10 days, the company may never fully recover from the loss. In fact, almost 50% of companies that suffer prolonged power outages are likely to go out of business within 5 years.[23]

Telephone outages can cause major havoc and destroy the reputation of a company. For example, the Midwest Stock Exchange, with security transactions of close to $75 billion last year, knows that even a brief interruption in its telephone service can cause losses in the millions of dollars. The company therefore has a backup exchange. "We consider the telephone system the highest priority system in the exchange. Even when computers are down, we can continue to do trading manually, provided we have our telephone system operating."[24]

Although the probability of a disaster is often at the core of cost-benefit analysis for disaster protection and recovery, this may not be the best approach.

TABLE 16–3
The extent of losses that a disaster can cause to a business.

Disaster's Price Tag:
- More than $3.8 billion annual loss in revenues and lost productivity
- More than 4 hours of downtime for each occurrence
- An average cost of $329,000 per occurrence in lost revenue and worker productivity
- An average of 355 worker hours lost per occurrence
- A loss of 38.1 million worker hours annually
- A loss of $444 million in wages annually

Source: Stratus Computer Inc., Marlboro, Massachusetts, based on a study of 450 information executives at Fortune 1000 companies. Adapted from Edwards, John. "Be Prepared," *CIO,* March 15, 1994, p. 70.

The first question should not be "What is the probability of a disaster striking?" Instead, it should be "What is at risk if a disaster does in fact strike?" The following questions should drive home the dangers of a disaster much more poignantly and realistically than a cost-benefit model:

- What will be the loss in revenue if a given disaster strikes?
- How will the competitive position of the firm be affected?
- How will suppliers, creditors, and stockholders be affected?
- How will the firm's customers be affected?
- What will happen to the financial health of the firm?

Another conventional approach to calculating the expected value of a disaster is to multiply the probability of the disaster by the estimated magnitude of the loss: Expected Value of Damage = Probability of Damage × Estimated Loss in Dollars.

In spite of the alarming statistics about disasters and their effects on a business, very few companies consider disaster avoidance and disaster recovery in their risk management plans. Top management often wrongly believes that the company is immune to disasters.

"An ounce of disaster prevention is worth a pound of disaster recovery cure. Physical disasters don't happen randomly. They are caused by preexisting, identifiable, disaster-prone conditions. Clearly, avoiding a corporate heart attack makes a lot more sense than the risk, pain, and expense of an attempt to recover after one strikes."[25]

Security Controls

In this section, we look at some measures that organizations can take to reduce security breaches. Note that we use the word *reduce*, not *eliminate*, since it is impossible to eliminate *all* security violations; crackers always appear to be one step ahead of security experts!

Computer security controls are policies, procedures, tools, and techniques designed to reduce security breaches and system destruction, to prevent errors in data, software, and systems, to protect systems from accidental, intentional, and natural disasters, and to continually enhance system security. Controls may be manual or automated. Figure 16–4 shows the four different types of controls: application controls, development controls, physical facility controls, and personnel controls.

Application Controls

Application controls are policies and procedures that ensure the security and quality of system applications in the organization (such as payroll and inventory management). Application controls cover four primary areas of data processing: input, processing, output, and storage.

Input Controls   **Input controls** are designed to prevent users from entering incomplete, erroneous, unauthorized, or inappropriate data. There are four different kinds of input controls: access privileges, input authorization, data validation, and data format.

Computer security controls
Policies, procedures, tools, and techniques designed to reduce computer security breaches and system errors. There are five types of controls: application, development, access, physical facility, and personnel controls.

Application controls
Policies, procedures, and methods established to ensure the security and quality of individual applications. Application controls cover four primary areas of data processing: input, processing, output, and storage of data, information, and programs.

Input controls
Ensure that input data are authorized, accurate, and timely by preventing users from entering incomplete, erroneous, or inappropriate data. Different kinds of input controls include: access privileges, input authorization, data validation, and data format.

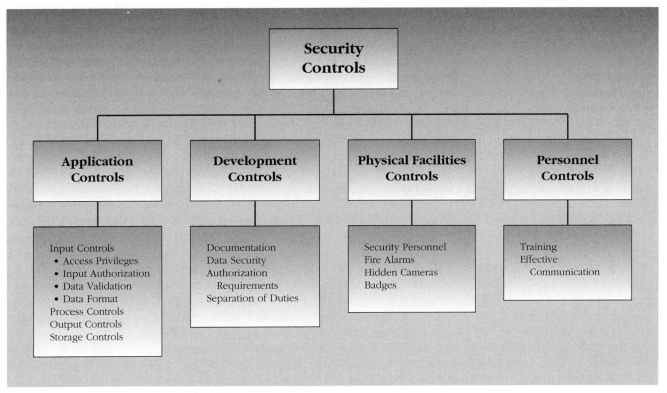

FIGURE 16-4

Some types of controls that a company can implement to secure its computer systems.

Access Privileges   Unique user IDs, aging passwords, smart cards, access control lists, and regular auditing and monitoring of potential security violations are some measures that organizations can take to ensure proper access privileges. Access privileges for vendors should also be closely monitored, since unscrupulous vendors can snoop around and gather intelligence on confidential data. Access privileges should be highly selective, closely guarded, and determined on a user-by-user basis or on a function-by-function basis, since most security breaches are committed by insiders who know the weak points in a company's network.[26]

Input Authorization   Data input must be authorized and monitored by appropriate authorities, failing which users with illicit motives may cause financial and legal problems for the company. For example, without proper input control, an unauthorized user can change payroll figures or other vital data.

In batch systems, where source documents are the primary source of data, input controls should monitor the movement of the source documents and the personnel who handle them. The source of each input should also be validated, particularly for critical systems or for those with major financial implications. For online systems, the primary source of input control is passwords.

Passwords, the most common type of authorization control, refers to a set of characters that acts like a key to unlock the system. Separate passwords can be used to access a system, an application, or even a file in a given application.

The success of this type of control depends on the ability of the user to create a password that is difficult to guess and to keep the password confidential. In order to ensure tight system security, many companies have policies that mandate the use of hard-to-guess passwords or randomly generated passwords, and require employees to change their passwords frequently. In recent years, with the increasing number of security breaches on the Internet, the idea of reusable passwords has come under close scrutiny and recommendations are being made that passwords be used only once, or that encrypted passwords be used, or both. Experts recommend that instead of a single word, a password should consist of a phrase, which is more difficult to break. Some companies use "firewalls," which are security filters that apply a number of criteria before giving a user access to the network.

For example, Security Dynamics, in Cambridge, Massachusetts, has created a SecurID smart card, which displays a new, unpredictable six-digit password every minute. A corresponding feature on the network ensures that the password on the user's card and the one on the host machine always agree. (A clock installed in the card is synchronized with access control hardware on the network). Security is further tightened by requiring the user to key in a secret personal identification number (PIN) so that in case the card is lost, the PIN will still prevent unauthorized users from gaining access to the system. The company claims that the odds of breaking into a system with SecurID are less than one in 14 billion.[27]

But some experts caution that passwords often convey a false sense of security and recommend that companies use the principles of I&A: identification and authentication. I&A requires the use of three things:[28]

1. *Something you know.* This would include things such as a password, a PIN, or a phrase.
2. *Something you own.* This would include such things as a smart card or an ID card.
3. *Something you are.* This would include things like thumbprints, retinal scans, handwriting, and signatures.

These three measures, combined together, can significantly increase the security of a system. Obviously, not all systems require such rigid access controls, but for critical systems they may be a necessity.

Data Validation   Data should be validated before it is processed. This can be done manually by two employees who compare data, or automatically by a computer comparing the input data with existing master files. There are also programs that automatically compare data values against pre-established values: a long distance phone number should be 10 digits long, and so on. Usually, such checks are made by the DBMS so that the same checks can be applied uniformly to all applications.

Several data validation techniques are commonly used to detect input errors. *Anticipation checks,* which compare input values with expected or anticipated values, are particularly useful for checking for nonblank values, such as an employee name on a payroll check. *Reasonableness checks* are controls that check whether input values are within reasonable limits: for example, hours worked per week cannot be greater than, say, 80. *Arithmetic proof checks* ensure that arithmetic operations are properly executed: the sum of two positive numbers cannot be negative, and so on.

Data Format   Input controls should also check the format of the data, ensuring that there are no missing values and that data are in the right format (integer versus decimal values, for example), the right size, and the right type (for example, telephone numbers should not include alphabetic characters). Though the type and extent of controls vary from organization to organization, and even from application to application, IS managers must establish and implement proper data controls. A distinction should also be made between policies that may be overridden under special circumstances and those that are strictly mandatory.

Controls are also necessary to ensure that all errors are corrected. Cumulative error lists that identify all errors in a certain application are useful for corrective action. Clearly, only authorized people should be allowed to correct errors and notification of error correction should be documented and forwarded to the proper authority.

Process controls

Ensure that data are processed using proper procedures and methods. Primarily designed to catch any errors that may have slipped through the input controls, they ensure that the right file or the most updated file is being processed, and that the results of data or file processing is accurate, reliable, and timely.

Process Controls   **Process controls** are policies and procedures that ensure that data are meaningful and reliable. These are designed to catch any errors that may have slipped through the input controls. For example, reasonableness checks can be incorporated into application processing so that any errors that may have gotten past the input controls are detected during processing. Other processing controls include ensuring that the right file or the most recently updated file is being processed and that the processing is accurate and timely.

Earlier in this chapter, we discussed some problems that an organization can face when its system is infected with a virus. What are some process controls that an organization can implement to protect itself from the dreaded virus? One of the most important steps toward eliminating viruses is to educate users about their effects and how to prevent them. In a recent survey of employees at a Fortune 100 company, 98% said that although they had heard about computer viruses, they were not sure as to what viruses do and many indicated that they had little or no knowledge of how to prevent or remove a virus.[29] Education is vital to prevent infection by viruses. Second, a simple yet highly effective measure is to restrict the movement of diskettes from one system to another; this greatly reduces the chances of spreading viruses from one machine to another.

Also, there are many off-the-shelf virus detection programs that can be activated when the computer is first booted up as a way to prevent virus infection. Other steps that organizations can take to prevent virus attack are to mandate that users change their passwords every 30 to 90 days, to establish strict guidelines for the use of "shareware," and to strictly prohibit access to "freeware" (software that is available at no charge).

Other process controls include frequent backups of important files. Making backups is creating duplicate copies of a file and storing them on a separate disk or medium, or even in a separate location. It is a way to protect files against accidental deletion, misplacement, and natural or man-made disasters. Take, for example, the case of the Rockland Community Action Council (ROCAC) administrative headquarters in Spring Valley, New York, where a fire started on a quiet Sunday morning. When it was put out later that day, seven PCs had gone up in flames and the CIO was convinced that the organization was ruined because its financial records, stored on those PCs' hard disks, were all gone. He suddenly remembered the fireproof filing cabinets, where some tapes had been stashed away. "My eyes nearly popped out when I realized the backup tapes were OK." The backup tapes contained all the vital records of the organization, which saved it from financial ruin.[30]

It is also strongly recommended that the original file be checked for viruses before backups are made. Organizations that are data-intensive keep a log indicating when each backup was made, to avoid any confusion or overwriting. With the spread of end-user computing, more and more organizations are shifting the responsibility of backups from the IS department to the end-user. When files are frequently backed up, the losses or damage from a virus are minimized, because only information generated since the last backup is lost or damaged.

Many organizations have written policies on the number and frequency of backups; some even state explicitly the penalty for failing to make backups. Although backups are vital, companies must perform cost-benefit analyses to determine which files are critical and to determine accordingly how frequently these files should be backed up (hourly, daily, weekly, monthly, semiannually, and so on).

Output controls
Ensure that output data are accurate and are delivered in the right format, at the right time, and to the right person. The number and rigor of the output controls depends on the criticality of the application.

Output Controls   The third type of application control is **output controls,** which ensure that system output is accurate and is disseminated to the right people at the right time and in the right format. The number and rigor of the output controls depend on the criticality of the application; for critical or proprietary applications, output controls are likely to be more strict and rigid than for noncritical applications. If the output is confidential, such as nuclear facility designs or medical research findings, control measures must be taken to secure the output from unauthorized parties.

In most cases, output controls include at least a periodic review of system output by authorized individuals who check the timeliness, accuracy, and format of the output, identify any exceptions (such as overtime being five times the usual value), and make sure that no unauthorized programs were accessed during processing.

Storage Controls
Designed to ensure that the storage devices on which data and programs are stored are protected from man-made and natural disasters. Passwords, access privileges, and backing up files are some popular storage controls.

Storage Controls   The fourth type of application control is **storage controls,** which ensure that the storage devices on which data and programs are stored are safe, secure, and well protected from natural and man-made disasters. Storage control mechanisms prevent unauthorized access to storage devices, as well as accidental or intentional deletion or manipulation of files. As you may recall, passwords and access privileges are two common and popular control measures that are effective storage controls. Backing up files is another control mechanism that helps organizations recover from damages to storage devices. Clearly, backup files should be stored on different devices from those that hold the original files, and in some cases should even be in a different location. File backups are discussed later in the chapter.

Development Controls

Control mechanisms for system security should not be an afterthought, but should be made an integral part of the development process, from product conception

Development controls
Controls that are built into the development cycle to ensure the security of information systems. These controls are set up so that security is not just an afterthought but is built into the system itself. Creating proper standards and documentation, ensuring the security and reliability of data, establishing proper authorization for changes or additions to requirement specifications, and separation of duties are some popular development controls.

to product delivery. **Development controls** are controls built into each phase of the development cycle. They include measures such as establishing development standards (guidelines for developing systems), creating proper documentation, ensuring the security and reliability of data, establishing proper authorization for changes or additions to requirement specifications, and separation of duties. Standards and guidelines for developing information systems were covered in Chapters 12 and 13.

Documentation   Proper system documentation is one way to control the quality of the development process and consists of detailed record keeping about the system, its logical and physical functions, its features, its interfaces, and any other elements that are essential to its smooth functioning and maintenance. Clear and well-written documentation should be developed for the entire system, for the various programs in the system, and for specific system operations. Documentation is an essential part of security control, because without it security experts may have to guess at the source, or even the indications, of a security breach. Moreover, when developers leave a project or leave the company, documentation is the only way to understand the intricacies and the possible weak links of the system so that proper security measures can be implemented. Though many developers view documentation as a boring task, it is so vital to the continued success of a system that some organizations hire a documentation specialist to ensure that all systems are properly documented and that the documentation is frequently updated.

Data Security and Reliability   Data security and reliability are another development control mechanism that prevents unauthorized access to data. They are particularly critical in real-time distributed systems. Some measures to secure data are preventing viruses, establishing access privileges, securing physical facilities, and implementing user IDs and passwords.

Authorization requirements
Control mechanisms to ensure that only authorized users gain access to the system and that once they gain access they only perform processes they are authorized to perform. This includes all activities related to input, processing, output, dissemination, storage, and maintenance of data.

Separation of duties
A development-related control mechanism that eliminates conflict of interest during system development that might compromise the security and reliability of the system.

Authorization Requirements   **Authorization requirements** are control mechanisms that allow only authorized users to access and use the system. These control all activities related to input, processing, output, dissemination, storage, and maintenance of data. Any installation of new programs and any system configuration should also require proper authorization.

Authorization controls are particularly essential for system changes, so that employees cannot accidentally or intentionally change applications—for example, payroll or employee benefits.

Separation of Duties   Finally, **separation of duties** is another development-related control mechanism, which reduces or eliminates conflicts of interest that can compromise the security and reliability of the system. For example, most organizations do not authorize system developers to give the final clearance on the quality and performance of the system. In other words, system testers should not be the same people as the system developers, because system developers have a personal stake in the perceived quality and reliability of the system.

In summary, there are four main types of development controls: documentation, data security and reliability, authorization requirements, and separation of duties. Next, we look at the third type of control—control of physical facilities.

Physical Facilities Control

The primary goal of physical facilities control is to protect the physical facilities that house the computer and other related assets from theft, unauthorized access, natural disasters, and vandalism, through measures such as posting security personnel, installing fire alarms, security alarms, and hidden cameras, and requiring users to wear badges or use smart cards to gain access to the building. Most facilities also include environmental control devices that monitor and control the air and the temperature in a building.

Although the reliability of physical support facilities is often overlooked, it is an important part of system security, particularly for real-time systems. Many support facilities were designed in the 1970s, when batch processing was the norm; when a system failed, the computer was simply shut down until the facility was restored. But today, many systems are 24-hour, real-time, mission-critical systems that simply cannot be interrupted.

In recent years, many computer failures have been attributable to failure of the support system, rather than of the computer system itself. For example, when an electrical fire broke out in the lower-Manhattan data center of Securities Industry Automation Corp. (SIAC) a few years ago, the New York and the American stock exchanges (NYSE and AMEX) came to a grinding halt and put transactions worth billions of dollars on hold for several hours. Although news reports attributed the disruption to the fire, the problem was traced to a faulty alarm system, which misinterpreted a blaze in the basement as a fire in the 14th-floor computer room and simply shut down the entire system.[31]

Personnel Controls

Many security breaches are caused by employees within the company, either because they lack knowledge about system security or because they have illicit intentions. In fact, as Table 16–4 shows, educating end-users about computer security is one of the top three security concerns of CIOs in the U.S.

"There's a bigger security problem with insiders than with terrorists or industrial espionage. You can't worry about protecting against external forces if you have not protected yourself from within. We've seen cases where a disgruntled employee has gone in and wiped out all the information on a server," says a security expert at Coopers & Lybrand.[32]

TABLE 16–4
Some of the leading security concerns of CIOs in the U.S.

Network security
End-user security awareness
Winning top management's commitment
Using access-controlled software
Distributed computing security
Integrating security systems
Monitoring user compliance with security policy

Source: Haber, Lynn. "Security: Users Still Struggle to Manage LANarchy," *Information Week,* March 7, 1994, p. 37.

Controls are only as effective as the people who implement them. Training system users and communicating security policies are two types of personnel control.

Train System Users   Losses from network security breaches are estimated to be in excess of $2 billion each year. This figure is expected to increase as companies move mission-critical data from mainframes to distributed environments and as the number of mobile users increases. Unfortunately, company employees are among the biggest threats to system data security. "The hackers you read about are by far the smallest threat. Many security breaches are caused by simple user errors."[33] Hence, a key ingredient to achieving network security is regular and extensive user training on how to secure systems and data. Also, employees must be educated on the consequences of poor security and the penalties for failing to follow company policies.

Establish and Communicate Security Policies and Procedures   Security policies and procedures, combined with extensive user training, should precede any investment in security products. Establishing the security policy for a company is the first and most important step. The security policy should contain a mission statement, identify the security responsibilities of each employee, and address, in very specific terms, the ways to protect system hardware and software.

Disaster Recovery Plan

One way a company can prepare itself to face natural, infrastructure, or operational disasters is to develop a well-thought-out and comprehensive **disaster recovery plan (DRP)** that specifies how a company will maintain information systems and services when a disaster strikes. The plan should clearly list and specify the specific situations that warrant the declaration of a disaster and should identify the specific courses of action that employees must take when a disaster strikes. All critical system elements must be included in the DRP. As Figure 16–5 illustrates, even though LANs are one of the fastest-growing segments of the computer industry, they are often not included in the DRP! The benefits of a well-thought-out DRP can be tremendous. When the Irish Republican Army bomb struck London's downtown financial sector, some of the top financial institutions in the world were seriously damaged. Yet the companies were able to operate within a matter of a few hours because of a sophisticated DRP.

Developing a Disaster Recovery Plan

Figure 16–6 shows the steps in developing a DRP. The first is to conduct a thorough analysis of the impact of a disaster on the business, called a business impact analysis or a business resumption plan. The more detailed the business impact analysis is, the smaller is the chance of overlooking critical elements during a disaster. The business impact analysis should clearly identify the situations that qualify as disasters, specifically name individuals who have the right and the responsibility to declare a disaster, identify the specific process by which a disaster will be declared, and identify and prioritize the critical processes, functions, and resources of the organization, which will be included in the DRP.

Disaster recovery plan
Specifies how a company will maintain its information systems and services if a disaster strikes. Specifies the situations that warrant the declaration of a disaster and identifies the courses of action that employees must take when a disaster strikes.

FIGURE 16–5

A large percentage of central
mainframes and distributed
computers are covered by disaster
recovery plans. The number,
however, drops significantly for
PC LANs and standalone PCs.

Sources: Comdisco Disaster Recover
Services; Panettieri, Joseph C. "Gimme
Shelter," *Information Week*, January
18, 1993, p. 26.

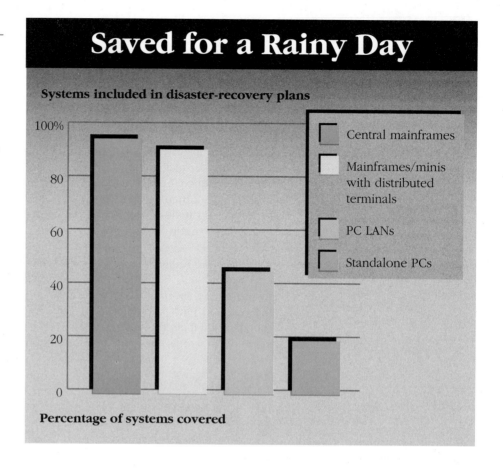

The business impact analysis is driven by the key question, "What would
we do if that key piece of technology were not there? The wrong answer is:
We pack up and take the day off. The right answer is: What did we do before
we got [that technology]? [Finding those alternatives] creates the sense that
'we're unstoppable.'"[34]

There are three steps to developing a business resumption plan:

1. Take an inventory of all corporate assets, functions, and resources that are
   essential to operating the business and prioritize them.
2. Identify the situations that qualify as disasters and the individuals responsible for declaring a disaster.
3. Develop the course of action that each employee in the organization must
   take to make the company operational after a disaster strikes.

A senior planning analyst tells how the business impact plan played a critical role when his company headquarters caught fire in the middle of the night.
Since the stability of the building was in question, the data center and technical
support could not become operational for another 3 days. But because the business plan was so well laid out, by 8:00 the next morning, the company had a fully
functional manual process in place. Had it not been for the local news, customers
would not even have known about the fire. The company's business resumption

FIGURE 16-6

The steps involved in developing a
disaster recovery plan.

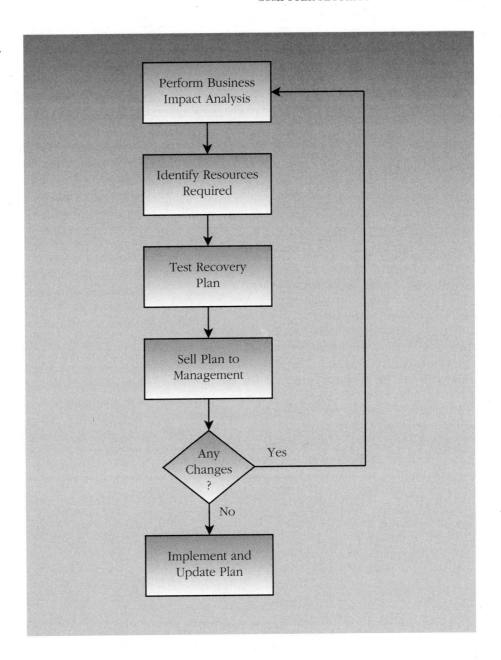

FIGURE 16-6

The steps involved in developing a disaster recovery plan.

plan moved it from a sophisticated networked system, with a PC on every desk, to a manual, paper-based system within a few hours.[35] Refer to the box, Diary of a Disaster Recovery, for an account of how an organization recovered from a disaster.[37]

The next step is to identify the resources required to recover from the disaster. These include money, time, personnel, and facilities that should be specifically dedicated to disaster recovery.

The third step is to test the recovery plan to make sure that it works and that no critical elements have been forgotten. During a disaster recovery test, every step in the plan must be practiced several times; the plan itself must be tested sev-

BUSINESS REALITIES
Diary of a Disaster Recovery

Here is an excerpt from an article that tells how an IS manager successfully walked his company through a disaster:

Charles Peruchini, director of information systems at aluminum wheel manufacturer Superior Industries International, was watching the national weather forecast at 4 A.M. on Monday, January 17. Then, at 4:30, an earthquake, registering 6.6 on the Richter scale, hit the suburbs north of Los Angeles. The $325-million company's data center, less than 5 miles from the quake's epicenter, was completely shut down for 2 days. Six U.S. sites depend on that data center for computing services, so Peruchini got into gear.

Without power and light in the data center and with debris scattered throughout, Peruchini began doing something he had only practiced before—setting up operations at an XL/Datacomp "hot site" in Anaheim, California, more than 60 miles away. He had contracted for the site in October. At 1 P.M., after conferring with plant managers in the midwest, Peruchini notified XL/Datacomp that he was declaring a disaster emergency. He located a backup tape of the operating system,

stored at an offsite data storage facility with Superior's security guards in a nearby company building. At 6:30 P.M., the "hot site" was ready to start loading the operating system and applications onto its AS/400 Model D70. But by 8 P.M., Peruchini had discovered that the 8-mm backup tapes of the application and data files could not be read without an 8-mm EMC tape drive similar to the one in the data center. The Los Angeles office of EMC located a Voyager unit at neighboring Del Taco, in Orange, California. At 10:30 P.M., Peruchini started loading his data center's manufacturing, financial, and distribution applications—all 99 of them. "I wasn't sure which were the critical ones. By noon the next day, all systems were go, except for the 19.2-Kbps modems that XL/Datacomp had sent to Superior's remote sites in Arkansas, Tennessee, and Kansas. At 3:30 P.M., we were finally in good shape. Power had been restored and the AS/400 there had been repositioned."

By this time, 2 days after the quake had hit, Superior's own data center was back up and running well enough for them to return. By 6 A.M. the next day, the data center's AS/400, surrounded by fallen ceiling tiles and debris, was processing data for Van Nuys and one remote plant. Four other Midwestern plants regained their links to the AS/400 at 10:30 A.M. after a long-distance line outage.[36]

eral times each year so that all employees know what to do if a disaster strikes. The plan should also be updated frequently to include new assets and new risks that increase the vulnerability of the firm. A DRP is good only if it is well tested, well understood, and well remembered.

The success of a DRP requires the commitment of top management and the cooperation of every department in the company. It is a serious error to think that DRP is the sole responsibility of the IS manager or that recovery mandates should come from the CEO. Also, disaster recovery is not a one-time commitment, but a long-term commitment of resources to keep the assets of the organization secure and protected. In spite of its obvious importance, CIOs and IS managers often have to struggle to get resources allocated for disaster recovery, especially during lean times.

Once the disaster recovery plan is drawn up, the next step is to identify the alternatives for implementing the plan. For example, a company can use the services of a disaster service bureau that provides temporary disaster recovery services, such as immediate access to time-sharing environments, access to utilities, and temporary personnel. Another alternative is to have reciprocal arrangements with other companies that use similar equipment and applications so that in case of an emergency one company can use the facilities of the other. However, it is very difficult to find another company that uses exactly the same system and the same set of applications and is not in direct competition with yours.

The third alternative is outsourcing disaster recovery operations to commercial vendors who provide a broad range of services, including providing backup systems and communications networks within 24 hours' notice of a disaster. Outsourcing vendors must be carefully chosen, because they can make or break the company in times of crisis and are expensive. Fees for commercial security vendors can range from a few hundred dollars per month to $50,000 per month, depending on the kind and quality of service they provide.

The fourth alternative is to build a backup site, which houses the same computer facilities and applications as the original site, along with backups of all data and programs. Clearly, this is a very expensive proposition that only large companies can afford. However, many companies lease or rent backup facilities that are at a safe distance from their facilities.

In 1992, an Irish Republican Army car bomb exploded in the heart of London's financial district. Although more than 35 firms had to seek alternative office space, things were not as bad as they could have been. The main IT centers for many businesses were housed elsewhere, and this, along with extensive contingency planning, allowed most firms to recover key business systems within a few days.

One of the hardest hit was the insurance and financial services group Commercial Union (CU), whose headquarters were seriously damaged. All facilities, including the main telephone switchboard, which handles 3,600 extensions, 500 terminals, and 100 word processors, were completely destroyed. But the company's data center was located 11 miles away near Croydon, at the south edge of London. On Saturday, a day after the bombing, the insurer devised an emergency plan to sustain critical operations. On Sunday, replacement terminals, fax machines, telephones, and other office equipment were ordered and delivered to various alternative sites around the city. Telephone services were rerouted from the company's central London telephone switch to the Croydon site. The company also set up 10 switchboards and a message back-up system to handle calls. With the help of IBM, it reestablished links between the new terminals at different sites and the mainframe in Croydon. By Tuesday, four days after the bombing, 631 of the 650 staffers were working at other offices.[37]

In summary, a company must carefully and continuously address the issue of securing its information systems. Table 16–5 summarizes some recommendations that we have provided in this chapter for developing secure computer environments.

 TABLE 16–5
Some recommendations for developing and maintaining secure environments.

- Security should be an integral part of the development process.
- A simple, secure system is always better than a sophisticated, vulnerable system.
- Sensitive and proprietary data should always be on the mainframe or the minicomputer, not on the PC.
- Stay with homogeneous platforms unless security tools for heterogeneous platforms become available.
- Be constantly on the lookout for new security tools and techniques.
- Pressure vendors to deliver customized solutions.
- Get upper management to understand what you are doing. If they do, you will get their support. If you get their support, you will get their money.
- Remember, that security is only as good as the weakest link in the chain.

Source: Haber, Lynn. "Users Still Struggle to Manage LANarchy," *Information Week,* March 7, 1994, p. 41.

 **Summary**

- **Why computer security is vital to the survival of a business.**

The increase in distributed environments, the exponential growth of information and information-related products, the increase in competitive pressures from all over the world, and advances in technology have all placed data among the most sought-after assets in today's competitive business environment. As our reliance on computers and information systems increases, the task of securing these systems also increases in criticality. A computer security breach is often viewed as a "corporate heart attack" because it can cause serious damage to the organization. The damage may consist of revenue loss, productivity decline, computer downtime, or loss of competitive status. Hence, computer security is vital to the growth, and even to the survival, of a business. Computer security is defined as a set of policies, procedures, tools, and techniques that an organization establishes to protect its computer assets from theft, security breaches, physical damage, and illegal access or manipulation. Computer security is a broad and encompassing issue that covers all the components of corporate computing: hardware, software, networks, physical facilities, data, and personnel.

- **The weak links in information systems that make them vulnerable to security breaches.**

There are several reasons why computer systems are vulnerable to security breaches. The increased complexity of information systems has made it difficult for organizations to develop rigorous security measures. The multitude of choices in system configuration is another factor contributing to the security challenge. Today, the number of hardware, software, and network choices is greater than ever before, making the task of the security expert more complex and challenging. Third, because of distributed computing, the number of employees working locally and remotely, nationally and internationally, on homogeneous and heterogeneous systems has increased significantly. It is therefore becoming a Herculean task to prevent illegal access and unauthorized manipulation of files in distributed environments. Fourth, hackers and crackers have become more sophisticated and persistent. A cracker is an individual who illegally breaks into a computer system or facility and steals passwords, mail messages, files, programs, and so on, for fun or for profit. Regardless of a cracker's motive, he or she can cause serious and irreparable damage to a company, its assets, and its reputation. Finally, in spite of all the warnings and horror stories, top management is still often reluctant to invest in system security.

- **Different types of security breaches.**

Security breaches can be broadly divided into five categories: hardware, software, networks, personnel, and natural or man-made disasters. Hardware breaches can be intentional or accidental. Cables, fax machines, modems, and cellular phones are particularly vulnerable to security breaches. "Sniffer" programs and computer viruses are the two primary threats to software. Networks are very vulnerable to security breaches. Particular weak links on the network include computers, improper access privileges, network cables and wires, lack of user training, and lack of well-thought-out security policies and procedures. Finally, disasters can cause security violations. There are three types of disasters: natural, infrastructure, and operational.

- **Security controls that organizations can implement to prevent security breaches.**

Computer security controls are established and implemented in order to reduce security breaches or even system destruction. Effective controls help to prevent system errors and protect systems from accidental, intentional, and natural disasters. There are five types of controls: application controls, development controls, access controls, physical facility controls, and personnel controls.

Application controls are policies and procedures that ensure the security and quality of individual applications in the organization. Some specific types are input, processing, output, and storage controls. Development controls are established so that the security of the system is addressed during system development itself and not as an afterthought. Some specific types of development controls are standards and documentation, data security, authorization requirements, and separation of duties. Access controls include passwords and other measures to make sure that access to data, programs, and systems is available only to authorized individuals. Physical security controls are measures taken to protect and secure the physical plant and the facilities of an organization. Finally, personnel controls are procedures to educate end-users about security measures and their criticality to the organization.

- **The importance of a disaster recovery plan.** One way a company can prepare itself to face natural, infrastructure, or operational disasters is to develop a well-thought-out and comprehensive disaster recovery plan (DRP), which specifies how the company will maintain the information systems and services necessary for its smooth operations after a disaster strikes.

The plan should clearly list and specify the situations that warrant the declaration of a disaster and identify the actions that must be taken by each employee when a disaster strikes. The four popular disaster recovery methods are: using a service bureau, establishing a shared contingency agreement, outsourcing to a commercial vendor, and building a backup site.

 Review Questions

1. Define computer security. Explain why computer security cannot be achieved through automation alone. Identify any three reasons why computer systems are vulnerable to security breaches. Explain why networks are so prone to security breaches.
2. What is the difference between hackers and crackers? Should an organization take measures to protect itself from both or just from one?
3. What is meant by security controls? Briefly describe the five types of controls.
4. What is meant by application controls? Briefly describe the four primary areas of data processing that are covered by application controls.
5. What are some data validation controls and how do they help to increase the security of input data?
6. What are development controls? Identify and describe the four types of development controls.
7. What is meant by separation of duties? Why is this essential for the development of reliable systems?
8. What is meant by access controls? What are some measures that companies must take to ensure that passwords provide the necessary security?

9. What are the three types of security breaches? Give an example of each.
10. Why are fax machines and modems particularly vulnerable to security breaches? What measures can an organization take to secure these two types of hardware?
11. What is a computer virus? What are some ways to prevent viruses?
12. What is a backup? Why are backups vital to computer system security?
13. What are some measures that managers can take to protect their networks from security breaches? Describe any two in detail.
14. Identification and authentication (I&A) requires three things. What are they? Give an example of each.
15. What is a disaster recovery plan? In particular, describe the business resumption plan and its overall importance to system security.
16. What are some steps involved in developing a disaster recovery plan?

 Discussion Questions

1. Automation alone cannot create secure systems. Computer security relies on common sense, good judgment, and high moral values. Discuss.
2. Contact the director of information services at your university. Find out whether the university has a disaster recovery plan; if so, describe the elements of this plan.
3. Winning the commitment of top management to allocate resources for security measures is one of the greatest challenges confronting IS managers. Develop a presentation to explain to the board of directors why investing in security measures is like preventing a "corporate heart attack."

ETHICAL ISSUES

Case 1: Monitoring Employees

One of the issues of system security is that today there are a number of tools that can provide managers (or others) with detailed information about users and their activities. This is one way to catch hackers, crackers, and others who may be violating the company's security policies. The power of technology provides opportunities both for using and abusing technology; the key to the successful use of monitoring devices is to distinguish between supervision and surveillance. This approach to security has raised a host of legal and social issues that have yet to be settled.

For example, although communication over public phone lines is considered private and can be monitored only by law-enforcement officials who have obtained a court order, communication over telephone lines at the workplace has no such legal protection. In fact, many managers believe that since their company owns those lines, they have every right to monitor the communications that pass over them—and their views are supported by federal law. The 1986 Electronic Communications Privacy Act prohibits phone and data line taps with two exceptions: law enforcement agencies and employers!

Reading E-mail and monitoring keystrokes, unlike monitoring telephone communications, has no legal precedent. This is causing a great deal of confusion and frustration, for both employers and employees. Therefore, at the request of the Justice Department, the Computer Systems Laboratory of the National Institute of Standards and Technology has formulated a set of guidelines about the legality of keystroke monitoring. This document, *Guidance on the Legality of Keystroke Monitoring*, states, "The Justice Department advises that if system administrators are conducting keystroke monitoring or anticipate the need for such monitoring, even for the purpose of detecting intruders, they should ensure that all system users, authorized and unauthorized, be notified that monitoring may be undertaken." But written notice alone is not sufficient. The Justice Department also recommends that system administrators add to every user's login a "banner" that gives "clear and unequivocal notice that by signing on and using the system, they are expressly consenting to have their keystrokes monitored or recorded."

The informed consent of users is vital to protect them from undue harassment. The Massachusetts CNOT (Coalition on New Office Technologies), a civil rights group, is formulating the CNOT Act, which would require businesses to tell employees what kinds of data will be collected about them, how frequently they will be monitored, how the employees can access and comment on these data in a timely manner, and whether the data collected will be used for evaluations or other actions by the personnel department.

In a recent study of 686 workers, there was overwhelming evidence that monitoring lowers employee productivity, increases turnaround, and decreases employee morale. Two thirds of the workers surveyed indicated that they felt monitoring made it difficult to take a break, even to go to the bathroom. Monitoring may deter workers from taking risks, making mistakes, doing unorthodox things, or using their creative energies.

At this stage, however, the issue goes beyond that of worker privacy, according to Alan Westin, professor of public law and government at Columbia University, in New York. It becomes one of human dignity.

1. Many managers believe that since their company owns the technology, they have every right to monitor any communication that takes place within that technology. Do you agree? Discuss.
2. If your company gave you written notice that you would be monitored and if a banner appeared every time you logged onto your computer, reminding you of the monitoring process, what, if any, objections would you have to being monitored?
3. Keystrokes are monitored in an effort to increase productivity. Why is there overwhelming evidence that keystroke monitoring has a negative effect on worker productivity?
4. Monitoring workers is not an issue of worker privacy but an issue of human dignity. Discuss.

Case 2: Worker Privacy

This case, illustrated by Figure 16–7, deals with policy issues regarding worker privacy. These issues are highly controversial and the Justice Department is looking at several legislative proposals to clarify the issue. Currently, one company in four has a privacy policy that covers monitoring or reading E-mail, listening to telephone calls, monitoring voice mail, gaining access to files on employees' hard disks, and monitoring users' activities on the network.

1. What is a privacy policy? Should companies disclose the existence of a privacy policy during recruitment?

2. Do you agree that privacy policies are necessary to protect the privacy of workers and clients? Are there other ways to protect worker and client privacy?

3. While 18% of employees said that companies should be allowed to monitor E-mail, only 10% approved of telephone and voice mail monitoring. What are some reasons why monitoring E-mail may be less offensive than monitoring voice mail or telephone calls?

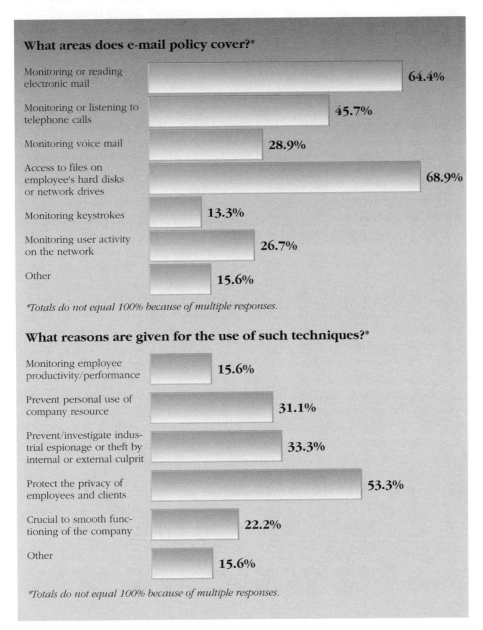

What areas does e-mail policy cover?*

Monitoring or reading electronic mail	64.4%
Monitoring or listening to telephone calls	45.7%
Monitoring voice mail	28.9%
Access to files on employee's hard disks or network drives	68.9%
Monitoring keystrokes	13.3%
Monitoring user activity on the network	26.7%
Other	15.6%

Totals do not equal 100% because of multiple responses.

What reasons are given for the use of such techniques?*

Monitoring employee productivity/performance	15.6%
Prevent personal use of company resource	31.1%
Prevent/investigate industrial espionage or theft by internal or external culprit	33.3%
Protect the privacy of employees and clients	53.3%
Crucial to smooth functioning of the company	22.2%
Other	15.6%

Totals do not equal 100% because of multiple responses.

FIGURE 16–7

Privacy policies are being intensely debated in computer circles, although only one in four companies has a privacy policy. This figure shows the different areas covered by privacy policy and the opinions of employees about such policies.

Source: Smith, Laura B., "Encryption, Monitoring, and E-mail Spur the Privacy Debate," *PC Week Special Report*, June 28, 1993, p. 202.

PROBLEM SOLVING IN THE REAL WORLD

Case 1: Is It an Angel or SATAN in Disguise?

Security Administrator Tool for Analyzing Networks (SATAN), marketed as a powerful, easy-to-use security tool, can easily become one of the worst security nightmares for an organization. Available free on the Internet since April 5, 1995, SATAN has caused heated debate in IS circles.

SATAN is a program that identifies security weaknesses in a networked computer environment by imitating the way an intruder would break into the system from a host computer that is not part of the site's LAN, thus giving SATAN the true flavor of a security breach. SATAN probes, identifies, and reports a wide range of security loopholes in a network, without in any way damaging it. The program provides recommendations to system administrators for eliminating security weaknesses.

At the core of the SATAN program is the inference engine module, which consists of several rule bases. The most critical rule base allows SATAN to deduce potential security problems based on historical knowledge about security problems. New rules can be readily added to this and to other modules. Another module runs a series of programs to probe the system and report the data.

Unfortunately, SATAN's strongest features are also its most dangerous. SATAN can easily be used as a learning tool for breaking into a networked system. If a cracker gets hold of SATAN, he or she can easily identify the weak points in the system and break into it even before the organization can close its loopholes. When the program finds a weak link in a system, it describes the vulnerability and explains how an intruder could capitalize on that weak link. Further, SATAN has an excellent, easy-to-use graphical user interface that allows even novices with no technical expertise to try the program. The World Wide Web browser interface is both a boon and a bane for network administrators, who find the product very easy to use but who are appalled that it is freely available on the Internet. Says one administrator, "With a free product, it's going to be the guys with extra time on their hands who will be out hacking and playing with it." Although SATAN only probes the system, administrators fear that a skilled programmer could easily use its source code (which is readily available) to break into or even damage a system.

SATAN codeveloper Dan Farmer, who has worked as the network security chief at Silicon Graphics Inc. (SGI), in Mountain View, California, acknowledges the dangers of SATAN, but says that such risks are part of providing security. SGI officials say SATAN contributed to Farmer's departure from their company because they did not agree that a product such as SATAN should be distributed in an indiscriminate manner. "We think instead it should go to network administrators in a controlled fashion," says a company spokesperson.

But some security experts disagree and say that the uproar is about nothing. "Any self-respecting hacker's tool kit already has all the tools that SATAN has, without the nice graphical front end," says one expert. This school of thought argues that solutions are available for all the vulnerabilities that SATAN detects, although some of those solutions may be expensive and call for reorganization of the entire network.[38]

1. If you were the CIO, would you recommend buying SATAN for your organization?

Case 2: The Clipper Chip

The Clipper chip is a new data encryption standard for the United States being proposed by the Clinton administration. Clipper is a microprocessor that, when linked to a telephone or data terminal, can scramble a conversation or document so it can be deciphered only by the intended recipient and the government. The catch is the Clipper chip's "back door" that permits federal agents to unscramble coded messages.

Clipper contains a secret algorithm, named Skypack, developed by the National Security Agency to protect unclassified, but sensitive, voice and data telephone communications. Users would be required to give the keys to unscramble encrypted information to two federal agencies to be held "in escrow" and used by law enforcement agencies in court-approved wiretaps. The key/escrow concept has merit but is considered to be fatally flawed in the Clipper proposal because the government would hold the decryption keys.

1. The FBI has to get permission from the Commerce and Treasury Departments before it can unscramble coded messages. Should businesses still worry about government interference?

References

Anthes, Gary H. "Internet Panel Finds Reusable Passwords a Threat." *Computerworld,* March 28, 1994, p. 50.

Bozman, Jean S. "Diary of a Disaster Recovery," *Computerworld,* Nov. 14, 1994, pp. 65–66.

Chaum, D. "Security Without Identification: Transaction Systems to Make Big Brother Obsolete." *Communications of the ACM,* vol. 28, October 1985.

Hoffman, Thomas. "Newark Airport Blackout Exposes Systems Flaws." *Computerworld,* January 16, 1995, p. 6.

Loch, K. D., H. C. Houston, and M. E. Warkentin. "Threats to Information Systems: Today's Reality, Yesterday's Understanding," *MIS Quarterly,* vol. 16, no. 2, June 1992.

Neumann, P. G. "Risks Considered Global(ly)," *Communications of the ACM,* vol. 35, no. 1, January 1993.

Rainer, R. K., Jr., C. A. Snyder, and H. H. Car. "Risk Analysis for Information Technology," *Journal of Management Information Systems,* vol. 8, no. 1, Summer 1991.

Schwartau, Winn. "Hackers, Sniffers, Worms, and Demons," *Information Week,* May 16, 1994, pp. 39–44.

Notes

1. Hoffman, Thomas. "Newark Airport Blackout Exposes Systems Flaws," *Computerworld,* January 16, 1995, p. 6.
2. Modified quote from "Toll Fraud and Telabuse: A Multi-Billion-Dollar Problem," *Information Week,* May 16, 1994, p. 48.
3. Violino, Bob. "Are Your Networks Secure?" *Information Week,* April 22, 1993, pp. 30–35.
4. "Breaking and Entering," *Computerworld,* March 7, 1994, p. 53.
5. Schwartau, Winn. "Hackers, Sniffers, Worms, and Demons," *Information Week,* May 16, 1994, pp. 39–44.
6. Danca, Richard A. "From A to Z: Privacy Policies Run the Gamut," *PC Week Special Report,* June 28, 1993, p. 208.
7. Haber, Lynn. "Security: Users Still Struggle to Manage LANarchy," *Information Week,* March 7, 1994, p. 37.
8. Anthes, Gary H. "Internet Panel Finds Reusable Passwords a Threat," *Computerworld,* March 28, 1994, p. 50.
9. Schwartau, Winn. "Hackers, Sniffers, Worms, and Demons," *Information Week,* May 16, 1994, p. 39.
10. Ibid.
11. Thyfault, Mary and Stephanie Stahl. "Weak Links," *Information Week,* August 10, 1992, p. 27.
12. Schwartau, Winn. "Hackers, Sniffers, Worms, and Demons," *Information Week,* May 16, 1994, p. 39.
13. Ibid.
14. Thyfault, Mary and Stephanie Stahl. "Weak Links," *Information Week,* August 10, 1992, p. 27.
15. Ibid.
16. Daly, James. "Virus Vagaries Foil Feds," *Computerworld,* July 12, 1993, p. 15.
17. Ibid.
18. Ibid.
19. Ibid.
20. Panettieri, Joseph C. "Gimme Shelter," *Information Week,* January 18, 1993, pp. 24, 26.
21. Horwitt, Elisabeth. "The $40,000 Bolt from Out of the Blue," *Computerworld,* May 25, 1993, cover page and p. 14.
22. Kass, Elliott M. "Playing with Fire," *Information Week,* April 2, 1990, pp. 48–54.
23. Ibid.
24. Stahl, Stephanie. "A Busy Phone User Gets off the Hook," *Information Week,* January 4, 1993, p. 35.
25. Murphy, Joan H. "Taking the Disaster out of Recovery," *Security Management,* August 1991, pp. 61–66.
26. Pepper, Jon. "The Bigger the Network, the Scarier," *Information Week,* Sept. 7, 1992, pp. 41, 44.
27. "SecurID Keeps Passwords Changing," *Computerworld,* March 28, 1994, p. 51.
28. Anthes, Gary H. "Without a Pass Phrase, You Will Fail," *Information Week,* March 7, 1994, p. 46.
29. Anthes, Gary. "Viruses Continue to Wreak Havoc at Many U.S. Companies," *Computerworld,* June 28, 1993, p. 52.
30. Chandler, Doug. "Disasters Underscore Importance of Having Backup for Vital Data," *PC Week,* August 29, 1988, pp. 83–86.
31. Kass, Elliot M. "Playing With Fire," *Information Week,* April 2, 1990, pp. 48–54.
32. "Are Your Networks Secure?" *Information Week,* April 12, 1993, p. 32.

33. Rounds, Martha. "Is Your LAN Data Secure?" *Software Magazine,* May 1992, pp. 27–29, 34.

34. "Technology Does Not Save the Day," *Datamation,* January 21, 1994, p. 12.

35. Ibid.

36. Bozman, Jean S. "Diary of a Disaster Recovery," *Computerworld,* Nov. 14, 1994, pp. 65–66.

37. Hunter, Philip. "London on Its Knees," *InformationWeek,* May 4, 1992, p. 17.

38. Wilder, Clinton, and Jason Levitt. "Cure or Curse?" *InformationWeek,* April 3, 1995, pp. 14–15.

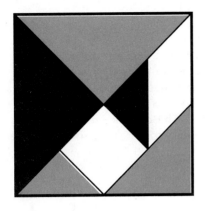

Business Ethics

Appendix A*

Overview

Recent business scandals suggest that business ethics should receive greater emphasis, both within corporations and within business school programs. Yet it is unclear just what business ethics really is—is the individual to be indoctrinated in someone else's view of what is right or wrong? Does business ethics mean that the business must be a charitable corporation? Or does business ethics mean that the corporation must function only within the law? About whom are we concerned when we talk about business ethics?

What constitutes ethical business practices is based upon the assumptions and values in the mind of the individual. Individuals make assumptions about the purpose of the organization. Individuals also hold values, the enduring beliefs that a specific mode of conduct or end state of existence is personally or socially preferable to another mode or end state. Assumptions and values together give the individual a sense of what is right and wrong, good and bad. The basis upon which individuals make assumptions and values.

The obligations and responsibilities assumed by an organization will be reflected in its mission, policies and strategy. The mission, policies, and strategy reflect current and past leaders' assumptions and values. Thus each organization will have a sense (if sometimes a small sense) of corporate responsibility. Moreover, crises or dilemmas also reflect their assumptions and values.

Because assumptions and values are inextricably intertwined with an organization's mission, policies, strategy and reactions, the question naturally arises whether a more socially responsible organization performs better financially than one that pays little attention to social implications.

Business Ethics

Business ethics is the consideration of "rightness" and "wrongness" of behaviors, decisions, or actions of people who work in business organizations (Carroll, 1989). The word, ethics, describes what ought to be. Moral standards are the group's or society's definition of "rightness" or "wrongness." So business ethics is the consideration and study of moral standards in business organizations.

*Reprinted with permission from *Business Ethics and Corporate Responsibility* by Susan J. Harrington, Ph.D., Kent State University, Stark Campus. Copyright by West Publishing Company.

Each poor decision is the result of a moral lapse (a decision that clearly violated a moral standard, such as stealing or cheating) or a poorly resolved moral dilemma (where the resolution of an ethical issue is not clear because there are two or more conflicting but valid sides to an issue). Yet each decision was typically made from the viewpoint of getting ahead. The call for greater business ethics suggests that there is a need for business ethics to act as a restraint on the capitalistic goal to achieve profits.

Business Ethics In a Capitalistic Society

Two managers may make entirely different decisions that each considers ethical. The manager who feels the organization exists to make a profit may work to enhance profits without regard to the social consequences, whereas the manager who values fairness or property rights would make different decisions based on his or her sense of what is right or wrong. The manager's assumptions concerning the role of an organization direct the manager in deciding objectives to be achieved and the rightness or wrongness of methods used to achieve them.

The assumptions in a capitalistic society that influence how people feel about right and wrong in business behavior have to do with property rights, explicit vs. implicit contractual agreements, and the responsibility of business toward its workers. Other assumptions include whether a firm will naturally use its power wisely and whether the firm is a member of a larger community.

An individual's assumptions and values influence the person's ethical theory used when resolving ethical dilemmas. The ethical theory used, in turn, is related to the individual's view of what corporate social responsibility is.

Ethical Theories

One assumption about the nature of business is that the organization exists to make a profit, presumably for its shareholders' benefit. The classical view holds that management's responsibility is to protect and augment the shareholder's investment in the firm. Using resources for anything other than augmenting the shareholders' wealth would be unethical.

The stakeholder view, like the classical view, also holds that the management's responsibility is to protect and augment the shareholder's investment in the firm, but it also assumes that there are other parties which have a stake in the performance of the organization. These other parties include, at minimum, employees, consumers, and suppliers.

Ethical Theories and Values

Individuals base their arguments on both their instrumental values (rightness or wrongness of behaviors used in achieving goals), their terminal values (goals to be achieved) and their application of these values to the work setting.

Corporate Social Responsibility

The idea of corporate social responsibility rests on two basic premises: (1) corporate legitimacy: i.e., business exists at the pleasure of society; its behavior must fall within the rules and guidelines of society and (2) moral agency: i.e., business acts as a moral agent within society and reflects and reinforces values (Wartick and Cochran, 1985). A moral agent is someone who is competent to understand the idea of "the good" for both himself or herself and for others, and to have a sense of duty in interaction with others.

The term, corporate social responsibility, has evolved since the 1950's as a concept to describe what society expects of organizations. The definition of corporate social responsibility has been vague because of differing values and assumptions, but Carroll (1989), building on others' definitions, has proposed a four part-definition: the economic, legal, ethical, and philanthropic responsibilities of business.

Economic responsibilities are included in the definition because of the corporate legitimacy concept: society expects business to be an economic institution that produces a product or service and strives to make a profit. Organizations are also expected to abide by laws and thus have legal responsibilities. Ethical responsibilities are those that society expects but are not codified into law. Philanthropic or discretionary responsibilities are voluntary and not expected by society. IBM's sending of executives to inner city schools to teach science and math would be considered philanthropic.

What is considered legal, ethical or philanthropic may differ from culture to culture. Even within a culture, economic, legal, ethical, and philanthropic responsibilities may overlap or change. For example, environmental issues, long ignored by business so as to reduce costs of production, are now subject to laws.

Corporate Social Responsiveness

The term Corporate Social Responsiveness (CSR) was coined to suggest that business can take a more dynamic, proactive view toward social concerns. The firm could take four approaches to being responsive: (1) reactive or "fight all the way" approach, (2) defensive or "do only what is required" approach, (3) accommodative or "be progressive" approach, or (4) proactive or "lead the industry" approach (Wilson, 1975; McAdam, 1973). A reactive approach suggests that the organization will resist investigations and fight compliance laws. Defensive managers will comply with the law while using the law as a shield. Accommodative managers will take some positive ethical actions to resolve problems. Proactive managers will attempt to identify problems before they happen and try to prevent them from occurring.

Corporate social responsibility and corporate social responsiveness are complementary concepts.

Corporate Social Performance

Corporate Social Performance (CSP) was created to describe what kind of social good an organization accomplishes. Moreover, each organization operates in an environment where specific social issues, such as environment, EEO, or employee safety, may be more relevant than for other organizations.

The interdependence of players in business breeds conflict, and conflict, in turn, breeds moral dilemmas that the managerial decision makers must face. Thus, embedded in such decision making are the individual manager's value judgments and the manager's own view of what ethical behavior is. For example, some believe ethical behavior is to maximize the return to all the shareholders, whereas others may believe ethical behavior is to maximize the return to stakeholders (Freeman and Gilbert, 1988). A manager's value judgments influence the selection of opportunities and objectives that are possible within time and resource constraints.

In addition, the selection of an implementation approach and attention to ethical implications of the approach emanates from the decision maker's value system. Moreover, corrective actions to insure that organizational outcomes are compatible with objectives are subject to value judgments and standards of behavior.

For example, managers' value systems determine how employees will be managed: e.g., whether employees are expendable, or whether an autocratic or participatory style may be used. Again, the manager's value system will be reflected in the treatment of employee issues, with guidelines emanating from the highest levels of the firm.

In sum, corporate strategy will most likely be related to the top management's own value system. Thus it can be hypothesized that the priority given to human and social issues in the mission and strategy of the firm will be strongly related to the CEO's own value system.

The question that arises from this discussion is whether those companies that are led by those with specific values or those companies which are concerned about social performance (have high CSP) excel and thus earn greater profits.

Relationship of Corporate Social Performance (CSP) to Corporate Financial Performance (CFP)

Only a few years ago a Public Broadcasting Service special report on ethics in American business noted that a majority of Fortune 500 managers believed that establishing an ethical culture within their corporations would lead to strategic competitive advantage (Public Broadcasting Service (PBS), 1988). Moreover, the Ethics Resource Center (1990) found that, of surveyed companies with a code of ethics, 53 percent said the motivating factor for issuing the code was "company growth," by far the leading reason for creating a code of ethics.

An informal survey by the CEO of Johnson and Johnson suggested that the market value of ethically-oriented firms grew at a greater rate than Dow Jones industrials as a whole. Similarly, "ethical" mutual funds (e.g., Pax World) that invest under specific guidelines have performed better than comparable mutual funds.

Overview

Because top level managers set the direction and atmosphere in the organization, their attention to and handling of ethical issues strongly influences the organization's ethical behavior. In other words, ethical conduct at the individual level translates into social responsibility at the corporate level.

Influences in Defining Corporate
Social Responsibility

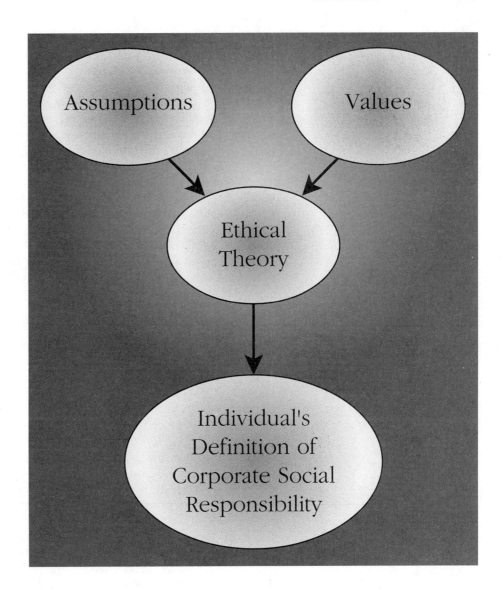

So it is appropriate to examine how managers make decisions, as well as the result of such decisions.

Management decisions affect what the organization is trying to accomplish. What gets accomplished is determined in part by the manager's competence to identify issues and evaluate consequences of alternate courses of action. Many issues involve an ethical component, and so within this process of identification and evaluation the ethical objectives of the corporation will be determined. The manager also directs how decisions will be carried out by establishing the firm's internal corporate culture and structure. How and what are accomplished influences both corporate social performances (CSP) and corporate financial performance (CFP).

Management decision making and ethical behavior are influenced by both individual characteristics and organizational factors. Qualities of individuals and their cognitive styles are thus important elements in how people resolve ethical dilemmas facing them in their jobs. Each person brings a unique set of characteristics to the decision-making process. So a manager's individual characteristics will have an influence on what is accomplished and how it is accomplished.

However, individual characteristics are not the sole determinant of ethical decisions. The types of issues and the existence of certain organizational factors direct or limit the alternatives that a manager can choose from. Issues, for example, may be slowly evolving or crisis-oriented, or may affect a few people severely or many people only slightly. Also, the organization may be limited in ability to respond by social, economic, technological, industry or regulatory constraints. Moreover, organizational structure and culture may limit alternate courses of action.

The nature of issues likely interacts with individual characteristics to influence decision making. The individual's cognitive style and belief system will influence how the individual handles issues varying in such attributes as magnitude of consequences or urgency. The interaction of the nature of issues and individual characteristics is particularly relevant to resolution of ethical issues.

Decision Making's Relationship to CSP and CFP

Top-level managers set the direction and atmosphere in the organization. Their key role is decision making. Many of their decisions involve ethical issues, situations where a person's actions, when freely performed, have harmful or beneficial consequences for others, usually at the expense of another. Management attention to and handling of ethical issues sets the tone for how the organization perceives its social responsibility.

A person making a decision involving ethical issues, the moral agent, may or may not realize that the decision involves an ethical component. The values and assumptions held by top-level management will determine which ethical theory is advocated and how an organization directs its attention. In other words, the values of top-level managers influence the organization's objectives and values.

Organizational values are important. Recall that one component of commitment is the employee's belief in the goals and values of the organization. Employees who have an affective commitment are loyal, have a deep concern for the organization's welfare, and have less absenteeism and greater productivity.

One approach used by Merck to communicate values is its mission statement: "profit derived from work that benefits society." As shown by this mission statement, top management's values are inextricably bound up in its decision making within the organization. For one, management decision making determines what is to be achieved. A manager's terminal values will thus be closely aligned with decisions concerning objectives. It is known that managers set up goals that are consistent with their image of themselves and their attitudes. Management decision making also determines how objectives will be achieved. Closely aligned with how decisions will be achieved will be the manager's instrumental values.

Management decisions affect how well the organization performs. Managers and organizations that excel are typically ones that do well at (1.) information gathering, (2.) intelligent selection of objectives (whats) and solutions (hows), and (3.) self-correction.

It is believed that a competent manager who excels at information gathering, selection of objectives and solutions, and self-correction is also more likely to consider all sides and consequences of a problem, and therefore may be more likely to consider the ethical implications of the decision. In sum, a manager who is more comprehensive in decision making will likely achieve better results, as well as consider ethical issues.

An Ethical Decision-Making Model

Because individuals, in particular, managers, are those who ultimately determine both social and financial corporate performance, it is important to understand how individuals evaluate ethical issues in a profit-seeking organization.

Ethical decision making is the process used by the individual to come to a conclusion or action that involves an ethical issue, although there is no empirical proof of precisely how ethical decision making evolves (Rest's (1986) model).

There are four components in the ethical decision-making process: (1) interpret or recognize the moral issue, (2) make a moral judgment, (3) establish moral intent by placing moral values above other personal values, and (4) follow through or engage in moral behavior.

Component 1: Interpret or Recognize the Moral Issue

In the first component of the model, interpret or recognize the moral issue, the person is, at minimum, realizing that what he or she may do will affect the interests, welfare, or expectations of other people. It is possible that the individual may not even recognize the ethical aspects of a decision. Of interest is that, in making decisions, managers may discount data that differs from their beliefs or challenges their values.

An example of misinterpreting an issue is when an individual may think that the organization supports unethical behavior, such as stealing competitor's customer lists, because superficially it appears to benefit the company. Other examples abound. One example is taking shortcuts that reduce safety to meet demanding project target dates; another, copying microcomputer software illegally, is widespread. Sometimes employees act without thinking about the behavior because of peer pressure or because others are doing it.

Component 2: Make a Moral Judgment

Making a moral judgment involves a person's convictions about what is right or wrong. These convictions vary drastically from person to person. For example, consider the difference in opinion between pro-choice and pro-life advocates.

The result of the moral judgment component is the individual's sense about what is right or wrong. Yet often individuals do not choose to do what they know is right. To abide by the individual's moral judgment, the individual must place moral values above other personal values, which is component 3 of the ethical decision-making process.

Component 3: Establish Moral Intent by Placing Moral Values Above Other Personal Values

Individuals can rank their values. Such a ranking implies that given a choice between a high-priority value and a lesser one, an individual will choose behavior leading to gratification of the high-priority value.

People tend to prioritize moral values over other values when faced with an ethical issue, although the precise reasons for this are unknown. Some possible reasons include learned social behavior, fear of punishment, perceived ability to achieve the desired result, self-integrity and identity as a moral agent, or an understanding of one's own stake in building a socially desirable world (Rest, 1986).

Component 4: Follow Through or Engage in Moral Behavior

Factors that influence whether the individual will follow through or engage in moral behavior can be both within the individual's control and out of the individual's control. An individual's perseverance and competence will influence the individual's success in carrying out intentions. On the other hand, events may occur that thwart the individual's effort, despite good intentions.

If an individual intends to engage in unethical behavior, social constraints may prevent the individual from following through. Social constraints will affect the relationship between attitudes (such as moral judgment and moral intent) and behavior (component 4, moral behavior).

Situations and Ethical Decision Making

In addition to issue characteristics, other factors influence ethical decision making. Situational characteristics are those factors external to the firm (e.g., regulatory environment), as well as those internal to the firm (e.g., corporate culture) that influence decision makers by providing different opportunities or alternatives for resolving issues. The external corporate environment is comprised of social, economic, technological, industry structure and regulatory components. These, in turn, affect the internal corporate culture.

Denison (1990), in several case studies, found that cultural change occurred in response to the demands of the external environment. Change was driven by a crisis of mission and strategy and the need to adapt, rather than any specific intent by management to change the culture.

Existing culture is influenced largely by what the organization's culture has been in the past. Culture is slow to change. Culture changes more frequently through the installation of new leadership rather than from a change in view by existing management.

Management Approaches to Clarifying Situations

Values therefore can be either espoused or enacted. Mission statements and codes of conduct are espoused values, whereas norms, modeling, and rewards and punishment are often enacted. To influence or change the ethical behavior in an organization, management must insure both espoused and enacted values are consistent with the desired behavior.

There are a variety of ways of creating an ethical organizational culture. Each of these can be related to the ethical decision-making process. For example, whistle-blowing procedures are a way of gaining awareness of an ethical problem (component 1 of the decision-making process). Ethics training addresses awareness as well as making a moral judgment (component 2). Changing the reward and punishment system may alter moral intentions (component 3) and thus moral behavior (component 4). By insuring that all four components are addressed, the organization is more likely to achieve ethical behavior within the organization.

An ethical organization may be one where there is an overt effort to manage the organization's culture (Reidenbach and Robin, 1991). This effort often encompasses many activities. At minimum, the CEO becomes involved and publicizes top management's ethical concern. Ethics training programs often use videos of the CEO discussing ethics, followed by discussions of case studies. Mechanisms and reporting procedures for dealing with employees' ethical concerns are put into place. Handbooks, policy statements, committees, ombudsmen, and ethics

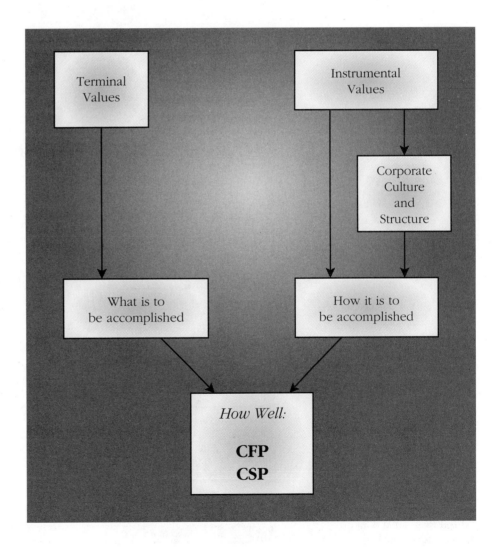

Management Values, Decision Making and Performance

**Issue Characteristics & Ethical
Decision Making**

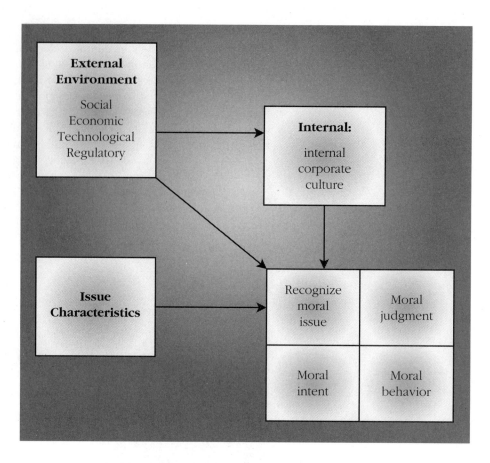

programs are established. In more advanced ethics programs, codes of conduct become more useful, rather than lofty ideals that are difficult to apply. In sum, a planned ethics program that addresses all aspects of ethical decision making is most likely to result in an ethical corporate culture.

1. Recognize moral issue	2. Moral judgement
3. Moral intent	4. Moral behavior

**Ethical Decision Making
4-component Model**

Supplementary Readings and Bibliography

Aupperle, K. E., A. B. Carroll, and J. D. Hatfield. 1985. An empirical examination of the relationship between corporate social responsibility and profitability. *Academy of Management Journal* 28(2):446–463.

Brummer, James J. 1991. *Corporate responsibility and legitimacy: An interdisciplinary analysis.* Westport, CT: Greenwood Press.

Carroll, Archie B. 1989. *Business & Society.* Cincinnati: South-Western Publishing Company.

Clarkson, Max B. E. 1990. Corporate social performance in Canada, 1976–1986. In *Corporation and society research: Studies in theory and measurement,* ed. Lee E. Preston, 281–305. Greenwich, CT: JAI Press, Inc.

Ethics Resource Center, 1990. *Ethics policies and programs in American business.* Washington, D.C.: Ethics Resource Center.

Freeman, R. Edward, and Daniel R. Gilbert, Jr. 1988. *Corporate strategy and the search for ethics.* Englewood Cliffs, NJ: Prentice Hall.

Freeman, R. Edward. 1990. Ethics in the workplace: Recent scholarship, In *International Review of Industrial and Organizational Psychology Volume 5,* ed. C. L. Cooper and I. T. Robertson, 149–167. Chichester: John Wiley & Sons, Ltd.

Friedman, Milton, 1970. The Social Responsibility of Business Is To Increase Its Profits. *The New York Times Magazine,* 13 September, 32, 33, 122–126.

Holmes, Sandra L. 1976. Executive perceptions of corporate social responsibility. *Business Horizons* 19 (3, June):34–40.

McAdam, T. W. 1973. How to put corporate responsibility into practice. *Business and Society Review/Innovation,* Summer, 8–16.

Public Broadcasting Service (PBS) and Ethics Resource Center. 1988. Ethics in American Business, aired November 17, 1988.

Reed, Lyman, Kathleen Getz, Denis Collins, William Oberman, and Robert Toy. 1990. Theoretical models and empirical results: A review and synthesis of JAI volumes 1–10. In *Corporation and society research: Studies in theory and measurement,* ed. Lee E. Preston, 27–62. Greenwich, Connecticut: JAI Press, Inc.

Regan, Mary Beth. 1993. An embarrassment of clean air. *Business Week,* 31 May, 34.

Smith, Adam. 1937. *The wealth of nations.* New York: Modern Library.

Soloman, R. 1985. *It's good business.* New York: Atheneum.

Ullmann, A. 1985. Data in search of a theory: a critical examination of the relationships among social performance, social disclosure, and economic performance. *Academy of Management Review* 10:530–577.

Wartick, Steven L., and Philip L. Cochran. 1985. The evolution of the corporate social performance mode. *Academy of Management Review* 10:758–769.

Wilson, Ian. 1975. What one company is doing about today's demands on business. In *UCLA conference on changing business-society relationships,* ed. George Steiner. Los Angeles: Graduate School of Management, UCLA.

Key Terms

business ethics   the consideration of rightness and wrongness of behaviors, decisions, or actions of people who work in business organizations

classical view   holds that management's responsibility is to protect and augment the shareholder's investment in the firm

Corporate Financial Performance (CFP)   traditional measures of corporate profitability (e.g., EPS, net income, or total sales)

Corporate Social Performance (CSP)   what kind of social good an organization is able to accomplish based upon the specific social issues it faces

corporate social responsibility   the economic, legal, ethical, and philanthropic responsibilities of business

corporate social responsiveness   the approach taken by business toward social concerns: i.e., whether business takes a more dynamic, proactive view

ethics   describes what ought to be and aims at establishing moral standards or rules for judging if something is right or wrong

moral dilemma   where the resolution of an ethical issue is not clear because there are two or more conflicting, but valid, sides to an issue

moral lapse   a decision that clearly violated a moral standard, such as killing, stealing, or cheating

moral standards   a society's or group's customs or practices currently used in situations where an action may harm any individual or group

terminal values   goals to be achieved

values   the enduring beliefs that a specific mode of conduct or end state of existence is personally or socially preferable to another mode or end state

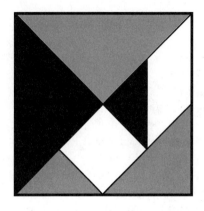

Glossary

Acceptance Testing Developers and users test the system under actual or simulated operating conditions to make sure that it is acceptable to users.

Accounting software General-purpose software that helps companies automate their accounting functions.

Agile manufacturing The activities of manufacturing environments that are dynamic and flexible enough to instantaneously produce customized goods and services in different quantities and effortlessly switch the manufacturing process from one product to another.

Antecedent The IF part of an IF-THEN rule. If the conditions in the IF part are fully satisfied, the system executes the actions identified in the THEN part.

AppleTalk A networking capability that is built into all Macintosh computers and can be used on twisted-pair wiring, coaxial cable, or fiber-optic cable, although it is most commonly used on twisted-pair.

Application controls Policies, procedures, and methods established to ensure the security and quality of individual applications. Application controls cover four primary areas of data processing: input, processing, output, and storage of data, information, and programs.

Application software Software designed to perform people-related tasks such as word processing, graphics, and so on.

Application-dedicated software Specialized or customized applications designed to meet the particular information needs of an organization.

Archie An information search tool for the Internet that identifies and indexes all files on anonymous ftp servers; user must know the file name, or at least part of it.

Arithmetic-Logic Unit (ALU) The part of the CPU that performs fundamental arithmetic and logical operations.

Artificial intelligence A field of study that designs and develops machines capable of performing tasks that would require intelligence if performed by a human being. AI is a branch of computer science that includes areas such as expert systems, robotics, natural language, speech recognition, and neural networks.

Assembler A program used to convert assembly language into machine language.

Assembly language A language based on mnemonics, or meaningful abbreviations of commands, such as *add, load,* and so on. It is the second generation of computer languages.

Attribute Each column in a relational table represents a field, also referred to as an attribute. Attributes are characteristics of an entity.

Audio conferencing Allows a group of people who are geographically separated to exchange verbal communications.

Audit trail A trail showing who corrected each error and when and how each error was corrected.

Authorization requirements Control mechanisms to ensure that only authorized users gain access to the system and that once they gain access they only perform processes they are authorized to perform. This includes all activities related to input, processing, output, dissemination, storage, and maintenance of data.

Backlog Information systems that are waiting to be developed because of lack of resources.

Backward chaining The inference engine begins with a goal, or hypothesis, and searches for data to support this goal. This method of reasoning is also referred to as goal-driven reasoning.

Baseband Transmits digital signals directly over the network; can transmit only one signal at a time. It

613

is one of the most common forms of transmission used in LANs. Both token-ring and Ethernet Systems use baseband transmission.

Batch processing There are two ways to process transactions: batch processing and online processing. In batch processing, transactions are accumulated over a certain period of over time, such as a day, a week, a month, or a quarter, before they are processed.

Bit An electronic signal that denotes a zero or a one; the smallest unit of representation in a computer.

Bits per second (bps) A measurement used to describe the speed at which a communication device sends and receives data.

Broadband Transmits multiple streams of analog signals over the network using frequency division multiplexing. Useful for transmitting large amounts of data over long distances.

Bus topology All computers on the network are connected through a single circuit to a central channel, or communication bus; each message is transmitted to all computers on the network, although only the targeted device will respond to the message.

Business intelligence Internal and external data that help a company assess and analyze the business environment and identify any possible opportunities or threats.

Byte A byte is made up of eight bits. Each character requires a byte of memory to be represented in the computer.

Cache memory A type of primary memory that is designed to increase the efficiency of the CPU. It is made up of memory cells that are used to store data and instructions temporarily.

CASE CASE is a tool that automates several phases of information system development. It graphically represents system requirements and automatically converts system requirements into program code.

CD-ROM Compact Disk-Read Only Memory, a special kind of optical disk that has excellent storage capabilities and stores different kinds of data, such as text, pictures, audio, and video.

Cellular phones As a cellular phone moves through space, each cell, or geographic area, through which it passes contains a base station with a radio transmitter, a receiver, an antenna, and a computer. The user's calls are handled using radio waves with a unique set of frequencies that are assigned to each cell.

Central Processing Unit (CPU) Also referred to as a microprocessor, this is a critical computer component that directs the flow of information among various input and output devices. The CPU is made up of the ALU and the control unit.

Centralized environment All computer facilities, systems, and resources are in one central location and other parts of the organization are linked to this central facility through telecommunication networks.

Channel Part of a telecommunication system that forms the link between message source and message sink for transmitting data.

Client A smaller computer, usually a PC or a workstation, that is on a network, shares some of its tasks and computing power with the server; both the client and the server share tasks and processes.

Client-server system A distributed system in which a server, such as a mainframe, stores commonly used data and programs. The client, usually a PC or a workstation, asks the server for data and programs.

Closed system A system that neither transmits any information to the outside world nor receives any information from the outside world. There are few, if any, closed systems in the real world.

Coaxial cable Consists of a central conducting copper core, surrounded first by a layer of insulating material and then by a second conducting layer of braided wire mesh. Used extensively in the cable television industry and in computer networks covering short distances.

Code reusability A significant benefit of OOPs that allows the same piece of code to be used for different applications.

Common carrier A company that furnishes voice and data communication services both to businesses and to the general public. AT&T, MCL, Sprint, GTE, and ITT are common carriers.

Communication satellite systems Commercial satellites that are launched into geosynchronous orbit at an altitude of about 22,300 miles above the equator. These are powered by solar panels and carry different types of signals, such as standard television programs, telephone transmissions, and high-speed data.

Compiler A system software product that reads a program written in a high-level language and translates it into machine language.

Computer graphics The graphical display of computerized information.

Computer literacy Working knowledge of computers, their components, and their functions.

Computer security A set of policies, procedures, tools, and techniques, to protect computer assets from accidental, intentional, or natural disasters. It covers all components of a company's computing environment: hardware, software, networks, physical facilities, data and information, and personnel.

Computer security controls Policies, procedures, tools, and techniques designed to reduce computer security breaches and system errors. There are five types of controls: application, development, access, physical facility, and personnel controls.

Computer virus A program that causes systems to behave in unexpected and undesirable ways. When the virus program is executed, it makes copies of itself and spreads from one system or application to another, either through networks or through shared diskettes.

Computer vision A field of study that endows computers with the ability to recognize objects.

Configuration The customization of a PC to meet the information needs of a particular user.

Consequent The THEN part of an IF-THEN rule. If the conditions in the antecedent are satisfied, the actions in the THEN part of the rule are executed.

Context diagram Provides a broad, abstract, top-down view of an entire system by identifying its major inputs, outputs, and processes.

Control unit The control unit is a part of the CPU that accesses data and instructions stored in the computer memory and transfers them to the ALU.

Cracker A computer thief who breaks into a system with the intent of stealing passwords, files, and programs, either for fun or for profit.

Creeping requirements New requirements that keep emerging throughout the development life cycle. These can seriously jeopardize system development.

Data The raw material from which information is generated. Data appear in the form of text, numbers, figures, or any combination of these.

Data communication carriers Telephone and telecommunication companies that provide telecommunication services to move data. There are two types of carriers: common carriers and special purpose carriers.

Data definition language (DDL) A language that is used to create and describe the data and define the schema in a DBMS. It serves as an interface for application programs that use the data.

Data dictionary A component of a DBMS that describes the data and its characteristics, such as location, size, and type of data. It is an electronic document.

Data flow diagram (DFD) A DFD is derived from a context diagram. It graphically portrays the inputs, outputs, data stores, and processes associated with each subsystem of the overall system. It breaks down the single process shown in the context diagram.

Data hierarchy chain The data stored in a database is organized in a hierarchy: databases, files, records, fields, bytes, and bits.

Data independence A system that lets a user access data based simply on the contents of the data and its associations with other data, without knowing the physical location of the data.

Data manipulation language (DML) The language that processes and manipulates the data in the database. Allows the user to query the database.

Data redundancy Occurs when data are duplicated in different files.

Database An integrated repository of logically related data that facilitates easy access and processing of data.

Database management system (DBMS) A set of programs that act as an interface between application programs and the data in the database. Support programs that work with the operating system to create, process, and manage data.

Database Model Represents the logical relationships among data elements in the database. Popular database models are hierarchical, network, and relational.

Decentralized environment Each individual site designs, develops, acquires, and maintains systems that meet its local needs.

Decision room Group members linked by a network of PCs that are located in a single room.

Decision support system (DSS) A set of well integrated, user-friendly, computer-based tools that combine internal and external data with various decision-making models to solve semistructured and unstructured problems. Among the functions of a DSS are "what-if" analysis, model building, goal seeking, and graphical analysis.

Decision table A simple graphical tool that depicts system logic. The table shows the conditions and the actions to be taken if the conditions are met.

Decision tree A graphical representation of the logic in a decision-making process and the sequence of decision points that constitutes the decision.

Dedicated marketing information system A system dedicated exclusively to the marketing functions of an organization. Business that cannot afford a dedicated system rely on their TPS for marketing information.

Deductive reasoning Reasoning that arrives at a specific conclusion based on a set of general principles and facts. Moves from the general to the specific.

Deep knowledge Includes general theories, principles, and axioms derived from books.

Derived information A function of an EIS that allows managers to find the cause or source of a certain problem through detailed data analysis.

Desktop publishing The production of office documents such as memos, price sheets, technical manuals, invoices, and newsletters.

Development controls Controls that are built into the development cycle to ensure the security of information systems. Creating proper standards and documentation, ensuring the security and reliability of data, establishing proper authorization for changes or additions to requirement specifications, and separation of duties are some popular development controls.

Direct access Also known as random access. A type of secondary storage in which any record can be directly accessed; this type of storage is essential for online systems.

Direct cutover During system implementation, the old system is removed and the new system is installed.

Direct distance dialing (DDD) Network that transmits voice and data.

Direct file organization Organization of files based on a unique key for each file, which is accessed directly through the memory address of the key.

Disaster recovery plan Specifies how a company will maintain its information systems and services if a disaster strikes. Specifies the situations that warrant the declaration of a disaster and identifies the courses of action that employees must take when a disaster strikes.

Distributed database Databases distributed over single- or multi-vendor hardware located in different geographic areas.

Distributed management Policies and procedures designed to manage the distributed systems in an organization.

Distributed systems Multi-vendor systems that reside on different types of computers, such as PCs and mainframes, that are linked by networks.

Document management systems Computer-based tools that allow users to access text and graphics, regardless of where they are located and in what form the data are stored.

Dot matrix printer The cheapest printer. It uses a rectangular array of 9 or 24 printing wires, or pins. The pins strike a ribbon and when the ribbon presses against the paper, it forms a character.

Drill-down A feature that allows the user to get information at any desired level of detail from an EIS.

DSS generator Comprised of programs such as data management tools, electronic spreadsheets, report generators, and statistical packages to facilitate system development.

DSS shell A program that is used to build a customized DSS. Has a skeletal version of a database, a model base, and an interface.

E-mail A system that allows people who are linked through a network to electronically communicate with each other, in written form, at any time, from anywhere in the world.

Electronic Data Interchange (EDI) A direct computer-to-computer exchange of data over a telecommunications network.

Electronic meeting systems Tools and techniques that allow groups of people, separated by time and distance, to exchange ideas, using audio, video, and other electronic media. Includes audioconferencing, videoconferencing, and groupware.

End-user computing (EUC) The design, development, and maintenance of information systems by system users, rather than by the IS department.

End-user management Managing end-users, who are vital links in an organization's information chain, to properly manage and maintain their information systems.

Entity A person, place, thing, or idea about which data is gathered.

Entity relationship diagram (ERD) A graphical tool that models the entities in a system and the relationships among them. An ERD is used primarily to model the data stores identified in the DFD; it depicts data without regard to the processes that affect the data.

Environment The world surrounding the system. The system is a subsystem of the environment.

Erasable Programmable Read Only Memory (EPROM) A computer chip with preprogrammed instructions. The instructions etched on this chip can be erased and reprogrammed using ultraviolet rays.

Ethernet A popular system that connects computers using coaxial cables. A typical Ethernet network has a maximum speed of 100 megabits per second (Mbps).

Evolutionary prototype A prototype that eventually evolves into a full-fledged system. Each iteration of the prototype builds on the previous version.

Exception report A report that identifies data that appear to be exceptional, where an exception is the difference between actual performance and expected performance.

Executive information system (EIS) A program that allows top managers to quickly retrieve, analyze, and disseminate data and information. Its functions include drill-down and derived information in addition to those found in most DSS.

Expansion slots Allows users to add features and capabilities to their computers, such as memory, sound cards, video cards, faxmodems, and other input and output devices.

Expert systems (ES) Software designed to capture the knowledge and problem-solving skills of a human expert. An expert system has three main components: a knowledge base, an inference engine, and a user interface.

Explanation module A module in an expert system that explains the problem-solving process in detail. Explanations can be either "canned" or customized to the user's level of sophistication.

External strategic systems Systems that are used primarily by a company's customers, clients, suppliers, or other external entities.

Fault-tolerant computers A computer with a backup mechanism to automatically isolate and reconfigure hardware that fails during systems operation.

Fax A technology that uses telephones, modems, and scanners to transmit text and graphics to an individual or organization anywhere in the world. The scanner in the fax machine scans the document at one end and at the other end, a built-in modem receives the message.

Feasibility study A careful analysis of the technical, economic, operational, social, legal, and strategic factors of a system to make sure that the system can be successfully developed.

Fiber-optic cable Consists of thousands of hair-thin strands of glass or plastic, bound together inside a glass cylinder that is covered by a protective sheath. Fiber-optic cable carries data signals in the form of modulated light beams. It is virtually free from all forms of electronical interference.

Field A meaningful group of characters. A record consists of fields; a field is made up of bytes.

File A file is a collection of records of the same type grouped together.

Financial and accounting information system (FAIS) A system that provides information related to the accounting and financial activities of an organization. Includes a large number of subsystems that address the operational, tactical, and strategic information needs of the business.

Floppy disks These are 5.25-inch or 3.5-inch storage diskettes made of polyester film with a magnetic coating, used mostly on microcomputers. They are reliable and portable and have fairly large memory capacities (between 720 kB and 2.88 MB). The 3.5-inch size is currently the most widely used.

Formal system A system that is designed and developed using well-established guidelines and principles. It helps to coordinate and to establish communications among different functional units and meet the overall information needs of a business.

Forward chaining The system begins by analyzing a set of data to solve a problem. Since data are the driving force behind this process, it is sometimes referred to as data-driven reasoning.

ftp File transfer protocol allows users to send or receive files from a remote computer.

Full duplex A data exchange device in which both parties can send and receive information at the same time.

Full-keyboard workstation system A GDSS that is set up in a room with group members at networked PCs. A group facilitator coordinates the responses of group members. A projector screen at the front of the room displays the inputs of group members.

Functional requirements System specifications identified by asking who, what, where, when, and how: Who are the users? What are their needs? Where, when, and how do they want the information?

Fuzzy logic A set of mathematical and logical principles that make it possible to use incomplete, inconsistent, and imprecise knowledge in an expert system.

General-purpose software Software that is mass-produced for a broad range of common business applications, such as word processing.

Geographical information system Powerful and versatile tools that allow users to generate and process information with a geographical point of reference. Data input, storage and retrieval, manipulation and analysis, and data output are its four main capabilities.

Goal seeking The process of determining the input values necessary to achieve a certain goal. This process can be viewed as the reverse of "what-if" analysis.

Gopher A menu-based interface that provides access to information residing on Gopher sites.

Graphical analysis A graphical depiction of data using charts, figures, and graphs. It is particularly useful in helping managers digest large volumes of data.

Group decision support systems (GDSS) Information systems that facilitate the free flow and exchange of ideas and information among group members while maintaining their anonymity. One type of DSS.

Groupware Communication tools, such as E-mail, voice mail, fax, and videoconferencing that foster electronic communication and collaboration among groups.

Hacker An individual who has the knowledge to illegally break into a computer system or facility, although he or she does not cause any harm to the system or the organization.

Half duplex A data exchange device in which two parties alternate sending data. In half-duplex mode, when one party has completed a transmission, control of the channel switches to the other party, allowing it to transmit data.

Hand-held computer A computer that is smaller than notebooks and used primarily to collect field data.

Hard disk A secondary storage device that actually consists of several disks, a read/write head mechanism, and an electronic drive interface.

Hashing algorithm A set of rules that are used to convert a unique key into a memory address in direct file organization.

Help desk A computer support facility that consists of a group of highly trained employees who are knowledgeable about hardware and software.

Hierarchical model A model in which the logical relationships among data elements are represented as a hierarchy using 1–M relationships.

High-frequency radio telephones Uses radio waves to transmit information over great distances. High frequency signals radiate from an antenna using ground waves and sky waves.

High-level languages Computer languages that improve on assembly language and machine language because they are English-like and require fewer instructions.

Home page An electronic description of an individual, institution, or organization. Home pages can be accessed through the Internet.

Host computer A large computer, often a mainframe, that sends and receives data over a network and performs a number of important functions, such as checking the data for accuracy, relaying error messages, and coordinating and controlling all data transmissions over the network.

Human resource information system (HRIS) A system that supports the planning, control, coordination, administration, and management of an organization's human resources. Includes a large number of subsystems that address the information needs of various human resource functions.

Imaging software Programs that scan data and information and convert them into digital images.

Imaging systems A type of document management system that converts paper, microfilm, microfiche, and electronic data into digitized images that can be printed, faxed, or viewed on a computer screen.

Indexed-sequential file A file in which data are stored in a sequence (similar to the sequential method), but in addition an index is created that shows the memory address of each piece of data.

Inductive reasoning Uses specific facts to arrive at general principles. It is more difficult than deductive reasoning, because a large number of facts have to be gathered and analyzed before generalizations can be made.

Industry Standard Architecture (ISA) Bus Type of electronical connection used in an expansion slot which transmits only 16 bits of data at a time at a speed of 8 MHZ and allows the CPU to communicate with peripherals.

Inference engine The inference engine is a component of an expert system. It is the control mechanism that applies reasoning to the knowledge in the knowledge base and decides what knowledge to apply and when and where to apply it.

Informal systems Systems created by ad hoc, informal work groups to support information needs that cannot be met by formal systems. These are powerful systems that meet unique needs and thrive in many organizations.

Information Data processed and converted into a form that is useful to the decision maker. Facts, principles, knowledge, experience, and intuition are applied to convert data into information.

Information literacy The ability to create and use information systems to achieve a competitive advantage. It includes computer literacy, business acumen, and problem-solving skills.

Information resource management (IRM) The process of managing all the components of an information system that collect, store, process, retrieve, and disseminate information. These resources include hardware, software, networks, systems, and personnel.

Information superhighway A network of networks that is fully scalable, with no central controlling entity, and cannot determine the user's profile.

Information system A system that creates, processes, stores, and retrieves information. The input to such a system is data; processed data becomes information.

Information technologies Tools and techniques that support the design and development of information systems; these include hardware, software, databases, telecommunications, and client-servers.

Inkjet A printer that uses a print head nozzle to spray drops of ink that form characters on a page.

Input controls Ensure that input data are authorized, accurate, and timely by preventing users from entering incomplete, erroneous, or inappropriate data. Different kinds of input controls include: access privileges, input authorization, data validation, and data format.

Integrated Services Digital Network (ISDN) Digital network which uses commercial telephone systems that allow users to transmit voice and data.

Intelligent support systems (ISS) Systems designed to assist intuitive decision making. Decision support systems, executive information systems, and expert systems fall into this category.

Internal strategic systems Systems that are used by employees within an organization and designed primarily to enhance internal productivity.

Internet Also called the Net, it is one of the oldest long-distance networks. Refers to a network of networks that links computer users all over the world. Serves as a repository of information on a wide range of topics.

Interorganizational Systems (IOS) Computerized information systems that are shared by more than one company.

Interpreter A system software that translates and executes one statement at a time.

Key A unique way to identify each record in a database.

Key field A field that serves as a unique identifier of instances of that record in the file.

Keyboard Most common and popular method of inputting data into a computer.

Keypad-response system A type of GDSS in which group members use hand-held keypads to communicate with each other. Group members are connected by a network of PCs that are located in a single room.

Knowledge acquisition The process of acquiring knowledge from a variety of sources, such as human experts, books, journals, databases, and electronic media. Acquiring knowledge from experts is a major challenge in the development of expert systems.

Knowledge engineers Professionals responsible for acquiring knowledge and representing it in the system. Besides good communication skills, knowledge engineers must have a good understanding of system development.

Knowledge representation The conversion of the knowledge and judgment of the expert into a form the system can use. There are a number of ways to represent knowledge in the system, including IF-THEN rules.

Laptops and Notebooks Computers that are battery-operated which provide mobile computing technology to be used any time and anywhere. Laptops are small enough to fit on the lap of a user; notebook computers are even smaller.

Laser printer A high-end computer printer, capable of printing 600 dpi or more.

Leased lines Telephone lines are leased to organizations for its exclusive use in setting up WANs.

Local area network (LAN) A network that links a number of independent electronic devices located within a relatively small area, usually with a radius of 1 to 10 miles. Usually connects devices within buildings and offices.

Local bus Gives peripherals direct access to the PC's CPU rather than having their signals arbitrated by ISA, EISA, or MCA I/O expansion buses.

Logical view The logical relationships among data elements in a database.

Machine language Language written at the primitive level of binary arithmetic. It was the first generation of computer language and was tedious and error-prone.

Magnetic disk Storage medium which provides direct access to data for both large and small computers.

Magnetic Ink Character Recognition (MICR) A device that can read magnetic characters found on a document; it reads data, but does not process data. Used primarily in banks.

Magnetic tape A popular secondary storage device, primarily used for storing historical data or for keeping backups of important files. It is a sequential storage device.

Mainframe A large, general-purpose computer with extensive memory and high processing speed. Mainframes are enterprise-wide systems that are ideal for transaction processing.

Management information systems (MIS) Well-integrated systems that meet the tactical informa-

tion needs of middle managers. These systems generate summary and exception reports.

Manufacturing information system A system that supports the manufacturing functions of purchasing, receiving, quality control, inventory management, material requirements planning, capacity planning, production scheduling, and plant design. Applies to both manufacturing and service environments.

Many-to-many (M–M) A relationship in which a record can have multiple parents and multiple children.

Marketing information system A system that meets the marketing information needs of an organization. These are primarily customer-oriented and work toward achieving the strategic sales and marketing plan of the organization.

Master file A permanent record of all transactions that have occurred in a company.

Metropolitan area networks (MANs) High-bandwidth WANs that link electronic devices distributed over a metropolitan area and are used for LAN-to-LAN connections, high-speed data transmission, backup network facilities, full-motion video, and image transmission.

Microcomputer Also known as personal computers (PCs). A compact, powerful, and versatile machine with memory and processing capabilities.

Microwave radio A popular unbounded medium that uses radio signals to transmit large volumes of voice and data traffic.

Minicomputer A small, powerful multiuser system with excellent memory capabilities and processing speed. It is less powerful than a mainframe but more powerful than a PC.

Mixed chaining The use of both forward and backward chaining to solve problems. Most expert systems are equipped to use both.

Model An abstract representation of reality. Models are an integral part of decision making.

Model management system A component of a DSS that stores and accesses models that managers use to make decisions.

Modules When a large program is broken down into smaller, more manageable units, these units are called modules.

Mouse A hand-held "point-and-click" input device that can be moved over a smooth surface to control the position of the cursor on the screen. Pressing the mouse buttons executes different commands.

Multimedia An interactive system that combines several types of media, such as text, graphics, animation, audio, and video. Most multimedia applications require a sound card, a video card, and a CD-ROM drive.

Multimedia systems Systems that can store, retrieve, and process various types of media, such as text, graphics, image, full-motion video, audio, and animation.

Multiprocessing system A multiuser system in which a number of processors, or CPUs, process data and instructions.

Multiprogramming A computing environment in which a number of users can run multiple programs on a single-CPU computer at the same time.

Natural-language interface A technology that enables computers to recognize and respond to the language in which human beings communicate with one another.

Network A system that transmits data to and from a number of locations that are geographically dispersed.

Network architecture A set of standards, or protocols, for telecommunication hardware and software.

Network model A model in which the relationships among data elements are represented by M–M relationships. It is a variation of the hierarchical model.

Neural networks Programs that model the capabilities of the human brain. They have excellent pattern-recognition capabilities and can also learn new information and behavior.

Nonprocedural language Language that focuses on *what* needs to be done, without specifying exactly *how* it should be done.

Object-attribute-value (OAV) Any piece of knowledge can be represented as an object-attribute-value triplet. The object can be a place, thing, person, or object. An attribute is a characteristic of the object; a value is the specific quality assumed by the attribute.

Object-oriented programming (OOPs) A powerful type of programming language that enhances the productivity of programmers and reduces software development time. Another significant benefit of OOPs is code reusability.

Office automation systems (OAS) Computer-based information systems whose primary purpose is to facilitate oral and written communication between individuals and groups. Examples of OAS are word processing, desktop publishing, voice mail, e-mail, videoconferencing, and multimedia systems.

One-to-many (1–M) A relationship in which each node can have only one parent, but can have multiple children.

One-to-one (1–1) A relationship between two entities.

Online transaction processing (OLTP) Data are processed as they are created; since there is no time lag between data creation and data processing, the information in an online system is always current.

Open system A system with a feedback mechanism that promotes the free exchange of information between the system and external entities.

Open system architecture A group of systems that communicate with each other. In such a system, files, programs, and databases can readily be transferred from one system to another.

Open systems interconnection (OSI) Network architecture that uses a seven-layered functional approach to achieve four primary goals: modularity, simplicity, flexibility, and openess.

Operating system The most important system control software, it refers to a complex set of software modules that manage the overall operations of a computer.

Optical Character Recognition (OCR) An input device that scans data from paper documents and converts it into digital form. The most widely used OCR is the bar code scanner, which scans patterns of bars printed on different products.

Organization-wide systems Systems that provide overall, comprehensive, long-term information about the entire organization. These systems integrate information from multiple sources to present a complete view of the organization.

Organizational structure Identifies the level of responsibility, authority, management, and scope of control of employees in the organization. There are two types of organizational structure: pyramid and task-based.

Output controls Ensure that output data are accurate and are delivered in the right format, at the right time, and to the right person. The number and rigor of the output controls depends on the criticality of the application.

Outsourcing Hiring outside professional services to meet the in-house needs of an organization. Using external agencies to create, process, manage, and maintain information systems and provide information-related services.

Parallel conversion The new system and the existing system continue to operate until all bugs in the new system are identified and eliminated. Most critical systems are implemented using this approach.

Parallel processing The processing of more than one instruction at a time. Multiple processors (or CPUs) are required for parallel processing.

Peer-to-peer relationship An arrangement whereby all devices on a network have equal status and privileges, as compared to a master-slave relationship, in which a central computer controls and coordinates all other devices on the network.

Pen-based computing Portable computers that use an electronic writing pad and a light-sensitive pen to input data into a computer. The writing is converted into digital input and stored in a file in the computer.

Personal information systems Systems that support the information needs of individual decision makers for solving structured, semistructured, and unstructured problems. PCs are a good example of such systems.

Phased conversion The new system is slowly phased into its operational environment by replacing parts of the old system with parts of the new system.

Physical view A view that shows how data is physically stored in a storage medium.

Pilot study Uses one department or business unit to test a system before installing it throughout the organization.

"Plug-and-play" A standard that allows different brands of hardware and software components to be "plugged in" and "play" on the same computer system. It allows users to run different kinds of software on different types of desktop machines from different vendors.

Pointers Data stored by a computer to establish links between records.

Primary storage The computer's main memory is called primary storage and is part of the central processor. It is made up of memory cells that are used to store data and instructions temporarily. There are four types of primary memory: RAM, ROM, cache, and registers.

Private branch exchange (PBX) An electronic switching device (or a special computer) that provides connections between the company's telephone lines and those of the local telephone company.

Procedural language Language that explains in a step-by-step sequence *how* a given task should be accomplished.

Process controls Ensure that data are processed using proper procedures and methods. Primarily designed to catch any errors that may have slipped through the input controls, they ensure that the right file or the most updated file is being processed, and that the results of data or file processing is accurate, reliable, and timely.

Production systems A subset of manufacturing information systems pertaining to the production of goods and services. Specifically addresses information needs relating to raw materials, equipment, manpower, and other issues related to production of goods and services.

Program A set of instructions given to a computer to accomplish various tasks. Written in a special computer language, called programming language.

Program flowchart Depicts the flow of logic in a computer program. It is built around the three software constructs of sequence, selection, and iteration.

Programmable Read Only Memory (PROM) Programmable Read Only Memory. Customized data and instructions, which are non-erasable, etched on a chip using special equipment.

Programming language A special kind of computer language, with its own syntax and grammar, that is used to write software.

Protocols Rules and formats that ensure efficient and error-free electronic communication.

Prototyping A system development methodology in which the system is iteratively developed using prototypes (models of the system). Also referred to as rapid application development (RAD).

Pyramid structure The pyramid structure is an organizational hierarchy with the CEO at the top and non-managerial employees at the bottom. Middle managers are somewhere between top management and non-managerial employees.

Quality information system Stand-alone or embedded systems that help an organization to achieve its quality goals. The quality plan is derived from the strategic information plan.

Random Access Memory (RAM) A type of primary memory that resides in the CPU and temporarily stores data and instructions.

Re-engineering Re-evaluating and radically redesigning the way in which a company does business; driven by the question, "Why do we do what we do?"

Read-Only Memory (ROM) Nonvolatile memory that resides in the CPU and cannot be changed except with special equipment or by the hardware vendor. Programs and instructions that are frequently used are etched in ROM.

Record A group of interrelated fields in a database. A collection of records is a file.

Reduced Instruction Set Computing (RISC) A new technology used by the PowerPC which processes instructions more quickly than older chips. It contains only those instructions that are fundamental to operating the computer.

Registers A type of special storage that holds data values, programming instructions, and memory addresses. Registers are located in the ALU and the control unit; they are volatile units of memory designed to increase the efficiency of the CPU.

Relational model Two-dimensional tables made up of columns and rows. Each column represents a field and each row a record. One of the most popular database models.

Relationship An association between two or more entities in a system is referred to as a relationship and is represented in the ERD as a diamond.

Repetition construct Allows the computer to perform a given operation a number of times until a certain condition is met.

Report writers Software packages that allow users to generate static questions.

Resolution The sharpness of an image. It is determined by the number of pixels on the screen.

Ring topology An arrangement whereby networked computers are arranged in a ring. The ring network transmits a message to all the nodes between the sending node and the receiving node.

Risk analysis A function of DSS and EIS that allows managers to asses the risks associated with various alternatives.

Robots Machines that are capable of human-like tactile perception and motor activities. Robots can perform routine tasks and more challenging ones. Robotics, the study of robots, is a branch of AI.

Rule-based systems One way to represent the knowledge and judgment of an expert within a computer system is by using IF-THEN rules. Systems that use IF-THEN rules are called rule-based systems.

Runaway projects Projects that are behind schedule and over budget.

Satellite communications Satellites, which companies lease or purchase, used to transmit data.

Schema A logical description of each piece of data in the database and its relationship with other data elements. It does not identify the actual value of the data.

Secondary storage Nonvolatile memory that resides outside the CPU on devices such as magnetic disks and tapes. Data is stored on secondary storage devices, retrieved, and put into primary memory, where it is processed, and then is transferred back to secondary storage. There are two types of secondary storage: sequential storage and direct-access storage.

Selection construct The computer must take a path when faced with a decision. The selection construct shows the computer how to decide the path to take.

Semiconductor A chip that is made up of several thousands of transistors fused together.

Semistructured decisions These decision fall somewhere between structured decisions, which are routine and repetitive, and unstructured decisions, which are unique and nonrepetitive.

Semistructured task Tasks that are partly structured and partly ambiguous, or unstructured. Semistructured tasks are often performed by middle managers.

Separation of duties A development-related control mechanism that eliminates conflict of interest during system development that might compromise the security and reliability of the system.

Sequence construct There are three constructs in structured programming: sequence, selection, and repetition. The sequence construct executes instructions one after another.

Sequential file organization The use of unique keys to sequentially store the contents of a file in the same sequence in which they were collected. Sequencing must be done before the file is created.

Sequential storage Data that can be accessed and retrieved only in the order in which it was entered.

Server A large central computer that serves as a repository of data and programs commonly accessed by a number of users.

Shell A set of tools and techniques that allows developers to build the prototype of a system.

Simplex Term for a data communication device that can either send or receive data, but cannot do both.

Single-computer system The simplest type of GDSS, designed primarily for single users. Uses a video display system through which each group member can communicate with the others.

Small Computer Systems Interface (SCSI) The 8-bit parallel I/O bus that "hides" the internal structure of the peripherals from the host computer and is the most popular bus today.

Source document The document that is generated at the source where the transaction occurs. A sales receipt is an example of a source document.

Spaghetti code Programming code that is so intertwined that it is difficult or impossible to follow its logic. When the modules in a program are not independent of each other, the programs that constitute the modules are likely to be written in spaghetti code.

Special-purpose carriers Also known as value-added carriers. Companies that add value to the basic communications services provided by a common carrier by providing E-mail, videoconferencing, correction of transmission errors, backup services, and network management.

Speech recognition Computer recognition of the human voice. The goal of speech recognition technology is to allow users to communicate with machines just as they do with other human beings.

Spreadsheets Programs that are used for applications involving numerical analysis, number crunching, graphical output, and "what-if" scenarios.

Star topology An arrangement whereby a central host computer receives messages from computers on the network and passes them to others on the same network. The most common example of star topology is the PBX.

Storage Controls Designed to ensure that the storage devices on which data and programs are stored are protected from man-made and natural disasters. Passwords, access privileges, and backing up files are some popular storage controls.

Strategic business plan A plan that identifies a company's goals as a means of achieving the organizational mission; also includes what is popularly referred to as swot analysis.

Strategic information system (SIS) A system that delivers information products and services that play a direct and prominent role in helping the firm achieve its strategic goals.

Strategic information systems plan (SISP) Identifies the information systems and technologies that are vital to support a firm's business strategy; derived from the strategic business plan.

Structure chart A graphical tool that shows the hierarchy of software modules and the relationships among modules.

Structured decisions Decisions that are routine and straightforward. By following a set of pre-established steps, a solution to the problem can be found. Such a problem does not require intuition or judgment, so the system returns the same solution every time.

Structured English (pseudocode) Describes the logic in a program using simple, easy-to-understand English phrases. It is widely used to document the processes that drive the program and is often used to supplement the DFD.

Structured programming Program development that takes a top-down view of the system and also breaks down the system into smaller, more manageable units, called modules. Structured programming is based on three simple constructs: sequence, selection, and repetition constructs.

Structured Query Language (SQL) A database language that allows users to query a database and receive ad hoc reports or planned reports.

Structured tasks Tasks that are routine, are easily understood, and do not require intuition, judgment, or experience. Lower-level managers often engage in structured decision making.

Structured tools Tools and techniques that support the various phases of traditional development methodologies, such as the SDLC. The four popular structured tools are the structure chart, the system flowchart, decision tables, and decision trees.

Subschema A subset of the fields and records in a schema. Subschemas provide a user-oriented view of the database.

Subsystem A unit within a system that shares some or all of the characteristics of that system.

Summary report A report that summarizes data from several transactions. This is one of the outputs of an MIS.

Supercomputers The fastest and largest computers available today, with large memories, high processing speeds, and multiple processors.

Surface knowledge Knowledge that comes from experience and consists of heuristics and rules of thumb.

Sustainable competitive advantage The ability of a firm to introduce a product, service, or technique that provides an ongoing benefit of competitive significance.

System A collection of interrelated parts that work together in harmony to achieve one or more common purposes.

System analysis A detailed problem analysis undertaken in order to understand the nature, scope, requirements, and feasibility of the new system.

System control software Programs that monitor, control, coordinate, and manage the resources and functions of a computer.

System definition The process of defining the existing problem, determining why a new system is needed, and identifying the objectives of the proposed system.

System design A roadmap that shows system developers how to convert system requirements into system features.

System development life cycle (SDLC) A traditional and popular development methodology for information systems. It consists of 5 phases: problem definition, system analysis, system design, system development and programming, and system testing and implementation.

System development software Software packages and programs that assist programmers and system analysts in designing and developing information systems.

System flowchart Uses symbols to describe the processes that convert input into output, the data required for each process, and the relationships among the processes.

System software Software that performs the basic functions necessary to start and operate a computer.

System support software Programs that support the smooth execution of various programs and operations of a computer.

System testing Testing the performance of the entire system, after unit testing has been successfully completed.

Task-based structure A structure in which a group of people required to accomplish a given task are brought together based on their skills rather than on their places in the organizational hierarchy.

Telecommunications media The means by which data are transmitted. There are two types of media: bounded and unbounded.

Telecommunications The transmission of data (text, images, voice, graphics, etc.) over different media from one set of electronic devices, also referred to as nodes, to another set of electronic devices that are geographically separated.

Telnet A command that connects the user to a remote machine located anywhere on the Internet. This allows the user to type commands to the remote machine, such as activating a program.

Throwaway prototype A prototype that is discarded after several iterations. This is a useful approach when state-of-the-art technologies are involved. System development begins with a clean slate based on the lessons learned during prototyping.

Time-sharing environment A way of allowing different users to use the CPU at the same time.

Token ring A frequently used arrangement of connecting computer equipment using twisted-pair cable.

Top-down approach Provides a view of the system from the highest level to the lowest. It moves from the general to the specific, and from the abstract to the concrete.

Topology The physical configuration of devices on a network. There are three popular network topologies: bus, ring, and star.

Touch Screen An input device that allows users to execute commands by touching a specific location on the screen.

Transaction file A file that contains information about transactions that are processed as a batch and that occurred in a given period of time.

Transaction processing systems (TPS) Information systems that record internal and external transactions. A TPS meets the needs of operational managers; the output of the TPS becomes the input to an MIS.

Transmission direction There are three directions in which data can be transmitted: simplex, half duplex, and full duplex.

Transmission mode There are two modes of data transmission over a network: synchronous and asynchronous. Synchronous transmission moves several characters at a time; asynchronous transmission, one character at a time.

Transmission rate The capacity of a communication channel, measured as the difference between the highest and lowest frequencies carried by the channel. The greater the bandwidth, the greater the amount of information that can be simultaneously transmitted over the channel.

Tuple Each row in a relational database represents a record, also called a tuple.

Twisted pair Two insulated stands of copper wire twisted together. When a number of twisted pairs are grouped together and enclosed in a protective sheath, they form a cable. Twisted-pair cable, one of the most popular telecommunication media, is used for phone lines and computer networks.

Unit testing The individual testing of each module of the system preparatory to testing of the entire system.

Unstructured decisions Decisions that are unique and nonrepetitive. Because they require intuition, experience, and judgment, there may be no one "best" solution and solutions may differ from one decision maker to the next.

Unstructured task A task that relies heavily on intuition, judgment, and experience. Top and middle managers often engage in unstructured decision making.

Upgrade The combining of parts of an existing PC with new components to enhance the PC's performance.

Usenet Provides users with electronic discussion groups or forums for gathering information on a wide variety of topics.

User interface Software that helps a user to interact with the computer.

Utility programs Programs that perform routine, repetitive tasks. Utility programs make it easier to use the computer.

Value-added networks (VANs) Public data networks that add value to basic communication services provided by common carriers by providing additional services, such as access to commercial databases and software, correction of transmission errors, e-mail, and videoconferencing.

Veronica An Internet-based, information search tool that locates all files on participating Gopher servers. User need not know the filename to retrieve the file.

Very high-level languages Also called 4GLs (fourth-generation computer languages), these are efficient, user-friendly, and English-like languages.

Videoconferencing A type of electronic meeting system that uses telephone, video, computer, and communication links to enable geographically separated decision makers to hear and see each other.

Virtual corporation A firm whose employers and employees are not limited by a physical work environment, but instead use communications technology to work from anywhere and at anytime.

Visual programming Programming languages that allow the user to visualize code and its impact on the system.

Voice mail The transmission, storage, and retrieval of spoken messages using computers. Eliminates many problems associated with telephones.

Voice recognition An input device that responds to the human voice to execute computer commands.

Volatile memory Memory that loses its contents when the power is switched off or fails.

Walkthrough An examination of each level of the structure chart to make sure that it accurately depicts the problem and the proposed system. Walkthroughs by developers and users help identify system errors early in the development process.

"What-if" analysis The process of assessing the impact of changes to model variables, the values of the variables, or the interrelationships among variables. This function is found in most DSS and EIS.

Wide Area Information Server (WAIS) A search system that accesses servers all over the world to locate files on specific topics and identify their addresses.

Wide area telephone service Similar to DDD except the organization pays flat monthly fee whether the service is used or not.

Wide-area networks (WANs) Networks that span large geographical areas, sometimes even countries; used for data and voice communications.

Word processing A computerized way to create, edit, and manage text.

Work-group information system A system designed to support group decision making. Such systems promote the free flow of information among group members.

Working memory A component of an expert system. It is a temporary storage area where the initial data, the intermediate results, and the problem-solving steps are stored.

Workstations Machines that are faster and more sophisticated than PCs and are equipped with a number of productivity tools that increase their efficiency.

World Wide Web (WWW) A hyper-text based Internet tool that allows users to display documents stored on any server on the Internet.

Write-Once, Read-Many (WORM) A special kind of CD-ROM: Write-Once, Read-Many. An optical disk that can be written to once, but read many times.

Index

A

A&P (Atlantic and Pacific Tea Co.), 170–71
Abbott Labs, 290
ABC accounting, 410, 411
Acceptance testing, 445
Access, 232
Access control software, 164
Accessibility, information and, 13
Access time, CD–ROM, 84
Accounting software, 140
Accuracy, information and, 13
ADP Automotive Claims, 100
Aetna Life & Casualty Co., 198, 227, 457
Agile manufacturing, 400–402
AIL Systems Inc., 87
Air Touch Communications, Inc., 410, 411
Allergan, 410
American Airlines, 62, 264, 526, 533–35
American Association of Retired Persons
      (AARP), 166–67
American Electronics Association (AEA), 403
American Express, 41, 49, 530
American Greetings Corp., 8–9
American Hospital Supply (AHP), 520, 523
American National Standards Institute
      (ANSI), 196, 225
America Online, 189
Anderson Cancer Center, 167
Antecedent, 341
Apple Computer, 102, 413–14
AppleTalk, 176
Application controls, 580–84
Application software
      commercial, 139
      dedicated, 137, 141–43
      defined, 137
      general-purpose, 137, 139–41
Arby's, 418
Archie, 194–95
Arithmetic-logic unit (ALU), 78
Armstrong World, 413
ARPANET, 186
Artificial intelligence (AI)
      branches of, 328–30
      defined, 56, 326, 328

Asea Brown Boveri Ltd., 377–78
Assembler, 119
Assembly languages, 119
AT&T, 164, 373
      Bell Labs, 121, 132
      Universal Card Services, 270–71
Attributes, 218
Audio conferencing, 372
Audit trail, 46
Authorization requirements, 585
Auto Alliance International (AAI), 407
Automatic teller machines (ATMs), 520, 531
Avon Products, 362

B

Backlog, 465
Backward chaining, 345
Malcolm Baldrige National Quality
      Award, 403
Baltimore Gas & Electric, 333–34
Banc One Corp., 90–91
Bankers Trust, 125
Bank of New York, 570
Bao Steel, 51, 52
Baseband, 176
BASIC, 119, 121
Batch processing, 47
Baxter Healthcare, 527
L.L. Bean, 394
Beaver Lumber Co., 309
Berners-Lee, Tim, 192
Biometrics, 215
Bits, 76
Bits per second (bps), 92–93
Blockbuster, 516–17, 518, 525
Borland International, 231, 232
Robert Bosch Ltd., 142
Boston Chicken, 131
Bounded media, 165–67
Bow Valley Industries, 270
Bridges, 163
British Airways, 239–40
Broadband, 176
Budget Rent-A-Car, 140
Buffer, CD-ROM, 85

Burnett, Leo, Worldwide Inc., 264
Buses, in personal computers, 103–4
Business goals, technology and, 9–10, 240
Business intelligence, 519
Business Research Group (BRG), 258
Bustopology, 179
Byte, 76

C

C, 119, 121
Cache memory, 79
California, Department of Motor Vehicles in,
      433
California Voter Foundation, 193
Campbell Soup, 395
Canada Trust, 335
Canadian National Railway, 124
CareNet, 44–45
Carneige Mellon University, 332
Carnival Cruise Lines, 171, 172
Carrier, 531
CASE. see Computer-aided software engi-
      neering
Cash, James, 146, 239, 240
Caterpillar, Inc., 365
CCA, 215
CD-Erasable (CD-E), 83
CD-ROM (compact disc—read-only memo-
      ry), 83–85
Cellular phones, 171
security issues, 577
Centers for Disease Control (CDC), 178
Centralized environment, 555–56
Central processing unit (CPU), 77–78
      in personal computers, 101–2
Ceridian Corp., 82
Channels, telecommunications, 162–64
Chase Manhattan Bank NA, 142
Chicago Tribune, 417–18
China, management information systems in,
      51, 52
Chubb's Health, 450–51
Ciba-Giegy International, 225, 226
Citibank, 520
Citicorp, 182, 529, 531

Classicomm Cable TV, 311
Client, defined, 261
Client-server (C/S) computing
    advantages of, 267–71
    architecture, 266–67
    defined, 261–62
    difference between local area networks
        and, 263
    disadvantages of, 272–73
    security issues, 273–75
    steps for developing, 264–67
    role of, 258–61
Clock speed, in personal computers, 102
Closed system, 26, 27
Coaxial cable, 165
COBOL, 119, 121
Code reusability, 122, 124
Color Tile, 333
Commander-EIS, 311, 312
Commercial Union (CU), 591
Common carriers, 164
Communication devices
    modems, 92–93
    types of, 92
    wireless, 168–72
Communication satellites, 170–71, 178
Communication systems, 367–72
Communication tools, Internet, 190–91
Community Redevelopment Act, 418
Compilers, 119, 136
Completeness, information and, 13
Comprehensive Research Information
        System (CRIS), 5
CompuServe, 164, 189
Computer(s)
    See also Hardware; Software
    benefits of, 75–76
    comparison of the types of, 101
    components of, 76–77
    hand-held, 99, 100
    laptops and notebooks, 98–99, 100
    mainframes, 95–96
    memory/size, 76
    micro-, 97–98
    mini-, 96
    pen-based, 100
    personal, 97–98, 101–6
    speed, 76
    super-, 94–95
    workstations, 96–97
Computer-aided software engineering
        (CASE)
    advantages of, 505
    background of, 503–5
    defined, 137, 482, 502–3
    disadvantages of, 505
Computer Associates International, 230
Computer Corp., 299
Computer ethics, commandments of, 28
Computer Ethics Institute, 28

Computer Fraud and Abuse Act (1986), 578
Computer graphics, 139–40
Computer literacy
    defined, 10
    versus information literacy, 10–12
Computer science, influence of, 6
Computer security. *See under* Security/
        security issues
Computer viruses, 577–78, 583
Computer vision, 329
Config, 442–43
Configuration, 98
Connecticut Mutual Life Insurance, 366
Consequent, 341
Context diagrams, 488–89
Control unit, 78
Coors Ceramics, 406
Copyright laws, software, 147–48
CorelDRAW, 139–40
Council on Competitiveness, 42
CPTrade, 259–60
Crackers, 574
Creeping requirements, 442
CSX, 365
Cyberdog, 189

D

Dailey, Andrew, 456
Dairymen's Cooperative Creamery
        Association, 289–90
Dallas, quality information systems in,
        405–6, 528
Dannon Co., 198
Data
    communication carriers, 163–64
    conversion of, to information, 13–16
    defined, 12
    entry errors, costs of, 215–16
    field, 217
    hierarchy, 216–18
    hierarchy chain, 217
    inconsistent, 46
    independence, 222
    invalid, 46
    key field, 218
    missing, 46
    organization of, into files, 218–20
    record, 217–18
    redundancy, 220–21
    representation of, in computers, 76
    retrieval, 242
    versus information, 12, 214–16
Database(s)
    advantages of, 222–23
    defined, 218, 221
    differences between files and, 224–25
    disadvantages of, 223
    distributed, 235–38
    entity relationship diagram and, 233–35

    tools, 242–44
Database management systems (DBMS)
    components of, 225–27
    decision support systems and, 292–93
    defined, 221–22
    importance of, 213–14
    primary functions of, 223
    principles of, 238–40, 242–44
Database models
    comparison of, 232
    defined, 227
    hierarchical, 228–29
    network, 229–30
    relational, 230–33
    relationships in, 227–28
Data conditioning system, 239
Data definition language (DDL), 225
Data dictionary, 227
Data entry, in transaction processing sys-
        tems, 45
Data flow diagrams (DFDs), 489–92
Data General, 310
Data management, information resource
        management and, 554–55
Data manipulation language (DML), 225–27
Data processing and revalidation, in transac-
        tion processing systems, 47–48
Data storage, in transaction processing sys-
        tems, 48
Data validation, 45–46, 582–83
Davidow, William, 360
dBASE IV, 231, 232
dbExpress, 299
DBMS. *See* Database management systems
DB2, 232
Decentralized environment, 556
Decision room, 304
Decision support systems (DSS)
    applications of, 288–91
    characteristics of, 288, 289
    compared to other systems, 316,
        345, 347
    components of, 292–95
    defined, 52, 288
    example of, 54–55
    functions of, 295–99
    generators, 300
    how it works, 53–54
    shells, 300–301
    success factors for, 312, 314–16
    tools for developing, 299–301
Decision tables, 497–99
Decision trees, 499–501
Dedicated marketing information system,
        395
Deductive reasoning, 339–40
Deep knowledge, 337
Defense Mapping Agency, Digital Nautical
        Chart project, 213
Deloitte & Touche, 183

Derived information, 312
Desert Sands Unified School District, 170
Desktop Management Interface (DMI), 98
Desktop publishing (DTP), defined, 59, 139
Development controls, 584–85
DHL Worldwide Express, 88
Digital Equipment Corp. (DEC), 96, 332–33
Direct-access storage, 80
Direct cutover, 446
Direct distance dialing (DDD), 177
Direct file organization, 219
Disaster recovery plan (DRP), 587–91
Disks,magnetic, 80–82
Disneyland, 85
Distributed databases, 235–38
Distributed management
    defined, 559
    information resource management and,
      555–59
Distributed systems, 556, 558–59
Document management systems (DMS),
    363–67
Documents, difference between reports
    and, 48
DOS (disk operating system), 129, 130
Dot matrix printers, 89–90
Douglas Aircraft, 363
Drill-down, 55, 312
Drucker, Peter, 307, 308
DSS. See Decision support systems
DuPont, 62, 97
DuPont Merck Pharmaceutical Co., 404

E

Economost, 523, 525
EIS. See Executive information systems
EIS ToolKit, 311, 312
Electronic data interchange (EDI)
    benefits of, 196–98
    costs of implementing, 196
    defined, 195
    implementation challenges, 198–99
    strategic information systems and,
      526–27
Electronic Data Systems (EDS), 463
Electronic Engineering Times, 348
Electronic Joint Venture, 560
Electronic meeting systems
    defined, 59, 372
    description of, 372–78
Electronic publishing and processing sys-
    tems, 363–72
E-mail (electronic mail), 59, 191, 367–69
EMISARI, 303
Employees
    deskilling of, 23
    mistrust by, 23–24
    productivity enhanced, 18
Encryption, 275

Encyclopaedia Britannica, 363
End-user computing (EUC), 451–55
End-user management
    defined, 560
    information resource management and,
      560–61
Engelbart, Douglas, 86
Enterprise information base and directory,
    239
Entity, 218, 488
Entity relationship diagrams (ERDs), 233–35,
    492–94
Environment, defined, 25
Equifax, 368
Erasable programmable read-only memory
    (EPROM), 79
Ernst & Young, 310
Error control, 45, 46
Error detection, 45–46
    software, 164
Erwin, Keven L., Consulting Ecologists, 579
Esprit de Corp., 461
Essential Information, 418
Ethernet, 176
Ethics, 27–28
    buying and installing software and,
      147–48
    E-mail, 369
Evolutionary prototype, 448
Excel, 139, 298, 299, 300
Exception reports, 49–50
Executive information systems (EIS)
    characteristics of, 311–12
    compared to other systems, 316, 345,
      347
    defined, 55, 307
    examples of, 309, 311
    growth of, 310–11
    packages, 311, 312
    success factors for, 312, 314–16
    types of information needed for decision
      making, 307–9
Expansion slots, in personal computers, 103
Expert systems (ES)
    applications of, 331–36
    characteristics of, 58
    compared to other systems, 345, 347
    components of, 56–57, 336–41
    defined, 56, 328–29
    example of, 57–58
Explanation module, 341
External strategic systems, 519
Exxon, 56
Eyegaze Computer System, 75

F

Fault-tolerant computers, 95
Fax (facsimile transmission), 59, 369–71
    security issues, 576–77

Feasibility analysis/study, 438–40
Federal Aviation Administration (FAA),
    326–27, 465, 466, 467
Federal Communications Commission, 175
Federal Express, 332, 333, 394, 521, 529,
    530, 531
Ferrell, O. C., 27
Fiber Distributed Data Interface (FDDI), 168
Fiber-optic cable, 165–67
Field, data, 217
File(s)
    defined, 218
    differences between databases and,
      224–25
    limitations of traditional, 220–21
    organization of data into, 218–20
File transfer protocol *(ftp),* 190
Financial and accounting information sys-
    tems (FAIS)
    defined, 407–8
    integrating financial and accounting,
      410–11
    types of, 408–10
Financial and accounting models, 294
First Union National Bank, 134, 135
Floppy disks, 81
FOCUS, 120, 300
Food Banks, 214
Ford Motor Corp., 83–84, 327–28
Formal systems, 7–8
Forrester, 272
FORTRAN, 119, 121
Forward chaining, 344–45
Fourth-generation languages (4GLs), 119–21
Frequency division multiplexing, 163
Frito-Lay, 377
Front-end processor, 163
Full-duplex mode, 163
Full-keyboard workstation systems, 304–5
Functional management, information
    resource management and, 559
Functional requirements, 440–41
Fuzzy logic, 344

G

Garbage In, Garbage Out (GIGO), 14, 215,
    287
Garrett Co., 146
Gartner Group, 273
Gateways, 163
GDSS. See Group decision support systems
General Electric (GE), 482, 504
    Plastics, 193
    Transportation Systems, 197
General-purpose software, 137, 139–41
General Services Administration (GSA), 83
Genesis Project, 41, 49
Geographical information systems (GIS),
    417–19

Global competition, 17–18
Global information systems, 467–69
Global networks, 184–86
Globex, 140, 529
Goal seeking, 298
Goldman, Steven L., 401
Gopher, 190
Grace Hospital, 85
Graphical analysis, 299
Greyhound Lines Inc., 96, 461
Group decision support systems (GDSS)
    advantages of, 305–7
    defined, 54, 301
    full-keyboard workstation systems, 304–5
    keypad-response systems, 304
    single-computer systems, 303–4
Groupware, 373–78
Grove, Andy, 188
Grumman Data Systems, 551
GTE Data Services, 124, 164

H

Hackers, 574
Half-duplex mode, 163
Hallmark Cards, 86
Hammer, Michael, 530–31
Hand-held computers, 99, 100
H&R Block, 530
Hard disks, 81–82
Hardware
    CD-ROM (compact disc—read-only memory), 83–85
    central processing unit, 77–78
    communication devices, 92–93
    floppy disks, 81
    hard disks, 81–82
    input devices, 85–89
    investment criteria for, 144–47
    magnetic disks, 80–82
    magnetic tape, 82–83
    output devices, 89–92
    primary storage, 78–79
    secondary storage, 80–85
    telecommunications, 163
Harley-Davidson, 125
Harper Group, Inc., 195
Harvard University, 268–69, 271
Hasboro, 271
Hashing algorithm, 219
Help desk, 456
HFSI, 552
Hierarchical database model, 228–29
Hierarchical structure, 19–20
High-frequency radio telephones, 171
High-level languages (HLL), 119
Hofman, J. Debra, 483–85
Holiday Inn, 266
Home Depot, 50–51, 82
Home page, 192–94
Home View Realty Search Services, 214

Honda of America, 440
Hong Kong, decision support systems in, 295, 296
Host computer, 162
Houston Astros, 221, 222
Hoving, Ray, 194
Human resource information systems (HRIS)
    competitive strategy and, 414, 415
    defined, 411–12
    developing, 414–16
    guidelines for selecting, 413
Human resource models, 294
Hurwitz, Judith, 262
Hyatt Hotels, 260–61

I

IBM, 62, 102, 103, 121, 133, 139, 176, 228, 232, 348, 574
IBM-SEMEA, 304, 305
ICI Films, 404–5
If-then rules, 341–44
Ikea North America, 398
Image retrieval and storage, defined, 59
Imaging
    defined, 365
    as a document management system, 365–67
    software, 140–41
Inconsistent data, 46
Indexed-sequential file organization, 219–20
India, decision support systems in, 291
Indianapolis 500, 226
Inductive reasoning, 340
Industry Research Council, 418
Industry Standard Architecture (ISA) bus, 103
Inference engine, 56–57, 339–40
Inferencing techniques, 344–45
Informal systems, 8
Information
    characteristics of, 12–13
    conversion of data to, 13–16
    data versus, 12, 214–16
    defined, 12
    format, 13
    overload, 23
Information literacy
    defined, 10
    versus computer literacy, 10–12
Information Management System (IMS), 228
Information presentation system, 239
Information resource management (IRM)
    components, 547–48
    defined, 546–47
    functions, 552–61
    objectives, 550–52
    principles, 548–50
Information Resources, Inc. (IRI), 232, 233, 290, 311, 312
Information retrieval tools, Internet, 190

Information search tools, Internet, 194–95
Information superhighway, 187
Information systems (IS)
    as an asset versus as a liability, 25, 61–62
    challenges in developing, 465–67
    characteristics of various types of, 61
    defined, 8
    developing cross-functional, 418, 420
    ethics and, 27–28
    financial and accounting, 407–11
    formal, 7–8
    geographical, 417–19
    global, 467–69
    growth of, 41–42
    human resource, 411–16
    informal, 8
    manufacturing, 399–403
    marketing, 393–98
    productivity and, 390–92
    quality, 403–7
    reasons for developing, 435
    risks of, 23–24
    types of, 21–23, 43
    versus information technologies, 8–10
    why organizations need, 17–19
Information systems, development methodologies
    comparison of, 464–65
    end-user computing, 451–55
    off-the-shelf software packages, 458–59
    outsourcing, 460–63
    prototyping/rapid application development, 448–51
    system development life cycle, 436–48
Information technologies (IT)
    defined, 8
    information systems versus, 8–10
Inkjet printers, 90
Inland Steel Industries, 550–51
Input controls, 580
Input devices, 85–89
Integrated Database Management Systems (IDMS), 230
Integrated services digital networks (ISDNs), 174–75
Intel Corp., 21, 75, 101, 191, 290
Intelligent support systems (ISS)
    artificial intelligence, 56
    decision support systems, 52–55
    defined, 52
    description of, 52–59
    executive information systems, 55
    expert systems, 56–58
    role and growth of, 285–86
Interep Radio Store, 370–71
Interfaces, CD-ROM, 85
Internal Revenue Service (IRS)
    depreciation cycles and, 146
    executive information systems at, 314
    expert systems at, 334–35
    imaging at, 366

Internal strategic systems, 519
International Data Corp., 97
International Foundation for Art Research, 358–59
International Standards Organization (ISO), 181, 403
Internet
 communication tools, 190–91
 defined, 186
 evolution of, 186
 information retrieval tools, 190
 information search tools, 194–95
 linking to, 188–90
 multimedia information tools, 192–94
 role of, 186–87
 security issues, 188, 572–73, 578
Internet Architecture Board (IAB), 187
Internet Engineering Task Force (IETF), 187
Interorganizational systems (IOS), 526–27
Interpreters, 136
Invalid data, 46
IRM. *See* Information resource management
ISS. *See* Intelligent support systems
ITT Hartford, 142, 164
ITT Sheraton Corp., 395, 397

J

Janus, 329
Japan, office automation in, 362
JBS and Associates, 140–41
Jewish Hospital Health Care Services (JHHS), 54

K

Kaiser Foundation Health Plan, Inc., 58, 331, 332
Kaiser Permanente, 555
Kaneb Services, 458
W. M. Keck telescope, 168
Keller, Erik, 402
Kemeny, John, 121
Kemerer, Chris, 532
Kentucky Fried Chicken (KFC), 116–18
Kenwood USA Corp., 177
Kerninghan, Brian, 121
Key, 234
Keyboards, 85
Key field, data, 218
Keypad-response systems, 304
Keystone Group Inc., 169–70
K.I.D.S. (Kid Identification Digital System), 366
Kinko, 373
Kiosks, human resources and use of, 417
Kmart, 176
Knowledge, role of, 327–28
Knowledge acquisition (KA), 337
Knowledge base, 336–38
Knowledge engineers (KE), 337

Knowledge representation, 56, 338, 341–44
Eastman Kodak, 460
KPMG Peat Marwick, 375, 376
Kurtz, Thomas, 121

L

Laptops, 98–99
Laser printers, 90
Leased lines, 177–78
Levi Strauss, 417
Lightship, 311, 312
Linguistics, influence of, 6
Local area networks (LANs)
 defined, 175
 description of, 175–77
 difference between client-server computing and, 263
Local bus, 103
Logical view of data, 224
Long Island Lighting Co. (LILCO), 87
Los Angeles Department of Public Social Service, 216
Lotus 1-2-3, 139, 298, 300
Lutheran General Systems, 268

M

McCarthy, John, 328
McCormick & Co., 377
McDonald's, 43
McFarlan, Warren, 5
Machine languages, 118–19
McKesson, 523, 525
Magnetic disks, 80–82
Magnetic ink character recognition (MICR), 89
Magnetic tape, 82–83
Mainframes, 95–96
Management information systems (MIS)
 compared to other systems, 316
 defined, 6, 9, 49
 description of, 49–51
 examples of, 50–51
 field of, 6–7
 reasons for studying, 16–17
Manitoba Public Insurance Corp., 311
Manufacturing information systems
 agile, 400–402
 benefits of, 402–3
 defined, 399
 developing, 399
Many-to-many (M-M) relationship, 228
Mapco, 526, 527
Marion, Pierre, 574
Marithe and Francois Girbaud, 10–11
Mark, 298, 299
Marketing information systems, 393
 benefits of, 398
 defined, 394–97
 developing, 397–98
Marketing models, 294

Marriott Hotels, 304–5
Mary Kay, 377
Massachusetts Department of Revenue, 14, 16
Master file, 47
Masters of Deception, 570–71
Material requirements planning (MRP), 399, 401
MCI, 164, 394
Media, telecommunications, 165–72
Meetings, problems with, 301, 302
Memory
 cache, 79
 primary storage, 78–79
 random access, 79
 read-only, 79
 registers, 79
 secondary storage, 80–85
 working, 340
Merced County (California), 57–58, 342–43
Mercedes-Benz, 240, 241
Meredith Corp., 441–42
Merrill Lynch, 522, 525
Metropolitan area networks (MANs), 179
Microcomputers, 97–98
Microfiche, 92
Microfilm, 92
Microsoft Corp., 125, 129, 132, 139, 232, 299
Microwave radios, 169–70
Middleware, 272
Midwest Stock Exchange, 579
Minicomputers, 96
Minitel, 519–20, 522
Minneapolis police department, 142
Minolta Corp., 141
MIS. *See* Management information systems
Missing data, 46
MIT, 310
Mixed chaining, 345
Mobile Oil, 214, 413, 417
Model building, 295–96
Model management system, 293–94
Modems, 92–93, 163
Modules, 494–95
Monitors, in personal computers, 104–6
Mooradian's Furniture, Inc., 141
Morris, Robert, 578
Motorola Corp., 60, 102, 240
Mouse, 85, 86
Mrs. Field's, Inc., 333
MS-DOS (disk operating system), 129, 130
Multimedia, as a document management system, 364–65
Multimedia information tools, Internet, 192–94
Multimedia systems, 60–61
Multiplexer, 163
Multiprocessing system, 129
Multiprogramming, 127–28, 129
Musical Instrument Digital Interface (MIDI), 91–92
Music Writer, 398

N

Nabisco, 199
NASA, 141–42
National Football League (NFL), 132
National League for Nursing, 177
National Science Foundation (NSF), 186, 187
Nationsbank Corp., 81
Natural-language interface, 329
NCR, 413
Nebraska State Patrol's Investigative Services Division, 284–85, 290
Neodata, 214
Nestlé Inc., 468
Network(s)
    architecture, 180–81
    defined, 160
    global, 184–86
    managing, 183–86
    security issues, 572–74
    topologies, 179–80
    types of, 173–79
Network control software, 164
Network database model, 229–30
Neural networks, 330, 347–49
Newark International Airport, 569–70
Newquist, Harvey, 336
New York City
    Board of Elections, 367
    transit police, 99
New York State, Education Department, 159
NOMAD, 300
Nonprocedural languages, 118
Nordstrom, 265
Nordstrom Valves, 142, 144
Norfolk Southern, 366
Northwest Airlines, 175
Notebooks, 98–99, 100
Notes, 376–77
NYNEX, 232, 338, 341, 578
Nypro, 406–7

O

Object-attribute-value (OAV), 341
Object-oriented programming (OOP), 121–23
Office automation systems (OAS)
    communication systems, 367–72
    defined, 59, 359
    description of, 59–61
    document management systems, 363–67
    electronic meeting systems, 372–78,
    electronic publishing and processing systems, 363–72
    tools, 361
Office of Emergency Preparedness, 303
Office of Management and Budget (OMB), 547, 548
Off-the-shelf software packages, 458–59

1-800-Flowers, 194
One-to-many (1-M) relationship, 228
One-to-one (1-1) relationship, 227–28
Online transaction processing (OLTP), 47
Open system, 26–27, 554
Open systems interconnection (OSI), 181–82
Operating system
    comparison of popular, 135
    defined, 125–26
    description of, 125–27
    environments, 127–29
    examples of, 129–34
    summary of functions, 128
Operations research, influence of, 6
Optical character reader (OCR), 88–89
Oracle, 231
Organizational structure
    defined, 19
    pyramid/hierarchical, 19–20
    task-based, 20–21
Organizations, why they need information systems, 17–19
Organization theory and behavior, influence of, 7
Organization-wide information systems (OWS), 22–23
OS/2 (Operating System/2), 133–34, 135
Output controls, 584
Output devices, 89–92
Output generation, in transaction processing systems, 48
Outsourcing, 460–63

P

Pacific Bell, 335–36
Paperwork Reduction Act (1980), 547–48
Paradox, 231, 232
Parallel conversion, 445
Parallel processing, 94–95
PASCAL, 121
Patricia Seybold Group, 265
Pattern Discovery, 347
Peer-to-peer relationship, 175
Pen-based computing, 100
Pennsylvania Hospital, 142–43
Pentagon, 121, 124
Pentium, 101–2
Pepsi-Cola North America, 462
PepsiCo International, 242, 243
Personal Computer Assets Management Institute, 456
Personal computers (PCs)
    clock speed, 102
    components of, 98
    description of, 97–98
    expansion slots and buses, 103–4
    how to buy, 101–6
    monitors, 104–6
    principles for managing, 455–58

processor, 101–2
    random access memory in, 102–3
    upgrading, 106
Personal information systems (PIS), 22, 23
Phased conversion, 446
Philip Morris, 468
Philips Electronics North America Corp., 83, 87
Phoenix Police Department, information system at, 459
Physical view of data, 224
PIDEAC (Personal Identification and Entry Access Control), 16–17
Pilot study, 446
Pioneer Hi-Bred International, 4–6
Pitney-Bowes, 97
Plug-and-play, 98
Pointers, 228
Political science, influence of, 6
PowerBuilder Enterprise, 124
PowerPC, 102
Price Waterhouse, 457
Primary storage, 78–79
Printers, 89–91, 92
Prisons, technology used in, 215
Private branch exchanges (PBXs), 173–74
Problem solving, steps in, 286–88
Procedural languages, 118
Process controls, 583–84
Processor, in personal computers, 101–2
Procter & Gamble, 467–68
Prodea Synergy, 124
Prodigy, 189
Production models, 294
Production systems, 399
Productivity, information systems and, 390–92
Program, defined, 118
Program flowchart, 497
Programmable read-only memory (PROM), 79
Programming
    object-oriented, 121–23
    visual, 123–25
Programming languages
    assembly, 119
    defined, 118
    high-level, 119
    machine, 118–19
    object-oriented programming, 121–23
    procedural versus nonprocedural, 118
    translating, 134–36
    very high-level, 119–21
Protocols, 180–81
Prototyping/rapid application development, 448–51
Pseudocode, 501–2
Psychology, influence of, 6
Public Service Gas & Electric, 347
Pyramid/hierarchical structure, 19–20

Q

Quality information systems, 403–7
Query support, in transaction processing systems, 48

R

Ralph's Grocery Co., 199
Random access memory (RAM), 79
in personal computers, 102–3
Rapid application development (RAD), 448–51
Raytheon, 122
RCA, 197
Reader's Digest Association, 212–13
Read-only memory (ROM), 79
Record, data, 217–18
Red Devil, 402
Reduced Instruction Set Computing (RISC), 102
Re-engineering, 530–31
Registers, 79
Relational database model, 230–33
Relevance, information and, 12
Repetition construct, 495–96
Report on the Effectiveness of Technology in the Schools, 75
Reports
difference between documents and, 48
exception, 49–50
summary, 49
Report writers, 227
Research Board, 273
Resolution, monitor, 104–5
Return on investment (ROI), 145–46
Revenue Canada, 504–5
Richardson Independent School District, 167
Ring topology, 179–80
Risk analysis, 298–99
Ritchie, Dennis, 121
RJR Tobacco, 197
Robots, 330
Rockart, John F., 483–85
Rockland Community Action Council, 583–84
Rockwell International, 578
Rosenbluth International, 371
Rule-based systems, 342
Runaway projects, 465–67
Russell Reynolds Associates, 411, 412

S

SABRE, 526, 533–35
Safeway Stores, 398
Salerno, Robert, 199
Santa Fe Railroad, 120–21
SAS, 120
SAS/EIS-Express, 311, 312
Satellites, communication, 170–71, 178

Schema, 224
Scotiabank, 123
SDLC. See System development life cycle
Secondary storage, 80–85
Secrets of a Super Hacker (Knightmare), 570
Securities and Exchange Commission (SEC), 95, 96
Securities Industry Automation Corp. (SIAC), 586
Security/security issues
client-server, 273–75
defined, 571
distributed databases and, 240, 242
fax machines and, 576–77
Internet, 188, 572–73, 578
network, 572–74
reasons for vulnerability, 571–74
software, 164
statistics on violations, 570
Security APL, 193
Security breaches, types of, 24
accidental/unintentional errors, 575
cellular phones, 577
decoding passwords, 576
intentional errors, 576–79
natural disasters, 579–80
sniffer programs, 579
viruses, 577–78, 583
Security controls
application controls, 580–84
backups, 583–84
data validation, 582–83
defined, 580
development controls, 584–85
disaster recovery plan, 587–91
passwords, 581–82
personnel controls, 586–87
physical facilities control, 586
Security Dynamics, 582
Selden, Paul, 395
Selection construct, 495
Semiconductors, 78
Semistructured decisions, 286
Semistructured tasks, 19
Separation of duties, 585
Sequence construct, 495
Sequential file organization, 218–19
Sequential storage, 80
Serfin Financial Group, 310, 311
Server, 261
SF Net, 160
Shanghai, geographical information systems in, 418, 419
Shearson Lehman Brothers, 123
Shell, 137
decision support systems, 300–301
Sherwin Williams, 311
Simon Wiesenthal Center, 60–61
Simple network management protocol (SNMP), 180–81

Simplex mode, 162
Singapore, electronic data interchange in, 197
Singapore Airlines, 335, 336
Single-computer systems, 303–4
SIS. *See* Strategic information systems
Small Computer System Interface (SCSI), 103–4
Snapple, 558
Sociology, influence of, 7
Software
application, 137–43
copying, 147–48
ethical issues, 147–48
investment criteria for, 144–47
making verus buying of, 143–44
off-the-shelf packages, 458–59
system, 125–37
telecommunications, 164
Software Publishers Association (SPA), 148, 456
Sosa, Glenn, 532
Sound boards, 91–92
Sound card, CD-ROM, 85
Source documents, 45
South Africa, multimedia in, 364
Southern Pacific Railroad, 369–70
Spaghetti code, 495
Spartan Stores Inc., 401
Special-purpose carriers, 164
Speech recognition, 329
Spreadsheets, 139
Sprint, 164
SQL. *See* Structured Query Language
Stalk, George, Jr., 399
Standardization. *See* Information resource management (IRM)
Standish Group International, 465–66
Star topology, 180
State University of New York (Buffalo), 168
Statistical models, 294
Storage controls, 584
Strategic information systems (SIS)
barriers to developing, 532–33
characteristics of, 523–27
compared to other systems, 517–18
defined, 17, 518–19
developing, 528–32
examples of, 519–23
information resource management and, 559–60
SABRE, 526, 533–35
Strategic information systems plan (SISP), 527–28
Structure chart, 496–97
Structured decisions, 286
Structured English, 501–2
Structured programming, 494
constructs of, 495–96
defined, 495
tools for, 496–501

Structured Query Language (SQL), 120, 225–27
Structured tasks, 19
Structured tools, 485–502
Subjectivity, information and, 12
Subschema, 224
Subsystems, defined, 25
Summary reports, 49
Sundstrand, 309
Sun Hydraulics, 125
Supercomputers, 94–95
Support tools, decision support systems and, 295
Surface knowledge, 337
Sustainable competitive advantage, 531
Switches, 163
Symphony, 300
SynOptics Communications, 402–3
System(s)
    characteristics of, 27
    closed, 26, 27
    components of, 26–27
    defined, 25
    open, 26–27
System analysis, 438–43
System control software, 125–34
System definition, 438
System design, 443–44
System development life cycle (SDLC)
    defined, 436
    limitations of, 447–48
    system analysis, 438–43
    system definition, 438
    system design and programming, 443–44
    system maintenance, 446–47
    system testing and implementation, 445–46
System development software, 125, 137
System flowchart, 497
System software
    defined, 125
    system control software, 125–34
    system development software, 125, 137
    system support software, 125, 134–36
Systems theory, general, 25–27
System support software, 125, 134–36
System testing, 445

T

Task-based organizational structure, 20–21
Tasks
    comparison of, 20
    semistructured, 19
    structured, 19
    unstructured, 19
Technology, business goals and, 9–10, 240
Technology management, information
    resource management and, 553–54
Telecommunications

channels, 162–64
components and connections, 161–62
defined, 160
electronic data interchange, 195–99
growth of, 159–60
hardware, 163
Internet, 186–95
media, 165–72
software, 164
strategic information systems and, 524–25
Telnet, 191
Telogy, 396–97
Terminal emulation software, 164
Texas Commerce Bank, 97, 98
Texas State Bank, 463
Textile/Clothing Technology, 401–2
Thiokol, 526
Third-generation languages (3GLs), 119
Thorn EMI, 96, 97
Throwaway prototype, 448
Time division multiplexing, 163
Timeliness, information and, 12–13
Time-sharing environment, 128
Token-ring network, 176
Tools
    to analyze and design systems, 488–92
    to convert program specifications into code, 501–2
    framework for selecting, 483–85, 486
    to represent processes in systems, 494–96
    to represent system data, 492–94
    structured, 485–502
    for structured programming, 496–501
Top-down approach, 485
Topologies, network, 179–80
Total quality management (TQM), 18, 395–97, 403
Touch screen, 85–86
Toyota, 185, 268
Toyota Vehicle Processors, Inc., 88–89, 90
Trademark Wizard, 125
Transaction file, 47
Transaction processing system (TPS)
    characteristics of, 50
    compared to other systems, 316
    data entry, 45
    data processing and revalidation, 47–48
    data storage, 48
    data validation, 45–46
    defined, 43
    description of, 43–49
    example of, 49
    output generation, 48
    query support, 48
    steps in, 45
Transmission control software, 164
Transmission direction, 162–63
Transmission mode, 162

Transmission rate, 162
Trans Union, 368
Travelers Insurance Co., 44–45, 134
Tribune Co., 146
TRW, 368
Tuple, 230
Twisted-pair cable, 165

U

Ucar Carbon Co., 51
Unbounded media, 168–72
Union Gas, 482, 504
Unisys, 52
United Airlines, 99, 531, 534, 535
United Behavioral Systems (UBS), 257–58
United Kingdom Taurus project, 465, 466
United Nations, 137, 138
United Parcel Service (UPS), 171, 194, 232, 531
U.S. Air Force, 309
U.S. Customs Service, 335
U.S. Department of Agriculture, 554, 555
U.S. Department of Defense, 186, 349
U.S. Department of the Treasury, 545–46, 554
U.S. Marine Corps, 178
U.S. Postal Service, 88, 142
United Technologies, 59
Unit testing, 445
University of California (Los Angeles) Medical School, 408
University of California (San Diego) Medical Center, 330
University of Pennsylvania, Medical center in Philadelphia, 141
University of Texas, 310
UNIX, 132–33
Unstructured decisions, 286
Unstructured tasks, 19
Upgrading, 106
Urban, Tom, 4–5
Usenet, 191–92
User interface, 57, 340
US West, 327
Utah, computer bulletin board in, 188
Utility programs, 134
UVB-Ware, 143

V

Value-added carriers, 164
Value-added networks (VANs), 179
Value Health, Inc., 168, 169
Vendors, use of multiple, 525–26
Veronica, 195
Very high-level languages, 119–21
Video board/card/graphics, 105
Videoconferencing, 59, 372–73
Video display terminals (VDTs), 89
    in personal computers, 104–6

Virginia Polytechnic Institute, 309
Virtual corporation, 360–62
Viruses, computer, 577–78, 583
VisiCalc, 139
Visual BASIC, 125
Visual programming, 123–25
Voice mail, 59, 371–72
Voice recognition, 86–88
Volatile memory, 7

W

Walkthrough, 497
Wal-Mart, 197, 199

Ward, Mike, 75
Wells Fargo Bank, 132
Western Publishing, 132, 133
"What-if" analysis, 297–98
Wide Area Information Server (WAIS), 195
Wide area networks (WANs), 177–79
Wide Area Telephone Service (WATS), 177
Windows, 125, 129–31
Windows 95, 131–32
Windows NT, 132
Wireless communication, 168–72
Wirth, Niklaus, 121
Wisconsin, database management in, 313
Word, 139

WordPerfect, 139
Word processing, defined, 59, 137, 139
Work-group information systems (WIS), 22, 23
Working memory, 340
Workstations, 96–97
World Trade Center, 238
World Wide Web (WWW), 192–94
Write-Once, Read-Many (WORM), 84

X

XCON, 332
Xerox, 333